Stanley I. Kutler

Looking for America

The People's History
Second Edition

VOLUME II
Since 1865

W · W · Norton & Company

New York/London

Library of Congress Cataloging in Publication Data
Kutler, Stanley I
  Looking for America. Second Edition.
  CONTENTS: v. 1. To 1865.—v. 2. Since 1865.
  1. United States—Social conditions—Addresses, essays,
lectures. 2. United States—History—Sources.
3. United States—Social conditions—Sources. I. Title.
HN57.K78 1979   309.1'73   79–1332

ISBN 0-393-95013-1

1 2 3 4 5 6 7 8 9 0

In memory of my grandfather:

an extraordinary man who

made some history himself

and taught it to me

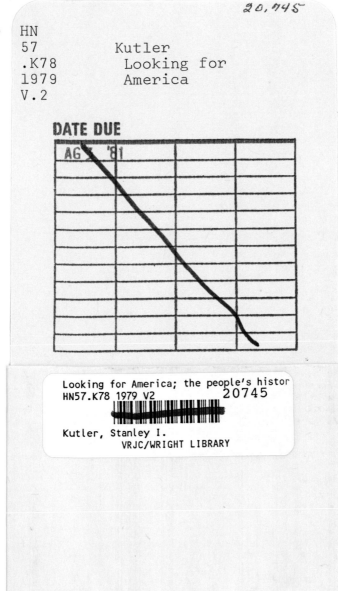

Preface:

Whose History?

Why is history so dull, so dry? students typically ask. Why must we know that the Missouri Compromise occurred in 1820, not 1821? What was "Bleeding Kansas?" Who really won the Battle of Bull Run? What was the AAA? the NIRA? the CCC? the PWA? the WPA? the CWA? What was Populism? Progressivism? the Square Deal? the New Deal? the Fair Deal? What were the terms of the Civil Rights Act of 1875? of 1957? of 1964? of 1968? What were three major accomplishments of James Polk's administration? Which president encouraged more antitrust prosecutions: Theodore Roosevelt, William Howard Taft, or Woodrow Wilson? Did Franklin D. Roosevelt "cure" the Great Depression? Is it perfectly clear that Richard Nixon was a crook?

Such questions, of course, are central to the collective history of the nation. When we understand the roles of prominent individuals and significant events, and when we locate time and place, we have a useful, necessary fix on the larger picture of development. But is that all? Must historical understanding embrace nothing more than past politics, abstract laws, and memorable slogans and statements of famous people?

Surely it is a pity that we so often select those aspects of the past for study. After all our attempts at determining the proper content of history courses, we must realize that history is a story about aspects of the human past. History can encompass the full range of the human experience: birth; work; conflict; love; marriage; prayer; taxation; ambition; failure; death. How could that be dull? We are social animals, naturally interested in what others have done or are doing, whether out of curiosity or in the expectation that we might learn more about ourselves by observing others.

I am often impressed by the crowds of young school children who regularly visit the museum exhibits in the State Historical Society in Madison, Wisconsin. What is it that they see? Clothes, military uniforms, tools, furniture, weapons, photographs, foods, medical instruments, building materials—all those things that illustrate how ordinary people lived and functioned. These displays have an enormous impact, and eager young faces reflect utter fascination.

To these children, this is the real stuff, the real attraction of the past, for it arouses an inherent interest in that broad range of human experience with which they can readily identify.

What, then, is the problem? Why have students found history courses dull? Why aren't the courses alive and meaningful to their lives? Perhaps because we too often fail to remember that ordinary people have been affected by the acts of prominent individuals and that they have been caught in the web of significant events—just as we are today. At the risk of appearing ambiguous, I readily admit that events usually are shaped and moved by the actions of uncommon people and, more properly, often by depersonalized processes. The past certainly cannot be depicted exclusively through the eyes of the proverbial common man or woman. But ordinary people do play roles imposed upon them by crucial events or larger political, social, and economic considerations.

King James I granted a charter for the settlement of Virginia, and John Smith, a truly extraordinary man, played a vital role in the survival of the colony. But who was starving? Who was in danger from Indians? What fears, what anxieties did they feel? Prominent politicians in the 1850s made much of "Bleeding Kansas," but who was bleeding? Why did people move to the territory? The westward movement was a truly important happening. But who went? Why? What did they experience? Immigration is another vital phenomenon. But who came to the United States? What problems did they encounter? What continually attracted them? Samuel Gompers talked about working conditions and the necessity for workers to organize, bargain collectively, and even strike. But how did ordinary workers relate to their new machines, and what was it really like for them to risk their jobs and strike? William McKinley and others justified the annexation of the Philippines in order to uplift, civilize, and Christianize our "little brown brothers." But we sent soldiers, not just missionaries, and they burned villages and tortured "traitors" who obviously had another vision of civilization and order. Franklin D. Roosevelt spoke of one-third of a nation as ill-housed, ill-clad, and ill-fed. But how did those people live? Martin Luther King said, "We shall overcome." We know a great deal about King; but who were the "we" and what were they doing? The Supreme Court under Earl Warren made notable, controversial decisions in the area of criminal justice; but the Supreme Court does not "make" cases. Whose life, whose freedom, whose interest was at stake?

Again, it is ordinary men, women, and children who find themselves caught in the process of history. They play their roles, they do their thing, and they leave an ever so tiny mark on the continuous sequence of time and events. But their marks should not be ignored, and should not be separated from those left by elites. Indeed, recognizing and understanding the contributions of ordinary people can only enrich, vitalize, and above all, personalize our knowledge of the past.

And so, in the following selections we will hear William Pond tell us what it really was like in Massachusetts Bay in 1631; we can hear Mrs. L.L. Dalton's self-conscious philosophizing on the frontier in Circle Valley, Utah, in 1876; we can hear the complaint of a semiliterate, fairly wealthy landlord who protested the requirement for indoor toilets in his row houses in 1912; and we can hear Reuben Dagenhart's account of what it was like for a twelve-year-old child in the mills. We can listen to ordinary people who pledged their lives, fortunes, and sacred honor to the American Revolution, and also to those who abandoned their homes and heritage because they did not believe in that revolution; we can listen to immigrants who came to America and saw their fondest dreams fulfilled while others experienced a nightmare; we can listen to young civil rights activists who in the 1960s found terror and brutality, not frolic and romance; and we can listen to the complaints and frustrations of young people looking for work in the 1970s. We can note the attempts of ordinary workers in Philadelphia in the 1830s who joined together to improve their lives; we can note the real joy and problems that freedom brought to ex-slaves; we can note the anxieties experienced by people who went on welfare in the 1930s and why some resisted doing so; and we can note the adventure and drudgery of men and women who found themselves caught up in war, whether in 1776, 1863, or 1968.

The experiences in this collection are not intended to reflect only those of a "bottom" element, or an "underside" in American life. These people represent, I believe, the wide range of diverse people who have filled the American past. They are white, black, red, or of varying ethnic character. Some are successful and fairly well-to-do in a material sense, although some are poor and have failed to achieve whatever goal they sought. Some are politically radical in outlook and aims, yet some approved of or expressed dissatisfaction with their lives without questioning the existing system.

There is no ideological focus to this work in the usual political sense. It would be easy to read the selections as a prolonged, unrelieved story of seaminess, violence, oppression, discontent, and alienation. But that would only scratch the surface of the experiences. I certainly do not intend to depict American life as exclusively ugly or sordid. What I wish to convey instead is a recognition that life has been a struggle for most people, whatever their involvement or endeavor. People relate to people, and sometimes they conflict; people relate to their government, and sometimes they conflict; people relate to their environment, and sometimes they conflict. The reality of past human experience is that life is hard, life is struggle, life is ceaseless toil; yet people are resilient, people endure—sometimes with pleasure and joy, sometimes with pain and tragedy.

A Note on the Second Edition

I am grateful for the opportunity to offer a revision of this work. The responses from colleagues and students to the first edition have been most heartening. Above all, they have reinforced my ideas about this approach to teaching history, ideas which I have tried to convey in the preface to these volumes. For this new edition, the format remains the same. I have altered some sections, deleted others, and introduced entirely new ones. In particular, the concluding sections of volume II reflect new social concerns—or more properly, a heightened awareness of persistent human problems and conditions. In general, the documents still tend to be experiential rather than analytical. Knowing and understanding human experience is, I believe, the essence of historical study. And that experience easily lends itself to endless forms of analysis.

For this edition, I have responded to a number of suggestions. I have been overwhelmed—and enormously pleased—by the letters from numerous instructors (and students) who have taken the time to comment on how well (or how poorly) individual selections "work." I hope they can see the impact of their criticisms. Again, I particularly must acknowledge Phyllis Torda and David Shepard for their dedicated assistance in gathering materials and illustrations. They have been diligent, imaginative, and loyal co-workers; more, they have been true friends through the years. Finally, James L. Mairs of W. W. Norton proves that being an editor and a friend are not mutually exclusive. I appreciate his intelligent, warm, and patient support for this project.

Madison, Wisconsin
October 1979

Acknowledgments

This project has been an exciting, profitable learning experience for me. The research has taken me into explorations of obscure, seldom used manuscript collections, and through seemingly endless volumes of state and local historical journals that publish valuable, but often neglected, documentary materials. Naturally, the editorial judgments have been mine. But as my citations indicate, numerous people have generously provided suggestions or their own treasured materials. Their responses to my queries have been overwhelming and gratifying. In particular, I wish to thank David Allen, Stuart Applebaum, Thomas Archdeacon, Tadashi Aruga, Steven Boyd, Anne Boylan, John Churchman, Donna Cord, Patricia Romero Curtin, Roger Daniels, Alan Dickson, Dennis East, Elaine Edelman, Kenneth Greenberg, Robert Griffith, Susan Grigg, Robert Halstead, Robert Hamburger, William Hanchett, Alan D. Harper, Jerzy Jedlicki, John Kern, Jesse Lemisch, David Levy, Diane Lindstrom, Clay McShane, Jacob Rader Marcus, Norman Markowitz, Daniel Nelson, Douglas Nelson, George Parkinson, Wilhelmena Robinson, Donald Roper, David Sartori, Harry N. Scheiber, Diane Sherman, John Shover, John Squibb, John Sutherland, Jon Teaford, Tom Terrill, Diana Vàri, Rudolph J. Vecoli, William Wiecek, and Bertram Wyatt-Brown. In addition, Miriam Feingold Stein led me to numerous sources, including those describing her own unique experiences and, from the start, has been especially encouraging.

The staff of the State Historical Society of Wisconsin is a historian's dream. Real professionals in the best sense, their courtesy is matched by their enthusiastic desire to assist. Josephine Harper, John Fleckner, and Eleanor McKay of the Archives and Manuscripts staff, George Talbot and the staff of the Iconography Division, and Susan Dalton of the Film Archives not only responded to my usual frenzied requests, but often led me to useful, unusual materials. I also appreciate the assistance of the Bancroft Library staff and the Regional Oral History Office in Berkeley, California.

For over a year, I have discussed—endlessly, they must think—this project with some of those beautiful people who make the Department of History at the University of Wisconsin a real community. Contrary to the prevailing non-sense, many good scholars are genuinely concerned with good teaching and, above all, how to involve and interest students in the study of the past. In this regard, I particularly acknowledge the aid and good advice of my colleagues, Paul Conkin, Thomas McCormick, Daniel Rodgers, Morton Rothstein, Stanley Schultz, and Richard Sewell. Paul Glad also listened, gave advice, and tried to teach me how to "read" photographs. Merrill Jensen's work—a standard for us all—constantly reminded me of the usefulness and significance of emphasizing the experiences of ordinary, anonymous people. As always, my law school colleague, Willard Hurst, offered his usual perceptive insights. Stanley N. Katz, my friend and sometime collaborator, does not have his name on the covers of these volumes; but, in various ways, he "collaborated."

Gerald Papke of Canfield Press has been a joy. From the beginning, he has pushed and stimulated me; but most of all, his enthusiasm and faith in the project have been extraordinary. Jerry Papke represents a vanishing breed: an editor who really is involved and interested in an author's work. Moreover, he provided splendid editorial assistance and he secured magnificent critiques from John Diggins, Estelle Feinstein, Peter Kolchin, Thomas K. McCraw, Myron Marty, Richard Ruetten, Kent Smith, and Thomas Wendel. Rarely do readers provide such conscientious, sensitive, and constructive criticism as they have; I hope they find their efforts have not been in vain.

I am enormously indebted to my research assistants. Vicki Metzel probably involved herself in the project nearly as much as I did. She diligently searched out my suggestions, provided ones of her own, transcribed materials, and regularly served as a sounding board. Phyllis Torda also helped compile materials and assisted during the hectic weeks of seeing the volumes through production. Karen McKim likewise offered significant research and biblio-graphical aid at various times. David Shepard's contribution in compiling the illustrations simply was indispensible and timely; I trust he realizes the extent of my gratitude. My Mother, the Unpaid Assistant and Family Historian, searched her "archives" for an important illustration.

Finally, five very special people did very special things for me: Sandy said something; Jeff helped proofread, among other things; David the Writer watched and smiled; and Susan and Andy kept asking, "Are you still making a book?" So there, I've made a book for all of them.

Stanley I. Kutler
Madison, Wisconsin

Contents

IV *Racism, Nativism, Imperialism: 1883-1916* **223**

I

After the War: The Freed Slaves and Reconstruction

CHAPTER 1

The freed slaves

Puttin' down ole massa

Jourdon Anderson's 1865 letter to his former master which discusses a possible return to the plantation, probably was composed by someone else—in all likelihood, V. Winters, a Dayton, Ohio, lawyer. Nevertheless, the letter usefully portrays what had to be deep-seated feelings and grievances present in the minds of many former slaves. Jourdon Anderson's calculations for back wages for thirty-two years of service obviously were sarcastic; yet on a more serious level, it is interesting to note the guarantees he demanded in exchange for regular employment, such as a stipulated salary, education for his children, and protection for his daughters against the "violence and wickedness" of the slaveowner's children. Incidentally, Colonel Anderson's request that Jourdon "come back" also tells us something about the white man's state of mind in 1865.

Dayton, Ohio, August 7, 1865.

To My Old Master, Colonel P. H. Anderson, Big Spring, Tennessee.

Sir:

I got your letter, and was glad to find that you had not forgotten Jourdon, and that you wanted me to come back and live with you again, promising to do better for me than anybody else can. I have often felt uneasy about you. I thought the Yankees would have hung you long before this, for harboring Rebs they found at your house. I suppose they never heard about your going to Colonel Martin's to kill the Union soldier that was left by his company in their stable. Although you shot at me twice before I left you, I did not want to hear of your being hurt, and am glad you are still living. It would do me good to go back to the dear old home again, and see Miss Mary and Miss Martha and Allen, Esther, Green, and Lee. Give my love to them all, and tell them I hope we will meet in the better world, if not in this. I would have gone back to see you all when I was working in the Nashville Hospital, but one of the neighbors told me that Henry intended to shoot me if he ever got a chance.

I want to know particularly what the good chance is you propose to give me. I am doing tolerably well here. I get twenty-five dollars a month, with victuals and clothing; have a comfortable home for Mandy,—the folks call her Mrs.

From Lydia Maria Child, *The Freedmen's Book* (Boston: Ticknor and Fields, 1865), pp. 265–267.

Cabins for freed slaves, probably formerly slave quarters.

Anderson,—and the children—Milly, Jane, and Grundy—go to school and are learning well. The teacher says Grundy has a head for a preacher. They go to Sunday school, and Mandy and me attend church regularly. We are kindly treated. Sometimes we overhear others' saying, "Them colored people were slaves" down in Tennessee. The children feel hurt when they hear such remarks; but I tell them it was no disgrace in Tennessee to belong to Colonel Anderson. Many darkeys would have been proud, as I used to be, to call you master. Now if you will write and say what wages you will give me, I will be better able to decide whether it would be to my advantage to move back again.

As to my freedom, which you say I can have, there is nothing to be gained on that score, as I got my free papers in 1864 from the Provost-Marshal-General of the Department of Nashville. Mandy says she would be afraid to go back without some proof that you were disposed to treat us justly and kindly; and we have concluded to test your sincerity by asking you to send us our wages for the time we served you. This will make us forget and forgive old scores, and rely on your justice and friendship in the future. I served you faithfully for thirty-two years, and Mandy twenty years. At twenty-five dollars a month for me, and two dollars a week for Mandy, our earnings would amount to eleven thousand six hundred and eighty dollars. Add to this the interest for the time our wages have been kept back, and deduct what you paid for our clothing, and three doctor's visits to me, and pulling a tooth for Mandy, and the balance will show what we are in justice entitled to. Please send the money by Adam's Express, in care of V. Winters, Esq., Dayton, Ohio. If you fail to pay us for faithful labors in the past, we can have little faith in your promises in the future. We trust the good Maker has opened your eyes to the wrongs which you and your fathers have done to me and my fathers, in making us toil for you for generations without recompense. Here I draw my wages every Saturday night; but in Tennessee there was never any pay-day for the negroes any more than for the horses and cows. Surely there will be a day of reckoning for those who defraud the laborer of his hire.

In answering this letter, please state if there would be any safety for my Milly and Jane, who are now grown up, and both good-looking girls. You know how it was with poor Matilda and Catherine. I would rather stay here and starve—and die, if it come to that—than have my girls brought to shame by the violence and wickedness of their young masters. You will also please state if there has been any schools opened for the colored children in your neighborhood. The great desire of my life now is to give my children an education, and have them form virtuous habits.

Say howdy to George Carter, and thank him for taking the pistol from you when you were shooting at me.

From your old servant,
Jourdon Anderson.

A"free"labor contract,1867

For every Jourdon Anderson, of course, there were thousands of ex-slaves who remained in the South. For them, the maxim, "The more things change, the more they remain the same," truly applied. The labor contract below was typical of the sharecropping arrangements devised in the chaotic days following the Civil War. While the Thirteenth Amendment had abolished slavery, these terms of labor actually fostered a system akin to medieval serfdom.

State of South Carolina
Fairfield District

Article of agreement between D. T. Crosby and the following freedmen whose names are hereunto attached.

1st The Said freedmen agree to hire their time as labourers on the plantation of D. T. Crosby from Jan 1=1867 to Jan 1=1868 to conduct themselves faithfully, honestly, civilly and diligently, to perform all labor on Said plantation, or such as may be connected therewith that may be required by the Said D. T. Crosby nor to leave the premises during working hours, without the consent of the proprietor. The Said freedmen agree to perform the daily tasks hitherto usually allotted on Said plantation. In all cases where tasks can not be assigned they agree to labor diligently ten hours a day.

For every days labor lost by absence, refusal or neglect to perform the daily task or labor Said servants shall forfeit fifty cents (50cts) If absent voluntarily or without leave, two dollars a day. if absent more than one day without leave to be subject to dismissal from the plantation and forfeiture of Share in the crop or wages as the case may be.

Said freedmen agree to take good care of all utensils tools or implements committed to their charge and to pay for the same if injured or destroyed also, to be kind and gentle to all work animals under their charge and to pay for any injury which they may sustain while in their hands through their carelessness or neglect.

They agree to be directed in their labor by the foreman, to obey his orders, and that he shall report all absences, neglect refusal to work or disorderly conduct to the employer Said employer agrees to treat his employees with justice

From Jesse Melville Fraser, ed., "A Free Labor Contract, 1867," *Journal of Southern History* 6 (November 1940): 546–548. Used by permission of the managing editor.

Head Quarters, District of St. Louis.

Office of Superintendent of Contrabands.

St. Louis, Mo., _Oct 10th_ 1863.

Tom Irvine a negro, aged _49_ years, _5 6_ height, _dark_ color, whose last master was _John O Brop_ of the County of _Phillips_ State of _Arkansas_ is hereby declared to be an emancipated Slave, and a free man, by virtue of the Proclamation of the President of the United States, made 1st January, 1863, under the provisions of the Act of Congress of 17th July, 1862.

By Order of Brig. General STRONG,

H. C. Filleborn
Capt. and Chief of Staff.

Witness:

H. V. Fisher
Chaplain and Superintendent of Contrabands.

Freedom papers for an emancipated slave.

and kindness, and to divide the crop with them in the following proportions, viz. Dink and three boys gets a portion of the crop one-third of the corn peas and potatoes gathered and prepared for market, and one-third nett proceeds of the ginned cotton or its market value, and Dink agrees to pay Barnet fifty five dollars in currency and a pair of shoes at the end of the year Dink also agrees to furnish, Barnet, with one peck of meal 2 ½ lbs of meat a week during the year. . . .

And I further agree to give Dink (one fifth) of the wheat crop harvested by them.

Said employer agrees to furnish animals, and to feed them, also waggons carts, plantation implements such as cannot be made by the laborers on . . . the plantation. All violations of the terms of this contract, or of the rules and regulations of the employer, may be punished by dismissal from the plantation with forfeiture of his or her share of the crop or wages, as the case may be.

The employer or his agent shall keep a book, in which shall be entered all advances made by him, and fines and forfeitures for lost time, or any cause, which book shall be received as evidence in same manner as merchants books are now received in Courts of Justice, and shall have a right to deduct from the share of each laborer all his or her fines and forfeitures also all advances made by him.

The laborer shall not sell any agricultural products to any person whatever without the consent of the employer until after the divission of the crops.

The laborer shall commence work at sunrise and be allowed from one to two hours each day for their meals, according to season of the year.

Witness our hands &c this
14 April 1867

Samuel Price [overseer?]

his
Dink X mark
makes

his
Barnet X mark
makes

Minors

his
Dal X mark
mak[es]

his
Wade X mark
makes

his
John X mark
makes

The drive for status

In the immediate aftermath of the Civil War, freed slaves and whites each sought the means to assume place and status in southern society. Both, of course, were conscious of a federal presence, as well as the possibility of further federal intervention. The following selection shows how each reflected that consciousness. First, a black man calmly called on the white community to recognize the need for reconciliation and to acknowledge the freed slaves' lawful rights. In response, an ex-Confederate officer emphasized the mutual interests of the two races, yet he strikingly warned that northern whites represented the outstanding barrier to reconciliation. The theme of "outside agitators" disrupting harmonious race relations endured as a familiar refrain for well over a century in the South.

On April 19, 1867, a general meeting of the citizens of Mobile was held relative to the new measures of reconstruction. Among the vice-presidents were men of all classes and color—as civil judges, bishops, clergy, physicians, citizens, etc., etc., of whom five were colored men. The only colored speaker on the occasion said:

"Fellow-Citizens: I feel my incapacity to-night to speak, after hearing the eloquence of those preceeding me. I received an invitation from the white citizens of Mobile to speak for the purpose of reconciling our races—the black to the white—to extend the hand of fellowship. You have heard the resolutions. You are with us, and I believe are sincere in what they promise. It is my duty to accept the offer of reconstruction when it is extended in behalf of peace to our common country. Let us remove the past from our bosoms, and reconcile ourselves and positions together. I am certain that my race cannot be satisfied unless granted all the rights allowed by the law and by that flag. The resolutions read to you to-night guarantee every thing. Can you expect any more? If you do, I would like to know where you are going to get it. I am delighted in placing myself upon this platform, and in doing this I am doing my duty to my God and my country. We want to do what is right. We believe white men will also do what is right."

The next speaker was a late Confederate officer during the war. He said:

"It is the first time for seven long years that we sit—and at first we sat with diffidence—under the 'old flag' and I cannot deny that my feelings are rather of a strange nature. Looking back to the past, I remembered the day (the 10th day of January, 1861) when I hauled down that flag from its proud staff in Fort St. Philip, and thought then that another flag would soon spread its ample folds over the Southern soil.

"But that flag is no more. It has gone down in a cloud of glory—no more to float even over the deserted graves of our departed heroes—one more of the bright constellations in the broad canopy of that firmament where great warriors are made demigods.

"But I did not come here to-night to tell you, men of Alabama, that my heart was with you—for you well know that as far as that heart can go, it never will cease beating for what is held dear and sacred to you. But I came here to speak to those of our new fellow-citizens, who are not seeking the light of truth.

"It is said that two races now stand in open antagonism to each other—that the colored man is the natural enemy of the white man, and, hereafter, no communion of interests, feelings and past associations, can fill the gulf which divides them.

"But who is it that says so? Is it the Federal soldier who fought for the freedom of that race? Is it even the political leader whose eloquence stirred up the North and West to the rescue of that race? No; it is none of these. It is not even the intelligent and educated men of that class, for I now stand on the very spot where one of them, Mr. Trenier, disclaimed those disorganizing principles, and eloquently vindicated the cause of truth and reason.

"Why, then, should there be any strife between us? Why should not our gods be their gods—our happiness be their happiness? Has anything happened which should break up concert of action, harmony, and concord in the great—the main objects of life—the pursuit of happiness?

"Where can that happiness spring from? Is it from the midst of a community divided against itself, or from one blessed with peace and harmony?

"In what particular have our relations changed? In what case have our interests in the general welfare been divided? Is not today the colored man as essential to our prosperity as he was before?

"Is not our soil calling for the energetic efforts of his sinewy arms? Can we, in fact, live without him? But while we want his labor he wants our lands, our capital, our industry, our influence in the commerce and finances of the world.

"And if, coming down from those higher functions in society, we descend to our domestic relations, where do we find that those relations are changed?

"Does not the intelligent freedman know that neither he nor we are accountable to God for the condition in which we were respectively born?

"Does he not know that, for generations past, the institution of slavery had been forced upon us by the avarice, the love of power of the North? Does he not know that to-day we have in him the same implicit faith and reliance we had before?"

A black view of race relations

Testifying before a Senate committee in 1833, an Augusta, Georgia, businessman contended that when ex-slaves "behaved themselves, and kept out of politics and attended to their business, they have done well." But he went on to charge that there was not much "hope" for blacks born since abolition as they often were given to "idleness" and "loafing." The concern for social control, for blacks to be kept "in their place," so to speak, dominated the white view of race relations following the war. While blacks usually tried to emphasize the more positive side of their dealings with whites, they were not oblivious to the underlying paternalism of whites, and all the tensions this raised. William J. White, a mulatto newspaper editor in Augusta, offered a typical response: one filled with optimism, yet extraordinarily sensitive to the enormity and subtleties of the problem.

Augusta, Ga., November 23, 1883.

. . . Question. You reside in Augusta, I believe?—Answer. Yes, sir.

Q. What is your employment?—A. I edit a newspaper—the Georgia Baptist, and run a printing-office. . . .

Q. You have had opportunities of looking into the condition of the laboring classes; now please give us any information you have acquired on that subject—what is their general condition; tell us whether they are bettering their condition, so far as you have observed; what relations exist between the white and the black people; in short, everything that you know on that general subject.—A. My opportunities for observation have been quite extensive. Soon after the war I was appointed an agent of the Freedman's Bureau and assigned to special duty, traveling through the State of Georgia, looking after the general interests of the colored population, with a special view to the proper discharge of the duties of local bureau officers and the organization and establishment of schools for the colored population, which were to be supported wholly or in part by appropriations made by the General Government. I held that position two years, which gave me an opportunity to get acquainted all over the State. Since that time my business has been such that my intercourse with those people has been to a greater or less extent kept up.

From *Report of the Committee of the Senate upon the Relations between Labor and Capital*, 48th Congress, 1885, 4: 785–793.

There has been a very marked improvement, I think, among the laboring classes in this section of country since the war, and that statement does not apply alone to the colored people, but it applies equally to the white laboring people. The poor white people throughout this part of the country are in much better condition now than they were in during slavery times. You will find fewer of those abject poor white people now and fewer rich ones. There has been a very large assimilation of the different classes of the white people. The poor have become a good deal better off, and the very rich have become poorer, so both classes have settled on a middle ground and constitute very largely what may now be considered a middle class. The same thing may be observed among the colored people, only that they were all poor, and whatever change has been made in respect to them has been on the upward grade. At the close of the war they had no property and no education.

The great need to-day of the laboring population, which, of course, is largely colored, is education.

The labor performed by the laboring population of this section of the country and of this State does not produce by at least 25 per cent, as much as it would produce were it intelligent labor. I think that accounts largely for the continued poverty of men who work very hard. This applies to a certain extent to both races, because there is a large percentage of the white rural population who have never had any education whatever, especially the older people. In recent years the young people, white and colored, are being educated, but formerly a large percentage of the population, both white and colored, grew up uneducated. Just here I will state that in my opinion the great thing to be done is to afford greater educational advantages to the entire population of this section of the country, and I think the Government ought to do it. There are two reasons why I think the Government ought to do it.

In the first place the Government has the means with which to do it without burdening the people, without increasing the tariff or increasing the internal revenue system, from the fact that there are millions of acres of public lands that are now being almost given away by the Government to foreigners. The Government gets comparatively nothing for those lands in the way of pecuniary compensation, while the lands become a fortune to the foreigners, who come here and get possession of them. Now, I believe that the Government ought to make these foreigners pay more for the lands, and that the money accruing from the sales of public lands ought to be used to educate the children whose parents are unable to educate them, and whose ignorance may be largely charged to the Government itself. Upon that ground I want to say to this committee that I am very strongly of the opinion that it is the imperative duty of the Government—that it is a debt which the Government owes to these uneducated people—to furnish assistance in procuring an education for them. Of course, I think that our State here ought to do what it can. We ought to do what we can for ourselves. Every State ought to tax the property of its people for educational purposes. That is not done now.

Georgia does not tax her property for educational purposes. The money raised for education here is raised in other ways, but I think the property ought to be taxed for educational purposes. . . .

. . . There is no money raised for educational purposes by direct taxation in this State. Now, as I have said, I think the State ought to tax the property of the people to some extent for the purposes of education—not heavily, it would not be necessary, for by a moderate tax a considerable amount of money could be raised. We have no free-school system in Georgia at present except in a few counties. The general school system of the State is only partially free during three months in the year; perhaps between one-half and two-thirds of the amount of money may be paid by the State, while the remaining proportion is paid by the persons who send their children to school during that period. Now, I think we ought to have a free-school system in Georgia, and if the State would levy a small tax upon property we could have such a system for at least three months in the year. Then I think the General Government ought to come in and supplement what the State may do with the full amount that would be required to give us an absolutely free-school system for six months in the year, which it could very well do. . . .

Q. You think the great need is more money? You think you cannot make any improvements in your school system without more money?—A. We cannot.

Q. And the best way to get the money required is by an appropriation from the Federal Government. Is that your idea?—A. I think the State ought to do more than it is doing for education, and then I think that the General Government ought to come in and supplement the efforts of the State with an appropriation in such way as they may decide to be most proper. I think it is a debt that the Government owes to this section of the country, and especially to the colored people, a debt that the Government ought to pay, especially now when it is so well able to do so.

Q. Well, that subject has been very fully discussed by the superintendents of education and the educational associations and conventions, and through the press, and there seems to be a general concurrence of opinion everywhere in favor of aid from the Federal Government to the States for educational purposes. Now, passing from that, what have you to say as to the relation between the two races here?—A. Well, the relations which the two races sustain to each other in Georgia are cordial enough. I think Mr. Hickman expressed this morning the idea of the great mass of the white people when he said that he liked the negro, and liked him as a negro. I think that is about the idea generally. Mr. Coggin said that the colored people were not exactly American citizens yet, and I think that is about the general idea of the white people here. As the two races stand related to each other in that way, their relations are entirely cordial as far as I know. The colored people are certainly friendly with the white people, and the white people are friendly with the colored people. Augusta is an exceptional city in that respect. The relations between the white and colored people in

Augusta are really more cordial than in any other place that I know of, and I am pretty well acquainted through the whole South. . . .

Of course, where it comes down to the matter of voting where there is a difference of opinion then there springs up a little friction; where there is no difference of opinion between the white and colored voters, for instance, if the colored men all go up and vote the Democratic ticket, then both races vote together nicely, but when they want to vote the other way there is some friction—considerable friction sometimes. . . .

Q. Is there not considerable friction between whites where they belong to different political parties and want to vote differently?—A. Oh, yes. . . .

Q. Is it the same kind of friction in both cases?—A. No, sir. You see the white people calculate on differing with each other, and they do not mind those differences, but they have never been used to being differed with by the darky, and they just cannot stand it. That, I suppose, as we look at human nature, is just as natural as can be. . . .

Q. Do you think that the white people will ever agree that there is any other race that is their equal?—A. Well, they are disposed in this country to be the lords of creation.

Q. Has there ever been, any country in the world where the white man was, that he did not claim to be superior?—A. I think that in the ages of the past there were a good many white men that submitted to slavery.

Q. Yes; but it was under standing armies.—A. Yes. Well, they were probably but little educated. It is hard to keep an educated people in slavery, whether they are white or black. On that point my views are that all men are alike under like circumstances. The man that comes to be a millionaire may have been born without a copper. . . .

Q. You are willing that these white folks here should vote, are you not?—A. Perfectly; and I always like to have them vote my way. Take a man who becomes a millionaire: he may have started out in life without a cent, but when he comes to be a millionaire he generally seems to forget where he came from, and gets to think that there is something about him which makes him better than other people around him. That seems to be human nature.

Q. How much white blood have you in your veins?—A. Well, sir, my impression is that I have fifteen-sixteenths.

Q. You are fifteen-sixteenths white. Now, do *you* have trouble about voting as you wish?—A. No, sir; the only trouble I have about voting is that they give me too much honor. They generally send four policemen with me to guard me, and I don't like it. No; I do not have any trouble at all about voting. We sometimes have a little cross-questioning, but I don't have any trouble. I have been right here for thirty and odd years, and I have been engaged in business since before the war. During the war, and before the war, I was an undertaker here and had charge and control of an undertaking business in which there was

$10,000 or $15,000 invested, and that brought me in contact with the white citizens all the time, and I can say that I have never had any trouble at all myself. . . .

Q. Don't you find, as a rule, what the intelligent colored people who have testified before us have stated to be their experience, that the intelligent and cultivated white men are the most friendly to the colored man, most disposed to assist him in elevating himself, and the first to recognize his rights and to aid him in maintaining them? Don't you find that that class of white men do exert their intelligence and their moral power instead of resorting to force?—A. Yes, sir; that is largely so, but at the same time I think the intelligent, cultivated white people adapt themselves to surrounding circumstances. For instance, the cultured and intelligent white people of Augusta would not tolerate lawlessness on the part of the whites toward the colored people. Their self-interest would prevent them from allowing anything of the kind, and they would not tolerate it; but in remote sections of the country the intelligent and cultivated white people, while they may not themselves take any part in this kind of violence, they tolerate it and do not try to prevent it when they could.

Q. Do you not find frequently that that condition of public feeling has been caused by the wicked leadership of bad white men misleading and deceiving these poor colored people?—A. I think it is the result of wicked leadership on both sides. I think the white people have a great many bad leaders.

Q. But they are white men who engage in creating these troubles on both sides, are they not?—A. Not necessarily.

Q. Has not that been the condition heretofore?—A. I don't think that is necessarily the case.

Q. Of course it is not necessarily the case, but has it not been the fact?—A. Well, I do not know as it has been, absolutely.

Q. I understood you to say that the colored people were misled in their ignorance, and they were misled by their leaders.—A. Yes, sir; but I did not say that they were misled by white leaders. I meant men—bad men, white and black. Without speaking of race, there are bad leaders in all of our political parties. . . .

The WITNESS. It has been stated here to-day that there is a very large number of vagrants in this city. Now, I am confident that the gentlemen who have made that statement are mistaken. Somebody spoke of the circus coming into town and of the great crowd of idlers that would gather about it. As to the crowd, that is a fact. If you get up a band of music and fill one of our squares with men and women dressed up in circus clothes you will see a pretty big crowd of children on the streets; not all children either; there will be a good many older people among them; but I think I have an opportunity of knowing more about the real condition of the people with whom I associate all the time than these gentlemen have, and I think they are mistaken in saying that we have a large number of vagrants here. Of course, it is true that there are idlers, and there are a good many white idlers. You will find some white men idling around the streets from one week's end to the other, and you cannot tell what they do for a living. You will have to follow them around until night to find out what they do, and of course there are some colored people of the same character. Still, I certainly think these gentlemen who have given that testimony are mistaken as to the number of colored idlers here, for I believe it will be the testimony of the police force that there are comparatively few colored idlers in Augusta. It is true that there are a lot of idle boys, and, as Mr. Lynch stated, the greatest trouble we have is from the sixteen-year-old boys. There are a good many boys of that age or near that age who idle around the streets, but still there is nothing like the number that has been represented here. I feel it my duty to mention this subject, and to say that I am satisfied that those gentlemen are in error about the number. Of course, in a city of 30,000 population, nearly half colored, there must be some colored idlers and white idlers too.

There is another thing that I want to call attention to. There are many reasons why some of the colored young men don't work more than they do. Is it not natural for a man or a woman to seek employment that will be most remunerative? An educated man, whether white or black, will seek employment by which he can use to the best advantage the education he possesses, and, if he can, will of course go into that kind of employment by which he can make more money than a common laborer can who gets perhaps $5 or $6 or $10 a month. A man who has any education will spend a good deal of time trying to do better before he will reconcile himself to going to work for a few dollars a month, especially in an occupation where the labor is purely manual. When a man's mind has been cultivated, and he is aware that by the use of that cultivated mind he ought to be able to make more money, he is not very likely to be content to work as a laborer. Now, if the larger and higher avenues of employment were opened up to these young colored people you would soon find that there would be fewer idlers among them. . . .

Emigration

Until the turn of the century, the freed slaves generally remained in the South and in the locale they knew so well. Many, of course, found themselves unable to move, saddled as they were with enormous debts incurred as a result of the operation of the crop-lien system and sharecropping. But a few found the means for leaving and, as evidenced by the following testimony, had few regrets.

Black exodus from the South: old style and the new.

Opelika, Ala., November 22, 1883.

JAMES H. WILLIAMSON, a colored man, was pointed out by the last witness as one who was about to leave for Texas, and he was interviewed as follows: . . .

Question. I hear that you are going to Texas?—Answer. Yes, sir; I am goin' to Texas. I have got tired puttin' on guano where it won't be no use.

Q. Have you any family?—A. I have eight children.

Q. How old are you?—A. Forty-five.

Q. How old is your oldest?—A. Twenty-three.

Q. How many boys have you?—A. Only two.

Q. What part of Texas are you going to?—A. Denton County, in the northwest.

Q. You are not going out there alone, are you?—A. My family went out there before Christmas.

Q. What does it cost to go there and back?—A. Sixty-five dollars.

Q. Have you got a house on your land there?—A. No, sir.

Q. How are you going to get through the winter?—A. I don't expect to go on the homestead until next year.

Q. Are many of the colored people leaving this part of the country?—A. Not many. A heap of them would go, but they are not able. They are principally mighty poor.

Q. You have worked hard here, I suppose?—A. Yes, sir.

Q. What has been your business?—A. Regular farming. I am a mechanic, too, a house carpenter.

Q. You have got some money together, of course, or you could not go to Texas?—A. Yes, sir; I have got a little.

Q. Well, you have taken care of yourself and this family of eight, and yet you have saved some money here?—A. Yes, sir.

Q. Has your wife been able to help you?—A. No; she has not been able to do much of anything in fourteen years.

Q. I suppose your children have helped you a little?—A. Yes; they have helped me.

Q. How much property or money have you got together?—A. I have got about $600 in money.

Q. How much land have you got bought in Texas—160 acres?—A. Yes; you get 160 acres, but you have got to go on to it and stay there five years before you can get a deed. You pay $17.50 and then you have to stay five years before you get the deed.

Q. But if you stay right there you will get it in the end?—A. Yes; but you have got to pay $17.50 and then after you stay there five years you get the deed, but if you move off before that time you don't get anything and you lose your $17.50.

From *Report of the Committee of the Senate upon the Relations between Labor and Capital,* 48th Congress, 1885, 4: 659–661.

Q. Then of course you and your family will stay there?

A. Yes, sir. There is a heap of people here that would like to go away because the land is so poor here.

Q. But can you not improve this land?—A. Well, where it has a clay foundation you can improve it, but where it is a piney wood the manure will sink right down. Lee County, about here, has a clay foundation; but 3 or 4 miles out you come on sand and the manure goes right through it.

Q. I suppose that you colored people are giving some attention to schools?—A. Yes, sir; but the schools are going down here. They aint near so good as they were about five years ago.

Q. What is the trouble?—A. Well, they don't pay; the county don't pay so much and the people aint able to pay. It requires all they can do to make a living. The schools run three months in the year now, instead of six, as they used to.

Q. Do you think this country is getting poorer?—A. Well, some of the people is improvin' and some not. My observation is that Lee County is goin' back, and Alabama generally is goin' back, and the colored people, I think, is worse off than they were ten years ago.

Q. How is the feeling between the whites and the colored people?—A. Well, there's two parties of them, white and black.

Q. Do you mean that they are not friendly between themselves?—A. In some instances they is; yet in some instances they aint.

Q. Do you have any trouble on account of your color?—A. Well, there is some trouble on account of color.

Q. Is that one reason why you are going away?—A. No, sir. For my part I find it as good here as anywhere I know. The reason of it is that they work and don't get no pay, and they become dissatisfied and quit. Then a heap of them takes to stealing—a heap more'n I ever knew before.

Q. How do you account for that?—A. Well, they are poor. A man don't get but 40 cents a day or 50 cents and board himself. Right in the busy time he gets 50 cents and board, but there is nothin' in this country for them to do until cotton hoein' time.

Q. When is that?—A. They commence about the 10th of May. After that they lay by in July, and then pickin' time comes in September.

Q. How much of the year do the women get a chance to work?—A. About five months.

Q. What can a woman earn when she does work?—A. $3.75 or $4 or $5 a month.

Q. What wages do they get by the day?—A. Twenty-five cents a day, and some 30 cents. They board them in cotton pickin' time. I hired my cotton picked and gave 40 cents.

Q. How much cotton did you make?—A. Twelve bales.

Q. How much did it cost you?—A. Pretty nearly half what it was worth. I have not made any money this year nor for the last two or three years. About

State Historical Society of Wisconsin.

Picking cotton in Mississippi, late 19th century.
State Historical Society of Wisconsin.

three years ago I got $400 or $500 ahead, but I thought I would lose it all if I staid here, so I am going out West.

Q. What are the others going to do who stay behind?—A. They are obliged to stay.

Q. Do you think they would go away if they could?—A. Yes, sir; a heap of them would go with me now.

Q. If you go out and do well there many of them will probably follow you?—A. Oh, yes, a heap.

Q. How are the young negroes doing?—A. Oh, they do not take any intrust. They do not lay up nothing ahead.

Q. How soon are you going away?—A. I expect to go Saturday of this week.

Q. How is it in respect to the domestic relations of the colored people? Do those who are married stick pretty closely together?—A. Some does and some don't.

Q. Do the colored people have any trouble from the whites in that respect?—A. No, sir.

Q. The white people do not interfere with the colored women?—A. No, sir; sometimes they does; but 'taint a general thing.

Q. Some say there is trouble of that kind and others say there is not?—A. Well, 'taint a general thing. But women that aint married—now there's a heap of trouble about that. Black women aint respected among the whites, and the reason is they make themselves unrespectable, because they haven't got any business, any work, and the men don't either.

Q. If they had employment, you think things would be better in that respect?—A. Yes, sir; but if a man wants to hire you, he won't offer you more than $6 or $8 a month. If I wanted to go to work for them, they would offer me about $6 a month and they would say, "Well, Jim, you're worth more than that, I know, but I cannot afford to give it," or, "Well, Jim, you're a good hand, and I'll give you $8 or $10 in the spring." Now, you see, I have a family to support, and I can't support them on that.

Q. You are in the prime of life, and must be about as good a hand as there is?—A. I am called as good as there is.

Q. And your wages would be only $8 or $10 a month?—A. Yes, sir; with board.

Q. And a house?—A. Yes; they furnish you a house.

Q. Do the people who hire you furnish you provisions for your whole family?—A. Yes, sir; they furnish them, but it comes out of your wages, provided you are paid.

Q. Do you mean that what the man furnishes you comes out of your wages?

A. No; he boards you and gives you $8 a month, but you have to feed your family out of your wages.

Q. How much will your board come to a week, or do you reckon it that way?—A. Sometimes it is higher than others, but at present the way we eat in this country, it would cost about 75 cents for meat and bread.

CHAPTER 2

The course of reconstruction

The vanquished whites: "no one can know how reduced we are"

In the immediate aftermath of the war, the white master class lay prostrate and stunned by the war's devastation. Many despaired of ever restoring a sense of normalcy to their lives and consequently left the country, with a sizable number going to South America and to England. For a brief time, during the early days of Reconstruction, there was a pervasive fear among such white southerners that their structured world of power and status had passed forever. Above all, the egalitarian schemes of the time aroused traditional white southern concerns of racial warfare. Edward Barnwell Heyward, who belonged to a wealthy South Carolina plantation family, had served in the Confederate army as a lieutenant in the engineers. He returned home embittered by his personal and physical losses during the war and, as reflected in the following letter to a northern friend, filled with deep pessimism toward the future.

Gadsden P. O.
S'Carolina
22nd Jan y 1866

My dear Jim

Your letter of date July 1865, has just reached me and you will be relieved by my answer, to find, that I am still alive, and extremely glad to hear from you.

I have myself, sometimes, thought that you had been among those who had joined the Army, and had given your life, for the cause, in which your nation, seems to much to pride itself, at this time; but I do not suppose so by your letter.

I am quite well, & have my family around me. During the war, I found time to get married again, and now have a most lovely woman, & baby eighteen

From Rodger E. Stroup (ed.), "Before and After: Three Letters from E. B. Heyward," *South Carolina Historical Magazine* (April 1973), 74: 100–102. Used by permission of the South Caroliniana Library, Charleston.

State Historical Society of Wisconsin.

"White geese" attacking Black schoolboy. Contemporary cartoon.

months old at my elbow. My daughter died during the war, and my Son is now a tall fellow who would astonish you by his size.

Our losses have been frightful, and we have, now, scarcely a support. My Father had five plantations on the coast, and all the buildings were burnt, and the negroes, now left to themselves, are roaming in a starving condition. Our farm near Charleston was abandoned to the negroes, leaving provisions, mules & stock. All is now lost, and the negroes, left to themselves, have made nothing, and seek a little food, about the city. Our Residence in the city, was sacked, and all the valuable furniture stolen and the house well riddled by shell & shot. Our handsome Residence in the country was burnt. The Enemy passed over all our property on the coast in their march from Savannah to Charleston, the whole country, down there, is now a howling wilderness. Up here, the Enemy came near, but did not find out my family, hid away in the woods and we have escaped. We live twenty miles from Columbia. Some of my relatives were there, during the occupation by Sherman, and suffered the terrible anxieties & losses of that dreadful event.

One of my Cousins at midnight, with her little children, in their night clothes stood in the street, and called Gen'l Sherman's attention to a soldier, at the moment setting fire, to her house across the street, and the man was arrested. The soldiers used some kind of combustible fluid which they splashed up on the houses, and those houses which escaped, show the marks on their side.

Such have been our sufferings and all was patiently endured. Our indignities have come since. We have lain down our arms and now submit.

I have served in the Army, my brother died in the Army, and every family has lost members. No one can know how reduced we are, particularly the refined & educated.

My Father and I, owned, near seven hundred negroes and they are all now wandering about like lost sheep, with no one to care for them.

They find the Yankee only a speculator, and they have no confidence in anyone. They very naturally, poor things, think that freedom means doing nothing, and this they are determined to do. They look to the government, to take care of them, and it will be many years, before this once productive country will be able to support itself. The former kind and just treatment of the slaves, and their docile and generous temper, makes them now disposed to be quite & obedient: but the determination of your Northern people to give them a place in the councils of the Country and make them the equal of the white man, will at last, bear its fruit, and we may *then* expect, them, to rise against the whites, and in the end, be exterminated themselves.

I am now interested in a school for the negroes, who are around me, and will endeavor to do my duty, to them, as ever before, but I am afraid their best days are past.

As soon as able, I shall quit the Country, and leave others to stand the storm, which I now see making up, at the North, which must soon burst upon *the whole* country, and break up everything which we have so long boasted of.

I feel now that I have *no country*, I *obey* like a subject, but I cannot love such a government. Perhaps the next letter, you get from me, will be from England.

I have, thank God! a house over my head & something to eat & am as ever always

yr friend, E. B. Heyward

P.S. Make my respects to your family.

White resurgence: "these people will have their own way"

The failure of the federal government immediately to establish a viable economic base for the freed slaves left them to their own devices, and from force of habit many returned to the slave quarters of their former masters. The documents below reflect views quite different from Edward Hayward's. The first is a military report written by a former Mississippi plantation owner who had volunteered to raise troops for the Union during the war. He offered a remarkably prophetic warning of southern white attempts to restore their predominance with a system he described as "more grinding and despotic than of old." The second selection is by a white officer commanding black troops in Mississippi. He observed that southern whites did not take seriously the then-unratified Thirteenth Amendment and, at the same time, schemed to install a new system of involuntary servitude. Both reports are significant for their emphasis on the need for massive federal intervention to relieve the plight of the blacks, including confiscation of large, white landholdings.

Vicksburg, Mississippi, July 8, 1865.

CAPTAIN: I have the honor to report that, in compliance with Special Orders No. 5, Headquarters Sub-district Southwest Mississippi, I proceeded to the counties of Madison, Holmes, and Yazoo, but that I did not reach Issaquena from the fact that the country between Yazoo City and that county has been so overflowed as to render the roads impassable.

I found a provost marshal of freedmen at Yazoo City—Lieutenant Fortu, who seemed to understand his duties well, and to have performed them satisfactorily. There was no officer of the bureau in either of the other counties. The whole country is in a state of social and political anarchy, and especially upon the subject of the freedom of the negroes, but very few who understand their rights and duties.

It is of the utmost importance that officers of the bureau should be sent to all the counties of the State to supervise the question of labor, and to insure the gathering of the growing crop, which, if lost, will produce the greatest suffering. In no case ought a citizen of the locality be appointed to manage the affairs of the freedmen: first, because these men will wish to stand well with their neighbors and cannot do justice to the negro; and secondly, because the negroes only know these men as oppressors of their race, and will have no confidence in their acts. The officers of the bureau should be especially charged to impress upon the freedmen the sacredness of the family relation and the duty of parents to take care of their children, and of the aged and infirm of their race. Where a man and woman have lived together as husband and wife, the relation should be declared legitimate, and all parties, after contracting such relations, should be compelled to legal marriage by severe laws against concubinage. Where parents have deserted their children, they should be compelled to return and care for them; otherwise there will be great suffering among the women and children, for many of the planters who have lost the male hands from their places threaten to turn off the women and children, who will become a burden to the community. The two evils against which the officers will have to contend are cruelty on the part of the employer, and shirking on the part of the negroes. Every planter with whom I have talked premised his statements with the assertion that "a nigger won't work without whipping." I know that this is not true of the negroes as a body heretofore. A fair trial should be made of free labor by preventing a resort to the lash. It is true that there will be a large number of negroes who will shirk labor; and where they persistently refuse compliance with their contracts, I would respectfully suggest that such turbulent negroes be placed upon public works, such as

From *Report of Carl Schurz on the States of South Carolina, Georgia, Alabama, Mississippi and Louisiana.* 39th Cong., 1st Sess., Senate Exec. Doc. No. 2, 1865, pp. 74–78.

rebuilding the levees and railroads of the State, where they can be compelled to labor, and where their labor will be of benefit to the community at large.

It will be difficult for the employers to pay their laborers quarterly, as required by present orders. Money can only be realized yearly on a cotton crop, because to make such a crop requires an entire year's work in planting, picking, ginning, and sending to market. The lien upon the crop secures the laborer his pay at the end of the year, for which he can afford to wait, as all the necessaries of life are furnished by the planter, who could not pay quarterly except at a great sacrifice.

The present orders recommend that the freedmen remain with their former masters so long as they are kindly treated. This, as a temporary policy, is the best that could be adopted, but I very much doubt its propriety as a permanent policy. It will tend to rebuild the fallen fortunes of the slaveholders, and re-establish the old system of class legislation, thus throwing the political power of the country back into the hands of this class, who love slavery and hate freedom and republican government. It would, in my opinion, be much wiser to diffuse this free labor among the laboring people of the country, who can sympathize with the laborer, and treat him with humanity.

I would suggest that great care be taken in the selection of officers of the bureau to be sent to the various counties. The revolution of the whole system of labor has been so sudden and radical as to require great caution and prudence on the part of the officers charged with the care of the freedmen. They should be able to discuss the question of free labor as a matter of political economy, and by reason and good arguments induce the employers to give the system a fair and honest trial.

Nowhere that I have been do the people generally realize the fact that the negro is free. The day I arrived at Jackson *en route* for Canton, both the newspapers at that place published leading editorials, taking the ground that the emancipation proclamation was unconstitutional, and therefore void; that whilst the negro who entered the army *might* be free, yet those who availed themselves not of the proclamation were still slaves, and that it was a question for the State whether or not to adopt a system of gradual emancipation. These seem to be the views of the people generally, and they expressed great desire "to get rid of these garrisons," when they hope "to have things their own way." And should the care and protection of the nation be taken away from the freedmen, these people will have their own way, and will practically re-establish slavery, more grinding and despotic than of old.

Respectfully submitted:

J. L. HAYNES,
Colonel First Texas Cavalry.

Railroad, Camp near Clinton, Miss., July 8, 1865.

SIR: I am induced by the suffering I daily see and hear of among colored people to address you this communication. I am located with my command four miles west of Clinton, Hines county, on the railroad. A great many colored people, on their way to and from Vicksburg and other distant points, pass by my camp. As a rule, they are hungry, naked, foot-sore, and heartless, aliens in their native land, homeless, and friendless. They are wandering up and down the country, rapidly becoming vagabonds and thieves from both necessity and inclination. Their late owners, I am led to believe, have entered into a tacit arrangement to refuse labor, food or drink, in all cases, to those who have been soldiers, as well as to those who have belonged to plantations within the State; in the latter case, often ordering them back peremptorily to their "masters."

One planter said in my hearing lately, "These niggers will all be slaves again in twelve months. You have nothing but Lincoln proclamations to make them free." Another said, "No white labor shall ever reclaim my cotton fields." Another said, "Emigration has been the curse of the country; it must be prevented here. This soil must be held by its present owners and their descendants." Another said, "The constitutional amendment, if successful, will be carried before the Supreme Court before its execution can be certain, and we hope much from that court!"

These expressions I have listened to at different times, and only repeat them here in order that I may make the point clear that there is already a secret rebel, anti-emigration, pro-slavery party formed or forming in this State, whose present policy appears to be to labor assiduously for a restoration of the old system of slavery, or a system of apprenticeship, or some manner of involuntary servitude, on the plea of recompense for loss of slaves on the one hand, and, on the other, to counterbalance the influence of Yankee schools and the labor-hiring system as much as possible by oppression and cruelty. I hear that negroes are frequently driven from plantations where they either belong, or have hired, on slight provocation, and are as frequently offered violence on applying for employment. Dogs are sometimes set upon them when they approach the houses for water. Others have been met on the highway by white men they never saw before, and beaten with clubs and canes, without offering either provocation or resistance. I see negroes almost every day, of both sexes, and almost all ages, who have subsisted for many hours on berries, often wandering they know not where, begging for food, drink, and employment.

It is impossible for me or any officer I have the pleasure of an acquaintance with to afford these people relief. Neither can I advise them, for I am not aware that any provisions have been, or are to be made to reach such cases.

The evil is not decreasing, but, on the contrary, as the season advances, is increasing.

I have heretofore entertained the opinion that the negroes flocked into the cities from all parts of the country; but a few weeks' experience at this station has changed my views on the subject, and I am now led to believe that those who have done so comprise comparatively a very small part of the whole, and are almost entirely composed of those belonging to plantations adjoining the towns. However, those who did go to the cities have been well cared for in comparison with those who have remained in the country. A small proportion of the latter class are well situated, either as necessary house-servants, body-servants, or favorites by inclination, as mistresses, or by necessity or duty, as each master may have been induced to regard long and faithful service or ties of consanguinity. Throughout the entire country, from Vicksburg to the capital of the State, there is but little corn growing. The manner of cultivating is very primitive, and the yield will be exceedingly small. I estimate that in this country fully one-half of the white population, and a great proportion of the colored people, will be necessitated either to emigrate, buy food, beg it, or starve. The negro has no means to buy, and begging will not avail him anything. He will then be compelled to emigrate, which, in his case, is usually equivalent to turning vagabond, or, induced by his necessities, resort to organized banding to steal, rob, and plunder. I am at a loss to know why the government has not adopted some system for the immediate relief and protection of this oppressed and suffering people, whose late social changes have conduced so much to their present unhappy condition, and made every officer in the United States army an agent to carry out its provisions. Were I employed to do so, I should seize the largest rebel plantation in this and every other county in the State, partition it in lots of suitable size for the support of a family—say ten acres each—erect mills and cotton gins, encourage them to build houses and cultivate the soil, give them warrants for the land, issue rations to the truly needy, loan them seed, stock, and farming utensils for a year or two, and trust the result to "Yankee schools" and the industry of a then truly free and proverbially happy people. Some other system might be better; few could be more simple in the execution, and in my opinion better calculated to "save a race" now floating about in a contentious sea without hope or haven.

I am, sir, very respectfully, your most obedient servant,

H. R. BRINKERHOFF,
Lieutenant Colonel 52d U. S. Colored Infantry, Commanding Detachment.

REGISTRATION AT THE SOUTH—SCENE AT ASHEVILLE, NORTH CAROLINA.—[SKETCHED BY A. W. THOMPSON.]

State Historical Society of Wisconsin.

Voting registration for freedmen, Asheville, North Carolina, 1867.

The politics and terror of reconstruction

The following selections reflect varied observations of the tense, tumultuous social upheaval that occurred in the South following the Civil War. They focus on problems generated by the freed slaves' attempts to participate as equal citizens in a reconstructed society. The documents illustrate the terror and unrest in Mississippi and Georgia that accompanied electoral contests in which federal military force tried to insure black participation. Not all segments of the society are specifically characterized here, but there are representatives of blacks, white radicals (or scalawags), and the military. The final selection is a sample of federal court confessions of members of the Ku Klux Klan in South Carolina who were convicted of attacks on blacks in 1871.

A Mississippi White Man and the Olive Branch

Hillsboro', Scott County, Mississippi,
January 14, 1869.

Sir:

The following observations with reference to reconstruction in Mississippi are respectfully submitted by one who has been a resident of this State since the surrender, and who, starting out with the olive-branch of conciliation, after careful and impartial study of the situation has arrived at the conclusions herein set forth:

As to my own county there was no pretence of a free expression of the voters at the election upon the ratification or rejection of the constitution. There was from the beginning a studied disregard of the merits of the issue, as of truth, and a feeling of terror created which few could resist. Merchants refused and granted favors according to political opinions; goods were refused for cash even, because proposed buyers were republicans; threats that republican freedmen should have no employment, and should be suffered to starve, were universal; and promises of provisions and employment to those voting the

From *Condition of Affairs in Mississippi,* 40th Congress, 3rd session, 1869, no. 52, part 2, pp. 274–275.

democratic ticket were equally extensive; certificates were sometimes given to freedmen for voting the democratic ticket, commending them to democrats for protection and employment; there were threats and warnings of violence for voting republican; prominent citizens publicly declared to crowds of freedmen that for voting republican the whites would be their enemies forever; numbers of white and black voted, through fear, against their wishes, and not a few of both went away to weep, literally, bitter tears for the humiliation; social and business ostracism and violence were threatened to whites; to vote the republican ticket was urged as a lasting disgrace to their innocent families; democratic committees were appointed professedly as challengers, but, in fact, these committees devoted their attention to watching for future persecution those who voted republican. On the part of whites there were apprehensions of personal violence, of loss of property by fire and in other ways, and of being broken up. To white men it was common to say, "You vote the republican ticket, and the back of my hand is to you as long as you live;" "We have no use for a man who votes republican;" "If you vote republican you are our enemy," &c.,&c. Republicans are held to be enemies to the people and country, and on this theory, if not restrained by federal power, every republican in the State would be driven out, or silenced in death or by intimidation. The writer was hanged in effigy at the county seat, only a few yards in front of the court-house, and "thus perish all Yankees" was the universal sentiment. The effigy was allowed to hang over the sidewalk of the principal street in town for a week, and I am not aware that leading citizens took any steps to take it down or to condemn the perpetrators.

On the part of the freedmen there was no threat, fraud, annoyance, persecution, or oppression to which they were not subjected. Taxes were collected pending the canvass, and these were a source of infamous frauds and impositions upon the freedmen. The damnable inequality in the assessment of taxes was made peculiarly effective. Real estate is made to pay about one-fiftieth less than capital, while the poor freedmen, without one cent of property, save the rags inherited from slavery, pay a poll-tax of from $8 to $15, often more than the real estate owner pays on 500 acres of land. One man in my county pays a State tax of only about $25 on 15,000 acres of land. The tax on the freedmen was persistently and defiantly declared by every white democrat in the county to have been imposed on them by and for the exclusive benefit of Yankees. Farmers, merchants, lawyers, ministers of the gospel, one and all, solemnly, sacredly, day by day assured the freedmen, on their hopes of heaven and on their honor as men, that these taxes were levied and collected by and for Yankee carpet-baggers! Hundreds of freedmen voted the democratic ticket on these assurances, and to this day they believe this blistering, sweeping fraud, for it was nothing else, and worked as wickedly, and with the same intent, as the fraudulent naturalization papers in New York or Philadelphia.

In this work local preachers were conspicuous, as they have been during all the troubles for years past. One preacher warned freedmen of the risk of violence if they voted republican. He said he would not harm them, but there were those who, in the woods, fields, or highways, would shoot them down. He was so anxious for secession that if the south did not secede he wanted Mississippi to secede; if Mississippi refused, he wanted Scott county to secede; and if Scott county refused, he declared his plantation should secede. During Sherman's march through here, in 1863, this preacher carried his shot-gun as a bushwhacker, but escaped with his life to become a base enemy of peace after the war. Another preacher, urging the work of "spotting" republicans during the election, as he phrased it, and believing defeat of the constitution to be the end of republican rule in Mississippi, triumphantly declared, "Old Tarbell will have to make tracks soon." Troops sent here at our request to protect us during election, talked openly and publicly of their desire to "shoot radicals and niggers," and democrats boasted of their good understanding with Gillem. There was in my county a complete reign of terror, and the election was a criminal farce—it was openly, glaringly, impudently so.

I have it from the lips of some of the best citizens of this county—men of character and of extensive business operations—that they acted with the democrats to save their persons from insult and violence, their property and business from destruction, and their families from starvation.

With suitable assurances of protection, necessary to both white and black, the evidence of hundreds will prove the foregoing to be scarcely a shadow of reality; in short, that the election was a base, deliberate, damnable swindle, which a general, looking through Andrew Johnson's eyes, could not perceive.

Without loyal juries, loyal officers, and loyal courts, complaints are idle. Indeed, men did not dare, nor dare they now, make complaints of the frauds and threats by which they were deprived of the privilege of voting according to their preferences.

That the constitution was rejected through fraud, threats, intimidations, and violence, or the fear of violence induced by those opposed, there is no sort of doubt.

Fear and Intimidation in Mississippi

Brandon, [Mississippi,] June 21, 1868.

Dear Sir:

I came here at the most exciting time probably that this place has known since the war; the democrats had a great meeting; among the speakers were Judge Potter; at one time I was in the court-house and saw him in the seats with

Ku Klux Klan raid, 1868.

colored men talking with them separately, causing them to promise to vote the democratic ticket. After this I learned a paper was circulated for them to sign, in which they promised to vote the democratic ticket, and about 100 names were received. The colored men were induced to do this by threats of being discharged, their supplies being stopped, and many were made drunk before this could be done. Supplies have already been stopped from those who would not promise to vote the democratic ticket. One man informs me his horse and wagon, valued at $150, is to be sold to satisfy an attachment for $9, on Saturday next, if not paid before; he has owing him $100 and over from white men; none will pay him, nor will the sale be stopped unless he votes democratic; but he is true steel and no signs of back down. Several colored men have had their lives threatened, and from the best information I can get there will be a row here unless a squad of troops are sent here to keep order. There is not a white republican in town; each register, clerk, judge of election, the sheriff and his deputies, are all strong democrats, and we may infer how much they will do in an event of that kind. It is now 11 a.m., and I go out at 1 p.m. Neither of the commissioners have arrived here yet; have not seen Myers or Brinson, but am informed that they are at work. I have colored men to go out to the other precincts if Evans or ——— do not come before I leave. The election will be held here on Thursday and Friday. No commissioner yet, 1 p.m., and I have to walk; the stable-keeper has failed to supply me—all of his horses went out yesterday and have not returned. I had one engaged at noon yesterday; don't know as it is intentional.

Since writing the above, and while out about ten minutes from my room, a K. K. K. warning was put under my door. Below is a copy, *verbatim et literatim:*

K. K. K.
DISMAL SWAMP.
11 hour.

2 D, × I ∧⎺.

Mene, mene, tekel upharsin. The bloody dagger is drawn; the trying hour is at hand; beware! Your steps are marked; the eye of dark chief is upon you. First he warns; then the avenging dagger flashes in moonlight.

By order of the Grand Cyclops:

⊥ I × T O.

Make a request of the post commander for the troops to be here on election days, or have them sent over on Wednesday, if possible.

Excuse haste, and my scribbling, mistakes, &c.

Respectfully, yours,

D. S. Harriman.

From *Condition of Affairs in Mississippi*, 40th Congress, 3rd session, 1869, no. 52, part 2, pp. 214–215.

The Ordeal of a Georgia White "Radical"

Lincoln County, [Georgia.]

Statement of Humphrey Curtis.

I reside in Lincoln county, at Tucker's Mills, about eight miles from Lincolnton. My name is Humphrey Curtis. Last Friday night, October 30, 1868, about midnight, some five or six persons disguised, four of whom I recognized as ——— and ———, a fifth, I thought was ———, came to my house and forcibly searched it, saying they were looking for my pistol. One of them struck me with his pistol on the forehead. They said there shouldn't a damned radical stay in the county. They took me from my house; and they had with them also two other men, named Abraham Brigsby and William Curtis. They made us take hold of one another and walk like soldiers, in single file. They marched us down to the mill, about half a mile from my house. They went into the mill and broke open my father's (William Curtis) box. My father is the miller, and had his things in the mill; they took out all his papers. They separated us, taking my father up the fence, Abraham over the fence, and leaving me where I was. I think we were about 15 paces apart; some of the disguised men going with each; two remained with me. I could not hear what was said by the others. They accused me of lying in wait to kill John Turpin and John Bussy; I denied it. They told me that I was not in as much danger as the others, to sit down by the mill; and they took Abraham and put a rope around his body and dragged him up and down the mill-pond, and they served my father in the same manner; then they took Abraham and my father on ahead, and told me to follow. They made me lie down in the mud with my face over the water, as though I was drinking; they let me get up. Then they made us all crawl upon the mill-dam on a log; they then told us all to get down into the water. Abraham made a plunge as though he was swimming or trying to swim off, and they all fired at him together. They thought that Abraham had escaped; they then commenced to coax him to come back, saying, "Come back and go home;" but Abraham did not come back. I saw Abraham try to climb up the bank, and then fall back dead. They then said to my father, "Old man, what can you tell us?" He said, "I cannot tell you anything." Then they said, "Farewell, old man," and fired upon him—I should think five or six shots, altogether. My father was killed instantly, and fell into the water. When I rose they fired on me; this was repeated three or four times. I got behind a rock, and they kept firing at me; then I crawled half in and half out of water, to a little island in the pond. I heard them say, "God damn him, he's gone." I must have fainted from bleeding, for I could not see anything then, and it was a bright moonlight night. When I came to I listened, and I

From *Condition of Affairs in Georgia,* 40th Congress, 3rd session, 1869, no. 52, part 1, pp. 59–60.

could not hear anybody. I laid there about one hour, and then I managed to get home, and in the night-time (Saturday night, October 31) some of my friends brought me down the river to Augusta. I have done nothing wrong that I know of, except I am a radical.

A true copy:

M. Frank Gallagher,
Brevet Captain U.S. Army, A.A.A. General.

The confessions of nightriders

AARON EZELL

I joined the Ku Klux Klan because they threatened me, and said they would whip me if I did not go into it; I have been on only two raids; there were three colored boys that we whipped; I was on the raid on Mr. Justice, at Rutherford; I joined the organization in March; I can read and write but a little; I am nearly forty years old.

Judge Bond. The sentence of the Court is, that you be fined ten dollars and imprisoned one year.

MONROE SCRUGGS

Why did I join the Klan? Well, I suppose, sir, it was for a want of sense; I have never been on but one raid; that was the one where Mr. Harris was whipped; I am going on twenty-one years old, but I can't neither read nor write; I work out for my living, hoeing; I did not know anything about the Ku Klux until I went on that raid, and I didn't want to go on another.

Judge Bryan, in passing sentence upon this prisoner, said:

The Court, in passing sentence upon you, looks upon your youth; you have not the responsibility of settled manhood, and it is but natural that you should have taken direction from those who were older than yourself, and you may have been impressed by the public sentiment around you. The Court seeks to find palliation for the enormities, the unmanly enormities, that have been committed. Striking men where men could not strike back to protect themselves, and where they had no redress or hope of redress; striking with masks on, and, therefore, striking without any responsibility! Whether these enormities

From *Proceedings in the Ku Klux Trials at Columbia, S.C. in the U.S. Circuit Court,* November Term 1871. (Columbia, S.C., Republican Printing Company, 1872), 777–781.

Klansmen in disguise.

have been committed on men, still more on women, they were wholly unmanly, and let me say utterly un–South Carolinian. Nothing could be so little characteristic of the State; nothing so calculated to bring disgrace upon the State; nothing so calculated to overturn and besmear its ancient, high and bright escutcheon. These stories afflict all men, but they peculiarly afflict him who now addresses you; I would be glad to regard them as exceptions; I must esteem them as in great measure exceptional, and I say to you, young as you are, you have brought reproach upon your State, and you have done wrong to its character. The greatest possible wrong that any sons of hers could do, would be to besmear and tarnish her ancient renown and reputation. In passing sentence upon you, we cannot but recollect your youth; we cannot but remember the disordered condition of the times; we cannot but recollect that the moral sense of our people, so recently engaged in war, and especially from the disorderly condition of things, may be, to some extent, blighted; we, therefore, feel justified in greatly modifying the sentence which has just been passed upon the prisoner who has arrived at full manhood. The sentence of the Court in your case is, that you be fined ten dollars and confined in prison for six months.

HENRY SURRATT

I joined the Ku Klux because they threatened to whip me if I didn't; I shouldn't have joined hadn't it been to have saved myself; I am about twenty years old; they threatened to whip everybody that didn't join the organization; I was never on nary a raid; I advised them not to go; I wasn't goin' to join them, but they said I would have to protect myself; they said I couldn't stay there if I didn't join them; that was in March; I have already been in jail about two months.

Mr. Corbin confirmed the statements of the prisoner.

Judge Bond. What are you going to do to protect yourself when you get home?

A. I don't know, sir; they have threatened us enough, I know.

Judge Bond. They will be likely to be quiet there in a month; and as you have been confined for two months, the sentence of the Court is, that you be imprisoned for one month.

The prisoner. I am quite willing to take that to have quiet there.

ANDREW CUDD

I am twenty-two years old; I can't read or write; I have been on two raids; on the raid that I went on, we whipped Jimmie Gaffner and Matt Scruggs; the chief of the Klan was Jonas Vassey; I shouldn't have joined the Klan, but they threatened to whip me, and they abused my folks right smart, and threatened to kill the girl that lived with me; they said if I didn't vote the Democratic ticket they'd give me five hundred lashes; one of my friends advised me to join it, for he said they would be sure to whip me if I didn't; I might have left, but I was so fixed that I could not get away; I had a family, and so had to stay with them.

Q. Are there churches in your neighborhood?

A. Yes, sir.

Q. Did all the members of the church belong to the organization?

A. Pretty much they did.

Judge Bryan. Did you join in whipping anybody yourself?

A. No, sir, indeed I didn't.

I have a wife and three children; pretty much all our Klan are here.

Judge Bond. The sentence of the Court in your case is, that you be imprisoned three months.

II

Life on the Closing Frontier: 1855-1890

CHAPTER 3

The Indian and
the progress
of civilization

The process of frontier settlement and expansion increased in tempo following the Civil War. The farmers' westward push and the great mineral discoveries of the period sharply renewed conflict with the Indians. The pattern was familiar: broken treaties, removal of the tribes to new reservations, and, finally, military repression. Indeed, without the full backing of the federal government and the army, the western settler, whether farmer or miner, would have had little opportunity for exploiting the land. Chief Seattle of the Puget Sound tribes clearly acknowledged the whites' superior force in a speech made in 1855 to the federal governor of the Washington Territory. Seattle's remarks were bitter, sarcastic, and pessimistic, yet also displayed the Indians' love of nature, reverence for life, and respect for traditions—all in dramatic contrast to the settlers' reckless use and plundering of the land. Robert Wright's reminiscences of frontier life in Kansas in the 1860s similarly portray the white people's contempt for their Indian adversaries. For Wright, life on the frontier was a great adventure "where every moment you were in terror of being attacked by Indians." Yet the Indians were just another element to battle, like the cold, the droughts, and the buffalo.

Chief Seattle Speaks

Yonder sky that has wept tears of compassion upon my people for centuries untold, and which to us appears changeless and eternal, may change. Today is fair. Tomorrow it may be overcast with clouds. My words are like the stars that never change. Whatever Seattle says the great chief at Washington can rely upon with as much certainty as he can upon the return of the sun or the seasons. The White Chief says that Big Chief at Washington sends us greetings of friendship and good will. This is kind of him for we know he has little need of our friendship in return. His people are many. They are like the grass that covers vast prairies. My people are few. They resemble the scattering trees of a storm-swept plain. The Great—and I presume—good White Chief sends us word that he wishes to buy our lands but is willing to allow us enough to live comfortably. This indeed appears just, even generous, for the Red Man no longer has rights that he need respect, and the offer may be wise also, as we are no longer in need of an extensive country.

There was a time when our people covered the land as the waves of a wind-ruffled sea cover its shell-paved floor, but that time long since passed away with the greatness of tribes that are now but a mournful memory. I will not dwell on,

From Clarence B. Bagley, "Chief Seattle and Angeline," *Washington Historical Quarterly* 22 (October 1931): 252–255. Used by permission of *Pacific Northwest Quarterly*. Material suggested by Diana Vari.

Blackfoot travois, 1880s.

nor mourn over, our untimely decay, nor reproach my pale face brothers with hastening it as we too may have been somewhat to blame.

Youth is impulsive. When our young men grow angry at some real or imaginary wrong, and disfigure their faces with black paint, it denotes that their hearts are black—and then they are often cruel and relentless, and our old men and old women are unable to restrain them. Thus it has ever been. Thus it was when the white man first began to push our forefathers westward. But let us hope that the hostilities between us may never return. We would have everything to lose and nothing to gain. Revenge by young braves is considered gain, even at the cost of their own lives, but old men who stay at home in times of war, and mothers who have sons to lose, know better.

Our good father at Washington—for I presume he is now our father as well as yours, since King George has moved his boundaries further north—our great and good father, I say, sends us word that if we do as he desires he will protect us. His brave warriors will be to us a bristling wall of strength, and his wonderful ships of war will fill our harbors so that our ancient enemies far to the northward—the Hidas and Timpsions, will cease to frighten our women, children and old men. Then in reality will he be our father and we his children. But can that ever be? Your God is not our God! Your God loves your people and hates mine. He folds his strong protecting arms lovingly about the pale face and leads him by the hand as a father leads his infant son—but He has forsaken His red children—if they are really His. Our God, the Great Spirit, seems also to have forsaken us. Your God makes your people wax strong every day. Soon they will fill all the land. Our people are ebbing away like a rapidly receding tide that will never return. The white man's God can not love our people or He would protect them. They seem to be orphans who can look nowhere for help. How then can we be brothers? How can your God become our God and renew our prosperity and awaken in us dreams of returning greatness. If we have a common Heavenly Father He must be partial—for He came to His pale-face children. We never saw Him. He gave you laws but had no word for His red children whose teeming multitudes once filled this vast continent as stars fill the firmament. No. We are two distinct races with separate origins and separate destinies. There is little in common between us.

To us the ashes of our ancestors are sacred and their resting place is hallowed ground. You wander far from the graves of your ancestors and seemingly without regret. Your religion was written on tables of stone by the iron finger of your God so that you could not forget. The Red Man could never comprehend nor remember it. Our religion is the traditions of our ancestors—the dreams of our old men, given them in the solemn hours of night by the Great Spirit; and the visions of our sachems, and is written in the hearts of our people.

Your dead cease to love you and the land of their nativity as soon as they pass the portals of the tomb and wander away beyond the stars. They are soon forgotten and never return. Our dead never forget the beautiful world that gave them being. They still love its verdant valleys, its murmuring rivers, its magnificent mountains, sequestered vales and verdant-lined lakes and bays, and ever yearn in tender, fond affection over the lonely hearted living, and often return from the Happy Hunting Ground to visit, guide, console and comfort them.

Day and night can not dwell together. The Red Man has ever fled the approach of the White Man as the morning mist flees before the rising sun.

However, your proposition seems fair, and I think that my folks will accept it and will retire to the reservation you offer them. Then we will dwell apart in peace for the words of the Great White Chief seem to be the voice of Nature speaking to my people out of dense darkness.

It matters little where we pass the remnant of our days. They will not be many. The Indian's night promises to be dark. Not a single star of hope hovers above his horizon. Sad-voiced winds moan in the distance. Grim Nemesis seems to be on the Red Man's trail, and wherever he goes he will hear the approaching footsteps of his fell destroyer and prepare to stolidly meet his doom, as does the wounded doe that hears the approaching footsteps of the hunter.

A few more moons. A few more winters—and not one of the descendants of the mighty hosts that once moved over this broad land or lived in happy homes, protected by the Great Spirit, will remain to mourn over the graves of a people—once more powerful and hopeful than yours. But why should I mourn at the untimely fate of my people? Tribe follows tribe, and nation follows nation, like the waves of the sea. It is the order of nature, and regret is useless. Your time of decay may be distant—but it will surely come, for even the White Man whose God walked and talked with him as friend with friend, can not be exempt from the common destiny. We may be brothers after all. We will see.

We will ponder your proposition and when we decide we will let you know. But should we accept it, I here and now make this condition—that we will not be denied the privilege without molestation, of visiting at any time the tombs of our ancestors, friends and children. Every part of this soil is sacred, in the estimation of my people. Every hillside, every valley, every plain and grove, has been hallowed by some sad or happy event in days long vanished. Even the rocks, which seem to be dumb and dead as they swelter in the sun along the silent shore thrill with memories of stirring events connected with the lives of my people, and the very dust upon which you now stand responds more lovingly to their footsteps than to yours, because it is rich with the dust of our ancestors and our bare feet are conscious of the sympathetic touch. Our departed braves, fond mothers, glad, happy-hearted maidens, and even the little children who lived here and rejoiced here for a brief season, still love these sombre solitudes and at eventide they grow shadowy of returning spirits. And when the last Red Man shall have perished, and the memory of my tribe shall have become a myth among the white man, these shores will swarm with the invisible dead of my tribe, and when your children's children think themselves alone in the field, the store, the shop, upon the highway, or in the silence of the pathless

Indian camp, Pine Ridge Agency, South Dakota, 1891.

woods, they will not be alone. In all the earth there is no place dedicated to solitude. At night when the streets of your cities and villages are silent and you think them deserted, they will throng with the returning hosts that once filled them and still love this beautiful land. The White Man will never be alone.

Let him be just and deal kindly with my people, for the dead are not powerless. Dead—I say? There is no death. Only a change of worlds.

Subduing the "Savages"

I came from the mountains in the spring of 1864 to Spring Bottom, on the Arkansas river. The Cheyennes, Arapahoes and Kiowas were committing many depredations along the Arkansas that summer.

Shortly after our arrival, my partner, Joe Graham, went to Fort Lyon after supplies to stand a siege, as we expected daily to be attacked, the hired man and myself remaining at the ranch to complete our fortifications. On the night of Graham's return I started for Point of Rocks, a famous on the Arkansas, twenty miles below our ranch, to take a mule which he had borrowed to help him home with his load.

The next morning at daylight our ranch was attacked by about 300 Indians, but the boys were supplied with arms and ammunition, and prepared to stand a siege. After they had killed one Indian and wounded a number of their ponies, the savages became more careful; they tried by every means in their power to draw the boys outside; they even rode up with a white flag and wanted to talk. Then they commenced to tell in Spanish, broken English, and signs, that they did not want to hurt the boys; they simply wanted the United States mail stock; and if it was given up they would go away. When this modest demand was refused, they renewed their attack with greater fury than ever before.

My wife and two children were with me at the ranch at the time, and, at the commencement of the fight, Mrs. Wright placed the little ones on the floor and covered them over with feather beds; then she loaded the guns as fast as the boys emptied them. She also knocked the clinking from between the logs of the building, and kept a sharp lookout on the movements of the Indians. Often did she detect them crawling up from the opposite side to that on which the boys were firing. Upon this information the boys would rush over to where she had seen them, and by a few well-directed shots make them more than glad to crawl back to where they had come from. This was long before the days of the modern repeating rifle, and of course they had only the old-fashioned muzzle-loaders.

For about seven hours the Indians made it very warm for the boys; then they

From R. M. Wright, "Personal Reminiscences of Frontier Life in Southwest Kansas," *Kansas Historical Collections: Transactions of the Kansas State Historical Society* 7 (1901–1902) : 53–59.

got together and held a big powwow, after which they rode off up the river. The boys watched them with a spy-glass from the top of the building until they were satisfied it was not a ruse on the part of the savages, but that they had really cleared out.

Graham then took my wife and two children, placed them in a canoe, and started down the Arkansas, which was very high at the time. The hired man saddled a colt that had never before been ridden, and left for the Point of Rocks. Strange as it may seem, this colt appeared to know what was required of him, and he ran nearly the whole distance—twenty miles—in less than an hour and a half. He was the only animal out of sixteen head that was saved from the vengeance of the Indians. He was a little beauty, and I really believe that the savages refrained from killing him because they thought they would eventually get him. He was saved in this manner: After the attack had been progressing for a long time and there came a comparative lull in the action, my wife opened the door a little to see what the Indians were up to, while the boys were watching at the loopholes; the colt observed Mrs. Wright, made a rush toward her, and she throwing the door wide open, the animal dashed into the room and remained there quiet as a lamb until the battle was over.

The Indians killed all our mules, horses, and hogs—we had of the latter some very fine ones—a great number of our chickens, and shot arrows into about thirty cows, several of which died. The majority of them recovered, however, although their food ran out of the holes in their sides for days and weeks until the shaft of the arrows dropped off, but, of course, the iron heads remained in their paunches; still they got well.

I had just saddled my horse, ready to start back to the ranch, when the hired man arrived, bringing the terrible news of the fight. He told me that I would find my wife and children somewhere on the river, if the savages had not captured them. "For my part," he said, "I am going back to my people in Missouri; I have had enough." He was a brave man, but a "tenderfoot," and no wonder the poor fellow had seen enough. His very soul had been severely tried that day. I at once called for volunteers, and a number of brave frontiersmen nobly responded; there were only two or three, however, who had their horses ready; but others followed immediately, until our number was swelled to about a dozen. A wagon and extra horses brought up the rear, to provide means of transportation for my wife and little ones.

When we had traveled thirteen miles, having carefully scanned every curve, bend and sand-bar in the stream, we discovered Graham, Mrs. Wright and the children about two miles ahead, Graham (God bless him!) making superhuman efforts to shove the boat along and keep it from upsetting or sinking. They saw us at the same moment, but they immediately put to cover on a big island. We shouted and waved our hats, and did everything to induce them to come to us, but in vain, for, as they told us afterward, the Indians had tried the same maneuvers a dozen times that day, and Graham was too wary to be caught with chaff. At last Mrs. Wright recognized a large, old, white hat I was wearing, and she told Graham that it was indeed her husband, Robert. When they reached the bank, we took them out of the canoe more dead than alive, for the frail, leaky craft had turned many times, but Graham and Mrs. Wright, by some means, had always righted it, and thus saved the little children.

A party went with me to our ranch the next day, and we witnessed a scene never to be forgotten; dead horses, dead hogs, dead cows and dead chickens piled one upon another in their little stockade. Two small colts were vainly tugging at their lifeless mothers' teats; a sad sight indeed, even to old plainsmen like ourselves. Both doors of the building were bored so full of bullet holes that you could hardly count them, as they lapped over each other in such profusion. Every window had at least a dozen arrows sticking around it, resembling the quills on a porcupine. The ceiling and walls inside the room were filled with arrows also. We thought we would follow up the trail of the savages, and while *en route* we discovered a government ambulance, wrecked, and its driver, who had been killed, with two soldiers and citizens, so horribly butchered and mutilated that the details are too horrible and disgusting to appear in print. They had also captured a woman and carried her off with them, but the poor creature, to put an end to her horrible suffering, hung herself to a tree on the banks of a creek northeast of where the Indians had attacked the ambulance. In consequence of her act, the savages called the place White Woman. The little stream bears that name to-day; but very few settlers, however, know anything of its sad origin. (It was on this creek, some years later, that the gallant Major Lewis met his death wound at the hands of the Indians, while bravely doing his duty.)

After the fight at Spring Bottom, I moved down to Fort Aubrey, where, in conjunction with Mr. James Anderson, I built a fine ranch. At that place we had numerous little skirmishes, troubles, trials, and many narrow escapes from the Indians. In 1866 I went to Fort Dodge. Now, one might be inclined to think that the kind of life I had been leading—the hard experience—that a person would be anxious to abandon it at the first favorable opportunity; but this is not so. It gives one a zest for adventure, for it is a sort of adventure that you become accustomed to; you get to like it; in fact, there is a fascination about it no one can resist. Even to a brave man—God knows I make no pretension to that honor—there is a charm to the life he cannot forego, yet I felt an irresistible power and could not permit myself to give it up.

Mr. A. J. Anthony and I bought out the Cimarron ranch, twenty-five miles west of Fort Dodge. The company of which we purchased were heartily tired of the place, and eager to sell, for two of their number had been brutally murdered by the Indians while attempting to put up hay. Anthony was an old "Overland stage messenger"; had seen lots of ups and downs with the Indians on the plains, and rather enjoyed them. So we got together some of the old-timers and went to making hay. Right there our troubles commenced. We both had seen a great deal of the Indians and their methods before; but we didn't realize what they could and would do when they took the notion. . . .

. . . Day after day the Indians would harass us in some manner, but they had not yet succeeded in killing any of our men, although they repeatedly ran off our stock, fired into and broke up our camp, until even the old-timers, men in whom we had placed the utmost confidence and depended upon in case of emergency, began to grow tired. They said it was too monotonous for them. I don't think they really understood the true definition of the word. Still we persisted, were hopeful, and continued to hire new men at from $75 to $100 a month for common hands; we had to have hay. We considered it no more than just to tell these new men, when we hired them, they would have to take desperate chances, and that was the reason we were paying such large wages. Well, the Indians finally exhausted us of our horse stock, and we had to resort to ponies; but they were too small and we got along very slowly. We were compelled to purchase a big span of mules of the United States mail company, for which we paid $600. Mr. Anthony was very proud of them, as he had often sat behind them when he was a messenger on the overland routes. They were named Puss and Jennie. The first morning they were sent to the haystack Anthony was in the corral stacking. After a while he came to the house, looking as proud as a peacock, and said to me: "Hear that machine? Ain't Puss and Jennie making it hum?" But the sound did not seem natural to me, so I grabbed a spy-glass and ascended to the lookout on top of the building. Sure enough, just as I expected, I saw two Indians come up, one on each side of the mules, pounding them over the back with their bows, and they were making it hum, while the boys in the camp were shooting as fast as they could load and fire, protecting the poor driver, who was running toward them for his life, with about two dozen of the red devils after him, whooping, yelling and shouting as they charged upon him. The two Indians who attacked the driver of the mowing-machine had watched their opportunity, rushed out of the brush on the bank of the river, and were upon him before he had the slightest idea of their presence, and running off with the mules. His two revolvers were strapped upon the machine, and he could do nothing but drop off behind from his seat, leave his weapons, and run for his life.

The government had ten men and a sergeant stationed at the ranch, on escort duty with the United States mail. One day while the men were at dinner, and a soldier was on guard outside, whom I suspected was asleep at the time, two Indians, who had stolen a couple of old mules from the stage station forty miles above rode by and fired at the sentinel, just for fun, I believe, or at least to wake him up, and then dashed down to the river, crossing close to a Mexican train. Quicker than thought they unsaddled their mules, threw them upon the backs of two freight horses that were picketed near, mounted them, and jumped off a steep bank five feet deep into the Arkansas and were over on the other side before the astonished Mexicans really knew what was going on.

The day before the same train had left a lame steer out in the sand-hills, and the wagon boss sent one of the hands back after it that morning. As soon as the two Indians crossed the river they spied the Mexican with the lame ox and immediately took after him. From the top of my building, with an excellent glass, I could plainly see their whole maneuverings. The savages circled around the poor "greaser" again and again; charged him from the front and rear and on both sides, until I actually thought they had ridden over him a dozen times, emptying their revolvers whenever they made a charge. They would only halt long enough to reload, and then were after him again. During all these tactics of the Indians, the Mexican never made any attempt to return their fire; that saved his life and scalp. They wanted to compel him to empty his revolvers, and then they could run up and kill him. Of course, from the distance, nearly two miles, I could not hear the report of the Indians' weapons, but I could see the smoke distinctly, and I knew that the Mexican had not fired a shot. Presently the poor fellow's horse went down, and he lay behind it for a while. Then he cut the girth, took off the saddle, and started for the river, running at every possible chance, using the saddle as a shield, stopping to show fight only when the savages pressed him too closely; then he would make another stand, with the saddle set up in front of him. After a few more unsuccessful charges, the Indians left him. When he had arrived safely at the train, they asked him why he had not fired a shot when the Indians rode so close to him. He stated if he had had a thousand shots he would have fired them all, but in crossing the river that morning his horse had to swim and his revolver got wet. (The cartridges were the old-fashioned kind, made of paper, and percussion caps the means of priming.) It was fortunate, perhaps; for if the Indians had surmised that his revolver would not go off, they would had his scalp dangling at their belts in short order.

I have seen with my glass from the lookout on top of my building at the ranch 200 or 300 wagons and 2000 head of mules and oxen, all waiting for the river to go down, so that they could cross; and I have watched a band of Indians charge upon them like an avalanche, kill the poor panic-stricken Mexican drivers as easily and unmercifully as a bunch of hungry wolves would destroy a flock of sheep. Then the savages would jump off their horses long enough to tear the reeking scalps from their victims' heads and dash away after fresh prey. They, of course, drove off many of the horses and cattle. Sometimes the owners would succeed in getting the majority of their stock into the corrals, and for days and weeks afterward the miserable mutilated oxen would struggle back to the river for water, some with their tails cut off close, some with ears gone, some with great strips of hide stripped from their bodies, others with arrows sticking out of them, the cruel shafts sunk deep into their paunches half way up to the feathers. The Indians did not care anything for the cattle as long as there was plenty of buffalo; they mutilated the poor creatures to show their damnable meanness. The horses, of course, they valued.

Once, while a train of wagons was waiting to cross, three or four of them having already made the passage, leaving the Mexican drivers on this side with the wagons loaded with loose wool, a lot of Indians swooped down upon them. When the men saw the savages, the poor defenseless wretches made for their wagons and concealed themselves under the wool, but the Indians followed them in and killed the last one with an old camp ax belonging to the train, afterwards mutilating their bodies in their usual barbarous manner. . . .

These constant skirmishes kept up till late in the fall; in November and December, 1868, the Indians made a treaty. . . .

The Sioux war, 1862: two views

The Sioux war in Minnesota offers a typical picture of stress on the frontier between the competing needs of the growing white settlements and long-standing Indian claims. The conflict erupted after the Sioux had agreed to a treaty ceding more lands, but found that dishonest government agents and traders reaped most of the benefits. Led by young dissidents, the Sioux raided white communities and within a few days killed over seven hundred settlers. The government dispatched troops to the area and finally suppressed the uprising by capturing over two thousand Sioux. Mass trials were held, and some three hundred Indians were sentenced to death. President Lincoln commuted most of the sentences, but on December 26, 1862, authorities hanged thirty-eight Sioux on a single scaffold. Big Eagle, a participant in the events, served three years of a ten-year sentence, after which he returned to Minnesota and converted to Christianity. His memoir, written some three decades after the war, is self-serving to some extent; nevertheless, it probably offers a fair summary of Indian grievances. The second selection is a letter from a woman survivor to her family in Norway. Guri Endreson, her husband, and children came to the "New Land" to settle and make a new life; instead they found "savages" who shattered their dreams and lives.

Big Eagle

I was born in the Indian village of my father near Mendota, in 1827, and am now sixty-seven years old. My father was Grey Iron, a subchief of the Mdewakanton Sioux. When he died I succeeded him as chief of the band and

From Kenneth Carley, ed., "As Red Men Viewed It: Three Indian Accounts of the Uprising," *Minnesota History* 38 (September 1962) : 126–143. Used with the permission of the Minnesota Historical Society.

adopted the name of his father, Wambde Tonka, which, as is commonly called, means the Big Eagle. When I was a young man I often went with war parties against the Chippewa and other enemies of my nation, and the six feathers shown in the headdress of my picture in the historical society at St. Paul stand for six Chippewa scalps that I took when on the warpath. By the terms of the treaties of Traverse des Sioux and Mendota in 1851, the Sioux sold all of their lands in Minnesota, except a strip ten miles wide on each side of the Minnesota River from near Fort Ridgely to the Big Stone Lake. The Mdewakanton and Wahpekute had their reservation up to the Yellow Medicine. In 1858 the ten miles of this strip belonging to the Mdewakanton and Wahpekute bands, and lying north of the river were sold, mainly through the influence of Little Crow. That year, with some other chiefs, I went to Washington on business connected with the treaty. The selling of that strip north of the Minnesota caused great dissatisfaction among the Sioux, and Little Crow was always blamed for the part he took in the sale. It caused us all to move to the south side of the river, where there was but very little game, and many of our people, under the treaty, were induced to give up the old life and go to work like white men, which was very distasteful to many.

Of the causes that led to the outbreak of August, 1862, much has been said. Of course it was wrong, as we all know now, but there were not many Christians among the Indians then, and they did not understand things as they should. There was great dissatisfaction among the Indians over many things the whites did. The whites would not let them go to war against their enemies. This was right, but the Indians did not then know it. Then the whites were always trying to make the Indians give up their life and live like white men—go to farming, work hard and do as they did—and the Indians did not know how to do that, and did not want to anyway. It seemed too sudden to make such a change. If the Indians had tried to make the whites live like them, the whites would have resisted, and it was the same way with many Indians. The Indians wanted to live as they did before the treaty of Traverse des Sioux—go where they pleased and when they pleased; hunt game wherever they could find it, sell their furs to the traders, and live as they could.

Then the Indians did not think the traders had done right. The Indians bought goods of them on credit, and when the government payments came the traders were on hand with their books, which showed that the Indians owed so much and so much, and as the Indians kept no books they could not deny their accounts, but had to pay them, and sometimes the traders got all their money. I do not say that the traders always cheated and lied about these accounts. I know many of them were honest men and kind and accommodating, but since I have been a citizen I know that many white men, when they go to pay their accounts, often think them too large and refuse to pay them, and they go to law about them and there is much bad feeling. The Indians could not go to law, but there was always trouble over their credits. Under the treaty of Traverse des

Iowa tribal chiefs and federal agents.

Sioux the Indians had to pay a very large sum of money to the traders for old debts, some of which ran back fifteen years, and many of those who had got the goods were dead and others were not present, and the traders' books had to be received as to the amounts, and the money was taken from the tribe to pay them. Of course the traders often were of great service to the Indians in letting them have goods on credit, but the Indians seemed to think the traders ought not to be too hard on them about the payments, but do as the Indians did among one another, and put off the payment until they were better able to make it.

Then many of the white men often abused the Indians and treated them unkindly. Perhaps they had excuse, but the Indians did not think so. Many of the whites always seemed to say by their manner when they saw an Indian, "I am much better than you," and the Indians did not like this. There was excuse for this, but the Dakota did not believe there were better men in the world than they. Then some of the white men abused the Indian women in a certain way and disgraced them, and surely there was no excuse for that.

All these things made many Indians dislike the whites. . . .

As the summer advanced, there was great trouble among the Sioux—trouble among themselves, trouble with the whites, and one thing and another. The war with the South was going on then, and a great many men had left the state and gone down there to fight. A few weeks before the outbreak the president called for many more men, and a great many of the white men of Minnesota and some half-breeds enlisted and went to Fort Snelling to be sent south. We understood that the South was getting the best of the fight, and it was said that the North would be whipped. . . .

It began to be whispered about that now would be a good time to go to war with the whites and get back the lands. It was believed that the men who had enlisted last had all left the state, and that before help could be sent the Indians could clean out the country, and that the Winnebago, and even the Chippewa, would assist the Sioux. It was also thought that a war with the whites would cause the Sioux to forget the troubles among themselves and enable many of them to pay off some old scores. Though I took part in the war, I was against it. I knew there was no good cause for it, and I had been to Washington and knew the power of the whites and that they would finally conquer us. We might succeed for a time, but we would be overpowered and defeated at last. I said all this and many more things to my people, but many of my own bands were against me, and some of the other chiefs put words in their mouths to say to me. When the outbreak came Little Crow told some of my band that if I refused to lead them to shoot me as a traitor who would not stand up for his nation, and then select another leader in my place.

You know how the war started—by the killing of some white people near Acton, in Meeker County. I will tell you how this was done, as it was told me by all of the four young men who did the killing. . . .

They told me they did not go out to kill white people. They said they went over into the Big Woods to hunt; that on Sunday, August 17, they came to a settler's fence, and here they found a hen's nest with some eggs in it. One of them took the eggs, when another said: "Don't take them, for they belong to a white man and we may get into trouble." The other was angry, for he was very hungry and wanted to eat the eggs, and he dashed them to the ground and replied: "You are a coward. You are afraid of the white man. You are afraid to take even an egg from him, though you are half-starved. Yes, you are a coward, and I will tell everybody so." The other replied: "I am not a coward. I am not afraid of the white man, and to show you that I am not I will go to the house and shoot him. Are you brave enough to go with me?" The one who had called him a coward said: "Yes, I will go with you, and we will see who is the braver of us two." Their two companions then said: "We will go with you, and we will be brave, too."

They all went to the house of the white man (Mr. Robinson Jones), but he got alarmed and went to another house (that of his son-in-law, Howard Baker), where were some other white men and women. The four Indians followed them and killed three men and two women (Jones, Baker, a Mr. Webster, Mrs. Jones and a girl of fourteen). Then they hitched up a team belonging to another settler and drove to Shakopee's camp (six miles above Redwood Agency), which they reached late that night and told what they had done, as I have related.

The tale told by the young men created the greatest excitement. Everybody was waked up and heard it. Shakopee took the young men to Little Crow's house (two miles above the agency), and he sat up in bed and listened to their story. He said war was now declared. Blood had been shed, the payment would be stopped, and the whites would take a dreadful vengeance because women had been killed. Wabasha, Wacouta, myself, and others still talked for peace, but nobody would listen to us, and soon the cry was "Kill the whites and kill all these cut-hairs who will not join us."

A council was held and war was declared. Parties formed and dashed away in the darkness to kill settlers. The women began to run bullets and the men to clean their guns. . . .

Guri Endreson

Harrison P. O., Monongalia Co.,
Minnesota, December 2, 1866

Dear Daughter and your husband and children, and my beloved Mother:

I have received your letter of April 14th, this year, and I send you herewith

From Theodore C. Blegen, ed., "Guri Endreson, Frontier Heroine," *Minnesota History* 10 (December 1929): 425–430. Used with the permission of the Minnesota Historical Society.

Sioux Massacre, 1861. Contemporary drawing.

my heartiest thanks for it, for it gives me great happiness to hear from you and to know that you are alive, well, and in general thriving. I must also report briefly to you how things have been going with me recently, though I must ask you to forgive me for not having told you earlier about my fate. I do not seem to have been able to do so much as to write to you, because during the time when the savages raged so fearfully here I was not able to think about anything except being murdered, with my whole family, by these terrible heathen. But God be praised, I escaped with my life, unharmed by them, and my four daughters also came through the danger unscathed. Guri and Britha were carried off by the wild Indians, but they got a chance the next day to make their escape; when the savages gave them permission to go home to get some food, these young girls made use of the opportunity to flee and thus they got away alive, and on the third day after they had been taken, some Americans came along who found them on a large plain or prairie and brought them to people. I myself wandered aimlessly around on my land with my youngest daughter and I had to look on while they shot my precious husband dead, and in my sight my dear son Ole was shot through the shoulder. But he got well again from this wound and lived a little more than a year and then was taken sick and died. We also found my oldest son Endre shot dead, but I did not see the firing of this death shot. For two days and nights I hovered about here with my little daughter, between fear and hope and almost crazy, before I found my wounded son and a couple of other persons, unhurt, who helped us to get away to a place of more security. To be an eyewitness to these things and to see many others wounded and killed was almost too much for a poor woman, but, God be thanked, I kept my life and my sanity, though all my movable property was torn away and stolen. But this would have been nothing if only I could have had my loved husband and children—but what shall I say? God permitted it to happen thus, and I had to accept my heavy fate and thank Him for having spared my life and those of some of my dear children.

I must also let you know that my daughter Gjaertru has land, which they received from the government under a law that has been passed, called in our language "the Homestead law," and for a quarter section of land they have to pay sixteen dollars, and after they have lived there five years they receive a deed and complete possession of the property and can sell it if they want to or keep it if they want to. She lives about twenty-four American miles from here and is doing well. My daughter Guri is away in house service for an American about a hundred miles from here; she has been there working for the same man for four years; she is in good health and is doing well; I visited her recently, but for a long time I knew nothing about her, whether she was alive or not.

My other two daughters, Britha and Anna, are at home with me, are in health, and are thriving here. I must also remark that it was four years last August 21 since I had to flee from my dear home, and since that time I have not been on my land, as it is only a sad sight because at the spot where I had a happy home there are now only ruins and remains left as reminders of the terrible Indians. Still I moved up here to the neighborhood again this summer. A number of families have moved back here again so that we hope after a while to make conditions pleasant once more. Yet the atrocities of the Indians are and will be fresh in memory; they have now been driven beyond the boundaries of the state and we hope that they never will be allowed to come here again. I am now staying at the home of Sjur Anderson, two and a half miles from my home. I must also tell you how much I had before I was ruined in this way. I had seventeen head of cattle, eight sheep, eight pigs, and a number of chickens; now I have six head of cattle, four sheep, one pig; five of my cattle stayed on my land until in February, 1863, and lived on some hay and stacks of wheat on the land; and I received compensation from the government for my cattle and other movable property that I lost. Of the six cattle that I now have, three are milk cows and of these I have sold butter, the summer's product, a little over two hundred and thirty pounds; I sold this last month and got sixty-six dollars for it. In general I may say that one or another has advised me to sell my land, but I would rather keep it for a time yet in the hope that some of my people might come and use it; it is difficult to get such good land again, and if you, my dear daughter, would come here, you could buy it and use it and then it would not be necessary to let it fall into the hands of strangers. And now in closing I must send my very warm greetings to my unforgetable, dear mother, my dearest daughter and her husband and children, and in general to all my relatives, acquaintances, and friends. And may the Lord by His grace bend, direct, and govern our hearts so that we sometime with gladness may assemble with God in the eternal mansions where there will be no more partings, no sorrows, no more trials, but everlasting joy and gladness, and contentment in beholding God's face. If this be the goal for all our endeavors through the sorrows and cares of this life, then through his grace we may hope for a blessed life hereafter, for Jesus sake.

CHAPTER 4

The buffalo hunt: profit and "sport"

The destruction of the prairie buffalo in the late nineteenth century was an ecological disaster of endless consequences. The buffalo, of course, was essential to the Indians, providing them with such necessities as food, shelter, and fuel. But beginning in the late 1860s, professional hunters ruthlessly slaughtered the great beasts, primarily for their hides. The hunters pursued their quarry for profit, a purpose somewhat understandable, notwithstanding the mindlessness and wastefulness of their work. Throughout the nineteenth century, American extravagance with natural resources amounted to a national scandal. And nothing more exemplified the situation than the "sport" of buffalo hunting from the security of a moving train. One observer commented that "it would seem to be hardly possible to imagine a more novel sight than a small band of buffalo loping along within a few hundred feet of a railroad train in rapid motion, while the passengers are engaged in shooting, from every available window, with rifles, carbines, and revolvers." So much for "sport," for the millions of Great Plains' buffalo were nearly extinct by 1885. The next selections offer memoirs from the 1870s by both the professional and the "sportsman."

W. S. Glenn, Buffalo Hunter

. . . About this time the hunt had grown to such an enormous business that J. R. Lobenstien [Loganstien], a capitalist of that time, and ram rodder of the buffalo hunt, . . . furnished the capital and contracts were sub-let for robe hides, dry hides, bull hides, etc. Merchants were furnished supplies, equipments, etc., [and] they in turn furnished smaller men, who kept up with hunters ready to supply them. An enormous amount of this business was done on time. As they had begun to make money out of it, they would supply any hunter who had a team and wagon. Now all this while the hunter was pegging away and it was not until afterwards that they got it down to a system to make it profitable over a scant living.

There was several methods to kill them and each one adopted his own course and plan. They would get together and while one gained a point from another, he, in turn, would gain a point from him. One method was to run beside them, shooting them as they ran. Another was to shoot from the rear, what was termed tail shooting: [always shooting] the hindmost buffalo and when a day's hunt was done, they would be strung on the ground for a mile or more, from ten to fifteen yards apart, and in this way the skinner had so much territory to go over he couldn't make wages.

From Rex W. Strickland, ed., "The Recollections of W.S. Glenn, Buffalo Hunter," *Panhandle-Plains Historical Review* 22 (1949): 20–26. Reprint permission courtesy of Panhandle-Plains Historical Society.

State Historical Society of Wisconsin.

Buffalo Hunting, 1870s.

We first noticed that the buffaloes always went around a ravine or gulch, unless going for water straight down a bluff; and as the buffalo always followed these trails a man on foot by a mere cut-off of a hundred yards could cut him off. That is why they was so far apart in tail-hunting, as it was called.

Hunting this way, the skinner and his wagon and team would have to travel to get in a day's work to make it profitable. Another method was to start out in the morning, which was most generally daylight both winter and summer. The hunter would start on horseback and when he came to a high place he would find out the direction of the wind, . . . and would then know which way to approach them. He would then proceed until he came to a bunch of buffalo, and if there was no ravine to get near, he would dismount, hobble or lariat his horse or turn him loose—whatever method he was used to—and proceed to crawl on his stomach so as to get near enough to shoot into the main herd. They would then run off two or three hundred yards, stopping to look back; if they happened to get wind of him at the second shot, they would not halt for a mile, and sometimes not for five. Sometimes the whole herd running would be moving for miles and in this way making his rounds [he] would often run or walk some twenty-five or thirty miles and come into camp from the opposite direction from which he had left his horse and would have to walk after him. This system was afterwards dubbed "tenderfoot" hunting and did not often pay expenses for either hunter or skinner.

Another method of hunting was to leave your horse out of sight after you had determined the direction and course of the wind, and then get as near as possible. If the herd was lying at rest, he would pick out some buffalo that was standing up on watch and shoot his ball in the side of him so that it would not go through, but would lodge in the flesh; as on many times it had been proven by men [who were] well hid and the wind taking the sound of the gun and the whizz of the bullet off, [that] if a ball passed through a buffalo the herd would stampede and run for miles. A buffalo shot in this manner would merely hump up his back as if he had the colic and commence to mill round and round in a slow walk. The other buffalo sniffing the blood and following would not be watching the hunter, and he would continue to shoot the outside cow buffalo; if there were old cows they would take them as there would be some two or three offsprings following her. If she would hump up, he would know that he had the range, and in this way hold the herd as long as they acted in this way as well as the well trained cowpuncher would hold his herd, only the hunter would use his gun. This was termed mesmerising the buffalo so that we could hold them on what we termed a stand, which afterwards proved to be the most successful way of killing the buffalo.

It was not always the best shot but the best hunter that succeeded, that is, the man who piled his buffalo in a pile so as to be more convenient for the skinner to get at and not have to run all over the country.

Beginning about the first of November and up until the middle of February, we were killing expressly for the robes. At this time of the year, all bull buffalo over three years old were separated from the cows and yearlings, going in herds by themselves, and were classed scrubhorn bulls, scarcely never seeing a cow in a herd of these scrubhorn bulls. The hunter could easily tell a cow herd at a distance from a herd of these scrubhorn bulls.

The hunter was hired by the piece: if robe hides were worth $3.00, [he was] given twenty-five cents for every one that he killed and was brought in by the skinners—was tallied up at camp. It was the camp rustler's business to keep tally of the number of hides killed each day. If the hides were worth $2.50, he [the hunter] got 20 cents; $2.00, he got 15 cents; $1.50, he got 10 cents; and $1.00, he got 5 cents.

All the cows shot at this season of the year were not classed as robes, as she would sometimes be poor and had not shed on the hip and flank, thus having a patch of dead hair and classed as a cow hide, and worth $1.50. The young bulls of three years of age were classed as spikes and equal to a cow hide. Smaller buffalo, such as small cows two or three years old, were classed as kips and were worth from 75 cents to $1.50, smaller yet from 25 to 75 cents, and were seldom shot except by accident, as a stray shot, or staying with their mother and standing around would be dangerous to leave on a stand.

. . . At the Doby Walls fight [i.e., the Adobe Walls, June 27, 1874], the hunters [used] all classes of guns, such as the Spencer, Springfield, Winchester and six-shooters, also all classes of buffalo guns, including a new sample 45, which Sharp had just sent out, . . . [Billy Dixon's famous long shot, so Glenn says, was made with the new 45-caliber Sharp.] Still some were not satisfied, so went outside and stepped off a 150 yards and commenced to pile dry bull hides ten in a bunch, and began to shoot with all four guns—as they went through so easily, they added more and continued to add until they had shot through 32 [hides] and one bullet stook in the thirty-third one and it proved to be the new gun. All had to have a shot with the new gun and as it gave entire satisfaction, they sent word back that this was the gun for the buffalo, and all of them ordered a gun. Sharp began to manufacture these rifles as fast as he could in various lengths and this gun, as it afterwards proved[,] was the cause of the extermination of the buffalo[,] as before this they had increased faster than killed out as it took too many shots to get a buffalo.

[Mean] While the hunter would be looking over his dead and wounded and cutting out the tongue, hump, and sometimes the tallow, it being the hunter's business to take these out while the buffalo was fresh, throwing them on some tree or rock where the wolves could not get them. In some instances if the hunter did good work the skinner could not keep up with him. Where the buffalo would be killed one day and skinned the next, [they] would be called stinkers. A buffalo left with his hide on will sour even in freezing weather, if skinned right after killing, would not smell for months if his entrails were removed.

I have seen their bodies so thick after being skinned, that they would look like logs where a hurricane had passed through a forrest *[sic]*. If they were lying on a hillside, the rays of the sun would make it look like a hundred glass windows. These buffalo would lie in this way until warm weather, drying up, and I have seen them piled fifty or sixty in a pile where the hunter had made a stand. As the skinner commenced on the edge, he would have to roll it out of the way to have room to skin the next, and when finished they would be rolled up as thick as saw logs around a mill. In this way a man could ride over a field and pick out the camps that were making the most money out of the hunt. . . .

We will now describe a camp outfit. They would range from six to a dozen men, there being one hunter who killed the buffalo and took out the tongues, also the tallow. As the tallow was of an oily nature[,] it was equal to butter[;] [it was used] for lubricating our guns and we loaded our own shells[,] each shell had to be lubricated and [it] was used also for greasing wagons and also for lights in camp. Often chunks as large as an ear of corn were thrown on the fire to make heat. This [i.e., the removal of the tallow] had to be done while the meat was fresh, the hunter throwing it into a tree to wind dry[;] if the skinner forgot it, it would often stay there all winter and still be good to eat in the spring and better to eat after hanging there in the wind a few days.

We will return to the wagon man[.] [There were] generally two men to the wagon and their business was to follow up the hunter, if they were not in sight after the hunter had made a killing, he would proceed in their direction until he had met them, and when they would see him, he would signal with his hat where the killing was. If they got to the buffalo when they were fresh, their duty was to take out all the humps, tongues and tallow from the best buffalo. The hunter would then hunt more if they did not have hides enough to make a load or finish their day's work.

A remarkable good hunter would kill seventy-five to a hundred in a day, an average hunter about fifty, and a common one twenty-five, some hardly enough to run a camp. It was just like in any other business. A good skinner would skin from sixty to seventy-five, an average man from thirty to forty, and a common one from fifteen to twenty-five. These skinners were also paid by the hide[,] about five cents less than the hunter was getting for killing, being furnished with a grind stone, knives and steel and a team and wagon. The men were furnished with some kind of a gun, not as valuable as Sharp's rifle, to kill cripples with, also kips and calves that were standing around. In several incidents [instances?] it has been known to happen while the skinner was busy, they would slip up and knock him over. Toward the latter part of the hunt, when all the big ones were killed, I have seen as many as five hundred up to a thousand in a bunch, nothing but calves and have ridden right up to them, if the wind was right. . . .

E. N. Andrews, Sportsman

Excursions over the "Plains" are becoming so common as to excite little or no attention. One can now ride over that broad expanse extending beyond the borders of civilization on the east, to and beyond the Rocky Mountains, in the most elegant coaches drawn by the untiring horse of iron.

In boyhood, when on some gunning excursion for game so infinitesimal as to be unworthy of mention, it was considered unwise to reveal a favorable resort, lest other Nimrods should go and steal our honors. But on the occasion referred to in this sketch, having had our views philanthropic enlarged a little, we shall not hesitate to tell, from actual observations, something of the Indian hunting-grounds of the Plains, which form the open porch to the mountains. It will, however, be as impossible to describe the scenes we saw, or the impressions produced, as it is for the poet fully to paint with words all the finer emotions of his soul.

Although these excursions are of common occurrence since the laying of the rails, and will ever continue so, yet to the writer the trip revealed scenes and events altogether new and striking, and such as can never be forgotten. We played a little on the border-lands; while the limitless area, where roam the Indian and his counterpart the buffalo, together with the wolf, the prairie-dog and the antelope, swift of foot, extends hundreds of miles farther westward, and thousands northward and southward.

Our excursion party, organized for the benefit of a church in that place, and numbering about three hundred, left Lawrence, Kansas, Tuesday, A. M., at 10 o'clock, October 6, 1868, by the Kansas Pacific Railway. Our train consisted of five passenger coaches, one smoking car, one baggage and one freight car. The two latter were used for the commissary, although on our way back the freight car was devoted to another purpose.

The Lawrence Cornet Band, which went along, entertained us upon the platform while our large company were undergoing the slow process of shipment. Our engine (all honor to her for having "done what she could") being of rather a consumptive tendency, drew us not very rapidly toward the Occident, especially along the inevitably upward acclivities which lay in her track toward the Rocky Mountains. . . .

There were seventy-five or eighty guns on board, and the writer bagged the first game, namely, one quail, while the train stopped near a plowed field. He does not boast of this, however, as most of the guns were rifles, while he had a shot-and-rifle combined—the right kind for a variety of game. . . .

It was now tea time; the day had been comfortable and pleasant. One of those rare sunset scenes which are not uncommon to the people of Kansas, greeted our sight, to describe which were impossible. Suffice it to say, that the golden

From E. N. Andrews, "A Buffalo Hunt by Rail," *Kansas Magazine* 3 (May 1873) : 450-455.

flood which extended eastward along the northern horizon, gradually ended in a distinctly violet hue, while the dark clouds above seemed to compress this evening glory, as they shut down from above, within the compass of a narrow space, making the scene more intense. But as joy and beauty are often accompanied by tears, so did not this day close without a change. We went on to Ellsworth, where we spent the night, arranging our seats, (for there were no sleeping-cars,) as best we could for a night's rest. At nine o'clock the wind had changed from south to north, and howled frightfully, as if to blow the cars from the track. The rain came, beating through every crevice; the lightning flashed, the temperature became quite cold, and there was a prospect of an uncomfortable night. But fires were kindled, and we rested as well as we could, with feet as high as our heads, while we wished for day.

At 5 o'clock A. M., on Wednesday, we left Ellsworth, near which is Fort Harker, and proceeded. The all-important question, revealing very plainly the thought and desire of all, was: "Where shall we see the buffalo?" "Are there any buffalo about here?" These and similar interrogatories were put to everybody we could find, especially to the colored soldiers or guards at the various water-tanks. When told that we should soon see the "animals," all were on the *qui vive;* the rifles were made ready; all eyes were strained lest some object should escape our notice. And it is no wonder that there was this hopeful expectancy, for most of us had probably never seen the bison, the mythic autocrat of the Plains! Nor did we anticipate a very near proximity to any large number of those animals. For one, however, I ardently desired to see a buffalo, a single one, at least, before the close of my mortal existence, especially since this is so peculiarly an American animal. . . .

We now arrived at Fort Hays and Hays City, the latter a poor gambling-place. Indeed, these frontier towns seem mostly to have been inhabited for the purpose of gambling with and thus robbing men coming in from the mines, or with cattle from over the Plains.

Here we were informed that there were plenty of buffalo twenty-five miles ahead! Could we believe it? We rolled onward on the iron track, but looked in vain on either side for the chief object of attraction. A few were seen in the dim distance; but this was an aggravation. We continued to shoot at prairie-dogs, and gathered, when the train stopped at the water-tanks, the cactus,—the kind called prickly-pear. There is also another kind, the sword-cactus, growing in this region. We met another train which had on board several quarters of buffalo-meat, also General Sheridan. But the latter seemed of little account to us buffalo-hunters, just then, since we had seen the tracks or evidences of the "animals." We were now told that ten miles farther on we should find them.

With minds still dubious on the subject, when near the 325th mile-stone, (counting from State Line on the Missouri River, where the road begins,) we began to see buffalo near at hand, or within a quarter of a mile of the track. But what a sight was gradually unfolded to our vision! In the distance, as if upon a gentle slope, we beheld at least a thousand buffalo feeding, though this was not a circumstance to that which followed. For ten miles vast numbers continued in sight; and not only for this short (?) distance, but for forty miles, buffalo were scattered along the horizon, some nearer and others more remote. In estimating the number, the only fitting word was "innumerable;" one hundred thousand was too small a number, a million would be more correct. Besides, who could tell how many miles those herds, or *the* herd, extended beyond the visible horizon? It were vain to imagine! Antelope and wolves continued to be seen here and there, the latter skulking near the carcasses of buffalo scattered all along the Plains near the track. . . .

Another thing noticeable: what gives to the telegraph-poles in this region that smooth, greasy appearance a few feet from the base? That is where the animals have rubbed themselves when passing. Thanks to you, O Telegraph Company, in behalf of the bison. This is a rare luxury for our shaggy-coated herds which inhabit where no trees are. But while noticing this appearance of the poles, a suggestive thought came into my mind. Is not this pushing and rubbing of the buffalo against the telegraph poles, in his onward march northward or southward over his own long-inhabited feeding-grounds, an effort of his nature to repel the encroachments of civilization, as fitly embodied in this pioneer agency of electricity? So it seemed. And is it strange that the herdsmen of these animals, the red men, should also refuse to stand and look with complacency upon the on-reaching iron trail of the white man, bearing the shrieking locomotive far out into the depths of his hunting-ground, and disturbing the quiet and sanctity of that boundless realm? Without apologizing for the cowardly depredations and hostile demonstrations of the Indian, who was then on the "war-path," we can yet see something that may, from his stand-point, look like a provocation sufficient to warrant all this hostility.

But to return to the actual sights and the sports of our party. At about 6:30 o'clock on Wednesday evening, October 7th, though not anticipating any sport at close quarters, (since we were told that on the morrow the train would return to the hunting-ground, so that we could have all day with the buffalo and hunt to our satisfaction,) when at the 365th mile-post we saw buffalo near at hand. Three bulls were on the left of the track, though nearly all that we had seen were on the right, or north of that barrier, while now on their southward course, feeding in their slow advance toward winter-quarters in Texas or New Mexico. Of those three noble wanderers, one was doomed to fall before the bullets of the excursionists. They all kept pace with the train for at least a quarter of a mile, while the boys blazed away at them without effect. It was their design to get ahead of the train and cross over to the main body of their fellows; and they finally accomplished their object. The cow-catcher, however, became almost a bull-catcher, for it seemed to graze one as he passed on the jump. As soon as the three were well over upon the right, they turned backward, at a small angle away from the train, and then it was that powder and ball were brought into requisition! Shots enough were fired to rout a regiment of men. Ah! see that bull in advance there; he has stopped a second; he turns a kind of reproachful look toward the train; he starts again on the lope a step or two; he hesitates; poises on the right legs; a pail-full of blood gushes warm from his nostrils; he falls flat upon the right side, dead. One of the remaining companions turns a farewell look upon the vanquished one, and then starts off over the prairie toward the herd. We had expected no such *coup d' essai* on that day, especially so late in the evening, and the pleasure and excitement were all the greater because so unexpected. The engineer was kind enough to shut off the steam; the train stopped, and such a scrambling and screeching was never before heard on the Plains, except among the red men, as we rushed forth to see our first game lying in his gore. The writer had the pleasure of first putting hands on the dark locks of the noble monster who had fallen so bravely. Another distinguished himself by mounting the fallen brave. Then came the ladies; a ring was formed; the cornet band gathered around, and, as if to tantalize the spirits of all departed buffalo, as well as Indians, played Yankee Doodle. I thought that "Hail to the Chief," would have done more honor to the departed.

And now butcher-knives and butchers were in requisition. "Let us eviscerate and carry home this our first captive without further mutilation, that we may give our friends the pleasure of seeing the dimensions of the animal." This seemed a good plan, and we proceeded to carry it out. After the butchers had done their work, a rope was attached to the horns, and the animal, weighing about fifteen hundred pounds, was dragged to the cars and thence lifted on board the freight-car, a few of our party climbing upon the top of the car, the better to pull on the rope. It was now getting dark, and as the head of that huge horned creature was being drawn up to the car-door, I thought I had never before seen any object that came so near my idea of the Prince of Darkness, as it seemed to look out over the crowd who were uplifting him.

"Monstrum horrendum, ingens!"

Our game being thus, after much effort, well bagged, we moved on again with a general feeling of immense satisfaction. "Glory enough for one day," thought we; "now what shall the morrow reveal?" . . .

CHAPTER 5

The mining frontier

From the days of Spanish conquests, dreams of riches from gold and silver lured many men and women to the frontier. The climax came in the late nineteenth century with the great mineral strikes in Nevada, Colorado, and the Black Hills of South Dakota. The following essays illustrate several important themes of life on the mining frontier. First, the reminiscence of the Leadville, Colorado, mining boom offers a vivid picture of the bawdy, chaotic character of mining towns. Lawlessness was rampant, and the community finally resorted to the support of vigilantes who practiced their own peculiar form of law and order. The search for precious metals also brought further encroachments on Indian lands, lands supposedly guaranteed by treaty—but this was only a small matter to eager prospectors. Second, John S. McClintock, author of the memoir of his days in the Black Hills, probably typified the venturesomeness and arrogance of his fellow pioneers. He dedicated his autobiography to those "who dared to leave their homes and enter upon a crusade in defiance of the protests of hostile savages and the mandates of the Federal Government, to brave the dangers, endure the privations and sufferings unto death, . . . to open to civilization vast areas of rich and unexplored regions."

Violence and Vigilantism in Leadville

I got into Leadville, Colorado, May 20, 1879, and found six thousand men in the camp and not one woman.

. . . Men were coming into the camp about as fast as they could get in over the one wagon road. July first there were forty-five thousand people in the camp, all men, and only one hundred and fifty women and children, and not a negro, Chinaman or Jap, but all grades of Americans, and about as many hard-boiled specimens and as hard-boiled as were ever accumulated on the same amount of territory before or since.

The things that actually took place there are unbelievable. I took in one hundred and fifty head of cattle and sold them from sixty to one hundred dollars per head; they were worth where I brought them from an average of twenty dollars per head. I sold them almost as fast as I could count them out and take in the money. I rushed back to the plains, sixty miles north of Denver, and gathered up a lot of work horses I had there and burned holes in the earth getting them into Leadville and got them to work as soon as possible.

Talk about money. People didn't seem to know what to do with their money or how to get rid of it fast enough. There never was nor never will be another

From John Lord, *Frontier Dust*, ed. Natalie Shipman (Hartford, Conn.: Edwin Valentine, Mitchell, 1926), pp. 79–91.

Gold Prospector, 1870s.

crowd as crazy as that rush of people to Leadville. They came on foot, on horseback, on wagons and on stage coaches. From thirty to thirty-five six-horse Concord stages each way, every day, and all coming in were loaded to the last man that could hang on. The travel going out was light, only men going back and forth on business. All baggage and express was brought in on wagons. The stages hauled nothing but passengers and mail. The road was so crowded that at times it was almost impossible to get over it. It was the same day and night. It was day all day and there was no night in Leadville.

I know you won't believe it but it is true. I went out of town for five days and where the timber stood thick as I went out, when I came back it was all built up solid. On both sides of a street that was full of stumps for a quarter of a mile there were stores selling goods, restaurants, boarding houses, offices and all kinds of businesses running full blast, and not in tents, but in houses. The entire country was covered with fine timber. The woods were full of saw mills cutting lumber, men as thick as fiddlers in Purgatory cutting house logs and teams hauling the lumber and logs as fast as cut.

I put my teams at contract work, furnishing mine timbers, except for a few teams of light cow ponies. I put them at job work. I gave a driver half after all expense was paid except the driver's board. And teams, horses, wagon and harness that weren't worth more than one hundred and eighty dollars, netted me as my share an average of twenty-one dollars per day. I had twenty-eight teams hauling timbers for different mines that netted me twenty-seven dollars and fifty cents per day per team. I never paid less than sixty dollars per ton for hay, and as high as three hundred. I never paid less than one hundred and sixty dollars per ton for oats and as high as two hundred and twenty dollars per ton. It cost seven dollars and fifty cents per day to run a timber team. I had one team hauling timbers to a tunnel that netted seventy-three dollars per day for five months.

I am not writing these things to let the reader know that I was making money, but to give you an idea of Leadville about this time. The tough element got so numerous and bold that they decided to run the town for their own benefit. In fact, they made it their business at the first election after the town was organized and chartered to manipulate the election absolutely. Then all appointive offices were filled by the men they wanted. That meant that the city was controlled by the saloons, dance halls, gambling houses, dead falls, hold-ups and hell dives, and no respectable, law-abiding citizen could get a law breaker arrested, no matter what the complaint. But if a citizen undertook to defend himself against a crook he was arrested quick and fined to the limit of what he could pay.

Things were run high handed. One of the leaders of the toughs was a fellow by the name of Frodsham. He was the brainiest, most reckless and fearless man of the toughs. He was interested in all manner of cussedness but his principal business was jumping mines, mining claims and town lots. He would go, or have some of his gang go, to a mine that was just beginning to produce ore or a desirably located mining claim or desirable town lot that some one was starting to build on, and put up a legally drawn notice location that antedated the location of the rightful owner. The whole country was government land and could only be gotten first by preëmption according to the United States laws. Then Frodsham would go to the owners of the property after a day or two and in very choice language—for he was an educated man—tell the owner there must be some mistake as he was working on his, Frodsham's, property. He was a hair trigger gun man and always ready, and if a property owner got mad and showed fight Frodsham always got the drop. He always kept in a perfect humor and was ready and very willing to show his location of prior date, and could always prove his case by plenty of witnesses who had seen the location notice put on the ground on the date written thereon. He would very politely inform the owner that if he didn't vacate he would be obliged to put him off by force, and he seldom failed to do it, as he had all the men he needed armed with Winchester rifles and forty-five six-shooters. . . .

Every morning from one to three or four dead men were picked up back of the dance halls and saloons, men knocked in the head or drugged for their money. No one was ever arrested or any effort ever made to find the guilty parties. Miners going back and forth to work were held up and robbed day and night, not one or two but dozens of them. It grew from bad to worse until the leading business men decided that the only salvation for decent people was to organize a vigilance committee.

But the city authorities got wind of the move and decided they had better do something. A day or two before the vigilantes were ready to act, Frodsham went to where an old man was building a house on a lot he had located and ordered him off. The old man refused to go, and Frodsham and his men began tearing the house down. The old man put up a fight and Frodsham shot him down in the presence of his wife and two daughters. To the surprise of every one, the police arrested him and the two men that were with him and put them in jail—the first tough that had been arrested and put in jail. There had never been but a few men in the jail and they were always the wrong ones. . . .

Another thing that was causing the city officials and police force to sit up and take notice was that it had been voted to move the county seat from Fairplay to Leadville. The sheriff had a state-wide reputation as a sure thing man with a forty-five six-shooter or a Winchester, and he didn't believe in wasting county time or ammunition shooting over the heads of toughs or anyone who tried to protect them. His deputies were all men of his own selection and had to come up to his ideas of what a deputy sheriff should be.

No one knew better than the city officials how all law and justice had been disregarded and how the city affairs had been handled during their administration. They feared that if the sheriff and his force were right there in the city, the people might appeal to the county authorities for protection and if they did there would be a mix-up that would certainly prove very unhealthy to somebody. They had waited too long. The dynamite was planted and the fuse lighted that was to blow their reign of terror out of existence.

The day after Frodsham was put in jail and the barber was shot was Sunday. But in Leadville there was no Sunday, and that night the vigilantes terrified every tough in Leadville by hanging Frodsham, his two men and the two hold-ups that shot and robbed the barber, to the frame-work of a kitchen that was being built on to the jail, and on the back of each of them was a big, white card which read in big, plain letters WE ARE THE LAW—WE ARE SEVEN THOUSAND STRONG AND WE MEAN BUSINESS. Signed, VIGILANCE COMMITTEE. On the breast of each was a similar card which read THIS IS A WARNING TO ALL MURDERERS, HOLD-UPS, THIEVES, MINE AND LOT JUMPERS AND TOUGHS IN GENERAL. DON'T IGNORE THE WARNING.

Monday morning, earlier than usual, there came out in a very large size daily paper, in small type, a whole page of names, and at the bottom was printed, "These and a great many others, well known to us, have twenty-four hours to get out of the Leadville mining district. Don't fail to go. Signed, Vigilance Committee." And they went.

Thirteen hundred and sixty went out over Weston Pass before twelve o'clock, and several hundred went out over Moquito Pass. The list of names included every city official from mayor down, police judge, chief of police, every alderman and every policeman; and of all the nice, quiet towns that was ever heard of Leadville was the quietest. There didn't anybody know who was who; no one could go more than two blocks after nine o'clock at night without being stopped by a vigilante and asked to show his card. If you had a card all right, go on. If you had no card or other satisfactory means of identification, you had to go to headquarters and were held there until you could be identified. A man could lay a twenty dollar bill on the sidewalk of the busiest street in the city and it lay there nearly all day and no one offered to pick it up.

There was a big, red-headed, red-faced, American-raised Scotchman named Red McDonald who ran one of the biggest and worst dives in the camp, called the Red Light Saloon, Dance Hall and Gambling House,—one of the "If we can't win your money with our sure thing games, we will knock you in the head, take your money and throw you out in the back alley" kind. More dead and insensible men had been picked up back of Red McDonald's place than any two other such places in town. His name, his two bar-tenders' names, and his floor manager's name were in the published list. Red made his boasts that damned if they could bluff him, he had heard dogs bark before now and didn't get scared. But it would have been better for him if he had got scared a little. The Red Light ran on as usual. Red began to crow about how he had called the bluff, saying, "I told you so."

Wednesday evening, a little after dark, I met Gus Irons, a particular friend of mine. We met on Harrison Avenue. Gus said, "Let's walk down Pine Street."

I said, "All right, something is liable to happen on Pine Street."

We walked past the Red Light saloon on the opposite side of the street and went on down three or four blocks, turned and walked back, and when directly in front of the Red Light, Gus grabbed me by the arm saying, "There they are."

Like ourselves, there was quite a crowd sauntering up and down Pine Street, mostly those that were wise.

What Gus called my attention to was about seventy-five men marching double file and when they got directly in front of the Red Light saloon they halted, right-faced, facing the saloon, and six men stepped out of the center of the file and marched into the Red Light. In not more than two minutes' time they marched out with Red McDonald, his two bar-tenders and the floor manager, all bare-headed, and in their shirt sleeves, except the floor manager; he had on a dress suit. They marched south toward the end of Pine Street. There was not a shot fired or a word spoken that I heard. The next morning they were all four hanging from the limbs of a big yellow pine tree just at the edge of the town. On their backs were cards that read, "WE ARE THE LAW. WE ARE SEVEN THOUSAND STRONG AND WE MEAN BUSINESS. VIGILANCE COMMITTEE." On their breasts there were cards reading, "HE COMMITTED SUICIDE." . . .

. . . [T]he sheriff and his deputies had moved in and opened up their office and gone into business. When everything seemed in smooth running order the Vigilance Committee disbanded. A city election had been held and an entirely new board of officials elected and a new police force appointed. That was in the early fall of 1879 and Leadville and the surrounding country have been as peaceable and law-abiding from that day to this as any place in the United States.

Whose Black Hills?

I embarked at St. Louis, Mo., for Fort Pierre, on a Missouri River steamer that was bound for Fort Benton, Montana. General Terry and his seventeen-year-old son, George, were on the same steamer, bound for the mouth of the Yellowstone River to meet General Custer. George and I became good friends and I afterwards wrote him at his home in New York all I knew about the Black Hills.

I arrived at Fort Pierre on the Missouri River two hundred miles east of the Black Hills, in April of 1876, the day after a wagon train had left there for the Hills, so I was detained for several days at that cheerless post, awaiting the arrival of the next wagon train that was en route from Sioux City.

There was quite a large number of Indians at Fort Pierre at that time, loafing around during the day and at night holding noisy demonstrations. Whether these were war dances, religious revivals, or political rallies, I was not informed.

From John S. McClintock, *Pioneer Days in the Black Hills,* ed. Edward L. Senn (Deadwood, S. Dak., 1939), pp. 45–52, *passim.*

Comfortably located in new tents at the mouth of Bad River at Fort Pierre, were about fifty men from the state of Pennsylvania. This party was thoroughly equipped with all the essentials for camp life and for home making, from tin cups to grindstones. Evidently they had started for the new gold fields on a purely business venture with probably no thought at the time of any contingency arising which might involve them in trouble with Indians over the right of way across the Bad Lands country, and they were wholly unprepared for meeting any such emergencies. This very important matter not having been previously considered they had neglected to bring with them a supply of war munitions which at that time were prime essentials in the settlement of Indian difficulties.

This party had intended to go on west with the wagon train but was deterred from doing so by hearing from another party of men to whom they had given shelter in their tents, some very discouraging reports of Indian activities. The party, which had just returned from Rapid City in the Hills, told some very shocking stories of seeing fresh graves all along the route to that place, and that as far up Rapid Creek as they had gone the graves of white men who had been murdered by Indians were seen on both sides. So the eastern men changed their plans and decided to build boats and go back down the river.

The men from Rapid City, whose business eastward was much more pressing, decided to float down on cottonwood logs. Two logs lashed together sufficed for two passengers. Although the "Big Muddy" was lashing its shores, it held no terrors for these men. I witnessed a touching departure. Four men on four short logs together with a heavy trunk, and below their boot tops in icy water, went whirling down the stream for their final destination, which I presumed was the Gulf of Mexico. Although I had at the time a fine Winchester rifle, I purchased another from them, as they were unable to take it.

While I gave but little credence to the exaggerated reports given out by the excited men who came from Rapid City, I learned before I reached that city that their stories were not founded wholly upon imagination. The Indians had really murdered a number of white men along the route and their graves were in evidence. At the time the men were at Rapid City the Indians were numerous and active in that vicinity, trying out the new needle guns with which they had been amply supplied either by Uncle Sam or other agencies. They were doing some very reckless and indiscriminate shooting, while engaged in their early spring roundup of American horses, which they were claiming by right of discovery and appropriation.

When the belated train from Sioux City arrived at Fort Pierre, I fell in with it, armed and provisioned for the summer, and was soon on my way to the Hills. Our train consisted of about twenty wagons and nearly one hundred men, no women or children. When strung out on the plains it certainly made a formidable showing. If viewed from distant hill tops, as it undoubtedly was, it might have been mistaken for General Crook's army.

Leadville, Colorado assay office, 1870s.

We moved along without incident for several days. There were two men on horseback who went far ahead of the wagons, as did also a very large footman, whose name was Campbell.

One afternoon, as we were approaching a point on the road known as Grindstone Buttes, we saw coming back towards us, abreast and at top speed, the two horsemen and Campbell. Their report was submitted in short order. They had discovered in a large valley beyond the bluffs an Indian village of considerable size, but had neglected to risk a second look in making an estimate of the number of its inhabitants. There was now but one thing to be done, and without parleying the train moved on.

On approaching the bluffs we realized that the picture had not been overdrawn by our scouts. There they were, the tepees looming up in the distance like shocks in an Iowa cornfield, yet we saw no Indians. In sizing up the village the most conservative estimate that I was able to make was one hundred braves. The situation, however, was not discouraging, as we had more than ninety men.

Our wagons were quickly thrown in a circle with the horses all inside. The captain of the train made a call for every man who had a gun to come forward. Previous to this call some of the knowing ones who were familiar with Indian tactics, gave out the startling information that the Reds, before our approach, had rushed across the valley and were then ensconced under the bluffs awaiting our descent into the valley. This would give them a decided advantage in executing their plans for a general slaughter of our party.

We disappointed them in this ruse and were now ready to line up over the bluffs. I gave my extra gun and ammunition to a young man who had none, and we fell into line. And now, to my great surprise and disappointment, only about one-third of our invincible force walked out into the open; and at least one-third had such an array of ante-bellum antiques and heirlooms for shooting irons, as I had never before seen.

Not until this time had I realized the gravity of the situation, of being right in the heart of the danger zone with not to exceed twenty-five effective rifles, with a good part of them single shots, to face at least one hundred warriors armed with needle guns. The situation was by no means exhilarating. I thought of the men who had gone down the river.

However, as we had no river to jump into and no woods to take to, our only alternative was to go forward to give battle. This we were proceeding to do and had crept up to within a few yards of the bluffs, all ready to rise up for the onslaught when two of our bravest, not to say foolhardy men, in their anxiety to get in the first shots, called out, "No Indians." Had there been any Indians there those two men would have gone over the wall with two of the best rifles in the outfit. The reds had given us the slip and the shock of disappointment to some of our militant heroes was keenly felt.

At this juncture three of the reds emerged from the village and came straight towards us. They were two very old men and a small boy. Through an interpreter we were informed that all their party, except themselves, had gone hunting back over the hill in an opposite direction from us. This information was of course accepted for what we thought it to be worth. It was my opinion and that of others, that they were in that locality for the purpose of doing the same as they had been doing on former occasions—ambushing and murdering small parties of white men. They were never known to attack a party of whites anywhere near their equal. They probably had been apprised by scouts of our approach and in view of our numbers had decided to retire back of their camp and watch our movements.

This opinion was confirmed by the fact that they made no attempt that night to stampede our stock. Evidently they were afraid to tackle us. However, had they known our actual fighting strength, they might have given up their search for jack rabbits and turned their attention to bigger game.

Here in our party were nearly one hundred men, no doubt as courageous as any who came to the Hills, who would have been nearly helpless in resisting an attack by any considerable number of Indians. This party was a fair representation of the throngs who came trusting to luck, by which nearly all were certainly favored, not only in reaching Deadwood, but in not being molested after their arrival. Our people, though numbered by thousands, were wholly unorganized and with a small percentage equipped with arms for making a good defense. The thought has many times occurred to me that it would have taken but a fraction of such a force as Sitting Bull hurled against Custer to clean up Deadwood and leave it in ashes.

During our trip from Fort Pierre to Rapid City, from four to six pickets were posted each night far out from camp. This was deemed necessary in order to give the sleepers ample time to prepare for action, the guards firing a warning shot should attack on the camp be made or a prowling Indian be spied. The names of these guards were called out in alphabetical order. Up to the last night before reaching Rapid City I had escaped this undesirable duty, but my name was called when the camp was made on Box Elder Creek right in the very heart of the danger zone. Here I put in more than half of the night, which was pitch dark, in watching near-by bushes and many other objects appearing to be human forms. Many times, with my Winchester at my shoulder, I watched for a movement, but as none was discernible I was spared the painful duty of killing a red man and arousing the sleepers. The following day our train pulled into Rapid City. Here we found hundreds of people who had just arrived from Cheyenne and Sidney. However, they were practically all on the move or preparing to move northward to Deadwood, the Mecca of all travelers. This was early in May.

As for myself, I was desirous, before going any further north, of seeing and examining, to my own satisfaction, the wonderful "Jenney's Bar" on Rapid Creek. So I stored my stock of eatables which consisted of more than one hundred pounds of crackers and other items of lesser importance, in a dirt warehouse. These I subsequently had brought up to Deadwood, by which time they had considerably appreciated in value and had also seemingly improved in flavor. After storing these goods, I walked into a store which was filled with customers and purchased some mining implements. While being waited upon, I inquired if there was any one present who was going up Rapid Creek. A dark complexioned man came up and said that he was going that way. I held a short conversation with the man who appeared to be a gentleman, as I afterwards found him to be. He gave his name as Edson and said that he came first to the Hills with the Jenney expedition in 1875 and that he came again and located a placer claim ten miles up the creek from Rapid City. He stated further that he believed that he had a good claim but as yet was uncertain as to its value.

So I very quickly decided to go with him as did also several others of our Pierre party. We had a team and all together we pulled up stream with Edson. A few miles from Rapid City he pointed out Jenney's Bar. There we tarried for a time while I tried panning from several of the most likely prospect holes of which there were many. . . . The results obtained from the pannings were but two to four light colors, so we passed on as all others before us evidently had done. We reached Edson's Bar at dark and went into camp. About four inches of snow fell that night and the next morning, Edson, who, I soon learned, was more of a hunter than he was miner, proposed to take our party a few miles northward where he said ranged a large herd of elk. This proposal was eagerly accepted by everyone excepting myself although I had a fine gun and was not a bad shot. I had come to prospect and not to hunt.

Leaving me behind, the party set out but not with the intention of annihilating the herd as each man agreed to restrict his limit to one elk. After their departure for the woods, I went quite a distance up and down the creek and scraped the bed rock in a number of the prospect holes along its banks, but without obtaining satisfactory results. So I very quickly decided that Rapid Creek was a failure for placer mining, and gave it up. I was now ready to again hit the trail to Deadwood. Our party of hunters returned to camp at dark. They, with but one exception, reported hard luck. However, by having one experienced hunter in the party, they were enabled to bring in one fine large elk that Edson had downed, so we were amply supplied with fresh meat to last us through to Deadwood. Early the next morning we bade farewell to our generous host and struck the Cheyenne trail for Deadwood. . . .

CHAPTER 6

Life on the prairie

cA cattle drive

Few events have been more romanticized that the cattle drives of the late nineteenth century. Novels, movies, and television programs have glorified the drive as high adventure, and the cowboy, of course, has been the ideal American hero. Actually, the drives were costly, dangerous, and above all, dull, hard work. The most famous cattle drives came out of the Texas plains to the railheads in Kansas. The selection here, however, is a diary of a seventeen-year-old "boy," William Emsley Jackson, who worked a herd eastward from La Grande, Oregon, to Cheyenne, Wyoming, in 1876. The tedious, harsh life of the drive, with the lack of grass and water and the constant stampedes, comes through clearly in Jackson's memoir. In addition, Jackson included comments on western life in the mid-1870s, such as the fear of robbers and outlaws, emigrant wagons going both east and west, Mormon settlements, and the desertlike character of the land. Jackson's opening remarks about the Fourth of July in the centennial year also reveal an interesting nationalistic consciousness.

1876 left La Grande May 23, Oregon to go with Lang and Shadl[e]y's cattle to Cheyenne, Wyoming. Overtook the herds on Clover Creek and went to driving with Lang's herd May 24, for $30.00 a month. Sold my cayuse to Dooney on Burnt River for $27.00.

June 23. Left Lang's herd and went to cooking for Cox at $40.00, being then on Salmon River. (Cox was foreman of the stock herd of 1400 cattle.) Dirt, dust and sage brush, no grass and no water all the way.

June 22 *[sic]*. Passed Salmon Falls on Snake River.

June 28. Passed Shoshone Falls on Snake River, height 215 feet. Was within seven miles of them and was greatly disappointed at not getting to see them. The cook could not leave.

July 1. Came onto Snake River again and struck plenty of good grass [and] considerable Juniper along the river. Sage brush decreases in stature and in quantity. Disagreeable experience with alkali dust, less frequent, but enough to leave its effects on the pages of this diary.

July 2. The Sabbath, and although this day is hardly distinguishable from any other by this crowd on this trip, we drive about two miles and lay over for the

From J. Orin Oliphant and C. S. Kingston, eds., "William Emsley Jackson's Diary of a Cattle Drive from La Grande, Oregon, to Cheyenne, Wyoming, in 1876," *Agricultural History* 23 (October 1949): 261–273, *passim.* Used by permission of the Agricultural History Society.

Emigrant wagon train, Great Plains, 1870s.

balance of the day. The drivers are cutting out and dividing the herds, putting all the large beef cattle into the other herd. Sage brush more scattering still, the vacancies being supplied with abundance of fresh bunch grass. We are now just opposite the Goose Creek Mts. off to the right, on which are large quantities of snow and considerable juniper timber. After sundown the mosquitoes are very bad, they keep us fighting with both hands.

July 3. Remained here till 4:00 o'clock and then moved one and a half miles up the road.

July 4. Grand Centennial Fourth of July. In a dry camp about two miles from the river. While we were eating breakfast there was discovered down to the left toward the river not more than 400 yards distant, a band of antelope. I counted nine. No one went after them. There have been quite a number seen during the last few days. Later we move up the river about three miles to a slou [sic] where a bridge is to be built across the Snake River, towards the construction of which $8000.00 have already been expended. Here we lay over the remainder of the day, and enjoyed the Fourth as best we could under the circumstances. There was some whiskey drunk by the crowd, but not to excess, a little fight between two of the natives occurred. Knives were drawn, but nobody hurt. Nothing very uncommon took place to commemorate this eventful day. Mosquitoes annoying as usual. Shadley started for Kelton this morning.

July 5. Arose early to begin the second century of our national career. Prepared breakfast as usual. Crossed Goose Creek. The herd went up the river and I made a circuitous route of seven or eight miles to make a net gain of two mi. It being 12:00 o'clock, we nooned. The mosquitoes are terrible. After dinner we moved 3 or 4 miles ahead and made a dry camp. The mosquitoes were so bad that we barely escaped being eaten alive, by losing a night's sleep and putting in the time fighting those blood-thirsty insects.

July 6. Moved on to Marsh Creek where there were 12 emigrant wagons camped. All bound for Oregon and Washington Territory. Bought a five-shooter of one of them for $8.50. Later met three more wagons[;] made a dry camp 3 mi. from Marsh Lake, though it was not very dry, for it rained on us all night and everything was wet, but no mosquitoes.

July 7. Got up in the rain. Went to the lake and nooned, the rain having subsided, and it was 20 mi. to the next water. We moved out about 6 mi. and made a dry camp—a wet drizzly afternoon—no mosquitoes or rain tonight but wet blankets to sleep in.

July 8. Got up just as daylight was showing in the east. Terribly cold and chilly. Never did crawl out of bed under more disagreeable circumstances, even when I had snow to contend with, sore faces and necks the result of our experience on the night of the 5th with those insects (mosquitoes) for which Snake River is noted, are still in evidence. We have a terribly rough and rocky road today, muddy in places and several steep pitches hard to get over. Met 8 emigrant teams, one of which had a yoke of cattle. They had a drove of loose cattle. Contrary to us, they are taking cattle there to stock the country while we are driving the surplus east. Later we came down onto Raft River overtaking Langs herd, and camped for the night. The other herd goes on, it being only about 3:00 o'clock.

July 9. We lay here until about 3:00 o'clock P.M.resting as they call it. But for me it means extra work, as it is always washday. Towels and old sacks to wash, beans to cook, notwithstanding the scarcity of wood, and then I had time to go fishing for about one and one-half hours. Caught 12 good ones from 6 to 12 in. in length. About twice as many were caught in the evening. (The Company furnished us with hooks and lines.) Crossed over and went out about 5 mi. and made a dry camp. This ends another Sunday.

July 10. Had breakfast by "sun up." Moved down to Fall Creek a distance of about 4 mi., by 9:00 o'clock, where we lay over till toward evening, catching some trout 6 to 14 in. long, the nicest ones I ever saw. Several were caught, but I was unlucky this time. There passed us today six travelers with about 6 horses. Met also 8 emigrant wagons, some of which were from Kansas. For the first time, we came into some juniper timber so I could have it for wood. Struck Snake about 1½ mi. below Fall Creek. We have been having a few very cold and chilly mornings for this time of year. An overcoat feels comfortable. This reminds me that we are getting pretty high up in the world. I write this while waiting for Cox to come and hunt out a place for camp. Today we received the intelligence from the Big Horn (through those immigrants) that the Indians have killed General Custer, two of his brothers and a brother-in-law, with the whole of his command, excepting five men, amounting in all to 300 men massacred. As to the truth of which we are not positive. Having come about 2 mi. we made a dry camp about 600 yds. from the river from which we carry water for camp purposes.

July 11. Drove about 3 mi. and nooned on the river about 2 mi. from Rock Creek No. 2. Caught lots of nice fish—different kinds—enough for dinner and breakfast. Moved on about 4 mi. over some terribly rough roads, passing through a narrow gap between high perpendicular cliffs. It is said that it was once a favorite place of attack for Indians, and that there are about 75 graves there, whose inmates have fallen by the treacherous foe. I noticed some of the Indians camped on a little stream about one mile from the river.

July 12. After traveling about 8 mi. we came to American Falls on Snake which have descent of about 50 ft. in 150 yds. Part of which is very rough. The river here is about 300 yds. wide. Here we met 13 emigrant wagons, most of which, I believe, were going to Oregon and Washington. Here we stopped for dinner and killed a beef—a yearling, and sold part of it to those pilgrims. Later drove on up to a stock ranch, filled barrel and bade farewell to Snake River.

Went about 1½ mi. and camped on the bluff along which we follow for some time. Here the mosquitoes were terrible, worse than we ever had them before, so thick that one might throw his hand out and strike a dozen at once. The boys went around with their heads tied up like they had the mumps, or some other contagious disease. Along about 10:00 o'clock they quieted down. . . .

July 19. A bunch of Indians, 6 or 7, passed us. Jeff came back without Shadley. He was not at the station. Plenty of snow within a mile of us. Crossed the divide and went down on the other side about 5 mi. Still in Snake basin. Here a road leading out into Montana makes a junction with ours. A drove of about 250 cattle came in on it and passed us. They were driving to New Mexico. This is a delightful country. Not rough and rugged as one might think to find it at this elevation, but it consists mainly of smooth rolling hills which are covered with grass and clumps of brush. But these hills would be called mountains in a less mountainous country. Sage brush is not much used for wood now, because it is not so common. Some small stuff in places. We are now in the place that we have been looking forward to with longing hearts, where there is plenty of good grass, good water, no alkali dust, nor sage brush; and we enjoy it greatly. All say that this is the best camp that we have had. . . .

July 21. While eating breakfast an accident happened which caused quite an uproar in camp. The horses which were to be used for the day had been caught and tied to the wagon, all on one side, when one of them went to pulling back. The others, thinking that something was wrong began pulling too. The result was that the wagon was upset and the contents badly scattered. This caused me to get a late start and so the cattle beat me to camp. Met five emigrant wagons today. Passed Lang's herd. Afternoon, went about 4 mi. and struck a dry camp. Just before dark Vidito, who had been out after some wood, a few hundred yards came running into camp with the report that a bear had been seen. So he and three others went in search of the animal, but they were so long preparing for the chase and it was so near dark that bruin was not to be found, and the hunt was abandoned.

July 22. A drive of 4 or 5 mi. brought us to a little settlement of Mormons, about three families (may be only one father). Passing which we came to the strongest kind of soda and mineral spring and farther on we came to beautiful springs of clear water where we nooned. . . .

July 26. Sun came out clear, but it is cool as is generally the case when one is in sight of snow. Back some better this morning. About 4 mi. out, nooned on the main road. Not much wood. Met 8 emigrant wagons—one a 4 ox team. Afternoon met 5 emigrant wagons. Can count about 30 individuals around their camp, which is about 150 yds. from ours. We came about 3 mi. since noon. While in camp here 4 more emigrant wagons arrived. Back feels better this evening. No rain today. Nice weather again, wood very scarce since we got out of the sagebrush country.

July 27. Sleep until I get ready to get up now, since I am not able to do anything. About 2 mi. drive brought us to another Mormon village, containing 12 to 15 dwelling houses. One mile more to noon camp. Met today, 18 emigrant wagons of which 6 were cattle teams of one yoke each and one of 2 yoke. They were from Ind. Ill. Mo. and Arkansas. Some bound for western Idaho and some for eastern Oregon. But the most of them were going to northeastern Oregon and Wash. Ter. A large emigration this year. Afternoon, after driving 3 or 4 mi. struck a dry camp. Met one emigrant team driving one horse and one mule—from Arkansas going to Walla Walla or thereabouts.

July 28. Three emigrant teams passed us while in camp—are being rushed right along now. Five herds of cattle between here and Georgetown. 2½ mi. brings us to Bennington, quite a thrifty little Mormon colony. Passed 6 more emigrant wagons. 4 mi. more brings us to another Mormon town known as Montpelier larger than any other that we have passed through. These people seem to live happily and enjoy themselves. Here are quite extensive settlements—farms and good houses. None appear to be exceedingly wealthy, but have all they need. All the mercantile business is done under the name of Zion's Cooperative Mercantile Institution. (Z. C. M. I.) This is a pleasant place during the summer—snow in sight the year round. The hardest part of the winter here is after Christmas. They have to feed the stock 3 months—pretty frosty, but I notice fine crops (or patches) of potatoes, beans, corn, oats; all late, but if winter holds off they will mature. We got good potatoes (old ones) raised here for $.50 a bu. Everything cheaper here than I have had it elsewhere on the trip. Butter $.18, Eggs $.15, and other things in proportion. (It was a luxury to get some of these things.) The principal occupation of the people of this region is stock raising. Across the river from here are several colonies or villages. Paris, the largest, is about 18 mi. from here. The valley is from 10 to 15 mi. wide. On the other side and above Paris is Bear Lake, which is said to be about 30 mi. long and 20 mi. wide, and deep enough anywhere to float a steamboat. It is about 15 mi. from here to the lake. Went 1½ mi. and nooned at a dry camp. Here we take a new cutoff which shortens our road 4 or 5 mi. Instead of keeping up the river, we turn to the left out into the hills and strike camp after a 4 mi. drive at a little creek. . . .

July 31. The last day of the great Centennial month. The day was signalized by our crossing the Ida. and Wy. Ter. line, which was marked by a stake every half mile. The boys say that they cannot see any difference between one side and the other. Passed two ranchers and met 8 emigrant wagons bound for the coast. Our road leads up the river bottom along the foothills. After a drive of about 5 mi. nooned on a little creek. Afternoon, on the road I took the team again myself and went to cooking, as my back feels able. Flies are bad again. Crowded now more than ever. Three herds in sight, 2 mi. up the river and we camped. Have *shewalla* (fish) for supper. Met one emigrant team.

August 1. We began another month with the impression that we should be on the road as long again as we anticipated being at the first of last month. I hope that we shall not see two more months on this trip. Passed an Indian camp of three wigwams belonging to the Snake tribe. Flies terrible again today. Almost impossible to keep the horses in the road. Three miles brings us to Smith's fork of Bear River. It is quite a large stream. Crossed and went out two mi. and struck a dry camp and nooned. Flies like man's flesh as well as horse's flesh. I omitted to say that there is quite a settlement at Smith's Fork. We left the main Bear River this morning. Afternoon, go out 3 mi. and make a dry camp.

August 2. Two miles brings us to a terribly steep hill about a mile in length and very rocky. The steepest hill that I ever ascended behind a team. Am now on top waiting for the herd to come up. I can see about a mile ahead a hill equal in length and magnitude to the hill just described, though I think it is not so rocky. The flies are not all dead yet, nor does their passion for blood cease. After going down hill for about a mile we noon on a little creek. Afternoon—Now comes the ascent of the second big hill—up about 2 mi. and very rocky in places. Descending, we pass through a little belt of fir and hemlock, a half mile further we struck a dry camp having gone about 3½ mi. since noon.

August 3. No water for cattle and a long distance before we come to any, on the road. After 1½ mi. we cross a little spring branch. Farther along the road we passed a grave on the headstone of which was carved:

MISS NANCY J. HILL
of
MONROE CITY MISSOURI
DIED IN 1852
Age 20 YR.

We have passed many graves on the road which I have taken no notice of. Passed one yesterday under the name of J. WILLIS. After descending a long, steep, rocky hill, we came down onto Ham's Fork of Bear Riv. About half way down the hill on the right hand side of the road we discovered a little grave. The inscription on the head board too obliterated to read. Ten emigrant wagons were camped down in a Gulch on the right, bound for Oregon and Wash. . . .

August 4. One month has already rolled by of the second century of the birth of our nation and talk of the Centennial is about ended. It will only appear in history for another hundred of years. Went down the river about 3 mi. and nooned. Passed two recent Indian towns of from 20 to 30 teepees and another just above camp of about 30. Perhaps all were made by the same band, which keeps moving down the river. (Only the poles were left standing.) We understand that these Indians are camped about 10 mi. below us, now. Passed 3 emigrant wagons bound for the north west. Had quite a lively thunder and rainstorm just after reaching camp. Afternoon. About 4 mi. brought us to night camp on a bluff of the river where we had to carry water up a very steep place, set it up ahead and then climb up after it. Sage hens, prairie chickens, and fish are plentiful through here. We have some to eat almost every day. . . .

August 11. On the road. Now for the first time in 3 yr. I see the smoke of the railway cars about 7 mi. distant. Begin to think we are getting back to America. We cross the river twice and noon at an old corral about 2½ mi. from the railroad. Afternoon. Moved up to within ¾ mi. of the station and struck camp on the river, and now for the first time since the spring of '73, I see a railroad train of cars—a passenger of 7 coaches bound east. We are now on the celebrated line of communication which connects the two oceans, the importance of which one can readily comprehend when one sees the six telegraph wires on both sides of the track and the 6 or 8 trains passing daily. This is very rough country for a railroad—up grade, down grade, over bridges, through tunnels and snowsheds.

August 12. Cross the creek, and a few minutes brings us to the great U[nion] P[acific]. Here we also strike Black's Fork, a tributary of Greenriver, which receives the waters of Ham's Fork a short distance above and which the railroad follows crossing occasionally. Here lies a train of 24 cattle cars on which Lang ships 400 head of beeves to Chicago. M. Shields and D. Clark in charge. Went down the railroad about 2 mi. crossed and nooned on Black's Fork. I should have mentioned that here we received ten Sharp's carbines and 90 pounds of cartridges, furnished by the company. We also have one Sharp's sporting rifle, one Henry rifle and one Winchester. Besides a number of the men have their own revolvers. P. M. Crossed the railroad again and went down about 5 mi. and struck camp on the river, after breaking the wagon tongue and driving about one mile without any. Here we repaired the wagon tongue with few tools to work with—an old ax with an edge like that of a mill pick, a file, and an old rusty brace and bit. However when finished we thought it was not likely to break again.

August 13. About 16 of the horses are gone. Two men are out after them. One man brings them in after following them 12 to 15 mi. After dinner moved on, crossed and re-crossed the river and camped, having gone about 5 mi.

August 14. Horses were all gone this time, but were brought in about 8:00 o'clock after being trailed clear over to Greenriver a distance of about 10 mi. The greater part of Lang's herd was also found across that river, having had a stampede. . . .

August 15. Seven miles brings us to Greenriver. Strike the river about ½ mi. below the city. This is the largest stream since leaving Snake R. it is 100 yards wide in places. Forded the river and went up to town for supplies. This is the largest and most important town since we started, having a round house, car works, six or eight stores, numerous saloons, and boarding houses. As one stands here and looks out beautiful scenery meets the eye. We are surrounded by rugged rocky hills which rise abruptly on every side to a height of hundreds of feet. Bare rock of a somewhat circular shape and flat tops projecting perpendicularly many feet above the lower hills are very prominent. P.M. Here we leave Greenriver, as does the railroad, and go up the famous Bitter Creek, which has been our dread during the previous part of the journey, and which is noted for its numerous bands of horsethieves and robbers. No grass and only the strongest alkali water, poisonous to man and beast. Hence, the name. . . .

August 27. Two mi. brings us to the summit of the Rocky Mts. This is Bridger's Pass. To an uninformed person it would seem nothing more than going over another hill. It does not appear to be so high, although we are aware that we have been traveling up hill for a distance of 1000 miles or more. There is plenty of snow in sight, apparently no higher than the road. I am ready to confess that the scenery here falls far below my expectations. Nothing more than a sagebrush region dry and barren, some dry scattering grass, and a little willow and cottonwood brush along the creeks and spring branches. Very little timber of any size. Here we stand on the summit of the great Rockies, on the rim of the great Mississippi Basin, the largest in the world, extending half way across the continent. And now we begin to descend the east slope of this great mountain range. Our waters henceforth are those whose home will be the Atlantic. We now bid farewell to the waters of the Pacific Ocean and the cool pleasant breezes from the southwest. After going down about 7 mi. we strike a little spring branch just below a grove of cottonwoods and willows where we noon. This being our nearest point to Rawlins, 18 miles from here. Cox takes a pack animal and goes to that place for supplies. P. M. A drive of one mile brings us to Pine Grove where lies the remains of another stage station. 2 mi. farther, after driving awhile on a less traveled road higher up the hills and to the right of the main road, having plenty of water in the barrel, we struck a dry camp, though there was plenty of water a few hundred yards back on the road. Grass is scattering and there is plenty of snow on the hills a short distance away. Cox failed to return. . . .

September 1. We begin the month on the fifteenth of which we had hoped to arrive at our destination—Cheyenne. We now see that we can reach it easily by that time and feel encouraged to think that our cattle-driving is so near an end. . . .

September 12. Up at 3:00 o'clock and have breakfast at daybreak, for we were driving from the bed ground again this morning. About daylight a fog began to settle down upon us, so that it was impossible to see more than 100 yards, which made horse hunting rather a poor business, and, although two men were after them, they were not found till the fog had partially cleared away, which was about 9:00 o'clock. Another sheep corral just above us on the creek. Overtook the herd grazing about 3 mi. from camp, and 10 mi. further found waiting the expected paymaster and the cattle drivers that are to succeed us, with their colored cook, who is to take my place. He was soon into the breadpan up to his elbows and we had dinner about 3:00 o'clock. P. M. After dinner we all received due compensation (?) for our summer's work. I received $145.00, amount of wages and money loaned after deducting all counter claims. It was so late in the day that all concluded to stay one more night. I helped about loading and hitching up, and we went out about a mile and made a dry

South Dakota sod-house, 1885.

camp. I am like that little darky now, "I'se free nigger" so don't do much but sit around.

September 13. Did not get up till after daylight, something very uncommon for this boy, and partook of considerable breakfast not cooked by myself, consisting of bread, bacon and beans, all poorly cooked. After breakfast we sat around till late, than bade good by to the boys remaining with the herd and took our leave on foot for the station one and ½ mile distant, Jeff, L. D. and I. The other three who were leaving, have horses and rode them back to the city. Shadley had agreed to pay our railroad fare back to Cheyenne. So we are now at the station waiting for the train which is due at 11:00 o'clock. Here is a section house, telegraph office and water tank 20 mi. from Cheyenne. About half past 10:00 we jumped aboard a freight and landed in the city about 2:00 P.M. fare $1.00. Took a square meal at Ocean Wave restaurant for .25 cents, after which took a shave, a shampoo and a bath, and put on some clean clothes. I left my watch at a jeweler's and wandered around through town the balance of the day, looking at the curiosities and works of art. Cheyenne is quite a large, flourishing town of probably 8,000 population and is the most convenient shipping point for the Black Hills. It is connected with Custer City by a mail and stage rout[e] and telegraph. We cannot get a train today, so lay over till tomorrow.

September 14. We remain here in Cheyenne till 3:00 P. M. when we take the train for Omaha. . . .

A new life: agricultural settlement

Charles and Nellie Wooster typified the prairie settler of the post-Civil War period. From the time that Charles left their home in Michigan until his wife joined him in Nebraska nine months later, their correspondence reflected the anxieties of departure, domestic separation, and settling in a new land. Charles's decision to leave was clouded with uncertainty from the outset, for he had no clear idea whether he would land in Minnesota, Kansas, or Nebraska. He simply knew he had to create a new life for himself and his family. The Woosters's letters truly offer a slice of frontier life as they comment on the potential danger of Indians, land claims, capital investments, the building of a new house, and, of course, the loneliness of two people forced apart by circumstances. Mrs. Wooster died five years after she joined her husband. Charles Wooster lived until 1923, having had an active career as a newspaper editor and local politician in Nebraska.

Chicago, March 12, 1872
9 p.m.

My Little Wife

I have been here about 24 hours, as you see by the date of this. I found that I could gain no time by starting towards Minnesota before 5 this afternoon. I have been running about town most of the (day) and have learned nothing worth mentioning. I went to the Office of the Prairie Farmer this forenoon. Saw a man there from Minnesota who had been there twenty years and after talking with him and some others and thinking the matter all over again concluded that I would not go to Minnesota at all. This evening I accidentally met a young man who has just returned from southwestern Kansas. He says everything is awful high there and gives a discouraging account generally. Having concluded not to go to Minnesota I have made up my mind to go to Nebraska and shall look for a place with a house and some improvements. I have half a mind to say I will not write again until I find a permanent stopping place, but still I may. I shall leave here within an hour and shall reach Omaha about 10 tomorrow p.m. . . .

Bye Bye

I think of you all the time and hope to see you soon

Charley

Silver Creek, Nebraska
[March]14 6 p.m.

This is a station city or village consisting of the depot, a grocery hotel, and one dwelling house. . . .

It [the country] is as much different from anything that you ever saw in Michigan as can possibly be imagined. What I shall do here I can not possibly say. I do not intend to be in a hurry. I shall probably remain here . . . some time and then perhaps [go] to Grand Island . . . You must make up your mind not to get homesick when you come, find what you may. If we find any peace or happiness on this earth, I suppose at least 99 per cent of it will be within our own home. . . .

From William F. Schmidt, ed., "The Letters of Charles and Helen Wooster: The Problems of Settlement," *Nebraska History* 46 (1965): 121–137. Used by permission.

Silver Glen, Merrick Co., Nebr.
March 27, 1872

My Little Wife

. . . Although there are Indians to be seen here, almost every day, they are very peaceable and are much more afraid of the whites than the whites are of them. In fact the white people do not fear them at all and I have yet to learn of a woman or child who stands in the slightest dread of them. . . .

When they wish to enter a house they will come and look in at the windows until someone notices them and then if the door is opened they will step right in without further invitation. They most always ask for something to eat, but if one doesn't wish to be troubled with them it is only necessary to refuse and send them on their way.

There is no danger here of raids from wild Indians for the country is settled many miles beyond and the wild Indians are far away . . . So don't give yourself any concern about Indians. You will stand in no more danger of them than in Michigan and when you have been here a little while you will not be a bit afraid of them. . . .

Charley

Silver Glen, Merrick Co., Nebr.
March 31, 1872

Little Wife

. . . This suspense is rather trying, but still I think things will come out all right in the end. I don't refer to my claim in this for there I apprehend no trouble, still there is always a *chance* for trouble if one does not go upon his land and stay there. I am well pleased with my land and believe there is no better in the country. If I have average luck I know that I shall make a nicer home of it than any other one in the country. Most people you know don't have much of an idea of beautifying their homes. They only look out for the "almighty dollar." I believe that while I am making the dollars I can just as well make a great many other things to add to our enjoyment that are usually lost sight of and that too without any additional expense, in fact I believe that in the end there would be the most money in this very course. . . .

Bye bye

Charlie

Silver Glen, Neb.
July 21, 1872

My dear little Wife,

  This morning I arose quite early, put my house in order, breakfasted upon a couple of cold pancakes. . . .

  I hope you will follow your own advice to me and not allow yourself to feel discouraged. . . . We cannot tell what may be in store for us. Let us do the best we can and not attempt to war against fate. I have some of the best land there is in Nebraska and it is admitted to [by] all who know it. *I will keep it,* and sooner or later we shall surely embrace each other in our "little home." . . .

  I do not want to put you in a sod house. It would be too bad for such a nice little wife.

  I do not fear the Indians, and if it were not for you I would not care how quick they came.

Bye bye love

Charley

Silver Glen, Neb.
July 28, 1872

My dear little Wife

  I do not know what to say to you. You inform me that you are coming this fall. I certainly hope you will do so for it is very unpleasant for me to live alone and do my own house work, no less so perhaps than for you to be without any fixed place in Michigan. But these are only a part of the reasons why we wish to be together. It seems to me however that it would not be very wise for us to undertake to go to keeping house when we have no money even to pay your fare here saying nothing about freight, the cost of enough furniture to enable us to live at all which would be 50$ at least, the incidental expense of living and things which it would be necessary to have to supply our table which the farm will not afford. Fuel would necessarily cost something. How could we live without a cow? A good one would cost 50$—a second rate one might be had for 40$. In the spring if I did not have a team and some farming utensils a little money would be almost a necessity. How should we get the seeds that I had intended to, for hedge plants, fruits and forest trees? True my corn crop ought to be worth 200$, but whether I could realize anything on it would be a very doubtful question . . . You can estimate our resources and the necessary expenses of settling up here as well as I can.

If I said I could live cheap here alone, it has been proved that I was correct for since the 26 day of April, living, fuel, cooking utensils and all probably has not cost me 10$. I have had no butter for two months and I do not use more than a pound of pork in a week. Of course it would be expected that I should supply you in Michigan as well as myself here. Both together would be more than keeping house here . . . As I said, I have some good land and I intend to keep it. The more I see of some other places the more I think of my own. I can prove up on it next spring and then I could raise money on it if I wish to, though I do not wish to if possible to avoid it. As heretofore I shall *try* to get along as well as possible but, if in so doing my feet should slip from under me and I should slide into hell, I should endeavor to endure the fry with all fortitude. . . .

Bye bye

Charley

Silver Glen, Neb.
August 28, 1872

My dear little Wife

. . . I think I shall get a yoke of oxen and a secondhand wagon. I think of going down about Columbus to look for them. I can not go till I do four or five days more in haying. I do not want to pay over 150$ for them both.

It will be better for me to get them at first if I get them at all as I shall need several days team work preparatory to building. The material for the house will cost altogether 150$, and I am in hopes that I shall be able to do so much of the work myself that it will not be necessary to pay out much for work.

I have bought the heifer I spoke of in my last [letter] and shall pay for her—40$—in a day or two . . . I would not have bought the heifer now, but I was afraid some one else would get her. She is the only one I have seen that pleased me and is, I think, the best one I have seen or heard of.

Charley

Adams, Mich.
Sept. 29, 1872

My dear Charley,

I rec'd yours of the 22 and sent a short note to you in reply, so as to have it be sure and reach you before it was too late to have the bedroom come in front instead of the buttery. And I wouldn't have you fail to do this for a large sum of money; the flowers etc., will be in the front yard no doubt, and I want my bedroom to be in the pleasantest place possible, and for a thousand reasons, figuratively speaking. I want the bedroom in front, and you will no doubt have it built there; and then another thing *please* don't fail to have a back-door and if it is going to cost so much that you will not have money for a door I will stay in Mich. enough longer to earn money for a door; oh! I do want a back door so much! ... You will never be sorry to have a back door and to have the bedroom in front. I shouldn't want to let hired men go into any buttery to wash in the sink (you may though, bless you!) and I don't want the washdish to be in the frontyard, and I expect to have a little standard or something of the kind fixed on purpose for the washdish to stand on while one is washing and then it can be hung on the side of it. . . .

[Nellie]

Silver Glen, Nebr.
October 2, 1872

My dear Nellie

... I am very sorry that I cannot follow your suggestions in regard to the house, but I cannot possibly. Don't "fly off the handle" now but reserve judgement until you come. Things will look very different from what you expect, and I am fully persuaded that you will like my arrangement better than your own. We will have things nicer than anyone else. Now you see. Your flowers will be in front of your bedroom and it will not look out on back yards. If you were on the ground today you could not for your life tell which was the *front*. There are two sides either of which might be considered as such. I cannot possibly give you anything like a true idea of these things.

I intend to plaster if cold weather does not overtake me and it shall not if hard work will prevent it. I shall leave the pantry till you come, and then you can have it finished to suit yourself.

Bye bye

Charley

Silver Glen, Neb.
Oct. 23, '72

Little wife:

I will write a few words today noon so that Mr. Alpaugh can mail the letter tonight. He is at work down at the house now. We shall about get the frame up today. Weather continues fine and I am in hopes he will be able to stay till the house is enclosed. I am getting very much "demoralized" and shall probably go to the devil if you don't come pretty soon. My clothes are all in pieces and many of them are so dirty that I should be ashamed to take them away to be washed.

It will probably not be best for you to start untill the things come, but be ready so that you can start any day. I think I will write a letter telling you to come and leave it with the Agent to be mailed immediately on the arrival of the things. If you get such a letter you will *know what it means.*

It may be of interest to you to know that the people here have seen fit to elect me Justice of Peace. I qualified last night.

Bye bye Little Baby

Charley

Silver Glen, Neb.
Nov. 4, 1872

Little Wife

We did not do a thing on the house last week but commenced again today. I hope to get it enclosed this week and then we *can* live in it. I would do most anything to have you here.

I could not have a stove in my sod house, because it is covered with hay. I can make my self tolerably comfortable nights and daytimes. I hope to work hard enough to keep warm . . .

Bye bye

Charley

Silver Glen, Neb.
Nov. 24,·1872

Little Wife,

Thursday I went to the station partly in hopes of meeting you. I did not know but you would come notwithstanding my letter. Friday night I went again and instead of yourself I found a letter from you. I am sorry you were feeling out of gear. I am sure I have tried to do the best I could. I wanted you here, but what could I do? My means were insufficient, and whenever I did get money it was not enough to meet demands. My expenses have been greater than I anticipated and now I find myself with a house but not a dollar to furnish it. A few days ago I had 60$ with which I intended to get furniture, but unexpectedly I was obliged to get about 20$ worth of stuff for the house when I supposed I had enough. The charges on the goods were upwards of 18$ and yesterday I went to Columbus . . . and spent 27$ or thereabouts for a pump, inside doors, door hangings, etc.

. . . You see then that we have no money and no prospect of getting any for an indefinite length of time unless it can be borrowed. It seems as though some of your brothers or all of them might have money the[y] should be glad to lend . . . and wait till we could pay. If not we must work in some other direction. As I told you . . . I can prove up on my place and give that as security if it's considered necessary, and that would be worth many times all we shall need to borrow.

. . . It is perhaps useless for me to say more. I am sorry for you, sorry for myself and sorry for the devil. . . .

. . . Come now if you can. Let us enjoy again each other's love. The future must provide for itself.

Charley

Silver Glen, Neb.
Dec. 3, 1872

Little Wife

. . . The floor is nearly laid now and two or three days work ought to be sufficient, especially if the pantry is not finished before you come, and it probably will not be as I wish you to have it done after your own heart. If I had money, I could be ready for you in three days and so I can in two or three days at any time after getting money. . . .

Your little chickens are no more for this world, some skunks dug in while I was away and eat them all, their mother, two or three other hens and two or three other chickens. I caught one of the skunks in a trap and am trying to catch another. . . .

What fine times we shall have when you come.

Bye bye

Charley

Hillsdale, Mich.
Dec. 9, 1872

My dear Boy

I'm now soon coming to you and am not going to be fooled out of it much longer, for although I have had a pretty hard time to find money, I have succeeded *at last* just as I gave up all hope and had gone to bed with a nervous sick headache. You must be pleased and not frown at me for taking the money in the way I have for it is all the way I can get any at present.

[My father] signed a note with me to get the money from Lawt Thompson. I should not have known that Lawt had any but Cousin Mart unbeknown to me asked him if he had some and would let you have it with pa for a signer and he said he would. So this morning pa came up to Lawts with me, and Lawt drew the note and I signed Chas. Wooster to it and pa signed H. P. Hitchcock . . . He had only 70$ to let so I took that for six months at 10 per ct. and now you will be pleased than other wise won't you? and don't for Gods sake send it back. . . .

I am going to start a week from tomorrow (Tuesday) so prepare for my coming and don't you write and say that the floor is not quite laid yet, for if it isn't I can soon hammer it down. . . .

Write to me as soon as you get this for I want one more letter from you before I go so I can carry it in the cars for company. . . .

Bye bye, for now I'm surely coming even if you write me the house is burned to ashes. Bye.

Nellie

Silver Glen, Nebraska
Dec. 13, 1872

My Little Wife,

Yours of the 9th was rec'd today.

I am very glad that you are coming at last, and am not at all displeased with your manner of raising the money. Your father was very kind. . . .

It will probably take Mr. Alpaugh most of next week to finish the house; I shall probably go to Columbus Monday and get things as to make ready for you. Things will not be in very good condition to receive you, but we will try and make ourselves comfortable.

On the road, whatever information you may need you can get of the conductors. Ask them any questions. At Chicago go get your ticket for Omaha. You perhaps might get one to Columbus, but do not do so, as your baggage would stop there and occasion some trouble. At Omaha there is an old grayheaded man who acts as policeman about the station. It would be best for you to let him have your check and he would claim your baggage for you. There is usually a great crowd of men and you could not well attend to it. Have him show you the car and take a seat as soon as convenient as they are often crowded. If you let him take your check, take the number of it with your pencil before doing so. It is his business to attend to the wants of passengers. I spoke to him about you and he said that if you would speak to him he would see that every thing was all right. I will of course meet you at Silver Creek.

. . . Charley's little love is coming to stay with him and then all her troubles will be at an end.

Charley

ℱeminism on the frontier

The toil, the loneliness, and the isolation of life on the frontier doubtless exacted a toll from the human psyche. Life was hard and probably few people could afford the time or emotional energy for self-examination. Moreover, the late nineteenth century was not necessarily noted as a time for consciousness-raising. This excerpt was taken from an 1876 autobiographical sketch by Mrs. L. L. Dalton, who lived in Circle Valley, Utah. The document, unfortunately, only implicitly comments on the drudgery and difficulty of everyday life, but it is unique for its quality of self-analysis. In the light of today's highly publicized concerns with feminism, Dalton's thoughts should remind us of the timelessness of the human condition and human problems.

Settlers clearing land, c. 1905.

... Thus I advanced my knowledge of the common branches, but my great ambition to gain a liberal education is still ungratified. In the early days of Utah, the struggle for bare sustenance was so severe that there was little time or opportunity for anything else; but I am thankful it is so much better now. I am truly thankful for every advantage I did enjoy, and wish I had improved them better; but there are times when my heart faints within me as I think of my God-given talents rusting away for want of polishing; and I do believe there is no sin in coveting that which is my neighbor's when I see others slight their privileges and trifle away those inestimable opportunities for which I have been almost consumed with longing. And it is most humiliating to see boys and girls in their teens acquiring greater proficiency than all my tedious years of self culture have enabled me to gain. But I am glad they are not limited to my meager opportunities, and I console myself for all that I lack, with the hope and determination that my children shall have a large part of that which I sought but never found.

From my childhood I have done considerable thinking, and long years ago pondered questions which puzzle me still. As long ago as I can remember I longed to be a boy, because boys were so highly privileged and so free. Thousands of things for which I heard girls gravely reproved, met only an indulgent smile when done by boys. They could go when and where they pleased, alone or otherwise, without a thought of danger or impropriety. Education was offered to them accompanied with bribes, promises and persuasions, while doled out to girls grudgingly as something utterly wasted, and expected to be of no future use. Well I remember my disgust when I asked a gentleman teacher if in his opinion, I was sufficiently advanced in mathematics to study algebra with profit, and he replied that it would be wasted time for me ever to study it, because I already had more learning than was necessary for a good housekeeper, wife and mother which was a woman's only proper place on earth. However, it is but justice to him and myself to say that he has since warmly commended my efforts at self culture and the good I have done as a teacher.

Often have I winced under the unconcealed contempt for "females" expressed by masculines of all grades from the urchin in pinafores to the finest scholars and ablest statesmen of the world. For these and many reasons in my youth and "blissful ignorance" I longed to be a boy; but I am now thankful that I belong to a more respectable class of society. ...

Not for all their boasted "supremacy," "superiority" and extensive advantages would I have women come down to their low moral level. Intellectual acquirements, fame, power, ... and even their self conceit added, are as feathers in the scale against moral purity; and since undeniably there are vastly more good women than good men on the earth, who will dare decide that it would not be better for all potent custom to allow two or more of these good women to marry one good man, than to condemn them whether they would or not, either to live single or to wed a man a thousand fathoms beneath them? I never could see a spark of justice in that rub, unalienable as the laws of the Medes and Persians, that unless married, a woman passing to middle age must be severely condemned, while there is so little in the conditions of matrimony and its male candidates to tempt a refined and noble minded woman. . . . Even while polite attentions from gentlemen were in themselves pleasant, I always felt a sort of guilt in accepting for my personality what I know was rendered merely to abstract youth and beauty; and much disgust at the thought that my quick intellect, my honest heart, my high aspirations, all the sterling worth that was really of myself, were never considered in this glittering realm of pleasure to which I was beckoned. What girl that ever paused to think she was caressed . . . merely for her youth and freshness, things not in the least due to herself, and which advancing time will soon take from her, and that then she will surely be forsaken by this society through no fault of her own, could even become enamored of its fleeting pleasure and hollow praise? I never was. Although the metrical movements of the dance in time to the rhythm of sweet music were very pleasant, I could grow tired as of any other kind of music, but I have seen girls who professed never to tire of dancing. I have often looked on while the beautiful girl, radiant of youth and happiness, with their devoted partners whirled through the dreamy waltz or sprightly cotillion, and mused on the possibility of one of these lovely and carefree maidens, become a woman and perhaps wife of one of these same adoring youths, wearing out not only her youth but her very life, drudging from morning till night to keep his house in order, and from night till morning with his ailing baby, only to be looked on by him as an inferior being, designed by Nature to serve him. He will also think her a lucky woman to have won so superior a man as himself to take care of her; and he will talk about supporting her as if she did not perform more actual work and do more real contriving in twenty four hours than her lord and master in a week. I wondered how any man could have the effrontery to ask, or any woman the supineness to lay down the scepter and crown of girlhood to assume the yoke and burden of wifehood. My prayer was then as now that the time may come speedily when women will know and hold themselves at their true worth; when their eyes will be opened to the degradation of wasting their spotless lives on worthless and depraved men; when by the extent of their knowledge of life as it is and as it should be, by the depth of their contempt for men who lead unholy lives, and by the firmness of their resolution and the dignity of their self respect, they shall compel men to come up to their standard of morality and with them seek something still better, or be outcast from the Eden of woman's association. Since there is nothing in Nature to prevent woman from sharing all the good things of this world, I am proud and thankful to see her beginning to burst the bonds of that iron handed custom which has so long warned her not to touch, and asserting her co-heirship with her brother man. I am not so unjust as to make no exceptions to all the sweeping assertions I have been making. I know all women are not good and true, nor all men tyrannical and unjust. I could mention the names of several men pledged heart and soul to the . . . work of woman's emancipation from her long bondage; and one at least of my acquaintances is a far more ferocious antagonist of woman Slavery than I. From him I received the first antidote draught to cure my misanthropy and disgust of life. He it was who first showed me wherein Religion is not leagued with women's oppressors; who first assured me with a man's lips that woman has as good a right to her individuality and her free agency on the earth as her brother man. So you see . . . that for his sake, did I never know another liberal minded, large hearted man, I could not, and would [not] wish to condemn the whole race. I shall give honor where honor is due, and while waiting for the good time coming when all men and women shall be free and equal, put in my feeble oar wherever I can in her service.

III

The Impact of
Industrialism:
1883-1917

CHAPTER **7**

Business and labor

State Historical Society of Wisconsin.

Skilled metal artisans, late 19th century.

A New England textile mill manager

Thomas L. Livermore managed the Amoskeag Manufacturing Company, a Manchester, New Hampshire, cotton textile mill employing nearly six thousand persons. He represented the developing managerial class of American industry, his previous experience having been as a patent lawyer in Boston. In his testimony to the Senate committee investigating capital and labor in 1883, Livermore forcefully presented the industry's viewpoint, claiming his workers were contented and well paid. He denied the need for unions and argued that they interfered with the employee's "freedom of contract," that is, the right of workers to negotiate their individual working conditions. Livermore also highlighted the industry's concern for overproduction and its dependence upon a protective tariff.

Manchester, N. H., October 12, 1883.

Question. What is the capacity of the mills to manufacture, and what do they manufacture?—Answer. The mills under my charge use about 40,000 bales of cotton a year, and produce between 55,000,000 and 60,000,000 yards of cloth, at a cost of between $5,000,000 and $6,000,000 per annum.

Q. You mean that is the cost of the production of the cloth?—A. That is the cost of the cloth.

I should add that, in addition to manufacturing cloth, I carry on for the company the management of the water-works which run the mills in this place, and also the construction of buildings and structures relating to manufacturing establishments, and in that capacity have employed and dealt with many hundreds of laboring people.

Q. That is, outside of the number of operatives?—A. That was included in the 5,500 to 6,000. It is a varying number on that account.

The cloth manufactured by our company is mainly cloth manufactured out of yarn that has been dyed. We dye this yarn. The articles are ticks, denims, cheviots, awnings, and ginghams. Besides this we make canton flannels which are not dyed.

The cost of the labor is about 30 per cent. of the total cost of the goods. That labor amounts to about $1,500,000 a year.

From *Report of the Committee of the Senate upon the Relations between Labor and Capital,* 48th Congress, 3 (1885): 3–25.

New England mill, 1880s.

The amount of capital employed, and of plant in the mills, and for quick capital, is about equal to the cost of the yearly product. It takes about as much money for quick capital as it does for establishing the plant and running the mills—after our fashion of running them. As I understand it, those mills which do not have quick capital have to borrow it and pay interest upon it, in order that they may be successful.

I have here a memorandum of the wages which we have paid, taken from the rolls of two of our large mills (embracing, the one the coarsest and the other the finest work that we make) in the month of July last, which was a fair month to make an estimate from, and is the latest month in which we have run full time, inasmuch as low water has interfered with our operations since then. Our average wages—the average wages of all employed in the mills—for the different departments are as follows: For carding, males, $1.29; females, 95 cents. For spinning, males, $1.61; females, 95 cents. For mule spinning, $1.09. For dressing, $1.28.

The average for the mule spinning and dressing is for both males and females together, as I have not been able readily to separate them. The same is the case with those that I am now about to give: For weaving, $1.34; in the cloth-room, $1.25; dye-house, $1.42; carpenters and mechanics, $1.73. This last item is of people not employed in the mills, but outside the mills, in repairs of the mills.

The average which I have given includes the wages of children as well as adults; as, for instance, some mule spinners get $1.65, and upwards per day, but the wages of the boys in the room bring down the average. So in dressing, the wages of some of the men are $1.50 per day, but the wages of the boys and women bring down the average; and so of the carpenters and mechanics. Some of them get $3 a day, but apprentices and beginners get less, and that brings down the average. . . .

Q. What rate of prices do the women, children, and apprentices receive? It varies, no doubt, very much.—A. It varies very much. There is a wide scale, but in some of these departments women earn as much as $1.25 and $1.35 a day, and the children run all the way from 40 cents a day upwards, depending upon their age and capacity. Some of the men weavers earn as high as $1.67 a day.

As to the cost of living, I would say that we have a pretty accurate gauge of that in our boarding-houses. The company maintains a number of substantial brick buildings which it lets to boarding-house keepers at a very low rent, upon the condition that they shall charge to women in the employ of the company fixed rates for board and lodging, which are agreed to by the company. At the present time, this rate for women is $2.25 a week for board and lodging; so that, for instance, the women in the carding and spinning departments who average 95 cents a day will earn $5.70 per week, and they are boarded and lodged for $2.25 per week, which leaves to them $3.45 a week, out of which they must pay for their clothing, which is not necessarily expensive, and the rest they can save if there are no extra calls upon them. Besides these boarding-houses, the company maintains seven hundred tenements of a substantial character for families, which it lets to its employés for about $1 a month per room. Many of these tenements have from four to six rooms, so that the rent of the families occupying them is from $48 to $72 per annum. All these boarding-houses and tenements are kept in repair and policed for sanitary purposes by the company. . . .

Q. What is about the average cost of these houses?—A. About $1,500 a tenement.

Q. The rent of them is less than 5 per cent. on the price?—A. The net rent to the company, deducting repairs and taxes, is about 3 per cent.

Q. State what is the location and what are the sanitary conditions of the houses as to ventilation, cleanliness, &c.—A. These houses are situated upon good land, which is well drained. They are supplied with water from the city water works, and I think they will compare favorably with private dwellings in point of ventilation, warmth, and health generally. Of course, the cleanliness of the interior depends upon the family occupying the houses for the time being, but we endeavor to exercise an influence which will promote cleanliness on the part of the families.

The Amoskeag Company is peculiarly situated in having a large body of land in this city which is not occupied by dwellings, and which it allows its employés to cultivate for the nominal rent of $1 per annum, where they find it convenient to cultivate garden patches. . . .

Q. What is the general health of your employés?—A. I think that the general health may be said to be good. It is the desire of the mill-managers in this part of the country, generally, I believe, to light, heat, ventilate, and care for their mills generally so as to make them as healthy and agreeable as circumstances will allow; for other considerations not taken into account, the best mill in this respect would produce the best and the most cloth. Bad ventilation and discomfort generally has, I think, a palpable effect upon the quantity and character of product of the mill. The operative working in a well-lighted, well heated, and well ventilated mill would retain his strength and spirits to the end of the day, when one working in a mill which was not well lighted and heated and ventilated, would flag toward the end of the day, and not be at his best as a laborer.

The hours of labor in the mills here, for those who work the longest are from 6:30 a. m. to 12 and from 1 to 6:45 p. m., and on Saturday until 4 p. m.; making an average of about ten and three-quarters hours per day for each of the six working days of the week. But large numbers of the employés in the mill are enabled to finish their work sooner than the rest, and *they* average ten hours and some of them less per day.

I am informed, and have no doubt from my investigation that it is true, that forty years ago the hours of labor averaged fourteen and a half per day in the mills; that they were gradually reduced by the voluntary act of the mill

managers until they reached the limit which I have given as that of to-day. I
suppose this reduction was made possible, and was in a large degree due to the
improvements in machinery and methods of manufacture which enabled the
mills to keep up their product as time went on with reduced hours of labor. . . .

Q. What is your knowledge of the state of feeling among your operatives, as a
general fact, as to their satisfaction with their condition, their living, and their
wages, their contentment or discontent or distrust, or any want of confidence in
their employers? We want to get at the relation and state of feeling in point of
fact existing between the employers and employés.—A. I think that as a whole,
the working people in our employ are not discontented with their pay or their
condition. Of course, I suppose that every one on earth who is employed would
be glad if he could get more wages than he does get, but I think that, generally,
in this place, the people are contented to remain on the terms under which they
are employed. . . .

Q. Have you any labor unions here? What is the fact as to the number of your
employés who belong to labor unions?—A. I do not think that there is a labor
union in this city, and I do not think that there has ever been one here which
lasted. There have been several attempts to form unions since I have been here
by agitators from the outside, mainly from Fall River, I think, and from one
cause or another they have always failed.

Upon inquiry and investigation I have been led to believe that there has never
been more than one general strike in this place, and that occurred about thirty
years ago. I think that was a strike due to a change in the hours of labor, which
was instituted by the mills, and I believe that the strike failed. Since that time
there have been small strikes of detached portions of employés, but I never
heard of one resulting in success. Some three or four years ago I had a strike of
about one hundred of my dyers for higher wages. I thought that the strike was
unreasonable and refused to accede to the demands of the strikers, and the
result was that after staying away from their work about a week a large part of
them—one half or more—came and asked me to take them back in the employ
of the company. At that time I took pains to personally interrogate all of the
men who came to me, to inquire why they had taken that means of trying to get
higher wages, and I must say that with one or two exceptions they seemed to
have been actuated rather by the fear of being odd and the fear of the censure of
their fellow workmen than by any discontent of their situation. . . .

Q. What is your observation as to the length of time or the hours of labor
that the operative is capable of enduring without physical or other injury?—A.
My belief is that he can work ten and three quarter hours on an average without
injury, and I may say that in a limited degree I had some experience myself as a
youth, for I worked at a mechanical employment for a while; but of course my
judgment must be formed mainly from my observation here. If one goes upon
the main street here in the evening—Elm street—he will see the sidewalks
crowded as densely as Broadway, New York, by the mill operatives who have

finished their work and got their suppers and come out to promenade and see the shops and each other, and they seem to be merry and happy and laughing. I do not think that it is an exaggeration to say that you may often see on the sidewalks here in the evening thousands who have come out under those circumstances. Now, if it were the fact that they were prostrated and tired out by the hours of labor, they would not be out I think as a rule. . . .

Q. How would it operate upon the interests of the manufacturer, and how upon the working people, in your judgment, if hours could be reduced so that the machinery could be employed, say, for illustration sixteen hours a day, and two sets of hands employed, each working eight, would such a system as that be practicable, and, if so, what would be the effect upon the wages of each individual operative do you think?—A. I do not know whether it would be practicable. I can see objections to it, but whether they would be insuperable I am really unable now to say. The three chief objections to it which I see now are these: With two sets of hands running the same set of machinery it would be very difficult to place the responsibility for the care of the machinery upon either; that is a very important factor in maintaining a mill. Then it would be very difficult to find time to repair that machinery, and it would all have to be done in the night-time. You would have to keep a set of workmen in the night-time, which would be more expensive and troublesome. Then the risk of fire would be increased very largely by reason of the lighting of the mills at night. At the present time the insurers object to running the mills beyond 10 o'clock at night, for instance. . . .

Q. I asked the question because the suggestion has been made by many labor reformers, as they are termed, that even six hours, considering the increased productive power of machinery or of the human being and machinery combined, would be as long as laboring people ought to be expected to work—as long as the interests of society require that they should, and inasmuch as there are many unemployed people, a reduction of the hours of labor would give something to others to do. The question whether it could be made to work practically is the serious thing.

The WITNESS. I do not believe at all in such theories. I think that at least in a free country like this, with thousands of miles of land to be taken up in a vast area of country which is inhabited by people occupied in industrial pursuits, and the great variety of employments to be found in this country, it is perfectly safe for at least the life-time of this generation to leave the question of how a man shall work, and how long he shall work, and where he shall work, and what wages he shall get, to himself. It is as certain that wages in a country situated as ours is, will adjust themselves to the level required by the demand and the market, as it is that water will seek its level. I do not believe that any one has ever yet seen in this country a time when distress on the part of the laboring people was universal. It has occurred in certain industries and in certain places without any question, but, every time, the tremendous field which is afforded to the laboring man in which to find employment has come to his relief, and with a little foresight, a little forehandedness, and a little energy, he has been able to find some employment in which he could earn his living and a little more. . . .

Q. Won't you please tell us your experience with the question of child labor; how it is, and to what extent it exists here; why it exists, and whether, as it is actually existing here, it is a hardship on a child or on a parent; or whether there is any evil in that direction that should be remedied?—A. There is a certain class of labor in the mills which, to put it in very common phrase, consists mainly in running about the floor—where there is not as much muscular exercise required as a child would put forth in play, and a child can do it about as well as a grown person can do it—not quite as much of it, but somewhere near it, and with proper supervision of older people, the child serves the purpose. That has led to the employment of children in the mills, I think. . . .

Q. I was asking you about child labor, but there is a little "lead" in that direction in regard to which we have heard a good deal of testimony generally, though not from such witnesses as yourself, and their ideas on that subject it is well to give to the public—to the working people as well as others. You were going on to say that there was much work in a mill that children could perform without much more muscular exercise than they perform in play. Will you continue what you were about to say on that subject?—A. Yes. Now, a good many heads of families, without any question in my mind, were not sufficiently considerate of the mental and physical welfare of their children, and they put them to work in the mills perhaps too early and certainly kept them there too much of the time in former years, and the legislature had to step in and protect the children against the parents by requiring that they should go to school a certain number of months or weeks in a year, or else they should not be allowed to work in the mills; and at the present time there is a very severe law in this State applicable to children—I think some under twelve and some under sixteen. I do not remember the terms of it, but the child has to have a certificate of the authorities in control of the schools that he has been to school the time required by the statute before the mill manager is able to employ him. I think the mill manager is subject to a very considerable penalty for non-compliance with that law. In this city in our mills, and as far as I know in the rest of the mills, we have been very particular to observe the statute. I do not know how it is outside of the city. I suppose that it may depend a good deal upon public sentiment. If public sentiment supports the law, it will be enforced; if it does not, it will not be. I think public sentiment does support it here to an extent, although I think it extends a little too far in preventing children up to sixteen working in mills more than a given time. Mr. McDuffie suggests to me, what is the fact, that the city authorities here have an officer who makes it his business to go through the mills to see whether the law is complied with or not.

Now, I think that when it is provided that a child shall go to school as long as it is profitable for a workman's child (who has got to be a workingman himself) to go to school, the limit has been reached at which labor in the mills should be forbidden. There is such a thing as too much education for working people sometimes. I do not mean to say by that that I discourage education to any person on earth, or that I think that with good sense any amount of education can hurt any one, but I have seen cases where young people were spoiled for labor by being educated to a little too much refinement. . . .

Q. The great complaint that gets into the press and among the politicians is that the laborer does not get a fair share of the product of his labor. I understand you to say that they get about 30 per cent. of the joint product of the capital and labor?—A. Yes.

Q. Is that 30 per cent. upon the actual cost, or 30 per cent. on the market value?—A. On the actual cost.

Q. You, of course, make out your expense account, and you include the cost of labor?—A. Yes.

Q. And your profits you reach, of course, by deducting the expense account?—A. Our profit we reach by deducting the cost of manufacture from the market price plus the cost of selling.

Q. Have you any objection to stating the general net profit from your industry?—A. No, sir.

Q. What is the general net profit per cent. upon the actual cost of the product?—A. Since I have been connected with the mills it has been about 7 per cent. upon the amount invested. It has been about 14 per cent. upon the actual stock of the concern, but, as I have told you, there is about as much quick capital employed as the cost of the plant, and the cost of the plant about represents the capital stock. In other words, our mills and machinery are worth about $3,000,000, and our capital stock is $3,000,000.

Q. That is the active capital?—A. That is the capital stock borne on our books. We have then beside that a surplus of quick capital, amounting to about $2,500,000, which is employed in the business, nearly as much more as the capital stock.

Q. What dividends do you declare, and how often?—A. The dividends are ordinarily declared semi-annually. The regular dividend is 5 per cent. on the capital stock; 5 per cent. semi-annually.

Q. That is, 10 per cent. per annum?—A. Yes; but there have been during this time extra dividends, which have brought the total up to about 14 per cent. per annum upon the nominal capital stock. . . .

Q. Upon the $3,000,000?—A. Upon the $3,000,000. I should add that this includes a little profit due from a sale of land; for this company owned substantially all the land on which this city is built, before the city was started, and has sold the land to the people who have built here, and it still sells land; and there is perhaps 2 per cent. out of the 10 per cent. of the annual dividend due to the sale of land. In this connection it is proper for me to state, to prevent misapprehension, that in addition to this plant of the mills, and to this quick capital, the company has property in land, which I have not included in this statement, because it is not germane to the inquiry. . . .

cA Georgia textile mill manager

John Hill, a mechanical engineer for the Eagle and Phoenix Manufacturing Company in Columbus, Georgia, described the growing textile industry in the South for the Senate investigating committee. Like Livermore, he painted a cheerful picture of working conditions, particularly noting how manufacturing had contributed to what he believed were harmonious relations between blacks and whites. But Hill, a transplanted northerner, did emphasize the advantages of the cheap, quiescent labor force that could be had in the South—blacks, women, and children—and thus offered further inducements for the increasing industrial migration to the South.

Columbus, Ga., November 20, 1883.

Q. Please give us, now, some account of the condition of the manufacturing industry in the southern part of the country, the principal places where manufacturing is carried on in the South, and where its development is most advanced and is likely to become most important. . . . —A. The rise of cotton manufacturing in the South has been gradual and regular, and the per cent. of advance from year to year has been measured by the general condition of the industry during the time. At times when cotton manufacturing was profitable mills have been rapidly built. At other times, when the profits on manufacturing were reduced, the building of mills has about ceased. This is the same in both the North and the South. In 1880, 1881, and 1882 there was a very rapid advance in the manufacturing capacity of the South. The same is also true of the North. In 1876, when the Phoenix and Eagle Company resolved to spend something like $1,000,000 in cotton improvement, and we entered the machinery market of the North, this was the only cotton-mill of any consequence being built in the United States that year, either North or South. The

From *Report of the Committee of the Senate upon the Relations between Labor and Capital*, 48th Congress, 4 (1885): 582–597.

machine shops of the North were standing idle and machinery could have been purchased at prices of our own making and was offered to us on those terms. At the present time the prospects for manufacturing are not bright, and all the improvements of consequence now being made in cotton manufacturing are simply finishing up something that had been started. There are very few new enterprises in cotton manufacturing starting now in the South, but still a much larger per cent. than in the North. There are some factories now being projected and which will probably be built, but they are engaged in rather as local enterprises for the benefit of the local communities and in a small way, than as investments of money for direct profit. The measure of the future development of cotton manufactures in the South will be in exact proportion to the profit on the money invested in the business compared with investments in other industries. If capital finds it more profitable to invest in cotton manufacturing than in other enterprises, it will be so invested, but not otherwise. Therefore I say the future development of cotton manufacturing here, as elsewhere, is dependent entirely on the prospect of profit, for cotton manufacturing is simply a business and its extension depends upon the dividend it yields.

Manufacturing in the South is more profitable than in the North for certain kinds of goods, and those goods can be manufactured in the South and sold at a profit which will pay a fair interest on the money invested, when the same goods manufactured in New England, and sold at the same price, would yield no profit. To explain, I will say that the local advantages that we have here in the matter of freight, in the price of labor, and in climate (for this climate is more favorable for manufacturing than the climate of the North), and our cheaper motive power, both water and steam, gives us, on the whole, an advantage of something like one-half in the cost of domestic goods. As an example I may state that in our new Eagle and Phoenix mill it costs less than 1 cent a pound to pick, card, and spin a pound of cotton into No. 14 yarn. That is the cost of labor alone, omitting incidental and general expenses, which may probably be about equal in the North and in the South. In other words, the labor account here for working up a pound of No. 14 yarn is less than 1 cent. Now, the average freight on a bale of cotton from Columbus to the East is 1 cent a pound. The average freight on a bale of goods from Columbus to New York is 50 cents a hundred—half a cent a pound. We can therefore spin 1 pound of cotton yarn, No. 14, for ninety-six one-hundredths of a cent per pound, omitting the other incidental expenses (which, as I have said, are about equal at the North and South), and we can put that cotton yarn down in New York for 50 cents a hundred, half a cent a pound, making the cost 1.46 cents for freight and labor on a pound of yarn when laid down ready for sale in New York. It costs 1 cent and a half to put a pound of cotton in a cotton mill at Lowell, into the picker room, before any labor whatever is spent upon it. . . .

Q. How do the two sections compare as to the cost of living—the cost of food?—A. The consumption of food by the human frame is like the consumption of fuel by the steam engine, it is regulated by natural laws, and is in proportion to the power expended. The use of food is to generate blood and heat to sustain the system. Now, it requires three times or more than three times the strength in original elements of food to sustain a Laplander than it requires to sustain a native or an inhabitant of the island of Jamacia, and the same natural law which demands fuel in proportion to the power expended, also requires less food in a moderate climate than in a rigorous one, the difference being in exact proportion to the labor and the expenditure of heat. The proportion of food necessary to sustain a Southern operative is governed by this natural law, and as the average temperature at the South is much higher than at the North, the amount of food required to sustain that temperature is in exact proportion; therefore you see it does not take as much food here to sustain an operative as it does there.

Now as to the efficiency of labor in the two sections. The Southern operative is native born, while the average Northern operative is not. They have got more Canadian operatives in Manchester, N. H., than they have natives. Now, as it is a well-known fact to all who have studied the subject, the elements of mind, the general mental make-up and intelligence of the native American exceeds by far the average of like qualities in the lower classes of foreigners, the classes who immigrate into this country to work in mills. So in the same proportion are you likely to find the comparative intelligence of the Northern and the Southern operatives, the Southern being native and the Northern being a foreigner. There is more endurance in the constitution in a cold climate than in a warm one, and our advantage becomes a disadvantage in this respect, where it is a question of hard, heavy labor. Natural laws would therefore indicate that for heavy labor the Northern operative would be superior to the Southern, but while this is true, it is also true that a warm climate develops the human system earlier, and makes the action of both mind and body quicker than in a cold climate. The natives of warm climates are more impulsive, quicker to learn, and quicker in action, though not so enduring. This climate advances the period of manhood or womanhood fully a year and a half over the average climate of New England, so far as development is concerned. A man or a woman here in Columbus is as far advanced in physical development at fifteen years of age as a like person would be in Lowell at sixteen and a half years of age.

Now, for cotton manufacturing, capacity to endure hard labor is not a material point, because the labor is not hard. The motions required are quick rather than laborious, except in certain departments. In weaving there is probably about as much of one kind as the other, and, of course, weaving is a very important department. It may be stated as a general fact, therefore, that in this regard the advantages in the South are at least equal to those in the North.

In the matter of education the native American of the North averages superior to the native of the South, owing to the fact that for many years, covering the lives of all the operatives now in the mills of the North, the free-school system has been universal there, and the necessity of education has been generally and fully appreciated. In the South, while a free-school system does exist in this State, yet it is not so far advanced as the free-school system in New England; not so liberal; not so easy to be availed of. It furnishes less school accommodation in proportion to population, and there is less disposition on the part of the people to patronize it, and, generally speaking, owing to the very limited time it has been in existence, the advantages of our free-school system here have not been reaped by our people to an extent that will at all compare with the benefits that the New England system has conferred upon the people there.

But again, as compared with foreign help, the probabilities are that even in the matter of education our Southern operatives have the advantage. In Alabama, South Carolina, and other States, where no attention has been paid to the free-school system, the operatives have not had the advantages that they have in Georgia.

The hours of labor in cotton manufacture in the Eagle and Phoenix mills average eleven per day, but in many mills they average twelve per day. In New England, in some of the States, the law prescribes ten hours as a day's work. That is so in Massachusetts, but not in New Hampshire. . . .

I might state that all mill operatives having to do with the process of cotton manufacturing involving quick perception and manipulation are white. In portions of the work, where it is only a question of muscle, and where intelligence is not a necessity, the laborers employed are either black or white, the preference, where it comes to a matter of mere muscle, being given to the colored laborer. I refer now to rolling a bale of cotton in, tearing it open, tumbling around boxes and bales, and such heavy work. It has been found, and is a fact patent to all who have studied the question, that the employment of colored labor in the finer processes of manufacturing is a question which is mooted only by those who know nothing about it. . . . It may be regarded as a fact about which those who understand the question can have no dispute, that it will be many years before the present condition of things can be changed. There are places to which each of these labor elements is specially adapted. The supply of both races is about equal to the demand, and there is an opportunity for support and for fair and reasonable prosperity open to one race as well as to the other.

There is a good feeling existing between the employers and the employed, both white and black, at the South, which is not equaled in any other section of this country, or in Europe either. There are no strikes here, no rebellions of the laborers, no disposition on the part of labor to combine against capital, and no disposition on the part of capital to oppress labor. Everything is in harmony, and a state of harmony and of prosperity in this respect exists which is to be found in no other place in the civilized world to the same extent as in the cotton States of the South. That is caused by the fact that there is a liberality upon the part of the employers which dispenses justice to the employed willingly and cheerfully, and without compulsion. This fact is recognized by the employés, and where there is justice between capital and labor, and no oppression, there is, of course, no necessity for collisions, strikes, or animosities. . . .

Now, I will make another statement which will probably be interesting to people who do not live here. The cotton States of the South are the only portion of the United States where whites and blacks work together upon the same work at the same pay and under the same regulations, the only part of this country where the two races will work side by side, justice being rendered to each, and the laborers of both races working in harmony and in unison, without rebellion and with mutual good-will. I employed on mill No. 3 from fifty to seventy-five brick masons, and probably from fifteen to twenty rock masons. The men of both races were mixed, working side by side, black and white. They were paid equal wages, and there was perfect harmony between them and equal proficiency except in cases where special acquirements were necessary on special work, and, in one instance, for considerable length of time, a state of facts existed that could not exist in any other country in the world, viz, that the entire lot of laborers were superintended by a colored man. You can't see anything like that in New England, can you? But what I say of the harmonious relations between the laborers of the two races has particular reference to Georgia, and other States where the races have not been antagonized by violent political agitations in the past.

The CHAIRMAN. We haven't got the colored men in New England.

The WITNESS. Well, the two races wouldn't work alongside of each other there, would they?

The CHAIRMAN. I do not know; I never saw it tried.

The WITNESS. I have tried it in the North myself. You can't work whites and blacks alongside of each other at the North. It is not a question of equality. That question does not come up. The laborer of the South is not a politician, and does not study these questions. He is willing to render a day's labor for a day's pay. He does not wish to be placed upon an equality socially with the black man, but he is willing to work side by side with the negro or any other man who will render an equal day's work for an equal amount of money.

The CHAIRMAN. You state that as a fact which generally prevails here with reference to the white and colored laborers of this part of the country?

The WITNESS. Yes, sir; it is impracticable to mix the races in labor where there is close connection (like a gang of hands working together), because in that case the white men will always try to have the colored men do all the work. The two races will work side by side at equal work quite harmoniously, but they had better be in different brigades, except in such work as masonry, where every man is on his own hook, so far as his work is concerned, and not dependent upon any other man. The mason lays a brick, and he does not require to have any one else to help him put it in its place, as he would if he had to put a log or a stone in place. Working them together does not work well, because in such a case the darky is going to do most of the work and the white man is going to do the bossing. There is really no trouble here between the races if you will give them justice, and not insist on bringing up matters that do not properly enter into the matter at all. The colored man is the most desirable laborer I have ever known. I would rather have him than any other laborer of any race that I know of, and I have tried pretty nearly all of them, because I came here from the West, where the population is so mixed that you don't know where anybody comes from. The colored man is an excellent laborer, but then you must treat him with respect. There is no gentleman in the South, no man who is capable of properly managing colored laborers, who does not render them proper respect. No Southern man who understands the relation of the races, and no man anywhere who understands human nature, will undertake to humiliate an employé. The result of this feeling is that the term "nigger," and other such opprobrious terms, are never used by Southern employers, except by those who know no better; but, on the other hand, terms of respect, such as "colored man," "black man," "colored woman," "black woman," are always used and accepted, and no odious terms of comparison are employed. You will find that to be the case everywhere through the South. You will never find the term "nigger" used as applied to the colored man except in the North.

The CHAIRMAN. I beg your pardon, but since I have been here I have heard it used quite often. I do not think it is used by men in official or representative positions, but in the ordinary slang of the day I hear it used a great deal.

The WITNESS. Well, I make this statement in reference to labor here because it is contrary to what I supposed to be the fact before I came here, and contrary to what the average Northern man supposes to be the fact, the general idea at the North being that there is a broad line drawn between the races down here. It is to correct that impression that I make this statement in regard to the two races working together more harmoniously than I think they can be found doing anywhere else in the world. I am sure that in New York or Boston or Chicago, or anywhere else at the North, you could not put these white and these colored men to work side by side as you can here in Columbus. Put a white man to work alongside of a colored man on the walls of a Chicago building and treat them both as you do here, and you will be pretty certain to have a strike at once. The correctness of that opinion is established, I think, by the fact that the thing is never attempted at the North. You don't find white men and black men working together in the iron mills or the rolling furnaces at the North, but here they are all mixed up in that way. If you undertake to put whites and blacks to work together even in the coal mines in Pennsylvania, you would have trouble, but nothing of the kind occurs here. . . .

I have been simply calling attention to the fact that we can do here what you cannot do there; that is, we can work the two races together on the same work in harmony, and I say again that you could not do that in the mines of Pennsylvania, in the rolling mills of Pittsburgh, in the manufacturing establishments of New York, or upon the buildings of New York, Boston, or Chicago. You could not find or get up in any of those places the same harmonious feeling which exists here between the races to-day.

The CHAIRMAN. Then it is not really the race question at all. It is simply this, that such a large part of your working population is colored that if you should undertake to exclude them from your labor market there would be nobody to do the work, and therefore, there being sufficient employment for both races, they work quietly alongside of each other, neither feeling that it is necessary to compete with the other for employment.

The WITNESS. Well, always, both before the war and since the war, there has been a better feeling between the two races here than at the North. The question of race, the question of the color of a man's face, does not arise at all in reference to this kind of labor, but in the North it does come in, and the consequence is that you find it impossible there to work the two races together harmoniously as we do here. I simply state this as a fact not generally known by parties at the North who have not investigated it. . . .

It is only in the proper place that the two races can come together harmoniously. They don't come together in the dining-room, they don't come together in society, but there is a place where they can come together harmoniously, and that is right down on this basis where it is a question of labor, and where the common sentiment of the people is that the two races are equal. So far as regards this question of such labor as can earn 60 or 70 cents a day, there is perfect equality between white and black labor here in the South. But that does not mean at all social equality. It has nothing to do with politics or with social equality or anything of the kind. It means just 75 cents a day for a day's work, whether the laborer is white or black, or $2.50 a day for a black mason, and $2.50 for a white mason. We have two blacksmiths at work at the Eagle and Phoenix mill, one of them being white and the other black, and they are on an equality in wages and in work. One of them is a very intelligent white man and the other is a very intelligent colored man. The question of equality does not come up with reference to those two men at all. They are both just blacksmiths working at $2.50 a day each, and drawing that amount of wages at the end of the week, and that is all there is to it. We do not mix the races in the machine shop. It is done only where there seems to be a certain suitableness in it. We do it on our rock walls and our brick walls, and among our carpenters, and we pay each one at the same rate for equal work.

Q. And give neither race the preference in selecting the men to be employed?—A. If I want a man to do certain things I want a colored man every time, while, on the other hand, if I want a man to do certain other things, I want a white man. I don't know that it hinges on the question of the whiteness or blackness of the man's skin; it hinges rather on the adaptability of the man to do the particular work that is required.

Q. Now, what have you to say to us in regard to child labor in factories?—A.

Well, the child labor question is different here from what it is in the North, for
sundry reasons. In the first place, it is a lamentable fact that parents here do not
recognize the necessity of education to the extent that they do in the North. In
the North all the people, including all the laboring classes, think it a duty to
have their children educated, and the facilities which the free-school system
gives them for that purpose are very largely used. Perhaps the laws of the
Northern States regulate the matter somewhat; but laws are second to facts,
and if the sentiment of the people did not justify such laws they would not be
made. Then, too, a law that would be good in that regard in Massachusetts
would not be good for anything in Alabama. You must adapt your laws to the
State and conditions of society. Suppose you should pass a law in Alabama
that, up to a certain age, children should not work because they must go to
school; it wouldn't be good for anything; for the reason that, in the first place,
even if they did not work, they would not go to school, because the parents
would not want to send them, and also because if they did there are no schools
to which they could send them generally. Again, on the other hand, that is not
true of Georgia. Of course, I am now speaking only of the average. There are
many people here who would be very apt and anxious to educate their children,
and who would be very glad to send them to school. There are many who do
send their children to school wherever they have the opportunity, but there are
many others who do not; from want of thrift, or from the fact which does not
exist elsewhere in this country, that the devastation produced by the war has
swept away the material prosperity of the people and probably set them back
fifty years in that respect, and as a consequence they are unable to educate their
children as they would wish. For these reasons, and also because of the fact
generally admitted, that economy is not one of the strongest points of the
Southern people, there are a great many parents who would be glad to send
their children to school, but who have not the opportunity or the means, being
compelled to keep the children employed in procuring the necessaries of life.

In regard to the small children, more especially those in our spinning room,
they are worth all they are paid, and the fact is that the wages they earn are a
necessity for the support of the families from which the children come; so that if
they were turned out there would be suffering upon the part of those families
for want of that income. We do not really employ those children as a matter of
preference, but as a matter of necessity. When a family comes here and a portion of them go to work in the mill they are sure to make application for
employment for all their children who are of sufficient age to go to work in the
mill, and they persist in those applications until those children are employed.

Q. At what ages are the children employed?—A. About ten years, I believe, is
the youngest age at which we employ them.

Q. What do children of ten years and upward do?—A. They do this very light
work, attending the spinning and winding machinery—very light work. There is
no work that those children do that is sufficiently arduous to over-tax them or

to interfere with their health or development. Their work is all light, and the only thing that can tax them is perhaps the hours of labor. . . .

The sweatshop: three views

The garment manufacturing industry in the late nineteenth century especially highlighted the destructive and weakening effects of unrestrained competition. The tremendous influx of cheap foreign labor from southern and eastern Europe, which crowded into the large urban centers, transformed the nature of the industry. Previously, manufacturing had been done in factories, but under the banner of "efficiency," piece work was farmed out to small entrepreneurs who in turn employed whole families in crowded, unsanitary tenements. The following selections offer commentaries on the sweatshop from the perspectives of an employer, a worker, and a visiting physician who worked for New York City.

A Proprietor

Chicago, April 4, 1892

The committee drove to the sweating establishment of ———. This shop is located in the rear of a two-story frame building over a stable in which there are three stalls, one horse, a dog, a spring wagon, and a large manure pile, and is reached by a narrow, dirty passageway which leads to a rickety pair of steps, by which the shop is entered. There is a space perhaps 25 feet square between the front building and the stable, which the sweater chooses to call a "yard," but which in reality is nothing more than a garbage receptacle. The dirty rags, ashes, and decayed garbage, together with the foul odors that issue from two unkept closets, evidence great neglect on the part of the tenant as to the healthful and sanitary conditions of his surroundings.

The proprietor was brought forward and interrogated.

Q. How many people do you employ here?—A. When we have a full force, about 18.

Q. What do you make?—A. Ladies' cloaks.

Q. What hours do you keep?—A. From 7 a. m. to 6 p. m. Sometimes we work until 9 o'clock at night.

From *Report of the Committee on Manufactures on the Sweating System,* 52 Congress, 2 Session, (1893), viii-x; 92–94; xiii-xvii.

State Historical Society of Wisconsin.

Trade union poster protesting exploitation of female labor, 1908.

Q. When you have full force how many men do you employ?—A. About 10 men.

Q. How many women?—A. About 8.

Q. In what condition do you get the garments?—A. They come here already cut and I make them up.

Q. What is the average wages of the men per week?—A. About $15 a week.

Q. How much do the women get?—A. About $6. They get paid for extra hours.

Q. In regard to your work. Do any of your people take any part of it and work upon it at home?—A. No, sir; except sometimes in the busy season I give it out.

Q. Where do your help live?—A. Not far from here.

Q. What nationality are your employés?—A. Hebrews.

Q. What is that population in this city?—A. About 150,000.

Q. Are wages higher or lower than they were two years ago?—A. Lower. There are so many who want work.

Q. How much do you get for making this garment?—A. Eighty cents.

Q. How much did you get for making it two years ago?—A. About $1.25.

Q. Is the help paid less now?—A. Yes, sir.

The party then drove to the shop of ———, engaged in the manufacture of ladies' cloaks. He rents four rooms on the ground floor of a two-story frame house. The front room, which is used for working purposes, is about 20 by 30, and contains three large benches, one stove, three machines, fourteen chairs, a bed, and other articles of household goods. The other three rooms are occupied by the family.

Q. How many people do you employ?—A. Work is slack now, and we employ only 7 girls and 4 men.

Q. How many do you employ when you are rushed?—A. About 20, and sometimes more than 20.

Q. How much do the men get per week?—A. They work by the piece.

Q. How much do they make in a week?—A. $8 or $10. If it is good work they make $10 or $15. But now they would be glad to make $8, if they could, in a week.

Q. What are your hours?—A. From 7 to 6.

Q. How is it when you are busy?—A. Oh, we work sometimes until 10 o'clock.

Q. How much do the women make in a week?—A. $3 or $4 when work is slow, and $6 when work is good.

Q. How are wages now?—A. Not so good. We get less now.

Q. Who sleeps on that bed?—A. The steamer.

Q. Who is he?—A. Oh, he is a man who worked here. He is out of a job now, and we take him in for charity.

Q. Do you ever give charity to more than one?—A. Sure.

Q. How many have you had at one time sleeping in this room?—A. (By an employé.) Lots of them; the beds are put away.

Q. How many sleep in the other rooms?—A. Two in each.

Q. What nationality are most of your help?—A. Hebrew.

Q. What effect has the reduction in the price of making these cloaks on wages?—A. The girls get smaller wages than they did. . . .

We next visited the house of ———, who makes cloaks, Mr. ——— occupies four rooms, using the front, which is about 15 by 18, for the shop. He has a wife and seven children, who occupy three rooms in the rear of the shop. The first room back of the shop, which is about 10 by 12, is used for a kitchen. In this room there was a red-hot stove, two tables, a clothes rack, and several piles of goods evidently just received. A woman was making bread on a table upon which there were other articles scattered promiscuously about, such, for instance, as a baby's stocking, scraps of cloth, several old tin cans, and a small pile of unfinished garments. In the second room we found an old woman with a diseased face walking the floor with a crying child in her arms. This room had no carpet on the floor, and the only furniture therein, with the exception of the week's wash, was a wardrobe and bureau. The third room also had a bare floor, and contained simply two beds without any bedclothing. Mr. ——— and family, together with his working force, were confined to the use of one water-closet, which was not well kept and had only one key.

Q. How many people do you employ here?—A. About 5 girls and 7 men.

Q. How much are they making?—A. $5, $6, and $7 a week.

Q. How much do they make in the busy season?—A. About $15.

Q. What hours do you keep?—A. From 7 to 6. Sometimes we work a little longer, but not much.

Q. Are the prices as good now as they were sometime ago?—A. About 50 per cent less.

Q. How long have you been in business?—A. About four years, and they have been going down all the time.

A Cloak-maker

Chicago, April 5, 1892

Q. What is your full name?—A. Abraham Bisno.

Q. Where do you live?—A. 151 Johnson street.

Q. What is your occupation?—A. I am a cloak-maker.

Q. For what contractor do you work?—A. ([Given, but omitted here.]

Q. How long have you worked for him?—A. Three weeks.

Q. How long have you been in that business?—A. Eleven years.

Q. What kind of cloaks do you make?—A. I make good cloaks.

Q. That sell for how much?—A. From $15 to $30.

Q. Now, ten years ago what did you get for making a cloak like that?—A. The cloaks differ and can not be practically compared.

Q. How long have you been a competent cloak-maker?—A. Since the last eight or nine years.

Q. Say eight years ago, how many hours did you make per week.—A. I worked from seventy to seventy-five.

Q. How much did you actually earn a week?—A. I earned from $14 to $16.

Q. Now, five years ago how much would you make a week?—A. Five years ago the work was different. It was necessary to make better goods, and although I received smaller prices I earned as much because I had learned to work faster.

Q. Your answer would be, "I was able to do and did do more and better work, but my earnings per week were about the same?"—A. Yes, sir.

Q. How was it about two years ago?—A. The money that I received was less per week.

Q. Did you work the same number of hours?—A. No. I can say that I worked from sixty-five to seventy hours per week, and I produced more than what I produced before working seventy-five hours, and yet I earned a little less.

Q. How much less?—A. From $13 to $14 in the busy season, and we figured that we produced as much as $20 compared with six or eight or nine years ago.

Q. How many hours do you work per week now?—A. About sixty hours.

Q. How much do you make per week?—A. Eleven dollars.

Q. How much do you produce?—A. More still.

Q. So that the piece price has gone down?—A. Yes, sir. As I told you I am eleven years in this business. When I first started the sweat shops were not developed. There were only three sweat shops in Chicago when I started.

Q. What do you mean by a sweater?—A. A man who takes work out, who invests no money in the business and who risks nothing, and has but little to manage, and yet he gets a share of the profits of that certain commodity.

Q. I want to get here a definition of the "sweat shop." Your idea is a shop not built for the purpose of manufacturing, but a place where manufacturing is carried on by employes who a contractor employs, and this contractor going to no particular expense to do the business in a business-like way?—A. Yes, sir. I work in a shop for a manufacturer. The manufacturer runs his shop at ten hours a day only; but I, who have a desire to work longer than ten hours, take work home every night. The manufacturer says you can take the whole work home and produce it at home. He takes it home, and he has the use of his wife and children and neighbors. He employs others, and these are the germs of the sweat shop. Sweat shops are shops at home; and now they have grown by reason of employing more and more into a factory. These sweat shops are in basements and attics, and the nuisance was brought about because the people can work longer than in a factory.

Q. What is your suggestion as to the best way to remedy this evil?—A. When I started to work I worked for Beifeld & Co., who employed some two hundred to three hundred inside help. Beifield Brothers saw that sweat shops would pay him and his business, and he in proportion increased the sweat shops and diminished the inside help, so now he employs only about seventy-five people inside. Leigh Brothers employed about three hundred people inside, and now he employs none, but he has increased his business similar to Beifeld. I give you this information, and I can prove it.

Q. You believe that this tendency is not a good one?—A. I believe that it is working for the destruction of man.

Q. What have you to suggest for a remedy?—A. If I was a lawmaker I would make it punishable by a fine to produce cloaks in a tenement house. I would make it punishable by a fine to produce clothing in a tenement house.

Q. Would you compel the manufacture of clothing to be carried on in factories properly constructed and carried on for the purpose, and the abolition of child labor?—A. Yes, sir.

Q. How far is child labor carried on in this city now?—A. Very much.

Q. You have a school law here?—A. Sure, but it does not work.

Q. What are the hours in the sweat shops?—A. The man who works the longest has the key.

Q. How about the health conditions as you see them?—A. I think it works to the destruction of health. They work in bedrooms and in shops where there is nothing to breathe. A brother of mine worked for five years in one of these shops, and he died and left a wife and five children. Personally, I take care of myself, and yet if I was not to work in such shops I would live longer. . . .

Dr. Annie S. Daniel

New York, December 19, 1892

I am outdoor visiting physician for the New York Infirmary for Women and Children, and have been for the past eleven years. My work is to visit those people who are sick in their tenement houses—women and children only. In the past year I have personally seen 1,457 patients—women and children—in tenement houses.

Q. Mainly in what quarter of the city?—A. On the east side, mainly from Twenty-third street southward to Chatham Square, and from Mott street to the East River. . . .

Q. What, if any, changes have taken place within the last ten years in the character and locality of the population within the district covered?—A. Between Grand and Houston streets. Formerly, almost entirely either Germans, or Irish, or American-speaking people, American-born, this population is changed to Jews, Russians, Germans, Roumanian Jews, entirely. The best example of that is found in Ridge street, in which there is not a family, scarcely, that is not a Jewish family. The population from Houston street to Fourteeth street is more mixed, but is becoming Bohemian and Roumanian; especially is this so in Second street and First street. Below Grand street, west of the Bowery, the change has been that the Italians and Chinese have come in; east of the Bowery it is again Jews.

Q. Take the section below Houston street, north of Chatham Square and east of the Bowery, what proportion, offhand, would you estimate as of Hebrew descent; a large proportion?—A. Oh, yes; I should say 8 out of every 10 persons. It has especially been so within the last five years. Before that time the population would have been German, Irish, and American within this same quarter.

Q. What are the principal occupations of the people within the district covered by your work?—A. Almost entirely some form of making clothes.

Q. And aside from the general business of tailoring, or the making of clothes in one form or another, what general business is the next most important?—A. The making of children's clothes, children's little dresses, and women's clothes generally; not women's dresses, though.

Q. Underwear?—A. Yes; underwear and children's clothing.

Q. Now, the next most important?—A. Rather scattering. There are none that compare in importance with the ones I have mentioned. The making of neckties, that may be included in men's wear, but that is not a very prominent trade.

Q. What, then, do you mean by separate trades?—A. Branches of the business, at each of which is engaged exclusively a considerable number of workmen; for example, the pressing of seams alone is largely done by those who are particularly expert at this, and who do nothing else. The sewing on of buttons is similarly done by those who do this alone and could earn not nearly as much at anything else except by long practice. The making of the buttonholes is another trade. Even the pulling out of the threads is done by those who do nothing else, and who have gained peculiar skill in that branch. It is hard to express the extent of the subdivision of labor, and steadily it is increasing; that is, the scope of the employment of each workman appears on the average to grow less and less. It must be remembered, too, that the general occupation of tailoring is subdivided not merely for the different processes I have mentioned, but for each of the different classes of garments; for example, in the making of overcoats, most of the processes involved would be carried on by those who would each, not merely be incompetent to do any other class of work than that at which he or she is specially employed, but would not be able to do similar work on a different kind of garment; for example, pantaloons. And the case is similar with regard to heavy and light garments of the same class. Within the district which I have mentioned there is, however, comparatively little work done by those who receive the goods direct from the large manufacturers, and the proportion of this sort of work is rapidly getting less and less, and is practically confined to the Germans and a few of the Irish, who are skilled workmen, as I call them. The work within this district is done in small shops, and even more largely in families. For instance, the head of the family gets the cloth from the middleman, or the sweater, as he is called, and the man does the machine sewing and the pressing, the woman the hand sewing, and the children the pulling out of the basting threads—speaking only of coats now. In the case of pantaloons, the children sew the buttons on, children as young as 4 years of age. . . .

Q. Now, the next largest proportion of tailoring work; how is that done?—A. In small, so-called sweat shops; that is, in establishments not built or particularly fitted for the business, simply old dwelling houses, and employing less than 20 hands.

Q. Now, as to the hours of labor?—A. They work from twelve to fifteen hours in the families. It depends entirely on the amount of work they have. I have known them to work twenty hours out of the twenty-four steadily.

Q. That is, the head of the family?—A. The heads of the family, the man and woman; that is only during the busy season.

Q. To how great an extent is child labor used; is it rare or common?—A. Very common; wherever there is a child in a family where work is taken in the child is employed.

Q. Generally speaking?—A. Always; either directly or indirectly.

Q. And how about the hours as to child labor?—A. That depends entirely upon the work.

Q. For example, are children worked at night?—A. Yes; I have seen many of them working as late as 10 and 11 o'clock at night; that is, in families, not in the sweat shops.

Q. What are the general hours in the sweat shops?—A. From twelve upward. There are very few who work eight or ten hours unless work is slack. . . .

Q. Now, as to the general health of these people?—A. The general health is good. They suffer mostly from their occupation and from contagious diseases. Contagious diseases are very prevalent, especially scarlet fever, measles, and diptheria. The proportion of contagious diseases to all of the sickness in the locality is very large, say two or three times what it would be in an ordinary community.

Q. To what contagious diseases do you have reference?—A. Mostly scarlet fever, measles, and diphtheria; these three especially. Whooping cough is very prevalent. Indeed, in the crowded and almost promiscuous conditions under which they live, contagious diseases, though not particularly fatal in this district, are always prevalent and practically continuing epidemics, so much so that everyone has them, and I rarely find patients over 14 with scarlet fever or measles.

Q. How about typhus and cholera?—A. Well, I have had no cholera, but I have had typhus fever in my district. . . .

Q. What distinction do they make between the place where they live and the place where they work?—A. There is no distinction at all. You may find the work in the bedroom, or you may find it in the kitchen on the table, and people eating; you will find the food and the clothes on the same table; and you will find the clothes on the same bed with the sick child with the scarlet fever. . . .

Q. How in regard to wages and conditions; are they getting better or worse?—A. Wages are growing lower. The conditions are about the same, except that as the wages grow lower the people grow poorer, and the beggars are increasing.

Q. How long have conditions remained practically similar to those now remaining?—A. It has been at least five years—since the large influx of Jews and Italians. Those people who are working twenty-five years, for instance, those women, say that within the last ten years it has grown decidedly worse. My observation corroborates that.

Q. And especially within the last five years?—A. Yes. Immigration has made the conditions worse.

Q. What suggestions have you as to what can and should be done, if anything?—A. I believe that the only remedy is prohibition of all tenement-house work, even by members of the family.

Q. All household work?—A. All household work—all work in the living rooms of the tenement-house people.

Q. Now, as to contagion. Do you consider that any large proportion of the clothing made within the district mentioned is exposed to contagion?—A. In every case where there is a contagious disease in the family the clothing is exposed. I know, from my own knowledge, that the germs of disease have been carried several blocks in the clothing.

Q. Is clothing a favorable medium for attracting and carrying disease germs, or otherwise?—A. Very favorable.

Q. What, if any, particular diseases are most likely to be so carried?—A. Scarlet fever and diphtheria. In case of cholera that would be decidedly so.

Q. How about typhus?—A. Typhus and typhoid fever would be carried.

Q. What, if any, means are used to rid any of the work done from contagion or its dangers?—A. Nothing is done at all.

Q. How near was the limited district within which we looked last night to the locality where last summer the typhus developed?—A. It was right in the district. One place was within a block of a place we inspected. In the last two weeks three cases of typhus have been found in the general district, close to where this work is carried on.

Laborers and their machines: despair

The rapid mechanization of American industry heightened productivity, probably lightened physical labor, and certainly increased tedium and workers' dissatisfaction. Mechanization put less of a premium on workers' skills and people found themselves subordinated to the demands of their machines. John Morrison, a twenty-three-year-old New York machinist, described for the 1883 Senate investigators the changed conditions he had witnessed in his nine years as a worker. Morrison's thoughts on revolution may not have been widely shared, but his observations on class lines accurately reflected workers' perceptions of themselves in a time of declining demand for their skills.

New York, August 28, 1883.

. . . Q. Is there any difference between the conditions under which machinery is made now and those which existed ten years ago?—A. A great deal of difference.

Q. State the differences as well as you can.—A. Well, the trade has been subdivided and those subdivisions have been again subdivided, so that a man never learns the machinist's trade now. Ten years ago he learned, not the whole of the trade, but a fair portion of it. Also, there is more machinery used in the business, which again makes machinery. In the case of making the sewing-machine, for instance, you find that the trade is so subdivided that a man is not considered a machinist at all. Hence it is merely laborers' work and it is laborers that work at that branch of our trade. The different branches of the trade are divided and subdivided so that one man may make just a particular part of a machine and may not know anything whatever about another part of the same machine. In that way machinery is produced a great deal cheaper than it used to be formerly, and in fact, through this system of work, 100 men are able to do now what it took 300 or 400 men to do fifteen years ago. By the use of machinery and the subdivision of the trade they so simplify the work that it is made a great deal easier and put together a great deal faster. There is no system of apprenticeship, I may say, in the business. You simply go in and learn

From *Report of the Committee of the Senate upon the Relations between Labor and Capital,* 48th Congress, (1885): 755–759.

Promoting union labor-made goods, early 20th century.

whatever branch you are put at, and you stay at that unless you are changed to another.

Q. Does a man learn his branch very rapidly?—A. Yes, sir; he can learn his portion of the business very rapidly. Of course he becomes very expert at it, doing that all the time and nothing else, and therefore he is able to do a great deal more work in that particular branch than if he were a general hand and expected to do everything in the business as it came along. . . .

Q. Do you know from reading the papers or from your general knowledge of the business whether there are other places in other cities or other parts of the country that those men could have gone and got work?—A. I know from general reports of the condition of our trade that the same condition existed throughout the country generally.

Q. Then those men could not have bettered themselves by going to any other place, you think?—A. Not in a body.

Q. I am requested to ask you this question: Dividing the public, as is commonly done, into the upper, middle, and lower classes, to which class would you assign the average workingman of your trade at the time when you entered it, and to which class you would assign him now?—A. I now assign them to the lower class. At the time I entered the trade I should assign them as merely hanging on to the middle class; ready to drop out at any time.

Q. What is the character of the social intercourse of those workingmen? Answer first with reference to their intercourse with other people outside of their own trade—merchants, employers, and others.—A. Are you asking what sort of social intercourse exists between the machinists and the merchants? If you are, there is none whatever, or very little if any.

Q. What sort of social intercourse exists among the machinists themselves and their families, as to visiting, entertaining one another, and having little parties and other forms of sociability, those little things that go to make up the social pleasures of life?—A. In fact with the married folks that has died out —such things as birthday parties, picnics, and so on. The machinists to-day are on such small pay, and the cost of living is so high, that they have very little, if anything, to spend for recreation, and the machinist has to content himself with enjoying himself at home, either fighting with his wife or licking his children.

Q. I hope that is not a common amusement in the trade. Was it so ten years ago?—A. It was not; from the fact that they then sought enjoyment in other places, and had a little more money to spend. But since they have had no organization worth speaking of, of course their pay has gone down. At that time they had a form of organization in some way or other which seemed to keep up the wages, and there was more life left in the machinist then; he had more ambition, he felt more like seeking enjoyment outside, and in reading and such things, but now it is changed to the opposite; the machinist has no such desires.

Q. What is the social air about the ordinary machinist's house? Are there evidences of happiness, and joy, and hilarity, or is the general atmosphere solemn, and somber, and gloomy?—A. To explain that fully, I would state first of all, that machinists have got to work ten hours a day in New York, and that they are compelled to work very hard. In fact the machinists of America are compelled to do about one-third more work than the machinists do in England in a day. Therefore, when they come home they are naturally played out from shoving the file, or using the hammer or the chisel, or whatever it may be, such long hours. They are pretty well played out when they come home, and the first thing they think of is having something to eat and sitting down, and resting, and then of striking a bed. Of course when a man is dragged out in that way he is naturally cranky, and he makes all around him cranky; so, instead of a pleasant house it is every day expecting to lose his job by competition from his fellow-workman, there being so many out of employment, and no places for them, and his wages being pulled down through their competition, looking at all times to be thrown out of work in that way, and staring starvation in the face makes him feel sad, and the head of the house being sad, of course the whole family are the same, so the house looks like a dull prison instead of a home.

Q. Do you mean to say that that is the general condition of the machinists in New York and in this vicinity?—A. That is their general condition, with, of course, a good many exceptions. That is the general condition to the best of my knowledge.

Q. Where do you work?—A. I would rather not have it in print. Perhaps I would have to go Monday morning if I did. We are so situated in the machinist's trade that we daren't let them know much about us. If they know that we open our mouths on the labor question, and try to form organizations, we are quietly told that "business is slack," and we have got to go.

Q. Do you know of anybody being discharged for making speeches on the labor question?—A. Yes; I do know of several. A little less than a year ago several members of the organization that I belong to were discharged because it was discovered that they were members of the organization.

Q. Do you say those men were members of the same organization that you belong to?—A. Yes, sir; but not working in the same place where I work. And in fact many of my trade have been on the "black list," and have had to leave town to find work.

Q. Are the machinists here generally contented, or are they in a state of discontent and unrest?—A. There is mostly a general feeling of discontent, and you will find among the machinists the most radical workingmen, with the most revolutionary ideas. You will find that they don't so much give their thoughts simply to trades unions and other efforts of that kind, but they go far beyond that; they only look for relief through the ballot or through a revolution, a forcible revolution. . . .

Q. You say they look for relief through a forcible revolution. In the alternative of a forcible revolution have they considered what form of government they would establish?—A. Yes; some of them have and some of them have not.

Q. What kind of government would they establish?—A. Yes. They want to form a government such as this was intended to be, a government "of the people, for the people, and by the people"—different entirely from the present form of government.

Organizing labor: futility

Given the large-scale organization of industry, its nationwide character, and the declining need for skilled operatives, workers in the late nineteenth century confronted the obvious need for their own organization. The obstacles, however, were enormous, what with the massed resources and power of capital and management. In the next selection, Charles J. Chance, a journeyman currier and leather tanner from Somerville, Massachusetts, discusses some of the problems of labor organizers, particularly the very real fears raised by such employer weapons as blacklisting. Most revealing, though, is his recognition that laborers were afraid not only to organize but even to publicly discuss their condition.

Boston, Mass., October 19, 1883.

Q. Are you connected with any labor union?—A. Yes, sir.

Q. What is it?—A. The Tanners' and Curriers' Union of Massachusetts.

Q. How many members are there in that organization?—A. About 2,300; over 2,000 I would say. It is a new organization, not long in existence. It has been in existence only nine months.

Q. There have been such organizations of your trade in other States, I suppose?—A. Yes, sir.

Q. How many of them are there—you are organized by States, I presume?—A. Well, that I don't know; I couldn't answer that question.

Q. How many lodges of curriers, or organizations corresponding to yours, are there in the country?—A. That I couldn't answer.

Q. About how many curriers are there in the country, do you think?—A. I suppose about 20,000 tanners and curriers.

Q. Your trade is that of tanner and currier?—A. The trade is tanners and

From *Report of the Committee of the Senate upon the Relations between Labor and Capital,* 48th Congress, 3 (1885): 528–536.

curriers; yes, sir. In some places they have a combination and run tanning and currying both.

Q. Do you suppose one-half of the tanners and curriers of the country are included in organizations?—A. No, sir; not yet, through fear; there is one-half of them that are afraid to join any organization.

Q. Are nearly all of them that live in Massachusetts included in the Massachusetts organization?—A. No, sir.

Q. But there are about 2,300 you say?—A. About 2,000; it is something over 2,000; but say 2,000 for certain.

Q. Where are those 2,000, mainly?—A. Eleven branches of the union are situated in Boston, Roxbury, Charlestown, Somerville, Salem, Woburn, Stoneham, and Chelsea.

Q. You have something to say to the committee; you may proceed to state it now.—A. Before I commence on anything for the committee I would state that I am in a position now, but having taken an active part in forming the curriers' union, I have been either black-listed or something of that sort, so that it was almost impossible for me to obtain work, until this last two weeks, when I managed to get into a place where they had either never heard my name or not known as much about the union matters as other shops had known. When I started in, in the union matter, I was fairly situated in my family and home. Since, of course, I have had to run, and have run, in debt for that reason. I have been known as a good workman, and never had any bother in that way. The matter to be brought before this committee I suppose————

Q. (Interposing.) Before you come to that, let us know more particularly about your connection with the union, and in what way it has resulted in your failure to get work; when did you commence these efforts, and what did you do by way of organization; where were you when you began?—A. Here in Boston.

Q. Well, what did you do?—A. I started in speaking for the men to join the organization.

Q. Speaking to them in public meetings?—A. Yes, some of them.

Q. And calling meetings yourself, with others, I suppose?—A. Yes, we called meetings.

Q. Where did you call your first meeting?—A. The first one that I called myself was in Charlestown.

Q. Where—in what building or hall?—A. Well, I couldn't tell you exactly the name of the hall.

Q. How many were present?—A. There were present 28.

Q. All of your trade?—A. All of my trade; yes.

Q. What did you do—what did you say to them?—A. I didn't say a great deal. I gave them rules of organization of the union, as it was founded before I got into it, and encouraged them to join—to form a branch of the organization in Charlestown—which they did.

Q. What reason did you give them for forming such an organization?—A.

The reason we gave was that we may possibly get the men all together; that they would come to a fair understanding between themselves, and that in time we may regulate the prices of wages more evenly than at the present time.

Q. How could you do that?—A. We could do it, and have done it since the organization has been started; done it in several places by a unanimous movement of men, not in any hard manner, as by strikes or anything of that kind; there has been no severity used by any of them, but it was done in a legal manner, by the men waiting on the firms and coming to a settlement with them before there was any chance of strikes.

Q. Have there been any strikes?—A. There was one strike in Charlestown shortly after the organization was formed. The proprietors of the place, Hubbard, Buzzell & Blake made an attempt at reduction of wages and a demand for more work. The men refused to agree to it, and appointed a committee to wait upon them.

Q. They wanted the men to take less pay and do more work?—A. Yes. So the committee waited on one of the firm, and he gave them a very independent, "sassy" answer, and the consequence was that some of the men were discharged, and the rest, when they saw how matters were, left.

Q. How many men were there?—A. Eighty men went out at that time.

Q. You protested against either change—either more work or less pay?—A. Certainly. We didn't want to have any change, or to have the union brought in as the cause of it. We wanted to have the union first fairly started, and then to make any fair arrangement with them; but they undertook to break up the union on the start; that was their idea, and after they got beaten on that, they gave in to the strike, but since then they have discharged the eight men that waited on them as a committee.

Q. How long ago is that?—A. That is three months ago this month.

Q. Were you one of the committee?—A. I was. They have since discharged, as I say, those eight men that waited on them as a committee, and the member of the firm that I have spoken of promised faithfully that after things had been settled there would be no hard feelings between those men and him. But he has employed an incompetent foreman there, and the foreman is running the shop for himself—it looks so to the men, at any rate—either for himself, or on orders from the firm.

Q. You think, then, that the organization prevented the reduction of pay and the increase of work?—A. Yes, sir; instead of getting the reduction they received a half-dollar advance, and did less work.

Q. You attribute that to the organization, do you?—A. Well, not exactly to the organization, although part of the men were members of it. It certainly had some effect on the firm, as the committee waited on them and gave them the vote of the organization. Since that time, in places where there was work to be got, I was refused the work myself, for what reasons I don't know. I had no hard words with any of the firm or anybody else. . . .

Q. Is there any other point that you have on your mind which you wish to state?—A. Out here in Roxbury there is a shop running some 80 men, and the proprietor of the concern out there has threatened to break up the union, or the "clique," as he calls it, and he has commenced already to discharge men that have been belonging to the union.

Q. That is simply because they do belong to the union?—A. That is Quirin & Edwards' shop.

Q. Why do they want to break up the union; what reasons do they give?—A. That the men will be wanting to get more pay when they become organized.

Q. How do you know that they give that as a reason?—A. They have told the men that.

Q. They have themselves told them that?—A. Yes, sir.

Q. Do they claim that they are unable to give more pay?—A. No; and they have also demanded that the men do more work. That is where one-half of our Massachusetts curriers are making a mistake in regard to leather. They are driving the work out of the men, and they are making calf skins to-day that are not as strong as common cloth. . . .

—A. If I would leave union matters alone and go to work at my trade as a non-union man and work against unionism I could receive 20 a week steady.

Q. How is that; they could not pay all the union men that way, could they?—A. No, sir.

Q. How do you know you could have that?—A. Because I am a competent workman.

Q. But you have said that the highest wages paid were $14?—A. You have asked me if I could do better, and the answer is that in that way I could do better.

Q. How do you know you could do better—that you could get $6 a week more than equally skilled workmen?—A. I have had the offer.

Q. What did they offer you $20 a week for when others only get $14?—A. The idea they have is that they could break up the union if they could get some of the men that are good workmen and officers of the union to abandon it—that they will gain their object that way—and the chances are that if I did take the $20 a week it would be only for a week or two, until things would get straightened out for themselves.

Q. When the union should be broken up you think you could not get $20?—A. No, sir; I couldn't get 20 cents then.

Q. You would be on the black-list again?—A. Sure.

Q. Are there any other points in the case?—A. I don't know as there is, except the matter of some of the men complaining about the human skins; quite an item, that.

Q. Is there anything else that you know of that bears upon the way things work between the employers and the trades-unions—any efforts to break the unions up—any means for doing it? You have spoken of the means used to get you away from the union.—A. Yes, sir. They have used the same means in Hubbard, Buzzell & Blake's, in Charlestown—they have sent those men out. And at Roxbury, at Quirin's, they have done the same thing. There is a shop at Woburn where they have done the same thing; in fact, it has been done all around. As soon as there has been a union started, the men have been discharged.

Q. What is the prospect of their breaking the unions up—or are the unions progressing?—A. The unions get stronger every day, sir.

Q. "The blood of the martyrs is the seed of the church," is it?—A. Yes, sir.

The CHAIRMAN. It has proved so in England, we have found from some witnesses who have testified already.

The WITNESS. There are men that would be willing to come here and testify, but, like myself, they know that as soon as they get here they are done for. I have spoken to several of them, but they are all afraid. They are union men, but are afraid to come out in public and give any voice to their wrongs. It is a general feeling that all workingmen have; and I believe that I will be the only tanner and currier that you will find to come before you. There may be one or two more that would come if they could possibly get together, but as a general thing they have all got this fear in them. They have been asked about this human-hide tanning that has been carried on here in Massachusetts for eighteen years, and they are afraid to acknowledge it. . . .

A strike: desperation

Labor strikes in the late nineteenth century were risky ventures. No federal or state laws existed to guarantee workers the rights to organize, to bargain collectively, and to strike without fear of reprisal and loss of jobs. The great strikes of the period—the railroad strike in 1877, the Homestead steel strike in 1892, and the Pullman strike in 1894—resulted from desperation, from a feeling of the utter hopelessness of confronting the power of organized capital. The following account by John S. McClelland, a Western Union telegrapher, reveals some of the sense of futility that marked labor activities of the period.

New York, August 13, 1883.

Question. Where do you reside?—Answer. In Hoboken, N. J.
Q. What is your occupation?—A. I am an operator.

From *Report of the Committee of the Senate upon the Relations between Labor and Capital,* 48th Congress, 1 (1885): 121–127.

Q. How long have you been engaged in that business?—A. About fourteen years. . . .

Q. . . . Tell us about the Brotherhood of Telegraphers, about the strike, and the causes of it so far as you know them, the rates of compensation paid to telegraph operators, and whatever you know about the subject generally.—A. Probably I could give you more information by being questioned from time to time as I proceed, but I have no objection to beginning, as you suggest, with a general statement. . . . Now the causes leading to this strike are indirect and direct. In the first place, in my opinion, the indirect cause of the strike was the presentation of or the determination on the part of our organization to present certain petitions to our employers. That was the indirect cause of the strike, but that need not necessarily have caused a strike. The direct cause of the strike, in my opinion, was the insult offered to our executive committee by the officials of the Western Union Telegraph Company. In all probability there would not have been a strike if the officials of the telegraph company had shown even the slightest willingness to confer with that representative committee, and to seek a settlement of the differences that were well known to exist between the company and its employés. So far in the course of this examination the fact has never been brought out that the telegraph company *did actually know* that the gentlemen of that committee were thoroughly representative men. Some time before the strike, after the meeting of our convention in Chicago was made known generally, Mr. Eckert, of the Western Union office in this city, sent a long letter to Superintendent Clowry, in Chicago, calling his attention to the fact that these demands were under consideration by the brotherhood; thus showing to the public and to us that he was quite familiar with the fact at least as long ago as last March that these demands were to be made. Then, too, we know as a fact that the officials of the company have known all along that these grievances existed and that we were preparing to seek redress, and we know also that these officials have been preparing themselves to resist any attempt on our part to secure the redress of our grievances.

You asked . . . something about the relation the salary question bore to the strike. In my opinion, the salary question is only a very secondary consideration. We banded ourselves together as individuals for the purpose of bettering our condition, socially, financially, or in any other way that we saw fit or saw an opportunity to do it, and we considered that we were entitled, under the laws of this country, to obtain for ourselves, if we could, greater advantages or privileges than we have been enjoying. We found that we were denied certain rights that were generally accorded to other people in the community. In the first place, we found that we were compelled to labor seven days in the week, while people in other branches of industry have to labor only six, and in some cases only five and a half days. We desired to have, and we thought we were entitled to have, one day in seven allowed us for rest, recreation, improvement of mind and body, or any other use to which we chose to put it. We asked—and this shows our willingness to assist the company to prevent its business from being disarranged—that in case it became necessary for us to work on the Sabbath, or in case a sufficient number of employés were willing to work on that day, they should receive extra compensation for such extra labor. It did not necessarily follow that a man who did not want work on the Sabbath day should be forced to do so.

In connection with that subject, I think it can be clearly shown to this committee, if proper time is given, that there is no necessity whatever for telegraph offices being kept open upon the Sabbath day at all, or at least if there is any such necessity it is a very slight one, and the real business that is done on that day can be transacted with about one-hundredth part of the number of employés that have generally been engaged in Sunday work. We know very well that a large proportion of the telegraph business that is now transacted on Sunday relates to purely secular matters, and could just as well be transacted on Saturday night or on Monday morning. The proportion of really urgent business that requires to be done on Sunday, such as death messages or other messages of emergency, is very small. . . .

Q. What proportion of work is done on the Sabbath in comparison with the amount done ordinarily on week days?—A. Not over a quarter, or probably less than that; I mean in a large office.

Q. And you think that perhaps 80 or 90 or 95 per cent. of that work is secular work, which could be done as well on Saturday or Monday?—A. Yes, sir; at least from 80 to 95 per cent. of it is of that character. To return to the question of individual action for the redress of grievances, individuals by themselves, that is singly, have endeavored from time to time to obtain better rates of remuneration, rates which they felt they were entitled to.

Q. Before you go to that point I want to get a little further information as to the sort of work that is done on the Sabbath. You distinguish between that which is work of necessity and that which is secular work. How do you make that distinction?—A. I draw the distinction between work of necessity and business work at the death or sickness line. No business transaction do I consider necessary on the Sabbath day.

To proceed with what I was about to say in regard to attempts by individual operators to have their grievances redressed, individuals have tried from time to time to better their condition by making appeals to officers of the company, but in nearly all cases they have been rebuffed or put off or denied even an answer. To make my statement more definite and practical on this subject, I will say that I have on a dozen or perhaps fifteen occasions held conversations with my direct manager on this particular point. I have asked him all manner of questions relating to it, and have found him utterly unable to give me any satisfactory answers. I have asked him what encouragement there was for a man who desired to be faithful and efficient in the performance of his duties to the company, what encouragement there was for such a man to remain steady and reliable and faithful to his duties, and his answer was, "None whatever. If you get tired of this position we can fill it with another man at $70 or $65 a month." That is another of the evils of the service, that when a man getting what we call a high salary is removed or vacates his position it is usually filled by a man at from $5 to $10 a month less; and if that second man leaves in his turn, the position is usually filled at a rate of from $5 to $10 lower still. These are grievances coming under the first clause of our complaint. We asked also, that the lady operators should receive equal pay with the gentlemen. That point, however, has been pretty well covered already, so that it is not necessary for me to go into it here. We ask also that eight hours shall constitute a regular day's work.

In asking that we allow the Western Union Telegraph Company the advantage of two hours more daily than their own chief officer has publicly admitted to be a reasonable day's work for a telegraph operator. The former president of the company, Mr. Orton, is on record as having sworn before a committee like this, on a certain occasion, that no telegraph operator could perform more than six hours' work per day with justice to himself or to the company. Mr. Orton was a man who grew up from the ranks, and who knew what a telegraph operator could do, and he placed the limit of an operator's usefulness to the company or to himself at six hours' work per day. It is a well-known fact that the work is very wearing on both mind and body, much more so than ordinary physical labor, and that operators as a rule do not live even to the prime of life. It is a very rare thing, indeed, to find a man in the business with a streak of gray in his hair. The operators are frequently carried off by consumption, generally caused by close confinement and the positions they have to take while at their work. Owing to the peculiar nature of the business, drawing the attention of the mind to the instrument and the rapid rate at which the sounds have to be distinguished and transcribed on the paper, and owing also to the position that a man must assume, sitting steadily and writing all day, the ordinary and proper exercise of the respiratory organs is prevented; and as a matter of fact you will find that when a man is what we call being "rushed" he hardly breathes at all—respiration almost ceases. . . .

Q. I suppose the telegraph operators are at this disadvantage, that there are but comparatively few corporations engaged in the business, and therefore very little competition for their services, so that when an operator gets out of employment there are only two or three companies to whom he can apply for work?—A. Yes; competition exists only to a very slight extent, but there is always a demand in the one great corporation.

Q. But there is no competition between the telegraph corporations?—A. No; because the one great corporation, the Western Union, swallows up all competing lines as fast as they are constructed. . . .

A yellow dog contract

Employers possessed formidable power to discourage unionization. They used strikebreakers, company police, and labor spies in addition to formal legal resources. Courts readily issued injunctions to halt strikes, employers retained the best legal talent, and workers were compelled to sign "yellow dog" contracts as a condition of employment. The essential feature of the contracts required workers to agree that they would not join a labor organization. In times of economic distress, workers had to sign or go without work. This was the "freedom of contract" between employer and employee that was so much a part of the prevailing economic and legal ideology. Courts consistently upheld the validity of yellow dog contracts until Congress made them illegal in 1932. The following contract was imposed in 1890 after a brief strike in a Stamford, Connecticut, lock manufacturing establishment.

Labor and Capital are Co-Partners; neither can prosper
without the other; the injury of one should
be the concern of both.

CONTRACT

BETWEEN

THE YALE & TOWNE MFG. COMPANY,

AND

. . . .

THE YALE & TOWNE MANUFACTURING COMPANY, as one of the parties of this contract, hereby agrees with the other party hereto as follows:

(1.) To punctually pay all wages or other earnings.

(2.) To have due regard for the rights and the reasonable convenience of employees.

(3.) To exercise reasonable care for the health and comfort of employees in all sanitary arrangements.

(4.) To give due consideration and prompt reply to requests, properly presented by employees, relating to matters which affect their welfare, and which are within the Company's control.

(5.) To fairly adjust with each employee, individually, the wages or other compensation, and to review this adjustment at reasonable intervals, if so requested.

From Estelle F. Feinstein, *Stamford in the Gilded Age: The Political Life of a Connecticut Town,* 1868-1893 (Stamford, 1973), 122k. Used by permission of the Stamford Historical Society.

(6.)   To give a certificate of honorable discharge, if so requested, to any employee entitled to it who has been not less than six months in the Company's service.

THE YALE & TOWNE MFG. COMPANY.

By ....

PAYMASTER.

IN CONSIDERATION OF employment by THE YALE & TOWNE MANUFACTURING COMPANY, and the covenants on the part of the latter herein set forth the person above-named hereby agrees with said Company as follows:

(7.)   To faithfully render the service which is undertaken and for which the Company pays.

(8.)   To conform to the shop rules and carry out instructions received from the Foreman or the Officers of the Company.

(9.)   In case any reasonable ground for complaint exists, to report the facts, first to the Foreman, and if no redress is thus obtained, to bring the matter, preferably in writing, to the notice of the Company, through the Paymaster or one of its Officers.

(10.)   To take no action of any kind, individually, or with others, tending to cause disturbance of the relations between the Company and its employees, because of any grievance, until the matter has been first submitted to the Company in the manner indicated in Article 9, and, if said request, so presented, is not granted, to take no action tending to harass or injure the Company until at least fifteen days shall have elapsed after such request has been presented to the Company without its taking action thereon.

(11.)   To withdraw and abstain, during the period of this contract, from membership in any organization whose rules would prevent the honorable carrying out of this contract.

(12.)   To forfeit to the Company, as liquidated damages, a penalty or fine equal in amount to one week's wages or earnings, in event of any violation of Articles 10 or 11 of this contract.

In Departments A and B, complaints under Articles 9 and 10 are to be made in the first instance to the Foreman or Contractor; if not acted on within three days, then to the Dept. Superintendent; if not acted on by him within three additional days, then to the Company as per Article 9.

....

STAMFORD, CONN., ... 189

Child labor

"It is worthy of particular remark that, in general, women and children are rendered more useful, by manufacturing establishments, than they would otherwise be." So argued Alexander Hamilton in his 1791 report advocating governmental encouragement of industry in the United States. And beginning with the growth of manufacturing in New England in the 1820s, factories regularly employed children who worked ten to twelve hours a day and performed tedious tasks for a fraction of the wages paid to adults. By 1880, children under fifteen constituted six percent of the labor force. During the next two decades, however, their employment dramatically dropped in northern states as reform legislation severely restricted the use of child labor. In the South, however, child labor in textile mills increased from slightly over 2,000 in 1870 to over 27,000 by 1905 because those states either refused to prohibit child labor or passed meaningless laws. Reflecting their weakened competitive position, northern manufacturers joined forces with social workers and organized labor to secure national legislation outlawing child labor. Congress passed a child labor law in 1916, but the success was temporary for the Supreme Court declared the law unconstitutional in *Hammer* v. *Dagenhart* in 1918. Congress provided another law a year later, but again the Court voided it. A constitutional amendment abolishing child labor passed Congress in 1924 but never was ratified by the necessary number of states. Finally, in 1938, Congress enacted virtually the same law it had in 1916, and this time, the Supreme Court upheld the law.

"It is not laborious work . . . ."

Nearly a century after Hamilton's support of child labor, Otto G. Lynch, superintendent of the Enterprise Manufacturing Company, an Augusta, Georgia, textile mill, nicely amplified his own support of the practice in testimony to the Senate Committee on Labor and Capital. Lynch discussed wages, working conditions, and he insisted that "circumstances made it necessary" for children to work. Of course, he noted no implications of the less-than-subsistence wages paid to adults, wages that virtually forced whole families into the mills.

Augusta, Ga., November 23, 1883.

. . . Q. How much help do you employ?—A. We have, I think, 485 on our pay-roll.

Q. How many of those are men?—A. I cannot answer that exactly; about one-seventh.

Child coal miner, 1902.

Q. The rest are women and children, I suppose?—A. Yes, sir.

Q. How many of them would you class as women and how many as children?—A. I think about one-third of the remainder would be children and two-thirds women. That is about the proportion.

Q. What is the average wages that you pay?—A. Eighty-two cents a day for the last six months, or in that neighborhood.

Q. What do the women make a day?—A. About $1.

Q. And the men?—A. Do you mean common laborers?

Q. Yes; the average wages of your laborers.—A. About $1 a day.

Q. What do the children make on an average?—A. About from 35 to 75 cents a day.

Q. You employ children of ten years and upward?—A. Yes, sir.

Q. Do you employ any below the age of ten?—A. No.

Q. About what proportion of the men in your employ can read and write; I mean who can read well enough to read the Constitution of the United States, or the New Testament, or a newspaper and understand what they are about?—A. I think about two-thirds of them can do it.

Q. What proportion of the women?—A. Not so large a proportion; I should think, probably, one-half of them.

Q. You think that one-half of the female operatives in your employ can read a common book, one of the novels of the day, or a history of the United States, and understand it?—A. I think that one-half of them may be said to know how to read, but that is a rough guess on my part.

Q. What proportion of the children can read or write?—A. Most of them can read. They nearly all go to Sunday school.

Q. Do they learn to read in the Sunday schools?—A. Yes, sir; if they have not learned elsewhere before they come to the mill.

Q. Then, reading and writing are taught in the Sunday schools?—A. Yes; reading is. I think a larger proportion of the children than of the grown people can read intelligently. . . .

Q. What is your experience as to the employment of child labor?—A. What do you mean?

Q. I mean is it a good thing according to your experience that children of from ten to fifteen years of age should work in the factories?—A. Yes, sir; I think it is.

Q. Do you think it is a good thing that they should work eleven hours a day all the year around?—A. I think it would be better for them if they were not compelled to work at all, but——

Q. (Interposing.) You would want them to work a part of the time in order to learn a business for life, would you not?—A. Yes, sir. Circumstances now force them into the mills. They come in with their mothers.

From *Report of the Committee of the Senate upon the Relations between Labor and Capital,* 48th Congress, 4 (1885): 748–753.

Q. I understand that as a matter of fact, in the present condition of these people it is a necessity that they shall have employment, and that the employment of the children of a family oftentimes prevents the whole family from becoming paupers; but setting aside this temporary necessity, do you think it well that children between the ages of say ten and fourteen years should be required to work more than about half the time in a factory?—A. Well, I don't know that I can answer that question satisfactorily. I don't know whether they should be compelled to work at all in the factory unless circumstances made it necessary.

Q. You think, I suppose, that it would be better for the children to have a chance to be outdoors?—A. Yes, sir.

Q. But the testimony is that many of those children seem to enjoy their work in the factory.—A. Oh, yes. It is not laborious work, and it is not continuous; there is more or less rest as they go along.

Q. Not much play, I suppose?—A. Some little; not much. Of course, we have discipline in the mill, but the labor is not continuous or excessive.

Q. Do the children remain in the mill during the whole eleven hours as the older operatives do?—A. Yes.

Q. How as to their chance of getting some education in your free schools?—A. Well, in individual cases they sometimes quit the mill and go to school—some of them do.

Q. For how long periods?—A. Indefinite periods. Some of the parents take their children out when they feel that they can do without them for a while and send them to school, and afterwards when it becomes necessary they send them back to the mill again. There is no rule about it.

Q. But most of them remain in the mill one year after another, I suppose?—A. Oh, yes; but they change a good deal out and in. . . .

"I don't know what month it is."

Child labor in northern states was subjected to more rigorous state regulation. The following selection from testimony before a New York legislative committee in 1896 indicates that there was some attempt to enforce prohibitory legislation. But the remarks by the immigrant child and his employer demonstrate again that necessity forced parents to send their children to work, and even to lie about the children's age and education to skirt the legal requirements.

Abraham Rose, having been called as a witness (not sworn) testified as follows: . . .

Q. You are not afraid of me, are you? A. I can't understand English.

Q. You are not afraid of me, are you? A. No.

Q. Will you tell me the truth in everything I ask you? A. I will.

Q. What is going to happen to you if you do not tell the truth?

(The examination of this witness was conducted with the aid of an interpreter.)

A. He knows that; he knows he will be punished if he don't tell the truth.

Q. Where do you live? A. Five Norfolk street.

Q. Where do you work? A. By Mr. Levi.

Q. Where is his place of business? A. Thirty-one Hester street.

Q. Where were you born? A. I don't know.

Q. Where were you born? A. I was born in Gallacia.

Q. Is your papa alive? A. Yes, sir.

Q. What does he do? A. My father is living and working; he is a peddler.

Q. How much does Levi pay you every week? A. He pays me two dollars a week.

Q. When do you go to work in the morning? A. At seven o'clock.

Q. When do you go home? A. At six o'clock.

Q. Do you get any time for dinner in the middle of the day? A. Yes, sir.

Q. Do you go home for dinner? A. I go home to dinner.

Q. Do you take dinner with your mother? A. I live with my mother, and my mother gives me to eat.

Q. What do you do with the two dollars you get every week? A. I give it to my mother.

Q. Does you[r] mother give you any money to spend? A. She don't give me nothing but one penny.

Q. One penny every week? A. Every week one penny.

Q. When were you confirmed? A. One year.

Q. Now, who told you to tell us that? A. Nobody told me.

Q. What synagogue were you confirmed in?—A. I was confirmed in Europe—not here.

Q. When did you come from Europe? A. About six months I am here.

Q. And is your father here only the same time? A. My father and mother came here with me. . . .

Q. Now, you must be 13 years old to be confirmed, must you not? A. I was 13 years old when I was confirmed. . . .

Q. How long have you been working for Levi? A. Two months and a half I am working for Mr. Levi.

Q. Did you work for anybody else in this country? A. Yes, sir; someone else.

Q. Who else—where does he live? A. His name was Levi too.

Q. Where does he live? A. In Montgomery street, but I don't remember the number.

From *Documents of the Assembly of the State of New York,* 119th session, no. 97, part 1, 22 (1896): 460–465.

Q. How much did this man pay you—the first Levi? A. One dollar and a half a week.

Q. And did you work just as long as you are working now? A. Yes, sir; I did.

Q. What do you do now—what is the kind of work you do? A. I am pulling bastings.

Q. And you do that all day long? A. Sometimes if there is nothing why I do nothing, but all the time there is nothing but bastings pulling.

Q. He keeps you busy all day long? A. There is only one finisher present and she can't give me work enough to pull bastings out.

Q. Can you write your name in English? A. I can read it in Polish.

Q. Can you write your name in English? A. I don't know whether I could or not.

Q. You can not, can you? A. No.

Q. Now, do you know what day to-day is? A. Yes, sir.

Q. What day is to-day? A. Monday.

Q. What month is this month? A. I don't know what month it is.

Q. Can you write anything in Polish? A. Yes, sir; I can write in Polish my name, my address, etc.

Q. Anything else? A. I can write a little, but not very good.

Q. Can you add up? A. I could, but I have forgotten.

Q. Do you know how much two and three make? A. Yes, sir.

Q. How much? A. Five.

Q. How much does five and seven make? A. Five and seven makes twelve.

Q. Were you ever in school in this country? A. No, sir; I was not.

Q. Who told you that you were 14 years old? A. I know that by when I was confirmed; I am 13 years old, and I am confirmed one year, and therefore I know I am 14 years old; that is the only reason I know I am 14 years old.

Q. Did you and Levi have a talk before you came down here to-day? A. No, sir; I have not spoken to Mr. Levi before I came here.

Q. Who told you how to get here? A. My boss brought me here.

Q. What did he say to you on the way down from the shop? A. A man brought me here to-day that came for me—a man that brought me here.

Q. You were down in the other building last Saturday, were you not? A. I was last Saturday with my boss in the other building.

Q. Did he say anything to you last Saturday? A. No; he said nothing to me last Saturday.

Nathan Levi, having been called as a witness and duly sworn by the chairman, testified as follows: . . .

Q. What is your full name? A. Nathan Levi.

Q. Where do you live? A. Thirty-one Hester street.

Q. Now, Levi, this little boy Abraham Rose who was on the stand is employed by you, is he not? A. Yes, sir.

Q. How old is he? A. His father told me—

Q. How old is he? A. I don't know.

Q. When did the father tell you that? A. He told me that.

Q. Talk so we can understand you. A. Yes, sir; when he came to me to work I asked him how old he was and he told me he was 14 years old, and I take him to work.

Q. He told you he was 14 years old; when was he 14? A. About ten weeks ago.

Q. Was he 14 years old just before the Jewish holiday? A. Yes, sir.

Q. Before what holiday? A. Ten weeks before; he came up to me to work and I asked him how old he was and he told me 14 years.

Q. Now, when was he 14 years old; did the father tell you that? A. No, sir; I don't ask him for that.

Q. Did you not ask the father to go before a notary public; you didn't ask him to swear to the boy's age? A. No, sir. . . .

Q. How long has he been with you? A. Ten weeks.

Q. How much would you have to pay a boy 16 years old to do the same work that this little boy is doing? A. All the same.

Q. You would pay a boy 16 years old two dollars, would you? A. For this work I don't pay any more. . . .

Q. Can you get a boy 16 years old to work for that? A. Yes, sir. . . .

Q. Did you ever have one? A. Yes, sir; I had a boy 16 years old.

Q. What was his name? A. I couldn't remember his name.

Q. When did you keep him? A. When I lived in East New York.

Q. When did you keep the boy that was 16 years old? A. Before my present boy came to me.

Q. So you had this 16-year-old boy about two months ago, did you? A. Yes, sir.

Q. What did he leave you for? A. I don't know why.

Q. What were you paying when he left? A. Two dollars a week.

Q. How old was he? A. Sixteen years old.

Q. How do you know he was 16? A. He brought me a ticket.

Q. He brought you a ticket, did he? A. Yes, sir.

Q. Why didn't you ask for a ticket from this little boy? A. I asked him for a ticket.

Q. You never asked for one, did you? A. I asked the father for a ticket.

Q. He has been with you for ten weeks? A. Yes, sir.

Q. Was there never a factory inspector in your place? A. No, sir.

Q. How long have you been doing business where you are now? A. Five years.

Q. And there never has been a factory inspector there? A. No, sir.

Q. Do you know what a factory inspector is? A. Yes, sir.

Q. There never was a factory inspector to see you? A. No, sir. . . .

Q. Do you know what can be done to you for employing this boy? A. No, sir; I don't know.

Q. Did you ever try to find out? A. No, sir.

Q. Do you know whether you have a right to employ that boy? A. I asked for a ticket.

Q. Do you know whether you have a right to employ that boy? A. If he is 14 years old then I can take him to work.

Q. Is that all you know; if he is under 16 years of age and can not write a sentence in English can you employ him? A. I don't know that.

Q. Did the factory inspector tell you that? A. No, sir.

Q. Has there ever been an inspector from the board of health where you are now? A. No, sir. . . .

A thankless child

Reuben Dagenhart was a fourteen-year-old boy when his father, backed by some textile manufacturers, successfully challenged the constitutionality of the federal law prohibiting the shipment of child-labor-made goods in interstate commerce. Nearly six years later, however, the twenty-year-old man had some second thoughts about his father's "success."

This is the story of an ungrateful child. The story of a lad for whom all the machinery of the American judiciary was turned to preserve his constitutional rights and, who, after six years, has not yet brought himself to give thanks.

The boy is Reuben Dagenhart, of Charlotte, N.C.

Six years ago, Federal Judge James E. Boyd, of the western North Carolina district, interposed the majesty of the law in Reuben's behalf. Some months later Chief Justice White and Justices Day, Van Devanter, McReynolds and Pitney did the same. They declared—and they made it stick—that the Congress of the United States could not take away from young Reuben Dagenhart his "constitutional" right to work more hours every day than a boy of 14 ought to work.

There may be another ungrateful boy in the picture—John Dagenhart. John, age 12, had his constitutional rights defended by the same courts to the extent that he was allowed to go on working in a cotton mill at an age when no boy should work at all in a cotton mill. But two days' roving through the cotton mill towns around Charlotte last week failed to find John, and readers will have to be content with the story of Reuben. This leaves out, also, the story of Roland H. Dagenhart, father of the boys, whose constitutional right to put them to work in the mills and to receive their wages each Saturday was upheld by the same upright judges.

From Lowell Mellett, "A Thankless Child," *Labor*, Washington, D.C., November 1923.

All that was found of Roland and the younger son after a search that followed their migration from Charlotte to Salisbury, from Salisbury to Kannapolis, from Kannapolis to Lowell and from Lowell to Gastonia, was the shabby little shack in the last-named town, the tiny "company" house, built on stilts, where father and son live.

Congress in 1916 passed an act that prevented the employment of a child under 14 in any factory and prevented the working of any child between the ages of 14 and 16 more than eight hours a day or after 7 o'clock at night or before 6 o'clock in the morning.

Congress didn't know the necessities of the cotton milling business. It didn't know the cost of keeping up the big and handsome Manufacturers' Club in Charlotte, for instance. Charlotte is a pure-minded town—no movies on Sunday, scarcely any soda fountains open: two years ago you couldn't even buy gasoline on the Sabbath.

Working in one of the mills were the Dagenharts. In addition to the father and sons there was a daughter, but she was 16, earning her dollar a day, and Congress had said nothing about girls of 16. So the suit, when the manufacturers had it arranged, read like this: "Roland H. Dagenhart, and Reuben Dagenhart and John Dagenhart, Minors, by Roland H. Dagenhart, Their Next Friend. vs. W. C. Hammer, U. S. District Attorney." It was to enjoin the District Attorney from enforcing the law made by Congress.

The federal court down there, Judge Boyd presiding, issued the injunction. Appeal was taken and the United States Supreme Court sustained Judge Boyd's view. True, Justices Holmes, McKenna, Brandeis and Clark disagreed with the other five. They couldn't see where anybody's constitutional rights were being violated by keeping kids out of cotton mills until they were 14 years old and limiting the hours they might work until they were 16. But Judges White, Day, Pitney, McReynolds and Van Devanter thought the act unconstitutional. Their decision meant that the Dagenhart boys could work in that cotton mill as long and as hard as their little hearts desired.

And should not the Dagenhart boys be grateful for that?

Well, Reuben isn't.

I found him at his home in Charlotte. He is about the size of the office boy—weighs 105 pounds, he told me. But is a married man with a child. He is 20 years old.

"What benefit," I asked him, "did you get out of the suit which you won in the United States Supreme Court?"

"You mean the suit the Fidelity Manufacturing Company won? (It was the Fidelity Company for which the Dagenharts were working.) I don't see that I got any benefit. I guess I'd been a lot better off if they hadn't won it.

"Look at me! A hundred and five pounds, a grown man and no education. I may be mistaken, but I think the years I've put in in the cotton mills have stunted my growth. They kept me from getting any schooling. I had to stop school after the third grade and now I need the education I didn't get."

"How was your growth stunted?"

"I don't know—the dust and the lint, maybe. But from 12 years on, I was working 12 hours a day—from 6 in the morning till 7 at night, with time out for meals. And sometimes I worked nights besides. Lifting a hundred pounds and I only weighed 65 pounds myself."

He explained that he and his sister worked together, "on section," spinning. They each made about a dollar a day, though later he worked up to where he could make $2. His father made $15 a week and infant John at the time the suit was brought, was making close to $1 a day.

"Just what did you and John get out of that suit, then?" was asked.

"Why, we got some automobile rides when them big lawyers from the North was down here. Oh, yes, and they bought both of us a coca-cola! That's all we got out of it."

"What did you tell the judge when you were in court?"

"Oh, John and me never was in court! Just Paw was there. John and me was just little kids in short pants. I guess we wouldn't have looked like much in court. We were working in the mill while the case was going on. But Paw went up to Washington."

Reuben hasn't been to school, but his mind has not been idle.

"It would have been a good thing for all the kids in this state if that law they passed had been kept. Of course, they do better now than they used to. You don't see so many babies working in the factories, but you see a lot of them that ought to be going to school."

"What about John? Is he satisfied with the way things turned out?"

"I don't know. Prob'ly not. He's not much bigger than me and he's got flat feet."

"How about your father?"

"Oh, he's satisfied, I guess. But I know one thing. I ain't going to let them put my kid sister in the mill, like he's thinking of doing! She's only 15 and she's crippled and I bet I stop that!"

CHAPTER 8

The varieties of protest

State Historical Society of Wisconsin.

Women's suffrage parade, Washington, D.C., 1913.

Competition: illusion or reality?

Competition allegedly was the law of life in the free enterprise system; in actuality, many business people sought to curtail it and reach accommodations whereby the largest and strongest firms dominated the marketplace. In the late nineteenth century, the formation of trusts or marketing agreements among a few large producers developed in key, essential industries and commercial activities. Increasing protests from small business people and publicists representing a consumer point of view contributed to periodic congressional investigations, and finally culminated in the passage of the Sherman Anti-Trust Act of 1890. The following testimony by George Baurmann, formerly an accountant for a meat-packing firm, describes the cartel arrangements among the Big Four of the industry.

Washington, D. C., Friday, February 1, 1889.

... Q. What is your business?—A. Dressed beef has been my business for the last four years.

Q. Have you been engaged in the business on your own account or in somebody's employment?—A. I have been in the business on my own account and also in employment.

Q. In whose employment, and how long?—A. In the employment of Nelson Morris & Co. for three years.

Q. Are you in their employment now?—A. No, sir.

Q. State in what capacity you were employed.—A. I had charge of their dressed beef department; the books and the account of sales of the dressed beef which was shipped out.

Q. State whether you know of any combination between dressed-beef concerns in Chicago.—A. Yes, sir; there is a combination.

Q. How long has it existed?—A. Since last May a year ago.

Q. Were you in the employ of Nelson Morris & Co. prior to that time?—A. Yes, sir; I had been in their employ for a year previous.

Q. Did you know the extent and nature of their business?—A. Yes, sir.

Q. State whether there has been any increase in their business after that com-

From Senate Select Committee on the Transportation and Sale of Meat Products, *Report,* 51st Congress, 1st session, 1890, S. Report No. 829, pp. 182–188.

bination was made?—A. They have increased since I first went in their employ about three times the dressed-beef business alone.

Q. Who consitute this combination; who are in it?—A. Armour & Co., Swift & Co., Nelson Morris & Co., and George H. Hammond & Co.

Q. Do they all live in Chicago?—A. The three first firms are in business in Chicago. Hammond is in Hammond, Ind., just over the line, with head offices at Detroit.

Q. What is the nature of this combination? What are the terms of it?—A. They have a pool which is based on the business that each firm had done from the first day of January until the first day of May. They make out weekly statements of the total amount of the weight of beef on each Saturday night. This is taken Monday morning to the headquarters down town. The packers' representatives say Frank Vogel, of Nelson Morris & Co., or Eddie Morris, of Nelson Morris & Co., Mr. Armour, or some representative of his, the secretary of Swift & Co., or Mr. Louis Swift, and a representative of Hammond & Co., meet each Tuesday in the Grand Pacific Hotel, in Chicago. These meetings have been held since the agreement between them up to the present day. They take statements with them of the price of beef received in the different cities, telegrams, etc., which are submitted and gone over at this meeting.

Q. Do they bid against each other for beef that is sold in Chicago?—A. No, sir. They have a combination in Chicago. They set the price of beef. It is killed, say, to day, and the cost of it is figured the same day. The next morning a certain price is put upon it.

Q. If a man takes a lot of beef cattle to Chicago and offers them for sale at the stock-yards, does he get more than one offer from these concerns?—A. No; there is no competition in the purchase. If one of the firms sees a bunch of cattle which he wants he immediately notifies any other firms if they should come there and attempt to purchase them.

Q. He tells them he has a bid on the cattle?—A. Yes, sir; that he has a bid on them; and they frequently wait until after 3 o'clock before making any purchases in order to break the price.

Q. Then the man who brought the cattle there has to keep them over night at great expense in order to sell them?—A. Yes; he has to pay another day's yardage and also for feeding them, which is very expensive. They charge very high, a dollar a bushel for corn and a dollar a hundred for hay.

Q. At the yards?—A. At the yards, and you can not buy outside of the yards at all.

Q. Why not?—A. They are not allowed to buy hay outside of the stock-yards or to feed cattle outside the yards. If the cattle are in the yards they have to buy from the stock-yards company, and these packers are all stockholders in this company—the Union Stock-yards and Transit Company.

Q. These packers are all interested in the yard?—A. Yes, sir. Mr. Nelson Morris, I think, has the biggest amount of the stock.

Q. What is the way in which these packers operate as to selling dressed beef now in cities?—A. Take Washington, for instance. They have an understanding here between each other that they will sell beef at such and such a price.

Q. Dressed beef?—A. Yes, sir; dressed beef. The price was the other day when I saw it 7 cents. They are selling the same beef in Richmond, Va., for 5 and 5¼ cents.

Q. Have you been to Richmond lately?—A. I was there Monday, Tuesday, and Wednesday.

Q. Is there more than one of these packers with places of business in a city, or does each one take a city and leave the others out?—A. No; they all go into a city.

Q. How does that happen?—A. They had beef-houses, you see, before this combination took effect.

Q. And just kept them up?—A. They just kept them up. It would be too apparent if they dropped these houses and if one firm shipped beef all to one place. It would just advertise the pool.

Q. They want to keep up the appearances of competition?—A. They want to keep up appearances . . . .

Q. I understand you to say that you managed this dressed-beef business for three years for Nelson Morris & Co.?—A. Yes, sir.

Q. You state that this combination exists. Do you know of returns being made out weekly by Nelson Morris & Co.?—A. Yes, sir.

Q. Just state how they made them out. What was the operation?—A. They have an agreement similar to the nail trust, which is on the basis of apportionment of the shipments, the poolage from the 1st of January to the 1st of May. They would ship so much each month. If they went over that amount that month they were to pay a certain sum into the pool; if they shipped under that amount they received from the other firms the benefit.

Q. So as to equalize the business?—A. Yes, sir; so as to equalize the business. These checks are sent out weekly and received weekly, but they are kept altogether in initials and in fictitious names, so that a party going through the ledger would never discover it unless he was familiar with the business of the firm.

Q. Are all the parts of the beef utilized by these dressed-beef men?—A. There is nothing wasted at all. There is not a thing that goes to waste. The carcasses are shipped as dressed beef. The meat on the head and neck is ground up and used for bologna sausage. The horns and pates are used for glue. From the hoofs they press out neat's-foot oil. The intestines, the round, middle, and bung guts, as they call them, are used for sausage casings, and the offal is used for fertilizer.

Q. So every part of the beef is utilized?—A. There is nothing that goes to waste whatever. Even the water that is in the animal is boiled and used for fertilizer.

Q. Explain the operation by which bologna sausage is made?—A. The bologna sausage is made out of this cheap meat. The lump of meat on each side of the head and neck and what inferior meat they may have in stock is thrown into a hopper and ground up. That is transferred into a finer hopper and ground finer and mixed with potato flour, which is imported from Germany. They put in spices and it is thoroughly seasoned. Some fat is also thrown in to give it the appearance that there is pork in it. It is then taken over to the sausage-stuffer and stuffed into the sausage casings. The meat is in its raw state. After it is put into the sausage casings and tied up it is dipped for a few moments in hot water in order to partially cook it, and then for a few hours it is put in the smoke room. The next day it is boxed and shipped as first-class bologna.

Q. Do these packers buy any diseased cattle?—A. They constantly buy them, but they have an inspector at the yards who is supposed to attend to his business. However, they can slaughter diseased cattle outside the yard. They have other slaughter-houses.

Q. Outside the yards?—A. Yes, sir; outside the yards.

Q. There is no inspection beyond that?—A. There is no inspection at those houses. I know of one case where Nelson Morris & Co. slaughtered, at Flannagan & Hoff's, a lot of lumpy-jaw cattle. . . .

Q. Prior to the making of this combination of which you speak between these packers, was the dressed-beef business very profitable in Chicago?—A. No, sir.

Q. It was not?—A. No; it was very uncertain. They would sometimes make money on a car, but the losses were more frequent than the profits.

Q. What was the cause of that?—A. It was the active competition.

Q. Competition between these packers?—A. Competition between these packers.

Q. Since this combination has been made have they made money?—A. Yes, sir. I have known them to make as high as $800 on a car.

Q. Nelson Morris & Co.?—A. Yes, sir. . . .

Q. You have known them to make $800 on a car?—A. Yes, sir; on a car of beef. . . .

Q. The firm of Nelson Morris & Co. is one of the largest there, is it not?—A. Yes, sir; it is one of the largest. They kill from 1,800 to 2,000 cattle a day.

Q. Have these packers agents out through cattle regions?—A. No, sir; they sometimes send a man through Indiana, Illinois, and Kentucky to purchase first-class native cattle. They will also buy cattle for their own account and send them down to the Phoenix distillery and feed them there.

Q. That fattens them very rapidly?—A. Yes, sir; that fattens them very rapidly. They use them for Christmas beef. Nelson Morris also is a stockholder in that concern. That is also a trust. That distillery belongs to the Western whisky trust.

Q. The Phoenix distillery?—A. The Phoenix distillery. C. B. Greenhut is the treasurer.

Q. One trust helps the other?—A. Yes, sir. They also have a combine on cuts.

By cuts I mean ribs, loins, rolls, butts, tenderloins, and clods. They have a combine in seven States. They all sell at one price. There is no competition at all. . . .

The WITNESS. Heretofore they have just loaded up a car at their own pleasure; say, they would put in 28,000 pounds and bill it 22,000 pounds and make 6,000 pounds freight. The railroad kept fighting them on weight. They would weigh the cars. These refrigerator cars are all owned by the firms; they use their own refrigerator cars. They had no weight upon them, and they could put any weight they pleased in them, because the railroad companies did not know the weight of the car until it was returned and they could weigh it on their track. So they finally came to some agreement. This slip here is to give the correct weight. Last summer during the railroad fight—the Grand Trunk fight—they shipped cars of dressed beef to New York as low as $10 a car. That was the regular price. While the regular rate at 65 cents would be $130, the icing would be $3, and it would come altogether, icing, transfer, and salt, to about $138. They shipped there for months at $10 a car, but never made any difference in the price of their beef.

Q. You do not know what are the terms of the agreement referred to in the form?—A. No, sir.

Q. When did you leave the employment of Nelson Morris & Co.?—A. I had such a big fight with them I have forgotten about just when. . . . It was the 26th day of October. . . .

The farmers and the railroads

Given the exclusivity of rail transportation, western farmers in the late nineteenth century found themselves at the mercy of the railroads. Beginning with the Granger Laws of the 1870s, states attempted to regulate freight rates and various discriminatory abuses of the carriers. But the problem was national in scope and required national action. For nearly two decades, Congress periodically considered various regulatory proposals, and finally responded in 1887 with the Interstate Commerce Act that established a federal regulatory commission and prohibited certain practices. The testimony by Datus E. Meyer, a Minnesota farmer, was typical of the complaints heard by congressional committees prior to passage of the 1887 law. Railroad abuses may have been national in scope, but the self-interest of farmers was not necessarily uniform. The letter following Meyer's statement was written in 1887 to the newly formed Interstate Commerce Commission and indicates that some eastern farmers saw the situation in a different light.

Datus E. Meyer, Western Farmer

St. Paul, Minn., June 25, 1885

The CHAIRMAN. You have some definite ideas on this subject of regulating and controlling railroads, State and interstate, perhaps. Will you proceed, as we are a little short of time, and give them to us as quickly as you can.

Mr. MEYER. I will do so. There is a very wide discontent among the smaller farmer of the State in regard to those matters, arising both from discrimination and what they consider extortion. To illustrate what I mean by that, I can produce you freight receipts that will show where car-loads of stuff have been brought from Springfield, Ohio, to Saint Paul at a charge of $65 a distance of about 800 miles, and carried to Saint Vincent, a distance of about 400 miles, and charged $155. That we exhibited in the legislature last winter while I was a member.

The CHAIRMAN. What road is that on?

Mr. MEYER. On the Manitoba. There were other freight receipts exhibited there, showing that where a car had been charged, I think, $45 from Chicago to the transfer out here by Saint Paul, from there to Alexandria, a distance not exceeding 175 miles, $72 was the charge. There were other receipts showing the same abuses in different localities as great as that. Then there were discriminations proved, such as this (Mr. Dalrymple alluded to them to some extent): They absolutely refused to allow a small farmer to have a car at all, in which to load his corn and ship it away, unless he put it through that elevator system that he refers to there.

Senator PLATT. Is there any difficulty about giving a farmer a car to load?

Mr. MEYER. Yes, sir.

Senator PLATT. Is it difficult for a railroad to do it, or is it impracticable?

Mr. MEYER. No, sir; it is not impracticable. They have switches on which we could load our cars, but they absolutely refuse to allow us to have cars, on account of having given the exclusive privilege to those elevator lines that Mr. Dalrymple was speaking of here. We could not get them for any price at all. That was common in the northwestern part of the State. It is referred to in the railroad commissioners' report of last year.

Another thing that was practiced, and was brought to our notice in the legislature, was this: They have what they call a transit-rate system in the southern part of the State. If I wanted to ship grain to Milwaukee I would have to pay the rates clear through to Chicago before they would allow me to ship at all. Then they would give me a ticket for the difference between Milwaukee and Chicago, and I would have to sell that ticket for whatever I could get for it.

From U.S. Senate, Select Committee on Interstate Commerce, *Report,* 49 Congress, 1 Session, S. Report No. 46, Part 2 (1886), 1335-1337. ICC Correspondence, File No. 418, National Archives. Material suggested by John Churchman.

These abuses have caused the farmers to think that they are very much abused in the matter.

You know how hard farmers are to organize; and yet there are over three hundred secret organizations in this State, organized for the purpose of obtaining redress in that matter.

There is another thing that small farmers feel abused over a great deal, it is this, they feel that they are required to pay interest on a much larger sum of money than a road costs. I believe, and I have been among the farmers a great deal, that I can say I have never heard a farmer express a desire to cripple a road in any way whatever. The only desire they have is to be protected in their common-law rights in these matters. They think they ought to have protection; and they look to Congress to give them some relief in these matters.

The CHAIRMAN. What proportion of the traffic in this State is State traffic and what proportion is interstate traffic?

Mr. MEYER. I think there is a much larger proportion of it State traffic than interstate, in all probability; and yet not so much after all, for this reason, that nearly all of our machinery and goods comes from out of the State into it; and any extra rates such as I have referred to as was charged on machinery and other things of course is taxed on the cost of the machinery; and the farmers who consumed them have to pay extra cost. They feel very much aggrieved over the matter.

Senator PLATT. Were these discriminations or unreasonable rates that you speak of on machinery?

Mr. MEYER. Yes, sir; they were principally on machinery. That to Saint Vincent was on machinery; that to which I referred as going to Alexandria, I believe was on machinery also. It is common to all goods that we consume. I can bring freight receipts if I have the time, or I can send them to your committee, substantiating these facts.

Senator PLATT. I have no doubt they exist, for we have heard of them frequently.

Mr. MEYER. We feel that they charge us extra rates on our grain for short distances. For instance, we ship from Saint Cloud to Minneapolis. They charge us when they ship through the elevator (besides which we have to pay the elevator charges) from 7 to 8 cents per bushel for a distance of 75 miles. That would be about 12 cents per hundred for a distance of 75 miles. We think that is an extraordinary price.

The plan of discriminating, and charging more for a short than for a long haul near competing points, is almost universal. I will allude to a case that has been brought to our notice at Mapleton in this State. Last year a merchant there shipped salt from out of the State to Mapleton. They charged him, as I recollect it, nearly 50 per cent. more for shipping it to Mapleton than they do from Mankato, a distance of 12 miles further on. This was brought to my notice, and I am calling it up from recollection. He thought he could get some relief by shipping his salt first to Mankato and then shipping it to Mapleton, but the railroad company, finding out what he was attempting to do, charged him the difference between the prices that they would have charged to Mapleton. So that he made no money by the operation.

Senator PLATT. Would you make the same rate per mile for a long distance that you do for a short distance?

Mr. MEYER. No, sir; I would not.

Senator PLATT. Do you think the disparity between the long distance and the short distance is altogether too much?

Mr. MEYER. Yes, sir; in many cases it is. There have been instances brought forward here where it would be a hardship to a railroad not to allow it to carry freight; and yet I do not believe that those isolated instances should be allowed to break the rule. I believe that the people should have some protection in these matters. I tell you that the feeling through the country among the small farmers and dealers, who suffer, is much greater than you think. Take men who are very wealthy (like Mr. Dalrymple, who gets special rates which this small farmer does not get), and they believe in them. If you could get a rule laid down by which the small farmer believed he was getting justice he would be contented; but as soon as he feels that he is not getting justice there is great discontent, and that discontent will grow.

Mr. Drake alluded to the fact of their passing some laws here. That was just before a period of great depression. And the reason those laws were repealed was largely due to the fact that the railroads, either from being crippled on account of the general depression of business or otherwise, were unable to afford any good relief; and the whole matter seemed to be broken up at that time. That seemed to be the difficulty. The next legislature did repeal those laws. But last winter there was a very strong feeling in favor of re-enacting some laws that would protect the people in their common-law rights. That is all they are asking for. They are not asking to cripple the railroads or to do an injury to them in any way. They want them to have a reasonable rate on the actual amount of money that they have invested, but they want their own rights protected.

Senator PLATT. They want reasonable rates and no improper preferences?

Mr. MEYER. No improper preferences. That is all they ask for.

The CHAIRMAN. They have the right now to go into court and sue if they are charged an unreasonable rate?

Mr. MEYER. That is true. But suppose a farmer sues under the common law. The railroads have their attorneys hired and paid all the time, and they can carry that suit on until an ordinary farmer is ruined. He cannot contend with the railroads.

The CHAIRMAN. What would you have done?

Mr. MEYER. I would put a commission between the farmer and the railroads that would see that he obtains justice. That is what I would have done, and what the farmers desire shall be done. You can depend upon that.

Senator PLATT. And if a railroad charged an unreasonable rate to a farmer, or gave undue preferences, and it was ascertained by this commission, and the railroads still insisted upon doing it, you would have some provision that the Government should prosecute the case at the expense of the Government and not at the expense of the individual?

Mr. MEYER. Exactly. I very much would desire such a law, and that is a kind of law that is very much desired by the farmers.

Robert B. Howland, Eastern Farmer

Union Springs, N. Y., April 16, 1887

Interstate Commission
High Court of National Jurisdiction

You have the best legal talent of the Land to remind you of the vested rights of the Corporations, of all their grievances, of all their needs.

There is another interest entitled to consideration. They will not appear by attorney and still they represent a large capital.

Agriculture represents a fundamental factor in the national Commonwealth. When farming is depressed all enterprise feels its effect.

In settling up the West, we offer lands free to all, the taxes are light, the first settlers from Europe come with few wants, with little culture, with strong muscles and great powers of endurance.

The farmers in the East have lands for which they have paid a full value in money, or give a high rent or high rates of interest, they have to pay high taxes to meet the wants of high civilization. The land pays an undue proportion of these taxes, wages are high, discrimination in freights have all been against them.

What is the result? Their farms are encumbered, they are discouraged, land is concentrating in the hands of the few. In New England lands are going back into wilderness. The number of freehold farmers are diminishing everywhere in the East. Price of land is down to ½ what it was.

If any interest needs freight discrimination it is the eastern farming interest.

Everything favors the West. Population in the old 13 states outside of the towns has not increased has dwindled in 50 years. A rigid pro rata freight per mile is needed to save a large fundamental interest in the East.

In the interest of these farmers the word is: Stand firm to the essential principle of the law. Give it a conscientious trial and let it defend the older interests of the East. These interests are nearly crushed by all that handicaps their efforts.

From one who has been for forty years a farmer in New York State.

The protective tariff: whose protection?

Debates over the nature and extent of the protective tariff dominated American politics in the late nineteenth and early twentieth centuries. The tariff was an article of faith for much of American industry, as indicated by the previous examples of manufacturers' testimony. Undoubtedly, it served a genuine need: to protect some industries from foreign competition and, in turn, to protect American workers. Opposition naturally came from advocates of free trade. But the following song, entitled "Tariff on the Brain," which appeared in a Populist weekly newspaper in the 1890s, indicated that to some people, tariff battles were a sham masking more real, more pressing, issues in the society.

Come all you honest people,
Whoever you may be,
And help the honest workingmen
Resist monopoly.
'Tis headed by the brokers—
They deal in bonds and stocks;
They cite us to the tariff
While they're getting in their knocks.

CHORUS

Tariff on the brain! Tariff on the brain!
Look out for politicians
Who have tariff on the brain.

The goldbugs, knowing Grover
To their scheming would agree,
They put him in the White House,
Their agent there to be.
They robbed us of our silver
And grabbed up all our gold—
They cite us to the tariff
And leave us in the cold.

From *Kansas Quarterly* 1 (Fall 1969): 87–88. Used by permission.

CHORUS

They've a scheme to throttle labor
And monopolize the land,
To make of us a servile herd
While they are rich and grand.
Their schemes cause want and hunger,
And they may get foiled perhaps;
Or will our fair Columbia
By their greediness collapse?

CHORUS

Coxey's army

Mass demonstrations have periodically occurred throughout American history. During the depression of the 1890s, numerous popular protests called for governmental action to relieve unemployment. The most notable was organized by Jacob S. Coxey who, in June 1894, led a group of marchers from Masillon, Ohio, to Washington, D.C., to call upon Congress for a program to finance public works projects—an idea largely regarded as absurd at that time. When the five hundred marchers reached their destination, they were attacked by the police and arrested for walking on the grass of the Capitol's grounds. The following popular songs satirized and ridiculed the government's excessive response.

For Tramping on the Grass

S. S. King, Kansas City, Kas.
(Tune: "Tramp, Tramp, Tramp ")

Vanderbilts have railroad schemes
That through Congress they would pass;
And they crowd the halls like bees about their hives;
And they get just what they want
As they legislate for class,
And they get applause while tramping on our lives.

From *Kansas Quarterly* 1 (Fall 1969): 72–75. Used by permission.

CHORUS

Tramp, tramp, tramping on our lives;
    Wake up, boys, it's coming day,
    And beneath the sunny skies
    We will cultivate the votes,
And in sunshine they will find us making hay.

    Carnegie, the Scottish lord,
    Growing great on tariff tax,
He can always pass the bill his brain indites;
    And he never feels content
    Till he breaks our burdened backs,
And they worship him while tramping on our rights.

CHORUS

    Shylock and his forces go
    Down to buy some law and men,
And the things they want are done without a pause.
    Silver falls beneath their blow,
    Bankers get on top again,
And defy us while they're tramping on the laws.

CHORUS

    Coxey's band at Washington,
    Shelter'd 'neath the stripes and stars,
As the Commonweal of Christ they onward pass;
    And they plead for labor's rights,
    But are thrust behind the bars,
For the desp'rate crime of tramping on the grass!

CHORUS

    Vanderbilt and Carnegie,
    Shylock and our Morrill, too,
They have trampled on our lives, our rights, our laws;
    But our eyes are open now,
    And some tramping we will do,
As we make our hay and boom along the cause.
CHORUS

The National Grass Plot

Anonymous
(Tune: "Star Spangled Banner")

Oh, say, can you see, by the dawn's early light,
That grass plot so dear to the hearts of us all?
Is it green yet and fair, in well-nurtured plight,
Unpolluted by the Coxeyites' hated foot-fall?
Midst the yells of police, and swish of clubs through the air,
We could hardly tell if our grass was still there.
But the green growing grass doth in triumph yet wave,
And the gallant police with their buttons of brass
Will sure make the Coxeyites keep off the grass.

State Historical Society of Wisconsi

Coxey's Army encampment.

The Pullman strike

The strike of the American Railway Union against the Pullman Company in 1894 produced one of the sharpest, most traumatic labor-management conflicts in American industrial history. Workers for Pullman lived in a company town and rented company-owned houses—supposedly the model of an enlightened industrial town. As Pullman's business declined during the depression years of the 1890s the company cut workers' salaries several times, without any corresponding reduction of rents or dividend payments to stockholders. After some workers were fired for protesting, the American Railway Union, headed by Eugene V. Debs, supported the workers' cause and refused to handle trains carrying Pullman cars. The railroads responded by attaching such cars to mail trains, thus having a pretext for appealing to President Grover Cleveland for federal troops. The troops plus a federal court injunction against Debs and the union finally broke the strike. For many businessmen, the strike fulfilled their worst fears about labor unions; for Debs, who went to jail, the crushing of the strike made him a formidable, lifelong opponent of the capitalist system. The documents below offer comments from several workers who appeared before a federal commission investigating the causes of the strike. Their remarks testify to the worst excesses of Pullman's system of paternalism.

Testimony of R. W. Coombs

August 16, 1894, R. W. Coombs, being first duly sworn, testified as follows:

1 (Commissioner WRIGHT). State your name, residence, and occupation.—Ans. R. W. Coombs; No. 526 Stephenson street, Pullman, Ill.; car carpenter by trade.

2 (Commissioner WRIGHT). How long have you been employed as a car carpenter?—Ans. I have followed the business for near twenty years; at Pullman for the past ten years.

3 (Commissioner WRIGHT). What class of cars do you work on?—Ans. In the freight department on refrigerator cars, gondola cars, and cabooses.

4 (Commissioner WRIGHT). Are you a member of the American Railway Union?—Ans. Yes.

5 (Commissioner WRIGHT). How long have you been a member?—Ans. Since last February.

From U.S. Strike Commission, *Report on the Chicago Strike of June-July 1894* (Washington, 1895), pp. 438–441, 454–455.

6 (Commissioner WRIGHT). State what wages you received as a car builder a year ago, and what wages you received in April last.—Ans. A year ago I made about $2.25 per day at piecework; I received 17½ cents per hour; last April I was not working as a car carpenter; I was inspecting for the company; but in March, 1894, my wages as a car carpenter was about 68 cents per day at piecework.

7 (Commissioner WRIGHT). Was that reduction gradual or sudden?—Ans. The cut commenced in November, 1893; prior to that the car carpenters received on the average from $2.10 to $2.25 per day at piecework; in November, 1893, was the first reduction we had and the cut came all of a sudden. I have here what I copied myself out of a ledger of the Pullman company that was gotten up by the general timekeeper of the freight department.

8 (Commissioner WRIGHT). Does that give the earnings from November last down to the time of the strike?—Ans. I will give it to you. We built cars there in lot numbers. Lot No. 1515—that was a Santa Fe stock car; that was built in 1888. Now, in November, 1893, we built the same kind of a car with the latest improvements upon it; in 1888 a car carpenter received $13 for his work on such a car; a truck builder received 90 cents, and a truck laborer 31 cents; hanging the brakes, $1.20; delivering, forging, and casting, $1.05; delivering lumber to the car, 88 cents; framing the car, 40 cents. Now, I will give the prices for the same kind of a car with the latest improvements, in November, 1893, which was the first cut we had that we felt; the car carpenter received $7 for his work—that is a reduction of $6 right on the jump; the truck builder received 60 cents; the truck laborer, 9 cents; hanging the brakes, 64 cents; delivering, forging, and casting of car, 35 cents; delivering lumber to the car, 21 cents; framing the car, 12 cents; making a total of $9.01.

9 (Commissioner WRIGHT). Has there been a reduction since November last?—Ans. Yes, sir.

10 (Commissioner WRIGHT). What would the expense of building that car have been in April last at the prices then paid?—Ans. We finished those cars about the 7th day of September, 1893.

11 (Commissioner WRIGHT). Give the reduction after that, if any, in the same class of work.—Ans. We have not been building a class of cars of that kind in 1894 yet.

12 (Commissioner WRIGHT). What would the price have been had you built any?—Ans. If we had built any more of them in 1894 I don't think we would have got anything for it; I don't know but what we would have to have paid the company for the privilege of building them.

13 (Commissioner KERNAN). After November, 1893, during the time you continued to work until the strike, what further reduction, if any, was made? —Ans. Well, I will say this: The car we struck on was what is called a Wickes patent refrigerator car; those are the cars the freight-shop men refused to work on; I don't know whether it was a stirke or not, but the boys refused to work;

at the time the boys quit there their wages averaged them about 81 cents per day. The very best car builders, men who had had experience of from twelve to fourteen years, could not make over 81 cents per day.

14 (Commissioner KERNAN). In May, 1893, what would they have been paid for that same class of work?—Ans. Prior to November, 1893, they would have been paid at the rate of about $2.10 per day.

15 (Commissioner KERNAN). In November, what would they be paid for that work?—Ans. Just about what I have stated.

16 (Commissioner WRIGHT). Do you rent a house in Pullman?—Ans. Yes, sir.

17 (Commissioner WRIGHT). What do you pay for it, and how many rooms are there?—Ans. I have been paying $15.71 per month.

18 (Commissioner WRIGHT). How long have you been occupying that house and paying that rent?—Ans. For the past four years.

19 (Commissioner WRIGHT). Has the rent been the same all the time?—Ans. Yes, sir; $15 for rent and 71 cents for water.

20 (Commissioner WORTHINGTON). How much did you have left last February from your earnings after you had paid your rent?—Ans. Just about $3.50 in the month of February after I had paid my rent.

21 (Commissioner WORTHINGTON). What is the size of your family?—Ans. A wife and two children.

22 (Commissioner WRIGHT). How many rooms in your house?—Ans. Five.

23 (Commissioner KERNAN). Is it a separate house by itself?—Ans. No; it is what is called a flat. There is a family that lives right over me who pay the same amount of rent.

24 (Commissioner KERNAN). What yard room is connected with it?—Ans. There is a back yard about 25 by 40 feet, and the family above and my family use the same yard. There is no front yard whatever.

25 (Commissioner WRIGHT). What would the same accommodations cost you of like size in some place other than Pullman?—Ans. I could go over to Roseland and rent a house with from five to seven rooms, with a nice yard to it, both front and back yard, with the same water we pay Pullman for, at from $9 to $12 per month.

26 (Commissioner WRIGHT). Have you any views relative to the prevention of strikes?—Ans. Yes, sir; I have.

27 (Commissioner WRIGHT). Please state them.—Ans. If the men at Pullman had had proper treatment there would never have been a strike. If our general superintendent in the freight department had listened to what a great many of us asked him to do, and had done it, there would have been no strike. I lay that strike altogether down there on a man named John Pearson, assistant superintendent of the freight department; he was the cause of the whole strike and nothing else, on account of his treatment of the men; his language and abuse to them drove them to what they did. I have heard him use very

abusive language to his men, and during the last two months before the strike, while I was inspector for the company, I was told that if a man did not do what I told him to do to take a club and knock his damned head off.

28 (Commissioner WRIGHT). By whom were you told that?—Ans. I was told that by John Pearson, assistant superintendent.

29 (Commissioner WRIGHT). Are you an applicant for work now at Pullman?—Ans. Yes, sir.

30 (Commissioner WRIGHT). On what conditions can you return to work there?—Ans. Under no conditions can I work there again. Harvey Middleton says I took a very prominent part in the strike. I asked Mr. Wickes one day if any of us had committed any great depredations sufficient to bar us from working for the Pullman company. Mr. Wickes said, "Not that I know of; you have all conducted yourselves like gentlemen; you have not destroyed a flower in our flower beds or broken a window pane." I asked him why we should be debarred from working there again. He said he didn't know as anything, but Mr. Middleton insisted I should never work there again. The day I took my tool chest out of the shop I had hardly got it out before he told me, "Now get away from here, and we don't want you here any more."

31 (Commissioner WRIGHT). Are you in arrears for rent?—Ans. Yes, sir; I think I owe those people about $117 for house rent.

32 (Commissioner WRIGHT). Have they taken any steps to collect it?—Ans. They have been at my house two or three times in the past two weeks after rent, but they have taken no legal steps that I know of.

33 (Commissioner WORTHINGTON). If I understand you correctly, you think there would have been no strike at Pullman on account of the inadequacy of the wages if it had not been for the conduct of this man Pearson?—Ans. I don't believe that there would. I believe he was the cause of all of it. . . .

Testimony of Mary Alice Wood

August 18, 1894, Mary Alice Wood, being first duly sworn, testified as follows:

1 (Commissioner WRIGHT). State your name, residence, and occupation.—Ans. Mary Alice ·Wood; No. 302 Stephenson street, Pullman, Ill.; from December, 1893, to May, 1894, I worked in the electrical department at Pullman.

2 (Commissioner WRIGHT). Are you a member of the American Railway Union?—Ans. I am.

3(Commissioner WRIGHT). Are you one of the strikers at Pullman?—Ans. Yes, sir.

4 (Commissioner WRIGHT). Have you sought to get back into the employ of the company?—Ans. No, sir; I have not, because I could not live on the wages I could get there.

5 (Commissioner WRIGHT). What wages did you earn in June, 1893?—Ans. I did not work there in June, 1893.

6 (Commissioner WRIGHT). I mean from the time you commenced to the time you quit?—Ans. My wages were the same, because I only started there about Christmas, 1893; I got $1 per day and paid the Pullman company $7.73 for rent.

7 (Commissioner WRIGHT). You have no knowledge of the rate of wages paid prior to the cuts of last fall?—Ans. Yes, sir; I worked in Pullman some two or three years ago, and I know the girls then made $2 and $2.25 per day, seldom less than $1.75 when I left there; prior to May, three years ago, I earned from $1.75 to $2.25 per day.

8 (Cmmissioner WRIGHT). Is there anything further you desire to state?—Ans. Yes, sir; my father, prior to eight years ago, was employed as a watchman at the Fulton street gate in Pullman, and on the 15th of July, 1886, or 1887 I believe it was, there was a man named Pearson attempted to leave the shops with a box of tools without a pass; the company's orders were strict to take a pass from anyone leaving with any article. Father demanded that he give him a pass; he would not do it and struck father in the face with a hatchet or something—I did not see this, but there are witnesses who did see it, one of the witnesses who saw it was William McLean, he is in New Jersey somewhere now, I don't know his address; a doctor in Pullman attended father and he was brought home; Lieutenant Kane arrested the man; he took a change of venue to a South Chicago police court, and he was acquitted, because they said no man had a right to stop him from taking his tools from the shop, either with or without a pass. Inspector Hunt, at that time captain of police, requested mamma to come up to Chicago with witnesses and they would have the man indicted, but when they got here the grand jury had adjourned and when it met again Pearson had left the town, and there was nothing further said about it.

I wanted mamma to bring a case against the Pullman company, but she had no money and they had everything and she did not do it. Father did not die at once, but he did not recover enough so as to get back his position, although he got employment in the paint department after a while. He was not able to work, and it was only through Mr. Canady's kindness that he was able to hold it at all; when he was able to go to the shop it was all right, and when he was not it was all right, and he died the 30th of May following.

9 (Commissioner WRIGHT). What has this matter to do with this strike we are investigating?—Ans. It has nothing to do with the strike, but a great deal to do with the Pullman company. . . .

The political plight of women

In most parts of the United States in this period, women were second-class citizens. For most concerned women, gaining the right to vote represented the key to equality. The granting of suffrage, of course, depended entirely on the political will or whim of men. The following selections illustrate both the forcefulness of the suffragists as well as the determination of their opponents. First, Helen Potter of New York City boldly and indignantly describes the political plight and powerlessness of women to the Senate committee investigating capital and labor in 1883. In the second piece, Doris Stevens recalls the demonstrations of the suffragists in Washington, D.C., in 1917. Although a number of states had adopted women's suffrage, President Woodrow Wilson adamantly opposed a national amendment until late in 1918. For their activities in the nation's capital, Stevens and her friends were jailed. Here she relates her experiences as a "political prisoner."

Helen Potter: "If you were a woman. . . ."

New York City, September 19, 1883

. . . A woman who sews for me on One hundred and fifth street has a corner lot which she has worked for for twenty years and paid for. She pays $23 tax on that little corner without any exit; it goes nowhere. She has bought it, however, on her wages as a sewing-woman at a dollar a day. There is a church in this city that cost $2,000,000 and is rolling in wealth, and it is not taxed at all, while this poor woman is taxed $23 a year for her little corner; and yet this church sets up to teach her morals and says she is a miserable sinner.

Q. Whose chances would you take for the future, this woman's or those who belong to that church?—A. Well, sir, there are very few people in this world who have the strength of character to say what they think, and I do not know that I have; so I will keep still. I have been connected with churches a great portion of my life, as I was so placed in business that it was necessary and proper that I should go to church as an example to others, having been connected with colleges and schools. The churches tell me that I am an inferior being, that I

From *Report of the Committee of the Senate upon the Relations between Labor and Capital,* 48th Congress, 2 (1885): 627–632.

must obey the laws, and be tried by the laws, but I have nothing to say about making the laws, and they say I must stay at home and mind my business, but as I have no home to stay in, I cannot stay; that is, I have no husband and children, and that is what they expect us to have, whether we can or not.

[Q.] You give some very forcible facts, and some strong opinions as to how the law ought to be and how it ought to be executed.

The WITNESS. The church tells me that I am not made for myself; that I must obey man; but I have not seen the man that has the right to command me, and therefore I do not obey. Therefore, I am breaking the moral law all the time, because I cannot obey anybody. My father is old, and is out in the West, and my brother is dead, and I have no husband; so I have nobody that I can obey, but if I did obey a man I should expect him to be responsible for my actions; if I did anything wrong he should suffer the penalty; otherwise he might tell me to murder somebody and I might be hung for it.

The CHAIRMAN. That would be a good way of getting rid of you. You have certainly stated some very startling facts.

The WITNESS. It is really an important question—this of the condition of women in our community. When I was a young girl I had some ambition, and when I heard a good speaker, or when I read something written by a good writer, I had an ambition to do something of that kind myself. I was exceedingly anxious to preach, but the churches would not have me; why, they said that a woman must not be heard, and to-day, to show the prejudice against us poor creatures, who are really slaves, public sentiment is such that the reporters in public meetings will report nothing that a woman says. . . .

. . . Any woman that wants to vote cannot get into the newspapers. We are so placed that we get no hearing. Churches tell us to stay at home. But what is the home of these poor girls? Take a girl who works from seven in the morning until six at night in these large stores—behind counters all day—when she gets back to her home, where does her home lie? It is to be found in some tenement house, with 30 or 40 other families. There is no base-ball club for her, no bowling-alley for her, no gymnasium, no reading-room, no art gallery open on Sunday, no anything for this poor girl when she is at liberty—nothing but a den where there are 30 or 40 people huddled together; she has not even facilities for bathing. How can she grow up to be a great and good woman? Men can go to concerts and entertainments, but women have to wait for invitations. The church tells us this poor girl should go home—perhaps to a drunken mother or a vile father. Where is her home? Will the church provide a home for her? If you gentlemen were in our places you would feel our degradation with a feeling such as no pen or tongue can describe. . . .

Q. You surely do not mean to say that this is a picture of the condition of the women of New York generally?—A. I say it is the picture of those who have not money enough to take care of themselves—who have not money enough to get any better homes.

Q. Do not men go to these same homes and live in that same condition of poverty?—A. Yes, they do. I have spoken on a broader basis than sex. I speak of the whole human family. . . .

I had not intended to touch on the woman question, because it is really a matter of adjustment, I think, before women can become educated and established and have ways opened for them. We will have to submit to that. I do not say it in any bitterness, because humanity is always the same. There are grand and noble men and women everywhere, and there is no distinction in that regard. But if you gentlemen should take a whole day to think it over, and each of you imagine yourself a woman, with all woman's relations and limitations, I think you could understand it. Take a whole day to it and think it over, and reflect how, if you were a woman, you could not do thus and so—you could not do so many things that are within the grasp and scope of man's power in the community.

Q. They do not treat women so badly anywhere that I know of, unless it may be, as you say, here in New York. I acknowledge that things are very bad, certainly, if that is the way they treat their women. But the suffrage question would not help that.

The WITNESS. Do you think, sir, that if I were a member of the board of health, I should permit the sanitary conditions that I have referred to to exist as they are? Why, if you should go and ask these people at our city hall here to do their duty in regard to these sanitary conditions, they would simply tell you to go home and mind your own business.

Q. Do you mean that women have no political influence?—A. Well, I suppose every human being has an influence, but in our case it seems to be so little that we can accomplish nothing. What can we do?

Q. You can make a man vote the way you want him to.

The WITNESS. Where is mine?

Q. Well, if you have not got one it is your fault; you must not blame that on the men.

The WITNESS. Well, I will not go into that question. But, in all seriousness, I think it would take perhaps two or three hundred years to get women into a condition, as voters, to thoroughly understand or resort to the tricks of men in politics. It would take that time to "educate" them. . . .

The only unpleasant result that I should anticipate from woman's suffrage is that which might possibly occur from a union of the church and the state. Ninetenths of the church members are women. They are more devotional, more religious, and more moral than men. I say this, too, with all respect to men, for I think there are most excellent men. Women forming, however, a large proportion of the religious element would naturally place the power more or less in church hands, and there would be perhaps a tendency toward the union of church and state, which a republican form of government should avoid; indeed I do not know but that every other form of government should also avoid it.

Q. You think that by virtue of her being better————

The WITNESS. [Interposing.] More religious, say.

Q. That it would therefore be dangerous to give her the ballot?

A. Well, it is in that regard only that I see any reason for doubt. I certainly think it would clean our streets, and I think it would purify politics, at least for the next two hundred years. It would take about that time to get women to understand the tricks of politicians as at present practiced. I do not think that women would be injured by it. Men and women are raised in the same family, they go to school together, they marry together, they go to church together, and why they should separate just at that point I do not quite see. It does not contaminate a woman to sit side by side with a man in her own family, or in the church, or at the theater; why should it do so to step up to a box and drop in a ticket stating her wants.

There is a woman in this city who pays taxes on perhaps a million dollars' worth of property, but she has no vote. A man across the street, who cannot read or write, and who shovels dirt for the plants and flowers and wheels a wheelbarrow in the garden of this same lady, has a voice to say whether a street shall go through her property, and whether her house shall be torn down or not. This woman came to the city of New York thirty years ago, with 20 cents in her pocket, and by her own skill and knowledge of values, and business capacity, has become worth a million of dollars through real estate in this city. Yet she has not a chance to say one word as to the taxes she shall pay or as to the disposition of her property.

Q. Is that the lady who was here yesterday, Miss King?—A. Yes, sir; she has no voice, as I have said, in the disposition of her property, or whether she will have in this city more water works, or less, or whether we shall have to suffer all the inconveniences that result from bad laws and a bad political system, while this Irishman across the street, who works for her, can say what shall be done with her property. Put yourselves in that condition, and see how you gentlemen would like it. She is not a married lady; there is no law to compel her to marry, and if she chooses to remain single why should she not be permitted to have the same right of disposition as to her property that a man has? . . .

Q. Do you think the only reason for that is that they want the suffrage?—A. Yes, sir. They want the power, and I do not blame them. . . .

Q. Why do you think that the suffrage is not extended to women by men—what is the true reason, the radical reason, why men do not give up one half their political power to women?—A. Well, it may arise from a false notion of gallantry. I think most men feel like taking care of, and protecting the ladies. They do not stop to think that there are in New England alone 150,000 unmarried women, who can have no help, as things are. It would be all very well, perhaps, if all women had representatives, and if all had a generous, straightforward honorable man to represent them. But take the case of a good woman who has a drunken husband; how can he represent her? He votes for liquor and for everything he may happen to want, even though it may ruin her and turn her out of doors, and even though it may ruin her children. If the husband is a bad man would it not be better for that woman to represent herself? . . .

Q. What effect do you think the extension of the suffrage to women would have upon their material condition, their wage-earning power and the like?—A. They would get equal pay for equal work of equal value. I do not think a woman ought to be paid the price of an expert, when she is not herself an expert, but I believe there would be a stimulus for a woman to fit herself for the very best work. What stimulus is there for woman to fit herself properly, if she never can attain the highest pay, no matter what sort of work she does? If women had a vote I think larger avenues of livelihood would be opened for them and they would be more respected by the governmental powers. I do not say it with regard to myself particularly, but I do not see any reason, for example, why it would not be just as proper for me to sit down and copy deeds in a nicely carpeted, well-ventilated room, out of sight of the world in the register's office, or similar offices. Why could not I do that and be entirely respectable and retain all my moral qualities, as well as a man? There is no such place open at present for women. There are over six thousand municipal offices in this city, and not one for a woman, no matter how much taxes she pays. . . .

Doris Stevens: Criminal?

Finding that a Suffrage Committee in the House and a report in the Senate had not silenced our banners, the administration cast about for another plan by which to stop the picketing. This time they turned desperately to longer terms of imprisonment. They were, indeed, hard pressed when they could choose such a cruel and stupid course.

Our answer to this policy was more women on the picket line on the outside, and a protest on the inside of prison.

We decided, in the face of extended imprisonment, to demand to be treated as political prisoners. We felt that, as a matter of principle, this was the dignified and self-respecting thing to do, since we had offended politically, not criminally. We believed further that a determined, organized effort to make clear to a wider public the political nature of the offense would intensify the administration's embarrassment and so accelerate their final surrender.

It fell to Lucy Burns, vice-chairman of the organization, to be the leader of the new protest. Miss Burns is in appearance the very symbol of woman in revolt. Her abundant and glorious red hair burns and is not consumed—a flaming torch. Her body is strong and vital. It is said that Lucy Stone had the "voice" of the pioneers. Lucy Burns without doubt possessed the "voice" of the modern suffrage movement. Musical, appealing, persuading—she could move the most resistant person. Her talent as an orator is of the kind that makes

From Doris Stevens, *Jailed for Freedom* (New York: Boni and Liveright, 1920), pp. 175–178.

for instant intimacy with her audience. Her emotional quality is so powerful that her intellectual capacity, which is quite as great, is not always at once perceived. . . .

She had no sooner begun to organize her comrades for protest than the officials sensed a "plot" and removed her at once to solitary confinement. But they were too late. Taking the leader only hastened the rebellion. A forlorn piece of paper was discovered on which was written their initial demand. It was then passed from prisoner to prisoner through holes in the wall surrounding leaden pipes, until a finished document had been perfected and signed by all the prisoners.

This historic document—historic because it represents the first organized group action ever made in America to establish the status of political prisoners—said:

To the Commissioners of the District of Columbia:
As political prisoners, we, the undersigned, refuse to work while in prison. We have taken this stand as a matter of principle after careful consideration, and from it we shall not recede.

This action is a necessary protest against an unjust sentence: In reminding President Wilson of his preelection promises toward woman suffrage, we were exercising the right of peaceful petition, guaranteed by the Constitution of the United States, which declares peaceful picketing is legal in the District of Columbia. That we are unjustly sentenced has been well recognized—when President Wilson pardoned the first group of suffragists who had been given sixty days in the workhouse, and again when Judge Mullowny suspended sentence for the last group of picketers. We wish to point out the inconsistency and injustice of our sentences—some of us have been given sixty days, a later group, thirty days, and another group given a suspended sentence for exactly the same action.

Conscious, therefore, of having acted in accordance with the highest standards of citizenship, we ask the commissioners of the District to grant us the rights due political prisoners. We ask that we no longer be segregated and confined under locks and bars in small groups, but permitted to see each other, and that Miss Lucy Burns, who is in full sympathy with this letter, be released from solitary confinement in another building and given back to us.

We ask exemption from prison work, that our legal right to consult counsel be recognized, to have food sent to us from outside, to supply ourselves with writing material for as much correspondence as we may need, to receive books, letters, newspapers, our relatives and friends.

Our united demand for political treatment has been delayed, because, on entering the workhouse, we found conditions so very bad that, before we could ask that the suffragists be treated as political prisoners, it was necessary to make a stand for the ordinary rights of human beings for all the inmates. Although this has not been accomplished, we now wish to bring the important question of the status of political prisoners to the attention of the commissioners, who, we are informed, have full authority to make what regulations they please for the District prison and workhouse.

The commissioners are requested to send us a written reply so that we may be sure this protest has reached them. . . .

The commissioners' only answer to this was a hasty transfer of the signers and the leader, Miss Burns, to the District jail, where they were put in solitary confinement. The women were not only refused the privileges asked but were denied some of the usual privileges allowed to ordinary criminals.

State Historical Society of Wisconsin.

Campaigning for women's suffrage, Wisconsin, 1912.

CHAPTER 9

The varieties of reform

Housing for workers

Living in the company house

In many factory towns, employers provided living quarters for their workers and families. At times, employers required the workers to live in company-owned housing as a condition of employment. In such cases, workers again found themselves subject to the whims and unchecked power of their employers. The following selection offers some workers' views on the horrors of company housing in Fall River, Massachusetts, in the early 1880s. Included also are some self-serving remarks by two manufacturers.

. . . A spinner who was employed in one of the mills that bore the reputation about town of having some of the worst houses said in substance:

"The tenements throughout the city are in a very poor condition. The reason why I live in this one is because I am compelled to. Compulsion is used by this mill, and whether the manufacturers have the legal or the moral right to keep us in their houses I do not know; but I think it is wrong. The sink is in the corner of this room, which we use as our living-room, dining-room, and kitchen. The closets in the yard are very bad, and their odor is the reverse of pleasant. There is a hydrant in the yard to which we all have to go for drinking-water, having none in the house that is fit to drink. Shortly after 6 o'clock any night you can see a line of men, women, girls, and boys waiting their turn, laden with pails, to get the water to use for drinking and cooking. In England I never knew what a tenement house was. No matter how poor the man, he always rented a little house that he called his own, which he occupied with only his own family. The tenement house is purely an American notion, that we English people do not admire, and when we are compelled to live in such houses, whether we like it or not, the burden is all the heavier to bear. Then in England the law always steps in and restricts the construction of any house where the rooms, and especially the sleeping apartments, are less than 10 feet in height. This room you are in is less than 8 feet, and in the upper stories I understand that it is still lower, so that if they should build dwelling-houses for operatives as they do in Lowell, the builders would save enough on the lumber to steal another floor." . . .

A spinner in one of the Central Mills, who had a very neat-looking tenement, thought that nearly all of the mill tenements were unfit to live in.

From *Report of the Committee of the Senate upon the Relations between Labor and Capital*, 48th Congress, 1 (1885): 63–65 (quoting Massachusetts Bureau of Labor Statistics, *Report*, 1882, p. 272).

"But," said he, "you take whole families, like mine, who work in the mills, and what benefit do they derive from a home? They are only there at night to sleep, and on Sunday, and to such one kind of a house is as good as another. There are no corporation boarding-houses, only tenements; and I do not think there is any large boarding-house in the city. This is explained by the fact that the help is composed mostly of families, while in Lowell and Lawrence there are more of the single help. Boarding is a distinctly American notion. You could not bring over an entire cargo of single English women to work in the mills, for the girls in the old country go out to service—become domestic servants. Your American girl, however, goes into the mill; she wants to feel at 6 o'clock that she is free for the balance of the night. Americans are very few in Fall River; but I think that if the mills had American help to deal with they could get on much better, for the American is proverbial for his submission."

This same man said:

"Rents are very high here, and range from $7 to $15 per month. I pay $8.50 and make, on an average, $9.50 per week. My wife and two children increase this to about $29 a week. The reason I do not live anywhere else is because the manufacturers require that the operatives shall live in their houses, and I am not so foolish as to risk being discharged and put on the black-list merely because the rooms are small; they are large enough for me, and I can save more money in this way to live on when wife and I get too old to work." . . .

The manufacturers, as a rule, spoke strongly in favor of their houses. One said: "Our tenements are very good indeed. They were built ten or twelve years ago and must be in good condition; we try to keep them so, at all events. The help take fair care of them. Of course there are exceptions. The intemperate do not; they do not care; they get intoxicated and use their rooms as though they were barrooms."

Another said:

"They are not as good as we would like to have them, but good enough for the operatives." . . .

Tenements and urban slums

The new immigrants in the late nineteenth century generally settled in large eastern urban centers or factory towns. Working for barely subsistence wages, they lived accordingly, packed into small apartments in large tenement buildings. Sanitary conditions were abominable, and safety provisions almost nonexistent. Helen Potter, apparently a social worker or visiting nurse, here comments on the housing blight in some of the ghettos of the lower east side in New York in the 1880s. Her remarks also give us some insight into the impact of family employment and slum conditions on the raising of children.

New York: lower east side immigrant settlement.

New York, September 19, 1883.

... The WITNESS. First, in order to have a good sanitary condition we should have plenty of water, which we have not. The water in the highest parts of this city will not flow above the second floor at its best. There is not a sufficient supply to protect the people and to keep them cleanly, to say nothing of affording protection from fires. We read columns in the newspapers about the protection of large store-houses of rich goods, but not a word about the condition of the poor people who have not water enough to get a bath, or even in some cases to wash their faces.

Human beings are crowded together in hundreds in the tenement quarters, 20 or 30 or 40 in a room, without water to keep themselves in a normal condition, to bathe themselves or keep themselves clean.

Q. What is the size of such rooms as you speak of, where so many people live?—A. There is a school building on the corner of Fourth street and Avenue C in which there are 300 pupils, and there is only one place where they can get water, and that has to supply also a store and a stable, and if the store or the stable wants water the children have to go without it. At No. 310 Houston street there is sometimes no water in the house at all, and when there is it has to be brought in from the yard for the large number of people who inhabit the tenement, so that the indolent, the inefficient, and the poor, especially the children, are suffering from the want of a good water supply. At No. 110 Ridge street is a rookery, an alley that people crowd into and mass together, without a sufficient water supply. People cannot be moral if they cannot be clean. The first step to everything that is good is cleanliness. At 161 Lewis street is another large tenement house without water supply sufficient to the needs of the people. And so far as cleaning the streets is concerned, or using water to clean their apartments, it is totally impossible to get a sufficient supply to do it. I cannot go into the technical details as to pipes, &c., or where we are to get the water supply from, but with all the brains that are to be found in the metropolis of the United States it seems to me that water enough might be found somewhere in the vicinity and arrangements made to conduct it here, so that poor people might keep themselves and their children clean.

There is a heavy tax also on any unusual use of water when the reservoirs are low; and every house pays $10 for the use of water. I should estimate that we need at least double the present water supply for sanitary purposes, to say nothing of fires. If all the goods in the city were in danger, we would need twice as much as that, in order to secure cleanliness to the people.

The second condition necessary for the advancement of the poor people is pure air. We have not pure air in a large part of this city, and the reason for that

From *Report of the Committee of the Senate upon the Relations between Labor and Capital*, 48th Congress, 2 (1885): 621–626.

is bad drainage—bad sewerage—and nuisances in the shape of garbage and refuse matter from the manufactories, which render impure the water which surrounds the city.

The garbage of this city is dumped into the harbor, ruining the harbor by filling it up, as this stuff must accumulate at the bottom, and when it is stirred up by the machinery of vessels passing around the city it produces a very offensive odor—an odor that is offensive to all people, no matter how low their condition. On the old maps of the city there are shown creeks of running water, and, in building up the city, these creeks have been filled up with garbage and built over. Some of the most fashionable parts of this city are built over filled-in ground, some 30 or 40 feet deep. On Fifty-seventh street and Fifth avenue there is 40 feet of garbage, and there is no subdrainage. The result of this is that when the tide comes in the water is backed into these old creeks or vats, and the cellars and basements become damp and in many instances flooded. In Harlem this is often the case. Do you desire me to speak as to anything outside of this city?

The CHAIRMAN. Yes, anywhere.

The WITNESS. Well, in Toledo Ohio during the present spring flood, the sewerage being similar there, when the floods came up they brought matter from the sewers into the basements and around the walls. The walls and boards had to be scraped to get it all off, so bad is the sewerage and drainage system of the cities of the country. There is really no one subject more important to the health of the country, nor one so much neglected.

Q. That condition must be known to the officials of the city government?—A. It is. It must be known to them.

I want to speak particularly of some of the special nuisances in New York. The dumping of the garbage in the harbor around New York has affected the bathing, and makes it very disagreeable to people who resort to Coney Island and places around the city for bathing purposes in the summer time. There is a factory on Long Island where a refuse is given forth which is bad enough when you are a mile away from it without going any nearer to ascertain exactly what it is like. It is clear to thinking people that the garbage of this city should be taken out upon the ground and placed between the sun and the earth, where it will help the earth; the soil needs it. The reason why this is not done is strange; it is past my comprehension. Mr. A. T. Stewart, the rich merchant, who recently died in this city, and also his successor, Mr. Hilton, offered to clean the streets of New York City and take all the refuse out of the city, free of expense, on their own barges, if the city would allow them to do so; but the city would not allow them to do so. Farmers in the vicinity of New York have endeavored to obtain this garbage to enrich their lands, but they have not been allowed to take it. Why, it is against the law for a person to dispose of any portion of the refuse of this city, even if it is upon their own grounds and produced from their own homes. I could not sell, on my own place, a barrel of refuse, or even give it away or take it out of town and put it on my own ground if I wanted to do so. Why that is so I do not know. Within a stone's throw of this place there is garbage that has been there three years, so that the things that have been thrown into it have become skeletons. No one has ever seen those streets but the folks who live there, for the tax-payers do not go there, and ladies do not go there, and the municipal officers evidently do not go there, and when you ask them to go down and see to matters in that neighborhood they have a headache or are otherwise indisposed. Property there has depreciated to such an extent that within a stone's throw of the city hall property is almost valueless, it is in such a bad condition. Miss Susan A. King, who was here yesterday, but did not give evidence, told me to say to the committee that she was acquainted down there, and had property there, and had dealt in real estate there sufficiently to know the quarter. She said that she had taken some of the city officers and insisted upon their going down there to visit these quarters, and they have never been heard of since. She does not advise the committee to go down there un-protected, as it might not be safe; but if they will appoint a time she will escort them. She thinks she might pilot them through safely. Then, there is Thompson street, and Mulberry street, and Bayard street, and Baxter street, and Chinatown, and Irishtown, and Italiantown right within reach of a short circle of the city hall. At No. 200 Mulberry street is situated the headquarters of the bureau of police, and actually of the board of health, and how they can escape seeing all these unsanitary conditions is wonderful to me.

In Baxter street in one room there are eight families, composed altogether of forty-two people, and three-quarters of them are so destitute of clothing that they cannot go into the street even to beg. . . .

Q. Where is this room; is it above ground or under ground?—A. Well, it is a basement, a half-cellar, and, when the tide comes in the water is eight inches deep on the floor; they have to put scantlings and slabs across to put their clothes on. One small stove is all that can be found in that enormous room to warm a whole crowd of people in the cold weather. . . .

Q. Do you say that there are eight families in one room?—A. Yes, sir.

Q. What is the size of the room?—A. It is a large room—a whole basement. It is, perhaps, longer but not as wide as this room—it extends back. . . .

Q. Do you know how the people who live there employ themselves?—A. I think they are rag pickers, mainly. I say that the houses for the poor in this city are too dark, too damp, too much crowded, too poorly ventilated, and have altogether insufficient water, and hence are too vile to live in. I refer to the tenements for the masses. Who it is who owns these houses I do not know. I have been told that some of these tenements—places of the lowest order—are owned by people like the Astors. How they can ride in their carriages, and dress in silk and velvets, or sleep peacefully at night while they permit their tenants to have such dwellings, I cannot understand. I suppose we are obliged here to speak within the limits of what the law can help; but the law could oblige builders to make buildings strong enough so that they would not tumble down, and to make them dry and substantial; and I suppose that the department which has charge of the sewerage in the cities could manage so that the sewerage system would be more efficient than it is. I suppose, too, that the building department could compel builders to have means of ventilation so that these houses would be habitable, and that they could compel them to have proper lights and windows and communication with the outer air, and the law could certainly compel them to put more than a small four-pane window in a place large enough for forty people to get into, to say nothing of their living in it.

The law should compel builders, also, to have plenty of fire escapes, and not allow buildings to be made in such a way that at the tops of hotels, and in corridors, and away off in remote and inaccessible parts of great buildings in great cities should be found the poor working girls who are forced to sleep there, and are sometimes burned up in consequence. They should make these tenement houses without paper on the walls; they should paint the walls smooth and clean, so that dirt and dust could be washed off and not remain for insects and disease to germinate in. They should also be prohibited from painting with poisonous greens or using papers colored with poisonous greens, where little children may be, for they may gnaw the paper or paints.

In each tenement, there should be a "nursery," a room in which there should be air and sunlight in plenty, where the children of the inhabitants of the house can be left in charge of a general governess or nurse while the mothers go out to work. Every tenement should have such a room, not a living room, but a large play-room for the children. I went into a little alleyway, a short time since, and up some stairs, and I heard a faint cry but could see no place from which it came. I asked a woman I met where that cry came from. She said, "from *there*," pointing to a place where I could see nothing. After some conversation and examination I found that she had pointed in the direction of a little window of four very small panes of glass that opened into a hall. I said "What is in there?" and she said it was a little child only three weeks old. I said, "where is its mother?" she says, "she is out washing." I asked her if there was no one who had charge of the little baby, and she said that nobody had charge of it; its mother had to go out to work, there being no other alternative but starvation for both the mother and child. I got upon a chair and looked in through this little window and there was a little baby three weeks old lying upon a pile of rags for a bed, having no clothing on its little body, and the mother not to be in until night-fall. The child was evidently tired out with crying, for its cry was faint and hoarse, and it was enough to make any one cry to hear it. How can we get good strong men or women out of children who are brought up in that way? . . .

The landlord and housing reform

The revelations of unsanitary and unsafe conditions in tenement housing led to demands for reform. In the late nineteenth and early twentieth centuries, municipalities and states passed new building codes requiring increased maintenance expenses for property owners. Landlords either complied, balked, or rebelled at the new regulations. And maybe, as the following selection indicates, housing problems could not have been cured merely by restrictive legislation. The letter, anonymously written to the Philadelphia Housing Commission in April, 1912, pointed out some of the problems from a landlord's perspective. The letter's semiliterate quality illustrates the writer's educational deprivation: as evidenced by the last statement, the writer was not also financially deprived.

Your objet is good but allow me to give my experence i am the owner of a lot of Small houses all in the Slums my experence we have less trouble with the houses that are not drained as that class of peopel dont know and dont want to know how to use a toilet they are always stoped up and full of filth in this case i find the Old Time Well the Best of all for those peopel they cant Stop the Well up and the Old time Well is for the good of health I have had toilet cleaned the next day they had it stoped up again and full of filth and bad Smell the Old Time Well never fails to hold all no one can have things cleaned for that class the easiest way is the best the old time Well is my choice Thearmost all of my closets are drained but i think i Will Sell Out all that are drained as they are to much trouble in the Slum Section i dont think that any of you peopel have any idear of What a property owner is up against With hopper Closet and a Slum tenant buy a few houses and try it and you Will Soon find that the Old Style Well is the best for the tenant i Wont have to much to Say as i am going to Sell Out a part of my 67 Small houses but will hold all that are not drained and if i am compeld to drain them i will sell them then to.

> Yours trouly
> a friend
> kindly receive this as a friendly letter
> as i mean no effence whatever.

From Housing Association of Delaware Valley Papers, Temple University Urban Archives, Temple University, Philadelphia. Used by permission. Material provided by John Sutherland.

The world's oldest profession

Following the Civil War, industrialization and the growing squalor of urban areas brought in their wake a vigorous, open revival of prostitution. Indeed, in the 1870s, there were serious proposals for "reglementation," that is, the practice of licensing and segregating prostitutes, and subjecting them to regular health examinations as in European cities. Few subjects evoked such an emotional, sustained response. Reformers who before the Civil War had been "out of style," suddenly found a new cause after the war and the abolition of slavery. For the next forty years, a steady flood of publications, lectures, and governmental investigations alerted the nation to the menace of "white slavery" and the horrors of prostitution.

The madam and the prostitute: "The last resort . . . is the sporting house."

The following selections, taken from testimony to the Wisconsin legislative committee investigating white slavery and prostitution, offer statements from a madam and a prostitute. Their remarks provide not only revelations into their own lives, but also some interesting observations of the society in which they operated.

Statement of WXS. . . . "I am forty-six years old. I was a school teacher before I was married. I have been twice married. My first husband died. I left my second husband because of his unnatural desires, which were repugnant to me. He has since died. My resources finally were so low that I had to look around for something to do. I did not care for school teaching, for which I had been fitted in my younger days. One day I answered an ad, which led to my becoming housekeeper in a sporting house. This was the first time I had ever been in a resort. I knew, however, what I was doing. For the first month I worked gratis, but to make things easier for me, the woman in charge gave me the cigar privilege, that is the profits from the sale of cigars. The woman had taken a liking to me, after the first month, and she gave me $10.00 a week and the cigar privilege, which sometimes netted $4.00 or $5.00 a night. It was a $5.00 house. The patrons were generous. I do not care for drink; I never frequent

From *Report and Recommendations of the Wisconsin Legislative Committee to Investigate the White Slave Traffic and Kindred Subjects,* 1914, pp. 181-184.

saloons and palm gardens. Soon I had about $300.00 saved, and when the woman who ran the house decided to leave the city and offered the house to me, I took it. It was simply a matter of a livelihood for me.

"I never have had intercourse with men promiscuously. I will not say that I never have had, but never promiscuously; never for money. I received the money that other people have taken in, but I never have sold my own body.

"I sold out my house in M . . . . . . and went to San Francisco, but had only been there about a year when the earthquake left me penniless. I got free transportation to Chicago, and was there offered a house in M . . . . . . I borrowed money from friends and took the house. I made wonderfully good money.

"I have never made less than $10,000 a year, but I have saved little, for there isn't a more charitable lot of people in the world than the sporting women. I gave not a cent to the police, but to charitable organizations, sisters of religious organizations, the Salvation Army, beggars, friends, and people in distress.

"I usually had from six to eight girls in my house. It was a $2.00 house. The girls got 50% of the earnings, and they paid no board. Unless I was certain that girls could take care of themselves, they had to be examined, and no man can ever say he got diseased in my house.

"Girls do not usually have their first relations with men for pay. Most of them have been betrayed. And many, many—I will not say a majority, but many, many of the girls have been married. I have known times when most of the girls in my house were girls who have been married. They were mistreated by their husbands or were there for some other cause; but, of course, that is no reason for people being in a house.

"I never paid to have girls brought to my house. I treated them well, and I could get all I wanted. As to having agents soliciting trade for my girls, I will say, no, nothing of the kind.

"The mentality of the girls is all right, but you will find as a rule they are not educated girls. The educated girl was the exception. The Catholic religion seems to predominate among the sporting girls, though I cannot say why. I know that a majority of the girls that have lived with me have been of the Catholic religion. There must be something lacking in their training, and yet they are more religiously trained than the other denominations. They have more religion trained into them, and yet they seem to fall.

"If drink were taken from these places, they would go outside and get it, and I have found it is very much better if you have girls in your house and they want a bottle of beer, to let them have it. I never cared very much about selling drinks, because I don't like to have my girls drink. When the liquor was taken out of the houses here, I cannot say that my business decreased to any great extent, because I presume I never catered very much to the drinking element. I never sold very much drink. I used to accommodate the girls. I always had it in the house and used to accommodate my girls more than I did the men. If a girl wanted a bottle of beer I would let her have it. Most of the girls liked to drink. I have had girls that did not drink at all. I have had girls that always set their glasses back on the tray, and I have always done that myself. I don't care for drink and I don't care for the effects.

"If I could have my way of running a house, and I wanted to run a house—which I hope I may never wish to do again—I think the way I would like to have things done would be if a man really feels the call of nature and feels that he must have that, to have him come in and get what he wants and walk out. I don't believe in all this entertainment. That is what draws the business. You know those kind of houses—in fact all houses—have been that way when they had those entertainments. It was a lot of "Hurrah Boys," and maybe nine out of ten men that come in only wanted to have some music and dancing, unless they wanted to buy a drink.

"I have never contributed to any campaign fund. The only contribution I ever made was for the building of the . . . . . .

"I never intend to run a place of that kind again. I wasn't in the business when they closed the district. I had left the line over a year before that, and at that time I was touring the world. I had been gone all that time.

"My patrons were both married and single men, about evenly divided,—half and half.

"If I had my life to live over, I would be an old maid school teacher. I would never know a man. If I had only known in the start all I know about men now, I never would have looked at a man. I would still be teaching little children. It is hard to tell what the feeling of women who have been prostitutes is. You know sometimes people may say they do it because they want to do it, and they would not do anything else if they could, and maybe that is what the tongue is saying and in the heart there is something entirely different. You know sporting women have good hearts.

"Sometimes men brought their sons to my house as patrons. They called on me and asked if I would give them a girl that was perfectly safe; said they preferred that to masturbation.

"In order to make it as difficult as possible for girls to fall, I would suggest that the first thing would be to eliminate the dance halls, because there girls go and men are only waiting for their prey. The class of men that go to those dance halls are only waiting to make some virtuous girl their prey. That is the first thing I would do. I think it is one of the most harmful amusements there is for young people.

"The dance itself is all right,—but not those public dance halls. There are so many young girls who go there, and that is where they get their first drink, their first invitation to go with a man, and these men are past masters in the art of winning young girls. If I had a daughter, I don't know what I would do. I think

I would keep her constantly—if I could afford to, I would have her with me, I would take her around and give her enough amusements so she would want to be with me. I would be almost afraid to trust her away from me. If my daughter had lived, I would probably never have been a sporting woman. If parents made more companions of their boys and girls, they would be better."

Statement of MXE. . . . "It has been quite a while since I went wrong.

"All I got was $2.50 a week. I was employed in a hotel down in . . . . . . I went out to Central Park and took a drink of beer, and some fellow said, "Let's go down to the red light district. It looked good to me, the lights and everything, and I went down.

"You don't understand. It is not us people you want to look out for. Get out on the streets where the saloons and dance halls are. Those are the places where the poor innocent ones are. I have heard children go past my house and heard them talk worse by far than I have heard anyone talk in my own house. Those young children,—those are the ones to get after. I have sat in my house, close to the sidewalk, since it was closed up, and have heard young girls going by on the street, and have felt like going down and licking them."

When asked what should be done with girls who wished to reform, the witness replied, "I would like to ask this. Would you employ many or any of my girls who had to leave the house? Would you not fire me the first time your son looked at me? You would think that even if I wanted to be good,—it does not make any difference how good I wanted to be,—would you not say to me, 'I cannot keep you; my son, perhaps, would go with you.' Where do you want us to go? We are not going to any old "Home" to live. We have had better homes than that. It is not difficult to get out of a house,—but what are you going to do when you get out. These women are not going to employ me in their homes; it does not matter how good I am. Perhaps their husbands or their sons will come home and say to her, 'What do you want her here for? She is one of the fallen women?'

"It goes right back to the home. Mothers wait too long before telling their daughters things. I think that anyone who really and truly wants to reform can go out and work. She does not have to be sent to a "Home."

"I think the boy is really more to blame than the young woman. The man will take the girl out and tell her how much he loves her, and pretty soon he has the best of her, through promises of marriage. He says, 'Well, now if anything happens, I will marry you.' Pretty soon, maybe, the girl will be coaxed again, and the man will tell someone else that he was out with Jennie Jones, and the next evening the other young fellow will go out. 'Charlie says he was out with you last night',—and the first thing the poor girl is gone. She is thrown out of her home. She is in bad at home. You are not going to employ her, because she has a bad name. Where is the woman going? The last resort for her is a sporting house. She is not going to lie out here in the street, is she? The man has no punishment at all. He can go to your . . . . . . Club, or to your churches and can marry the daughter of the richest man in the city; and he really is to blame for this poor girl's going wrong. The ladies will pat him on the back and put him up for the highest office in the city. It has been done. There should be a fine for a man going with a woman, the same as for a woman going with a man. The man may go to the legislature. Where does the woman go? The last resort for her is the sporting house."

"Enforcing" the law

The crusade against prostitution resulted in allegedly strict state, and later federal, laws to prohibit the practice. Enforcement, however, was another matter. Did communities really want the practice stopped? To what extent were law enforcement officials prepared to force obedience? Certainly there was no lack of zealous prosecutors or police officials who sought public favor by vigorous enforcement. On the other hand, this statement of a Wisconsin sheriff in 1914 typified the uncertainty of some public officials on the subject and their perception of public wishes.

. . . I have had information that there were three houses of prostitution running in this city. There have been no complaints, and they are not objectionable here. As to why I did not close these houses, let me say that we have about six hundred Greeks in this city who are single, three or four hundred Lithuanians, and about as many Austrians. A large number of the foreign people we have are single men, and I think by closing these houses it would make the city worse than it is. I admit that if a crime is being committed you do not need a complaint, but in these cases no complaints ever come to me at any time. My advice is that I think if we did close the houses, we would have a worse state than we had before. I don't think I could better it any by doing my duty. I understand that half of the prostitutes' earnings, in this city, is paid to the madam they live with, and I know a felony is being committed when a person receives these moneys, and he is subject to punishment in the penitentiary. My justification to the people of this county for permitting this crime to continually be committed here is to protect others. If stealing were going on I would not consider the effect on the other parts of the city, but would certainly stop it. I think that public sentiment wants it to run, and that justifies me to a certain extent, in violating my oath of office.

From *Report and Recommendations of the Wisconsin Legislative Committee to Investigate the White Slave Traffic and Kindred Subjects,* 1914, p. 149.

Social misfits
and their cure

Industrialization and urbanization in the late nineteenth century seemed to inevitably accentuate the presence of what the following essayist called the "flotsam and jetsam of the social stream"—the criminals, paupers, alcoholics, and insane. Some argued that social misfits arose from environmental conditions; others, however, maintained that heredity was the cause—a most convenient explanation at a time when theories of racial superiority were very much in vogue. Dr. G. Frank Lydston, a Chicago surgeon, forcibly advanced this second view. No sentimentalist, Lydston opposed the usual forms of punishment and instead advocated castration as the more humane and more effective solution for society's ills. The popularity of genetic solutions to problems increased through the first decades of the twentieth century, although the actual practice of such solutions generally was confined to the treatment of imbeciles.

Among all of the advances in sociologic science which may fairly be attributed to modern scientific medicine, nothing is more prominent than the philosophical treatment of the crime question. The attempt to reduce criminology to a rational and materialistic basis has constituted a great step in advance—one which marks a distinct epoch in scientific sociology. The science of criminology is comparatively new, and its study, in this country particularly, has only recently become popular. But it is my impression that just at the present moment the study of criminology needs to be saved from some of its overenthusiastic friends and from the misdirected zeal of certain *dilettante* scientists and alleged criminal anthropologists. The second exception which I would take to the trend of scientific thought upon the crime question is that we are too much concerned with the criminal of to-day or the cure of the individual criminal, rather than with the very remote conditions which produce criminality in him, and which conditions will inevitably produce criminality in his descendants, as well as in many individuals who are more or less remotely related to his criminal stock.

In the consideration of the theme which I take the liberty of presenting herewith, it will be necessary to indulge in some general considerations of the causes of, and remedies for, crime. In the first place, the proposition is ad-

From G. Frank Lydston, "Asexualization in the Prevention of Crime," *The Medical News* 68 (23 May 1896) : 573–578.

State Historical Society of Wisconsin.

Eugenics demonstration, early 1900s.

vanced that society is responsible for its own criminals, and in a less degree for its paupers, inebriates, and insane. These are the flotsam and jetsam of the social stream. They are, so to speak, the excreta of society, the retrograde products of social metamorphosis, bearing the same relation to the social body that certain excrementitious products of physiological metamorphosis bear to the animal body. The sources of these products should be considered, and the aberrations of the social body which produce them corrected, else no measures of repression of resultant evils are likely to be successful. I believe that the conditions producing these excrementitious social products are more amenable to measures of correction, and less inevitable, than what I have presumed to term the analogous conditions in the human body. In the case of the animal body, we are aware that certain excrementitious products of physiological change are absolutely necessary. We, however, deny the necessity of allowing these products to remain in the animal body and contaminate it or be placed in a position to injure other animals after discharge from the body. Is not the same true with regard to the social body? All of the conditions which produce the criminal class are furnished by society. Society's method of cancelling its debt is to punish the criminal after he has arrived at a point at which he menaces the safety, comfort, and commercial interests of society. At no time before, is cognizance taken of the results of the poisonous stream of criminality as it sweeps through some particular part of the social system, and an attempt made to correct them. Is this logical? Would it not be far better to turn the stream harmlessly aside, dam it at its source and antidote its contained poisons, if such a course be possible?

Society begins its self-contamination at the marriage-license window. The foundation-stone of society is the matrimonial relation. Its assumption is the most important step that a human being can possibly take, and upon the conditions which surround it depends some of the most important interests of our social system. Taking this into consideration, and laying aside the interest of the individual, is it not surprising that no effort at the regulation, control, or supervision of the marriage relation is made by society? The license window is a place where the honest citizen and the criminal, the sane and the insane, the diseased and the healthy, the pauper and the millionaire, the learned and the ignorant, may meet upon common ground—for the important consideration of $1.50. The criminal, the insane, the epileptic, the syphilitic, the consumptive, and the drunkard are legalized to go on producing their kind, the number of their progeny being limited entirely by the sweet will and physical capacity of the individuals. That the product of the factory of degenerates set in operation by licensing such people, is a menace and a burden to society goes without the saying. Has society a right to protect itself against its own vicious offscourings? I believe it has. I think the time will come when it will be no longer possible for our army of degenerates to procure licenses to marry. *I believe that it should be, and one day will be, a crime for a person in the active stages of venereal disease to marry and almost invariably infect innocent persons.* There can be no greater crime against the individual than inoculation with contagious disease—a disease which, perhaps, may outlast several generations and carry affliction to unborn innocence.

I am well aware that sentiment is strongly against the regulation of matrimony, still, sentiment has been no bar to the demand for a license and for the performance of the marriage ceremony by the proper parties afterward. Why should it be a bar to demands for proper qualification on part of the prospective candidates for matrimony? To reduce the question to its ultimate by very material and substantial argument, society should govern matrimony upon business principles. It should protect itself against the danger and expense of breeding an army of paupers, lunatics, criminals, and diseased persons. A life insurance company which should be governed by sentiment, would not be very highly regarded from a business standpoint, nor would it be likely to endure. Why should not society handle this question from the standpoint of a huge co-operative insurance association?

The prospective criminal once born, what does society do to prevent his becoming a criminal? Practically nothing. The child of poor but honest parents, is allowed to run the streets and contract evil habits or vicious associations. Result, eventually a criminal or a prostitute in a large proportion of cases. The child with hereditarily criminal propensities is allowed to follow the same course. The diseased degenerate child, whose parents are unable to care for it, is allowed to be exposed to all manner of vicissitudes, and unless fortunate enough to be cut off by death at an early period, eventually becomes a burden upon the community. What is the remedy at present instituted for this condition of affairs? Society punishes the vicious child after a criminal act has been performed, and sends the diseased one to a hospital to be supported by the public after he has become helpless. Even to-day, the child who has committed its first offense is thrown by the authorities into contact with older and more hardened criminals—to have its criminal education completed. We have millions for sectarian universities, millions for foreign missions, but no dollars for the redemption of children of vicious propensities or corrupting opportunities, who are the product of our own vicious social system and should be the wards of the State. But this is expensive. Yes, possibly,—for the time being,—but within a few generations a diminution in expensive processes of law and of costly penal institutions, would make the plan a most economic one in the long run. . . .

In the consideration of such a vital question as the management of the criminal class, the sentimentalist and his natural ally, the preacher, have joined hands on the question, and to them the world has looked for the reformation for which it has waited in vain. Such practical treatment as the question has received has been chiefly in the direction of devising ways and means to punish the criminal, the building of penal institutions and scaffolds, with the expensive law machinery which leads thereto. And then society has set about devising ways and means to save the elect from its own laws, and has split hairs to such an exceeding degree of fineness that there lies between the thieving corporation or the absconding millionaire, and the petit larceny fellow, who steals to live, an impassable gulf, one at least, across which Mammon alone can build a bridge.

Society makes crime; manufactures its own criminals, and winks at the violation of its own laws in high places. It gives the criminal all facilities; the best of inducements for carrying on his avocation, and then threatens to punish him if he follows the path cut out for him. Above all, society gives the criminal a chance to breed. Crime, as I have said, seems to be more profitable, safe, and comfortable on the average, than honest labor. What have our preachers, moralists, sentimentalists, and law-makers accomplished? They have spent the energy and money of the people for nothing. Every penal institution, every expensive process of criminal law, is a monument to the stupidity and wastefulness of society—an expenditure of money and energy to cure a disease which might be largely prevented. We have millions for courts of law and penal institutions, but nothing for the salvation of the children of to-day, who will be the criminals of the future. The first and worst injury that society inflicts upon the criminal is, allowing him to be born. The criminal has a good and just cause against us.

The principal remedy for the conditions which tend to manufacture criminals out of young children, consists in making them wards of the State, where it shall be shown that their parents are unable or unwilling to care for and educate them properly, or where it shall be shown that the children are vicious, either personally or in association, and above all, in cases in which the children are of criminal parentage. *The management of these children should begin before they commit criminal acts.* They should be taken charge of and placed in suitable institutions in which physical, as well as intellectual and moral training are followed. The first duty of the State to the degenerate, is to make him a healthy individual and give him the physical capacity necessary to enable him to become a useful citizen. If the child is exposed to evil influences and sources of corruption, it is the fault of our social system, and one which should be corrected. Good morals shoud not be expected from diseased children. The moral sense is the product of a healthy brain, and to be healthy the brain must be fed with good blood, a condition which is not possible in the case of the young waifs or neglected children whom we see about our streets. . . .

Habitual criminals, certain murderers, and rapists, should be emasculated. This serves three purposes: (1) The rational punishment of the individual. (2) A powerful moral influence upon other and prospective criminals. (3) The criminal is prevented from perpetuating his kind. . . .

There is one feature of castration which makes it far superior to capital punishment in most cases. Executions do not punish, and are but an evanescent lesson to others. A few castrated murderers, habitual criminals, and rapists scattered throughout the community, would be most efficient aids to the criminal memory.

Oliver Wendell Holmes once said: "If you want to reform a man, begin with his grandfather." I offer as an amendment that if you want to reform the criminal, castrate both his grandfather and grandmother. There is but one substitute: Take the children of to-day, who will be the grandfathers of future generations and make useful citizens of them. And yet, this failing, asexualization comes into play. . . .

In conclusion, I desire to say that the advocates of castration demand it—not for all criminals, but for habitual and incurable types, for rapists, and possibly for some murderers. As far as the latter are concerned, their execution is useless. Let them choose between scientific experimentation under anesthesia, and castration. They might expiate their crimes by benefiting scientific medicine. As for capital punishment, away with it!

With regard to sexual crimes, asexualization is of very practical importance to the people of the South, among whom such crimes, particularly on part of the ignorant Southern negro, is of especial frequency. This was one of the important points brought out by the discussion before the Medico-Legal Society. It is to be understood, however, that the discussion of this subject applies to all sexual criminals of whatever color; the negro criminal of the South is especially considered, because he has been very prominent, not only with reference to the frequency of the crimes which he has committed in this direction, but because of the barbaric treatment which he has received in certain communites as a method of punishment. . . .

Nowhere in the history of civilization has the futility and barbarity of capital punishment been so well shown as in the punishment of negro rapists in the South. The negroes who perform the acts under consideration are the lowest and most ignorant of the race. They cannot read the newspapers, and it is conceivable that a negro may be hanged or burned at the stake without the negroes of the adjoining county becoming apprised of it. The lower-class negro is subject to attacks of *furore sexualis,* which completely remove any inhibitory impressions which he may have received, even though in his rational moments he knows that swift and terrible vengeance will be meted out to him for the crime of rape. He is usually a religious fanatic who sees the gates of Heaven yawning wide to receive him just beyond the scaffold. Those gates are ever hungry for the fruit of the gallows-tree, and your negro fanatic needs no priest or clergyman to bid him *bon voyage.* The Zulu crops out in his not very remote descendant on such occasions. Death is no punishment, and its moral effect is but transitory on those about him. What a rapist needs is an ever-present object lesson, and one which puts the criminal beyond the power of further criminal acts of like nature.

A negro clergyman of education, in commenting on my paper on this subject, said: "The conceded superiority of the white race has much to do with rapes committed on white women by the negro. Art, literature, and religion combine to inflame the passion of the negro for white women. Your fairies, nymphs, goddesses, and angels are all white. Did you ever hear of a black angel? The result is an inflamed passion and an exaggerated curiosity on the part of the negro."

It is my opinion that a few castrated negroes scattered throughout the South would do more good than a multitude of executions. The colored clergyman whom I mentioned, suggested that the offender's ears should also be cropped, that he might be easily recognized. . . .

The repression of the criminal class is a question which should be dealt with from a practical standpoint. Sentiment, if exhibited at all, should be in behalf of honest people, not the criminal. The maudlin sentiment which impels fashionable women to present bouquets and frosted cakes to imprisoned criminals may yield to the pressure of the new method of criminal correction. Like all other diseases the disease of crime is one which is more rationally treated by prevention than by curative methods. Will not the law-maker join hands with the medical practitioner and endeavor, even at the sacrifice of his own interests, to prevent the diseases which he treats?

The police and corruption

Graft and corruption inevitably accompany any political system, whether it be autocratic or democratic. The buying and selling of political offices became commonplace in the post-Civil War era. Reformers focused much attention on the installation of a civil service system, designed to reward merit and secure public officials from corruptible political influence. But reformist zeal often proved self-defeating. The following selection, written by an anonymous New York City policeman, reports of the persistence of bribery and corruption in law enforcement. Most interesting, however, is his argument that "fool laws made for the benefit of old women who don't understand human nature"—for example, restrictions on gambling, prostitution, and liquor—created an environment that made such practices almost inevitable.

When I was a youngster one of my favorite games was what we children called "Cops and Thieves," we used to play it all over Cherry Hill where I was born, and many a time I stayed from school to enjoy the sport of chasing the

From "From the Policeman's Point of View," *The Independent* 55 (8 January 1903): 146–150.

other boys down the cellars and over the roofs and through the alleys and streets, for I was always a "cop," and it was my business to catch the "thieves."

We children who were always in the street knew the regular policemen, and had a great admiration for them, seeing that they could make the grocer take his wagon away, or could enter a house and arrest a man who was raising a disturbance, and were more than a match for even the greatest fighters that we had in the tenements. They seemed to us to be men of great power who could do as they pleased with other people, and, of course, we did not know that they had officers set over them whose orders they had to obey. So as I grew up I wanted to be a policeman, and I watched all the members of the force very closely in order to get their ways.

Those were the days of Tom Gould, Billy McGlory and Harry Hill. The police were pretty openly hand in glove with all the gamblers and divekeepers, and late at night one could find them all over town sitting in the dives in uniform, drinking and running things. There are no such times now, whatever may be said. . . .

That the candidate for the New York police force must understand the four fundamental rules of arithmetic; he must be able to spell words in the Rule Book and in common usage; he must be able to take down simple sentences from dictation; his memory must be good; he must know the city streets and prominent buildings; have a good understanding of the Rules and Regulations of the Police Department and be able to define terms used in the Rule Book and in police work.

Six months after I had entered the school I was examined by the Civil Service Commissioners and passed with 81 per cent. physical and 83 per cent. mental, and a month later I was appointed by the police commissioner. That was in November, 1898.

I was assigned to duty in the precinct where I lived, and reported to the captain, who put me on probation for 30 days. Each week day I attended the police school of instruction, where I kept up athletics and learned drill and rules, and each night I went out with a policeman, who "broke me in" to the duties, and whom I assisted in making arrests. . . .

The influence of the politicians over the police force has been growing weaker all the time, and some of the sergeants and captains now refuse to take orders from the district leaders.

The politicians' "pull" is founded on the fact that they make the Mayor who makes the Police Commissioner. So when they elect a Mayor they ask for a commissioner who will suit them, and when he is in office they can make it very hot for a captain who tries to enforce blue laws. They can move the captains around, putting one who does as he is told in a place where he can make $30,000 a year in addition to salary, and another in a place where he cannot make a cent extra.

So if a policeman disturbs "good people who are paying tribute" the district leader complains to the captain of the precinct, and if he does not mend matters a complaint of the captain is made to the commissioner. But this seldom happens. The patrolman who insisted on enforcing all the laws would be an idiot. He would not last a month, and would be thrown out a broken and disgraced man. His officers and comrades would see to that.

There isn't any reason why a patrolman should enforce the fool laws about gambling and excise. They're against nature, and he knows it, and has no sympathy with them. How far this business of protecting people who violate law goes I don't know. It used to include pickpockets, tin horn gamblers with brace games, bunco men, green goods and knock-out-drops operators, and burglars—pretty nearly all sorts of regular operators. It isn't anything like as complete now as it used to be. Still there are pickpockets now operating about the Bridge, and how could they do it unless the police were fixed?

Some are let work and some are taken in, and there must be a reason for the difference of treatment. Pickpockets, like detectives, work in couples, and I've known one to come up to a pair of plain clothes men, and say:

"The other fellow has $150."

One of the detectives collars the other pickpocket, and says: "I guess I'll have to take you up to the station house and 'mug' you (take photograph for Rogue's Gallery)."

"Can't we fix it up," says the pickpocket. "I have $75."

"All right," says the detective, and takes the $75 and the pickpocket trots on. Soon he hears footsteps behind him, and another detective catches him. "Hey! What are you doing here? I'll have to take you in," says the second detective, and the pickpocket is collared again, and has to give up the other $75 to get off. He goes away kicking himself.

Now, what did the first pickpocket get for betraying his partner? He must get something, for thieves have to live, and it costs money to support their families. The city isn't paying their salaries. It seems to stand to reason that the detectives must pay them by allowing them to work, and I suppose with the other criminals as with the pickpockets. But I don't pretend to know, and I'm sure that no one man knows all ends of this business of "protection," there's so much secrecy even between those most deeply engaged in it. I hear that Byrnes did all his detective work through "crooks," giving each other away. He did not pay them in money, so he must have paid them by letting them work.

Since the last election we have had in office commissioners who could not be used by politicians to punish a man for doing his duty, and that's all right so far as it goes. But the men and their officers know perfectly well that the politicians are only down for the moment, and that they are coming back to power, so why should policemen make trouble for themselves by opposition to the present system.

Every man on the force knows that the people don't want the laws enforced. The Mayor concedes that, and promised "a liberal enforcement," which means no enforcement.

That's the way that we patrolmen look at the matter, so we go with the tide, taking what comes and not seeing any more than is good for us to see.

As I went around with the experienced policeman during my probation he taught me all the ropes, and explained that the greatest danger for a young man was from the temptation to arrest people who were "putting up."

"If you do that," he said, "the sergeant will work you forty-eight hours at a stretch, and finally break you."

It didn't take me long to find out that the sergeant could keep me on the go till I dropped if it suited him. That was when I went on regular duty at the end of a month. I arrested a saloonkeeper who forgot me, but who had put up for the wardman and the inspector's man. I got a hint to leave the man alone after that, but I wanted to make him understand that I had something to say as well as the big fellows. I took him in again for violating the Sunday law. He was discharged. Soon after that I came off duty and went on reserve. I went upstairs to the dormitory to sleep, having been on patrol for sixteen hours. I had not been in bed ten minutes when the sergeant called me down to the desk, and sent me out to see about some boys annoying householders ten blocks away. It was a fake report. When I came back he sent me out to a fire, and after that he found another special call to keep me busy till I had to go on patrol again. There are plenty of these special calls at a busy station house, and the sergeant can always make some if he wants them. I squared matters by apologizing to the saloonkeeper.

Before I got on the force I had heard that policemen made a deal of money in addition to their salaries, and after I got fairly to work I found that I was in it. . . .

. . . Every man that's promoted has to pay for it. I know absolutely of my own knowledge that the commissioner got $1,000 for making ——— a captain, and when the others in the department heard of it they said that the commissioner was a cheap one for cutting rates like that.

Of course, when promotions are paid for the money has to come from "put ups." In Manhattan as much as $10,000 has sometimes been paid for a captaincy, but that is nothing if a man gets the right kind of a precinct where he can make from $20,000 to $50,000 a year. As I get them the rates for protection in Manhattan have been as follows per month:

Pool rooms, from $300 to $500; saloons, from $10 to $40; gambling houses, from $100 to $2,000; disorderly houses, $20 to $100; push carts, $2 per week each.

There's plenty of other "graft" that I don't know about; for instance, the detectives down in Wall Street make a lot of money somehow.

The push cart pedlers' money is collected by one of themselves. He goes among the carts and marks the stand of the man who has paid with white chalk, and the stand of the man who has not paid with blue chalk. The ignorant pedler does not notice.

Along comes the policeman on post and looks at the carts. When he sees a blue mark on a cart he with his club pokes the back off the pedler that owns it, moving him on while he lets his comrades stand. . . .

The most I ever made on any post was $156 a month. That was downtown in Manhattan on a beat that was about a mile and a half long. Every saloonkeeper on my post used to put up $5 a month for me and my partner in addition to the money given to the captain's agent—the inspector had no one collecting. There were twenty-five of these saloons and five gambling places, three of which gave me $10 a month, while two paid $5. From the women I and my partner, who patrolled the beat when I was off, got a total of about $75 a month. Of course, there were many who tried to do business without paying, but they soon found themselves in a hole because we enforced the law against them. Some patrolmen have made as high as $250 a month.

Beside the presents of money which naturally make policemen feel kindly disposed toward the givers there is free liquor. It is everywhere offered to the policemen, and it trips a good many of them up. The fool law is also responsible for this, because if it wasn't a fool law it would not have to be violated, and then the liquor dealers would not have to make themselves solid with us.

After a man has been on the force a little while he knows all the people who are "putting up," and grows to be very friendly with them. There are twenty places on my beat where I can tap at a side door and get a drink, and there are nearly as many where I can go in a back room and sleep while some one watches to give me warning if the roundsman comes in sight. So the temptation to take it easy and have a good time is very great, and on bad nights the policeman need not patrol his post unless he wants to.

If a policeman is anything of a good fellow he will prefer to favor his friends rather than strangers, so when there is any trouble between a liquor dealer or gambler and some ordinary citizen he inclines to decide against the ordinary citizen. That's the way that people sometimes get the idea that policemen accept money for protecting robbers.

New York policemen are just as honest as any other set of men, and this system of bribery is not their fault. It is the fault of the fool laws made for the benefit of old women who don't understand human nature. The laws pretend to try to abolish gambling and disorderly houses and to close drinking places on the only weekly holiday. That is all hypocrisy. Men always will gamble and drink. In the great cities of Europe there is a license system. If that were in force here it would put a stop to police bribery. . . .

The shame of the cities

Municipal corruption provoked the most protest from middle-class professionals and business people in the early twentieth century. "The Shame of the Cities"—a characterization used as the title of Lincoln Steffens's series of essays—not only insured the maintenance of political power through voting frauds by organized machines, but also created an intricate system of graft and influence. While the system certainly had advantages for business people trying to "get along," it frustrated many and led to their participation in the various political reform crusades of the period. Richard Spillane, a manufacturer who employed nearly three hundred people in an unnamed eastern city, here recounts his dealings and persistent battles with lower echelon city officials. Typical of the reform language of the period, Spillane deplored "the inefficiency, the sloth, the carelessness, the injustice, and ... the graft of city administrations."

. . . My factory is in one of the great cities on the Atlantic seaboard. It is near the water. I own the land and the buildings which I occupy. Some few years ago my neighbors and I were informed that the city was going to condemn a portion of our land in order to open up a thoroughfare to the water. It was only a short strip, about six hundred feet in length. I was a bit interested, because I knew that, as my property was adjacent, I would be likely to have an assessment for the improvement. The matter was taken up in due course by the authorities, and a commission of three was appointed to condemn the six hundred feet of land. The first time this commission met I attended the session. The three gentlemen were on hand promptly at the hour set. They took their seats, and one of them, acting as spokesman, said:

"The first business before this commission is to elect a chairman, and second to elect a secretary."

They proceeded to do so. Then the secretary read the order creating the commission and some other papers pertaining to it, after which the chairman announced that the next thing before the commission would be to examine the map of the property that was to be condemned. The map was not ready, and he instructed the secretary to have it prepared in time for the next meeting. The chairman then looked at his fellow-members and remarked that, as there seemed to be no other business before the commission, he would entertain a motion for adjournment. The motion was made and carried and the commission adjourned to meet again two weeks later. The session had lasted fifteen minutes. For each session each commissioner received a fee of ten dollars.

I was present at the second meeting of the commission. The map was ready and was examined by the three gentlemen. After an informal talk the chairman said that it would be necessary for them to go in person and examine the property, and, if it was agreeable to all, they would do so two weeks later. They then adjourned. The session had lasted eight minutes.

From Richard Spillane, "Driven from the City: A Business Man's Story of Persecution," *Outlook* 102 (16 November 1912) : 573–578.

I attended various other meetings of the commission, some of which lasted ten minutes, and some twenty or twenty-five. So little was done and so little progress was made that I grew weary and discouraged. I inquired of the Assistant Corporation Counsel, who was looking after the legal end of the commission's work, how much the assessment on my three hundred feet of property would be. He replied that he could not tell exactly, but, judging from past performances, it should be about $1 a front foot, or $300 in all. I remarked that, if that was the case, I would not bother about coming to any more meetings of the commission, as I was willing to pay $300 for the improvement, and that I could spend my time to much better advantage in my factory than in attending the commission's meetings, which seemed likely to be protracted.

It was nearly two years later when that commission ended its labors. It took them all that time to condemn that six hundred feet of property. The fees of the three commissioners amounted to $1,900. Most of the six hundred feet of land was owned by two estates, one of which got about $23,000, and the other a little in excess of $20,000. Presently I received notice that my three hundred feet of property was assessed $5,900 for the improvement. I was astounded. I went to the Assistant Corporation Counsel and asked him if he recalled the conversation I had had with him in the early stages of the commission's work. He replied that he did remember perfectly, and I then asked him how he reconciled that $5,900 assessment with his idea of $300. He replied that you never could tell what assessors would do, that I had no recourse. He remarked that I might as well be a good fellow and save myself a lot of bother by paying the assessment, or I would be penalized for sixty days after the assessment was entered on the books; interest at seven per cent would be charged.

I went to see my lawyer. I told him that the $5,900 assessment was a rank injustice, and he agreed with me. He said that he did not know very much about that section of the law, and advised me to consult an attorney whom he named who made a specialty of it. I went immediately to see this attorney. He was a very dignified and pompous gentleman. I appreciated, of course, that as I had been sent to him by another lawyer the two would divide the retainer between them. So I told this gentleman at the start that I did not propose to pay for his opinion. If he wanted to take the case on the terms I would outline, I would be glad to engage him; that I would give him $10 for listening to my story, but no more unless he was willing to take up the case. After I had related the circumstances, he asked me to come back in two weeks; but I protested at this delay, saying that the case was a simple one, and that I wanted action in less time than that; in fact, that I wanted to know whether I should pay the assessment or fight it. He said that he would communicate with me as soon as he could.

In two or three days he telephoned me to come to his office. He opened the interview by stating that he would require $500 immediately as a retainer. I reminded him of what I had told him at our first interview. He appeared somewhat chagrined, and replied that there was only a fair chance that the assessment could be upset, and that the best he would do would be to charge me $100 for his opinion, $500 as a retainer, and 50 per cent of whatever reduction he was able to obtain in the assessment. I replied that I thought his terms were excessive, and that there were other property-owners in the neighborhood who were assessed as heavily as I, that he could get their business also, and that the best I would do would be to pay him $100 down, $150 if he got the case re-opened, and 25 per cent of whatever reduction he secured in the assessment. He turned on me with great scorn and said that he was not accustomed to receiving instructions from persons who came to him with cases, and that he would have nothing further to do with the matter.

I went back to my office and thought the thing over. I worried about it, more or less, for a week or so. Then I got a notice from a title company that held the mortgage on my factory property that the assessment of $5,900 had been levied, that it had to be paid within sixty days, and that if I did not pay it they would be compelled to foreclose the mortgage. I went immediately to see the head of this title company, whom I knew, and explained the situation to him. I told him that I intended to attack the assessment in court, and pointed out the injustice that not only I, but other manufacturers in the neighborhood, had been subjected to in the matter. A title company is a very cold proposition. The gentleman with whom I was talking said that my statements were very interesting, but that the title company would foreclose the mortgage if I did not pay the assessment or give them a bond of $5,000. I replied that I could easily furnish such a bond, and would hand it to him the following day.

When I went to the bonding company's office, I found that they did not do business in that particular line, and that, in fact, none of the surety companies would furnish me with such a bond as I required. I could get bonds for honesty, against burglars, and lots of other things, but not against the outcome of a suit of the kind I was going to bring. Somewhat crestfallen, I reported my lack of success to the title company man. He replied that it would be satisfactory if I gave a bond backed up by a deposit of $5,000 to the credit of his company. I went to my bank, explained the situation, and got a receipt for a deposit of $5,000, which I took immediately to the title company. The man there glanced at it and handed it back to me, remarking that the $5,000 must be deposited actually with the title company, and that they would allow me two per cent per annum interest while it was so on deposit. I answered that I was paying five per cent at the bank for the money, and I thought it was a pretty tough hold-up scheme. The title man answered calmly that I would either have to pay the assessment or deposit the $5,000 with them, or that they would foreclose. So I put up the $5,000.

I suppose most men would have let the thing end then and there, and would have paid the assessment, but I am somewhat of a fighter. I went to another lawyer, a man of a good deal of prominence, who was holding a city office at the time. His term was about to expire, and he was going to resume his law practice, which had lapsed somewhat in his absence. I told him my story and made him the proposition that I would give him a retainer of $100, $150 when he got the case reopened, and 15 per cent of whatever reduction he secured in the assessment. He laughed at me. I left his office, and three or four days later he called me up on the telephone and asked me to see him. I did so. He said that he had been looking into the matter, and believed that there was a loophole by which he could upset the assessment. He wanted $150 down, $150 for reopening the case, and 25 per cent of all that he saved me. I stuck to my original proposition, which he finally accepted.

This lawyer succeeded in having the assessment set aside as excessive and unwarranted. That made it necessary for the whole matter to be taken up by the authorities. I was delighted. With the court order in my hand, I went to the title company and asked for the return of my $5,000. It was refused. Some other assessment will be put on the property, they said, and meanwhile we will hold your $5,000. And they held it.

But that assessment case was worth fighting about. When they dealt out the next assessments, mine was $600. I paid my lawyer his 15 per cent, his $100 retainer, and the $150 additional, but I saved about $4,000. Against that saving of $4,000 I had to charge up months and months and months of worry and trouble. . . .

Cities, if they only would realize it, are a good deal like landlords. A good, sensible landlord uses every effort to attract, to please, and to keep his tenants. The manufacturers are the life-blood of a city. They are among its best-paying tenants. A bad, corrupt, or careless city drives them away. It is like the landlord who makes his house undesirable for his tenants. Small towns and cities, as a rule, have active, wide-awake, pushing boards of trade or chambers of commerce. In big cities there is no end to the number of civic organizations. A good many of them ostensibly are for the purpose of attracting new industries and seeing that their comfort is looked after once they are located. As a matter of fact, I do not know of a single such organization in my city that accomplishes anything worth while. They pay good salaries to a staff of clerks who do just enough to hold their jobs. But I never would think of taking any of my troubles to the Chamber of Commerce or to the Manufacturers' and Merchants' Association. I did once, and had about the same experience that I had when I went into that branch city department to find out about the electric wiring permit.

The small city, like the owner of a new house, is eager to get tenants and to keep them. The big city has so many tenants that it is careless. It is so great that it doesn't fear competition. It seems to think that its vacant spaces will be filled up anyhow, and that those who are established won't dare move. It's the little places that offer the best inducements.

I have found it futile to complain to the government of the big city where I have been in business and paid taxes for so many years. Its officials change rapidly. Before you can get any satisfaction of your grievance there is a new set and you have to begin all over again. There is as much delay as there is in the courts.

I've grown tired of this state of things. So have other big manufacturers in my neighborhood. I have been talking with a number of them. We have sent experts to other places—small towns that seem to have good transportation facilities by land and water. We have been inviting propositions, and have a lot of them. Also we have been looking for a large tract of unimproved land that will meet our needs. If we find what we want we'll all move in a body and build a new city—one of our own, that we'll run on a business basis. We'll attract still other manufactories. The State laws are made for our protection and for the protection of our employees. We'll have just as few . . . ordinances as we can get along with. Then perhaps we'll be able to get along without the incessant trouble and annoyance that we have had to endure for so many years and which we'll have to keep on enduring to the end of the chapter if we don't move.

Leisure and pleasure

Improving the quality and efficiency of life was a dominant theme of the reformist mood that characterized the Progressive movement in the early twentieth century. At this time, the saloon was a vital social institution where people (mostly men, of course) could congregate, relax, and enjoy the company of others. For most reformers, however, saloons also were dens of iniquity where husbands and fathers succumbed to the temptations of liquor and squandered their salaries, all to the neglect of their family and social responsibilities. The following essay proposed the alternative of public "rest rooms," that is, places where people of both sexes and all classes could congregate for rest, amusement, and nonalcoholic refreshment. The idea, of course, paralleled the growth of neighborhood settlement houses in New York, Chicago, Cleveland, and other large cities, but these institutions particularly catered to immigrants and served as a conduit for assimilation. The public rest-room concept described below represents the forerunner of municipally created and sponsored community centers which now exist in all classes of cities across the nation.

From A. D. Davis, "Rest Rooms in Cities," *The Municipality* 1 (February 1901): 17–20.

The building of rest rooms, in the cities of this state, is a new movement, and, judging from the excellent service which they have and may be made to render, they should receive the favorable consideration of every city in Wisconsin. In the larger cities, like Chicago and Philadelphia, the department stores have provided waiting rooms. Marshall Field and Wanamaker have such rooms in their stores. While these accommodate large numbers, they, as a rule, reach only customers and do not serve the needs of properly furnished rest rooms. These objections hold also for hotels, saloons, railway and street car depots. It can not be doubted that rest rooms, in which refreshments are served and having on their tables choice games and reading matter, would supply a need felt in our large cities.

In Wisconsin we are not interested so much in solving the needs of large cities as we are in those having less than 35,000 population. It is largely true, however, that municipal problems are similar irrespective of the population or nationality. This article is an attempt to answer the question: "What is and may be the service of rest rooms to the cities of our state?" . . .

So far, there has been established in this state two rest rooms, one at Eau Claire, in July, 1899, and one at Chippewa Falls in January, 1901.

The one at Chippewa Falls consists of one room located in the business portion of the city. The room is heated with steam, has city water, and is lighted with gas; the water and gas are donated. It is furnished with tables, easy chairs, couches, pictures, etc. On the tables are found some of the best magazines, the local and daily papers. The room is kept by a matron who receives $12 a month. The rent is $15 a month. This is the total expense, as the furniture, reading matter, and other incidentals are donated by the public. These expenses are borne by the merchants who have made monthly subscriptions, and the money is collected at the end of each month. The room is under the management and control of the Woman's Club. The average number of people daily accommodated is about twenty-five.

The Eau Claire rooms are much better. This is to be expected from their longer experience and larger population. The rooms are located in the central part of the city. There is a sitting room furnished with easy chairs, a writing desk, and a table on which are found the daily papers, the leading magazines, and other reading matter, all of which are donated. Back of the sitting room is a lunch room with tables, dishes and a gas stove. On the second floor there is a well furnished toilet room and a lounging room with rocking chairs, couches, settees, cradles, etc. The rooms are in charge of a matron, and are open from 8 A. M. to 6 P. M. The expense amounts to $700 a year, $50 is donated by the Woman's Club and the remainder by the leading business men in sums ranging from $1 to $50 a year. Since the opening, the average daily visitors have been 70, number of daily lunches eaten 30, and average number of packages cared for 38. The rooms are under the management of the Woman's Club. In this respect the rest rooms follow the true line of progress, since it belongs to the individual to initiate and to the city to adopt when convinced of the need.

These rooms serve all classes of people, the farmer, the trader and stranger from the neighboring town, and the business man. They furnish a comfortable place for the farmer's wife to rest while waiting for him to finish his business. They are especially serviceable to mothers with small children who formerly were compelled to wait in the stores where they felt, and often rightly so, that they incommoded others. The wives and mothers are relieved from much care and worry by the comfort of these rooms. Through amusements, refreshments, and various kinds of reading matter, they may be made to serve the waiting or loafing farmer who now often goes to the saloon and spends money which the merchant should get.

The large number of daily lunches in the Eau Claire room show another excellent service. Farmers from a distance cannot do their trading and return home between meals. They cannot eat their lunches in the stores without inconvenience both to merchants and themselves, and experience shows that, as a rule, farmers do not take their meals at hotels or restaurants. Some have no objection and do go to saloons which often have good accommodation and serve cheap lunches. These rooms furnish a convenient place where they may eat their lunches and have a warm cup of tea or coffee; and so far as they induce from the saloons those who otherwise would go there to loaf or lunch, they serve a good purpose.

The trader and stranger from a neighboring town who must wait an hour or more for their train find here a pleasant place to rest, and they will in time, doubtless, assist in drawing trade from near towns. . . . During conventions and public occasions they serve both the city and visitors in caring for baggage, lunches, etc., and providing a place where people may lunch and rest. Thus they assist the business man and help build up the city. The willing contributions, which the merchants make, are ample proof of their services. . . .

It is generally believed by social reformers that the saloon is a social necessity until a satisfactory substitute is found. It is possible that, in providing dining, waiting, amusement, and toilet places, rest rooms may at least partially supplant the saloon as a social institution. Much can be done by placing toilet rooms in the Y.M.C.A. and public buildings. By keeping the rest rooms open at night when farmers do not need them, they may be made to serve the laboring men who are the best customers of saloons. They should, however, be made as attractive as the saloon. They should have smoking apartments, on the tables should be placed the best reading matter, cards, and all kinds of games, and refreshments should be served. In brief, rest rooms, to serve the laborer, should have all the attractions of the saloons without the evils of intoxicating liquors. The proper charges could be made for refreshments and games so that the laborer would not feel that this was a service of charity.

IV

Racism, Nativism, Imperialism: 1883-1916

CHAPTER 10

The nadir for black Americans

Blacks and the new paternalism

The premise of black racial inferiority had governed race relations in the South since the arrival of the first slaves in 1619. Before the Civil War, John C. Calhoun of South Carolina eloquently argued the virtues of slavery and the superiority of white civilization. Appropriately enough, then, these remarks made after the war by his grandson, John Caldwell Calhoun, an Arkansas cotton planter, offer a useful introduction for gauging post-Reconstruction white attitudes. While Calhoun acknowledged that in some respects, the ex-slaves' conditions had improved since abolition, he underscored the inherent inferiority of blacks and the necessity for white guidance.

New York City, September 13, 1883

... Q. Speaking of the personal feelings between the white and colored races in different parts of the South, how have those feelings been in the State of Arkansas as compared with the same in other States, now and hitherto?—A. I do not know that I could draw any distinction. I do not think it is particularly different in Arkansas from what it is in any of the other Southern States.

Q. In the testimoney before the Exodus Committee, of which I was a member, many of the witnesses testified to a better condition of things, so far as they were concerned, at that time (it was in 1879, I think,) in Arkansas than in some other Southern States.—A. I think the same rule that applies to almost all the walks of life governs there, which is that it is a matter of interest; and I do not see why there should be any difference of feeling in any other State from what there is in Arkansas. The interest of the laborer and the interest of the white man are identical; they must take care of each other.

Q. Do you think the feelings between the planter and the colored laborer, as a rule, are more amicable and friendly than on the part of the small white farmers toward the negro population; how is it in that regard?—A. I think that the white farmer is not so dependent upon the negroes as the large planter is for his labor, and he is not brought so much in contact with the negro laborer as the large proprietor. Probably he has not the same experience with him; but if a small white farmer became a planter and would have to employ laborers I do

---

From *Report of the Committee of the Senate upon the Relations between Labor and Capital,* 48th Congress, 2 (1885) : 186–187.

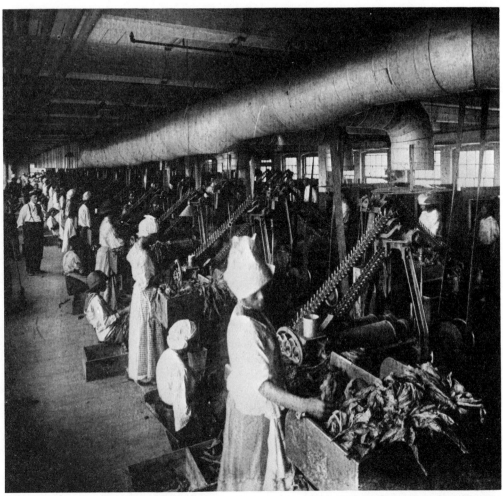

Valentine Museum, Richmond, Virginia.

Richmond tobacco factory, female and child labor.

not know that there would be any difference in his treatment from that of an ordinary planter.

Q. Mutual relations depend very largely on mutual interests there as everywhere else, of course?—A. Yes.

Q. What is the moral condition of the negro population now as compared with what it was before the abolition of slavery?—A. I think from the end of the war—from emancipation on, probably—the negroes became demoralized; they naturally would. A great many of them went off to cities and towns who had been in the country before and were not subjected to evil influences; were not led off by temptations and all kinds of extravagance. I think, therefore, the demoralization was very much greater in their morals. Their morals are not as good as they were before the war; but I think that as the negro begins to accumulate some little property, and feels the responsibilities of citizenship resting upon him, and begins to acquire information, his morals improve along as he becomes able really to take care of himself and to think for himself.

Q. Taking the colored population as a whole, so far as you know them, are they in a material and mental and moral condition getting better or getting worse?—A. Decidedly getting better.

Q. In every respect?—A. Yes, sir.

Q. Your account of them is mainly of a very hopeful character?—A. It is. I do not wish to be construed, however, as comparing the future prosperity of the negro if left to his own resources as he is to that of an industrious white man, because he has not got the same qualifications. I think that the negro, with his surroundings, his character, and his habits, will make strides toward improvement; but that he will improve to the same degree that a white population would, placed under similar circumstances, I do not think.

Q. In other words, you think there is some natural difference in the qualities of the two races?—A. I do.

The new order: a white view

Robert B. Kyle, an Alabama lumber mill owner, was more representative of the emerging, dominant white oligarchy of the "New South" than Calhoun. He blatantly stressed black people's inferiority, finding them lazy and unreliable. In his testimony, Kyle bemoaned what he saw as the destructive consequences of freedom, particularly in that they fostered the notion that "freedom means freedom from care and responsibility." While the lumberman complained that older blacks did not want their children to work as hard as they had, and that they seemed primarily concerned with education and improvement for their children rather than hard work, he paradoxically insisted that blacks had no pride. Kyle challenged his congressional inquisitors to provide a national governmental solution for "arousing" black pride; yet Kyle and others like him for the next eighty years regularly opposed any federal intervention in behalf of blacks.

Birmingham, Ala., November 12, 1883.

... Q. What is the relative proportion of whites and blacks in your part of the State?—A. In our section the blacks are from one-fifth to one-sixth of the population. For instance, our county votes about 2,800, and the negro voters are from 450 to 500.

Q. What is the feeling between the whites and the blacks in your part of your State, so far as you have observed it?—A. It is entirely harmonious. There is no trouble between them at all.

Q. Has there ever been any?—A. There never has been any.

Q. What is the condition of the laboring population there, white and black?—A. Do you mean those engaged in agriculture, or the other laboring population.

Q. You may state first the condition of the agricultural laborers.—A. Well, sir, I cannot say that they are prosperous; they are just about making a living, and that is about all they are doing.

Q. Is there any reason why they are not prosperous?—A. No reason, excepting want of industry. That is the only reason I can see.

Q. What is the system of cultivation generally?—A. It is gradually improving a little. They are using more improved implements within the last two or three years, and to that extent there is a change for the better. Men who exercise a proper amount of industry and judgment in the management of their farms are doing pretty well, but those who do not are not doing well, which I suppose is the case in all parts of the country.

Q. In view of the natural conditions and advantages of that portion of the State, what ought to be the success of the farmers as a class?—A. In my judgment, it ought to be good, as good as anywhere in the world. Everything is there that is requisite to make a prosperous, growing country, except active and well applied industry, but that they do not have to the extent that they ought to have it. ...

[O]ur agricultural labor is concentrated upon cotton to a considerable extent; then, too, it is not as efficient as it ought to be; for instance, in the plantation that I cultivated there are about 650 acres of open land. The last crop that we

From *Report of the Committee of the Senate upon the Relations between Labor and Capital,* 48th Congress, 2 (1885) : 13–27.

made with slave labor on that plantation, we made 315 bales of cotton, and an abundance of corn and meat to supply the place. Since the war, with free labor, we have never made a hundred bales of cotton or corn enough to supply the place.

Q. You have given us those very striking facts and drawn a very striking contrast; now, what is the philosophy of it?—A. The philosophy of it is that you cannot rely upon the labor.

Q. You gave a while ago as a reason for some of the evils which you mentioned the lack of proper industry; what is the cause of that lack of industry. You may as well give us the philosophy of that also, as you are about it?—A. I cannot tell you what is the cause; it is the want of a proper—let me see how I would word that—well, sir, I think it is owing to the fact that a very small amount of labor will make the necessaries of life in this part of the country, and there is very little ambition to accumulate, and consequently very little industry.

Q. That statement applies to the white population inhabiting the mountainous sections of the State; how is it with the colored population there and elsewhere throughout the State?—A. My observation has been pretty general throughout the State, and in my judgment, what I have stated applies with more force to the colored than to the white people.

Q. I suppose the illustration which you cited of the labor on your own plantation is a case of colored labor?—A. Yes, sir; it was entirely colored labor before the war; now it is mixed.

Q. Which do you think is the better laborer on the farm?

A. Well, the white man is more reliable. For instance, you rent your land to a negro, and if he suspects his crop is not going to be as good as he anticipated, he will just pick up and quit; whereas a white man, under the same circumstances, in nine cases out of ten, will wait and work it out, even though he sees he is not going to get anything out of it.

Q. That is really a case of greater integrity and conscientiousness on the part of the white man, rather than a case of greater efficiency as a laborer?—A. Yes, sir; that is it.

Q. What do you take to be the reason of that state of affairs, with reference to the negro? He was formerly a slave, and then, you say, he worked well; now, however, he is unreliable as a worker, although now he is working for himself. What is the reason of that?—A. Well, it is owing to a deficiency in his mental and constitutional organization, I think. That is how I look at it. I have been raised with the negroes, and I think I understand them pretty well.

Q. I understand that, and I am asking you these questions because you are a man who has had large opportunities to observe and to judge.—A. Well, sir, I am answering you honestly. I have been very largely in connection with the negroes all my life, as a matter of course, and I am satisfied that they are deficient in the appreciation of moral obligations. For instance, they don't regard the obligations of a contract as they ought to—neither those that are educated nor those that are not educated—they do not seem to have a proper appreciation to do what they have agreed to do, and therefore you cannot rely upon them as a race. That is my observation of the character of the negro, in all the varied relations of life in which I have seen him—working on the plantation, working in the saw-mill, working on steamboats, everywhere—a want of appreciation of the obligation resting on him to carry out his contracts.

Q. Well, as a race, of course, they made no contracts until recently?—A. No, sir; not until recently.

Q. Do you think that as the colored man becomes accustomed to deal upon the contract system he may develop this sense of obligation? What seems to be his tendency in that regard?—A. My idea is that it will take several generations to develop that quality in the colored man. The present generation of negroes, born since the war, all of whom have more or less smattering of education, seem to have the idea that freedom means freedom from care and responsibility, the idea that education will supply all the wants of life without labor; in other words, they all expect to be school teachers or preachers, or to hold office, and to have an easy time. They do not seem to realize the fact that nothing is got in this world without work. They may go on in that way for a generation or two, and they may gradually learn that they have got to work, and education may benefit their children, but so far, it has not resulted in giving those people any sense of the necessity for industry, or appreciation of moral obligations.

Q. They do not understand that education is simply a means of enabling them to work to better advantage?—A. No, they do not seem to appreciate that at all. That is the great problem in this country, what is to become of us when we lose the efficient labor that was trained in slavery. When that generation of laborers is dead and gone, what is to become of the country?

Q. That is really a serious question here, is it not?—A. That is the question in connection with the labor system in this country.

Q. I think you must be quite right about that, but I understand you to say that your observation applies as well to the white men as to the colored?—A. Not to so great an extent. As you get off from towns and railroads and villages, you find that the white men are not paying much attention to education, but when you bring them into contact with business life, they seem to understand the importance of educating their children, so that they may be able to do business. The remoter sections of the State, those farthest removed from lines of travel, are still living with darkened eyes and do not appreciate the necessity of educating their children, but they have been waking up for the last few years.

Q. You would naturally expect from the difference between the two races that the white people would rally first, and come first to an appreciation of the new condition of things?—A. Yes, sir; and I think they are doing it.

Q. Do you find any inclination on the part of the colored men to acquire property?—A. Very little indeed; only in isolated cases. I have a few men who have been working with me since the war almost continuously, who have acquired homes and have paid for them, and are doing pretty well, but they are men who were slaves.

Q. Those are men that were slaves, and that had the habit of working already formed when they were set free?—A. Yes, sir.

Q. How is it with the younger men?—A. I don't recall one of the younger men who has accumulated anything since the war. Those who have accumulated are the older ones, men who were, perhaps, from twenty to twenty-five years of age when the war closed. In fact, they are the only reliable class of laborers that we have among the colored population.

Q. The young colored man is the serious difficulty here, it seems?—A. Yes, sir; he is the serious difficulty now with us.

Q. What does he do?—A. He works a little, and the balance of the time he spends in playing base-ball, and in amusements generally about the towns.

Q. His vice is simply idleness?—A. Simply idleness.

Q. Does he tend in any degree to drunkenness?—A. Well, you know that the love of whisky is a prevailing thing in the race, and the young ones will, of course, learn to love it as well as the old ones; but the most marked disposition of these young men is to amusement and idleness.

Q. Is this young colored man willing to take hold again and work when his money is gone?—A. Yes, sir; he will work on short jobs; he does not want a long job, though.

Q. How many of these young colored men of, say, between the ages of sixteen and thirty, save anything in the course of a year?—A. Not 2 per cent. of them, I should say. . . .

Q. Do those older ones, the parents who had learned to work before the war, fail to understand that their children must work also, or do they try to train them in industrious habits?—A. They really seem to feel that if they can keep them from working they are doing them a very great favor.

Q. Then they too have the idea that freedom means idleness?—A. Yes, sir; They don't want their boys to work as they have worked. That is their prevailing idea pretty generally.

Q. And you think the education that the younger ones receive in reading and writing excites a still stronger feeling on their part that they are not designed for common manual labor?—A. Yes, sir; their idea is that the object of the education they receive is to enable them to make a living without work, without labor.

Q. I think you mentioned to me, in conversation, an incident which illustrates that view; do you remember it?—A. Yes, sir; I was down at Marion, and the president of the college there was settling with an old colored man for some hay that he had bought, and while the president was back getting change, I had a little conversation with the old man. I told him that I was very sorry to see that section of the State in such dilapidation, and I asked him what was the matter with the people. "Well," says he, "I'll tell you, boss; these young niggers won't work." "Well," said I, "what is to become of the country when you old-time fellows are all dead?" "I tell you, boss," said he, "it looks mighty bad." I then asked him, "What is the reason they won't work?" "Well," said he, "I'll tell you; my boy, Jim, went to school, and when he comes home and gets into these plow-handles, to help me to do the plowing, he says, 'Look-a-here, dad, you didn't send me to school to learn how to plow.' " Now, that is an illustration of the general idea and the general feeling among them, and this old man thought that after the old-time niggers were all dead, the result would be that the young ones would "get an education, and go to the penitentiary."

Q. You say that those among the colored men who have acquired real estate are the old-timers?—A. Yes, sir; none of the younger ones that I have any knowledge of have acquired a dollar's worth.

Q. How is it about the young negro women?—A. They are not doing much. They are trying to live without labor. It is a very difficult matter to get house servants at any price.

Q. What wages do house servants receive in your part of the country?—A. From $5 to $6 a month, and, of course, board and a house to stay in.

Q. Are your house servants there mostly colored?—A. Yes, sir; they are nearly all colored. It is a very rare thing to see a white servant. My wife says she would not have felt so bad about the results of the war if it had only left her her negro house servants. . . .

Q. The successful conduct of business enterprises depends upon the working people, and they are practically independent of you?—A. They are. If we could get good reliable labor to immigrate into our country we might develop very rapidly.

Q. What occurs to you that might be done to bring about that change?—A. I cannot tell.

Q. It is evident that if the spur of necessity—actual hunger—could be brought to bear upon your laboring people, that would educate them to some sense of the value of their time and their opportunities.—A. The trouble about that is that if a man goes into a mine as a miner he will get 50 cents a ton for mining ore, and will make from $1.50 to $2.50 a day, according to his skill, and that money which he earns in one day will feed three or four indolent sons and daughters at home, and you cannot bring white men down here to compete with that labor. The white man feels degraded in attempting to do so. A native Southerner would not feel half the sense of degradation in competing with the colored man that would be felt by a man brought from a distance. Consequently I do not see how we are going to get an immigrant population into our country with this colored population already in the country. It is the darkest phase of our condition here.

Q. You have got to develop a sense of increased wants among these people?—A. Yes, sir. What few wants that they have now are very easily supplied.

Q. Yes; but if you could create in them an ambition to satisfy the wants that are incident to a higher degree of civilization they would have to go to work, would they not?—A. Yes, I suppose so.

Q. Is there any way of arousing their pride or their cupidity?—A. I do not see how you are going to do it. That is a problem that perhaps you gentlemen at Washington may work out some day.

Separate and really equal? A black response

Long before the Supreme Court's decision in *Plessy* v. *Ferguson* offered national legal approval of the idea of separate but equal facilities for blacks and whites, segregation existed as a fact of life in the South—as it did in certain institutions in northern states. Although southern blacks had little opportunity to resist Jim Crow laws, particularly after they were disfranchised, some insisted that the bargain of "separate but equal" reflect reality. C. H. Johnson, for example, candidly acknowledged the fears that restrained blacks from speaking out; yet he forcefully presented his own views. He insisted that blacks "wanted to be treated right" and that if segregation were to be imposed, then conditions had to be equal. But Johnson almost uncannily anticipated events of the next half century when he maintained that the dominant white society simply would not fulfill the promise of equality.

Columbus, Ga., November 20, 1883.

. . . Question. Where do you live?—Answer. In Columbus.

Q. How long have you resided here?—A. About twenty-six years.

Q. What is your business?—A. I am porter in an auction and commission house.

Q. What pay do you get?—A. About $25 a month.

Q. Have you a family?—A. I have a wife, but no children.

Q. Have you any real estate?—A. No, sir.

Q. Are you able to save anything from your earnings?—A. Yes, sir; I can save a little now and then, but it is very seldom that I see a place to save anything.

Q. Is your wife able to do any work?—A. Yes, sir; she can do some, but she is sickly.

Q. She is not able to help you much, then?—A. No, sir; not much.

From *Report of the Committee of the Senate upon the Relations between Labor and Capital,* 48th Congress, 4 (1885) : 635–638.

Q. Go on, now, and make any statement that you desire to make?—A. Well, I think that the condition of our people, as a general thing, has been stated very fully to you, and I do not see where it is necessary for me to go over the same ground that has been gone over to you.

Q. Do you feel as though your people had had a fair chance to be heard by this committee?—A. I do.

Q. You think there is nothing they want to say to us that they have not had a chance to say?—A. I do not think there is anything. I think they have talked very plain about the condition of the colored race in this city.

Q. And you think they have said all they want to say?—A. Well, I won't say that they did that. There are some things, probably, that they wanted to say that they did not say.

Q. Why didn't they say them?—A. Well, it is just like as it was in time of slavery. There was a great many things that they would have liked to have done, but for fear, and they have got that same feeling now, a great many of them have, and they want to say things, but they are afraid of the white people; afraid that the white people will say to them afterwards, "Look here, John, you remember the sort of remarks you made before that committee. I am done with you now." That is the case with some of the colored folks; they are afraid to say what they want to say; but I aint of that sort. Whatever I want to say I am going to say it. Unfortunately I am not an educated man, but I think, in my own judgment, I would have been a help to my people if I had been educated, because I see a great many things going on among them that I think they ought to be advised about that they need advice about, and I do not think anybody else but a colored man could take hold of it and work it like it ought to be worked to their interests, because every man, and every nation, and every race, is bound to look out for their own people. A white man is a white man, I don't care where he is. If it is in a manger a white man looks for a colored man to look up to him as a white man and to respect him as a white man.

Now, speaking of education, I have heard a good deal about it here, enough about it. If you could give it to us all together to get us all up as high as you all are, that would be best. But then, of course, that is a long way off. But speaking of education, I think the first thing our race ought to consider, and the first thing they ought to learn, is to respect themselves, and then when they do that they will certainly command respect from everybody else. That is the way I look at it. Now, as a general thing, our people do not do that, not in Columbus here, and the reason why they do not do it is that they are so poor and get such little wages for their work, that they are ready any time to be bought up by dimes and quarters and fifty cents, or by a five-mile ride, with whisky thrown in, at any election. They allow themselves to be bought up in just that way. Now, there is where I think the colored man ought to come in and give us advice about such matters as that, for I don't believe that any man that would do that would ever be respected by a white man, or by any colored man either, that respects himself. I do not think that any man that does things like that demands respect or ought to have it. I have been living in Columbus now for about twenty-six years. My native home was in Atlanta. I have not got the time to tell you all that I would like to say about some things, but will make it short, and I will say this: As far as the feelings that have been existing here among the colored people and the whites, I think we have got a very good feeling among us. I have not seen any signs of bad feeling among the whites and the colored people. It is true that a great many thinks they are not treated right in some things. I think I am right about that. I may be wrong, though, but I do not think I am.

The great trouble with us poor colored people is that we need more power. Where are we going to get it? That is the question, as I look at it. We need more power, and if we have not got the power, there is no use to talk about negroes sitting on juries, and all that sort of thing. If we do not have the power to put them there, we cannot do it; that is all about it. There is no use to go asking a man for a thing that he don't want to give you, for he aint going to give it to you unless he is obliged to do it. I don't say that the negro would give his fellow-man any more justice than the white people give us. I do not believe he would give him justice any more than the white jury would—that is, than some white juries would—for I believe there is some people here that would give a colored man just as much justice as a colored jury would, and may be a little more, because I tell you right now there is feelings that has always existed among the colored people to pull down amongst them that is higher than others. That is the great trouble with them, and I believe that white juries would give a colored man as much justice, but I think that if you mix them up on the juries, and had one for white and the other for colored, a colored man that was in trouble would think that he got justice from that kind of a jury whether he did get it or not, and I believe the races would think so as a general thing. That is the reason why they would like to have it, and I don't know but they would be right.

It is true that we do not have any strikes among us here. We have been getting along peaceably. We have not had such a thing as a strike here for a long time. There is no spirit among the people to get up such a thing. We have got along very quietly, I believe, as a general thing.

I was speaking about the respect that the colored people ought to have for themselves, and I may say that I think the white people, some of them, love the colored folks most too much down here, anyhow. I am afraid it will get so after awhile that there aint going to be any colored race, and then the white man and the black man will get too close altogether. I believe I have about as many white friends as any colored man here. I have never had any one deny me a favor that I asked of him—that is, any one that was able to grant it—and I believe I am about as well known in this city and in the country here as any man around Columbus. I have been staying at a public house so long that both white and black people, men, women, and children, all know me. I have got a good many that come to me for advice as to what is best for them to do, and so on, and I do not know anything that would do any more good than to get that power that I was speaking about. But then where are we going to get it? They have been talking a good deal here about money to educate the children—the young generation. I think myself that the first thing we have got to do is to go to work to get up the money and to get power to do what is right. That is the way I look at it.

Q. What form of power do you mean?—A. I don't want anybody to understand me to say that I am advocating the cause that has been existing for some time around over the country about the civil rights bill. I don't see that we are just exactly prepared to stand the pressure that that civil rights bill would put upon the colored people if they had it in existence. That is the way I am thinking about it. I think this, that we want the power of having social equality amongst us, as a general thing, in the city and in the country around, and there is a great many things that ought to be looked after that cannot be—that there can't be nothing got done about except we have the power to do it. . . .

Q. What do you mean by social equality?—A. I mean that when we go into places that a man has a right to go into, we want to be treated right. Suppose I get on the cars, for instance; I want to be treated fairly. As I said about the civil rights bill, if I get on the cars to ride from here to Montgomery, or to Atlanta, although I pay the same fare that you pay—they make me do that—I do not have the same accommodations. Now, I think that if I have to pay the same fare that you pay I ought to have a right to ride in the same car that you ride in.

Q. Suppose you have one just like it, won't that do?—A. Well, if it is just like it; still, it may not be the car that I want to ride in, because I ought to have a chance to ride in ary one I wanted to. I think if they are going to make a law not to allow a colored man to ride in a first-class car they have no right to make him pay first-class fare. That is the trouble between the colored man and the whites about this civil rights bill. I myself do not care anything about the civil rights bill; but then, as I said about social equality, I think we ought to demand our rights in that respect. . . .

Q. Suppose you have a car just as good as the one the white folks have, but are not allowed to go into their car, will that be satisfactory?—A. But that is not going to be done. They are not going to make a law of that kind.

Q. But if that was done, would it satisfy you?—A. Of course, I do not want to mix up with white people, because I do not really think it would be right.

Q. If they have a right to mix with you, you have a right to mix with them, haven't you?—A. That's it.

Q. But suppose the matter were fixed in such a way that you could not mix with each other?—A. If you owned this house here, and a man rented this room from you, and paid you $10 a month for it, and then if I came to get a room, and you said to me, "I am going to put you down in the kitchen, and I will make you pay me $10 a month," I would know that that was not right.

Q. That would be a different case. I am supposing a case where the accommodations provided for the two races are just the same, and neither has the right to go into the car devoted to the other.—A. Well, if you give me just as good a room right next door as the other man, and to pay only the same rent, I would be satisfied. But don't allow a man to come in over my wife, or any other lady that respects herself as a lady, swearing and spitting and cursing around. That is not allowed you in white cars, and I do not blame them for not allowing it. But if a man don't contend for his rights he will never get them. That is how I look at it. When I pay for anything I like to get it. When I go uptown and buy a woolen blanket, and when some other man goes uptown to buy a woolen blanket, and the storekeeper sells him a cotton blanket, because he is ignorant, and makes him pay the same price I pay for mine, that is not treating him right. All I want is just what I pay for, just what is right, and I do not want to kick up a fuss with any one, or with the white people about getting in amongst them, or being with them, because I do not believe it is right that we should be mixed up and always be together in every place, and such things as that; but I think that if a colored man is paying the same fare on the railroad that a white man pays, he has just as much right as the white man has to proper accommodations. I do not care whether it is on a railroad or on a boat. I think about it in this way, that if a man is in a hotel and a colored man comes along and pays the same fare that the white man pays, he has the same rights as the white man. . . .

Black labor: a plea for organization

Like their northern counterparts, southern black laborers saw organization as their salvation. To be effective, however, labor unions had to be organized along biracial lines. But the ingrained prejudice of white workers, as well as that fostered by employers bent on driving a wedge into the common interest of a working class, again frustrated black ambitions. The following letters to Terence V. Powderly, Grand Master Workman of the Knights of Labor, the most prominent national labor organization in the late nineteenth century, portray the plight of the black worker. The first letter is from a black organizer, while the second apparently is from a white man who recognized that exploitation of blacks similarly reduced the standards for whites.

T V Powd

The Order in the South must of necessity be composed largely of the Negro race. The great bulk of the labor in this country is performed by colored hands, against whom a cultivated prejudice (akin to hate) is most intense. Ridiculous as it may appear to men of broader intelligence there are toilers with wt. skins, whose lot is in no sense superior to that of the black slave's, who will not join the Order because of the prejudice that has been instilled into them against the Negro. They have not yet learned the great lesson that greed makes no distinction in the color of the victims of its robbery.

Again, there are shrewd, calculating politicians who act solely with a view to personal gain, or to endeavor to control the colored vote. The greatest difficulties, so far, the Order has had to contend with have come from the contentions raised by this class of men in their struggles for leadership. In some localities the effect has tended largely to injure the Order, but it will grow upon the ruin of all such characters. It is a most encouraging fact that the colored people make good knights—they are exceedingly watchful of their liberty—and a strong and powerful org. of them is only a question of time.

Our State Master Workman, Bro. G. Y. Mott, works faithfully and earnestly, and with good results, though at times strongly antagonized. He is a mechanic—a worker with his paint brush—and a good one. Yet I am told that a few days ago he was "relievd" of a job on a banker's property, with no reason assigned, other than his "insurrectionary movements among the Negroes." This, I consider, the best indorsement he could get, in the estimation of working people.

In Bro. J J Holland, I am persuaded you will find an able and efficient Lieutenant, especially for work in the South.

Yours fraternally,
J A Bodenhamer

The Eastern Marble Works
W D Stuart, Proprietor
Dealer in Tenessee Variegated Marbles
Furnished, Sawed & Rough Blocks in Wholesale to Dealers
Owing Mills.

Whitesburg, Miss.
Aug 18, 1890

TV Powd. G MW
Scranton Pa.

Dear Sir;

I am mngr of this business—have been such for about 20 mos. When I first took charge there were branches in Columbus, Miss. Decatur, Ala. Chat-

From Philip S. Foner, ed., "Documents: The Knights of Labor," *Journal of Negro History* 53 (January 1968) : 75–76. Letters from the Terence V. Powderly Papers, Catholic University Library. Used by permission.

tanooga, Tenn, as well as here. During the past 5 yrs. I have traveled over much of 9 So. Sts, & Been in a position to note the lamentable condition of labor; so I feel able to address you on this very vital subject—labor in the South. Of course, the great distracting source is negro competition. The negro is forced to accept 50 to 75 cents per day & that forces the wt man to take about the same. These wages will not enable a wt or black to ed. his children or feed them such food as will nourish body & brain properly. The poorer classes are becoming grosser every day because of their diet of corn meal and "sow-belly" from the beginning to the end of the years. In the name of charity for poor man, can not something be done to right this terrible wrong before oppressed labor endeavors to right it with force & thus increase the evil? I have evolved a partial remdy; but you may done more in the way of thinking on this line than I & more to the purpose. Standing at the head of a frt. org as you do, can you do, can you not start some reform? This dreadful competition of cheap labor in the so. must sooner or later very seriously effect the prices of wages in the north, and almost chivalize our great masses. I will be glad to aid in any movem, to better the condition of labor in the so. but not in an open way unless it be in connection with an orgzed effort; for to move in the matter is to stir up the most intense prejudices of the wts. & to combat with the dense ignorance of the blacks & "poor wt. trash," & which of the 3 would be most to overcome is hard to say. In self defense the Knights ought to move in the matter at once. . . .

Can I be of service to you in bringing about some greatly to be desired reforms? Hoping that your efforts to advance the cause of labor may fully succeed, I am yours Truly,

C. C. Mehurin

Peonage: the new serfdom

Although the Thirteenth Amendment had prohibited involuntary servitude, many areas in the South developed the system of peonage which bound ignorant, defenseless blacks to plantation owners or forced them to work for local governments. The practice involved leasing convict labor to either private or public contractors to work off fines or jail terms. The period of labor regularly exceeded the value of the penalty, either in money or time. The first selection is a semiliterate peon's complaint to William Ambrecht, the United States attorney for the Southern District of Alabama. The second is Ambrecht's summary of the facts of the leading peonage case, in which the United States Supreme Court subsequently decided in favor of the peons.

Finklea, Ala., Jan. 20th, 1911.

Dear Mr. Armbredth [sic],

Mobile, Ala.,

I hope if your please that you will do something to stop these Monroe County Officers from putting me in jail and taking away every thing that I have on earth, for nothing, all because I failed to work the road one day in Monroe County when in the first place I live in Conecug County, in the second place I am over fifty years old, they have already collected from me 85,60 and still claim that I owe them $42,50, is there anything that you can do as an officer to stope them from treating me that way. have I no rights that the courts will respect. I appeal to you as an officer of the law to do something to keep these men from putting me in jail for nothing except what they call failure to work the road, they have already kept me in jail five months for this so called offence, of not working the roads one day, in Monroe County when I live in Conecuh, and I am over fifty years old.

Please let me hear from you,

Respectfully,
Andrew Salter,
Colored.

Attorney General,
Washington, D.C.

Dear Sir:—

I enclose herewith copies of indictments which were returned by the Grand Jury involving peonage in Monroe and Conecuh Counties, Alabama.

Cases 4086, United States against J.A. Reynolds and 4080, United States against Gideon W. Broughton should be considered together. Ed Rivers, the peon, was at the May term 1910 of the County Court of Monroe County convicted of petit larceny and was fined $15. and a judgment was rendered for that amount together with $43.75 cost. J.A. Reynolds confessed judgment with Rivers and Rivers entered into a contract with Reynolds to work out the debt at the rate of $6.00 per month. This contract is set out in the second count in the indictment in case 4086. Rivers worked for Reynolds from about the 4th of

From Department of Justice File No. 155322, National Archives.

May until about June 6th, 1910, and then ran away; thereupon, as appears in the third count of the indictment, Reynolds made an affidavit charging Ed Rivers without a good and sufficient excuse failed to perform his contract with Reynolds. Rivers was arrested upon a warrant issued by Judge I.B. Slaughter after the making of the affidavit by Reynolds; Rivers was convicted and fined the further sum of One cent (1¢) together with $85.05 costs, and thereupon G.W. Broughton and M.L. Metts confessed judgment with Rivers and Broughton paid the fine and costs, and Rivers agreed to work 14 months and 15 days at the rate of $6.00 per month. This is all set out in the third count of the indictment.

The theory upon which I have proceeded in this indictment, is, that when Rivers was convicted in the May term 1910 of a criminal offense, the State of Alabama had the right to impose either fine or imprisonment upon Rivers, and had the right to commit him to jail for non-payment of the fine. However, it seems to me to be a sound proposition that when Reynolds confessed judgment with Rivers and paid the fine, which the State through its Court had imposed upon Rivers, that thereupon the power of the State of Alabama to punish Rivers was exhausted, and that the payment of the fine by Reynolds to the State upon request of Rivers constituted a simple contract debt, due by Rivers to Reynolds for money paid by Reynolds at Rivers request: and that thereupon Reynolds had all the rights against Rivers of a simple contract creditor, but that he had no right to compel Rivers to work out the debt, which Rivers owed Reynolds by reason of the payment by Reynolds of the fine imposed upon Rivers. If I am right in my construction of the law, it is likewise clear that if Reynolds threatened Rivers with arrest if Rivers did not work out the debt, and that Rivers performed services for Reynolds against his will to work out the debt, and the said service was performed against Rivers will, but because he was coerced and intimidated by the threat that he, Reynolds, would have Rivers arrested if he did not perform service, Reynolds was guilty of peonage. It is upon this theory that the second count of this indictment is drawn.

If my construction of the law is proper, then it seems to me to be likewise clear that if Reynolds, after Rivers left his employment, made an affidavit charging Rivers with failure and refusal to perform his contract service and thereby caused Rivers to be arrested, he caused an arrest for holding Rivers in a condition of peonage, and is likewise guilty under that phase of the law. The third count of this indictment is drawn to cover the arrest.

After Rivers was arrested upon an affidavit made by Reynolds, which is copied in the third count of indictment 4086, Gideon W. Broughton confessed judgment with Rivers in the sum of $87.06, being the amount of Rivers One cent (1¢) fine and $87.05 costs, and thereupon Rivers contracted to work for Broughton for 14 months and 15 days at the rate of $6.00 per month. Under this contract he went to work for Broughton, and Broughton likewise threatened that if Rivers did not continue to perform service, he would have him arrested. Rivers service to Broughton was not voluntary, but was forced by threats of arrest. On the 19th day of June 1910, Rivers ran away from Broughton; the second count in indictment 4080 against G.W. Broughton charges Broughton with holding Rivers in a condition of peonage upon the same theory that the second count in indictment No. 4086 charges Reynolds with holding Rivers in a condition of peonage.

When Rivers ran away from Broughton about the 19th day of June 1910, Broughton caused W.L. Metts to make an affidavit charging that Rivers failed and refused to perform labor under his contract, and thereupon Rivers was arrested and convicted and fined $300.00 together with $112.80 cost, making in all $412.80, and in default of the payment of such fine, was sentenced to hard labor for the County. The third count in this indictment charges Broughton with causing the arrest of Rivers to be returned to a condition of peonage upon the same theory that the same count of indictment 4086 charges Reynolds with causing Rivers arrest to be held and returned to a condition of peonage.

It does not appear in the indictment, but it is true that Reynolds was sent to hard labor for the County for more than a year. In order to bring him before the Grand Jury I had to get an order from the Court directing that he be brought here. He was brought here in chains with shackles riveted on his legs. After he gave his testimony before the Grand Jury, the Marshall took him back to the turpentine camp where he was performing hard labor for the County. Immediately after his return to the turpentine camp, a writ of habeas corpus was sued out and thereupon Rivers was released; he was given money and clothes. At that time the sentence of hard labor imposed upon him by the County Judge, Slaughter, had not expired. I do not know why he was released, unless it was that the officials of Monroe became alarmed when they learned that Rivers had been brought as a witness before the Federal Grand Jury and concluded that he should be turned loose. The treatment of Rivers is typical; he was convicted of petit larceny in May 1910, and the punishment imposed by the Court was only $15.00 and costs, amounting to the sum of $43.75, making a total of $58.75. Had Rivers gone to jail at that time his term of service would not have, in all probability, exceeded two months; instead of that, by means of successive confession of judgment by Reynolds and Broughton, Rivers in June 1910 found himself indebted in the sum of $87.06 and under contract to work 14 months and 15 days. He tried to get out of his troubles by running away, and as the result, found himself confronted in June 1910 with fine and costs amounting to $412.80 and sentenced to hard labor for more than a year in default of the payment of this fine and cost. . . .

Lynching: maintaining social order

Segregation was the legal device for preserving the South as a "white man's country" and for keeping blacks in their place. Lynching, however, was the time-honored extralegal method and, as in other times in American history, it was justified as necessary for the maintenance of law and order when established procedures did not function as the community desired. The first selection is an eyewitness account of the capture and torture of a black man and his wife. The man had been apprehended in the belief that he had killed a white planter in Mississippi. The letter to the editor of a national magazine is a defense of lynching by a white man who had recently moved to the South and who described himself as "a convert in reference to the negro question."

When the two negroes were captured, they were tied to trees, and while the funeral pyres were being prepared they were forced to suffer the most fiendish tortures. The blacks were forced to hold out their hands while one finger at a time was chopped off. The fingers were distributed as souvenirs. The ears of the murderers were cut off. Holbert was beaten severely, his skull was fractured, and one of his eyes, knocked out with a stick, hung by a shred from the socket. Neither the man nor the woman begged for mercy, nor made a groan or plea. When the executioner came forward to lop off fingers, Holbert extended his hand without being asked. The most excruciating form of punishment consisted in the use of a large corkscrew in the hands of some of the mob. This instrument was bored into the flesh of the man and the woman, in the arms, legs and body, and then pulled out, the spirals tearing out big pieces of raw, quivering flesh every time it was withdrawn. Even this devilish torture did not make the poor brutes cry out. When finally they were thrown on the fire and allowed to be burned to death, this came as a relief to the maimed and suffering victims.

From Mary Church Terrell, "Lynching from a Negro's Point of View," *North American Review* 178 (June 1904): 854. Quoting an account in the Vicksburg, Mississippi, *Evening Post*.

To the Editor of The Nation:

Sir: A recent editorial in the *Nation* concerning the burning of a negro in Waco, Tex., for murder and rape on a white woman leads me to write you this letter for publication. Let me say, however, that your editorial was not that wild denunciation that one so often sees in our Northern papers against lynching.

I was born in New York, educated in a Middle Western college. I never crossed the Mason and Dixon line till I was twenty-eight years old. During this time I thought Southern people who lynched and burned negroes for rape were barbarians, and deserved the same torture they dealt to the negroes. To date I have been living in the South fifteen years; and now I'm a convert. I have found that the average Southern man knows more about the North than the Northern man does about the South. There are reasons for this: The North is richer and greater in many respects than the South, and when a man of the South has the time and means to travel he goes North. The Northern man goes abroad. Look up the enrolment of students by States in our Northern colleges. You will find students from Southern States in surprisingly great numbers, especially graduates. Apply a similar test to the Southern colleges; many excellent institutions do not have a single student from the North. Southern merchants, bankers, educators, and even farmers and other business men, spend from a few weeks to a number of years up North. The same percentage of Northern people does not thus become acquainted with the South by visiting it.

I say I am a convert in reference to the negro question. I have lived in the North among negroes, but they were of the better class; they were more intelligent and refined than those of the South. Their superiority was due, in the main, to two factors, viz.: (1) they were, to begin with, the thriftiest, most moral and intelligent, of the Southern negroes that had moved from the South, or the descendants of such; and (2) they were so few in number that they were swept by the current of the Northern will and social pressure. Since I had never heard of a case of rape on a white woman in our community, I thought the negroes and whites of the South ought to get along equally as well. But circumstances are far different in these two sections. In many sections of the South negroes greatly outnumber the whites. When such is the case, negroes are inclined to be troublesome and insolent to the whites. I got a taste of this contempt for white minority some years ago in a South Carolina town, where I had frequently gone as a travelling salesman. I walked in company with two other white men to a commissary store in the suburbs. On the way out we met a large negro that I had often seen about the commissary. He politely gave us half the sidewalk, and spoke to us. An hour later I returned alone, and met the same negro and a companion. The former tilted his head proudly into the air, and, whistling a brazen tune, jostled me from the walk.

From "Letter to the Editor," *The Nation* 102 (22 June 1916) : 671.

It may be bad to lynch, but is it not far worse for a dehumanized fiend, swelling with bestial lust, to lay his cursed hands on a pure, defenceless woman to satisfy his animal nature? Mr. Editor, you have never had a sister, a wife, or a child outraged by a beast who has all the privileges of respectable men.

Think how you would act and feel if the life, and that which is a thousand times more sacred than life, of your dearest one were forever blasted at the hands of the Southern woman's worst enemy. Five years ago I beheld a sight the like of which I hope I may never live to see again. A doctor friend asked me to go with him to a country home; for I might be of service. An honest-faced, intelligent young farmer met us at the gate. Tears were streaming down his cheeks, and he was suffering great anguish of mind and heart. In the house his beautiful wife lay a writhing, groaning mass on the bed. The shock was too much for her. After medical attention, she somewhat regained herself, but only to think of her poor baby—for the outraged girl was only eleven. The wife and mother cried, begged wildly for help, caressed her husband, and worked herself into a feverish exhaustion. In the little girl's room we beheld on the bed the body of a murdered child, with golden hair, tangled and clotted with her own dying blood. A grewsome cut on her left cheek yawned to the bone. Her throat was black and swollen from the strangler's hand. Two of her front teeth were broken off. The most horrible sight cannot be spoken for print; but the child was eleven, and the negro a large man of twenty-five, and he resorted to laceration with a knife. This is by no means an exaggerated case. There are others equally as bad.

If that had been your only child that had been raped and murdered by a trusted farm hand, and he had been lynched that night by your neighbors—would you have sat down next day and written an editorial against *lynching,* or against *raping?* 'Tis exceedingly strange that whenever a negro is lynched for rape, our Northern papers are filled with editorials about the *awful* crime of lynching. Yet I have never read one editorial protest against the rape fiend. Your silence on the thing would indicate that the life and character of a pure woman are not so sacred as the life of a vulture that preys upon the vitals of society.

Some people seem to think lynching is for the negro alone. He happens to select premeditatedly his manner of dying. Let the white man commit rape, and he will meet a like fate. I believe that the sacredness of woman is so divine that whoever seeks to outrage her deserves a punishment more awful than that accorded to a common murderer. Just as the carcass of a pirate dangling from the arm of a ship was a warning example to other men of piratical intentions, so is the lynched rape fiend a warning sign to those who think they may tamper with the character of a woman. The righteous indignation of a community in speedily and awfully punishing *the* heinous crime is not to be too hastily criticised by those who do not know conditions, and who have never felt the pangs of hell in having a loved one ruined.

Let us be honest and unprejudiced. The Southern people are actually human beings. They are from the same stock and race as the Northern people. Let your criticism be constructive, and not condemning. Devise plans to prevent the negro from causing the South to wreak vengeance on him, and then black bodies hanging from telephone poles will be as rare as dead pirates hanging from the yard-arms of present-day ships. Lynching is a horrible disease. Remove the cause, and the disease disappears. Try to feel and think in your time about the negro situation in the South as the great Lincoln did in his time, when he said: "I have no prejudice against the Southern people. They are just what we would be in their situation."

J. T. WINSTON.

Bryan, Tex., May 26.

Liberian exodus: the "best and last chance on the earth"

For some black Americans, the idea of migrating to Africa offered the only real escape from racism, oppression, and poverty. The American Colonization Society, which had originated in 1817 largely as an alternative to slavery, continued to function in the late nineteenth century. While the idea of "back to Africa" had a modest appeal before the Civil War as a means of escaping slavery, the colonization program rarely attracted more than five hundred new settlers per year in the three decades after 1865. For most freed slaves, the North was a more obvious, indeed desirable alternative. Americans who had settled in Liberia, however, regularly wrote public and private letters to encourage new immigrants. After 1865, the Liberians particularly emphasized the need for farmers in order to open the interior of the country. The following letter from Liberia is strikingly similar to those written by immigrants who had come to the United States and then encouraged relatives and friends in their native land to follow them. Similar, too, is the descriptive mixture of opportunity and hard work that awaited new settlers.

From *Liberia*, Bulletin No. 7, American Colonization Society (November 1895), pp. 35–37.

Greenville, Sinoe County, Liberia,
July 20, 1895.

Messrs. Merity Hill, W. F. Smith
    H. P. Roberson, and J. W. McArthy, Macon, Ga.

GENTLEMEN: Your joint letter of May 22, 1895, has come to hand and the contents have been well considered. While I feel it a duty to give you an early reply, I must confess that I find no little trouble to make up an answer that will convey to your minds just what is necessary for you to understand.

I beg to say that Liberia is still the open door for the oppressed Negro from every clime. Her climate is congenial to his health. Here he can develop in body and mind. It is said that Liberia is poor; but, pray, what makes a country rich? Has it not been energy, industry, and enterprise that has brought the United States to her present standard of wealth—produced her corn, wheat, rice, tobacco, beef, pork, cotton, sugar, manufactures, etc., and made her what she is today? And may we not ask, Has the Negro had no part in her successful development? Has not his muscles tilled the ground, planted the seed, and harvested the crop which rewarded the owner, emptying into his lap increased wealth yearly? Now, if the Negro could do all this for another, why may he not do it for himself? In Liberia he may have a coffee farm, a sugar farm, a rice farm, a ginger or an arrowroot farm, if he has the energy and does not mistake the idea of freedom. No dependent man can be said to be free. Liberty was never intended to be the cradle of idleness, but should tend to promote industry, frugality, temperance, and high aspirations for the best things, to obtain which we must labor.

I am anxious to see immigrants coming to Sinoe, ind Liberia, but not men who have sworn eternal hatred to the hoe, the axe, and habits of industry. We need learned men, but not men who think themselves everything. We need doctors, teachers, lawyers, mechanics, merchants, men who will adapt themselves to the situation of the country, hopeful men, men who will look to the future when by their labor and toil they may transmit to those succeeding them a progressive and happy home. We want no drunkards, no paupers, no infirm, worn-out, and sickly people. . . .

I came from Savannah, Georgia, in 1849, and have been contented with my crabs, shrimps, lobsters, mullets, trout, crokus fish, oysters, tarpons, cavallas, snappers, and other fish found in our waters, and, thank God, I still have energy to take them from thence when I need them. The forests abound with deer, the air with birds. Why should a man not live in such a country? . . .

As to lands, Liberia furnishes each head of a family soon after its arrival with a town lot and thirty acres of land for farming. Thirty acres of land will take sixteen thousand coffee trees and leave ample room for vegetables and breadstuffs (annual, nay constant, crops). Now, sixteen thousand trees after five years will yield, at the lowest calculation, each tree one and a half pounds, which at present market price, sixteen cents per pound, will bring to the owner in gold $3,840. Suppose he uses half of this to carry on his work and support himself and family, he will still have $1,920 to keep against the day of sickness. Remember that to gain this point you cannot stick coffee plants in the soil and leave what you plant to be dwarfed, choked, and killed out by the weeds, grass, and insects. Coffee needs attention. The time lost promenading the streets and talking politics should be given to the farm if you mean productiveness. While waiting for your coffee to grow and to produce, you may plant rice, corn, eddoes, potatoes, pease, sugar-cane, &c. All these yield you annual returns, from which you can draw support until the coffee trees call you to reap the happy reward of your energy and patience. Coffee trees taken care of last for forty years in Liberia. May you not, therefore, make them a bank of your own?

Many Negroes in America are still waiting and hoping for equality there, which they will never enjoy beyond their visions and dreams. Thank God, I am here in the Fatherland and scarcely hear of your troubles. I am housed in Africa.

Africa is now being divided out by Europe. Since the Negroes will not take it, the white man will. Liberia, in western Africa, alone is ruled by Negroes. Her unfurled banner, the stripes and lone star, proudly command respect. She is, however, in need of reinforcement. And who should respond to the call quicker than the American Negro? Believe me, he may wait, hope, and delay, but should our lone star set to rise no more he will lose his best and last chance on the earth.

It is well for those coming to Liberia to bring provisions, medicines, clothing, beds, shoes, soap, money, tools, axes, hoes, rakes, cooking utensils, and, God knows, they should bring industry.

Respectfully yours,

Z. B. ROBERTS.

CHAPTER 11

A nation of new immigrants

"In Sweden, I would have been a hired hand"

Most accounts of immigration stress the "pull" aspects of the phenomenon—that is, the attractions and opportunities of the New World. But "push" considerations of poverty or persecution in the Old World formed part of the equation for emigration. The following statements by Swedish immigrants in 1907, given to a Swedish government commission surveying emigration, typify immigrant success stories. Through the years of heavy immigration, a small number of people returned to their native lands either for reasons of disillusionment or sentimentality. Most had little desire or reason to leave the United States, although they retained great affection for their homeland. The statements below summarize some Swedish immigrant experiences in this country, and also reveal interesting attitudes toward attempts to discourage emigration by distorting the facts and realities of American life.

E. C. S., Pennsylvania. Emigrated 1871. From Östergötlands län.

I was born in October 1850 in Östergötland. My father was a charcoal burner and had nine children. The croft was large enough so that he could keep a cow every other year, if he bought a little straw. For the croft he had to provide a hired man and a hired girl to the manor during the busiest time of the year. And so his lease was revoked and he came to America and is now ninety-two years old. The first thing I remember is that we lived in a little cabin in the greatest poverty. Around the age of seven I had to go out and rock children's cradles, that was my first occupation, and then herd geese, pigs, and sheep. In this way I worked for the manor until my fourteenth year, when I was confirmed. I also had a little schooling, nine months altogether, two days one week and three the other. The children were too many, so that boys and girls had to go every other dfay. After my confirmation, I hired out to a big crofter. My wages were set at twenty-five *riksdaler*, a pair of boots, two shirts, and a pair of mittens per year. Then I came to another crofter, where I got herring five times a day and had to be at the manor at four o'clock in the mornings and quit at eight-thirty in the evenings, and then go a mile and a half home to

From H. Arnold Barton (ed.), *Letters from the Promised Land: Swedes in America, 1840–1914* (Minneapolis, 1975), 276–79, 286–89. Used by permission of the University of Minnesota Press.

Immigrants in night school, 1920s.

get a little oatmeal and milk and four hours' sleep.

In 1871, on the fourth of April, I left the old home and landed in New York on 4 May. Now I was at last in the promised land, without family, without friends, and almost without money. Here I wandered back and forth like a deaf-mute. I had a ticket to Chicago and now set off for there, and then through some mistake of the railroad personnel I was sent the wrong way, so that I had to stay alone over a Sunday at Niagara Falls. There I got locked in the station house from Sunday morning to Monday morning. I showed my ticket to a hackney driver and he took me to another station, from which I got a seat to Chicago. Here there were cries from all sides: Come along to the Emigrant Home, but I had been warned about Chicago's emigrant runners, so I followed no one but took my knapsack and went off alone without knowing where. After wandering around for a while I caught sight of a sign on which there was written: Carl XV's Hotel. . . .

Here I stayed until the following day, when a gardener, P. from Rosehill, came and wanted to hire people. He offered sixteen dollars a month, room, and board, plus a dollar extra if we provided our own bedclothes, which we promised to do. I together with many others were given places in a hayloft, and since we were all emigrants it didn't matter so much for we could not speak an English word. When we were to get paid at the end of the month, instead of seventeen dollars which we had been promised, we got eight dollars, some ten dollars. I myself got twelve dollars since I did not want to stay on, and that I had no desire for, since Mr. P. used too much of Chicago's garbage to feed his emigrants with, and he was too stingy to let us go to get a drink, and he didn't want to keep a water boy, but we had to stretch out on the ground and drink out of marshy water holes, wherever we could. So. P. became a millionaire, and we who worked for him caught sicknesses of various kinds. I for my part got the ague. And so I wanted to see if I couldn't find America such as I had heard it described before I left home, and so I made my way back to Chicago and Carl XV's Hotel.

Now we were recruited through an employment agency to go to Wisconsin and work on the Wisconsin Central Line. In wages we were to receive $2.50 a day and a free trip, which was to be taken off our first pay. Instead of $2.50 which we were promised in Chicago, we were now offered $1.75 per day, with food and lodging at $20 a month. Our quarters consisted of some logs rolled together with a little straw inside on the bare ground. We arrived there on a Wednesday evening, worked Thursday and Friday; on Saturday morning it rained, and then almost the whole work gang made off for town and we took out tickets for Chicago again. Once back in Chicago we returned again to Carl XV's Hotel.

Now my ague, which I had gotten at Rosehill, had fully developed and we were now at the end of June. One day, when I began to shiver, I went outside the hotel wall and sat down. . . . Now I was in the worst situation I had ever been in in my whole life, sick and without money or acquaintances, with two hundred *riksdalers'* mortgage on my muscles for my journey over. Like a sleepwalker I wandered up and down the streets of Chicago. Was this really the highly praised America?

I finally left Chicago and made my way to Pennsylvania, where I worked on the railroads for about four years; then I entered into matrimony with a girl from my native place. She had a little money, and I had saved up a little so that we bought a little farm of 20 acres where we settled down, bought three cows, a horse, and a few implements. This farm we kept for two years, then we sold it; we bought another of 120 acres for $1,000, sold 50 acres of it, and that made me free of debt. Now we worked on this for a couple of years and then there was a sawmill nearby which was for sale and we bought it for $2,000. Now I sawed timber both for myself and for others so that in two years I had paid for the sawmill, but then it burned down and I had no insurance. I rebuilt it right away and began sawing again.

Now, I began buying up larger and smaller pieces of land with timber, and that went fine. My old farm was sold, a larger and better one bought, a general store started, town properties purchased, and then I started building houses in the towns of Youngsville and Jamestown, New York. So today I have 300 acres of land, a good farm, good sawmill with a planing machine; two stores, eight houses in the towns, and ten leaseholders who pay me an annual income of $900. Meanwhile we have brought up eight children, of which some are married. I pay an annual tax of $175. My assessed value is approximately like this: my farm $3,000, woodland $2,500, sawmill with equipment $3,000, horses and other livestock and farm implements $15,00, lumber on hand $3,000, town property in Youngsville $10,000, in Jamestown, New York, $2,500. If I had stayed behind in Sweden, I would have been a hired hand, at the very best a crofter.

L. F. L., Minnesota. Emigrated 1891. From Norrbottens län.

Born on a medium-sized farm in one of Norrbotten's coastal parishes thirty-odd years ago, with a strong desire to learn, which I early had the chance to satisfy, already as a boy I acquired a strong lust for adventure. I had not, however, thought much about a trip to America, even though I had been in touch with several returned Swedish Americans and though my sister had emigrated to America in my sixteenth year, in the fall of 1889.

But at a book auction at the courthouse in the fall of 1890 I bought a batch of books, and among them I found one with the title *The Truth about America*. I have long since forgotten the author's name, but it was apparently one of your predecessors in the movement to prevent emigration.

This book contained a mass of the most ridiculous lies about America, of the same kind as the stories one reads from time to time in our conservative newspapers back home, with which they think they can frighten the simple

Swedes, as when they frighten small children with the boogeyman. They forget that the average Swede knows just as much about American conditions as authors and journalists. The book in question, as I said, painted America in colors as somber as ever any medieval priest could paint the Evil One's abode. This caused me and others who read the book to reflect over what motives could lie behind such a book, and we came to the conclusion that it must be above all to frighten people out of emigrating, and secondly to make the little man satisfied with conditions in Sweden. How successful this was is shown by the fact that all the farm boys in the village to whom I lent the book kept me company over to America the following spring. There were of course many other causes besides, which helped us to decide to leave: the idiotic class differences, lack of the vote, military service, etc. The economic situation was the least important reason, for all of those who went from my home village that spring were from well-to-do farm families.

Although I have now been in this country for sixteen years I still follow the course of events back home and take great interest in the welfare of my homeland. The Swedish American newspapers, of which I read a half dozen, every week include a couple of pages of news from Sweden as well as special correspondence on the events of the day. If the Swedish newspapers would publish half as much about Swedish America, perhaps they would judge us more fairly at home. I have never visited Sweden since I came here, but I feel a deep love for the land where my cradle stood, where my old father lives, and where my mother's remains lie at rest. I have forgotten all that was hard at home and have only the happy memories of childhood left. . . .

Because I do not want my illusions to be crushed, I have never since visited Sweden.

My life here in America has gone through many changes. My "dog years" were especially hard for a youth who was not used to working for others. I worked at sawmills, in the forest, on farms, at a newspaper press, etc., was a census taker and a policeman, until nearly fifteen years ago I got the position in the postal service which I now have. It is not a high position, but under the same circumstances I could never have gotten anything like it in Sweden. My salary is $900—over 3,300 *kronor* a year. When it is considered that when I took the examination for the position I had not gone a single day to an American school and still made a grade of 97 per cent, that is not so bad. My working time is six or seven hours per day.

It could thus never occur to me to leave this position and return to Sweden, where a person who has not acquired academic degrees has no chance to get a position in public service. . . .

The reasons why it would be impossible for Swedish Americans to get along well in Sweden are many: the ridiculous "title sickness" and silly class system, the groveling of the low and the arrogance of the high, the antipathy against Swedish Americans and "self-made men," the bureaucracy and pedantry, the complicated system through which the wealthy seek to keep political power, the forced militarism, and the whole system that makes it impossible to acquire through one's own work as good an income as that mass of good-for-nothings who have managed to obtain certain academic degrees from the state and the commune to do nothing. I consider it fruitless to work against emigration or to try to bring about a remigration of Swedish Americans as long as conditions at home are the way they are. Both Swedes and Swedish Americans have greater demands on life than the ruling class in Sweden is willing to fulfill. Let them therefore go their way. You can surely fill their places with Slavic and other lower kinds of people with smaller requirements and more suitable for your present system, for to expect the ruling class to change the system for the benefit of the little man is expecting too much.

The Chinese: violence

Antiforeign prejudice frequently had resulted in violence. Among immigrants, few experienced more cruelty and subjugation than Orientals—first the Chinese, and later the Japanese. Large numbers of Chinese had been lured to the United States, first during the gold rush, and then in the 1860s as coolie labor for railroad development in the West. After that, they tended to congregate in ghettos in west coast cities, particularly San Francisco and Los Angeles. There they posed an economic threat to white laborers, and animosity toward the Chinese attained bitter proportions by the 1870s. The following eyewitness account of the anti-Chinese riot in Los Angeles in October 1871 reflects the violent manifestation of that hatred.

As a result of the gubernatorial message of 1854, the state senate appointed a committee . . . to investigate the "Chinese evil." An exhaustive investigation was had; and, read in the light of latter days, the report of that committee proves the far-seeing judgment of those who made it. The report declared:

The Chinese are destructive to the best interests of the state and dangerous to its peace. They come not as freemen but as serfs and hirelings of a master. It needs no Solomon to predict the result: disputes will take place and blood will flow, to be followed by the expulsion of a population who will be driven from the state by violence instead of law. . . .

For some time prior to the 28th of October, 1871, the Chinese quarter of Los Angeles had been in a state of agitation, growing out of a dispute concerning the ownership and possession of a Chinese woman. "Chinatown" was then, as now, divided between distinct clans. One of those clans claimed the woman, Quangk Cow, by name. A rival clan disputed the claim and spirited Quangk

From P. S. Dorney, "A Prophecy Partly Verified," *Overland Monthly,* new series, 7 (March 1886) : 230–234.

away to Santa Barbara. The first claimant, however, utilized the machinery of the courts, and the county of Los Angeles was put to the expense of bringing the woman back to answer a buncombe charge of larceny. Upon her arrival, Quangk Cow was immediately bailed out and fell into the hands of her original masters. This result created intense excitement among the Celestials, and a carriage containing the leader of the successful faction and the disputed woman was surrounded and fired upon in broad daylight and in the heart of Los Angeles by a band of infuriated highbinders. . . .

For two days that portion of the city cursed by the presence of the Mongols was in a state of war. Every house was barricaded and the crack of revolvers and the bursting of bombs reverberating throughout the city kept the people in a constant state of anxious excitement. Crowds gathered at the intersection of Commercial and Los Angeles Streets, and some of the most daring ventured as near the Mongol quarter as Carillo's or Caswell's corner; but they were quickly dispersed by a shower of bullets from the pistols of the Mongolian shooters.

Business and travel in and about the Chinese quarter being wholly suspended, the authorities resolved to quell the disorder. To this end the police made a raid upon the fighters late on the afternoon of October 28. This show of authority had a singular effect upon the Chinese. The storm of internecine fury instantly lulled. Upon all sides a peculiar cry went up; the fighters, as one man, united in opposing the police; and, taken wholly by surprise, the "peelers" were routed in a moment.

The town was now thoroughly moved. A feeling of deep alarm, not unmixed with fear, spread abroad. Places of business and residences adjacent to the scene of war were closed and abandoned, and an immense concourse of anxious spectators collected at the intersection of Main and Aliso, and of Commercial and Los Angeles Streets.

The police prepared for another charge and were joined by a few citizens, among whom was "Bob" Thompson, a well-known and very popular character. The second charge was better calculated and more determined than the first but was met as before; the police were again routed, leaving behind them Officer Bilderrain, desperately wounded, a Spanish boy shot in the foot, and citizen Thompson writhing in the agonies of death. A third charge resulted only in bearing off the wounded. The boy and Officer Bilderrain were taken to their homes, while Thompson was borne to a drugstore on Main Street. It was now between 6 and 7 o'clock in the evening, and a vast multitude were assembled in front of this store.

About 8 o'clock the death of Thompson was announced. The announcement was received in sullen silence; but in a moment the crowd melted away, and Main Street was deserted. In another moment, armed men were seen hastening, singly and in clusters, from every street and avenue, all heading toward Chinatown. The whole city seemed moved by one grim and tacit purpose—men streamed down from the hills and swarmed from the suburbs, while "Sonora" poured forth a horde of swarthy avengers. Businessmen closed their shops and joined the gathering clans, and in less than fifteen minutes after the announcement of "Bob" Thompson's death, the cracking of rifles, the roar of shotguns, and the rattle of small arms proclaimed the investment of Chinatown.

About 9 o'clock the first Chinese was captured. He was armed with a hatchet and was taken while attempting to break through the cordon of whites that surrounded the Chinese quarter. A dozen hands clutched him, and a hundred throats hoarsely shouted: "A rope! To the hill! To the hill!"

A man, then and now of standing and influence, dashed into a neighboring store and presently emerged, shaking aloft the first rope—a smooth, kinky, brand-new coil.

As the maddened men surged up the hill (Temple Street), the little ill-favored prisoner, borne bodily along, was stabbed in the back and side and was dead as a doorstep before General Baldwin's corral was reached, to the gate-beam of which the dead man was hanged. While the rope was being fastened to the neck of the corpse, two burly human beasts held it erect, while an Irish shoemaker known as "Crazy Johnson" stood guard, revolver in hand. . . .

By this time, Chinatown, wholly surrounded, was in a state of siege. Mounted men came galloping from the country—the vaquero was in his glory, and the cry was: *"Carajo la Chino!"*

Among the Spaniards whose boldness and vigor attracted attention that night was Vasquez, afterward famous as a bandit, and Jesus Martinez, his chum and relative. Chief among the Americans, plying a Henry rifle until excessive labor clogged its mechanism, the writer observed a certain high official; and in the van of the fight, one of the city fathers—a member of the City Council and a Wells Fargo official—valiantly struck out from the shoulder. A young Israelite, heavy-framed and coarse-featured, and a German known as "Dutch Charley" were prominently active and cruel. "Crazy Johnson" seemed to represent all Ireland; while Jacques, a Frenchman, shirtless and hatless, and armed with a cleaver, reveled in the memory of the Pont Neuf and the Sans Culottes. Jacques was the fire-fiend of the occasion—time and again Chinatown was ablaze—and Jacques with his cleaver was always found pictured in the glare.

After the assault became general, the Chinese never returned shot or blow; but securely barricading every avenue of approach, each like a badger retired to his den and in sullen silence awaited his fate. But few attempted to escape, and all who made the attempt fell riddled with bullets. Not far from eleven o'clock the Main Street side of Chinatown fell into the hands of the besiegers, and, led by Jesus Martinez, the assailants scaled the low adobe walls and mounted to the asphaltum roof. This achievement was hailed with deafening cheers by the crowd below.

The condition of the Chinese had now become wretched indeed. The "Quarters," it will be remembered, were an old Spanish hacienda one story high, with an open courtyard in the center. Martinez and his companions, armed with axes as well as firearms, cut holes in the asphaltum roof, through which the cowering creatures below were shot in their hiding places or hunted from room to room out into the open courtyard, where death from the bullets of those on the roof was certain. Within or without, death was inevitable. The alternative was terrible. As each separate wretch, goaded from his covert, sought in his despair the open space, a volley from the roof brought him down; a chorus of yells telegraphed that fact to the surrounding mob, and the yells were answered by a hoarse roar of savage satisfaction.

A simultaneous rush from Los Angeles Street forced the doors upon that side, and the work of real diabolism began. Men were dragged forth, many of them mortally wounded, and hurled headlong from a raised sidewalk to the ground. To the necks of some of the most helpless the mob fastened ropes and, with a whoop and a hurrah, rushed down Los Angeles Street to the hanging place, dragging some writhing wretch prone upon the ground. More of the doomed and bleeding miserables were jerked along by as many eager hands as could lay hold of clothing and queue, cuffed and cursed in the meantime by the infuriated multitude. A boy was thus led to the place of slaughter. The little fellow was not above twelve years of age. He had been but a month in the country and knew not a word of English. He seemed paralyzed by fear—his eyes were fixed and staring, and his face blue-blanched and idiotic. He was hanged.

Close behind the boy followed the Chinese doctor; a man of extreme age, well known, and reputed wealthy. The doctor begged piteously for his life, pleading in English and in Spanish; but he might as well have pleaded with wolves. At last he attempted to bribe those who were hurrying him to his death. He offered $1,000—$2,000—$3,000—$5,000—$10,000—$15,000! But to no purpose. He was hanged, and his $15,000 was spirited away none the less. At his death the old man wore a valuable diamond ring upon his left index finger, but when his corpse was cut down it was found that the left index finger had been wrenched from its socket, and finger and ring were gone.

One very tall Chinaman, while being hustled to the place of execution, endeavored from time to time to strike aside the hands that clutched him, accompanying his efforts with spasmodic ejaculations, such as: "All light, me go, me no flaid!" When this man was brought to Goler's (a blacksmith and wagon-maker's shop, the awning of which served as a gallows), the mob [was] in a state of frenzy over the famine of rope. "Rope, more rope!" was hoarsely howled upon all sides, and—let humanity blush—a woman, a married one, and a mother, rushed to appease the human tigers with her clothesline. This woman kept a boarding house on Los Angeles Street, directly opposite Goler's shop.

Goler's awning being filled with pendant dead, a large wagon of prairie schooner kind was made to serve as a gallows tree. With the clothesline the tall Chinaman was swung from the driver's seat of the prairie schooner. The man being very tall, he could not be swung wholly clear; his toes still lightly touched the ground. Among oaths and derisive cries of "Rise 'em, Riley!" desperate efforts were made to swing the man clear of the ground but to no purpose. The act of sickening brutality by which—the writer being witness—the victim's death was, in the fury of the moment, compassed is not fit for these pages. The murderer, "Dutch Charley," a tinsmith by trade, was afterward sent to San Quentin from San Bernardino County for the murder of a squaw.

Charley's act was the crowning horror of that horrible night. It revolted even the baser brutes who had urged him to its commission. Brutality had sickened itself. The babel of passion was hushed and abashed, and in sullen silence the mob fell to pieces and slunk away in the night, like a gorged and tired beast.

It was midnight, and a body of men appointed by the sheriff cut down the dead—twenty-three in number. Nearly all had been dragged through the streets at the end of a rope, and all were found shot and stabbed as well as hanged. Such was the first completed act of the drama prophesied by the senate of 1854.

The "lecherous Jew"

From the mid-seventeenth until the late nineteenth century, Jewish immigrants found America a veritable paradise, relatively free from the legal restrictions, the violence, and the role of convenient scapegoat that had been their lot in the Old World. But anti-Semitic attitudes and propaganda flourished as part of the general development of nativist sentiment toward the new stock of immigrants that flooded the land after the Civil War. Typical was the work of Telemachus Thomas Timayenis—an odd-sounding name for a representative of nativism—who, in several pamphlets, portrayed the traditional notions of the cunning, exploitive character of Jews. In this selection, Timayenis emphasized an old theme: the "Jew lecher," as Timayenis called him, who threatened the purity of nice, innocent Christian girls.

"In all matters pertaining to corruption and pollution, in matters that defile moral character, the Jew stands unequalled."

—THE ORIGINAL MR. JACOBS.

Next to his lust for money, the strongest passion in the Jew is his licentiousness. This, like every other vicious trait of which the Jew is possessed, takes a peculiarly prominent and objectionable form.

The average Jew is disgustingly bawdy in his talk, and interlards his conversation with filthy expressions and obscene words. On the verandas at summer-resorts, in hotel-corridors, in the lobbies of theatres, on steamboats, on railway-cars, and in public places in general, the Jew indulges in this repulsive peculiarity, to the great annoyance and disgust of respectable Christian women and decency-loving Gentile men. This was one of the habits which made him so objectionable at summer-resorts, and has led to his practical exclusion from

From [Telemachus Thomas Timayenis], *The American Jew: An Exposé of His Career* (New York : Minerva Publishing Co., 1888), pp. 81–87.

almost every first-class summer-hotel in the land.

The boldest and most offensive of that class of persons who lounge about the prominent thoroughfares of our principal cities, and are known as "street mashers," are Israelites. Overdressed, with mincing gait and dandified mien, these Jew "mashers" are daily to be seen strutting up and down the leading streets, ogling, with amazing effrontery, every woman who passes them by. Young girls of tender age are especially marked by these Jew "mashers" as their particular prey. Some years ago, in San Francisco, the attention of the police was directed to a band of Jew "mashers," who made a point of following up the girls of a certain public school on their way from the classroom to their homes. These Jew scoundrels, wherever they were unable to make a girl's acquaintance, would follow her up in pairs, talking together in the most disgusting manner, so as to be overheard by the objects of their pursuit. Some of the children's male relatives, assisted by the police, finally succeeded in very effectually disposing of this band of wretches.

Almost any afternoon, in Kearny Street, San Francisco, knots of Jew "mashers" are to be seen hanging around the corners, and ogling the women who pass. Some of these fellows have not merely lascivious propensities in view, but have their sharp and restless eyes open to any possibilities of blackmail that may present themselves. Some years ago, a young married woman who had been foolish enough to allow one of these foppishly dressed Jew scoundrels to make her acquaintance, was so mercilessly blackmailed, although her conduct had in no way passed into the bounds of criminality, that the unfortunate woman was driven into an attempt at suicide. The truth then leaked out; and she and her husband never again lived happily together, and eventually drifted apart.

Upon one occasion, a young lady, while passing the corner of Park and Kearny Streets, was addressed by one of these Jew Lotharios of the street. Gazing upon the Jew dude with a pitying look, she drew a fifty-cent piece from her pocket, and threw it at his feet, exclaiming,—

"You miserable thing! you don't look as if you were half fed. Go and buy yourself something to eat with that."

The Jew masher gazed for a moment at the coin as it lay on the sidewalk, and then the instincts of his race conquered him. He stooped, picked up the money, and pocketed it. A quick and efficacious way to get rid of the Jew masher is to throw him a little money. It will engross his attention, and secure a release from his importunities.

In Eddy Street, San Francisco, a Jew dentist established himself some time ago in business. One day, while a lady was under the influence of an anaesthetic in the dental chair, this scoundrel, taking advantage of her helpless condition, committed certain improprieties. The lady regained consciousness more quickly than he anticipated, and he was discovered. She went home, and told the whole story to her husband. The latter, arming himself with a stout rawhide, compelled his wife to accompany him to the dental parlors. Arrived there, he laid the lash lustily over the Jew's head and shoulders,—flogged him unmercifully. The Jew coward made no attempt at defence. He simply writhed and squirmed and screamed, like the whipped cur that he was. Finally, lest his humiliation should not already be sufficiently complete, he fell down on his knees before his assailant, grovelling before him, kissing his feet, and imploring him to desist the castigation. Then, still abjectly kneeling, he confessed his attempted crime in terms of sickening servility, and implored the wife's forgiveness. What a disgusting spectacle! But let all Jew lechers be treated likewise. . . .

In the same city, a big scandal was occasioned some years ago by the misconduct of a daughter of the wealthiest shirt-manufacturer on the Pacific Coast,—an Israelite,—with a Chinaman who was a servant in her father's household. What became of the offspring of this scandalous intrigue cannot be definitely ascertained, but the father offered a hundred thousand dollars to any young man of decent antecedents who would make the girl his wife. His offer was confined to Gentile young men, he having a longing for a Gentile son-in-law, but he found no takers. Had he been less discriminating in his choice, and been satisfied with a Jew son-in-law, he could doubtless have married the girl off in twenty-four hours. What slip in maidenly virtue, what dishonor, would not the Jew gladly hug to his breast for the sake of a hundred thousand dollars? A hundred thousand dollars! Joost t'ink of it, Moses!

In many of the factories operated by the Jews throughout the country, the life of an honest girl therein employed is made simply a hell, by reason of the Jews' predominant lechery. Instances in support of this assertion have turned up by scores within the past ten years. In Newark, N.J., some time ago, a number of factory-girls demanded the discharge of a certain Jew foreman, upon the ground that he was in the habit of systematically insulting them by indecent proposals and actions. The Jew employers refused to discharge the Jew employee, whereupon the girls struck. As they were preparing to leave, this Jew foreman came into a room, one flight up, where a number of the girls were putting together their effects. The sight of him evoked quite a storm of indignation and rage; and, seizing upon him, the girls forced him to the window, and, disregarding his shrieks, threw him out headlong.

In Paterson, N.J., similar charges were preferred against another Jew foreman; and not long ago, in New York, the officers of the Society for the Prevention of Cruelty to Children neatly trapped a Jew employer who was in the habit of inducing little girls under fourteen to remain after work-hours, and debauching them. Similar instances of the workings of Jew lechery might be quoted from all over the country, at tedious length.

The Jew drummer is one of the most assiduous patrons of houses of prostitution throughout the country. Without the Jew clientele, it is safe to say that fully sixty-six per cent of the houses of ill-fame in the various cities of the United States, excepting, for certain obvious reasons, New York and Chicago, would be compelled to go out of existence. Not only is the Jew a liberal patron of these houses of prostitution; but such is the insatiability of his carnal appetites, and to such an extent does he give rein to his lasciviousness, that his debauches only too frequently exceed the ordinary limits of lust. Those certain hideous and abhorrent forms of vice, which have their origin in countries of the East, and which have in recent years sprung into existence in this country, have been taught to the abandoned creatures who practise them, and fostered, elaborated, and encouraged, by the lecherous Jew!

The melting pot

Despite the violence and venom of nativist attitudes, many of the new immigrants persisted in idealizing life in their new homeland. Those who had fled their native countries because of religious or political oppression passionately sought to adapt themselves. This anonymous selection is from an essay submitted for competition in a contest entitled "What America Means." It was written by a young Russian Jewish woman who allegedly had studied English for only a year, and it reflects her desperate desire for Americanization. It is interesting, too, how she belittled the political radicals among the new immigrants whom she believed—quite correctly—had stigmatized their fellow refugees. The essay is reprinted with the original grammatical and spelling errors.

What did I myself look forward to when I left my home, my mother and my little sisters? My way was hard, harder then many of those emigrants, because I was all alone, no help from any one could I expect, and I was not very big, never worked before. I had just graduate from high school when decided to go away. What made me take the hardships of the long way? Not the looking forward made me go, but the looking backward made me search a new life and struggle a hard battle.

Yes it was hard it is hard still now to bear the homesickness, loneliness, among strange people not knowing the language doing hard worke without a minute of joy. But when I look back into my childhood without a single spot of gladness in it, always under a terrible fear—fear of "goim" (gentiles). I think that there is not anything harder than hardships of childhood.

I remember myself in my fear-mood—frightened by stories of massacres, unable to go to sleep for fear that gentiles may come and kill my mother and

From *The Immigrants in America Review* 1 (June 1915): 70–71.

father, as they killed my aunt and her husband. I could see in my imagination their mishaped bodies, swiming in blood, and I almost screamed of horror, when I saw myself left all alone in the big world and no one to care for me and stand for me before the gentiles. What can be worse a sight than a child with a frightened and hating soul? And that what I was.

Now when I meet italians, russians, jews here in America I see the great meaning of that country for us. We who in Castle Garden were still the same poor, desolate emigrants of Europe after a struggle with life, became winners of the battle, we have new ideas of freedom, we think with pride that in seven years we will be "Americans" and citizens and we are proud of our new country (that) because it is so much better than our old country and that it wellkomed us, and we try to be worth it and go to schools to study civics and all do hard work which makes our country just a little better. America means something to an American it means more to us immigrants for this meaning is new and holly and wonderfully dear to us.

When I meet the American children in white dresses and pink ribbons going to school to teachers whom they love and who love them and try to make their studies as interesting as possible, I see myself and my chums going to school as to a trial, in gray uniforms, black aprons, coming there to repeat words of a strange catechism which was forced into our heads. While young American learn in school how to love and respect your people and your government, 'so wise, so free,' so practical, we were forced to devine our kings who are so cruel so dull and so unsensible. But triying to force into us seeds of patriotism, they raised hatred in them, for teachers who offend us, calling "zudovka" (dirty jew) such teachers are unfit to stand as tutors of growing minds and certainly mislead more than one of the young generation.

In about five month after I came to America, I entered a hospital to take up training for a nurse. I could not speak English at all for some time, but when in a month I aske questions America opened to me through my patients. There were immigrants unable to speak, even to each other because of the mixture of all different nationalities and languages, Americans of all ranks who were sometimes cross and impatient to the little foreighn nurse. America opened to me through the Irishmen and Italians hurt in a saloon fight and others their countrymen who were sick because they worked a whole day at hard labor in factories and outside and then went to school to study civics in night school, for their ambition told them, that they ought know their civil duties to a country in which they worke with a shovel diging sewers and laying tracks.

That what I learned during my short life in America: America means for an Immigrant a fairy promised land that came out true, a land that gives all they need for their work, a land which gives them human rights, a land that gives morality through her churches and education through her free schools and libraries. The longer I live in America the more I think of the question of Americanising the immigrants. At first I thought that there is not such a question as that, for the children of immigrants naturally are Americans and good

Americans. America is a land made up of foreigners and the virtues of American life is the best Americaniser. The first generation of American immigrants can't be Americanized much for they were raised in different ways the mod of living is different. And yett how much it is when they love America and are such patriots. I remember I took care of an old russian women, I was the only one who could speak to her in the hospital and we always had great conversations while I was fixing her up. Once she was telling me about her husband. On her face was a half sarcastic, half glad smile when she was criticising the way her husband acts. He was getting childish, she said, why only the other day the school teacher gave the boys a book about Washington and the granfather heard them reading it. He pinned a paper flag on his hat and playing on a 5-cent horn lead the march of boys who were singing "Washington o, Washington, the father of our country." "Something wrong with him" said my patient, but it seemed to me that it was a righted wrong, for a man that never knew the patriotic feeling before became a purest, patriot now. No one tried to teach him be a patriot he came to it by himself.

How often the children of Americans call the immigrants "pollack" and "Diego" and only torment their Americanising, because they loose their confidence in Americans. Here is a way for Americans to help foreigners become Americans: teach their own children to respect those people that struggle such a hard battle.

There is only one kind of immigrants who need for their Americanising something besides sympathy. Those are anarchists and other political parties who do not realise the greatness and wisdom of American government, because they have no idea of morrailty. They come from Europe in a state of unbelieve and immorality because the church, administration and schools of Europe by forcing them to have certain false ideas of false virtues killed their best feelings in them. They need to be restorted a fallen building and the first thing they need is to build under themselfs a foundation of moral ideas, believe in God and their country.

"In America it is no better...."

The United States, of course, was not paradise for all new immigrants. However necessary their migration, many never adjusted and accepted their new life. Indeed, through the first four decades of the twentieth century, a significant number returned to their native land, disillusioned or made bitter by their experiences. The following excerpts from letters of Polish immigrants particularly illustrate the difficulties and cynicism of people who had led a marginal existence in the Old World and did not find life noticeably easier or different in America.

February 15 [1904]

DEAR BROTHER ADAM, AND ALSO DEAR SISTER AND BROTHER-IN-LAW AND YOUR CHILDREN:

We are in good health, thanks to our Lord God, and we wish to you the same.

Now, dear brother, I think well [intentions are good] about you. If work were good you would already be in America. I have had no work for four months now, and I wait for better conditions. If the conditions don't improve by Easter, we will go back to our country, and if they improve and I get work, I will immediately send you a ship-ticket, and you will come. There will probably be hard times in America this year because in the autumn they will elect the president. If the same remains who is now, then all will be well, but if they elect a democrat, then there will be hard times in America, and those who have money enough will go back to their country. You will learn [all] in another letter. Hold out a little, until I bring you to me or until I come myself to you, and then we shall suffer together. Inform me about your health and success, and what kind of winter you have, because we have great cold and snows. I have nothing more to write, I send my good wishes and low bows to brother and to the Wolskis. With respect,

Your brother,
RACZKOWSKI [FRANCISZEK]

January 10 [1909, 1910, or 1911]

DEAR SISTER:

. . . I received the letter with the wafer and I thank you for thinking of me, dear sister. Now, dear sister and brother-in-law, don't be angry if I don't write to you very often, but I don't know how to write myself and before I ask somebody to write time passes away, but I try to answer you sometimes at least. You ask me how much my boys and my man earn. My man works in an iron-foundry, he earns 9, 10, 12 roubles [dollars] sometimes, and the boys earn 4 or 5 roubles. My dear, in America it is no better than in our country: whoever does well, he does, and whoever does poorly, suffers misery everywhere. I do not suffer misery, thanks to God, but I do not have much pleasure either. Many people

From F. Zaniecki and W. I. Thomas, *The Polish Peasant in Europe and America* (Chicago: University of Chicago Press, 1918). 2: 188–189, 220. Used by permission.

in our country think that in America everybody has much pleasure. No, it is just as in our country, and the churches are like ours, and in general everything is alike. I wish to know with which son grandmother is. Write me. And who is farming on that land after Rykaczewski? Perhaps we shall yet meet some day or other, dear sister. I should like to see you, and my native country. I have nothing more to write, I kiss you both and your children. I wish you a happy and merry and good New Year. May this New Year bring you the greatest happiness possible. We wish it to you from our heart. The children kiss auntie and uncle and their cousins.

We remain, well-wishing,
H. J. Dabrowskis

Assimilation: two views

Assimilation for the new immigrants was difficult in the face of native hostility and the handicaps of alien languages and cultures. Among the first generation of immigrants who adapted fairly well there were many who still saw their loyalty and character split between their old and new countries. Stoyan Christowe, a Bulgarian immigrant, eloquently discussed the process of adaptation as he experienced it—an experience that left him "half an American." His subsequent visit to Bulgaria only reinforced that feeling, for his native land still had enormous appeal to him; yet, he quickly grasped the truth of the old proverb, "You cannot go home again." The second selection portrays the problems of immigrant or second-generation children who became alienated from their parents because of the latter's persistently "foreign" ways.

Half an American

As I try to recall my earliest impressions of America, first come to mind the rotten tomatoes which native urchins hurled against us poor frightened immigrants as we trudged morning and evening from our quarters to the foundries and back. My impulse then was hatred for all Americans, whom I considered as omniscient giants before whose energy and ingenuity nature herself bowed. My first desire was to accumulate as much as possible of the proverbial American gold and beat it back to the old country.

From Stoyan Christowe, "Half an American," *Outlook and Independent* 153 (4 December 1929): 530–531, 555–557.

A Knowledge of English
is the Gateway
TO
American Life
American Citizenship
American Ideals

Promoting English for the "melting pot."

Some, the more frugal and labor-loving ones, did precisely that. Through severe economy they saved a thousand dollars or so in the course of a few years and returned to the villages to resume their honored positions as masters of houses and families. There they augmented their properties by buying another vineyard, a couple more meadows; swept away the decayed thatch from the roofs of their houses and covered them with gleaming red tiles.

But the majority of us stayed. We soon got used to the tomatoes, even took for granted an occasional egg. We knew we were foreigners and we were not slow in perceiving that while in our own country the word foreigner connoted guesthood, in America it carried an implication of contempt. We had come to stay and avail ourselves of the riches. No one likes a guest that has come to stay permanently.

We lived in clusters in the large cities and contemplated the American world through the windows of our coffee houses. Physically we were in America; mentally and spiritually in the old country. If ever an American ventured into our coffee houses we all stirred like the bees in a hive into which a slug has made its way. There was just as much excitement caused by the strange visitor as if he had visited our native village. We had created a world of our own within that greater world into which we only occasionally ventured.

This great world which encompassed ours was to me an immense confusion. Of its complicated pattern I could not discern a single stitch, much less begin to perceive the pattern itself. Filled with fright, I thought of the little native world with which I was intimate and whose mysterious life was not a mystery to me. Did I not help promote that life? I knew the grass grew in the meadows because we watered it; the grapevines sprouted and leaved profusely because we pruned them in the spring and weeded out the hampering growth from amidst their roots; the corn grew because we plowed the field and planted the seed there.

But here everything seemed purposeless and inexplicable. For ten hours every day I stood harnessed to a monstrous machine and bored holes into pieces of steel. I did not know whence those steel pieces came, how they were called, why I was punching the holes in them, where they were going from me, of what eventual use they would be. The whole city in which I lived was like that. People went about hurried in all directions. To what purpose, I could not divine. The whole of America was like that in those early immigrant days.

But gradually I began to perceive a faint rhythm in the cacophony and to discern a certain measure and line in the catastrophic disorder which surrounded me. The mist began to clear away and the mighty structure of America loomed before my vision like a lofty vague mountain at the earliest dawn.

As the American world took form before my eyes and slowly revealed itself to me, a dimness about the world I came from began to settle in my mind. The traditional names of the heroes of our land began to seem the names of heroes of a mythical world and to be crowded out of my memory by names which would once have sounded strange to me. More and more America revealed itself, intriguing me farther and farther into amazing labyrinths and captivating me with the crude sorcery of steel and iron, until I began to see beauty where I had once seen only frightful ugliness.

There started then to awake in me a fevered passion to become part of the magnificent, resplendent scheme which unfolded and grew before me. I studied the language with maniacal zest; read newspapers and magazines and books with the avidity of a fanatic. I read out loud billboards, posters, signs of all kinds, names of companies and corporations, names of streets and squares; and every word, every name opened new vistas to me. I was becoming saturated with Americanism.

More and more America captivated me. It alone was great; everything else was puppetry. The glare of this fantastic civilization blinded me to the achievements of any other nation. Europe was but a museum with its people the porters and guides in it. America was the living world, where men breathed, worked, created, built, sought the solutions of the mysteries of nature and harnessed the universe. I passed through a phase of blind provincialism; a sort of spell emanated from outward things coloring my vision and judgment.

In my passion to liken myself to the Americans, to rub out from my personality all foreign traits and characteristics, I suffered agonies. I would not content myself with straight and safe English. Americanisms, native idioms and localisms would give a certain authenticity to my own Americanism. And I was not cautious in their use; with the result that often I made myself ridiculous, saying things entirely different from what I intended to say. Once in my college days a fellow student and I passed on the campus two lovers. I noticed as they came by us that the young man was holding the girl so awkwardly that she walked with difficulty. My intention was merely to remark to my friend on the unnatural way in which the young man was holding his companion and I could well have said, "What a stupid way to hold a girl!" but precisely what I said was, "Say, that fellow's got that girl in a bad shape!" My friend laughed uproariously, but genially, and I with him. In those days I was not very self-conscious about my mistakes. I knew that my whole being was in process of change, that I was in a state of turmoil. My English was in ferment.

Years have passed since then. And I am now a different person. Still I often ask myself these questions: What has been the result of this long and blind gestation in the womb of America? Have I become an American? Has the storm in my being lulled now that I have spent two-thirds of my life in a struggle for readjustment and adaptation? The one answer that pounds in my mind most is this: Despite the readiness and zeal with which I tossed myself in the melting pot I still am not wholly an American, and never will be.

It is not my fault. I have done all I could. America will not accept me. I shall always be the adopted child, not the real son, of a mother that I love more than the one that gave me birth. It is hard for a man with ingrained native traits and characteristics to remake himself in the course of one generation. There is still something outlandish about me; mannerisms and gestures that must strike as odd one born and bred here; tints and nuances in my speech that must betray my foreign birth soon after I open my mouth to speak.

I once believed that America demanded complete surrender from those who adopted it as their mother. I surrendered completely. Then I discovered that America wanted more—it wanted complete transformation, inward and outward. That is impossible in one generation.

Then what is my fate, and the fates of the thousands who fall into my category, or, should I say, into whose category I fall? What are we? Are we still what we were before we came to America, or are we half Americans and half something else? To me, precisely there lies our tragedy. We are neither one nor the other; we are orphans. Having forsaken our own mothers to become the foster children of another, we find ourselves orphaned. Spiritually, physically, linguistically, we have not been wholly domesticated. And at the same time we have rendered ourselves incapable of resuming life in the old country.

While I am not a whole American neither am I what I was when I first landed here; that is, a Bulgarian. Still retaining some inherited native traits, enough to bar me forever from complete assimilation, I have outwardly and inwardly deviated so much from a Bulgarian that when recently visiting in that country I felt like a foreigner and was so regarded. . . .

Now I do not claim that America openly demands uniformity of the immigrant that has come to stay. The federal authorities when granting citizenship rights do not put one through a form of examination designed to ascertain whether he has attained to these qualities before they grant him his papers. But though the demand has not taken such concrete form it is nevertheless there palpably and none perceives it better than that immigrant who has been inoculated with the fever for Americanization. I have seen in the homes of foreigners certificates of American citizenship framed like college diplomas and hung on the walls. I have heard the owners of these diplomas of citizenship speak disparagingly of their own peoples and lands and exalt everything American, except prohibition. A kind of Americamania dominates their feelings and attitudes. Yet to the Americans themselves, I mean not the Americanized but the whole Americans, these proud citizens are Greeks or Bulgars or Polaks; not infrequently, Dagos, Wops, Bohunks.

What then eventually happens to these people? Do they continue living in a shroud of deception, or do they sooner or later see through the illusion and tire of their fidelity to America? At length I believe every immigrant begins to think of the old country. Many return with the thought of looking things over and remaining there. But they immediately find that while they have not made of themselves whole Americans, they have become so different from their own people and their mode of living has undergone such a drastic change that the prospect of resuming habitation in their native lands depresses them. There by their own people they are regarded as Americans and are looked upon with a not too approving eye. In America they are foreigners. What are they? They speak well neither English nor their mother tongues. . . .

In Bulgaria I am not wholly a Bulgarian; in the United States not wholly an American. I have to go through life with a dual nationality. When in the United States I long for the sleepy villages and the intimate life of the Balkans. When I am in the Balkans I dream of America day and night. An American made motor car seen on the street, an advertising poster announcing the showing of a motion picture made in the United States, anything closely or remotely connected with America is enough to send thrills through my spine. I was taking an afternoon nap in the house of a friend in Sofia and upon waking was told that I had been talking in my sleep. "What did I say?" I inquired, afraid of having revealed some secrets, with which one's head is always filled in the Balkans. "Nothing much," they comforted me, "You just kept blabbering about America!"

And shall I forget my joy upon my return to America! I was downright foolish. I felt like a child at the sight of his mother from whom it had been separated for months. Without unpacking my things, I left my room at the hotel and for nearly two hours walked up and down Broadway like a man possessed. Everything that my eyes beheld, I felt like embracing within my arms.

But here I am. A year has barely gone by and I am ready to embrace a Balkan donkey with fraternal affection. Yet I cannot leave America, though I am but half an American.

A Sense of Shame

I am sixteen years old and I was a freshman in high school when I quit . . . We live in an American neighborhood, and there were hardly any Jewish boys in my class. We used to live in a Jewish neighborhood, but we moved so I would keep away from the gang. So my mother figured it out.

I don't like to bring my American friends around. They were born here and so were their parents. My mother speaks 'English' to them, and they make fun of her. When I ask her to leave them alone she says: 'They are only goyim (Gentiles), ain't I good enough to entertain them?' Sure, she 'entertains' them—at my expense. My father won't allow us to play ball on the lot. He says it's a waste of time and a disgrace to make such a lot of noise over nothing. He was raised in Poland. But then he don't believe in sweatshops either, but has never been anything but a cutter in a sweatshop. It's awfully embarrassing to bring any American friends to the house. In New York it was different. We lived on the East Side, and those who were not Jews were something worse than that,

From Pauline V. Young, "Jim's Own Story," *Survey* 59 (15 March 1928): 777-778.

and we did not care. My brother was raised there and he even went to Hebrew School, and to *shuhl* [the synagogue] with my dad.

I hate to stick around here with no friends and nothing to do. My mother reported me to the judge of the Juvenile Court. He told me to stay off Augusta Street, and I did for a couple of days, but I was not going to be lonesome all by myself, and when I started to long for the guys, I ditched school and went out there to join them.

They sure are a slick bunch, and we have a lot of fun together. We can play ball all we want to, besides there are many playgrounds in that neighborhood, and the directors are congenial fellows, but we don't stick around there all the time. We like to see the city, we like to go to the beaches. Some of the boys have a car and we drive around the city and sometimes go to the beach. We don't plan our doings, some one hits upon an idea and we all act on it. Sure we have to follow the leader. You got to, if you want to stick around a gang. Our leader is slick and smart, and his orders are worth taking. He is sure of himself, he plays fair and divides even. He is naturally boss.

I got in trouble many times while with the gang. I was in Juvenile Hall several times. The longest I ever stayed there was two months. That was for truancy. But when I went back to my old school I started ditching school again. I did not like the teachers nor their subjects. It's pretty bad business to have a court record, the school knows about it, the guys tease you, and your parents worry and nag. Once I was arrested for fishing in a lagoon in a park. We didn't know we could not fish there, and we landed in Juvenile, but the night watchman looked us over and said: 'There ain't no use bringing them kids here, you just make criminals out-a them, and besides we ain't got no room.' And they let us go. Once a bunch of boys got arrested for trying to get money from milk bottles to go to Venice and have a good time. It costs at least a dollar to have fun. It costs fifty cents to rent a bathing suit. Sure, I have one but it got many rips and is the New Yorker kind. My mother figures that if I don't like that suit I won't go to the beach, but she has another guess coming. Then when you are at the beach you want to have fun at the Fun House, or at a show and some food. My parents don't believe in beaches and never go swimming. I don't like to stay home, and my parents don't understand what boys need, and they expect me to be old-fashioned and go to *shuhl*.

I have never taken very much stock in religion. I don't see any sense in it. Our Sabbath begins Friday at sunset, but my father works in the shop all day Saturday. Oh, he sighs and hopes to be in the land of the 'faithful' before he dies, but that don't help him any. I don't see why a faithful people should suffer and be laughed at like we are. My parents nag me to go to *shuhl* on holidays. They make many sacrifices to keep their traditions, but they don't mean anything much in my life. It's different with my brother, he got a start in New York in a Jewish community, but I can't be friends with Gentiles at school and at work and stick up for European ways too. That's just why I don't like to stay home. I don't want to hurt my parents and I can't follow their advice. . . .

Ethnic pride and preservation

Whatever the alienation of some second-generation children, a strong sense of ethnic identification and pride persisted within various groups. Lodge and fraternal associations maintained native cultural traditions, particularly as individual ethnic groups clustered in relatively small, tightly knit communities in urban areas. Interestingly, this also involved secondary struggles within larger groups. For example, there was a tense, at times bitter, rivalry between established German Jews and the new Jewish immigrants from eastern Europe as they differed in language, culture, and religious customs. Among Catholics, new arrivals, such as Poles and Italians, bristled under the dominant Irish hierarchy of the church. This next selection reflects some of this hostility.

A few months ago Archbishop Ireland said that the Catholic churches in our country, the United States, should be Americanized. This was an insult to all Polish parishes in Chicago as well as in the United States. Polish priests in Chicago are greatly opposed to the demands of Archbishop Keane and Bishop Eis to have all sermons spoken in the English language.

Polish people are greatly opposed to this form of Catholicism compelling Polish Catholic people to listen to sermons spoken in the English language, when the majority of older people do not understand it.

If this request is fulfilled, the Catholics will demand that the Germans, Italians, and all other nationalities do likewise. This question was raised by Archbishop Keane against the Poles. For what reason? Are the Polish parishes getting too rich? Are they expanding too fast or is it that the Irish want to dominate the Catholic world? Can't the Polish Catholics have as much freedom as the other nationalities? Isn't the United States a land of Freedom? It is, but that is no reason that the Irish should have more preference than any other nationality.

The *Dziennik Chicagoski* was the first newspaper to take up the fight on behalf of us Poles. This newspaper wants to remind us Polish parents that if our children grow up and cannot speak their native tongue, the whole blame will rest on the shoulders of the parents. Therefore, now is the time to stand up and fight for your religious rights. In another article this paper pointed out that according to the rules of the church and the Bible, no one can restrict the use and

From "The Use of Polish in the Church" *Zgodat* (December 20, 1900). Works Progress Administration, *Chicago Foreign Language Press Survey* (Chicago, 1942).

teaching of any language in Catholic schools and churches. What did Archbishop Keane and Bishop Eis think of this idea?

It is true that Bishop Eis said in one of his speeches that the children in this country speak the English language better and more correctly than their own native tongue, but this is largely due to the fact that they came in contact with children speaking this language either in school or at play, while their native tongue is spoken mostly at home.

We Polish people should not trouble ourselves too much with the affairs of the French, the German, the Irish, or any other nationalities in regard to the church, but take care of our own interest. What are these countries doing to help Poland win back its freedom? Nothing. They want us Poles to be under the rule of other countries so they can do what they wish with us. Do they want to do the same with us Poles in regard to the Catholic religion?

The Polish National Alliance took up the fight here and is doing everything possible in its power to awaken within the Polish people the urge to fight for their rights and their native language.

Polish churches were built with the hard-earned money of us Polish people, who donated wholeheartedly; schools were erected, monuments in memory of Polish noblemen and heroes. Our museum and national treasury is a hundred times dearer to us Poles here than the museum and national treasury in Rappersville.

By this time the *Polish Courier* printed an article: "We haven't any right to fight if we have nothing to fight for, but the Polish people would be blind if they didn't fight to protect their own name and nationality. We know that the existence of the church depends on the support of the people and their donations. We must and should do our utmost to protect and prolong the life of the Polish Catholic churches. It is our life, our backbone; without it we are lost. No other nationality in this city can boast of as many churches, Catholic schools, amusement centers, and Polish clubs and societies as the Poles. Be proud of them; we need your support."

The Polish priests are doing their utmost to make the Polish parents realize the worth of this fight. They do not compel the Polish parents to force the children to attend Polish parochial schools; it is up to them whether their children learn the Polish language or attend Polish schools, but this is a minor factor in comparison with the fight that we are confronted with at the present time. We are fighting to continue the use of the Polish language in our sermons, because it is our solemn duty.

Nevertheless, we feel that Archbishop Keane and Bishop Eis will realize what it means to the Polish people to forbid them to use their native language; we feel that eventually this matter will be dropped.

CHAPTER 12

What we do at home is reflected in what we do abroad

Wounded Knee: "It was a good winter day...."

The Battle—or Massacre, depending upon one's angle of vision—of Wounded Knee ended three centuries of warfare with the Native Americans. More than 150 Sioux, including 44 women and 18 children, were slaughtered by the Seventh Cavalry, the same troop that had been humiliated fourteen years earlier in the Battle of Little Big Horn. The events at Wounded Knee have since become a symbol for the brutality and savagery of the years of struggle that led to that inevitable tragic day in South Dakota in December 1890. Black Elk, a holy man of the Ogalala Sioux, was there and later recalled the events. Was it more than coincidence that the final opposition to continental conquest just preceded the overseas imperialist adventures that developed during the next several decades?

. . . It was now near the end of the Moon of Popping Trees, and I was twenty-seven years old (December 1890). We heard that Big Foot was coming down from the Badlands with nearly four hundred people. Some of these were from Sitting Bull's band. They had run away when Sitting Bull was killed, and joined Big Foot on Good River. There were only about a hundred warriors in this band, and all the others were women and children and some old men. They were all starving and freezing, and Big Foot was so sick that they had to bring him along in a pony drag. They had all run away to hide in the Badlands, and they were coming in now because they were starving and freezing. When they crossed Smoky Earth River, they followed up Medicine Root Creek to its head. Soldiers were over there looking for them. The soldiers had everything and were not freezing and starving. Near Porcupine Butte the soldiers came up to the Big Foots, and they surrendered and went along with the soldiers to Wounded Knee Creek where the Brenan store is now.

It was in the evening when we heard that the Big Foots were camped over there with the soldiers, about fifteen miles by the old road from where we were. It was the next morning (December 29, 1890) that something terrible happened. . . .

In the morning I went out after my horses, and while I was out I heard

From *Black Elk Speaks: Being the Life Story of a Holy Man of the Ogalala Sioux*, by John G. Neihardt (New York: William Morrow & Co., 1932), pp. 257–268. Copyright 1932, 1959, 1961 by John G. Neihardt. Used by permission of the John G. Neihardt Trust.

Wounded Knee: after the battle.

shooting off toward the east, and I knew from the sound that it must be wagon-guns (cannon) going off. The sounds went right through my body, and I felt that something terrible would happen.

When I reached camp with the horses, a man rode up to me and said: "Hey-hey-hey! The people that are coming are fired on! I know it!"

I saddled up my buckskin and put on my sacred shirt. It was one I had made to be worn by no one but myself. It had a spotted eagle outstretched on the back of it, and the daybreak star was on the left shoulder, because when facing south that shoulder is toward the east. Across the breast, from the left shoulder to the right hip, was the flaming rainbow, and there was another rainbow around the neck, like a necklace, with a star at the bottom. At each shoulder, elbow; and wrist was an eagle feather; and over the whole shirt were red streaks of lightning. You will see that this was from my great vision, and you will know how it protected me that day.

I painted my face all red, and in my hair I put one eagle feather for the One Above.

It did not take me long to get ready, for I could still hear the shooting over there.

I started out alone on the old road that ran across the hills to Wounded Knee. I had no gun. I carried only the sacred bow of the west that I had seen in my great vision. I had gone only a little way when a band of young men came galloping after me. The first two who came up were Loves War and Iron Wasichu. I asked what they were going to do, and they said they were just going to see where the shooting was. Then others were coming up, and some older men. . . .

In a little while we had come to the top of the ridge where, looking to the east, you can see for the first time the monument and the burying ground on the little hill where the church is. That is where the terrible thing started. Just south of the burying ground on the little hill a deep dry gulch runs about east and west, very crooked, and it rises westward to nearly the top of the ridge where we were. It had no name, but the Wasichus sometimes call it Battle Creek now. We stopped on the ridge not far from the head of the dry gulch. Wagon guns were still going off over there on the little hill, and they were going off again where they hit along the gulch. There was much shooting down yonder, and there were many cries, and we could see cavalrymen scattered over the hills ahead of us. Cavalrymen were riding along the gulch and shooting into it, where the women and children were running away and trying to hide in the gullies and the stunted pines.

A little way ahead of us, just below the head of the dry gulch, there were some women and children who were huddled under a clay bank, and some cavalrymen were there pointing guns at them. . . .

I had no gun, and when we were charging, I just held the sacred bow out in front of me with my right hand. The bullets did not hit us at all.

We found a little baby lying all alone near the head of the gulch. I could not pick her up just then, but I got her later and some of my people adopted her. I just wrapped her up tighter in a shawl that was around her and left her there. It was a safe place, and I had other work to do. . . .

By now many other Lakotas, who had heard the shooting, were coming up from Pine Ridge, and we all charged on the soldiers. They ran eastward toward where the trouble began. We followed down along the dry gulch, and what we saw was terrible. Dead and wounded women and children and little babies were scattered all along there where they had been trying to run away. The soldiers had followed along the gulch, as they ran, and murdered them in there. Sometimes they were in heaps because they had huddled together, and some were scattered all along. Sometimes bunches of them had been killed and torn to pieces where the wagon guns hit them. I saw a little baby trying to suck its mother, but she was bloody and dead. . . .

When we drove the soldiers back, they dug themselves in, and we were not enough people to drive them out from there. In the evening they marched off up Wounded Knee Creek, and then we saw all that they had done there.

Men and women and children were heaped and scattered all over the flat at the bottom of the little hill where the soldiers had their wagon-guns, and westward up the dry gulch all the way to the high ridge, the dead women and children and babies were scattered.

When I saw this I wished that I had died too, but I was not sorry for the women and children. It was better for them to be happy in the other world, and I wanted to be there too. But before I went there I wanted to have revenge. I thought there might be a day, and we should have revenge.

After the soldiers marched away, I heard from my friend, Dog Chief, how the trouble started, and he was right there by Yellow Bird when it happened. This is the way it was:

In the morning the soldiers began to take all the guns away from the Big Foots, who were camped in the flat below the little hill where the monument and burying ground are now. The people had stacked most of their guns, and even their knives, by the tepee where Big Foot was lying sick. Soldiers were on the little hill and all around, and there were soldiers across the dry gulch to the south and over east along Wounded Knee Creek too. The people were nearly surrounded, and the wagon-guns were pointing at them.

Some had not yet given up their guns, and so the soldiers were searching all the tepees, throwing things around and poking into everything. There was a man called Yellow Bird, and he and another man were standing in front of the tepee where Big Foot was lying sick. They had white sheets around and over them, with eyeholes to look through, and they had guns under these. An officer came to search them. He took the other man's gun, and then started to take Yellow Bird's. But Yellow Bird would not let go. He wrestled with the officer, and while they were wrestling, the gun went off and killed the officer. Wasichus and some others have said he meant to do this, but Dog Chief was standing right there, and he told me it was not so. As soon as the gun went off, Dog Chief told me, an officer shot and killed Big Foot who was lying sick inside the tepee.

Then suddenly nobody knew what was happening, except that the soldiers were all shooting and the wagon-guns began going off right in among the people.

Many were shot down right there. The women and children ran into the gulch and up west, dropping all the time, for the soldiers shot them as they ran. There were only about a hundred warriors and there were nearly five hundred soldiers. The warriors rushed to where they had piled their guns and knives. They fought soldiers with only their hands until they got their guns.

Dog Chief saw Yellow Bird run into a tepee with his gun, and from there he killed soldiers until the tepee caught fire. Then he died full of bullets.

It was a good winter day when all this happened. The sun was shining. But after the soldiers marched away from their dirty work, a heavy snow began to fall. The wind came up in the night. There was a big blizzard, and it grew very cold. The snow drifted deep in the crooked gulch, and it was one long grave of butchered women and children and babies, who had never done any harm and were only trying to run away.

"Is America any better than Spain?": black soldiers in Cuba

Black soldiers comprised a significant part of the standing army. In the Spanish-American War, they fought with great distinction in both Cuba and the Philippines. In Cuba, for example, black troops played a crucial role in the Battle of San Juan Hill that made Theodore Roosevelt and the Rough Riders national heroes. The irony of black soldiers fighting for Cuban freedom was not lost on the men themselves. Their treatment in embarkation camps in the South, and their observations of the lack of a color line in Cuba, led some to question their place in American life. At the same time, as one of the following letters indicates, they for the most part remained willing to fight and die in defense of the nation's "flag and honor."

Troops debarking for Cuba, 1898.

Hon. H. C. Smith
Editor, *Gazette*

Dear Sir:

The Ninth Cavalry left Chickamauga on the 30th of April for Tampa, Fla. We arrived here (nine miles from Tampa) on May 3. From this port the army will sail for Cuba. We have in this camp here and at Tampa between 7,000 and 8,000 soldiers, artillery, one regiment of cavalry (the famous fighting Ninth) and the Twenty-fourth and Twenty-fifth infantries. The Ninth Cavalry's bravery and their skillfulness with weapons of war . . . is well known by all who have read the history of the last Indian war. . . .

Yesterday, May 12, the Ninth was ordered to be ready to embark at a moment's notice for Cuba. . . . We are here waiting for the order to march. Possibly before you shall have been in receipt of this communication, the Ninth, with the Twenty-fourth and Twenty-fifth infantries and eight batteries of artillery will be in Cuba. These men are anxious to go. The country will then hear and know of the bravery of these sable sons of Ham.

The American Negro is always ready and willing to take up arms, to fight and to lay down his life in defense of his country's flag and honor. All the way from northwest Nebraska this regiment was greeted with cheers and hurrahs. At places where we stopped the people assembled by the thousands. While the Ninth Cavalry band would play some national air the people would raise their hats, men, women and children would wave their handkerchiefs, and the heavens would resound with their hearty cheers. The white hand shaking the black hand. The hearty "goodbyes," "God bless you," and other expressions aroused the patriotism of our boys. . . . These demonstrations, so enthusiastically given, greeted us all the way until we reached Nashville. At this point we arrived about 12:30 a.m. There were about 6,000 colored people there to greet us (very few white people) but not a man was allowed by the railroad officials to approach the cars. From there until we reached Chattanooga there was not a cheer given us, the people living in gross ignorance, rags and dirt. Both white and colored seemed amazed; they looked at us in wonder. Don't think they have intelligence enough to know that Andrew Jackson is dead. . . .

The prejudice against the Negro soldier and the Negro was great, but it was of heavenly origin to what it is in this part of Florida, and I suppose that what is true here is true in other parts of the state. Here, the Negro is not allowed to purchase over the same counter in some stores that the white man purchases over. The southerners have made their laws and the Negroes know and obey them. They never stop to ask a white man a question. He (Negro) never thinks

From Cleveland Gazette, May 13, 1898; (Milwaukee) Wisconsin Weekly Advocate, January 18, 1900. Both letters are reprinted in Willard B. Gatewood, Jr., *"Smoked Yankees" and the Struggle for Empire, 1898-1902* (Urbana, University of Illinois Press, 1971), pp. 27-29; 233-235.

of disobeying. You talk about freedom, liberty, etc. Why sir, the Negro of this country is freeman and yet a slave. Talk about fighting and freeing poor Cuba and of Spain's brutality; of Cuba's murdered thousands, and starving reconcentradoes. Is America any better than Spain? Has she not subjects in her very midst who are murdered daily without a trial of judge or jury? Has she not subjects in her own borders whose children are half-fed and half-clothed, because their father's skin is black. . . . Yet the Negro is loyal to his country's flag. . . .

The four Negro regiments are going to help free Cuba, and they will return to their homes, some then mustered out and begin again to fight the battle of American prejudice. . . .

Yours truly,
Geo. W. Prioleau
Chaplain, Ninth Cavalry

Editor
Wisconsin Weekly Advocate

Just before our departure for the States I will write you once more. I am very glad to state that the health of the regiment is good and it is with regret that I state that we will return to Texas. . . . I am tired of being in the South and receiving such treatment as we have generally received in the South, for that section I can pass by, and I am sorry to state, Mr. Editor, that our recruiting officers have not been as careful as they might have been, for the last recruits our regiment got since the war have not been up to the standard. Give us men who are an honor to the race. . . . No better boys ever shouldered a gun than those boys fresh from schools or factories of the South and East; and they proved their valor upon the battle field, for a good soldier is very obedient, no matter how harsh discipline is; and when they were discharged it was with regret that the older soldiers saw them go; but of course as long as everything remains as it is in H Troop, it will be hard to keep a good class of men. It takes months of hard training to make a soldier, not always abuse and to keep from them what is justly due a soldier—which I shall state more about in my next letter. The troops are expecting to leave here within the next three or four days and I am afraid that many will suffer from chills and fever as they did when they returned from Cuba in '98. Then it was summer. Give me Cuba rather than any section of the South. . . .

. . . Cuba, if everything remains at peace, should be the home of the colored man. Here you have everything to come for; it is not far from the States; and I am sure that if . . . prominent colored men should go to Cuba, they would go to Cuba, not far away to Africa. It does not require much work to farm, and it is just as healthy, with proper sanitary conditions, as America. This place was in a terribly filthy condition; no wonder people died of fever and other diseases so fast. Then Americans who came to the island eat too much of its fruit. It is impossible for them to eat this without having the fever, and the mango which is so tempting after being in the sun after falling from a tree twenty minutes, is about a sure case of yellow fever. Keep out of the rain as much as possible until you are acclimated. Your chances are just as good as the native for health. Mr. Editor, you find the colored man in all kinds of business and trade; all colors working together in the greatest harmony. I have heard a great deal against the Cubans, but could the American Negro say as much, and not submit as the American does, to about everything: and I only hope the time will come when they will call a halt and strike back; and if our general government don't protect you, protect yourself. There have been Americans who came to this island and tried to . . . draw the color line, but the Cubans would not submit to such treatment and cleaned up the place; and if they will only take lessons from the Cuban, America will then be the land of the brave and free and not until then. It is only a question of time when it will come, if the South is not more just to the American blacks. It is with regret that we are about to return to the States and to the South, but thank God my time is not long to remain and when I soldier again my regiment or troop will never be stationed in the South. I cannot risk all and receive no credit and [have] . . . all my rights taken from me because I am black. . . .

Respectfully yours,
John E. Lewis
H Troop, Tenth Cavalry

"Civilizing"the Philippines

Following victory over the Spanish in 1898, the United States acquired a new colonial empire. The question of annexing the Philippine Islands, however, aroused bitter debate within the nation. The pro-imperialist forces successfully argued their case in terms of national interest, and equally important for a nation believing in the ideals of the "American Mission," they emphasized the need for the United States to "civilize" its "little brown brothers." Actually, when the war had started, there had been an active Filipino independence movement against Spain, and Filipino leaders were less than gratified with the American annexation. Consequently, we inherited a widespread insurrection and guerrilla war. After three years of fighting and over eight thousand native deaths, the task of "civilizing" was over.

William Howard Taft, the civilian governor of the islands, referred to the insurrectionists as "traitors," a curious choice of terms for people who did not subscribe to the United States Constitution. The unorthodox character of such wars (as we were to learn again in Vietnam sixty years later) provoked horrible atrocities on both sides. In this selection, former Sergeant Leroy E. Hallock described the "water cure" torture used to gain information, and the burning of native villages.

Washington, D. C., Saturday, May 3, 1902.

. . . Q. Where was your regiment stationed during the period you were in the Philippine Islands?—A. The first three months I was stationed at Iloilo. After that the headquarters of the company was Leon, Panay.

Q. Did you see any cases of water cure or torture applied to the natives?—A. Yes, sir.

Q. Where?—A. At Leon.

Q. State the circumstances, please.—A. There were about ten or a dozen natives captured that were thought to be implicated in the murder of one of the members of our company.

Q. O'Hearn?—A. Yes, sir.

Q. It was stated in one of the reports that he was roasted over a slow fire and then hacked to death with bolos.—A. That is the confession of the natives; yes.

Q. And these men were captured who were believed to have had something to do with that?—A. Yes, sir.

Q. Now you may go on and state the circumstances.—A. What led to the capture of these natives, it was reported that Captain Glenn or some soldiers under his orders gave the water cure to a native and he confessed and told who the others were that took part in the killing of O'Hearn, and these members of our company captured these natives and gave them the water cure, and they confessed it.

By Senator BURROWS:

Q. Confessed to what?—A. To having a part in the killing of O'Hearn.

Q. Having had a part in it?—A. Yes, sir.

By the CHAIRMAN [Senator Lodge]:

Q. Who inflicted this punishment upon the natives?—A. The members of Company I.

Q. Were they ordered to do so?—A. Yes, sir.

Q. Who ordered them to do so?—A. The first sergeant.

From U.S. Senate, Hearings before the Committee on the Philippines, *Affairs in the Philippine Islands*, 57th Congress, 1st session, 1902, part 3, pp. 1969-1979.

Q. Who was the first sergeant?—A. Januarius Manning.

Q. Do you know him?—A. Yes, sir.

Q. Is he now a resident of Boston?—A. Yes, sir.

Q. You may state any details you wish in regard to the treatment of these natives.

Senator ALLISON. You saw this?

The WITNESS. Yes, sir.

By the CHAIRMAN:

Q. You saw the water cure inflicted?—A. Yes, sir.

Q. Did you take part in it?—A. No, sir.

By Senator RAWLINS:

Q. Who was in command of this company at that time?—A. Alexander Gregg.

Q. How many troops were at Leon at the time this occurred?—A. About half of the company, I should say.

Q. Was Captain Gregg there at the time?—A. Yes, sir; he was there at the quarters.

Q. How far from the quarters was this torture inflicted?—A. Less than a hundred yards.

Q. Did all the command know about it at the time?—A. Yes, sir.

Q. Captain Gregg knew about it?—A. I don't know how he could help knowing it.

Q. You say that a member of your company had been reported killed?—A. Yes, sir.

Q. That information, I understand you to say, was derived from Captain Glenn?—A. I think a detail of our company was out looking for O'Hearn and they made a detail under Captain Glenn, and they got some native and gave him the water cure and he confessed and gave the others away and told who took part in it.

Q. That was, as you understand it, the result of the application of this torture; as a result of that torture some native, to relieve himself, stated he had taken part in the killing of this soldier?—A. Yes, sir.

Senator ALLISON. I object to Senator Rawlins putting words in the mouth of the witness—"to relieve himself." He said nothing of the kind.

By Senator RAWLINS:

Q. I am asking if that was not what was reported to you; that, as a result of this torture, this native stated he had participated in this killing?—A. Yes, sir.

Q. And named about a dozen other natives?—A. Yes, sir.

Q. And these twelve who were also reported by Captain Glenn to have been named by this native after the water cure had been given to him, where did they live?—A. In the vicinity of 5 or 6 miles from our quarters.

Q. Five or six miles from the army?—A. Yes, sir.

Q. And upon that information they were arrested?—A. Yes, sir.

Q. And brought to Leon?—A. Yes, sir.

Q. And they were taken out and the water torture applied to each of them?—A. Yes, sir.

Q. You may state whether it was given to them more than once.—A. It was given to them on two different days; it was given to them on August 21, 1900, and on August 23, 1900, to the best of my recollection.

Q. And what was the purpose of subjecting them to the torture?—A. To see if they had participated in the murder of O'Hearn.

Q. The first day they did not get all the information they desired—was that it?—A. Yes, sir.

Q. And so the torture was repeated the following day?—A. Yes, sir.

Q. And on the following day, as I understand you, these persons who were subjected to this torture confessed that they participated in the killing of the soldier?—A. On the 21st and 23d of August.

The CHAIRMAN. Was this 1900?

The WITNESS. Yes, sir.

By Senator RAWLINS:

Q. What was the effect upon these natives of giving this water cure?—A. They would swell up—their stomach would swell up pretty large—and I have seen blood come from their mouth after they had been given a good deal of it.

Q. And on the second day, do you know what information they gave; how was it obtained?—A. No, sir; only that they confessed to having had a part in it. . . .

Q. What was done with these 12 men after they had been subjected to the water cure?—A. They were confined there in the guardhouse. Some of them escaped and some of them were killed while trying to escape.

Q. How many of them were shot to your knowledge?—A. I should say five or six.

Q. You know of five or six of them having been shot?—A. Yes, sir.

Q. How soon after the infliction of the water torture?—A. I could not state the exact time. It was before we left there.

Senator BEVERIDGE. Shot while trying to escape?

The WITNESS. Yes, sir. . . .

Q. While you were there were there any villages burned?—A. Yes, sir.

Q. How many?—A. I was only present at the time one was burned; but I have known of as many as half a dozen being burned.

Q. How large were these villages?—A. The one that I witnessed being burned I should say was three or four thousand people; that that many people lived there. . . .

Q. Do you know of these towns being burned simply by hearsay?—A. I witnessed one of them.

Q. But the others; do you know of their being burned simply by hearsay?—A.

I know of their being burned by the members of the company talking about them.

Q. Can you name the member of the company who told you about that now?—A. I could not name anyone that told me, but I can name several that were present.

Q. Can you name anyone who told you?—A. No, sir.

Senator BEVERIDGE. I object to any testimony on this subject that is hearsay.

By Senator RAWLINS:

Q. I will ask the witness this. You observed the flames in the distance, did you?—A. The smoke; not the flames.

Senator BEVERIDGE. Is this direct examination?

Senator RAWLINS. This is cross-examination.

Q. And you saw the smoke of the villages that you did not see being burned?—A. I saw smoke from this town of Tubungan when that was burned.

Q. Have you been over the ground where these towns were, that you learned were burned? Have you been over that ground since they were burned?—A. Yes, sir.

Q. And what have you observed there at those towns; were they left or were they burned?—A. They appeared to be deserted; everything was burned, houses and shacks, with the exception, perhaps, of a few on the outside of the town, on the roads or trails that would not be burned, that were close to the town. . . .

Q. What became of these people who inhabited these towns that were burned?—A. I think they went into other towns. They didn't build up the towns at all.

Q. They did not attempt to rebuild the towns?—A. Not to my knowledge.

Q. Do you know whether or not they were permitted to rebuild these towns that were destroyed?—A. I could not say.

Q. Do you know of any attempt on the part of the natives to rebuild any town that was destroyed?—A. No, sir.

Q. Did you know of any natives around Leon who were begging for food?—A. Yes, sir. They have a market day there in those towns once a week, and on that day a good many beggars would be around.

Q. You may state to what extent the burning went in the case of these towns that were burned—whether it extended to food and household articles and things of that description.—A. Yes, sir.

Q. Did it so extend?—A. The one that I witnessed being burned, they did not have time to get anything out to speak of; they might have had time to get what valuables they had out, but they did not have time to move their furniture or food.

By Senator ALLISON:

Q. You only witnessed the burning of one town?—A. Yes, sir.

Q. And that was done rapidly?—A. Yes, sir.

By Senator RAWLINS:

Q. This burning you have described and the infliction of the water torture—you may state whether or not it was a matter of common repute among the soldiers with whom you came in contact that those things were practiced.

Senator BEVERIDGE. I object. We have had that question up two or three times.

The CHAIRMAN. I think the witness is entitled to say whether the thing was a matter of common repute.

The WITNESS. It was reported that if the soldiers wanted to get any information out of the natives they gave them the water cure, and in any town where there was any evidence of being insurgents the town was burned.

By Senator RAWLINS:

Q. Then, as I understand it, that was a matter of common repute; the inflicting of this water torture and the burning of these towns was a matter of common repute?

Senator ALLISON. If you understand it, you do not understand it from the witness.

Senator RAWLINS. I asked the witness whether or not it was a matter of common repute, and he said it was reported among the soldiers that whenever they wanted to get information they applied the water torture, and when they obtained the information and they found that a town contained insurgents they burned the town. Let it rest at that.

Senator ALLISON. I think that is right. . . .

By Senator RAWLINS:

Q. That you have no information about it except by hearsay, as I understand it; that is, what the others told you?—A. What the members of the company talked about and told to each other.

Q. All you know about it is what the others told you?—A. I was not a witness to it.

Q. How many men of your company had been killed during the entire time you were stationed at Leon in Panay—you were there all the time?—A. Yes, sir; on the island of Panay.

Q. How many men were killed?—A. Two men.

Q. Two men altogether?—A. Yes, sir.

Q. How many natives were killed during the same time by American soldiers?—A. I could not state the number.

Q. About how many?—A. It would be very hard for me to tell.

Q. Give us a general idea, if you can.—A. Well, if we got into a skirmish we could not tell how many men were killed or wounded.

Q. Were there a good many killed?—A. There were more killed than there were Americans.

Q. How many do you know of yourself having been killed?—A. Do you mean altogether in the fights we had there?

Q. Yes.—A. That the regiment participated in?

Q. That your company participated in—yes; the regiment.—A. In the neighborhood of 200 or 300, I should say, for a guess.

Q. How many fights did you yourself participate in?—A. Three, I think, sir.

Q. And in those three fights how many natives were killed?—A. In the neighborhood of 200, I should say.

Q. How many Americans were killed in those three fights?—A. I should say 20. . . .

In pursuit of "niggers" and "outlaws"

A black soldier fighting in the Philippine insurrection complained of the sacrifices blacks made "for a cause so unpopular among our people." The racist connotations of the war were inescapable, and probably most white soldiers felt a similar contempt for the natives as the marine sergeant who in the following selection described them as "niggers." In the light of later Vietnam experiences, the sergeant's closing comments on command responsibility for the behavior of field troops are particularly interesting.

. . . The 9th Infantry, Co. C had been massacred at the Isle of Samar, farther south than we had been, and as the Army got cold feet, they called for the Marines to get there and clean the place up. The 9th Infantry, Co. C were on too friendly terms with the native women and had them spend a lot of time around the quarters. On September 28, 1901, when the natives had got ready, the women were all in the quarters eating supper with the men, and their arms were laying around. The signal was passed and the natives rushed in upon them, while the women threw themselves on the men so they could not get their arms in time to save themselves. The niggers killed 59 of Co. C, and the few that were saved made their escape by water and got to Catabalogan where General Smith had his headquarters. I don't know what he did at the time, but we were hurried there to do the cleaning up. We stopped at General Smith's headquarters, and I went there with Major Waller for our final orders, which he gave us. The order was to kill and burn everything that we carried out except the women and children. Major Waller then proceeded to Samar to carry out the orders. We got there about noon of October 6th, I think, when we were met by all the

From Harry C. Adriance, "History of the Life of a Soldier in the Philippine Islands. . . . " Typescript (Madison: State Historical Society of Wisconsin) pp. 18–22. Used by permission of the director.

natives who gave us a fine welcome and took their boats and helped us get our supplies ashore, as they thought that the best way to make friends, and give us the same dose later on which they came near doing in another way, but they failed. We put out a guard as soon as we landed, and I guess they thought we were afraid of them, but the Marines always protected themselves first and talked afterward. We had a scout guide with us who proved his worth later on. After letting them have a good look at us carrying our arms with us everywhere we went, they left and we proceeded to get things ready for our comfort, when we got a chance. We got our things landed and stored away, and after having a fair meal we turned in, with a good guard stationed with a Colts Automatic, at the main way of the town. We had the first good rest of the trip, but not removing our clothing, belts or guns. . . .

We began to take short trips inland where we tried to catch the leaders, but we found them gone as they had been notified when we left and where we were going, but we soon found the one who was giving the news. . . . We made a number of trips under Captain John A. Day and Captain Bearse, but never had results. Finally our scout found there was a bunch of niggers up the river, and we prepared to go after them. We put a 3 inch gun and two Colts on some boats towed by a steam launch from a ship anchored there, and with the men from the ship we made quite a showing. We left a strong guard behind to protect our quarters when we started up the river. We had not gone over a mile when the bullets began to fly and we put our guns into action with our 3 inch firing ahead and the Colts clearing the brush on the shores. They soon took french leave, but we found some good ones left behind. Only one of our men was wounded slightly. We kept this up for a while, when we saw a block house on a hill which one 3 inch shell scattered, and a couple left to tell nothing. We found a fine place to view the country here, which was poor and mountainous, and nothing being cultivated.

After having a rest and a bite to eat, we set out to return. While on our way, we sent a few more shots as a reminder that we were still on the job and would call sometime later, which we did with success, and took a few prisoners, which we could use in keeping the place clean around the quarters and the Officers' building, which was located on the hill about 200 yards from us. After a few trips to other places, our scout found there was a cavern around the shore about a mile away, where the natives met often. The natives officers were there and would be there the next day, so Major Waller sent a lot of us over under darkness and laid in wait for them, when they arrived about 10:00 A.M., and we gave them a grand welcome. After getting all the news we could from them, the scout found a Macabee he knew, and we spared him for future use, as the scout said he was our friend, but we always had him where we could see him. We left about 15 leaders of the niggers' army where they could always be found. We returned to camp well paid for our hard trip.

About the latter part of October we made a trip to a village in the mountains where they were said to be located. With one day's rations and a load of bullets in our haversacks, led by Major Waller, we went up the river by boat, landed and made the boats fast so we could return that night. . . . On the way down the river, we were nearly there, when we saw a boat coming with a native waving a white flag. We were going to shoot, but the Major stopped us and said we would see what was up and to keep an eye on the shore, as there may be a trap. The native told us that the natives had made an attempt to capture the guards and quarters and then to have caught us on our way down the river. We forgot our troubles at once and hurried to get at them for revenge. It took all the power the Major had to stop us. On reaching camp we saw nothing wrong until we saw the prison in the place full of niggers, about 150 men, women and children, with the president at the window. The president was the ruler of the people and always kept tabs on all our doings, so he could send a signal when we were going out and they could get away. We found out he was the boss when they massacred the 9th Infantry and was trying the same on us, but failed, as he did not take the Marines seriously. The next day business began. The women and the girls and boys under 16 years were turned loose and were told to get as far away as possible and to be quick about it, which they did. The chief was then brought out and was given a real third degree. He admitted that he was the one who had caused all the trouble and begged for mercy, which he got later on. After getting all the locations of the outlaws' places, Captain Day was put in charge of the finishing details which were to be carried out about a half mile from camp. With plenty of volunteers, they had a clean trip and returned empty handed. After a few more trips, the Major got the report that the island was safe and clear, when in short time we were relieved by the Army, who need not be afraid as there was no longer any danger and we were ordered to Cavite, where there was a Court Martial for the Officers who had carried out the orders of the Department, General Smith. He said he never gave any such orders, and I was one who heard him give them. The Major was cleared from all charges and that was the end of it, but I am sure it hurt his chances of becoming our next Commandant, which it did. . . .

Victor's justice

The following excerpts from War Department reports reveal in stark simplicity the brutalizing impact of the Philippine insurrection on both sides. These records summarize the court-martial trials of soldiers for offenses against the natives and the military commission trials of insurrectionists "for cruelty to soldiers in violation of the laws of war." The records, however, reveal the special nature of a victor's justice in that Filipinos and Americans, who had committed similar crimes, were charged with quite different offenses and received vastly different sentences.

Memorandum in regard to trials of Filipinos by military commissions for cruelty against soldiers, January 1, 1900, to March 13, 1902.

NAME	OFFENSE AND DATE OF ITS COMMISSION	SENTENCE			REMARKS
		Death	Life	Years	
Raimondo Hermanes, a native	Murdering Q. M. Sergt. Albert Votrie, Company K, Thirty-ninth Infantry, U.S.V.; assaulting with intent to kill Corpl. Isaac Evans, Company K, Thirty-ninth Infantry, U.S. V.; and assaulting with intent to kill Pvt. Edward Behring, Company K, Thirty-ninth Infantry, U.S. V., at Bagbay, Luzon, P.I., Feb. 2, 1900.	Yes	—	—	Commuted to imprisonment at hard labor for 20 years.
Nicacio Leonor, a native	Murdering Q. M. Sergt. Albert Votrie, Company K, Thirty-ninth Infantry, U.S. V.; assaulting with intent to kill Corpl. Isaac Evans, Company K, Thirty-ninth Infantry, U.S. V.; and assaulting with intent to kill Pvt. Edward Behring, Company K, Thirty-ninth Infantry, U.S. V., at Bagbay, Luzon, P.I., Feb. 2, 1900.	Yes	—	—	Commuted to 20 years.
Juan Tuson, a native	Murdering Q. M. Sergt. Albert Votrie, Company K, Thirty-ninth Infantry, U.S. V.; assaulting with intent to kill Corpl. Isaac Evans, Company K, Thirty-ninth Infantry, U.S. V.; and assaulting with intent to kill Pvt. Edward Behring, Company K, Thirty-ninth Infantry, U.S. V., at Bagbay, Luzon, P.I., Feb. 2, 1900.	Yes	—	—	Commuted to 20 years.
Macario Estrella, a native	Assaulting with intent to murder Serg. Charles W. Ray, Company I, Twenty-second U.S. Infantry, at San Fernando, P.I., Mar. 15, 1900.	—	Yes	—	
Vicente Prado, a native	Murdering two Americans, Anthony Gurzinsky, Company C, Thirteenth U.S. Infantry; other party, name unknown, Apr. 2, 1900; murdering two Igorrotes, names unknown, May 3, 1900; murdering Fruto M. Flavia and his son Francis, May 3, 1900.	Yes	—	—	

From U.S. Senate, Hearings before the Committee on the Philippines, *Affairs in the Philippine Islands,* 57th Congress, 1st session, 1902, part 3, pp. 2070-2074.

Memorandum in regard to trials by courts-martial and military commissions of persons in or connected with the Army in the Philippine Islands for offenses against natives, showing offenses, sentences, and remarks (if any) in reviews of proceedings touching subject of cruelty to natives.

NAME AND ORGANIZATION	OFFENSE AND DATE OF ITS COMMISSION	SENTENCE			REMARKS
		Dishonorable discharge	Forfeiture of pay and allowances	Confinement	
Geo. F. Townsend, Company B, Twenty-third Infantry.	Assaulting native in shop with intent to do him harm. Oct., 1898. (62d A. of W.)	No	$30	3 months	
Jas. A. Rusher, Company B, Twenty-third Infantry.	Entering house and demanding money and striking native over eye. Nov., 1898. (62d A. of W.)	No	$60	6 months	
Will F. Scholtz, Company H, Twenty-third Infantry.	Taking fish from natives and selling same for $40 Mexican. Collecting toll from Chinaman to amount of $1. (62d A. of W.) March, 1899.	Yes	Yes	1 year	
Oliver Smith, Company A, Twentieth Infantry.	Larceny of 67 cents from native. (62d A. of W.) March, 1899.	No	$40	—	
Walter Turnbull, jr., Company I, Fourteenth Infantry.	Assault and battery by wounding native woman on head with bayonet, Feb., 1899, and creating disturbance in native shop by assaulting proprietor while drunk, March, 1899. (62d A. of W.)	Yes	Yes	3 years	
John R. Roberts, Company I, Twenty-ninth Infantry.	Larceny of pocket knife from native; value, 7 cents Mexican; June, 1899. (58th A. of W.)	No	$30	—	
William W. Morgan, Company M, Twentieth Infantry.	Larceny of $40, property of native, Mar., 1899. (58th A. of W.)	Yes	Yes	18 months	
John C. Lund, Company G,	Larceny of watch of native, May	Yes	Yes	2 months	Confinement remitted.

Gunboat diplomacy in Mexico

An aggressive economic interest animated American activities both in the formal empire and in areas where the United States sought special favors or control. During the second decade of the twentieth century, American oil companies actively exploited the rich oil fields in Mexico. Special privileges were gained (often by bribery) from the Mexican government and the companies had the overt diplomatic and military support of the United States government. The following report by the commander of the cruiser U.S.S. *Annapolis*, stationed on the east coast of Mexico, commented on radical labor activities by the Industrial Workers of the World (IWW) in the oil fields. The report may have been somewhat exceptional, for Captain Louis Richardson registered a complaint against the oil companies' repressive labor policies and the lack of tact by American diplomats in dealing with Mexicans. His concern, of course, merely represented a different, yet perhaps more effective, means of insuring a steady flow of oil vital to American needs.

The city of Tampico is very quiet at the present time. The I.W.W's have been squelched and I do not apprehend any trouble at present from German activities. There is some restlessness amongst the employees and a tendency on the part of the employers to give the demands of labor very little consideration.

I have talked with the oil company officials and endeavored to pursuade them to use some diplomacy in dealing with bona fide labor questions, suggesting that when a labor committee made demands that it appeared to me that it would be good policy for them not to flatly refuse to consider the demands but for them to investigate carefully the increased costs of various commodities that the workman and his family required; to investigate the bearing and manner of the various foremen toward the Mexican laborer; the condition and quality of food that was served, and the sanitary conditions where the workmen were employed, and instead of a flat refusal, to prepare an impersonal reply based upon the above investigations, stating that they were very much interested in the welfare of the workmen and that steps had been taken to improve conditions where the complaint seemed to be just, etc. In other words, to take a conciliatory attitude. I fear, however, that the oil companies are not inclined to do so as they feel that the United States will step in if unsatisfactory conditions arise, and as the local head of one company said to me in the

From Record Group 80, Louis C. Richardson to Navy Department, 31 August 1917. Records of the Department of the Navy, National Archives, File 4225/175. Material provided by Mr. Robert Halstead.

presence of the heads of five other companies, that they would assist in shutting down the oil business for a month if they thought the United States would intervene.

The local Mexican officials, I am confident, will stop any strike that is conducted by I.W.W's or German influence. To what extent they will interfere in a bona fide strike for higher wages or better living conditions I am not prepared to say but I am sure they will co-operate almost to any extent to keep the port open. . . .

I have had several long talks with the American Consul and believe that I have succeeded in getting him to change somewhat his attitude towards the Mexicans. I advised him that we all appreciated the beautiful spirit of hospitality that the oil men showed us and that we could continue to accept it, but in accepting it we must guard against letting their point of view and their prejudices dominate us in handling situations that arise; that we must remember that this is Mexico and that the local officials and Mexicans should be treated in the same manner as we would treat officials of a first class power, so far as courtesy goes, and that we must try to carry out, as far as we know, the policy of the administration. I am satisfied that the American Consul is now endeavoring to work along these lines, notwithstanding the fact that he is greatly prejudiced (or at least has little like for the Mexicans).

As set forth in the first paragraph of this letter , I have endeavored to get the oil men to correct certain abuses, and at the same time handle the Mexicans, especially the laborers, in a conciliatory or diplomatic manner. The Mexican workman is very sensitive and as a rule are illiterate but they realize that they are no longer Peons and they resent any abusive talk to them by American foremen. A great many of these foremen are very aggressive and with little education and little patience or liking for Mexican laborers and are not as careful as they should be in talking to their workmen. A little bit of courtesy goes a long way towards handling the Mexican and the ignorant class are very much like children. They take offense at small things and will do almost anything for you if you have a kindly disposition. However, this statement would be incomplete unless I called attention to the inherent racial dislike that does exist. The large mass of Mexicans are at heart jealous and envious of the white man's superiority and this fact is used by the Mexican politician when he wishes to arouse the masses against a foreign nation, but under ordinary conditions when the people are not lead by a politician, kindness and diplomacy will win them and cause them to give you a kind of worship.

I believe the policy of friendliness and courtesy causes them to co-operate with you in every way possible and avoids numerous annoyances that could be put in your way, but one must be wide awake and remember that when very important questions arise that will effect the popularity of a leader he will no doubt side against you in order to retain his prestige and power; in other words, if the popular feeling is very strong in the opposite direction to which you wish to lead the leader, you will find that the leader will not be with you. . . .

V

Patriotism, Normalcy, and Social Tensions: 1916-1929

CHAPTER 13

War and loyalty

Preparedness and World War 1

Before the United States formally entered the war against Germany and the Central Powers in April 1917, Woodrow Wilson's administration sponsored a vigorous campaign of "preparedness," designed to significantly expand the military forces and to shore up the nation's defenses. Wilson's support for preparedness accompanied his utilization of "Americanism" themes by 1915. Thus, insistence on an uncritical acceptance of national policies neatly coincided with the drive to strengthen national power and military readiness. This selection typifies the appeals for sacrifice, energy, and patriotism which flooded the popular press of the day.

In my home we are always glad when you emphasize the fact that "preparedness does not mean preparedness for war, but really preparedness against war for peace." Every time it is put, in editorial or special article, it must strike some perhaps doubtful reader with a new significance.

What a pity that the thing is called preparedness at all! The very word seems an invitation to attack. It constantly requires explanation. True, it is short, and brevity in a title always attracts; but peace insurance seems to us to express it better.

For, after all, it is only that. And until our daily prayer that His kingdom come on earth as it is in heaven is farther along the road to fulfillment we shall need peace insurance.

That we invest in this kind of security doesn't mean, as others have pointed out, that we are going to hasten into war, any more than "taking out" fire insurance means that we are about to burn our house down, or life insurance as a preliminary to worse. There are, of course, persons who plan thus, but not the average, respectable citizen; and the average, respectable nation but reflects its citizenry. . . .

There is far more sympathy, I believe, among women for a rational preparation for defense than is supposed in some quarters.

True, many of our thoughtful women are convinced that we shall have peace only if we stand before the world unarmed, thus proving our desire to molest no

From Margaret Shaw Graham, "Another Woman's View of Preparedness," *Outlook* 112 (9 April 1916): 892–893.

country and to be let alone. But I have never heard one of these advocate abolishing the municipal police system, imperfect though it is. Neither do I know a single peace-without-insurance woman who fails to put her valuables, if she has any, in a safety vault and lock up her house at night. Even these advocates realize in some connections that, until all men are educated up to their moral standards, their property and their lives must have some degree of tangible protection.

The majority of women with whom I talk, however, seem to see clearly that our best hope of real peace must come through the power to base our demands for peace upon our ability to maintain peace. They believe that by "taking out" such insurance we become, not a great aggressive force, but rather a great potential power. It is what President Wilson once termed the Recall, "the gun behind the door." It may never have to be used. It probably won't be if it is known to be there. But if it is needed we have only to remember Washington to appreciate its value.

If in his day there had been such a "gun," the Revolutionary War would have been shorter, the suffering of our men and the loss of life considerably less.

This peculiar type of myopia from which Americans suffered in Washington's day has been strikingly evident in every war since. The result, as every reader knows, has been unnecessary sacrifice of life and property. Yet some of us have not learned the lesson.

I sometimes fear we Americans think ourselves better than we are. I doubt very much if we are so good that we can impress that fact by mere words upon aggressive nations in such a way as to hold them awestruck and inactive; that this country, splendid as it is, is yet good enough or strong enough to convince the world at large, by simple argument, that heaven on earth has come!

In a letter from Mr. [Theodore] Roosevelt is stressed the point mentioned in the beginning of this one, that preparedness against war is the best means of averting war. I like particularly his thought that if it is impossible to avert war save at the cost of dishonor, women like certain types he mentions, as well as their sons, will face the dangers of battle just as women face other perils they cannot escape. And he adds:

"It is our duty individually and as a Nation to avoid all quarrels, to avoid every species of brutality, of wrong-doing, of wanton offense, to try to inculcate gentleness and fair and upright dealing as between man and man, nation and nation; but it is also our duty to keep ourselves masters of our own souls, and possessed of those stern virtues, for the lack of which no softness of manners, no gentleness of nature, and, above all, no soft and easy course of life, will in any way atone."

Let me add (and it is not so much another story as at first appears) that the women who are interested in Preparedness are likewise interested in the way Congress is going to bring it about. Housekeepers for the most part, considering oftentimes, as many must, how to make both ends meet, they are not exactly dazzled by the way in which the business end of Congress conducts some of its departments. If certain of the slipshod, haphazard methods which result in duplication and unnecessary expense are reformed at Washington, many thousands of dollars now being wasted can go toward adequate Preparedness.

The loyalty mania

Wars and foreign policy repeatedly have divided American society. In the War of 1812, the Civil War, the Philippine insurrection, and the Vietnam adventure, the nation fought with bitter internal cleavages that consequently brought about repressive governmental measures. World War I probably offers the best (or worst) example of such policies. Despite a formal declaration of war by Congress, deep divisions existed in the nation, with opposition to the war led by radicals, pacificists, and certain ethnic groups, most notably Irish and Germans. Administration propaganda, as well as the formal policies of government agencies, strengthened the hand of quasi-official groups such as the American Protective League and the Loyalty Legion which sought to root out "disloyal" elements. In Wisconsin, whose Senator Robert M. La Follette perhaps was the most outspoken public opponent of the war, the Loyalty Legion was most vigilant. Citizens with Germanic names, such as the writer of the first letter, found it necessary to conspicuously display their loyalty and submit to the pressure for conformity. The second letter reflects the animosity and impatience felt by "patriots" toward war critics and dissenters such as La Follette.

September 1, 1917

My dear Mr. Bloodgood:—

Will you kindly enroll me as a member of the Loyalty Legion organized in this state a few days ago?

I am delighted to give expression in this way to my desire to support my country and my government loyally and devotedly in this national crisis and I should like to volunteer for any work which you may find it expedient for me to do and which I am able to perform for the good of our nation.

From Loyalty Legion of Wisconsin, Correspondence and Miscellaneous Papers (Madison: State Historical Society of Wisconsin). Used by permission of the director.

University of Wisconsin professors march in Loyalty Day
parade, 1917.

There are a few objectors, very vociferous sometimes, who seem to be doing their best to bring disaster and ruin upon us and I have not infrequently been humiliated by finding it necessary to suggest that I did not agree with their activities though I carried a German name. I hope that my association with the Loyalty Legion may relieve me from this hereafter and that I may be helpful in furthering your work in even a small way.

With my kindest regards and congratulating you upon having been chosen to head this splendid work, I beg to remain

Yours very truly,
A. P. Wettstein

September 1st 1917

Dear Mr. Bloodgood:

... It has always been my opinion that it is not so much the rank and file of the people who have caused the State of Wisconson to fall into disrepute, throughout the Country, as it certainly has done.

The men higher up and the mis-Representatives in Washington are more responsible on account of their prominence and the advertising they get in the Daily Newspapers.

The people themselves are indirectly responsible, however, as they virtually endorse these conditions by electing such renegades and allowing them to continue in office.

One thing which ought to help is the action the Governor has taken in regard to the meeting of the Peace Council which should not be allowed in this State under any circumstances and particularly in this City.

It is about time for a court martial, a brick wall and firing squad for some of these traitors, the higher up the better.

Yours truly
R. A. Dousman

P.S.

Another thing which has done much to establish Milwaukee as a German or pro-German City is the Slogan of the Schlitz Brewing Co. "The Beer that made Milwaukee famous"; Infamous rather.—

Americanizing workers: the "home-stake"

The war generated a variety of enthusiasms, fueled in part by a sense of national community and a generally raised level of prosperity. The following essay, written by a professional architect, used the occasion to advocate the mass-scale design and construction of low-cost houses. The seemingly altruistic message for privately owned housing was tempered by a more substantial appeal for a means to promote industrial harmony. Using the jargon of the times, the "home-stake" in America was seen as a resolution for industrial conflict—or the so-called labor question.

As Lloyd George said in his great speech at the American Luncheon Club, "In some centuries the history of the world moves but a day, at other times it moves centuries in a day." This is one of those times. We are living in an era of great achievements. Less than six weeks ago Russia was the most parental of autocracies; the change in Russia is but little more rapid than changes in our very midst.

One of the greatest and most significant of these is summed up by the word "Americanization." That is a new word, a word minted by the war, but it is firmly planted and will produce a wonderful harvest. It has many angles and relations, but the most significant and important of all of them is its relation to the profession of architecture and the business of building. "Next to the job-stake, the home-stake in America is the big, vital, Americanizing influence." That dictum of a foremost authority challanges the profession altruistically just as it must interest the profession selfishly.

"How best to house our workingmen and their families" is not solely a material question. It has its emotional and sentimental side. What! Sentiment in the question of housing workmen? Yes, and again yes! Every man, wage-earner or professional man, has his emotional, sentimental side, and this we must respect if we are going to live as a family in harmony.

The secret of industrial harmony is contentment. The nursing of civic pride develops community spirit. Having that, we will see our economic and industrial trials fade away. Give a man a comfortable home, in which he has not only a pecuniary interest but a proper pride, and you summon to the sur-

From William Hart Boughton, "One Way to Solve a National Problem," *The Architectural Review* 5 (April 1917): 27.

face those better elements which every human being possesses, and which in the past have been stifled largely by miserable housing conditions.

Like all proper sentiment in business, this side of the housing question is intensely practical. One of our greatest industrial troubles has been the continual shifting of our laboring population. With nothing to tie them to any locality, with no interest in their surroundings, lacking any incentive to settle down and help make a community bigger and better, their nomadic tendency has been an inevitable result. They have lived from day to day, always ready to move to another city for the only inducement the employer has held out,—a few more dollars each week.

Give this laboring population a suitable, comfortable home, with its little garden, which they can eventually own, and what results? Americanization in its broadest sense. And that's sentiment. But also, the nomadic instinct has been crushed—and that's business. Practical? Why, man, it's a greater solution of the labor question than this country has ever known. The home-stake will deprive the job-stake of its allurement. Manufacturers will have to compete for each other's workmen in terms of something else than merely higher wages. And in thus creating normal, healthful living-conditions, the manufacturer has infinitely raised the worker's efficiency. Little time will be lost as the result of sickness. It is well established that the old, and still present, conditions encourage vice; raising the moral tone of the whole community fortifies its good health. The workman is not only there to stay, but he is a vastly more productive workman. He has proved that the sentimental and the practical sides of the housing question are inextricably associated, mutually inter-dependent.

And if that is the case from the manufacturer's view-point, how much more so is it the case for us architects and for the whole building-world in general! The tests of design and construction which apply to industrial housing are simply those which must be faced and squarely met in home-building generally.

Loyalism and vigilantes

The efforts to insure national conformity and loyalty often resulted in vigilante methods and violence. The Industrial Workers of the World—the so-called Wobblies—particularly felt the brunt of loyalist activities during the war. Much of the IWW leadership, and probably a good deal of the rank and file, opposed the war for class and ideological reasons. Feared and despised in peacetime, they offered an easy target for their enemies after the outbreak of the war. The government vigorously prosecuted large numbers of Wobblies and the Immigration Bureau detained many of them who had alien status. This account recounts the sworn testimony of the secretary of the Tulsa, Oklahoma, local who witnessed the beating, tarring, and feathering of his union brothers on November 9, 1917.

On the night of November 5, 1917, while sitting in the hall at No. 6 W. Brady Street, Tulsa, Okla. (the room leased and occupied by the Industrial Workers of the World, and used as a union meeting room), at about 8:45 P.M., five men entered the hall, to whom I at first paid no attention, as I was busy putting a monthly stamp in a member's union card book. After I had finished with the member, I walked back to where these five men had congregated at the baggage-room at the back of the hall, and spoke to them, asking if there was anything I could do for them.

One who appeared to be the leader, answered 'No, we're just looking the place over.' Two of them went into the baggage-room flashing an electric flashlight around the room. The other three walked toward the front end of the hall. I stayed at the baggage-room door, and one of the men came out and followed the other three up to the front end of the hall. The one who stayed in the baggage-room asked me if I was 'afraid he would steal something.' I told him we were paying rent for the hall, and I did not think anyone had a right to search this place without a warrant. He replied that he did not give a damn if we were paying rent for four places, they would search them whenever they felt like it. Presently he came out and walked toward the front end of the hall, and I followed a few steps behind him.

In the meantime the other men, who proved to be officers, appeared to be asking some of our members questions. Shortly after, the patrol-wagon came and all the members in the hall—10 men were ordered into the wagon. I turned out the light in the back end of the hall, closed the desk, put the key in the door and told the 'officer' to turn out the one light. We stepped out, and I locked the door, and at the request of the 'leader of the officers,' handed him the keys. He told me to get in the wagon, I being the 11th man taken from the hall, and we were taken to the police station.

November 6th, after staying that night in jail, I put up $100.00 cash bond so that I could attend to the outside business, and the trial was set for 5 o'clock P.M., November 6th. Our lawyer, Chas. Richardson, asked for a continuance and it was granted. Trial on a charge of vagrancy was set for November 7th at 5 P.M. by Police Court Judge Evans. After some argument by both sides the cases were continued until the next night, November 8th, and the case against Gunnard Johnson, one of our men, was called. After four and a half hours' session the case was again adjourned until November 9th at 5 P.M., when we agreed to let the decision in Johnson's case stand for all of us. . . .

From *Liberator*, 1 April 1918, pp. 15–17.

Johnson said he had come into town Saturday, November 3d, to get his money from the Sinclair Oil & Gas Co. and could not get it until Monday, the 5th, and was shipping out Tuesday, the 6th, and that he had $7.08 when arrested. He was reprimanded by the judge for not having a Liberty Bond, and as near as anyone could judge from the closing remarks of Judge Evans, he was found guilty and fined $100 for not having a Liberty Bond.

"Our lawyer made a motion to appeal the case and the bonds were then fixed at $200 each. I was immediately arrested, *as were also five spectators in the open court-room,* for being I.W.W.'s. One arrested was not a member of ours, but a property-owner and citizen. I was searched and $30.87 taken from me, as also was the receipt for the $100 bond, and we then were all placed back in the cells.

In about forty minutes, as near as we could judge about 11 P.M., the turnkey came and called 'Get ready to go out you I.W.W. men.' We dressed as rapidly as possible, were taken out of the cells, and the officer gave us back our possessions, Ingersoll watches, pocketknives and money, with the exception of $3 in silver of mine which they kept, giving me back $27.87. I handed the receipt for the $100 bond I had put up to the desk sergeant and he told me he did not know anything about it, and handed the receipt back to me, which I put in my trousers' pocket with the 87 cents. Twenty-seven dollars in bills was in my coat pocket. We were immediately ordered into automobiles waiting in the alley. Then we proceeded one block north to 1st Street, west one-half block to Boulder Street, north across the Frisco tracks and stopped.

Then the masked mob came up and ordered everybody to throw up their hands. Just here I wish to state I never thought any man could reach so high as those policemen did. We were then bound, some with hands in front, some with hands behind, and others bound with arms hanging down their sides, the rope being wrapped around the body. Then the police were ordered to 'beat it,' which they did, running, and we started for the place of execution.

When we arrived there, a company of gowned and masked gunmen were there to meet us standing at 'present arms.' We were ordered out of the autos, told to get in line in front of these gunmen and another bunch of men with automatics and pistols, lined up between us. Our hands were still held up, and those who were bound, in front. Then a masked man walked down the line and slashed the ropes that bound us, and we were ordered to strip to the waist, which we did, threw our clothes in front of us, in individual piles—coats, vests, hats, shirts and undershirts. The boys not having had time to distribute their possessions that were given back to them at the police stations, everything was in the coats, everything we owned in the world.

Then the whipping began, A double piece of new rope, ⅝ or ¾ hemp, being used. A man, 'the chief' of detectives, stopped the whipping of each man when he thought the victim had had enough. After each one was whipped another man applied the tar with a large brush, from the head to the seat. Then a brute smeared feathers over and rubbed them in.

After they had satisfied themselves that our bodies were well abused, our clothing was thrown into a pile, gasoline poured on it and a match applied. By the light of our earthly possessions, we were ordered to leave Tulsa, and leave running and never come back. The night was dark, the road very rough, and as I was one of the last two that was whipped, tarred and feathered, and in the rear when ordered to run, I decided to be shot rather than stumble over the rough road. After going forty or fifty feet I stopped and went into the weeds. I told the man with me to get in the weeds also, as the shots were coming very close over us and ordered him to lie down flat. We expected to be killed, but after 150 or 200 shots were fired they got in their autos.

After the last one had left, we went through a barbed-wire fence, across a field, called to the boys, collected them, counted up, and had all the 16 safe, though sore and nasty with tar. After wandering around the hills for some time—ages it seemed to me—we struck the railroad track. One man, Jack Sneed, remembered then that he knew a farmer in that vicinity, and he and J. F. Ryan volunteered to find the house. I built a fire to keep us from freezing.

We stood around the fire expecting to be shot, as we did not know but what some tool of the commercial club had followed us. After a long time Sneed returned and called to us, and we went with him to a cabin and found an I.W.W. friend in the shack and 5 gallons of coal oil or kerosene, with which we cleaned the filthy stuff off of each other, and our troubles were over, as friends sent clothing and money to us that day, it being about 3 or 3:30 A.M. when we reached the cabin.

The men abused, whipped and tarred were Tom McCaffery, John Myers, John Boyle, Charles Walsh, W. H. Walton, L. R. Mitchell, Jos. French, J. R. Hill, Gunnard Johnson, Robt. McDonald, John Fitzsimmons, Jos. Fischer, Gordon Dimikson, J. F. Ryan, E. M. Boyd, Jack Sneed (not an I.W.W.).

This is a copy of my sworn statement and every word is truth. . . .

A clear and present danger?

Official repression of dissent took a variety of forms during World War I, with probably the most notorious being the Espionage Act of 1917 and Sedition Act of 1918. Under the former, Socialist leader Eugene V. Debs was convicted for saying that the people should "resist militarism, wherever found." The Sedition Act, similar to the long-discredited Federalist act of 1798, made it a felony "to utter, print, or publish disloyal, profane, scurrilous, or abusive language about the form of government, the Constitution, [or] flag . . . or by word or act oppose the cause of the United States." The most famous test of this act came in *Abrams* v. *United States* (1919). Jacob Abrams and others had published pamphlets that denounced Wilson for intervening in the Bolshevik Revolution and called for resistance to that policy. The Supreme Court sustained Abrams's conviction, contending that the pamphlets tended "to excite . . . disaffection, sedition, riots, and . . . revolution." In dissent, Justice Oliver Wendell Holmes scoffed at the government's fear "of a silly leaflet by an unknown man," and argued that it did not constitute a clear and present danger to the security of the United States. One of Abrams's leaflets—that "unknown man," or "puny anonymity," as Holmes also characterized him—follows.

President Wilson with his beautiful phraseology has hypnotized the people of America to such an extent that they could not see the hypocricy of it until it is no longer possible not to "see."

Yes, we, the Workers of America, have been duped—duped by the wonderful speeches of President Wilson. Although most of us did know the corruption of all the capitalists and rulers, be they Kaizers, Czars, Kings or Presidents, yet we have almost revered the attitude that "our" President had taken toward OUR COUNTRY, the country which now is the only country of the proletariat. We really thought that he would not consent to intervention, or in other words, that he would keep his hands clean of this dirty business of destroying the Russian Revolution, the real proletarian revolution.

And here lies the hypocricy of it. The President of the United States had not the courage to come forward straight and openly and say "We, as well as all other capitalist nations of the world, cannot have this revolution in Russia prolonged. We also are dead afraid of this proletarian government, which, when once in full power, will destroy capitalism forever and will spread its dangerous doctrines all over the world." No, he kept his policy secret, but instead fed us on pretty empty phrases, and in the meanwhile American troops were already landing in Russia and were allying themselves with the other nations in the destruction of the Russian freedom, the real freedom of the working-class, and not the so-called democratic "freedom."

Yes, while we were being hypnotized here by the sweet lullaby of the President, the monarchs of this land were combining with the monarchs of all lands in this bloody work of crushing Russia, thus furthering the cause of imperialistic and militaristic Germany as well. Is not the government of Germany just as afraid of this wave of the proletarian spirit as all other nations? And consequently by intervening in Russia, the allies are furthering the cause of Germany as well as their own. They are all combined, these blood-dogs of all nations—foe or no foe—when it comes to fighting their common enemy, their deadliest enemy—the awakened proletariat of their respective countries.

From *Abrams* v. *United States*, 250 U.S. 616 (1919). Briefs and Exhibits.

State Historical Society of Wisconsin.

Book-burning, 1917: "Here Lies the Remains of German
in Baraboo High School."

And thus all together the capitalists of this world are united in destroying what is just the beginning of the real proletarian social revolution.

Will we, the workers of America, allow this "intervention" without a murmur? Will we remain deaf to the cry of our brethren over the sea? Will we not raise an arm to stop it? Will we just sit hand-folded and look on how they, the hypocrites of this country, in unison with those of all other lands, are combining to make an end to our revolution, the Russian Revolution?

WILL WE AWAKEN TO THE FACT THAT WE HAVE BEEN DUPED?

WILL BE RISE IN OUR MIGHT AND REFUSE TO PARTICIPATE IN THIS BLOODY BUSINESS?

WILL WE ONCE'AND FOR ALL MAKE A STOP TO THIS SHAMEFUL HYPOCRICY AND ANNOUNCE THAT WE KNOW ALL AND MEAN TO BLOW BACK?

While the guns of Europe are raging and the blood of youth is spilling like water on the altar of capitalism, the statesmen of every country are making plans how to "assist" Russia, but what we known to be, how really to ruin Russia.

Germany is restoring order in Russia; the allies with the United States are preparing to go to Russia and make a government for the Russian people. In other words, all without exception—the allies as well as the Central Powers—are helping Russia.

But thinking into this matter more profoundly, we come to the conclusion that the allies, who pretend to fight for democracy; that the Central Powers, who say they are fighting for their existence, are all forgetting their own fights and are starting for Russia, ready to put their whole strength for that fight.

Germany is tearing parts of Russia; the allies with Japan are ready to conquer Siberia, while shedding crocodile tears and making holy faces like "Billy Sunday" to make believe that they are helping Russia. And all this combined action is but to one end—to try and destroy the revolution. Germany is trying to make a new monarchy in Russia; the allies—a republic, like the United States. All in order that they may be able to put their iron clutches on the throat of the Russian proletariat, and exploit them as they are exploiting their own people in their own lands. They are trying their best to make Russia safe *for slavery*.

Will we allow that? "No," shall be our answer. We, the toilers of America, who believe in real liberty, shall pledge ourselves, in case the United States will participate in that bloody conspiracy against Russia, to create so great a disturbance that the autocrats of America shall be compelled to keep their armies at home, and not be able to spare any for Russia.

And furthermore, all those who are trying to agitate to invade Russia shall know that we are ready to do to them what they are preparing to do to Russia.

If they will use arms against the Russian people to enforce their standard of order, so will we use arms, and they shall never see the ruin of the Russian Revolution.

Aliens and national security

The trials of the International Workers of the World (IWW) rank-and-file and prosecutions under the Espionage and Sedition Acts, among other repressive governmental acts, were followed by mass roundups and deportations of radical aliens. After the Bolshevik Revolution, a left-wing splinter group of the Socialist party formed the American Communist party, composed largely of immigrants, many of them not yet naturalized. The anti-German fervor of the war, coupled with a suspicion of the pacifist tendencies of the left, produced a flurry of official repression. A. Mitchell Palmer, Woodrow Wilson's attorney-general, focused on the dangers of the Communist Internationale which included, he said, "the I.W.W.'s, the most radical socialists, the misguided anarchists, the moral perverts and the hysterical neurasthenic women who abound in communism." The infamous "Palmer raids" led to the arrest of over six thousand persons. Aliens particularly suffered, for they were arrested without warrants, taken to Ellis Island (or some other federal detention center), and then held incommunicado pending deportation. The following letter—written to the radical leader Elizabeth Gurley Flynn—describes the plight of one dedicated radical who was incarcerated on Ellis Island.

Ellis Island, N.Y. III. 14.20
Room 210

   Miss Eliesabeth G. Flynn
   Secr. Workers Def. Union
   7 E. 15 Str. New York

   Dear Comrade.

Little over a year ago I met you in the Lobby of the Rand School and told you that I was leaving New York. . . . However, I did not know at that time that there was a warrant issued against me here and that the Immigration Authori-

From Elizabeth Gurley Flynn mss., State Historical Society of Wisconsin. Used by permission of the director.

ties here were after me. Seven months later, going home from work, I was arrested in San Francisco; my Arrest being ordered by the Washington Federal Authorities on the same N.Y. Warrent. The Charge against me read that, while addressing a Memorial Meeting in N.Y., commemorating the Death of Jakob Schwartz, killed by the Department of Justice, I have threatened with a World wide Revolution, that will knock in the gates of this country, and at another meeting 10 days later, celebrating the First Anniversary of the Second Russian Revolution I have [eulogized] the Chicago martyrs and that I was a Dangerous anarchistic Agitator. Of course It makes no difference how true or untrue those Charges against me are. However, I was kept 3½ months imprisoned in S.F., but having had the luck of having friends in S.F., especially E. D. Nolan, so 10,000 was put up for me in Cash Bond, and I was released. Immediately after my release I got to work and brought in some new life in the S.F. Soviet of Russien Workers. This Soviet never did, nor does at present bother about Conditions in America. It has existed and exist for the sole purpose of educating the Russians in America and keeping them informed about conditions in Russia. I was elected as Publicity Committee for the Soviet and we started to do good work. The Capitalist Press of S.F. gave us very good and sympathetic write-ups. The Soviet arranged a Mass Meeting, attended by over 1000 Russian Workers. It adopted Resolutions: Challenging the Government to assigne Place and Time, where We, all Russian Bolshevieks could come and register for Voluntary Deportation. Stating, that we, all Russians in America are Bolshevieks, and stand by the Russian Soviets. The 7 Febr. I addressed this Meeting. The 9 Febr I received a letter from the Immigration Dept which ordered me to surrender on the 11 Febr., which I did. They held me in the Immigration Prison in S.F. until the 15, then boardered me on a Transportation Train and shipped me to Ellis Island. The Voyage, which lasted 4 days, was the rottenest imagineable. A certain rascal by the name Russel was in Charge of the Transport. I wrote all the Facts about this Trip to Hells Island in a letter to Miss Fitzgerald. I wish, that you obtain it and make Public, as much of it, as you can. When I got here I felt very delighted. I thought, that I was going to Russia. But, the way it looks now, I have deceived myself. I've been here over three weeks. And the way it looks I shall stay here for good, unless some actions will be taken. All they wanted to was to get me away from S.F., where they thought I was a dangerous "Agitator," and quieten me down. It doesn't seem to me, that they are going to send any Russians out of the Country While every Immigration Prison is packed with Russians. I assume, that there are not less than 3000 Russians imprisoned all over the Country, anxiously awaiting the day of their Deportation, except those who are at large on bonds. Now, if the Defense Union is willing, to eliminate the suffereings of those incarcerated, for Gods sake, stop spending Money on Lawyers. Use every cent you have for Publicity, for only Publick Pressure will compel the Immigration Officials to act. It is all right to have a legal Defense, when one can appear before Court and clear himself. While our cases are left entirely in the hands of the burocratic Officials in Washington, those "Gentlemen" know no Justice. The only thing they do fear is Public Opinion. I would suggest, that a large Mass Meeting be arranged, under the name of the Russians in N.Y. Not as a Radical Meeting, but a Russian Meeting, protesting against the Imprisonment of the Russians in America, and *demanding* Mass Deportation for the Russians. The expenses of the meeting could easily be raised at the Meeting itself, with some profit for the expenses which the Def. Union has by supplying the Russians with Clothing and other necessary things for their voyage, which, by the way all my friends imprisoned greatly appreciate. But, if Lawyers are to be retained, instead of paying Money for writs of "hocus pocus," fighting our Deportation, let them file such writs to demand immediate Deportation for all Political or Class War Prisoners. This is not only my Opinion, but the opinion of all Political Prisoners on the Coast in Immigration Prisons as well as here on Hells Island, I would also suggest, that a Bulletin or Leaflet be issued, containing all the facts of brutality, which we have to face in the different Immigration Prisons all over the Country. I am also sending a Copy of a Telegram I received last week from the S.F. Soviet.

Bernard Sernaker
Care of Departation Dept.   Ellis Island, N.Y.

National Association of Manufacturers' poster promoting
industrial harmony, 1918.

CHAPTER **14**

The 1920s: cultural change and conflict

Black migration: to the new promised land

The exodus of southern blacks to northern cities increased after the turn of the century and then greatly accelerated because of new industrial opportunities during World War I. For most blacks, their reasons for moving and resulting problems were similar to those of immigrants from foreign lands. The following letters, some written to the *Chicago Defender*, a black newspaper, and some written to family members, offer a microcosm of the migration process. Included are letters inquiring about work opportunities in the North, letters expressing despair over living conditions in the South, and finally, letters relating both pleasant and unhappy experiences in new homes. The move to northern urban centers such as Chicago, Cleveland, or Pittsburgh created profound changes for these southern blacks, changes as striking and traumatic as those felt by any foreign immigrant.

Dallas, Tex.,
April 23, 1917.

Dear Sir: Having been informed through the Chicago Defender paper that I can secure information from you. I am a constant reader of the Defender and am contemplating on leaving here for some point north. Having your city in view I thought to inquire of you about conditions for work, housing, wages and everything necessary. I am now employed as a laborer in a structural shop, have worked for the firm five years.

I stored cars for Armour packing co. 3 years, I also claims to know something about candy making, am handy at most anything for an honest living. I am 31 yrs. old have a very industrious wife, no children. If chances are available for work of any kind let me know. Any information you can give me will be highly appreciated.

New Orleans, La., 4/24/17

Dear Sirs: Being desirous of leaving the South for the beterment of my condition generaly and seeking a Home Somewhere in Ill' Chicago or some other

From Emmett J. Scott (comp.), "Letters of Negro Migrants of 1916-1918," *Journal of Negro History* ('uly, October 1919), 4:290-340; 412-465.

A newly arrived southern black family, Chicago, World War I.

prosperious Town I am at sea about the best place to locate having a family dependent on me for support. I am informed by the Chicago Defender a very valuable paper which has for its purpose the Uplifting of my race, and of which I am a constant reader and real lover, that you were in position to show some light to one in my condition.

Seeking a Northern Home. If this is true Kindly inform me by next mail the next best thing to do Being a poor man with a family to care for, I am not coming to live on flowry Beds of ease for I am a man who works and wish to make the best I can out of life I do not wish to come there hoodwinked not knowing where to go or what to do so I Solicite your help in this matter and thanking you in advance for what advice you may be pleased to Give I am yours for success.

P. S. I am presently imployed in the I C RR. Mail Department at Union Station this city.

Newbern, Ala., 4/7/1917.

Dear Sir: I am in receipt of a letter from ——— of ———, ———, in regards to placing two young women of our community in positions in the North or West, as he was unable to give the above assistance he enclosed your address. We desire to know if you are in a position to put us in touch with any reliable firm or private family that desire to employ two young women; one is a teacher in the public school of this county, and has been for the past six years having duties of a mother and sister to care for she is forced to seek employment else where as labor is very cheap here. The other is a high school pupil, is capable of during the work of a private family with much credit.

Doubtless you have learned of the great exodus of our people to the north and west from this and other southern states. I wish to say that we are forced to go when one things of a grown man wages is only fifty to seventy five cents per day for all grades of work. He is compelled to go where there is better wages and sociable conditions, believe me. When I say that many places here in this state the only thing that the black man gets is a peck of meal and from three to four lbs. of bacon per week, and he is treated as a slave. As leaders we are powerless for we dare not resent such or to show even the slightest disapproval. Only a few days ago more than 1000 people left here for the north and west. They cannot stay here. The white man is saying that you must not go but they are not doing anything by way of assisting the black man to stay. As a minister of the Methodist Episcopal Church (north) I am on the verge of starvation simply because of the above conditions. I shall be glad to know if there is any possible way by which I could be of real service to you as director of your society. Thanking you in advance for an early reply, and for any suggestions that you may be able to offer.

With best wishes for your success, I remain,
very sincerely yours.

Chicago, Illinois.

My dear Sister: I was agreeably surprised to hear from you and to hear from home. I am well and thankful to say I am doing well. The weather and everything else was a surprise to me when I came. I got here in time to attend one of the greatest revivals in the history of my life—over 500 people joined the church. We had a Holy Ghost shower. You know I like to have run wild. It was snowing some nights and if you didnt hurry you could not get standing room. Please remember me kindly to any who ask of me. The people are rushing here by the thousands and I know if you come and rent a big house you can get all the roomers you want. You write me exactly when you are coming. I am not keeping house yet I am living with my brother and his wife. My sone is in California but will be home soon. He spends his winter in California. I can get a nice place for you to stop until you can look around and see what you want. I am quite busy. I work in Swifts packing Co. in the sausage department: My daughter and I work for the same company—We get $1.50 a day and we pack so many sausages we dont have much time to play but it is a matter of a dollar with me and I feel that God made the path and I am walking therein.

Tell your husband work is plentiful here and he wont have to loaf if he want to work. I know unless old man A——changed it was awful with his sould and G——also.

Well I am always glad to hear from my friends and if I can do anything to assist any of them to better their condition. please remember me to Mr. C——and his family I will write them all as soon as I can. Well I guess I have said about enough. I will be delighted to look into your face once more in life. Pray for me for I am heaven bound. I have made too many rounds to slip now. I know you will pray for prayer is the life of any sensible man or woman. Well goodbye from your sister in Christ.

P. S. My brother moved the week after I came. When you fully decide to come write me and let me know what day you expect to leave and over what road and if I dont meet you I will have some one ther to meet you and look after you. I will send you a paper as soon as one come along they send out extras two and three times a day.

Pittsburg, Pa., May 11, 1917.

My dear Pastor and wife: It affords me great pleasure to write you this leave me well & O. K. I hope you & sis Hayes are well & no you think I have forgotten you all but I never will how is ever body & how is the church getting along well I am in this great city & you no it cool here right now the trees are just peeping out. fruit trees are now in full bloom but its cool yet we set by big fire over night. I like the money O. K. but I like the South betterm for my Pleasure this city is too fast for me they give you big money for what you do but they charge you big things for what you get and the people are coming by cal Loads every day its just pack out the people are Begging for some whears to sta If you have a family of children & come here you can buy a house easier than you cant rent one if you rent one you have to sign up for 6 months or 12 month so you see if you dont like it you have to stay you no they pass that law becaus the People move about so much I am at a real nice place and stay right in the house of a Rve. ——— and family his wife is a state worker I mean a missionary she is some class own a plenty rel estate & personal Property they has a 4 story home on the mountain, Piano in the parlor, organ in the sewing room, 1 daughter and 2 sons but you no I have to pay $2.00 per week just to sleep and pay it in advance & get meals whear I work so I think I shall get me a place whear I work next week the lady said she would rather we stay in the house with them & give me a room up stairs than to pay so much for sleeping so she pays me eight Dols per week to feed now she says she will room me so if I dont take that offer I cant save very much I go to church some time plenty churches in this plase all kinds they have some real colored churches I have been on the Allegany Mts twice seem like I was on Baal Tower. Lisen Hayes I am here & I am going to stay ontell fall if I dont get sick its largest city I ever saw 45 miles long & equal in breath & a smoky city so many mines of all kind some places look like torment or how they say it look & some places look like Paradise in this great city my sister in law goes too far I stop here I will visit her this summer if I get a pass I cant spend no more money going further from Home I am 26 miles from my son Be sweet Excuse me for writeing on both sides I have so much to say I want to save ever line with a word and that aint the half but I have told you real facts what I have said I keps well so far & I am praying to contenure & I hope you & your dear sweet wife will pray for me & all of my sisters & Bros & give Mrs. C. my love & sis Jennie & all the rest & except a barrel ful for you and Hayes Pleas send me a letter of recommendation tell Dr., to sign & Mr. Oliver. I remain your friend.

Business: an American religion

"The business of the United States is business," declared President Calvin Coolidge in the mid-1920s. The condition of business and the concerns of business people offer one of the leading themes of the decades. Indeed, the pursuit of profit truly was a religion and business people were the prophets and saviors of society. Edward E. Purinton, a popular lecturer on business efficiency, here offers a typical song of praise for the business civilization of the 1920s. Purinton celebrated business as the common denominator for life itself—it was at once a game, a science, an art, an education, an opportunity, a philanthropy, and above all, a religion.

Among the nations of the earth today America stands for one idea: *Business.* National opprobrium? National opportunity. For in this fact lies, potentially, the salvation of the world.

Through business, properly conceived, managed, and conducted, the human race is finally to be redeemed. How and why a man works foretells what he will do, think, have, give, and be. And real salvation is in doing, thinking, having, giving, and being—not in sermonizing and theorizing. . . .

What is the finest game? Business. The soundest science? Business. The truest art? Business. The fullest education? Business. The fairest opportunity? Business. The cleanest philanthropy? Business. The sanest religion? Business.

You may not agree. That is because you judge business by the crude, mean, stupid, false imitation of business that happens to be located near you.

The finest game is business. The rewards are for everybody, and all can win. There are no favorites—Providence always crowns the career of the man who is worthy. And in this game there is no "luck"—you have the fun of taking chances but the sobriety of guaranteeing certainties. The speed and size of your winnings are for you alone to determine; you needn't wait for the other fellow in the game—it is always your move. And your slogan is not "Down the Other Fellow!" but rather "Beat Your Own Record!" or "Do It Better Today!" or "Make Every Job a Masterpiece!" The great sportsmen of the world are the great businessmen.

The soundest science is business. All investigation is reduced to action, and by action proved or disproved. The idealistic motive animates the materialistic

From Edward E. Purinton, "Big Ideas from Big Business," *Independent* 105 (16 April 1921): 395–396, 412–413.

method. Hearts as well as minds are open to the truth. Capital is furnished for the researches of "pure science"; yet pure science is not regarded pure until practical. Competent scientists are suitably rewarded—as they are not in the scientific schools.

The truest art is business. The art is so fine, so exquisite, that you do not think of it as art. Language, color, form, line, music, drama, discovery, adventure—all the components of art must be used in business to make it of superior character.

The fullest education is business. A proper blend of study, work, and life is essential to advancement. The whole man is educated. Human nature itself is the open book that all businessmen study; and the mastery of a page of this educates you more than the memorizing of a dusty tome from a library shelf. In the school of business, moreover, you teach yourself and learn most from your own mistakes. What you learn here you live out, the only real test.

The fairest opportunity is business. You can find more, better, quicker chances to get ahead in a large business house than anywhere else on earth. The biographies of champion businessmen show how they climbed, and how you can climb. Recognition of better work, of keener and quicker thought, of deeper and finer feeling, is gladly offered by the men higher up, with early promotion the rule for the man who justifies it. There is, and can be, no such thing as buried talent in a modern business organization.

The cleanest philanthropy is business. By "clean" philanthropy I mean that devoid of graft, inefficiency, and professionalism, also of condolence, hysterics, and paternalism. Nearly everything that goes by the name of Charity was born a triplet, the other two members of the trio being Frailty and and Cruelty. Not so in the welfare departments of leading corporations. Savings and loan funds; pension and insurance provisions; health precuations, instructions, and safeguards; medical attention and hospital care; libraries, lectures, and classes; musical, athletic, and social features of all kinds; recreational facilities and financial opportunities—these types of "charitable institutions" for employees add to the worker's self-respect, self-knowledge, and self-improvement by making him an active partner in the welfare program, a producer of benefits for his employer and associates quite as much as a recipient of bounty from the company. I wish every "charity" organization would send its officials to school to the heads of the welfare departments of the big corporations; the charity would mostly be transformed into capability, and the minimum of irreducible charity left would not be called by that name.

The sanest religion is business. Any relationship that forces a man to follow the Golden Rule rightfully belongs amid the ceremonials of the church. A great business enterprise includes and presupposes this relationship. I have seen more Christianity to the square inch as a regular part of the office equipment of famous corporation presidents than may ordinarily be found on Sunday in a verbalized but not vitalized church congregation. A man is not wholly religious until he is better on weekdays than he is on Sunday. The only ripened fruits of creeds are deeds. You can fool your preacher with a sickly sprout or a wormy semblance of character, but you can't fool your employer. I would make every business house a consultation bureau for the guidance of the church whose members were employees of the house.

I am aware that some of the preceding statements will be challenged by many readers. I should not myself have made them, or believed them, twenty years ago, when I was a pitiful specimen of a callow youth and cocksure professional man combined. A thorough knowledge of business has implanted a deep respect for business and real businessmen.

The future work of the businessman is to teach the teacher, preach to the preacher, admonish the parent, advise the doctor, justify the lawyer, superintend the statesman, fructify the farmer, stabilize the banker, harness the dreamer, and reform the reformer. Do all these needy persons wish to have these many kind things done to them by the businessman? Alas, no. They rather look down upon him, or askance at him, regarding him as a mental and social inferior—unless he has money or fame enough to tilt their glance upward.

A large variety of everyday lessons of popular interest may be gleaned from a tour of the world's greatest business plants and a study of the lives of their founders. We suggest a few.

1. *The biggest thing about a big success is the price.* It takes a big man to pay the price. You can measure in advance the size of your success by how much you are willing to pay for it. I do not refer to money. I refer to the time, thought, energy, economy, purpose, devotion, study, sacrifice, patience, care that a man must give to his lifework before he can make it amount to anything.

The business world is full of born crusaders. Many of the leaders would be called martyrs if they weren't rich. The founders of the vast corporations have been, so far as I know them, fired with zeal that is supposed to belong only to missionaries. Of all the uncompromising, untiring, unsparing idealists in the world today, none surpass the founders and heads of the business institutions that have made character the cornerstone. The costliest thing on earth is idealism.

2. *Great men are silent about themselves.* Conversely, the more a man talks about his personality, his family, his property, his position, his past, present or future achievements, the less he usually amounts to or will ever become. We had to spend weeks of hard work to obtain personal interviews with the heads of the International Harvester Company.

They prefer the forge to the limelight. They do not want free "publicity." And they refuse to make oral statements that might be misquoted or misunderstood; they insist that all facts and figures for publication be checked with utmost care, sometimes through a dozen departments, to prevent the least inaccuracy. . . .

3. *The best way to keep customers is to make friends.* Of all the assets of a

business concern the chief is goodwill. To gain this, you can afford to spend as much as to manufacture or sell your product.

Now a fundamental rule in creating goodwill is to benefit the customer in a way he does not look for, does not pay for. The Western Electric Company offers to teach any woman the principles of household efficiency, mailing on request literature without charge. The science of managing a home indicates the use of electrical appliances, but the company wants to teach the science whether it sells the goods or not. . . .

4. *Only common experiences will unite the laborer and the capitalist.* Each must get the viewpoint of the other by sharing the work, duties, and responsibilities of the other. The sons of the families of Swift, McCormick, Wanamaker, Heinz, du Pont have learned the business from the ground up; they know the trials, difficulties, and needs of workers because they *are* workers; and they don't have to settle agitations and strikes because there aren't any.

Further, by councils and committees of employees, management courses for department heads and foremen, plans of referendum and appeal, offers of stock and voting power to workers, employee representation on the Board of Directors, and other means of sharing authority and responsibility, owners of a business now give the manual workers a chance to think and feel in unison with themselves. All enmity is between strangers. Those who really know each other cannot fight.

5. *Every business needs a woman counselor.* Better, a wcman's advisory board. Nearly all manufacturing and merchandising relates somehow to the interests of womankind.

Before E. M. Statler built his latest hotel in his big chain of hostelries, he consulted the housekeeper and matron of his masterpiece house, Hotel Pennsylvania, the world's largest inn. He wanted to know the precise arrangement, equipment, and service that women guests valued most. He knew that no man could tell him.

There could be written a book of business revelations that would astonish the world. Over and over, at critical times in the development of national corporations, the hidden hand of a woman has held the huge concern at balance, or swung it in the right direction. You can no more run a business without a woman's intuition than you can run a boat without a keel.

6. *The great new field for professional men is corporation work.* Teachers, doctors, lawyers, editors, psychologists, chemists, bankers, engineers, even philosphers and ministers now find pleasant, permanent, lucrative employment as heads of departments in famous business houses.

. . . More and more, business will demand the knowledge and skill of scientists and artists of many kinds.

7. *The pleasure of money is not in having or spending it.* The pleasure is in getting it—and giving it away. Money rewards the exercise of keen brains and quick wits, but the real fun is in the exercise. I don't know of a single self-made

millionaire who puts money first. There is always something bigger and better than money in his mind.

As for his heart, that is where he *gives* the most. The heart of Judge Gary is in the manifold benefits he creates for the employees of U.S. Steel. The heart of John Wanamaker is in the John Wanamaker Foundation, a beneficial organization for Wanamaker workers, and in the international Sunday school forces that he set in motion. The heart of Julius Rosenwald is in the schools he established for poor boys and girls, and the relief work he founded among the Jews. . . .

8. *A family heritage of wealth alone is the worst kind.* Most parents think they are good to their children if they leave a large bankroll, easily accessible. Others foolishly magnify the bestowal of a college education, or social position, or some other inheritance not earned, and not valued because not earned.

Founders of great business enterprises know better. They bequeath to their sons a personal equipment of aims, principles, and methods which make real men of the scions of wealth. . . .

9. *Age is nothing to a live man.* When a person gets old the calendar is not to blame—he was born dead from the heart out and the neck up.

John H. Patterson was of middle age before he really started the National Cash Register Company. He had no experience in the business either, having been a country storekeeper without personal knowledge of engineering or manufacturing. But he got a purpose—and forgot everything else. Whoever does that is young till he dies. It is never too late to make a fresh start in life. . . .

10. *The most powerful preacher is, or can be, the lay preacher.* The business manager of Gary, Indiana, the world's largest industrial city, preaches nearly every Sunday. He is called upon by the pastors and priests of churches of a dozen different faiths and nationalities whose members are employees of the U.S. Steel Corporation to address the congregations in some helpful, appropriate way. Because he is a fine businessman, with power, skill, and money back of him, the men of the city want to hear what he has to say. And because he is a gentleman—kind, thoughtful, and sympathetic—the women of the church listen gladly to his lay sermons.

I look forward to the day when professional sermonizers will be considered a relic of past incompetence, and in their place will be men who are personal vitalizers and organizers.

11. *Charity must be cleansed of poverty and sentimentality.* You are not kind to the poor when you merely give them food, clothes, or money. You pauperize them when they most need energizing, organizing, and reorganizing.

A leading official of Sears, Roebuck & Company hates "welfare work." He says the company won't do any. Why? Because (1) the company refuses to pose as a philanthropist, socialist, or fairy godfather; (2) a self-respecting employee hates being "welfared" by his employer: (3) charity and business don't go together; (4) the majority of welfare workers are officious, crude, paternalistic, and unscientific, out of place in business; and (5) employers need welfare work, perhaps of a different kind, as much as employees, and a one-sided program of such voluntary philanthropy is unwise and unfair.

This man claims that whatever improves the health, happiness, homelife, or future progress of the worker improves the work and should be considered a straight business proposition. He believes that commercialism should include idealism and fraternalism, but without mention of the fact.

12. *Industry will finally be the savior of the community.* We hear much about a decadence of morality and increase of crime. Now the person who gets into mischief and goes astray was doing nothing, or the wrong thing, or the right thing badly. Put everybody in the work he loves, teach him how to do it well, and treat him and reward him fairly; then you take away the chief components of wrongdoing, which are idleness, irresponsibility, loneliness, and curiosity, aided and abetted by a consciousness of misfitness. Thomas A. Edison remarks that he never had time to break a moral law.

. . . Happiness for a human being lies in his work, or nowhere. And the way to make people good is to make them know they are good for something. . . .

"*The noble experiment*"

In 1919, following years of agitation; pressure, and intense lobbying, the states ratified the Eighteenth Amendment to prohibit the manufacture and sale of intoxicating liquors. But the battle against "Demon Rum" was far from over, for public controversy continued to rage over the merits of prohibition and attempts to enforce it. The amendment's opponents insisted that it was unduly coercive of individual liberty and that it bred crime and general contempt for law as it was unenforceable. Its advocates, however, remained convinced that prohibition could uplift and improve society. The following essay by an Iowa social worker typified the belief that future generations, free from the evils of liquor, would reap benefits from the law.

In 1904 when I became resident director of Roadside Settlement in Des Moines, the House stood directly across the street from the Wayside Saloon and occasionally a Wayside patron mistakenly stumbled into our front door. A year later Roadside moved to the South-east Bottoms, a plat in which the first deed of conveyance stipulated that no saloon should ever be located on the

From Flora Dunlap, "Settlement vs. Saloon," *The Survey* 58 (15 May 1927): 197–200.

land. So we were not again neighbors of a saloon, but for ten years we were neighbors of all the products of the saloons. Drunken men were the commonest sight on the streets, as were haggard women and ragged, undernourished children.

One street intersection, just outside our district, had a saloon on each of the four corners, the next had three, and practically every intersection passed by our neighbors on their way to work had one or more saloons, with others between intersections. A flaunting red-light district lay between us and the downtown section. . . .

At the state referendum on suffrage in June, 1916, I was president of the state suffrage organization and the executive secretary was living at Roadside also. We went to the polls early to vote on a bond issue, having of course no vote on the suffrage question. Although Iowa was at that time legally dry, most of the election board seemed slightly tipsy. One member, who belonged to one of our gym classes, was very friendly and insisted we should vote on suffrage. He pressed the special ballot on us both and was puzzled and disappointed that we showed so little enthusiasm for our own cause. The before-mentioned member cursed us loudly and vehemently and as we left the room attempted to rise, apparently to follow us, but he was so drunk he fell headlong and as we passed out we left him stretched at full length on the floor, uttering denunciations of women who wished to move out of their divinely appointed "spere."

After 1920 I served in the same precinct in every election for three years, and never in that time was any man who served with me in the slightest degree under the influence of liquor. So quickly did the old order pass! Its passing may be credited to woman's suffrage or to prohibition or to both.

Prohibition came into effect in Iowa under state enactment in 1916. There had been county and local option laws for years and these were constantly being strengthened and extended. Des Moines saloons were closed under local option some months before state prohibition went into effect, and some men still secured liquor. It was said over and over again, then as now: "There is more drinking than ever. Prohibition does not prohibit. It is far better to have the licensed saloon than the bootlegger."

With the passing of the saloon in our neighborhood, families who had no furniture began to collect a few pieces. Bedsteads and mattresses were seen where before there had been heaps of rags. Children who had stayed away from school for lack of suitable clothing became more regular in attendance. More shoes appeared to have been bought for the feet that wore them. Women who had been unable to attend neighborhood gatherings for lack of proper attire appeared in new dresses. Men who had never been seen publicly with their wives and children escorted them occasionally to Roadside parties.

True, some of the old drinkers had occasional sprees, but liquor was high in price, not easily obtained and dangerous to life. A bootlegger acquaintance said to me in 1916: "All you say about the danger is true. I know I am a damned fool to sell the stuff but I am not such a double damned fool as to drink it." A few months later his widow came to arrange for day-nursery care for her three small children while she went out to work. Speaking of her husband's death, she said: "It was just his own carelessness that killed him. He drank a bottle of liquor that his partner told him was genuine. You can't trust nobody on the pedigree of liquor." . . .

A good many times between 1918 and 1924 members of settlement groups have come to the house under the influence of liquor. Usually they have left quietly when told their presence was undesired and apologies have been made later. Usually they seemed to have had only a limited supply of liquor and to recover from it in a few days. Most of them are men from twenty-five to thirty-five years of age who began to drink in pre-prohibition days. I know only an occasional younger man who has acquired the habit since 1915. . . .

As I recall the Bottoms of 1904, I know that the lives of its people have been revolutionized. How much of this revolution is due to prohibition I do not know. But I do know that the shuffling drunkard I saw stumbling along Scott Street a month ago is exactly as sodden and degraded as the drunkards who stumbled along that street twenty-two years ago, and I know that all the helpful forces of modern life, material and immaterial, can do nothing for a man whose brain and body are paralyzed by liquor.

There is illegal drinking and selling in the Bottoms as there is in so many communities. Who is most to blame I do not know. I do know that if the city, county, state and federal forces charged with enforcement of the law were working cooperatively instead of uncooperatively and were supported by the citizens who are law-abiding, the prohibition law would be enforced. Even with partial enforcement, drunkenness in the Bottoms twenty-two years ago and drunkenness there today is as smallpox was before and since men have learned the use of vaccination.

Prohibition follies

The prohibitionists insisted on total abstinence from all forms of liquor; consequently, strict enforcement of the law became extremely difficult given the widespread demand for alcoholic beverages. The federal government's Prohibition Bureau was understaffed and repeatedly conflicted with local authorities. It also felt great pressure to make highly publicized raids on speakeasies to offer evidence of its vigilance. The following reminiscence by a federal prohibition agent in Alameda County, California, who worked in conjunction with District Attorney Earl Warren, recounts the difficulties of enforcement and some of its cynical purposes.

Customs agents after capturing bootlegged Mexican liquor,
Texas, 1928.

... The still was the source of supply, and the federal government and the Prohibition agents, by and large, were out after the source of supply, that is, the stills and the cutting plants and that sort of thing.

However, the general public, at least the WCTU, the churches, etc., was making such a ruckus and hollering about the bootleg joints so that you *had* to go in there and make a big splurge, knock off a few bootleg joints and satisfy the general public and the church folks, see. But I can point out to you this, that if we knocked over one great big still like this, that was turning out several thousand gallons of 190 proof alky a day at the source of supply, we were doing a better job even though it took us a longer while to locate and to make a powerful enough case to satisfy the federal court. We did more good that way than going out and knocking over dozens of these bootleg joints a night!

But here again you came into the proposition, why did we do it? Well, here's Earl Warren, here in Alameda County, a very vigorous prosecutor, a politician responding to the church and WCTU folks. Therefore, he's got his own active staff set up to go out and raid these places. The federal courts were charged with the responsibility, regardless of how large or small it was; that is, to enforce Prohibition.

In the spirit of cooperation with Mr. Warren and with his people, we would get together and we'd go out and we'd raid these places, or if I and my crew went out alone and raided the place we would turn the case over to the state. Because the federal government wasn't in the business of making money from the fines, turning a case over to the local court was never questioned. It is still a fact that in the small towns like Benicia, Emeryville, Oakland, and many others, they depended a heck of a lot upon these fines they received from these Prohibition cases to help them in their expenses of government. They never admitted it then and many deny it now, but it's the truth.

For instance, we went up and we raided in Benicia. Then we turned all the cases right over to Benicia court. The Judge'd come down in the middle of the nighttime, and he waxed eloquent. He dispensed judgments in all directions. Everybody who'd come in was guilty and then he had a set fine of $250 or whatever it was. This is in Depression days and that's a pretty good size of money. It didn't take many of these bootleggers to build the coffers of the city up to the point where it paid the judge's salary for a year, you see, and it helped out. They appreciated it. That let them off the hook because their local authorities hadn't initiated this action against the local citizens, the Federals did it.

They viewed this—the bootlegger himself, that is, this bootlegger who'd been taken into Benicia or Vallejo or Emeryville court, whatever it was—they viewed it very much the same way as the city fathers did, that it was the same as a

From Lloyd Jester, "Reminiscences of an Inspector in the District Attorney's Office." Oral interview, Regional Oral History Office Bancroft Library. Published by permission of the Director, The Bancroft Library, University of California, Berkeley. Material provided by Miriam Feingold Stein.

license. They figured, well, they could stand—they call them "busts" now to-day, but in those days we called them "knockovers"—they could stand so many knockovers a year, pay their fines the same as buying a license, and think no more of it.

But if you arrested them more than three times, they'd start screaming like a banshee. They would say things like, "Gee, you're getting me all the time! Why aren't you getting so-and-so?" But they didn't mind coming in and paying up a fine once in a while. What they feared most was more than three convictions on one place, which meant facing a chance of abatement.

I remember one time we had a fellow by the nickname of "Peanuts." I don't know what his real name was. He was a bartender. He tended bar for the Fegonis' during Prohibition. He'd done so for many years. Well it was no fun arresting "Peanuts" towards the end, because you could just as well knock at the front door and say, "Peanuts, come on out. I'm going to take you in and book you." And he'd do it! So there was no sport in it anymore, and I suppose that that's why "Peanuts" went so long between arrests! I don't know. . . .

A bootlegger's tale

The "Noble Experiment" ultimately came to an end with the repeal of the Eighteenth Amendment in 1933. Prohibition, of course, never succeeded. The de-mand and market for intoxicating liquors continued and organized criminal elements provided the goods. Bootleggers and gangsters flourished, but competi-tion among them resulted in soaring crime rates and violence. The dangers—and profits—of trafficking in liquor are recalled here by a Minnesota bootlegger more than thirty years after repeal.

Q. Rumor has it that back in your early days you were tied up with the prohibition and the bootlegging game.

A. Oh, yes. In fact I suppose I sold forty or fifty thousand dollars worth of liquor upstairs in this building. . . .

. . . I had no idea of going into it, but I had a 1914 Ford, which was quite a luxury in them days and three young fellows come one morning—I will not mention any names—and said, "We know where there is a barrel of pure grain alcohol, and we'll steal it if you will haul it away for us, and we'll give you a

From oral interview with Frank Schmidt by Robert Krueger, 20 December 1967, Stillwater, Minnesota (Madison: State Historical Society of Wisconsin). Used by permission of the director.

fourth of it." Well, I had to figure out and get some planks to roll it up into the back seat. When I got there, instead of one, they had two barrels—a hundred gallons. "Well," I says, "go and hide it." So we went out on the farm. One of the boys had an uncle out on a farm. We buried it in the ground, and then they wanted to sell it. The boys wanted some money. So I raised some money and bought the three of them out at quite a discount, and then I started to peddle it and sold the hundred gallons at about, oh, I guess at about $50 or $60 a gallon. . . .

. . . I would go south in the winter time for my health and just cut down and stop the bootlegging. Went down and took the baths of Hot Springs, Arkansas, to preserve my health. They done me an awful lot of good. Of course, now I'm too old, and I don't take them at all on account of I have no breathing left—no lungs left. . . .

Q. You indicated that you continued in the bootlegging business. After that initial hundred gallons, what was your source of supply for additional bootlegging?

A. I run whiskey from Canada. . . .

Yeah, for the high-class trade in St. Paul and Minneapolis. After a couple runs, my car stopped five or six bullets, and a couple of the sheriffs or constables had me pegged. There was only one road, the Jefferson Highway, and I quit that.

Q. How would you make the contacts within this bootlegging business?

A. Well, different ways. They contacted me; it would get around. . . .

If you had some real liquor, why it got around.

I did buy some alcohol from Chicago through St. Paul. . . . [T]hat was handled mostly by Capone. I was the first one to go over to St. Paul and tell some of the boys there that they were knocking off them cars over there in St. Paul. I said, "Why not have them whole carloads of barrels of alcohol come to Stillwater, and then truck it over to St. Paul?" . . . They thought that was a pretty swell idea, but of course I never even let my wife know so she couldn't tell anybody what was going on.

Q. Well, you were operating on quite a large scale then?

A. Oh, yes. It was mostly wholesale.

Q. And tied in with some, shall we say, rather questionable characters in the Twin Cities and Chicago.

A. Very much. Very much.

Q. Well, how long did you continue in this bootlegging? Can you remember any outstanding incidents that happened at that time? You mentioned that after having five or six bullets pumped into your car, you decided to abandon the Canada run. Did you have any other close calls?

A. Well, I had one, but I don't want to talk about that because I still carry the bullet.

Q. You still carry a bullet from this experience?

A. I didn't know, it was so long ago. But, every once in awhile, it would kind of fester a little, but it's way in. I forgot all about it 'til I was in Hot Springs, Arkansas, sitting on a chair. I had a little apartment down there. The leg broke off the chair, and I fell to the floor. The lady had insurance, and they called a doctor right away, and the doctor come, and he says, "You got to go have some X-rays taken." So I went to the Medical Arts Building in Hot Springs, Arkansas, and they took a lot of pictures. I saw the next day when I went back to get the proofs that the doctor looked kind of funny at me. When I come home to my room, in come three detectives and here the print—the X-ray pictures—showed I had a bullet in me. They wanted to know where I got shot, and when I got shot, and why I got shot. . . . So I told them I forgot all about that, it was so long ago. This fall made that old sore open up a little.

Q. . . . On TV now and in occasionally reading about the days of prohibition, we'll see or hear something about the highjacking of car loads of alcohol or truck loads of alcohol. Was there any of that in the Stillwater-St. Paul area?

A. Oh, yes, yes, there was a lot of that around, and when we started to unload here, I used to be in on it and get part of the load—five or ten barrels of alcohol. Finally the highjackers got wise and now the fellows from St. Paul—the big dealers over there—now the Federal men don't shoot; those highjackers shoot. They actually carried extra men with shotguns. . . .

The bootleggers carried guns to shoot the highjackers, and so then, of course, the highjackers got wise and they run them off the road. Then, of course, there was no use unloading because they had Stillwater pegged. The Federal men had them pegged, and we couldn't unload here no more.

Q. Did they really bother you very much? Was the enforcement effort strong, or how was this stressed?

A. Well, I was raided where I lived. I had a vacant apartment on the other side and had a little chicken shack in there. Four Federal men come over, and I was carrying the bottle, and I run across the hall into this apartment and broke the bottle right on this radiator. When I broke the bottle, a fellow named, well, I better mention no names, anyway one of the Federal men, a kind of informer, swung on me. He was a big heavy-set guy, and I swung back and I knocked him out. When I come over from trial, when I got to the Federal Building, two or three other agents swarmed around me and I kept swingin' and every time I hit one of them why . . . (I used to keep in pretty good shape. I had a punching bag in the basement that I punched and skipped rope everyday for ten or fifteen minutes, maybe twenty minutes) . . . when I got to the Federal Building for trial, I got in the hallway and met some of the Federal men that raided me. They said, "You shouldn't be no bootlegger. You should be a prize fighter!"

Q. What was the quality of this "liquid refreshment" that you were handling and dispensing? Was it of quite high quality?

A. Oh, yes, I wouldn't buy cheap; I'd buy the best. Mostly was alcohol. . . .

. . . I had my fights, plenty of them; and whenever some fellows come into town and tried to cut prices, I'd give them ten minutes to get out of town. . . .

. . . I remember one time a couple young fellows came. I told them to get out. They'd believed me and they went so fast, they got out as far as Lake Elmo and run into the ditch. Both of them got hurt.

Q. Why were they so afraid of you? Other than the fact that you were a big man and kept in shape, why were they truly afraid of you? . . .

A. I didn't hold anything over them. They weren't too afraid of me; they just let me alone. If you know that a man carries a gun, and he's been in the Army and knows how to use it, you ain't going to pick on him. You're going to pick on somebody that ain't so handy with his gun or his fists. . . .

Social change and the automobile

Few technological innovations have had the mass impact of the automobile, both socially and ecomically. By the 1920s, the horse, the carriage, and the dirt road had passed from the everyday scene of city and most of rural life. The automobile made obvious economic contributions as well as offering improvements in communications. But it also altered lifestyles and created new social problems, as described below. While the author observed the growing omnipresence and dominance of the automobile, he did not reflect on the social costs and hazards that troubled later generations.

After wandering along twenty thousand miles of foreign strands I am back in my old home town and I can't seem go get my bearings. There's a lot missing besides the folks I used to know.

The town is still named Rochelle. Not that French Rochelle of which the poet sang: "*And thou Rochelle, our own Rochelle, proud city of the waters!*" This, my town, is just plain Rochelle, Ill., population 3,310, seventy-five miles west of Chicago on the C. & N. W. and the C. B. & Q. railways—and the Lincoln Highway.

It has required days of stumbling around once familiar streets cluttered up with motor cars to discover that the Lincoln Highway, offspring of the automobile, has transformed my town. And as one of an army of old-timers who

From Earl Chapin May, "My Town and the Motor Car," *Collier's* 75 (January 3, 1925): 17–18.

State Historical Society of Wisconsin.

More fuel; more pleasure. 1920 advertisement.

have returned this year to some one of ten thousand similarly transformed Rochelles I marvel at the march of progress.

Like my fellow old-timers I gaze fondly at photographs of the town that was, hop into a handy motor that whizzes me over regions once remote—then return to gaze again at pictures of the family phaeton and the local express. My old Rochelle was a corking town! Now it is hopelessly motorized. There are motors, motors everywhere and hardly a horse to drink at the once popular public fountain!

In the sparkling days of its youth Rochelle was a busy mart for horse fanciers. There were four bustling sales barns—Henry Earl's, Henry Carpenter's, George McMann's, and Jimmy Boyle's. There were artfully appointed livery stables, too, where traveling men or local swells hired favorite sorrels or steady-stepping roans and jogged the country roads for profits or pleasure. Those stables are motorized now.

Cherry Street, then as now lined with stores, was the scene of daily equine display. With Scar Thompson, Bunk Beebee, Loppy Boynton or Stub Crandall at the halter straps, heavily fetlocked Clydesdales, dapple-gray Normans, broad-backed Belgians or trim-built Morgans scampered up and down between rows of box wagons, top buggies, canopy tops and hayracks. Abe Klee, with his heavy cane, and other professional buyers from New York or Chicago selected or rejected the horses displayed while Doc Dodge, Henry Hodge and others of our hoursemen lined up along the street and cracked a lusty whip. Rochelle sold its eight thousand horses a year then. It sells less than a hundred a year now. And it's a bigger town now too. . . .

The mud's all gone from my home-town thoroughfares. And gone are the fifty loads of manure garnered from four hundred feet of our best business street—the one between Bain's Opera House and Johnny Flynn's cigar store —during Mayor Wilbur McHenry's spring house cleaning of 1902. We shall never see their like again, not on the motor-mad streets of Rochelle.

Gone, also, are the sales barns that handled eight thousand horses a year. Where Boyle's barn once stood is a $50,000 motor agency. The concrete home of the Hi Way Tire Shop occupies the site of Henry Earl's Horse Emporium. Johnson's famous brick business block opposite the post office is the local home of touring cars. . . .

Where the millinery shop stood at the corner of Washington and Holland streets is a vast and ornate oil station. Two blocks south, where the "Rigister" used to come from the press every Friday, is another oil station, equally vast and ornate. A half mile north, where I used to hunt birds' nests, are two more oil stations, gaudy by day, glaring by night. The town is reeking with oil and shiny with steel.

The Rochelle Cornet Band no longer gives its summer concerts at Washington Street, head of Cherry. It has been relegated to Town Hall Square a half block from the main-traveled roads. But even there on Wednesday nights the motor cars are massed so closely you can hardly squirm through. The city fathers have to take the new fire truck out of the town hall and leave it on a side street so the boys can make a run if the fire whistle blows. Our old hand-drawn hose cart has been sold for junk.

During one of these concerts I asked Ross Harter, in his twenty-fifth year as Rochelle's Official Announcer, about these and other matters. Ross had just informed our assembled thousands that "on next Wednesday night the band will play at the dedication of Memorial Park."

He chewed the quid on my questions, leaned against Police Chief Hodge's new sedan, and explained:

"The Lincoln Highway Commission won't let us block traffic at Washington and Cherry streets any more. There are too many tourists going east and west on the Lincoln Highway—which is cement from Chicago to the Mississippi, you know. It's nothing for the fellows sitting in front of Flynn's cigar store to count five thousand cars turning this corner on Lincoln Highway. They counted 13,907 in thirty-six hours once this summer. Rochelle is on the north and south Meridian Highway through Illinois too.

"There's six hundred cars owned in Rochelle. But you could count eight hundred parked in and around this concert now. There's more than that here for the Saturday-night shopping. Herb Bain actually tagged seven hundred and fifty-one Saturday night. And say, you mustn't call it 'Washington Street' any more. It's Lincoln Highway, the Great Motor Route!"

That change in the name and character of my native street hurts. . . .

Our "new house" was built away out—at the corner of Washington and Chapin streets, on the site of the old baseball grounds, two blocks upstreet from our "old home." It is at 604 Lincoln Highway now. Farmers' cars surround it on shopping nights. A hundred automobiles pass it now where a dozen rigs rattled by in the dirt-road days. It's a noisy place. And it used to be so restful.

The tile factory, our first infant industry, has disappeared, but the big new Whitcomb Works turns out gas engines for the world. The commercial club is selling stock for a new accessories factory. After driving the town dray twenty-two years, Johnny Unger has retired in favor of a younger man and a motor truck.

The Morgan & Heintz Building, from whose upper window "the man was hanged when Rochelle was Hickory Grove and the railroad had just come through," has been replaced by a modern bank building. It is the first business block erected in Rochelle in ten years for other than garage or motor sales purposes. The bank handles the motor-car contract business.

My old swimming hole in Kyte Creek below the slaughter house has been ruined by the drainage commissioners. But just a block away Braiden's Quarry, once our source of limestone and ice, has become Lake Clara, with swarms of summer motorists buzzing around its community bathing beach.

Folks motor for miles to take a plunge. Hundreds from the near-by free tourists' camp, where the city dump heap used to be, bathe in Lake Clara each mellow day. The water's fine. I've tried it.

Our folks no longer march in slow processions across the C. & I. tracks to Decoration Day exercises or appear as "prominent citizens in carriages." All our citizens, prominent and otherwise, ride in motor cars now. Our laundress tells me she couldn't get along without her car.

Sunday was the Sabbath in the horse-drawn days, with a simple, quiet program. Church in the morning, big Sunday dinner, nap or a jog of six miles to Steward and back in the afternoon, cold supper, church in the evening, a bit of reading and bed.

Now we're off in someone's car by Sunday sun-up, doing a double century to Lake Geneva, Janesville, Freeport, Clinton, or other distant dinner place and getting home long after dark—with a date to motor to Sterling for dinner the next night or to Beloit the night after that, and later in the week to Belvidere or Elgin. There's no rest for the pious or wicked. The folks are riding, riding, riding. . . .

For always there are cars, cars, cars. Now and then I hear the distant clackety-clack of hoofs on well-bricked streets. That, I know, is "Andrew Binz, with his horse and buggy." The ancient Andrew, alone, imposing, reminiscent, is true to his traditions.

Yesterday I saw a solitary surrey moving slowly down Lincoln Highway. I shall not see Andrew's horse and buggy or that surrey if I come back again. The town is moving too fast, keeping pace with a motorized world.

Technology and women's life on the farm

Mechanization was not an unmixed blessing for farmers. While their workload was lightened significantly, farmers more than ever found themselves subject to overproduction and the caprice of the free marketplace. Farm women, however, found that the introduction of labor- and time-saving conveniences drastically altered their lives, releasing them from tedious drudgery and affording them time for self-improvement and recreation. The innovations described below are commonplace today, but in their time they represented a significant change in daily living patterns.

From "The Labor Savers I Use," *The Farmer's Wife* 25 (February 1923): 301*ff*.

Saving Every Minute

First comes my kitchen cabinet, standing five feet from and in front of the stove and containing everything that is needed for baking. I can prepare anything for the oven without taking a step till the cake or pies or biscuit are ready to slip into the oven.

Next comes my built-in woodbox that can be filled from the shed and forms a nest in my kitchen beside the firebox end of the stove.

With my five babies, all under five and one-third years of age, the bathroom on our first floor is a blessing. Two springs piped into a concrete reservoir supply the house and barn. The hot water tank is connected with my range.

And my laundry tubs! Such backache and time savers as they are. Mine are in the kitchen and covered as a table when not in use for washing. With no tubs to fill and empty, washing does not seem like washing. I had rather be without my hand-power washer than the tubs.

My husband had acetylene lights put in, so all the time I once used cleaning and filling oil lamps is now used for other work. With the outfit is the hot plate which makes summer cooking more comfortable.

I have an ironing board on a standard and a gasoline iron so I can iron when and where I choose.

One year I spent almost a day pitting cherries but never again! I bought a pitter and an apple parer. They not only do better and much quicker work but my five-year-old boy can operate them as well as I. Doing every bit of my own work, sewing for all of us even to the making of the children's coats, I must plan to save every minute I can so as to have a little time for reading and other things I enjoy.

By using my bread-mixer, it takes seven minutes to knead bread and have it set to rise.

I must also mention my mop wringer, dust mop and sweeper.

Winter used to mean spending a goodly share of each day carrying "chunks" from the woodshed to keep two heaters going. Now we have a pipeless furnace, all wood for it in the cellar and a much warmer house.—Mrs. L. L.S., N.Y.

Quartette Of Life-Savers

When our laundry bill steadily mounted higher till we were paying two dollars every week for clothes not always well washed, we decided something had to be done. We had a gasoline engine but no wash room, just a back porch too small for engine and washing machine.

A washing machine with engine directly beneath the tub settled that problem as it occupied no more space than an ordinary tub. Less than a year's laundry bill bought it. It not only took the drudgery out of washing but gave us *clean* clothes and saved money.

An old piano stool and a gasoline iron made the combination I thought out that saves so much time and energy and money on ironing days. I found that I could iron as well sitting as standing; the iron was always the right temperature; and no time was lost going to the stove for hot irons. One pint of gasoline is sufficient for a big ironing making the fuel cost almost nothing.

The Home Economics Clubs of this country have formed testing circles for trying out a number of labor-saving devices. I am using the wheeled table or kitchen jitney and have found it such an efficient maid that my boy is going to make me one at school.

The dishes and silver and all the food can be wheeled in at one trip and at the close of the meal one load of used dishes goes back to the kitchen instead of four or five as usual. Counting ten steps from kitchen to dining room (both are small) and at least five trips from one to the other, there is a saving of three hundred steps in one day in the preparation and clearing away of meals.

On ironing day this jitney is close at hand and as the clothes are ironed they are piled on it then wheeled to their proper places.

My kitchen is so small that there is not room for a drain board at the sink but why should I worry? I have a large dish dryer with galvanized dripping pan underneath so I can use it on my kitchen cabinet. I wipe glasses and silver but dishes and cooking utensils are scalded and dried by evaporation. Counting just one-half hour saved in a day, in one week's time I am three and one half hours to the good.

These four articles constitute my much prized quartette of labor savers. Since the foremost women specialists of the American Medical Association agree that a large per cent of the women who die are the unnecessary victims of the strain of housework, I think I may call them life-savers for they eliminate so much of the waste energy that is expended in housekeeping.— Mrs. J. E. T., Wash.

A "Ten Cent Counter"

Perhaps it is putting it too strongly to say I could not keep house without my list of desirable articles, because I did keep house without many of them the first years of my married life. But I was buoyed up by the joyfuyl anticipation of possession as soon as I could afford them.

I believe I shall put my wire dish drainer first on the list because it is such a help and costs so little and is in use three times every day. Next I like my double boiler, and my steam cooker and fireless cooker make a great labor-saving team. Our meals are properly cooked and in short order with these.

My "ten cent counter" as the family calls it, is another great convenience. It is a small shelf that holds kitchen utensils such as funnels, measuring cup, potato ricer, paring knives, putty knife (a fine thing for cleaning sticky kettles), butcher knives and brushes. Underneath is a string of hooks upon which hang large spoons, meat fork, pancake turner, tea strainer, dairy thermometer, egg beater, ladles, corkscrew.

My kitchen cabinet is another standby that I should hate to do without and the food chopper that I keep in it is a convenience that I should greatly miss.

An oil stove helps me many times when it is hot or I am too hurried to wait for the fire to catch. My oil mop is a great help in my cleaning also.

Last but not least I want a few blooming plants on my kitchen window shelf and a few pictures if only cut from magazine covers—a bit of woods or some scene that widens the walls of my kitchen, takes me in fancy away from the daily grind and feeds and refreshes my inner self so that I can be sweet and patient to those that depend upon me for the love and comfort that only a home can give. I often pin a bit of verse or a few lines of prose that appeal to me to my window shelf over my work table that it may be my inspiration when I look that way. These last mentioned helps I *know* I could not keep house without.—Mrs. W. A. H., Ia.

Needs One More

The household help I value most is my mop-wringer, a box-like contrivance of galvanized iron, which fits on the edge of a pail. One side is flexible and provided with a handle and presses the water out of the inserted mop. Boiling water or lye can be used if necessary. There is nothing to get out of order. I paid $1.50 for it sixteen years ago. I could not get it for that now.

Perhaps my food-grinder takes precedence of my bread-mixer. I run squash or pumpkin through instead of laboriously pressing them through a colander. I use it to make orange marmalade which took two hours or more to shred with knives. While I feed the little machine, my husband rushes the peel and pulp through the food chopper in fiften minutes. Mince meat and sausage too are done in quarter the time it takes to chop in a bowl.

With a bread-mixer, the bread takes five instead of twenty minutes as in the old way. I do not touch it with my hands until I mould it into loaves.

My kitchen cabinet is an old-fashioned one, with two large bins and two drawers but no back or shelves. I keep flour in one bin and cereals and groceries in the other.

Then my egg-beater, one with a wheel. *Swish! swish!* and in one minute four or six eggs are well beaten.

I have a long-handled dry mop which can be washed and resprinkled with any dusting oil; it saves me grovelling under the beds and is woe to cobwebs in the high corners; also a soft broom with a shorter handle which is much superior to the stiff brooms for gathering dust on to a dustpan. Another useful thing is a steel for sharpening knives which I have learned to use. I am independent of the men folks for this now. I can remember the time when I sharpened knives on the edge of a crock!

My washing machine is simply a galvanized iron tub, fitted with a funnel-like dasher. It is the best thing I have found for washing flannels or heavy bedding. I also have an ingenious clothes horse which folds up. My father-in-law made it. It holds a lot of clothes. Besides this, I have a large reel outside for drying clothes.

My latest help is a vacuum cleaner, which, if used once a week, obviates the necessity of taking up carpets so often. With the addition of a bent nozzle one can clean couches, chairs or bed mattresses. It certainly is surprising what dirt I can remove with it.

When I find an instrument for dressing fowls, I shall be happy. Perhaps that is asking too much!—Mrs. D. J., N. Y.

Blessed Water

The running water in the house! What a constant cause of thankfulness! What a joy to use all I need and want! And I can not bear to waste it unnecessarily even yet, for memory of former days has left scars so deep. It is foolish for me to say, "I *could* not keep house without it" for I have; and I'll not say, "I *would* not," for circumstances alter cases. One does so much for love and for necessity. But I will say, "I would much *rather* not keep house without it!"

Have you ever, in utter need, heard the clank of the dipper against the sides of an empty water pail? I remember hearing that dismal sound when my little girl, sick and feverish, was crying a drink. Not a drop of cold water in the house for a craving child! The men from the hayfield had drunk the last drop and left the empty pail. The spring was downhill, a long, long way in the hot sun. I could not leave the child, so I took an umbrella for shade, a can for the water and carried her down to the spring.

How delicious it must have tasted on that feverish tongue. Then came the long slow walk back up the hill, with the water and the child, who fortunately was quieted enough to manage the umbrella.

The water from that same spring is in our pressure-tank now but to me *water* is the most necessary, the biggest item in the country household for saving the time and strength of the whole family. Other things shrink into insignificance beside that all-important one.

There is my washing machine. It doesn't *seem* as if I could put through by hand the big washes I have done in the machine. I think I have succeeded where my friends have been disappointed in theirs because I have followed implicitly the directions accompanying it.

My mop wringer! I can remember my mother scrubbing floors on hands and knees with the old scrub brush, or later wringing the heavy, wet mop. My heart is truly thankful, I hope, for the things I do not have to do. I only wish I could share with so many of my neighbors who have not.

I must mention one other labor saver—the Little Maid In The House. She amuses the baby; she runs upstairs and down on errands for me; she sets the table; she is dish washer and drier. She is indeed a constant joy and interest. Could I keep house without her? I would much rather not!—Mrs. H. W., Maine.

Science v. religion

The introduction of Charles Darwin's theories of evolution in the nineteenth century sparked a sharp conflict with many elements of organized religion, particularly Protestant fundamentalist sects which insisted on the purity of biblical authority regarding human creation. The general push for cultural conformity in the 1920s heightened the conflict, and several states passed laws prohibiting the teaching of evolution in public schools and universities. The most notable example occurred in Tennessee and resulted in the 1925 "monkey trial" in Dayton. Despite the conviction of John Scopes, a local schoolteacher, the trial largely discredited the antievolutionists and thereafter their campaign was thwarted in most states. The following letter by E. A. Birge, a university scientist, to his Congregationalist pastor, was in response to a personal attack by William Jennings Bryan. Bryan, then in the twilight of his career, led the anti-evolution crusade and later appeared as a prosecutor in the Scopes trial (Clarence Darrow appeared for the defense). Birge argued that Bryan had introduced a false, unnecessary, anti-intellectual tension between science and religion.

My dear Mr. Worcester:

There was printed in the Capital Times of Feb. 7 a long letter from Mr. Bryan, largely devoted to my alleged errors regarding religion.

From *Wisconsin State Journal*, February 17, 1922.

You know my religious ideas, as your predecessors in the First Congregational church have known them for the past 40 years; but since I am and have long been an officer of the church, and since Mr. Bryan's criticisms obviously assail my right to such a position, I think it not improper for me to send you this statement. . . .

I was fortunate in deriving my religious training from both my father and mother. It would be hard to tell which of them had the more influence on my life, but it is certain that my father had an influence on my religious thought not only greater than that of any other person, but also greater than that of all other persons combined. He had a singularly religious nature. He lived and walked with God in a higher sense of those words than anyone else that I have known; and, like most such men, his fellowship with the Father expressed itself in faith and in life rather than in talk. I owe it to him that when, as a raw youth, I began to look at the world for myself and to form a working philosophy of life, I did so under the guidance and inspiration of the central ideas of the bible. From the first I was taught to look to such truths as that which St. Paul packs into the five words, "All things are of God." I quote this as the shortest expression of a fundamental belief expressed in the bible over and over again in many ways and in many places, and a truth that is central both in the old and the new testaments. The preacher furnishes an equally brief statement in the older revelation, in the words, "God that doeth all."

This truth my father believed—and taught me to believe—not as one of those things that are in the bible and are therefore to be accepted as true in a vague and general sort of way. On the contrary, he believed it as did the writer of Job, as did the author of the one hundred and fourth psalm; he accepted it as St. Paul believed it and as our Lord taught it, that is, as one of the most fundamental of the working beliefs of religion. So it was for him and therefore for me a central truth for the interpretation of thinking and of life, and it enters into both in many directions and on countless occasions. Let me follow it out along one line only—that of God's truth about the work of God—of relation to the world about us, especially the world of life. That relation offers no difficulty to one who accepts the statements that I have quoted from the bible and which it repeats in more specific form in scores of places. I can not quote a tenth of the passages which apply specifically this general truth about the work of God—of whom and through whom and to whom are all things.

If we look to the plant world, St. Paul tells us that we sow a "bare grain" and that God "giveth to each seed a body of its own." Our Lord told us the same truth in a paraable when he said that God "clothes the grass of the field."

As to the animal world, I wish I could quote in full the one hundred and fourth psalm, which tells us how God is sending forth His spirit to create each of the inhabitants of the sea from Leviathan to the "creeping things innumerable both small and great;" that each of these creatures wiats on God for its food, thrives as God maintains it, falls when "God hides His face," dies when God takes away its breath; and as they die, God again "renews the face of the earth." This psalm and others like it give us in larger and more general terms the same teaching which our Lord, according to His custom, gave us by concrete illustrations when He told of God's relation to the feeding of the birds, to the fall of the sparrow, and to the clothing of the flowers. It is the same doctrine that St. Paul sums up in the phrase, "He giveth to all life and breath and all things."

And the bible deals with man in the same way. "Thine hands," said Job, "have framed me and fashioned me together round about"—not man in the beginning, nor man in a general way, but—my body, with its skin and flesh, bone and sinew, in all its organs and tissues, was framed by God's hands, just as my mind came direct from "the breath of the Almighty."

Do I need to quote more in order to show that St. Paul's teaching merely falls into line with that of his predecessors when he tells us that God "giveth all things to all"?

You will not be surprised, then, to have me say that much of the religious discussion about evolution puzzled me, just as Mr. Bryan's handling of the subject would puzzle any boy whose good fortune it had been to receive an education like mine. For while these critics were deeply concerned to have people believe that there was a direct relation between God and nature, in the remote past, they never seemed to think that such a direct relation exists today. The writers of the bible, on the other hand, believed that God is always at work in the world about us in a way as immediate and as direct as possible. They believed that God today is doing all things, and their faith in His past working was a result of their vision of His present activity. These preachers of my youth asserted that all religion depends on our believing that "original creation" came directly from God. The bible tells us that religion depends on our finding God doing all things immediately about us at all times, so that in Him we "live and move and have our being."

Still further, you will see that one who believes these words of St. Paul would find it hard to get excited over God's relations to nature in the distant past. If I "live and move and have my being" in God today,—if—to use present day terms—my environment, physical and spiritual, is God, if God today is giving to me and "to all life and breath and all things," it does not need much argument to show that He was the same and did the same at every time and at all times and for all creatures in the past.

So with regard to science. Some of the preachers of my boyhood found science "atheistic" because it tried to tell how things are done in the world. But the bible tells us not only that God gives "to each seed its body" but also that "the earth bringeth forth fruit of herself." There is no contradiction in these statements which are only the same thing stated from different points of view. All religion is contained implicitly in the first just as all science is an enlargement of the second. The critics of my youth were much disturbed by statements of the second type and no doubt some people may smell irreligion or worse in it today. But no one who believes for himself that he "lives and moves and has his being" in God can be disturbed by this or by any statement of science. He has learned that if he wants to know how God gives a seed its own body he must ask the botanist; if he wants to know how God "sends forth His spirit and creates" any "creeping thing" of the waters he must ask the zoologist; if he wants to know how God's hands "framed and fashioned" his body he must learn from embryology how "the bones do grow in the womb of her that is with child."

These are all questions of fact and are to be answered from a knowledge of the facts and in no other way; and this is equally true whether they have reference to the present or the past history of life.

I do not write this letter as a full statement of my ideas on either religion or science. But I think that you may fairly learn from it how it has come about that I have taken part both in the religious and the scientific activities of the world in which I have lived, with no thought of conflict or even division between them. I have never found it necessary to justify religion to science or to excuse science to religion. I have accepted both as equally divine revelations, and both as equally wrought into the constitution of the world. I have believed that wisdom and might are God's and I have equally believed that science reveals to us how that might and that wisdom are expressed in the operation of the world. This has been my faith for the past 50 years or more and I am hardly likely to abandon it now.

There are two specific points to which I may give briefer notice. Mr. Bryan seemed to dislike especially my objecting to his uniting religion to a "discredited scientific hypothesis." I think that the history of the church gives good ground for my objection. In the 15th century people were told that the doctrine of a round world was "atheistic." The same term was applied to geology in the late eighteenth and early nineteenth centuries, and in the late nineteenth century evolution was in like manner called "atheistic" by men of whom Mr. Bryan is a belated follower. Who today looks back with pride upon those earlier attempts to keep back science by the authority of religion? Or was the cause of religion advanced when men were told that the only way to hold their faith in God was to unite their faith with the belief that the earth is flat and that the sun and stars revolve about it? Did such teachings help religion in the past and is there any good reason to think that Mr. Bryan will succeed where his predecessors have failed dismally during four centuries?

The fundamental error of all these people was in making religion depend at all on specific scientific theories, whether right or wrong. For, however correct scientific theories may be today, they may be changed tomorrow and will probably be almost unrecognizable a century hence. If, therefore, religion is tied up with any such theory it is likely to be discarded by people when the theory has to be changed. Such an attempted union may not hurt science, and ordinarily it does not; but it is sure to hurt religion, and I have a right to protest against such injury. . . .

The harmful effect of such teachings was clearly seen in many of those who used to oppose evolution. They told us that we bear the image of God because of God's work in the creation of a remote ancestor; but they never thought of telling us that God sent forth His spirit and created in His image you and me and every baby that ever was born. They had to look far back in the history of the world before they could see that the hand of God was at work to frame and fashion man, and they talked like those who had never found the God who is daily and hourly giving to all of his life and breath and all things.

It was the presence in Mr. Bryan's speech of this attitude of mind that called out my protest to him. For I am sure that we must accept, as basal among our religious beliefs, the teachings of the bible derived from prophet and poet, from apostle, and from our Lord, that "all things are of God" today, that the past came from His hand just as the present is coming, and that our faith in the future is our faith in a present God.

Old wine in new bottles: the revival of the Klan

While traditionalists in America regarded evolutionary theories as one kind of threat to treasured values, they responded with equal vigor to their perception of danger from the growing power of "foreign" elements. The 1920s witnessed a strong revival of nativist, xenophobic, and racist sentiments, particularly by rural Protestants. In the South, and now significantly in widespread areas of the nation, the Ku Klux Klan reemerged as an accepted authority for the keeper of native values and traditions. Crosses were burned, nightriders intimidated blacks, but most important, the Klan utilized public forums to speak out against the dangers of race mongrelization, Popery, Jews, and other foreign influences. Undoubtedly, the Klan's power contributed to the defection of some southern states from the Democratic party in the election of 1928, when Al Smith, son of Irish immigrants and a Catholic, was the party's standard-bearer. And throughout the nation, the Klan disseminated anti-Catholic publicity, surely contributing to Smith's over-

From *The Ku Klux Klan,* Committee on Rules, House of Representatives, 67th Congress, 1st Session, pp. 15–27.

whelming defeat by Herbert Hoover. The following comments by a former Klansman summarize the purposes of the Klan and some of its activities in New York City.

Mr. CAMPBELL. Mr. Wright, will you state your name to the stenographer?

Mr. WRIGHT. C. Anderson Wright. . . . I was formerly a member of the New York klan, king kleagle, assigned as chief of staff of the invisible planet, Knights of the Air. Gentlemen, I urge an—

Mr. CAMPBELL (interposing). When were you a member of the klan?

Mr. WRIGHT. When was I a member?

Mr. CAMPBELL. Yes.

Mr. WRIGHT. Up until the 14th of this month; I mean last month.

Mr. CAMPBELL. The 14th of last September?

Mr. WRIGHT. No; this October.

Mr. CAMPBELL. This is October.

Mr. WRIGHT. I mean the month before that, September.

Mr. CAMPBELL. You were a member up to the 14th of September last?

Mr. WRIGHT. Yes, sir.

Mr. CAMPBELL. State again what empire or part of the empire you had jurisdiction over.

Mr. WRIGHT. The aeronautical unit known as the Knights of the Air.

Mr. CAMPBELL. What was your jurisdiction?

Mr. WRIGHT. The whole United States in this department.

Mr. CAMPBELL. Who appointed you?

Mr. WRIGHT. Edward Young Clarke, the imperial kleagle.

Mr. CAMPBELL. From Atlanta?

Mr. WRIGHT. From Atlanta. I was stationed in Atlanta. . . . I was in the Air Service, and I am a reserve in the Army to-day. Through that I was interested in aeronautics, I joined the klan in New York and was very much interested in it at that time, as I was in other fraternal orders of which I am a member, and thought it was a very good thing until I got to Atlanta. . . . I was unassigned and was automatically placed in charge of the Knights of the Air as chief of saff. It was an affiliated branch. I have documentary evidence to prove that. . . .

Mr. CAMPBELL. Is there an open roster of the members?

Mr. WRIGHT. No, sir. They have a very elaborate file system in Atlanta in the imperial palace; each member in each klan is kept in a certain division of very expensive steel files; each drawer is pulled out and it has a list of the members card by card, but those are not accessible to anybody but the secretary of the order, the imperial secretary.

Mr. CAMPBELL. You say there was a class of 200 when you were initiated?

Mr. WRIGHT. Yes, sir.

Mr. CAMPBELL. Were the members of the class made known to their friends?

Mr. WRIGHT. No, sir; nobody knew who was in the class, as everybody was afraid of the thing; they did not know what it was all about, and the men who were putting on the work were very timid. Mr. Clarke [the Imperial Kleagle] came to New York for the occasion to officiate at the conferring of this first degree. It was done in the Masonic Temple in New York City, in one of lodge rooms. Clarke tells about how he put on the first class and how he fooled the police of New York City. He has boasted many times that a captain of the New York police force went into the order at this time, and that Enright had his squad looking for Clarke all over New York and these members; that this captain of police sent this squad, which was the bomb squad in New York, off in another direction while the men were sent notice to meet at this Masonic Temple room, where the degree was conferred. Everybody was a stranger to each other that night, and the ceremony was kind of bungled without question, and after everybody was getting very nervous and just about ready to go out, finally three robed figures appeared in the regalia of the klan, and after they had obligated everybody by going through a very short part of the ritual and the oaths they removed their masks, and these men were Edward Young Clarke, the imperial kleagle; William Coburn, who was at that time in charge of the work here in Washington, D.C., in your city here, and later became the supreme attorney of the order, and the last time I heard of him he was grand goblin on the Pacific coast; the other man was Lloyd P. Hooper, who was the organizer, salesman, and field worker. He had seen the possibilities of the name Ku-Klux Klan and had gone to Atlanta to negotiate and had come back here with authority to organize the Ku-Klux Klan. . . .

Mr. CAMPBELL. What were your instructions with respect to whom you should regulate and how, and how you were to serve the klan or uplift the community?

Mr. WRIGHT. My instructions as a klansman were simply starting in and giving the Jews the dickens in New York. Their idea was this, as preached by Clarke and Hooper in my presence, with several other prospective members whom I brought up, that the Jew patronizes the Jew, if possible: therefore, we as klansmen, the only real 100 per cent Americans, will only patronize klansmen. Now, the idea was this, to simply organize everybody that was of their belief and religious belief into this order and they would practice not only moral clannishness but also practical clannishness; in other words, a klansman would be compelled to buy from another klansman if possible. That was how it was explained to us by Hooper. He did not really know much about it at that time; he was simply out for the money he could make out of it, and that was also explained by Clarke. They said, "In New York City here we have all the Jews; they are controlling New York; we will get under here and when we have 10,000 members here, if we do not want a certain man to do a certain thing, if this man receives 10,000 letters or telegrams stating that he should not do this thing, he is not very apt to do it." In other words, if a member of the klan should be brought on trial before a certain judge or jury, if that judge or jury received 10,000 requests from New York to do a certain thing, they would be pretty apt to do it. That was their idea of gaining control of the courts.

Mr. CAMPBELL. What, if anything, were you told about the wearing of the mask, or were you told it was important that you should do that?

Mr. WRIGHT. You only wore the mask, according to imperial instructions, when you were in the klavern or klan, and then only when what they called the aliens or strangers or people to be initiated were present. Of course, in official parades it was up to the exalted cyclops. . . .

Mr. KREIDER. What was the object to be accomplished, or what were the duties of the aerial service?

Mr. WRIGHT. I will tell you what my idea is and what the ideas of the flyers of this country were. We saw that the Aero Club of America and other organizations were absolutely going out of existence: they were decaying; and we felt that we should get a fraternal order together of flyers to promote commercial aviation and give the boys a chance to fly. We are all reserve officers, or some of us are, and since we have been out of the Army we have never seen an airplane. If we take our reserve documents and go to a field to fly we are told there are no ships available, and we have to go through a certain medical examination, which is ridiculous, but we can not fly. So we got several together, and I will name a few of the men, including Reed Landis, one of our famous aces and son of Judge Landis, of Chicago; Jack Swaab, also one of our aces, who, by the way, is part Jewish, and Sydney Owens, who is an ace and lives in Philadelphia, and Maj. Biddle, also an ace and lives in Philadelphia. . . .

Mr. KREIDER. Did all the members of this organization, known as the Knights of the Air, have to be members of the Ku-Klux Klan?

Mr. WRIGHT. No, sir; but here is where the hitch came, as decided by Clarke; he said, "No man can become an officer of the Knights of the Air who is not a klansman; we will absolutely control the Knights of the Air through having only klansmen as officers." That was the first thing; and then Clarke decided that the equipment that the klan got should be placed in his name and not in the name of the Knights of the Air, his idea being to absolutely control it with an iron hand. As I say, out there it was talked over for two days what we were going to do, and he was very visionary, and he saw Edward Young Clarke controlling the air in America, without question or belief. . . .

Mr. KREIDER. Was this organization to be used later on or at any time to terrorize men?

Mr. WRIGHT. Oh, no. The Knights of the Air was simply started into being with the flyers as something to get us together, and was capitalized by Clarke as a money-making plan; that is all. I afterwards saw letters, after I left Atlanta, being sent out under the name of Mr. Cherry, who was a klansman, and an assistant over in the office, who had never seen an airplane, I think, to all the aero clubs and flyers throughout the country, saying what a great thing the Knights of the Air was; in fact, after I left there, there was nobody that I know of that was a flyer or a reserve officer in the Army. It was simply a case of Clarke's ideas being absolutely so that no man could conscientiously go into it as a reserve officer in the United States Army. There is no question about it. The whole Ku-Klux Klan is simply based on treason against the country, in this way, that they have planned and schemed and would have, if not publicly exposed, gotten control of practically every seat of government through their tremendous voting power. In the State of Texas to-day I venture to say that practically all the smaller cities are absolutely controlled by the klan from the mayor on down. Texas should be the headquarters of the Ku-Klux Klan and not Georgia, because in Georgia they all look upon it more as a joke—the Atlanta people. . . .

Mr. FESS. What is the purpose of the parades we hear about?

Mr. WRIGHT. The parades?

Mr. FESS. Yes; we have had statements about terrorizing.

Mr. WRIGHT. Well, the idea is this, which I can prove and will be very glad to file before the committee, by their own semiofficial organ, the Searchlight —the idea was simply to terrorize people by showing their strength. To cite an instance of that, in Dallas, Tex., they were having trouble there with a certain class of the building trades—I do not know just exactly what it was—and the klan decided they would hold a parade to show their strength. So it seems like it was all arranged with the city authorities and the parade was held in Dallas, and they marched down the street in full regalia, and about the time they appeared the lights were all extinguished, and the next day the people were back at work. This is cited in their semiofficial organ and in the press throughout the country. . . .

Mr. SNELL. What induced you to disclose the secrets of the klan?

Mr. WRIGHT. Why did I?

Mr. SNELL. Yes; anything special?

Mr. WRIGHT. Yes, sir. My reason was simply this: I have nothing against the mass of klansmen. They go into it in ignorance, and I knew that. My idea was not to expose so much race hatred, which would drive lots of people into the klan. In other words, there are enough narrow-minded people who would be glad enough to join an order against the Jews, Catholics, foreign born, and Negroes; but if you can show a man where he was simply taken in and made a goat of in order to get money out of him by selling all these mystic contrivances and show him how his money went and the men it was making wealthy and the women who was behind the whole thing and show him where the man at the head of the order was not receiving any money or the imperial treasury was not receiving any money, I figures the klansmen should know that and would be glad to know that, whether they had done any violence or anything else. In other words, I think to-day the more the papers preach on the Ku-Klux Klan as preaching racial hatred, the more members they are going to get, because there are so many narrow-minded people who will join, but when you can show them where their money goes and what a fool he is made and the character of the people getting it, then I think the klansmen of the country will realize and wake up to what they have gone into.

Mr. SNELL. That is, your only interest was to show the foolishness of the whole proposition?

Mr. WRIGHT. To show the people who were getting the money; that was it.

Mr. RODENBERG. And how they were being duped into this organization?

Mr. WRIGHT. To show how they were being duped and show up this woman who was really the power behind the whole thing. Also, the klan are preaching the chastity of the home and the purity of the womanhood of our country, when the real leading spirit of the klan, I found out absolutely, and the one behind the throne, was a notorious sporting-house keeper in Atlanta, which has been proven in court records, and the man who is the imperial kleagle, the real man who is the head of the order, and this woman were living in adultery together in Atlanta on a beautiful estate which has been bought with their supplies, and then I thought it was up to them to know who were running the klan and preaching morality, and so forth.

Mr. JOHNSON. Mr. Wright, something has been said somewhere in this testimony or in a letter sent to Members of the House by Mr. Terrell, their attorney, that Members of the Senate and House were members of this Ku-Klux Klan; do you know anything about that?

Mr. WRIGHT. Only by boasting. I have never sat in conclave assembly or klan lodge room with anybody I knew to be a high official of the United States Government or of any eastern department. I do know that the governor of Georgia was bitterly against the klan, the former governor of Georgia, Gov. Dorsey, and openly attacked it, and the prosecuting attorney of Atlanta admitted he was a klansman when this trial came up about this Lakewood tragedy.

Mr. JOHNSON. Did the imperial wizard or any of these goblins or cyclops ever tell you that Members of Congress belonged to the klan?

Mr. WRIGHT. Oh, yes, sir. It was openly boasted all the time, especially by Clarke, how they would soon control Congress. . . .

VI

Depression and War: 1929-1945

CHAPTER 15

The social impact of depression

The trauma of relief

The stock market crash in October 1929 immediately produced a general decline in a broad array of economic indicators. Gross national product, foreign trade, and wholesale commodity prices dropped sharply, and unemployment rose to unprecedented heights, peaking at over thirteen million in 1932. The traditional work ethic beliefs in initiative, opportunity, and perseverance clashed sharply with the realities of the times. For those who desperately sought work and failed to find it, bitterness and frustration with the "system" became an immeasurable social by-product. The lack of work was enough to depress one's spirit and sense of belonging as well as financial condition. Perhaps nothing jarred middle-class Americans more in the 1930s than the prospect or reality of applying for direct relief. The following article, written by a college graduate who described herself as a "member of the middle class," reveals the impact of going on relief for such people. The author describes the traditional values learned during her childhood—education, thrift, and cleanliness—that distinguished her from "them," that is, the poor, the lazy, the "submerged tenth" of society. But the Great Depression cut sharply across class lines. With her husband, an unemployed professional musician, the family finally had to apply for relief and she poignantly discovered what it was like to be one of "them." Dealing with relief authorities, the author also learned the demeaning, arbitrary character of bureaucratic forces that at times manipulate, if not totally dominate, the people they are supposed to serve.

"The submerged tenth." I remember when I was yet in pigtails how I sat reading in the stuffy parlor where Mother kept the shade drawn so the sun would not fade the furniture. I had found the little book in Father's library. It described in lurid terms how *they* live, suffering from hunger, squalor, dirt, and ignorance. The author took it for granted that the four were inseparable. She went on to explain how *we* must fulfill our Christian duty, not merely by feeding their hunger, but by inculcating our godly virtues of thrift, cleanliness, and education. My young heart was full of sentimental tinder and easy to set on fire. I thought then that I would grow up to be a social worker.

When I went to college I studied sociology. I was taught that hunger, squalor, dirt, and ignorance are the results of environment. Charity, therefore, is no

From Ann Rivington [pseud.], "We Live on Relief," *Scribner's Magazine* 95 (April 1934): 282–285.

solution. We must change the environment. In order to do this we have settlement houses, playgrounds, and social workers in the slums.

In the past year and a half I have again revised my opinion. I am no longer one of *us*. For all my education, my training in thrift and cleanliness, I am become one of *them*. My condition is shared by a large sector of the population. From my new place in society I regard the problems and misery of the poor with new eyes.

Two years ago I was living in comfort and apparent security. My husband had a good position in a well-known orchestra and I was teaching a large and promising class of piano pupils. When the orchestra was disbanded we started on a rapid down-hill path. My husband was unable to secure another position. My class gradually dwindled away. We were forced to live on our savings.

In the early summer of 1933 I was eight months pregnant and we had just spent our last twelve dollars on one month's rent for an apartment. We found that such apartments really exist. They lack the most elementary comforts such as steam heat, bathtubs, sunlight, and running hot water. They usually are infested with mice and bedbugs. Ours was. Quite often the ceilings leak. In our apartment the leaks became so bad that every time it rained we were forced to set kettles around the room to catch the worst of the deluge. Sometimes we had to wait half the night, sitting around in dry corners, before it was possible to mop up and go to bed.

What, then, did we do for food when our last money was spent on rent? In vain we tried to borrow more. So strong was the influence of our training that my husband kept looking feverishly for work when there was no work, and blaming himself because he was unable to find it. Another thing we did was to open a charge account at the corner grocery on the recommendation of our next-door neighbors. An application to the Emergency Home Relief Bureau was the last act of our desperation.

My husband took care of the actual application. I was then unable to walk the three miles to the public-school building that served as a relief station. We were so completely uninformed about the workings of charitable organizations that we thought all we need do was to make clear to the authorities our grave situation in order to receive immediate attention. I had some vague idea that our "superior qualifications" would bring us instant sympathy and help.

My husband came home some five hours later with an application blank in his pocket. All this time he had been waiting, he told me, with more than fifty other people.

We filled out the application with great care. It was an interesting document. I was surprised at the request for proof of two years' residence. What if we had moved here only a year ago and were in our present situation? What then? There must be plenty of people like that.

There were many questions to which we had no answer. "List property owned in full or in part." "Insurance. Give names of insurance companies."

"How much money have you now? In the bank?" "Have any persons, friends or relatives, helped you in the past year?"

The next morning my husband started early for the bureau. He returned at about two o'clock, very hungry and weak from the heat. But he was encouraged.

"Well, I got to talk to somebody this time," he said. "She asked me over again all the questions on that paper and more besides. Then she said to go home and wait. An investigator should be around tomorrow or day after. On account of your condition she marked the paper urgent." The next day we waited, and all of two days more. The fourth day, which was Saturday, my husband went back to the bureau. It was closed until Monday.

On Sunday morning the Italian grocer reminded me of our bill. "It get too big," he said. We cut down to one meal a day, and toast.

Monday brought no investigator. Tuesday my husband was at the bureau again. This time he came home angry.

"They said the investigator was here Friday and we were out. I got sore and told them somebody was lying."

"But you shouldn't. Now they won't help us."

"Now they will help us. She'll be here tomorrow."

Late Wednesday afternoon the investigator arrived. She questioned us closely for more than half an hour on our previous and present situation, our personal lives, our relatives. This time we certainly expected the check. But we were told to wait.

"I'm a special investigator. The regular one will be around Friday with the check."

My husband was in a torment of anxiety. "But we can't wait till Friday. We owe ten dollars downstairs now, and they won't let us charge any more. We have to eat something. My wife ———"

The investigator looked tired. "You'll just have to put them off. I must make my report. And there are other cases ahead of yours."

By Monday morning we had nothing for breakfast but oatmeal, without sugar or milk. We decided we must go together to the bureau and find out what was wrong. It seemed to us that my appearance at that time would lend emphasis to our plea. Therefore, as soon as we had finished breakfast, we borrowed carfare from our kind neighbors and started out.

We reached the relief station a good fifteen minutes before nine. . . . I watched the people around us. There they sat waiting, my fellow indigents. Bodies were gaunt or flabby, faces—some stoical, some sullen—all care-worn like my husband's. What had they done, or left undone, to inherit hunger? What was this relief we were asking for? Certainly it was not *charity*. It was dispensed too grudgingly, too harshly, to be that. I smiled bitterly as I remembered the grace my father used to repeat before meals: "Lord make us thankful for that which we are about to receive."

When our turn came to talk to one of the women behind the desks we were told that the checks had been held up for lack of funds and that we should go home and wait for an investigator "some time this week." We were not going to be put off in this manner. My husband told her, "We have to have something more than promises. There's no food in the house, and my wife can't live on air."

"Well, that's all I can tell you," said the woman. I went to the back of the room and sat down again. My husband stood near the desk, and between other cases he went up and talked further.

"If that's all you can tell me, who knows more than you? We're not leaving without a better answer."

The woman's voice rose. "You can't talk to me like that!" A guard was hovering near, ready, as I thought, to eject us.

"Then whom can I talk to? I want the supervisor." I came up and stood beside my husband. At last the supervisor was called.

"The checks will be out tomorrow night. You will get yours Thursday."

"And what are we to do till Thursday? Already, you made us a promise you didn't keep. We need food now, and we're not leaving till we know where it's coming from."

The supervisor did not seem enthusiastic about our staying longer. If I had not been so obviously pregnant, I think we would have been thrown into the street. As it was, he picked up the telephone and, with my husband's instruction, called Pete the grocer and asked him to honor our account for two days more.

"As I told you, you will have the check Thursday morning," he repeated as we left.

Sure enough, early Thursday afternoon the regular investigator arrived. He gave us a check for eight-fifty to cover two weeks' food. We had already spent two dollars at the grocer's since the supervisor's phone call, and this amount, of course, was counted off the check. But Pete was not satisfied.

"Gotta take off more. I poor too."

I shook my head. "Wait," I said. "We'll pay you, but not this time."

I looked around the little shop hungrily. A pregnant woman's taste for delicacies was accentuated by the days of semi-starvation. I was tortured by a great longing for fresh fruit.

"How much are the grapes?" I asked.

"No grapes," said Pete. "No grapes for you."

"But why not, Pete?"

"Grapes are luxury. You get beans, potatoes, onions. Poor people no eat grapes."

I was bewildered. But Pete meant what he said. He showed me a bulletin he had received from the Relief Bureau, listing the things allowed on the food checks of the jobless. I cannot remember all the regulations. The paper was too long and involved for that. But I do remember that only dried fruit was listed. The quantities of eggs, butter, milk, were strictly limited. No meat except salt pork, unsliced bacon, pig's liver and other entrails. Rice, beans, potatoes, bread, onions were the main items to be sold. I saw no mention of fresh vegetables. I was highly indignant. . . .

My baby was born one week later in a public ward where I was taken as an emergency case. The nine days' hospital experience is no part of this history, which deals with my adventures, as one of the city's unemployed, in obtaining food and shelter. But it is necessary to state in this place that I came home after nine days, ill and weak from inadequate care, bad food, and far too short a rest in bed. I came home with a dawning consciousness of my position, not as a unique sufferer, but as one of the mighty and growing mass who had somehow come to be cast aside as useless in the present scheme of things, cast aside in spite of the various skills and talents they may have possessed.

As summer wore away into fall we began to feel the effects of the inflation, so widely heralded in the newspapers as a harbinger of prosperity. Week by week the price of almost every food item rose steadily, a penny or two at a time. Since our relief checks remained the same, our diet became poorer and poorer. By the first of October we were down once more to one meal a day, supplemented by toast and coffee. We told our investigator about this, but to no purpose. He repeated to us that we were getting all that was possible, that he was forced to skip other cases entirely some weeks because he had not enough money at his disposal.

Gradually the more and more deficient diet began to tell on us. We did not lose much weight—the very poor usually eat plenty of starch—but we began to suffer from general debility, colds, minor infections. The baby, who had thrived at first, cried a great deal, especially during the night. Finally we had her weighed, and found that in the last month and a half she had not gained an ounce, in fact, had lost a trifle. After we made that discovery we curtailed our own diet even farther, in order to give her Grade A milk and orange juice.

We began to have other serious worries. Now the landlord was becoming a frequent and insistent visitor. He was a small, dry-faced individual, with a deceptive air of taking everybody into his confidence. For his benefit we invented all kinds of imaginary expectations of money. At last he gave us one week more in which to pay up all we owed him. He called again the next day. He stood in the doorway, dressed in his well-tailored suit, and explained dolefully that the bank was going to foreclose—all on account of us.

We admitted that we were on relief, and promised to ask for a rent check. He explained that such a thing was impossible. The relief was not giving out rent checks except after eviction. It would cost him fifteen dollars to evict us, and the check would be for only twelve. He would lose three dollars.

"Try to borrow," he said as he left, "or do something. I'll be back in a few days." When he was well out of earshot my husband and I looked at each other and burst into hysterical laughter.

"Poor landlord!" my husband cried: "He's almost as badly off as we are, just because we can't pay the rent!"

The city elections were approaching. We did not suppose that they would affect us in the least. What, then, was our surprise when the investigator brought us a rent check. It might or might not have been intended as a bribe for our vote. We were too cynical, at that time, to see any connection between economics and politics, and we refrained from voting. However, the check helped us for the time being to stave off the fear of eviction.

The problem of insufficient food was becoming daily more serious. I still held my baby to dry breasts before giving her the milk mixture. She was developing digestive troubles.

As the cold weather came on our apartment became more and more unbearable. The damp chill ate into our bones. The place had no heating facilities except a fireplace without a grate. The end of November we received a coal order from the relief, and by taking it to the nearest police station my husband could obtain coal, provided he carried it home, half a mile, on his back . . . .

Three days of nightmare we spent in that icy place while my husband searched out a shelter for us. At last, a friend who had a small steam-heated apartment in a slum even poorer than our own told us that he was leaving town and we might move into the place if we liked. The relief was paying rents for the winter, and the fifteen-dollar rental was within their budget for a family of three. We should be able to get a rent check by the time the first payment was due. Our friend would "lend" us the money for the moving bill.

The day before we moved we had dinner with our friend. We talked a long time after dinner.

"How much relief did you say you're getting," our host wanted to know. We told him.

"Is that all? It seems pretty small. We have a neighbor over here who's working as an investigator. I'll ask her to come in and give us the dope."

The neighbor was called and introduced. She took a pencil and did some figuring.

"You should be getting ten dollars," she said, "ever since early fall." She showed us how the amount was determined: "$1.65 a week for a man, $1.55 for a woman, $1.00 for a baby, add 15 per cent, then add 15 cents for soap; multiply by two. That should be the check."

"But why don't they give us that, then?"

She laughed. "Either your investigator was too lazy to figure, or, well, he may have been trying to make sure of his job. You see, the investigators are terribly overworked, and always afraid of being fired and having to go back to the relief allowance themselves. We're under pressure to give as little help as possible, to refuse relief on the slightest excuse, to miss some families with the checks occasionally. At the same time, if cases complain, the whole blame is thrown on us. So if we lie to people, or 'put the fear of God into them,' it's all in self-defense. The only ones who get what they're entitled to are those who know what is their quota and demand it, especially if they make their demands in an organized way."

After we moved we got our rent check, our ten-dollar food check, letters to turn on our light and gas, a weekly order for salt pork, butter, bread, and eggs, by demanding these things and demanding them fearlessly. About a month ago my husband applied for work under a musicians' project of the Civil Works Service. As yet he has not been notified of any work, though he takes the long hike across town several times a week, to be sure he is not being forgotten. It begins to look as if this, too, is a help only available to those making insistent demands.

Meanwhile we are still living on the relief. While our position in the new apartment is less desperate, the neighborhood is infinitely worse, and the uncertainty as maddening as ever. We feel ourselves always on the edge of a precipice, with nothing to save us, sooner or later, from the abyss. We keep wondering, questioning. What if our check does not come next week? What when the relief bureau stops paying rents for the summer? Will we be evicted? Will our family be broken up, our little girl taken away from us? After a time these questions reach out beyond our burning personal needs. What is the cause of our suffering? Whither is it leading us, and the increasing millions like us? What is wrong with the system, the civilization that brings with it such wholesale misery? My own voice is one of many that are asking, more and more insistently.

Make-work or dignity? the WPA

The idea of government as employer of last resort was one of the most controversial political questions in the 1930s. As the government instituted public works projects under the auspices of such agencies as the Civil Works Administration, the Public Works Administration, and the Works Progress Administration (WPA), critics charged that they were nothing more than boondoggles designed to gain political support for the Roosevelt administration. The notion of a lazy WPA worker, leaning on his pick or shovel, was widely publicized by the New Deal's detractors. On the other hand, supporters of public works projects argued that such work stimulated the econ-

From "I Build a Highway," *North American Review* 247 (Summer 1939): 241–250.

omy, gave dignity to workers which a system of direct relief handouts did not, and finally, the projects themselves represented substantial contributions for the society and the future. The author of the following selection, a WPA worker, was well aware of the criticism but eloquently defended the system as an alternative to relief payments, and he displayed a keen appreciaton of its future value.

Several months before this is written, on April 30, 1938, to be precise, I began to assist in the widening of one of the most necessary and important traffic arteries in the State of Ohio. Now I am not a road builder by training, temperament or profession. I am nothing more than one small unit of a battalion of workers equipped with picks and shovels who are at work on the reconstruction of that highway which is officially designated as WPA Project Number 16523-K.

As for my personal self, I am known to the WPA foremen, superintendents, timekeepers, accountants and paymasters as Number 83202. To the casual reader this may suggest the mechanism of Sing Sing or that of a chain gang in Georgia, but to me, a realist in my own right, it expresses nothing more nor less than the absolute prerequisite for the successful conduct of a highly intricate and essential accounting system.

Why did I become a part of this road-building industry? you may inquire. Well, it's like this. Along with millions of other writers, physicians, lawyers, plumbers, carpenters, architectural draftsmen, machinists, steel workers, automobile workers, painters, bricklayers and whatnot, I became excessively weary of waiting for Private Industry to employ my services since the débâcle of the year 1929. Not that we didn't want to work; approximately nine out of every ten of us are glad to go to work at "anything," even roadbuilding, since we are told that corporations, while showing a modest black balance for the final quarter of 1937 and the first quarter of 1938, are, nevertheless, "not hiring anybody; on the contrary, they are dismissing employees; retrenching, so to speak, because they are fearful of the policies of the Administration."

These mouthpieces of these same corporations are the same voices which come over your radio with re-echoes of "budget balancing," pointing out, incidentally, the terrific burdens of taxation under which our children and grandchildren will groan and sweat blood. Be all that as it may, most of us highway-builders ae not greatly concerned about our children's children at the moment. What concerns us most vitally is the inevitable urge for a cheese sandwich and a pint of cold milk during that midday period which members of the Chamber of Commerce term "luncheon." . . .

Well, now that we have been put to work, building roads among other things, you may ask us how are we doing in our new careers, accompanied, of course, by the inevitable question: do we actually *work* while we are on the job? Of course, I am as familiar as you are with the hundreds of cartoons which have appeared in hundreds of American newspapers which depict us, WPA workers, leaning on a pick at the side of a country road, or if the cartoonist becomes tired of showing us leaning on a pick, he portrays us in the act of leaning on a shovel.

As a matter of fact, my gentle reader, we do occasionally lean on our picks and shovels, but before I tell you why we do so, it is first necessary to tell you something about the manner in which we are going about the task of widening Cedar Road in the vicinity of Cleveland, Ohio, as covered by WPA Project 16523-K.

In the first place, there are more than one hundred of us excavating the dirt, slag, cinders, brick, sod, etc., which is the present formation of the roadbed to the right of the paved highway, proceeding east. After we have excavated miles and miles of this right side of the highway, I am told unofficially, we will return on our excavating tour on the left side of the road, going west. I do not know just how long this will take; besides, it is none of my business. That we are making noteworthy progress is obvious to anyone, even to any indignant taxpayer who happens to motor through our ranks at the speed of seventy miles an hour. For example, the concrete mixer and its accompanying pavement-laying gang are always right behind us, pouring in the cement, and it is our job to keep well ahead of them, which, of course, we do. And when I tell you that the concrete is poured in and dried at the rate of approximately a quarter of a mile every day in the week, excepting Sunday, you may readily comprehend that we are excavating and shoveling at a lively rate.

And oh, yes, about our leaning on picks and shovels, which I have conceded in the foregoing. I neglected to mention that our pick-digging requires an excavation exactly nine inches deep. The preliminary digging is done after the manner of constructing a small trench, and the final excavations must be graded evenly by the men with the shovels. Now when your pick wielder is tearing his laborious way through layers of mixed sod, gravel, slag, paving brick, assorted clays and the like, there is nothing more readily available for his partner, the shovel expert, than to stand by and lean on his shovel, which is simpler than balancing the shovel on his cranium or his nose after the manner of a vaudeville juggler.

You must try to bear in mind, even if it hurts, that the man or boy you observe leaning on his shovel has just completed the task of removing anywhere from ten to forty shovelsful of the aforementioned mixture from the same trench in which the pick wielder is now busily engaged. And if you hadn't whizzed past that same trench at such a dizzy rate of motoring speed, you might have witnessed the unholy spectacle of the pick wielder whom you saw at work pause after his pick had torn into the earth for the twenty-seventh time, and lean indolently on his pick while the shovelman went to work.

Perhaps some method may be discovered eventually by which the knights of the pick and shovel may be inducted into a work program of perennial activity, a picking and shoveling simultaneously in the same trench, or possibly the evolution of a superman wielding a pick and a shovel concurrently, a sort of an efficiency technique based on the perpetual motion principle; but thus far such a technique is regarded as physically hazardous, if not downright murder, in any civilized community.

With those labored explanations, if you still feel that WPA workers receive sixty cents per hour for one hundred hours per month in payment for standing at country roadsides, leaning on picks and shovels, well, in the paraphrased words of the late Edward S. Jordan, get yourself a job on some WPA project; just try it once, that's all I ask. Should Private Industry ever let you down, as it has me, and you find yourself working on my highway, I'll be glad to put you into touch with the most efficacious methods for the treatment of sunburn and pickhandle blisters known to medical science. . . .

Returning to my highway itself on Cedar Road, in the vicinity of Cleveland, Ohio, WPA Project Number 16523-K, reminds me that I have been asked frequently if it is a useful and a necessary project, and my answer invariably is "yes, it *is* a useful and necessary project, just as are almost all other WPA projects." Of course, the definition of "necessity" in the mind of the average citizen is always governed largely by what his individual needs and desires happen to be at the moment, and if he is a motoring citizen, as millions are (even some WPA workers, quite like impecunious industrialists, cut down on food expenditures to buy gasoline), he will appreciate my highway out on Cedar Road after our work of widening is completed.

In the not far distant future, our American motorist will enjoy several additional lanes of travel on that highway; he will not be obliged to hug the curb at the sight of an approaching motorist; he will not be forced to turn into the ditch as he so often has in the past; more motorists will arrive at their destinations, sound in mind and body. . . .

I do not know what proportion of the total sum expended on my highway is properly chargeable to direct expense and what proportion should be set up on the Government's books as a capital asset. However, the headlines in my newspaper lead me to believe that these necessary expenditures are all being charged to the item of Expense and if that is so, it seems to me that our Government at Washington needs more and better bookkeepers. The truth of the matter is that my highway, Cedar Road, is rapidly becoming a permanent asset to the people of America, just as Boulder Dam, the Panama Canal, Norris Dam, and any postoffice building are permanent assets. . . .

Relief: pride and prejudice

While some Americans could confront and adjust to the new realities of their condition, others stubbornly clung to their older values. For them, an acceptance of relief or public assistance meant degradation of their own sense of pride. Furthermore, while denying themselves anything beyond mere subsistence, many such people harbored deep resentment toward those who accepted relief and enjoyed luxuries. Thus in their own way, they, too, questioned the workings and viability of a system that apparently granted greater rewards to those "unwilling" to work. However distorted the perspective, it represented very real, deeply-felt prejudices that cut through the society.

... I am ... a member of a too-little-thought-of group, those who, by the skin of their teeth and a pride instilled into them for generations, have kept off relief, and who now, because of the increased cost of taxes and living expenses in general, are almost in the last ditch. ...

Perhaps I should tell you about my family first. There are just the three of us, a seventeen-year-old son, my husband and myself. My parents are dead, and my husband's mother is a widow, who barely manages to keep herself. In 1930 my husband had a job in a near-by town. My father died, leaving a little country place of fifteen acres, of poor soil, and much run down as to buildings, fences, and so on. However, we thought we could buy my brother's interest, and so have a home. We still lacked five hundred dollars of a complete payment when my husband was laid off. The layoff proved to be permanent. Since then he has been able to get work during the summer on the farms near us. We had two cows and have increased that to four.

During that time my husband has spent seven months in various hospitals, undergoing five serious operations. If he had sat down on relief to recover, I feel some of these operations might have been avoided. His pride wouldn't let him, and he had a feeling we might take something some other person needed desperately. As he was a World War veteran, we were spared the expense of hospital treatment, but we paid for the care he had to have from local doctors while at home. We had a sort of feeling we must, if we could.

Last summer he got a little over five hundred dollars in bonus money. It was already spent, practically. We cleared up our doctor bills, taxes and a number of small debts. He had to go to the hospital in August of last year and was there

From "A Letter from Illinois," *The Saturday Evening Post* 209 (17 April 1937): 27, 49, 52, 56.

until early November. Last spring we took a chance and rented a small farm on a share-crop basis. Because my husband became ill in the spring and we wanted to keep our son in high school, we had to hire the greater part of the work done in the early spring and after school opened in the autumn. We put about one hundred dollars into getting a start with poultry. I am telling you this to show you what we did with the money.

My boy is not lazy. If we had to take him out of school to work and help us, he would do his best. Last fall, when his father was in the hospital, he milked the four cows, separated the milk, did various small chores, before going five miles to school each morning. Evenings he reversed the process. On Saturdays he did all he could toward the farm work. He is not an extra-strong boy, but he made good averages in school—seventh in a class of seventy. I want to keep him in school at all costs. But here we are. His father has not done any work since early last spring. He has an incurable disease, which requires lots of rest and good food. I am untrained, except as a housewife. What shall we do?

We talk about relief as the girl and her loving parents must have talked of marriage to the villain in those old days when the villain always held a mortgage on the old homestead. It is something we will do if there comes a time when there is no other way. True, we might have let our debts go, and not have paid those who harvested and planted our crops or cared for my husband. But we have been brought up with other ideas, and debts hang heavy over our heads until paid.

So much for us. To show you plainly why we are puzzled about accepting relief, I must explain the feeling about relief in this community. And to do so I can only go into detail concerning those on relief. Otherwise you cannot understand. For here is a feeling that relief is a thing you are justified in taking, if you can get it. Recently I sat talking with three women, all of whom were on relief, and all of whom had recently done permanent waves. In the course of the conversation I remarked I had never had a permanent wave, and one of the women replied she thought a woman was a fool who neglected her looks. The others agreed. And if I wasn't a fool, I must have looked like one. . . .

I wish there was something I could do to earn money. I don't mind hard work, and I am willing to undertake anything to keep my family together. My husband may attempt to work this spring. It seems practically certain now that he must return this summer to the hospital for treatments. If he goes to work, it will only cause him to break down sooner.

I don't know what to do. We were brought up in a day when a man could share-crop forty acres, and, with the help of cows and chickens, make a good living for a family, but the tractor and the large-scale farming have ended that. I suppose that's what ended it. At any rate, it can't be done any more.

I wasn't trained to do anything except make a farmer a good wife. Two years ago my husband came home from the hospital just before Christmas. He had gone in August for a severe operation, came home in September, and had to return in November. We were up against it as hard as anyone ever gets, I believe.

While he was gone the second time, I got a job waiting tables in a tavern. I got paid only tips, but I could gather in from six to eight dollars a week. It was awful. I didn't dare make a customer angry. And some old fool who should have been home rocking his grandchildren was always patting me on the back or trying to hold my hand, and saying, "Let me buy you a drink, little girl."

If my husband had known, he would have been heartsick.

But we kept off relief. I drove five miles, in all sorts of weather, in an old car which was apt to stall at any time, and did on several occasions. I worked from eight in the evenings, seven nights a week, until one and sometimes two o'clock, mornings. I did my own housework, with my husband's help; even our laundry. I am still wondering if I was a fool. I believe I'd do it again. . . .

To be sure, Uncle Sam has spoiled his children. While I was at the tavern, a man and his wife, on relief, came in to get beer and sandwiches. They told me I was silly. "Get on relief and quit working here," they said. "The Government wants to get this money in circulation. Why, when they brought us meat and butter and eggs the first time, we told the truck driver we had those things, and he said to take everything offered us and sell the stuff we raised. He said they'd figure if we didn't need part of it we didn't need any, and that they had the stuff to distribute and had to do something with it."

But, oh, dear, I said I wouldn't write an article. I just want to tell you one more thing and I'll quit.

Not long ago a group of youngsters were playing cards at our house. Said I, "Listen to this story, and tell me what this man should have done. He was wealthy, owned a farm and a factory. One night he was attacked by robbers. Two men beat them off. He gave each a small sum, but later learned one of them was ill and in need, so set aside a small sum each month to help him. The other fellow, hearing of it, said this was unfair, so the rich man gave him an equal allowance. Soon after, he heard of an old man in the neighborhood who was in need. He decided to set aside a part of his income each month to help needy people, and he appointed a friend to take care of this matter for him. In time, he found it hard to get men to work on his farm or in his factory. His wife began to complain that she could get no one to help about the house. Imagine his surprise when he learned that many who were able to work had persuaded his friend to give them a monthly allowance from the fund he had set aside for charity. Now, what should have been done?"

There ensued a lot of arguments, all in good fun, and mostly beginning. Well, I'd have done so and so." I gathered they were about evenly divided. Half of them seemed to think the police should have been called, and those fellows made to work. The other half argued, "Why, that'd be a swell way to do. You couldn't blame them for getting all they could for nothing, if everybody else was. Why, heck————" and so on.

Funny, those kids arguing. Not much serious thought back of what they said. Not much back of what grown-ups do and say sometimes. I sat there grinning like Alice's Cheshire cat as they turned back to their game. But I didn't fade away, leaving the grin, as the cat did. Instead the grin faded away and left me. For I was suddenly looking at another angle. All those kids will vote, come next presidential election.

. . . Are we fools, not to take the easy way? Or will there come a time, if we can only hold out, when we shall be glad we didn't? What if we fight on and my husband is never able to work again? Will I wish we had taken the easy way for his sake? What of my boy? Should we have put away the bonus bonds toward a college education for him and let the Government care for us? I can see a way for us, and there must be ways for others. My husband took the examination when the mail route past here was open. He got second place. The man who has it has a fair real-estate business. Why couldn't my husband be given some light Government work like this mail route, which he is capable, both mentally and physically, of handling, instead of a pension? I can see similar ways for many of these folks on relief. Not to let any person have two jobs or too much farm ground. But I'm not a fairy godmother. I can't fix things. I can't help thinking, however, that many folks on relief aren't lazy and grasping. But won't they become so? . . .

Penny auctions: Shays's rebellion, 1933 style

Agriculture had been depressed long before the crash of 1929. Overproduction, the expenses of capital improvements, the decline of prices in foreign markets, and, in some areas, natural disasters, all combined to reduce farmers' incomes and to cause widespread distress in the agricultural sector. As the depression deepened in the 1930s, debt-ridden farmers regularly faced foreclosure. In a number of midwestern states, groups of farmers resorted to "penny auctions" in which friends would bid literally pennies for their neighbors' property and then restore the land and goods to the owners. As the following memoir portrays, there was an element of intimidation, and sometimes violence, in such proceedings. But these farmers hardly saw themselves as revolutionaries or radicals; rather, they considered themselves preservers of the traditional family farm. The farmers did not ask for the abolition of their debts but only for "more time to see [themselves] . . . through the depression years." A number of states passed mortgage moratorium

From Harry Haugland, "The Right to Live." Unpublished typescript (Iowa City: University of Iowa Library). Used by permission of Frances M. Haugland. Material suggested by John Shover.

laws that temporarily suspended debt payments. In this sense, the farmers' demands and needs were similar to those who had participated in Shays's Rebellion of 1787

Things really looked tough on this morning in August 1933 as I took a short-cut across the field to Ray's place. Each morning the sun appeared like a ball of fire which seemed to have but one purpose: to scorch the earth in the shortest possible time. This morning it had come up with a bit of cloud, and the distant rolling of thunder gave renewed hope that at least a little rain might fall. However it proved to be just another day, and, as one farmer described it, "Just like the politicians: a lot of noise, a blast of wind, but no results."

Ray's cornfield, fifty acres, stood curling in the sun. Six weeks earlier it had been waist high, spreading from row to row, a solid mass of rich green leaves waving in the sun. Now it would normally have been head high and setting ears, but instead it had shrunk to half of its former height and stood withering like an onion patch in the fall. . . .

Ray had telephoned me the evening before saying, "Be here at nine in the morning." I asked no questions. Everyone in the neighborhood knew what it meant when Ray called with his terse message, and they seldom failed to show up.

"Where to today?" I asked as we walked slowly toward the farm house.

"About sixty miles west and over the state line," he answered. "Damned bank took everything a fellow had and is going to have a sheriff sale at the fairgrounds. Can't see what the hell the bankers are thinking of, selling folks out at a time like this."

"One would think that cases like Joe's would be a lesson to them," I said. "Six dollars and seventy-two cents is all they got from the whole kaboodle, and all Joe wanted was to be left alone to work out of it. Now he's got his stuff and they can't touch it.". . .

He knew that the boys depended on him and a few others to lead them. The going had not been too rough up until now, as the sheriffs and other authorities had been local and could usually be induced to help in negotiating a reasonable and peaceful settlement between debtor and creditor. It had only on rare occasions been necessary to resort to penny sale tactics.

The aim of our organization was one of pure survival. All the farmer asked was more time to see him through the depression years. If they won, they had saved (temporarily at least) their home and means of livelihood, and the means of paying their just debts. If they lost, they would be no worse off. They knew they had nothing to lose, so they decided to fight. . . .

The creditor, in truth, had little if anything to gain by foreclosure proceedings, for a forced sale, even if legally conducted, seldom paid out over fifty cents on the dollar, and a deficiency judgment against a busted farmer could hardly be called a very liquid asset. . . .

The heart of the creditor was governed largely by his purse strings so when he was faced with the choice of (1) a legal sale which, at best, would net him a substantial loss in both money and popularity and could easily result in a total loss via a penny sale, or (2) a chance to work out to a 100% settlement in time, he was usually wise enough to allow time.

The business and professional men, even though they had existed lock, stock, and barrel on the farm trade, very often showed open resentment and even hostility toward "such doings," as they termed them. In retaliation, they were just as frequently reminded that they were not considered absolutely essential to any community if it came to mere survival.

Had not our grandparents, when they first settled this country, existed without buying or selling a great deal? They grew most of their food; wool from sheep furnished most of their clothing after grandma had processed it. A cow furnished milk while alive and meat and hide for shoes when dead. They built their log shacks or dug a cave. They made their own furniture and nailed together their own coffins. In all these things we could do the same if need be, though today it would be harder, for there is no longer any virgin territory worthwhile in which to settle down. Any such change today would be nothing short of revolutionary. . . .

A large crowd had gathered at the meeting place which was in town, two miles away. Each had brought a bag of lunch or a jug of coffee, so when it was all thrown together "grabteria" style, no one had to go hungry. Trucks had been arranged for with each rider chipping in for gas and oil. A surprising number were already there—from a radius of fifteen miles. Other neighborhood representatives would join us at various intersections along the highway. All the old standbys had arrived or were arriving momentarily. There was Clarence, Olaf, Big Bill, Oscar, Anton, Cris, Joe, Hank, John, Fred, Al, and Randy. Very little money was being spent, the first and foremost reason being that they did not have any. Besides that these town folks had not been too friendly, so let them keep their damn stuff. . . .

The sixty mile ride was uneventful. We entertained ourselves by calling to mind the outstanding events of the past year. . . . A creditor of some farmer had sent out a truck for a load of wheat. (Legal attachment papers had been served.) At 30¢ a bushel it would not make much of a dent in the indebtedness, but it made a serious hole in the wheat bin. A group of neighbors met the truck at the corner with the following advice: "Better turn around and go home; there ain't no wheat going out of here." In another instance, a truck had been loaded with flax and was half way to market when two automobiles passed and turned directly across the road. Two or three other cars followed, and in all 20 to 25 husky farmers stepped forward and, without a word being spoken, half of them climbed onto the rear of the truck to give weight on that end while the others picked up the front end of the truck by the bumper, gave it a right turn and ordered the astonished driver to "get that flax back in the bin." A truck load of 1500 chickens belonging to a produce house had been dumped at the outskirts of a small town, and every kid in the place came home with a free chicken supper. When the sheriff arrived at the scene and attempted to get the names of the culprits, he was told to look in the telephone directory. "You'll find them there." A trucker with a double deck of sheep refused to stop and got a six inch plank through his windshield. Another got a leather belt full of spikes thrown across the road in front of him. All of these acts of violence had been committed openly by these men and many others who, under normal conditions, wouldn't as much as harm a kitten. However, the gentlest creature becomes fierce when faced with the loss of his home or the means of maintaining that home, and that wolfish struggle for existence bred a peculiar desperation from the tenderest sentiments. The old bewhiskered farmer told his county sheriff, "Why a settin' hen will fight a 200 lb. man if he tries to drive her off her nest, and surely we'd be poor sticks if we wouldn't show the guts of a settin' hen." And to add humor to the setting, he began to sing, "I'm old, but I'm aw-ful-ly tough!"

Truck and automobile loads of men and some women joined the caravan at every highway intersection so that when they arrived at the state line, we were probably several hundred strong. As we approached town, we came upon a huge crowd of men and women in a field just outside the city limits. Here they had formed their little groups and were eating picnic dinners. Our folks gathered together; all the jugs of coffee and lunch baskets were opened, and anyone and everyone was invited to partake. . . .

After dinner a meeting was called and plans were discussed regarding lines of strategy. There was no point in trying to negotiate further, for all attempts to do so had failed. The farmer in question had made a mutual agreement with the bank for a division of all the farm chattels in lieu of the mortgage. He had voluntarily surrendered that portion of the property, feeling that he could struggle along with the remaining equipment and manage to live. A few days later the sheriff served papers attaching the remaining livestock and machinery in direct violation of the former agreement. The farmer might have been able to win in court, but he had no money to spend in court. Now the property was all at the fairgrounds and was to be sold at public auction that afternoon. We had decided on a penny sale with each item to be paid for in cash at the time of the purchase. It was up to everyone of us to watch and warn any person who seemed to be bidding out of line. Rumor had it that the sheriff anticipated trouble and had deputized a large number of local citizens. The fact that this caravan of cars and trucks with hundreds of men and women arrived simultaneously naturally confirmed their suspicions.

The crowd milled around restlessly through the barn housing the horses and cattle and over to the lot where the farm machinery was lined up in regular auction fashion. A group composed of key men from every community had met on the lot outside the town and discussed ways and means of handling various situations that might turn up—although everyone realized that each problem had to be handled in its own way as it presented itself. It was generally understood that nobody was to be identified as leader or foreman, for that would make such person vulnerable to arrest. The sheriff called the meeting to order and proceeded to give the warning that any interference with the due process of the sale would be dealt with according to law. Everyone was tense. Joking and bantering had ceased. The formerly jovial faces had suddenly become as hard as nails. Everybody stood silently waiting like men who wouldn't waste anything—not even words. I spied Ray a few feet from where I stood. His face seemed to be drawn like that of a tiger, ready to spring at anything that might come his way. Oscar, Big Bill, Eric, Carl; each held his position and appeared equally alert. The very situation we had long been afraid of was here. Could we meet it?

A ring had been formed around a grain binder, the first item to be offered for sale.

"How much am I offered?" called the sheriff.

For a moment there was a tenseness, a seeming foreboding of tragedy that made the seconds seem like minutes.

"I'll bid a nickel!" came a voice that broke the spell. It was Oscar who had spoken.

"Five dollars!" came from a fairly well dressed person who was obviously not a farmer. As he moved a little in the crowd, a deputy badge could be seen under his coat.

One of our older men, a farmer from my own county who will be recognized by anyone around this part of the state who may read this story, laid his hand on the shoulder of the bidder and said, "Plenty high, ain[']t it?"

Suddenly, and without warning, a shot was fired and the farmer dropped to the ground and lay flat on his face. But in a moment he rose up enough to shout, "Get him boys; he got me!"

The sudden turmoil was terrifying. Everyone seemed bent on getting over to the man who had fired the shot—another deputy and clerk at the sale. He had fired a tear gas bomb. Some went over the grain binder; others shoved their way around. There, facing them, was the deputy who had bid the five dollars. He was waving a revolver, and there were several others with billy clubs. Ray was right at my side. I don't know whether or not he saw me. The question which had so often come to our minds: "How will they react?" was being answered.

The crowd surged forward in spite of gun and billies. It was as though they considered them but toys.

Ray was in front of the gun. He spoke to the man who held it. His voice was low and cold. It sounded unnatural—almost frozen. "Put it up, you damn fool," he said; "No one is afraid of you. You might get one or two of us, but you'd never live to tell about it." As he spoke he kept advancing. A billy club seemed about to come down on his head. Apparently without taking his eyes off the man with the gun, he grabbed the billy by the knob. He jerked and the handle stretched out like a door spring. The band was still around the deputy's wrist, the leather strap hanging loosely from it. Ray's eyes had never left the man who was still holding the gun. "Drop it, I tell you," he said, reaching out for the barrel. The deputy was backing up. The gun barrel was turned toward the ground with Ray's hand on the barrel and the officer's hand on the handle. "*Will* you let go?" he said as he held the barrel of the gun in one hand and the business end of the billy in the other. "All right, you are asking for it!" and he brought the billy down with considerable force on the deputy's wrist. Ray had the gun. He handed it to one of his friends saying, "See if there are any bullets in it." Things were really happening—and fast. There were six bullets in the gun, and they were fired into the ground. The gun was immediately broken on the steel wheel of a manure spreader. The cylinder fell to the ground and was trampled under the feet of the milling crowd.

Now the crowd's attention was divided between the man who had been shot and the man who had done the firing. I stooped to pick up my neighbor who was still lying on the ground. His face was covered with soot from the cartridge, and there was a scent of tear gas in the air. It is impossible to describe my feeling of joy to learn that the shot had not been fatal. He had gotten the full charge of the bomb in his eye and had been partly stunned, and he was still in terrible pain. He was immediately taken down to the office of a local doctor who, upon examining the eye, found it in serious condition.

The deputy who had fired the shot had been dreadfully mauled by the members of the crowd, all of whom thought he had killed his victim. He also was taken to a doctor and possibly to a hospital for treatment.

The crowd finally settled down and everything became quiet again. It had all happened so quickly that only a matter of minutes had passed. The sheriff had been stripped of his gun and was lucky to be still in possession of his shirt and trousers. He mounted a stand and announced that the sale would be discontinued, but the enraged crowed was in no mood to discontinue anything.

He was ordered down from the stand and immediately taken into hand by a group of people who reminded him that he had started it and now he would finish it too. No sale had been made, so former bids were forgotten and the auction began anew. Three cents, five cents, and up as high as fifteen cents were bid on any one piece of machinery as the now docile sheriff was being led down the line from piece to piece.

Humor found its way back into the crowd, and wisecracks flew thick and fast. "Sell it, the damn thing is rusty," and a gang plow sold for eight cents. A wagon was found to have only one speed, so it was sold for a nickel. An old cistern pump was picked out of a pile of junk and the sheriff holding it up said, "How much am I offered?"

"The sucker is on the wrong end," someone shouted. A horse sold for eleven cents because harness marks showed he had been used. A bob-tailed cow brought six cents because someone warned that the sun would shine on her bag and sour the milk. A bull was said to be a "woman chaser" and sold for the first bid offered.

The entire lot of horses, cattle, and machinery brought the fabulous sum of $7.88.

Everything was removed the same day and distributed among friends in both states and several counties. These people saw to it that all of the property got back into the hands of the original owner.

The trips back home were uneventful, though it was past midnight before most of the folks got back to their places—and chores were still undone. . . .

"We do not know where . . . we will spend this coming night"

Before the Depression, most people living in the rural South led a marginal existence at best. The economic collapse of the 1930s left the area destitute, particularly for those who were tenant farmers and found all avenues of credit closed to them. Those who could work did so for a pittance. Consequently, for the first time since the Populist upsurge of the 1890s, exploited agrarian elements attempted economic and political organization. The most notable venture was the Southern Tenant Farmers Union, which originated in Arkansas in 1934. From the outset, whites and blacks allied in the cause, largely under local leadership. New Deal reformers in the Agriculture Adjustment Administration encouraged the movement. Socialist and Communist organizers from outside also attached themselves to the union—a fact immediately exploited by the landowning planter class. The latter, with their control of law enforcement officials, counterattacked with legal and physical threats, and even violence. The following affidavit of a union member testifies to the brutal harassment.

SWORN AFFIDAVIT OF WILLIAM H. STULTZ
Address, Parkin, Ark.

Wynne, Ark.
June 27th, 1935

My name in full is William Hence Stultz. I was born in Iron City, Tenn. Sept. 3rd, 1896. . . . I am an ex-service man enlisted in the regular army air service July 21st, 1919, and during the world war served in 22nd observation squadron A.S. as machine gunner and observer in France 1919 and 1920. I am married and have six children.

I am destitute upon the highways in Cross County together with my wife and six children, without a shelter, homeless, penniless, and I have no property neither real or personal, no income, and am without a job of any kind; that I am compelled by force of circumstances to face the elements of bad, rainy weather unprotected by shelter, other than furnished over-night by sympathetic neighbors, with children aged from 16 months to 12 years. And one of these children, the 16 months old baby, is sick. We are without a change of clothing because we are unable to carry any luggage because we have to carry the children, and our personal belongings and clothing is now at this time in the relief office at Wynne, Ark. On the night of June 26th, 1935 we found refuge in a house-boat of two tiny rooms three miles south of Parkin, Ark. near Sycamore Bend together with another destitute family of five. The father of this family whose name is D. Linville is lying flat on his back suffering from stomach trouble. . . . We do not know where on earth we will spend this coming night at this time. . . .

I am an evicted Share-Cropper, and was first evicted on Feb. 24th, 1934 by J. C. Cherry, Parkin, Ark. as a result of the acreage reduction program, and since then I, together with my family have been driven from place to place. . . . I received $21.00 per month FERA Relief from Feb. 1934 till July 1934 (Work Relief) and was then given a job at $3. per day building fences by the relief administration in Cross and Poinsett County which lasted for me until I was discharged in November 1934 because of membership in the Southern Tenant Farmers Union. Mrs. Harvey, County Relief Administrator, told me personally that, "Because of my union activities I could no longer get relief." And since then I have had no relief, living on the generosity of other Share-Croppers who understood my condition and whose condition was a little better than mine own, until I was again evicted from the farm of Joe W. Johnson, Truman, Ark. and was picked up on the highways together with my family by a passing automobile driven by Powers Hapgood, North Brookfield, Mass. and

From Southern Tenant Farmers Union Papers, Southern History Collection, Chapel Hill, N.C. Used by permission.

brought to the Transient Bureau in Memphis, Tenn. on July 22nd, 1935.

The relief officials in Memphis refused to provide for me and my family at first and told me I would have to go back to Truman, Ark. I explained that the relief officials there and in Cross County refused to give me any relief for my family, and they provided relief over the week-end to have time to investigate, which was provided reluctantly with many insults and abuses. Monday they told me a truck would call at the apartments where I was staying and take me and my family back to Parking, or Wynne, Ark. where I had formerly been on relief and had an established residence. I was assured by Mrs. Crim that arrangements had been made for us and that a house would be provided, but doubting her word I had Mr. Powers Hapgood call by long distance to make sure my family would have shelter, but Mrs. Lillian Harvey, Director of relief at Wynne, Ark. stated that no house had been provided, and that I was not wanted in Cross county because I was what she called "A Radical" . . . Where-upon, when the truck came to take us back I asked to see Mrs. Crim again to make sure that proper relief had been provided for me and my family, and I went to the relief office to see her and was met in front of the Tenn. Hotel by her and a police officer who informed me that I had the choice of either going to jail or accepting the transportation back to Arkansas, and she again assured me that a house had been provided for us and that we would be taken care of properly at Wynne, Ark. Under the circumstances I returned to Wynne, Ark. together with my family.

On arrival at Wynne, Ark. I was unloaded into the waiting room of the relief office. . . . Mrs. Lillian Harvey, Relief Director, came into the room and stated,

> "Mr. Stultz, you take your family and get out of the relief office.
> This is no place for a family, and you and your whole family are
> not wanted in Cross County, not even in the State of Arkansas."
> And we are not going to provide a house for you.

I ask her for a grocery order and she stated,

> "What do you need with a grocery order when you have no home"

Mrs. Proctor then came in and talked kindly and influenced Mrs. Harvey to give us a grocery order of $5.50 which is supposed to last us for half a month, and an order on the comissary for flower, meal, and beef. The groceries we could not take because we had no home and were afoot on the highway carring [carrying] our babies. . . .

Therefore, in view of the fore-going facts, we fathered our family together and begin drifting upon the highways afoot and as stated in the second paragraph, and we wandered fourteen miles on foot carring our babies until weary, hungry, and exhausted we came to the house boat mentioned herein.

A sit-down strike

Industrial laborers in the mass-production, basic industries particularly felt the ravages of the Great Depression. Most workers in steel, automobiles, and rubber, among others, were not organized into unions. The craft-, skill-oriented American Federation of Labor had either neglected or failed to include such workers for both ideological and practical reasons. Collective bargaining was virtually nonexistent in these industries for organized labor found itself practically helpless against the massed power and resources of the large corporations. But with the New Deal legislation of the 1930s, workers received governmental guarantees for the right to organize and bargain collectively, without fear of reprisal. Nevertheless, bitter organizational battles followed. U.S. Steel finally yielded in 1937, but the Ford Motor Company resisted unionization until 1941. Probably the most radical technique utilized by labor came with the famous sit-down strikes in the auto and rubber industries. In effect, workers claimed a vested "property right" in their jobs. They "occupied" the factories, refused to work, and prevented scabs from taking their jobs. The following memoir by Rex Murray the president of the General Tire local union in Akron, Ohio, recounts the 1934 sit-down strike in that factory, which incidentally is the earliest-known such strike.

. . . We attempted to bargain with them [the General Tire management] as soon as we got our [federal labor union] charter in 1933. [But] they refused to recognize the union as a bargaining agency. In fact they had set up what they called an employee representation plan, which in our opinion was a company union. When we would take an issue to the company which the company felt they could grant, they wouldn't grant it to the union, but they would call a meeting of their employee representation plan. And somebody would propose the idea and the company would grant it, and then they'd post notices on all the bulletin boards throughout the plant that the employee representation plan was granted thus and so. . . .

We checked what had happened in the rubber and other mass industries and how the companies had forced them to strike for recognition and then immediately go for a court injunction to prevent picketing or a very limited number of pickets if they were admitted at all. And they would insist that the law enforcement officials carry out the mandate of the injunction. And if necessary they would come in and bust a few heads and bust up the picket line, and there was your labor organization, gone up the river. We [also] talked to

From Daniel Nelson, ed., "The Beginning of the Sit-down Era: The Reminiscences of Rex Murray," *Labor History* 15 (Winter 1974) : 89–97. Reprinted by permission of Daniel Nelson, The Rubber Industry Oral History Project (University of Akron), and the managing editor of *Labor History*.

people who had first hand knowledge of what had happened in previous attempts to organize. I talked to such people as Wilmer Tate [secretary of the central labor union], W. H. Wilson, [A.F.L. organizer in Akron], Frank Petino [president of the central labor union], and Coleman Claherty.

[During these discussions Murray suggested the idea of occupying the plant.]

They thought I was off my rocker. Claherty in particular said I was crazy. I said to him, with all due respect, 'Sir, if you can find another method that will work and be effective and establish collective bargaining, I can assure you that the vast majority of the people in the plant will be back of you and support you.' [But] he didn't have no other methods, no other procedures. He'd exhausted all he knew.

[Murray also discussed his idea of the sit-down with the local union officials.]

They were in favor of it. They couldn't find a better method or a better procedure to follow, so they agreed with attempting to go this route. We [then] started a program of exchanging information with our key people—committeemen and officers in the plant—and we run a 'school' for a couple of weeks trying to anticipate what actions or what the company may try to do and try to build a counter offensive to offset it if it became necessary.

For example, if they brought the police in and it got to the point where we felt it was necessary . . . we could give them [the strikers] a signal and they would go to work, and they would work until the police left the plant and then we would shut it down again. This was the plan. . . . And if we got . . . [arrested] inside the plant it would be no different from insisting on our rights to picket outside the plant and being arrested outside the plant and being taken and thrown in jail. So this was a chance we had to take . . . We discussed the thing in detail from A to Z and tried to anticipate what action the company might take and what our counteraction might be.

The stewards were pretty well informed to keep [these plans] . . . under their hat and at the proper, opportune time these people would be given a signal what to do or what not to do. They explained to the rest of the people that a signal was to be given. It wasn't to be done unless the signal was given. [But the rank and file] was ready for whatever action was necessary to establish recognition, sit-down, walkout, or whatever. They'd go either way. We was going to try the sit-down method and if that didn't work we would discuss it further and decide what further course of action to pursue. . . .

I think they . . . [wanted us to strike] because they wanted a chance to bust it up. And that would have been the opportunity but they didn't get it. [The strike] started when I walked through the plant and gave [the workers] the signal to shut it down. That's when it started. And as fast as I could walk from one department to another, throughout the plant, that's when it went down. And one of the plant guards was following me from about the time I got to the second department, telling me I couldn't do it. 'You have to stay in your own department.' I said, 'I'll go back to my department in a little while!' and I just

Wisconsin farmers dumping milk in protest against low prices, 1934.

kept walking, one floor to the other. When I gave them the signal they pulled the switches and shut it down.

They just stayed there and they changed shifts, just like they was working. People who come to work next shift came right in the plant, sit down beside the machine. Those people went home and the next shift, right around the clock.

There was one guy that continued to work. I went to the foreman . . . and said there was one individual who apparently did not want to cooperate with the rest of the people. And to prevent trouble I would appreciate if he would say a good word to this individual. And the general foreman went to him and what he said I don't know but the machine shut down. [The other workers] played checkers, played cards, and things of this nature. Mostly just sitting around—bull session.

[The management] was confused and . . . didn't know what to do . . . Mr. [Charles] Jahant, who was the vice-president in charge of manufacturing at the time . . . made a request that he be permitted to talk to the people, and we said we'd cooperate with him and he would talk to the people if he wanted to but there'd be no vote taken. And he went through the plant, department by department, and the people listened to what he had to say and sat tight. And later he wanted all of them together and we arranged to have all the people who was off shift . . . come into the plant, and we had a meeting in the back of the plant, in a lot. People just stood up and he used the platform, the loading platform for the railroad cars. . . . And when he got through talking he tried to take a vote there and I stopped him. I told him there'd be no vote. In fact he even come right out and said 'Will those in favor of returning to work move to the right and those that wishes to continue the strike move to the left' and I stepped in and interrupted him . . . and said there will be no vote taken.

. . . [W]e marched out of there. We went directly from there to the East High School auditorium to hold our meeting. . . . And this is when . . . [the strikers] voted to establish a picket line in place of the sit-down in the plant. And we changed it from a sit-down strike to a . . . [conventional strike] outside the plant. . . . The people thought they would have a lot more freedom and it would eliminate considerable criticism that was developing because of the males and females both being in the plant, sitting down.

. . . I think they [the management] was confused and surprised that the people would strike together the way they did and support the union and . . . was afraid . . . [an effort to expel the strikers] would create some kind of destruction of property in the plant or violence and people getting hurt, and they didn't want to become involved in it. And perhaps there was one [other] point. . . They thought if they let . . . [the workers strike] for a few weeks and cool their heels that they'd change their mind and be willing to crawl back to work on their hands and knees . . . [But] this sit-down established a tremendous amount of confidence in the people . . . and . . . they would stick together and if necessary fight to win their ends. . . .

Labor violence: Memorial Day, 1937

While the sit-down strikes constituted a new departure in labor-management conflict, the decade witnessed countless episodes of traditional, bloody violence.
Perhaps the most famous occurred in Chicago, on Memorial Day 1937. Steel
workers and their families had gathered for a union rally after striking pickets had
been arrested at the Republic Steel plant. The strikers voted to send a mass picket
line to the factory, but after several minutes' "discussion" with the police, they
were attacked. Ten workers were fatally shot, thirty wounded by bullets, and over
sixty beaten badly enough to require treatment. Thirty-five police officers suffered
minor injuries. Senator Robert M. La Follette, Jr.'s investigating committee found
the police guilty of either "gross inefficiency," or "a deliberate effort to intimidate
the strikers." During the Senate testimony, one policeman charged that the
strikers were under the influence of marijuana. When asked how he knew this, he
said the strikers' eyeballs were red, their facial grimaces were frenzied, and they
kept shouting, "C.I.O., C.I.O." [Congress of Industrial Organizations]. The following
testimony by Harry N. Harper offers the perspective of a man who went to the
scene to deliver a message to his brother, a striker.

Testimony of Harry N. Harper

... Mr. HARPER ... The parade was formed on the street commonly known as
Green Bay Avenue. I was still looking for my brother, so I walked up an down
the sidewalk. I could not locate him. Then the parade started, and they proceeded through the prairie.

I was still standing on the side, watching the parade go by. I thought
probably I could recognize him, when an acquaintance called me to come over
in the parade. I went there, and he had with him his mother and his father. He
introduced me to them, and I inquired of him if he had seen him, and he said
no.

So I stayed in the parade. The parade marched down diagonally from where
the speakers' platform was, and had stopped about halfway down the prairie,
or probably a little more. I got out of the parade again and looked to see if I
couldn't find him, and walked up forward, and walked back. I couldn't find
him. So the parade started again.

From U.S. Senate, Subcommittee of the Committee on Education and Labor, *The Chicago Memorial Day Incident,* 75th Congress, 1st session, 30 June, 1–2 July 1937, part 14, pp. 4820–4821, 4959–4964.

State Historical Society of Wisconsin.

"Memorial Day Massacre," 1937. Republic Steel strikers and
police.

At this time I was not in the same position that I had left. I think it was just about 50 feet farther to the front end of the parade. The parade started up through the prairie, and they came up to the officers, who seemed to be formulating a semicircle, some through the prairie on the right, and on the left of Burley Avenue.

The parade stopped in front of the officers, and I saw a number of men in the plant. . . . I walked to the head of the line, and that was not close enough to distinguish anyone, so I walked up in front of the flag bearers, approximately a few feet to the left, and I spoke to an officer.

I told him I had a mission here, I had a message from my mother, that if I could possibly reach the office or get to the office of the Republic Steel Corporation, that I had enough identification in my pocket to identify me as a brother of Peter Harper. He shook his head no. I asked him if it would not be possible for one or two policemen to go along with me. It was just a shaking of the head.

Then an officer just a little to my left said to one of the men alongside of me, or a trifle to my back, I do not know who it was—cursed and said, "Stand back you (so and so), or I will fill you full of lead!" That remark made me stand up and take notice.

I looked at the officers' faces to my right and to my left. The faces were drawn, the lips quivering, and they seemed to be intoxicated with something that is hard for me to explain. Maybe if I used the interpretation of a football player that was waiting for the last signal to charge the line, that would express it. I think I displayed some fear, because one of the officers stated, "What are you afraid of?" I was on the verge of saying—I do not know whether I got it out of my mouth—I was going to say, or I did say, "I do not know. It must be in the air." I think before I got that last statement out of my mouth, it seemed to me like a blast of a whistle, and then all hell seemed to have let loose. Immediately I was struck on the side, my left side. I went down, I think, to my knees.

Senator LA FOLLETTE. The left side of your head?

Mr. HARPER. The left side of my head. It was very painful. The blood was gushing out of my face. It was running in my mouth. I went back and held my hand above my eye. I was in a crouching position so the blood would not strangulate me. It was running into my mouth. I tried to retreat and go back, but, as I was going back, I had vision in my right eye, but I had no vision in my left eye. There were shots fired, and I saw people in front of me going down. They were paraders that were in back of the flag, and in back of me. It seemed as though they were going down, as though being mowed down with a scythe.

I was wondering what was doing that, and I looked to my right. I saw the officers on the right with their revolvers drawn, not shooting in the air, but pointing point blank into that crowd. I do not know how far I ran. I saw a ditch, looked probably like a culvert. I fell into that ditch. The instinct of self-preservation came over me. I thought I was going to get some bullets in the back.

I lay there not very long. While I was lying there, to my left I heard a voice, stating, "Help me, buddy. I am shot." I said I was helpless. I was lying in a position like this [indicating] when a green ball of fire fell to my right, a few inches from my face. It was spitting blue smoke. It affected this eye a little [indicating the right eye] and it was choking me. I had to make one more futile attempt to go back—to go back. When I got up a terrible trembling feeling came over me and a sickening feeling in the pit of my stomach. I do not know whether it was the gas or the loss of blood, but I went back groping.

I lost the vision of the right eye. I called for help: "Help me!" Someone grabbed me, grabbed me under the arms. I could not go then. My legs failed me, and then I remember hearing them calling for more help, and then they carried me, and then carried me back. How far I cannot say. I could not see any more. I was taken and placed in a machine. I remember it being a machine. There were a few more fellows put in there with me. I heard their voices. One man that was put in alongside of me was moaning. One man directed the car to go to the hospital— "To the nearest hospital." He started the car. I heard the car in motion and felt it going, bumping. Where it was going I could not say.

Senator LA FOLLETTE. ... Did you subscribe to an affidavit under date of June 24?

Mr. HARPER. Yes, sir, Mr. Senator. ...

Senator LA FOLLETTE. I will read the balance of this affidavit. ...

And then that long journey started. Whether there were one or two officers, I cannot say who was there. But I am positive there was one man lying down on the floor of the patrol, if not two. And this gentleman who was sitting, I think he was shot in the leg, he was one of the strikers. He was begging the officers to take us to the nearest doctor or hospital but the officers refused. But I do think he made one stop. It might have been the South Chicago Hospital. I am not positive. I was begging them to give me first aid and told them I was in agony. The officers said, "We will take care of you"—so he slammed the door. I do not know whether anyone got out or not, but I do remember he slammed the door and started off. He said, "Shut up, you son-of-a-bitch. You got what was coming to you." So they proceeded to drive on. The driver seemed to be strange—he did not know where he was going or could not operate the motor. The motor was in poor condition. He stalled the motor several times. And this man who was still conscious and sitting on the seat, he was begging them to stop at a doctor's because these men were still breathing. He used a plural term—whether he meant me or the two people on the floor—you understand I could not see at the time.

We finally got there. It seemed like ages to me—and what I have heard since it was 3 hours. When we got to the Bridewell Hospital they opened the door and told me to get up. I said I could not. I had no control over my legs. I said, "I am terribly weak." I could not see; my left eye was out and my right eye was closed entirely, and my face was a mass of blood. Blood was trickling onto the floor, onto the bodies that were lying there. And my wife saw all my clothes—they were all soaked with blood. I did not move when he commanded me to get up. Then he said, "We will take this one on in. We will take the others to the morgue—no use bothering with them." There was no doctor to see whether these men were still breathing; they had been breathing for some time because this gentleman who was conscious and who was begging for first aid when we were near to the Bridewell, he said, "Oh, they stopped breathing."

Then they dragged me out by my legs. I bumped my back coming down. I made a futile attempt to get on my feet. I could not stand; I could not see. So one man, I do not know whether it was an officer or not, got me under the arms and dragged me up and down steps. Where I was going I did not know. Finally they had me in the building somewhere—I assume it was the Bridewell. They sat me down with no attention for quite awhile. Then someone came along and stripped me of all my clothing, so I sat there for another length of time—I do not know how long—before they brought clothing to me. I told them I was cold, freezing and shivering—they ignored me—and finally brought a little short jacket to slip on. And then they took me away. They finally washed the blood off my face. I do not know how many men opened both my eyes and looked at them and mumbled something. Then they bandaged my eyes and put me to bed. They left me that way. My head was bandaged up; at times I was delirious. My stomach had been abused. I do not know whether it was through abuse or gas bombs that made me deathly sick, or the loss of blood, but I could not see.

They sat food—very scant food—in front of me. They told me, here is your meal. I could not see to eat and when one of the other patients tried to help me he was sent back to bed with very abusive language. I could not eat. I pleaded for a glass of milk, which was denied me. I pleaded for them to contact my wife and relatives. They refused that. They absolutely gave me no attention whatsoever until Wednesday, June 2. They took the bandage off my right eye. I was able to see a very little at the time, due to the swelling in my right eye.

Tuesday night, June 1, it must have been about 8 or 9 o'clock approximately, they took me somewhere and made a futile attempt to stitch the lower lid of my left eye. The doctor or interne gave me a shot in the arm, and he took one stitch and then he walked out. It seemed like he was contracting a business deal in the next room. It seemed like ages before he came back in again. He asked me if I felt sleepy, and I said, "No." He took another stitch, which was very painful. I guess that was all he did to the eye, put back the bandage and put me to bed.

In the meantime, between the first and second stitches, one of the orderlies came in twice and asked me if the doctor was through. My eye was open, exposed all this time. I said I did not know. He said, "Gee, it is taking a long time to do this." Evidently he had been sent down to take me up. Then I was put to bed and I asked for a glass of water, which was denied me.

On Wednesday, after the bandage was off my eye, I was able to taste food, and the first bite of food was the day my wife came in and I was just in the act of eating, and she can probably tell more about conditions than I.

Furthermore, I did not move bowels from the time I came in to the time I left. I felt bloated and in pain. I asked for an enema. I was refused that.

When I left they gave me my clothes in a sack and told me to go into the washroom and dress. I do not know how I ever managed to get there and dress. I thought my wife would bring clean clothes, but they made me put on the bloody clothes I had. They sat me on a bench and told me to wait. My wife came up about a half hour later.

I do not remember from then on. I was taken home on Wednesday evening in a cab. I was taken from 7324 Maplewood Avenue to the Michael Reese Hospital in an ambulance. I also want to state that I went from 160 pounds down to 130 pounds.

When I went to the Michael Reese Hospital they washed out the eye, and the house physician, Dr. Kaufmann, gave me first aid, put in a solution, and also gave me an enema and cleaned out my system and gave me a hypo to put me to sleep. Dr. Kaufmann came in the next day and treated the eye, looked at it, and made arrangements for an operation of what was left. My wife had seen what was left of the eye and he contacted her and told her what had to be done. They consulted me. We agreed to it, and they operated on me on Saturday, June 5. They had to build up my strength, as I was too weak for an operation. The eye was knocked out and they removed the remnants of it. I have been receiving treatment every other day, and the doctor just committed himself to say what condition it was in when the first examination was made. Infection had set in my eye. Then Dr. Kaufmann said because of this he had to be very conservative in his operation. They refused all visitors at Michael Reese Hospital. I was at the Michael Reese Hospital about a week and a half. I left on Saturday, June 12, a week after the operation.

In the march on Sunday, May 30, I walked directly in front of the flags.

We stood there approximately 5 minutes. I heard no conversation between the other strikers and the police officers. There was a colored officer who said to one gentleman and I heard him—he said, "Get back, you son-of-a-bitch or I will shoot you full of lead." That statement made me feel uneasy, but I was too late. I think I could identify this colored officer.

I was not armed. I was dressed in my good clothes. I did not see any sticks, guns, or clubs. If I had seen any I would not have walked over with the crowd. If there had been a possibility of trouble I would not have gone over. I have a wife and child and there was nothing for me to gain by going there if there had been trouble. The crowd was jolly—they asked every one to come in and form a peaceful line. Women and children were in the parade. Men had their wives. Some of the boys had their sweethearts. There was no intention of trouble. I do not see why a man would take his wife, sweetheart, son, or daughter, father or mother to this parade if they had expected trouble. One man took his mother and father.

As I was talking to this officer, I sensed danger facing them. The parade was in back of me. It seemed that it was a planned attack. They were tense, waiting for some— just like a football player—waiting for a signal to go. I was still in conversation when the blast of the whistle was blown. It sounded like a police whistle. I was so close I could not pick the officer who—something struck me, whether it was a club, bullet or shot, I could not say. I went down and was trampled upon. I do remember seeing that the police had their guns out. I heard the shots and I looked to my right and they were coming forward with their pistols drawn.

I signed some paper at the Bridewell Hospital. I could not read it. They said it was necessary for me to sign this paper to be released from the Bridewell Hospital. I told them I could not see and he said that he would read it for me. He guided my hand. He told me I could not get out unless I signed it.

_____ _____

Subscribed and sworn to before me this — day of June 1937.

_____ _____, *Notary Public.*

Senator LA FOLLETTE. Is that a portion of the affidavit which you made?

Mr. HARPER. Yes, Mr. Chairman.

Senator LA FOLLETTE. Is there anything material to be added to the affidavit that I have read?

Mr. HARPER. Yes. Out of fairness to my wife and little youngster and our friends, when I was stripped of my clothing I heard the officers say, "Look for communistic literature." I had no communistic literature, I am sure, in my pockets, but I am positive that they found my wallet with my identification card, name and address, who to notify, and in case of an accident notify a priest. Neither one of these was done.

The statement I am about to make, as much as I hate to do it—as I said, it is out of fairness to my immediate family. Incidentally, I am of the same faith of some of these officers who were present at that horror of horrors. I was christened in the Catholic church, attended parochial school as a boy, was married in a Catholic church, and attended the Catholic church regularly. When I was a boy attending the parochial school I was taught the Ten Commandments. One of those commandments stands out uppermost in my mind today is, "Thou shalt not kill." I wonder if some of these officers have not forgotten that. . . .

The impact of reform: TVA

The creation of the Tennessee Valley Authority, with its vast network of dams, produced power, reduced flooding, and provided recreational facilities for what had been one of the most impoverished areas of the nation. The TVA is one of the New Deal's most enduring legacies. Four decades later, however, Justice William O. Douglas, one of the most prominent New Dealers of the 1930s, complained that the "TVA became a sacred white cow that did untold damage to the environment." Douglas particularly deplored the TVA's encouragement of strip coal mining and the resultant destruction of the natural wilderness. Nevertheless, the TVA offers a rare example of a reform which brought immediate social and economic change to peoples' lives, a change that most regarded for the better.

The following letter from an Alabama physician was in response to a form inquiry from the agency regarding the uses and benefits of its services.

June 10, 1936.

Mr. David E. Lilienthal,
T.V.A. Office,
Knoxville, Tennessee.

Dear Mr. Lilienthal :—

Some time ago I received a letter from you asking me to write what I thought of T.V.A. electricity. I have waited for words sufficient but they are all too feeble. T.V.A. electricity and rural electrification is by far the greatest thing that has ever come to man-kind in the rural districts.

I have been near Wilson Dam for the past 18 years and have seen enough power wasted to pay for its construction. While T.V.A. power has been the greatest blessing, I think the power trust's self-purchased right to make unreasonable profits out of users of electricity has been the worst curse. And I have seen enough of both to be somewhat of a judge. To illustrate : My office is in Tuscumbia and I have paid the trust as high as $6.00 per month for running a fan in my office. My home is on T.V.A. line south of Tuscumbia on the Jackson Highway. We have the following : radio, refrigerator, cooking stove, washing machine, iron, sewing machine, churn and lights for an eight room house at a cost of from $2.85 to $5.00 per month. This is wonderful. (We hope in the near future to have a completely electrified home.)

The power trust has done more to sap the vitality of the Nation than the hookworm. And I would rather be the most humble worker for the T.V.A. and do all I could for humanity for a few short years and die than to be the whole power trust and wiggle in its hookworm slime for a million years.

Pardon my effort to give you two pictures I have in mind : No. 1—The twelve years previous to President Roosevelt's Administration was a time that trusts and combines prospered and they bought men in high places (who preferred gold rather than honor) to aid them in their graft. I will only mention one that looks like a sell-out, but he's typical of that class, Our Happy Warrior of 1928. I see him as he fought for the New Deal and for the masses. I see him a few months ago when he was taking a little walk in Washington. I see him in con-

From Administrative Files, Public Relations Letters, TVA Archives, Knoxville, Tennessee. Reprinted by permission of the Director of Information, TVA. Material provided by Thomas K. McCraw.

sultation with the lords of finance. Later I see him at the modern feast of Belshazzar with a thousand of his lords of finance. As he stands in that royal palace hall I hear him lambasting the New Deal, lambasting the T.V.A., lambasting Congress, lambasting the President, lambasting his former speeches in '28 when he spoke the sentiments of his own heart. In this same hour came forth the fingers of a man's hand and wrote on the wall and Alfred saw the part of the hand that wrote and his countenance was changed and his thoughts troubled him. So the joints of his loins were loosened and his knees smote one against the other. And this is the interpretation of the writing "Thy political days are finished. Thou art weighed in the balances and found wanting, thy power has been given to another. . . . "

Picture no. 2 : From the time of the election of our last President to now is history. We see the works of the New Deal in all of its ramifications. Power dams being built, lines built in the rural districts, CCC reforestation, soil conservation etc. And after the November election I see the Grand Triumphant march of our New Deal President, one of the best the world has ever known, backed by a New Deal Congress, T.V.A. officers and men as they march back to Washington to finish the good work. And I see our great Nation, the greatest in the world, covered with a net-work of power lines as the water covers the seas. And when this is all finished I see our President and Congress backed by the T.V.A. officers and men and an innumerable host of home owners, housewives and citizens of our great Nation. And I see this host of people as they stand around the switchboard and I see our grand old Senator George W. Morris standing by our president (the man that has done more in this work than any other living man) I see him as he raises his hand and turns the switch that floods our great Nation with light and dispels the blackness of darkness forever for future generations. And I hear this innumerable host as they sing,

"My Country 'tis of Thee, Sweet Land of Liberty, Of Thee I sing."
And as this host of happy people march back home I hear the hum of machinery as this T.V.A. power turns the wheels of every conceivable machine for lifting the burdensome work of our homes. Then I hear them singing that grand old Doxology,

> "Praise God from Whom all blessings flow,
> Praise Him ye creatures here below,
> Praise Him above ye Heavenly Host,
> Praise Father, Son, and Holy Ghost."

This is no idle dream but can be the greatest reality that has ever come to man-kind.

Truly yours,
R. L. Montgomery.

CHAPTER 16

War: at home and abroad

The land of the free

The rise of Nazi Germany in the 1930s and its self-proclaimed designs for a new world order evoked a growing concern among many Americans. In the United States itself, pro-German groups openly paraded in Nazi uniforms. Their activities created certain tensions, but generally were tolerated given the prevailing ideas of free expression, fostered by the political activism of the depression decade. Meanwhile, anti-Nazi organizations multiplied, particularly after the German regime's policy of anti-Semitism resulted in more violent, repressive incidents after 1938. Numerous public officials and celebrities participated in anti-Nazi protests and there were calls for a boycott of German goods. These two letters were written to Melvyn Douglas, a well-known, popular movie actor of the period, and reflect negative, yet significantly different, responses to such protests.

Mr. Melvyn Douglas   January 3, 1938
Hollywood, California

Dear Mr. Douglas:—

A group of fans in our neighborhood and myself have decided to get together and write you a letter expressing our disappointment in you and the recent unfavorable publicity which you have gotten for yourself.

We never knew before that you are Jewish and needless to say you no longer hold the affectionate position in our esteem which you formerly held. We shall support in the future some leading man who is white. Then you and the Harpo Marxes, the Borros Morroses and the rest of your race can devote all of your energies to politics because that will be all you shall have to do.

We are all good Americans and as any good American we can have but little respect for Kikes. We therefore cannot visualize a romantic actor as a member of a despised race.

Yours very truly,
Twelve Ex-Fans (Female)

From Melvyn Douglas, Correspondence (Madison: State Historical Society of Wisconsin). Used by permission of the director.

[1939]

Mr. Melvyn Douglas,
Beverly Hills, Calif.

Sir;

I see by the paper where you presided at a meeting calling for an embargo of German goods as a reprisal for the persecution of the German Jews. Very few in this country will uphold Germany in her ruthless actions, but there are millions who firmly oppose involving ourselves by useing any ineffective plan which will only evolve more hate. If we want to help, let's take the refuges, otherwise keep still. Our history is not free from blimishes.

If you use the theaters to spread such prepagands of hatred, it will only be fair for the millions who oppose to form a boycott on the movies by refuseing to attend theaters involved. I am ready to start such a move in opposition. This is not a sanction of German policy. It is the American policy.

Truly,
[F.R.]
Brookville, Kan.

Isolationism and interventionism

From the outbreak of war in Europe in September 1939, to the attack on Pearl Harbor in December 1941, the American people bitterly debated this nation's role in world affairs. Public opinion polls and congressional votes demonstrated a sharp division between those who favored interventionism or all-out aid to the Allies, and those who demanded complete neutrality and isolation. The latter's motivation stemmed from a variety of considerations, including even sympathy for Nazi Germany (particularly after the German invasion of the Soviet Union), but the profound disillusionment and cynicism resulting from our experience in World War I perhaps were most influential. Noninterventionists argued that our sacrifices in 1917-1918 had been in vain, for the decadent Old World remained committed to the same selfish, aggressive designs that had produced so many wars. The emotional appeal of the first selection typified such attitudes. Others, however, insisted that German and Japanese aggressiveness represented a threat to the United States, as well as Europe and Asia. The second selection is a letter written to probably the most popular radio news commentator of the period and in it the writer remarkably anticipated the events that were to follow shortly.

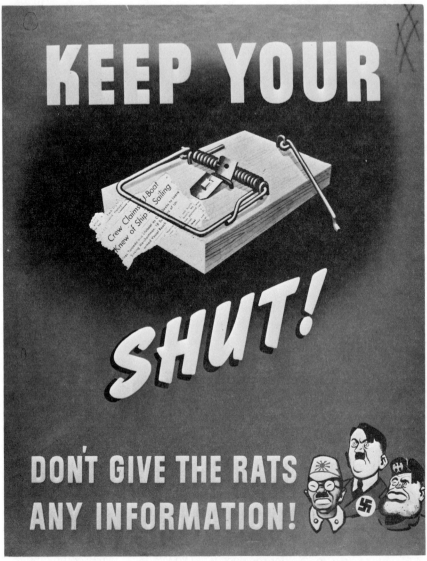

State Historical Society of Wisconsin.

World War II poster.

I am a mother who believed in America going into the last World War. I am a mother, one of 30,000 whose sons lie buried under crosses in France.

Our son was our only child. He was a boy everybody loved. He had a good job at sixteen; he had taught himself an electrician's trade. Then there was trouble on the Mexican border. Before his father and I knew it, Georgie had enlisted in the National Guard. He gave his age as twenty when he was only sixteen.

When he came back from the border we were about to go to war with Germany. Georgie told us he was going to enlist in the regular army and not wait to be sent with the National Guard. "I am not wearing this uniform for show," he said simply. His father and I thought him too young to go overseas. But it was no use. "If you don't give me your consent, mom and pop," he said, "I will change my name and go anyway, and then you won't know what unit I'm with." So we let him go.

One day, on February 13, 1918, I saw an army balloon flying low over our little house on Long Island. I could almost make out the faces of the balloonists and it seemed to me they had a message from Georgie. "I hope nothing has happened to our son," I prayed. Later the news came that he had died in a base hospital on that very day.

After that I threw myself into war work. I left my pots and pans on the stove and my chickens in the coop. I had only two things to comfort me. Theodore Roosevelt, to whom I am related through marriage, wrote me shortly before his own son fell in France, "May the heavens be kind and tender toward you." And Georgie, after hearing of my Red Cross work, had written me not long before he was wounded, "If anything happens to me I will die peacefully because I will know you will carry on where I leave off."

So I worked harder than ever, serving soldier boys in the canteen, knitting by lamplight, and selling Liberty Bonds.

Then we had peace and I carried on the work of the American Gold Star Mothers of the World War. Later, in 1924, I went to see Secretary of War Weeks. I begged him to have our boys' graves in France marked with marble crosses instead of perishable wooden cross-pieces. At first he did not understand why we mothers wanted crosses—why we would not be satisfied with small flat headstones.

"Mr. Secretary," I said, "is not the cross the symbol of sacrifice?" His own son, Secretary Weeks told me, had been in twenty-seven engagements and had been over the top nine times, but had happily come back alive. Now there were tears in his eyes, and he said, "You shall have your crosses, and we will mark the graves of the Jewish boys, if their families prefer, with the star of David."

I wonder how many people today remember those crosses in France, remember the great sacrifice those crosses symbolize. The boys who fell were pitifully young—most were eighteen, nineteen, or twenty years of age. They

From Mathilda Burling, as told to Dorothy Dunbar Bromley, "A Mother's Plea," *Current History and Forum* 51 (August 1940) : 48–49.

were too young to know what war was like. Too young to know how much of life they were giving up.

And who thinks today of the boys who came back insane, maimed, and crippled? Women who sat on their front porches knitting, and never went near the hospitals, did not know what war was. But I saw the horror of the boys who were raving mad in cages. I made myself look at the basket cases.

I can still see one boy with a beautiful face in an evacuation hospital in Staten Island. He had no arms or legs. He begged me not to let his mother know that he was still alive.

These are some of the sights which I cannot forget. Now, twenty-two years after our sons made the final sacrifice, Gold Star Mothers come to me and cry, "Mother Burling, do you believe my boy died in vain?"

If only I could honestly tell them their sons did not die in vain! But I cannot. I look at Europe today, sunk again in one of the wars they have been fighting for three hundred years. I hear talk all around me about our going to war once more to save the world for democracy. Even some ministers urge such a course—why, I cannot understand. They would talk differently if they had seen, as I did, American mothers kneeling at the graves of their sons in France.

It was God's will, we told ourselves then, that our sons should have been called upon to die for the peace of the world. That was in 1931 when we could still hope for peace.

Today how bitter is our disillusionment! The newspaper headlines might be copies of what was printed early in 1917. There is talk of universal military conscription, of a vast preparedness program. The President, it is true, has assured the American people that our youth shall not again be sent to die in a European war. But we Gold Star Mothers cannot forget that President Wilson was reelected on the platform, "He kept us out of war."

Many Gold Star mothers are now grandmothers. Others have younger sons born in war-time with a prayer in the mother's heart that this son might live to ripe manhood and comfort her in her old age. But we speak not for ourselves alone. We plead for the peace of soul of those millions of American mothers who have as yet had no cause to tremble at the sight of an unopened telegram in their hands.

We women of America love America. We will help defend our country. We will give our sons and menfolk to defend it should it be attacked. But we are aware that Chief of Staff General Marshall said not long ago that he did not apprehend an invasion of our shores. So why, we ask—and women, everyone knows, are the supreme realists—should we go to war abroad in the name of democracy, when, by the very act of fighting a totalitarian nation, we should have to resign ourselves to a regimentation which would be fascism under an American name?

It will be too late when war has been declared. Too late when your son comes to you, as mine did, and says simply, "Mother, I am going." It is we women who create young life, we women who wait at home. So I say to you mothers, you wives and future wives, raise your voices.

No war, remember, was ever fought without the support of women. Our sex has the numbers—if we will summon the courage—to turn back the tide of war hysteria which is rapidly sweeping over the country. We must write our Congressmen, we must write the President, we must form organizations in every community. If we would save our menfolk we women must act and act quickly.

Atlanta, 8/3/41

Dear Mr. Kaltenborn:

I have heard much criticism of the policies advocated by our Anti-American groups. I mean, of course, the so-called "Isolationists" (whose chief aim is to disorganize our government, undermine our resistance and maneuver this nation into an indefensible position) and our appeasers (whose chief aim is to surrender this nation and its people into the "tender" hands of the axis powers under the hope that their services will be recognized by the axis chiefs and they will be made puppet dictators or gaulieters over certain areas). But, I have neither heard or read a single intelligent discussion or analysis on the results of such policies had we decided to adopt them instead of the course we chose.

For instance, I would like to have you analyze for us the results—move by move—beginning with the "Isolationist" surrender of the Phillipines. . . . Let's suppose they had been successful all the way through, however. The Phillipines would have been "freed" immediately (years ago) and they would have as promptly been gobbled up by the Japanese. The Japs would have built strong naval, military and air bases in the Phillipines, with which to cut Britain off from her Far Eastern Empire and Britain would long ago have been defeated in the Far East. Meanwhile, still following the Isolationist leadership, we would have refused aid to Britain in Europe and the Atlantic. The British, German, Italian and American experts all say that without American help Britain would long ago have been defeated—very probably last September or October. Still following "Isolationist" policies, we would be about 132 war ships short of our present naval strength (with none building) and with an army of 65,000 half trained poorly equipped men, as, by isolationist vote it would still be today, and with an air force of about 1900 worn out antiquated war planes, we very likely could have defended this nation for a week if we had decided to even try a

From H. V. Kaltenborn Papers, Correspondence (Madison: State Historical Society of Wisconsin). Used by permission of the director.

hopeless defense. At any rate, our independence would have been gone a year ago, as we would have had the guns of the axis, plus the British navy turned against us. When the Japs ordered us out of Pearl Harbor and demanded that we withdraw from the Phillipines; that Britain withdraw from Singapore and surrender Australia, New Zealand, India, Burma, and Hong Kong as the price [of] peace it was not an idle threat, but a factual outline of the least offensive part of the plot the axis had underway. Then the isolationists, having failed in their efforts to maneuver this nation into a position that would have made any kind of defense hopeless and useless began their campaign for a "negotiated" peace that would have meant the surrender of all strategic bases from which to defend this nation, plus the handing over to the axis of the British navy and British resources, and, in the end, that would have accomplished the same end as an axis victory by arms. In either case, the independence of this nation would have been "sold down the river" by our isolationists. The mere fact that these results are so obvious is ample reason why the people should have them discussed on a nation wide scale so the people could see for themselves why we cannot afford longer to be mislead by those whose "good" intentions are the source as the trained "leaders" of sheep to slaughter except that our isolationists have more sense than the sheep leaders and they know where they are leading the people—at least, some do! To illustrate, I will tell you of a strange coincidence. I was getting lunch at a quick lunch counter and while eating a paper boy came by and I brought a copy of the noon edition. The place next on my left at the counter was vacant and I spread my paper there. A nice looking well dressed man who occupied the place next to my paper . . . referred to Mr. [Charles] Lindbergh. I said I believed Lindbergh to be a traitor and a tool of Hitler. He said "I don't believe he is. I don't think he has sense enough to be a traitor. I believe he is just a plain, ordinary fool, and I'll tell you why." He continued, "Whenever one man gets to believing that he knows more about military affairs and military strategy than all of our army experts, . . . and then knows more about naval affairs and naval strategy than all of the Admirals of the U.S. Navy combined, and more about aviation than the combined air force and more about government, than our entire staff of government officials, and more about finance and economy than all of our bankers and economists combined, it is proof that that mind is out of balance as there never has been and never will be a human mind able even to begin to grasp so great knowledge. "Therefore," he said "there is only one logical conclusion, and that is that a mind with such bloated ideas of its own greatness could only be the mind of a fool." On the other hand, he said he would concede that [Senator] Burton K. Wheeler is the most dangerous enemy this nation ever had, and that if we do go down to defeat it will be due almost entirely to Wheeler. He said Wheeler had so far managed to becloud every issue and keep the nation handcuffed and paralyzed, in spite of the fact that . . . almost anywhere you go, 99 times out of a hundred you can win the lifelong friendship of almost any intelligent man by

calling Wheeler "what you think he is" and he says the worse the name you call
him the better friend you have made of the man who hears it. He says if you
label him a straight out 22 K s.o.b. you have made a bosom friend for life. He
says Wheeler is the most wholeheartedly hated, loathed man in the world, so far
as Americans are concerned, even outranking Hitler and his cheap kind. These
things should be spoken of frankly. I hope you will do it!

[B. M.]

The home front: women at work

The military needs for the war at last solved the unemployment problems of the
Great Depression. The opening of defense plants in 1939-1940 offered ample opportunities for work. But once the nation plunged into actual war, the need for
military personnel necessitated tapping new sources for workers. Blacks, for example, found jobs in occupations that generally had been closed to them. Perhaps
most striking was the widespread use of women in the production of military
material. Factory work, of course, was nothing new for American women; but
they, too, found themselves in entirely new situations. The following account by a
woman working in a shipyard describes the entrance of women into defense
work, and the problems they encountered.

. . . Over and over for months I had heard from the radio the call for women
to enter war work. I had been delaying for one reason or another but I finally
recognized these arguments in favor of my going to the shipyards: my children,
now in their teens, were able to take some responsibility for our home; I wanted
to help out the war effort more than I had been doing through a few voluntary
services; and with living costs always going up and the children's education
looming ahead, we could use the money. So I had taken the aptitude test at the
U. S. Employment Office, had attended a defense class for shipfitters, and was
now on my way to an actual job at Richmond.

. . . When I reached the shipyards . . . I was borne along by the crowd and
permitted to enter through the guarded gate when I had shown my temporary
pass. I stood in a long line to receive papers; I stood in another line to receive

From Virginia Snow Wilkinson, "From Housewife to Shipfitter," *Harper's Magazine* 187 (September 1943) :
328–337.

State Historical Society of Wisconsin.

World War II poster.

tool checks (for every tool borrowed, a chip from your stack). At last some sixty of us women were herded to a personnel building, where a young man addressed us on safety precautions, the woman counselor for the day shift advised us about our clothing, and then, after a tour of the yard, we were divided into the trades for which we had been employed. The names of the welders were called and responded to. An escort was assigned to take them to their locations. The burners were selected, the flangers, the chippers, the checkers. Only a sparse group remained to be grouped as shipfitters' helpers—six women besides myself, Negro and white. Again we started out en masse; this time to a little cottage which was labeled "Master Shipfitter." The man upon whom the cottage door opened was small and harassed. We were presented to him a little apologetically, I thought, by our guide.

"What have you got there?" the shipfitter asked.

"Just a few shipfitter helpers, Mr. Jepson."

"Oh, my God! Women shipfitters. Why do they treat me like this? Women shipfitters. . . ."

. . . I was sent to work on a nearly completed hull in one of the concrete basins—a hull which had been constructed up to its weather deck. I found myself on the rusty black steel more amazed than ever before.

I was assigned to a leaderman working high on the side of the ship.

"You come along with me, duchess. I'll teach you how to make scuppers. Come on."

To "come on" meant to clamber over the side of the ship until I felt the scaffolding beneath me. The simplest way seemed to be to jump from the deck to the scaffold, for I was not going to be caught lagging behind the men here where I was the only woman on the side of the hull. Sometimes a worker would extend a hand of assistance. I refused to see it. I jumped from deck to scaffold, catching myself by a clutch at a handy pipe; I squeezed to the outer edge of the support to allow another worker to pass; I ran along the scaffold planks. All this in abysmal ignorance of where I was. It was hours later, I think, when my leaderman, standing beside me, tossed a little piece of wood or rag overboard and I heard no sound from it as it fell or lighted. I looked over and down, and down, and then crept by inches back to the security of the hull's side. No soft billowy water lay beneath us, but a great depth of brutal concrete.

"Do people often fall off the scaffold?" I asked, shaking.

"Not often," my leaderman assured me. "Only once."

I did not allow the firm surface of the hull to get out of my clasp for the remainder of the afternoon, not, that is, until later, when a piece of red-hot steel just skinned between me and the hull I was clinging to. It landed at my feet still glowing. I looked up at the men above me, who were preoccupied with the burning of a hole.

"Never mind, darling," the leaderman soothed. "I think they saw you."

But later I heard him berating these same burners. "You let a red-hot clip fall within an inch of her—what the hell you trying to do?"

The next day Mr. Jepson sent me out to an assembly way where I was entered upon the foreman's books as a shipfitter's helper. Here are made the double bottoms which hold water and oil for the ship's needs and for necessary ballast and, I suppose, give a second bottom when the first is missing. These units look much like the honeycomb of a wasp's nest—with the wasps still crawling about chipping, marking, and welding. They are built up off the ground about five feet on skids of heavy timber and iron. . . .

I walked along the skids and bumped into a man in tan, apparently an engineer. We talked.

"Tell me," I asked, "Do you think I have misjudged my job? Do you think if I keep trying I can find something to do?"

"Let me tell you," he said. "I have degrees from four different universities. I helped build Singapore and Pearl Harbor. And *I* can't find a job for myself."

I took my problem to Mr. Jepson.

"Can't you find a job with something for me to do?" I asked him.

"You've got a job, haven't you?"

"You mean I've been employed. But I can't go on taking money for doing nothing. I've got to respect myself or leave."

"My God, all day long they come in here wanting me to find them a job with more to do. What do you think I am? I can't revolutionize the industry. What people don't understand is that this is shipfitting. You can't build ships the way you do other things." He spread out his arms. "There are times while the work is getting laid out when few people are needed but then, after it shapes up, everyone around, and more, can be thrown on it. There just has to be a period of lull. If this were a peacetime activity the boss would be around with more work than anyone could do, shouting, 'Get the hell on to the job.' But by God, woman, this is war. What can you expect?"

Later, my foreman, answering the same inquiry, said, "The management does employ more men and women than it can put to work at once but they are here on hand, taking on new experience, learning new terminology—port, starboard, bulkhead, and vertical keel. Some will drop out but eventually the others will be drawn in on the job. Some of those will be no good. The others will build ships. You've got to have a lot of people to draw from in order to get even some good workmen. They shake the basket after a while and the capable come to the top."

"And the women?" I asked.

"And the women too have got to be used. The men don't like the idea; they voted against it in their unions; but they'll get used to women in time and think nothing of it. They used to feel the same way about women in the plate shop, but it's full of women now—they run the show—and there's no real hostility there toward them any more. Women haven't been seen much on ships yet but they'll be seen as the war goes on."

I was glad he mentioned the war. I had been wondering whether it was because there were no radio news reports here that no one spoke of the war, that great events shaping outside were diminished and pushed back from the consciousness of men. Was it because there were no clocks—for never a one could you find in the yard—that there seemed to be so little realization of the time that was so late? It was hard indeed to remember the urgency of the voices on the air, my own struggle against a sense of guilt and conscience, and the compulsion that had finally brought me to this job I was not doing. Should I leave? I remembered my husband's and children's absurd pride in my being here and decided to give myself two months to find something real to do.

. . . It must have been a fortnight or so later that I was given my first real shipfitting job . . . I was taught to put chocks on the double bottom. Chocks act as supports when the unit is turned over and put into the waiting hull. For weeks the craftsmen of our skids had worked on a huge section of double bottom, labeled XAK, which was at last passed as finished. It was prepared by the riggers to be lifted by the cranes—and then the whistle blew and we all went home. In the morning we learned that while the cranes were lifting the sixty tons—on the graveyard shift, mind you—the great weight suddenly broke loose and dropped, breaking a crane, smashing the roadway and concrete walk, and quite ruining the unit itself.

If the work in the basin on Hull 6 was not to be held up we had to rush a new XAK to replace the other. All hands were thrown upon it—even my hands. I was told to locate the chocks on the blueprint, to measure for them, to find the chocks, to get a welder to put them on, and to check to see that they were square. . . .

A few mornings later, as soon as we stepped upon the skids, we perceived that something new was astir. The shipfitting women—there were three of us—were called together.

"We're going to give you your own unit to work on together," the leaderman said. "XAK is your baby now. Study your print, square your frame lines down the vertical keel, and get the crane to bring you your steel."

Alice, our naive nineteen-year-old, glowed. "Golly," she said. "Really?" The colored girl was more sophisticated but we were all pleased.

"Let's be so accurate and careful that they won't be able to find a thing wrong. Let's check and recheck everything. . . . "

"We'll work it out together. If one of us makes a mistake we'll tell her and correct it and no bad feelings . . ." "We'll all stand and fall together on it." That was the way we talked.

I never saw such a change in three workmen as in these three girls. We became integrated persons working together on a project which focused all our interests. I noticed how quickly we ran our own errands, how conscientious we were in checking, how we abhorred sloppy measurements. For once we had been given responsibility, for once we had been put on our own, for once we had enough to do.

"When we finish we'll hold open house and invite you in to tea," we told our leaderman.

Our enjoyment was such that we did not notice that something was amiss until late in the afternoon. Then we became gradually aware of the hostility of the men. Our woman burner reported that they were "seething with resentment" that women should be given a unit to construct. The women checkers said, "You should just hear what we hear outside our checking shed, my dears." This was the first time I had come up against the hostility of one sex toward another and I could not believe it. The men had always been so decent, so respectful, so kindly. But this was the first time that we had been seen in the light of competitors. We had been amusing little creatures only too happy to take what crumbs of jobs were dropped to us.

Our leaderman said, "I know, but pay no attention. They'll have to get used to women shipfitters. Half these men may be in the Army this January. They might as well accept the fact that women will have to take their places."

Our woman checker said, "In September I was one of the first women ever to be admitted out here in the yards. You could have cut the resentment with a knife and spread it thick. But it's gradually being worn away."

The next day, with no explanation, our XAK, "our baby," was taken from us and given to the men. We had to stand aside and see the men working on what we felt was our project. Cora, whose boy friend was one of the group, said the men were afraid the assemblies would become like the plate shop—overrun by women. She took herself over to the unit where her friend was working, to lean against the steel. Alice took out her lipstick: "Oh, what the heck do I care so long as I get my dollar five an hour. But it *was* fun."

I tried to reflect that there must be another side to this thing. Maybe the men who were heads of families, straining to take care of several dependents, and who had known the bitter struggle for a living—maybe these men resented the fact that any eighteen-year-old could come out without a day's training, without a grain of tool sense or mechanical sense, and draw the same pay as they and rise at the same rate—even these girls who would go at once into debt for fur coats and "perfectly adorable" evening gowns. The pay was too high for the beginner, I knew—for the boy who had quit high school as well as for the girl. The experienced workman might easily feel resentment. But this I knew too; that the responsibility placed upon these girls had made them almost in one day into serious workmen. . . .

I had promised myself two months in which to find myself here in the shipyards but my probation was not to last so long. It seemed that we, the women, were being assimilated gradually, if slowly. For a while we had floated on top, undissolved, but the broth was big enough with a little stirring and stewing to absorb us all—or almost all. The great need was for experienced workmen, men or women; and time on the job, doing this and a little of that, adds up finally to experience. I was given more and more to do. (When I told my leaderman that I liked having more to do he answered, "Well, neither you nor I nor the shipyards are as new and green as we were; we're all getting under way.") Six weeks from the date of my arrival at the yard I was given a unit to handle by myself. I guess it was not so much but it was my own.

I measured for and located the steel material which was to go on this unit. I labeled it with chalk and engaged the riggers to lift it. I asked a flanger and a tacker to be on hand to put the steel in place and to tack (weld) it up. And then I stood while the crane—one of those beautiful gray cranes which trail steel through the air with a motion as graceful as the soaring of a hawk on an up-current of air—picked up the material and sped it to our unit. It wasn't so much, no more than anyone could have done, but I felt the keen exhilaration of getting under way. It was good, I thought, this working together on a ship.

Standing so elated, I felt a ripple of interest run from workman to workman. We all looked up and out to sea where a gray troopship was being towed past us silently. Our ship. My first day in the yard I had helped make a scupper for it and these other men and women standing grinning had made the double bottom.

"There she goes!" we said and watched it as it slipped away. Then I turned back to my work, for at last I had a job.

Concentration camps: American style

The Japanese attack on Pearl Harbor resolved the deep divisions among the American people. The war generated unity and determination and there was no need for wholesale governmental repression of individual liberties such as had characterized the Wilson administration's conduct in 1917-1918. Indeed, the degree of unity inspired such confidence that the Supreme Court declared compulsory saluting of the flag unconstitutional *(West Virginia Board of Education* v. *Barnette,* 1943). The one major stain on the record for maintaining civil liberty came with the forced evacuation of Japanese-Americans, aliens and citizens alike, from the West Coast and their confinement in "relocation centers." The policy evolved from long-standing prejudice against the Japanese combined with the fears of military authorities and the civilian bureaucracy. General John L. De Witt, west coast military commander, created his own logic when he argued removal was necessary because "the very fact that no sabotage has taken place to date is a disturbing and confirming indication that such action will be taken." No similar action was taken against German or Italian citizens, which is evidence in part of the racist tone of the removals. The following accounts offer the recollection of a white California woman who attempted to help the Japanese-Americans, a bitter protest from evacuees who refused to serve in the armed forces, and finally, a letter from a Nisei who did serve and tried to justify his action to his parents.

Aiding Evacuees

. . . The reason I got into any of this? I was talking to Bob Okamatsu who was on my husband's staff at the University YMCA. His parents had just been ordered out of their home in Alameda, which was the first area to be evacuated. (Bob is now working in a large grocery firm, in an administrative position, in the Middle West.) His family, his mother and father, two brothers and a sister, no, one brother and sister, were all very devout and active members of the Baptist Church and while his parents didn't speak any English at all, they went regularly to the Japanese Baptist Church.

I think it was probably because of that that I made a reference that I did in talking to Bob. I asked him if the people in the Baptist Church had indicated any wish to help his parents or anybody. And he said, "No, I suppose it's too soon." Or something like that, I don't remember exactly what he said. But I remember definitely saying to him, "Well, Bob what can the church people do? Do you think is something they *should* do?" And he looked at me and said, "Ruth, I think they've got to either put up or shut up."

I don't know how long it was after that—I think probably the next day, it might have been the same day, I don't know—I was talking to Mrs. Eric Bellquist, whose husband was on campus in the Political Science department, and who had testified for the Tolan Committee in behalf of loyal persons of Japanese ancestry in relation to a possible evacuation. Mrs. Bellquist and I discussed it, and we decided that certainly somebody ought to do something about helping those old people. Do two things. One, find a place for them to stay in the next zone, until they could find out what they wanted to do. Because this was an immediate thing. It had to be done right away, and then, help them with some of their personal belongings. Many of them didn't have children who were Nisei, didn't have anybody. And they were losing their household goods, for instance selling beautiful refrigerators for one dollar. You know, that sort of thing. And we felt that inasmuch as they had practically nothing they could take with them, were in a hurry and had no place to go, that was the first thing we could do—find them places to go.

So we got together a representative group of young students, university

From an interview with Ruth Kingman, "The Fair Play Committee and Citizen Participation." Regional Oral History Office, Bancroft Library. Published by permission of the Director, The Bancroft Library, University of California, Berkeley. Material suggested by Miriam Feingold Stein.

An elderly Issei in an American concentration camp during
World War II.

students—about half of them I would say, were from Stiles Hall, the University YMCA and the other half from the University YWCA. Lillie Margaret Sherman was the director of the YWCA and my husband Harry was the director of Stiles Hall. We talked to them and asked them if they thought it was a good project. They thought it was.

So, after planning it with the students, who, in turn, enlisted as many more students as they wanted or felt they needed, they then canvassed the entire southwest Berkeley area where Japanese-Americans or Japanese lived and the houses next to those houses where they might have been known. Because this was the second zone it was still open. The students tried to see if there were rooms where some of these old people could stay until they could find other places in the next zone. I don't know now, and I don't think we ever even kept track of how many were placed; but I would say there wasn't anyone who left that first prohibited area who wanted a place to stay that we couldn't place. And, as far as their possessions were concerned, that didn't seem to amount to very much. We didn't have to do very much about that until the next order came which cleared everybody out of Berkeley. They had to go back further into the state or further east still. Then personal property was a problem. And so we began scurrying around trying to find safe storage space. And this is where we went to church groups, asking if they had basements or attics where these things—just personal things, paper, clothes, and whatever—could be stored until the evacuees could send for them. And we insisted upon three copies of lists—everything being made available to us. We kept one copy and one copy went to the Army and one copy went to the evacuee. So that was the way it was. Our copies were kept in the safe of the First Congregational Church for years until I think they were thrown out because there was no point in keeping them any longer.

Then it wasn't very long until the order came for complete evacuation and the Berkeley people were ordered to Tanforan. All they could take was what would fit in one suitcase per person. Some of them had lived here all their lives. There were University students; there were doctors, nurses, lawyers, businessmen, as well as gardeners, maids, cooks, everything. Everything but blue-collar. I think there were no blue-collar evacuees. As far as I know, they were either white-collar or laborers. The laborers mostly were the Issei (Japan born). They had sent their children to college so the Nisei were pretty much white-collar. But they could carry only a suitcase, so we had to hurry around and find storage places for their other belongings.

Well, we did. Through the churches and through the women's faculty group—not as such, but women on the campus—wives of faculty members. We found basements and attics for the property of hundreds of families. Literally hundreds of families. And some of those things were kept carefully clear through the entire war till they came back. Others, upon request, were sent to their owners wherever they were. And then later, when the evacuees began to come back, but still didn't have any place to go, they would sometimes come and get some of their belongings a little at a time. . . .

. . . The Tanforan situation was, to say the least, disgracefully uncomfortable. . . . It was a race track and these people lived in the horses' stalls. And all of the remaining vestiges of the horses' occupancy were not necessarily gone. There would be a family, say of three, or four; father, mother, two small children, maybe a tiny baby. And, of course, one couldn't help but be a little ambivalent about this. You felt so sorry for them. I mean having to live that way when they were American citizens who'd never done anything but go to school—that sort of thing. I mean while we weren't worried about them we felt sorry for them. On the other hand, this was a job that the Army had been given to do and in American history there had never been anything like this. They were not equipped to handle men and women and babies. On a large basis like this, all in a hurry. They were not accustomed to providing for the needs of women and children.

One of the things that bothered the older women down there more than anything else and also when they got to Topaz, was that, as the Army calls them, latrines had no dividing curtains at all. Now this, for a Japanese woman, was just about as hard as anything she could ever be asked to undergo. So as soon as they could they tried to better this. The Army did try, and even in the face of criticism from people who were reading of the cruel treatment of American civilians who had been placed in prison camps by the Japanese in Singapore and elsewhere. They really tried, but they weren't equipped to do it. So the whole thing was pretty bad.

Well, anyway, they tried to set up schools, of course, immediately for the children. Both to keep them busy and to keep them up with their school work. School work being very important to them all. Of course, they had some accredited Nisei teachers there. They had some good art teachers. I remember Professor Obata was there. From the University of California Art Department.

And I remember, one of the things that they felt so much the need of, in addition to all textbooks, was the sort of thing that kindergarteners and young children use, art materials and papers and what have you. So one of the things that I did was to go to other parents of young children here in Berkeley, and rounded up several huge cartons of mostly used, but not too much used, color equipment and paper and dull scissors, the sort of things that children use. And then because they had an adult art class too, I remember I went to the California School of Arts and Crafts and they sent to Mr. Obata a huge crate of art materials that had been used somewhat but were perfectly useful. And so they were able to start something to keep their minds off of what they were, where they were, and what they were doing, among the adults as well as the children. . . .

A Protest

February 8, 1943

TO: The Editors of the Heart Mountain Sentinel

SUBJECT: Recent Draft Status of the Nisei Internees

. . . Certainly, we who have been interned in the various assembly and relocation centers could not have been unaware of the worldwide implications of the present war between the dictator and democratic nations. But we have also been aware of the minimum part being played by the Nisei as a group. It is general knowledge that our volunteers in the past have been rejected, and outside of a very few individuals, the very soldiers in uniform have been relegated to positions [of] menial labor, their fighting spirit curbed, their natural abilities overlooked.

Therefore, is it strange that there is a lassitude in our thinking, when it comes to actual participation in a war in which we can see no ultimate gain, either for ourselves or for our aged parents? The government has shown that it intends to follow the whims and caprices of public opinion rather than the cold light of statistics and proof. It has rejected us spiritually, economically and politically by surrounding us with barbed wire and armed sentries. It has passed us by in the needs of the country both in national defense and on the home front. It has allowed the growing suspicion that we are undesirable and dangerous to foster and spread until actual hostility is shown us wherever we have dared to relocate.

Now with the nation growing acutely aware of manpower shortages, and the need for capable young men desperate, the government has finally turned to us and asked us to volunteer our services. Volunteer, that is, not as an integrated part of the United States Army, but rather a separate corps.

What the actual intentions of the government are, are very obscure. Whether it intends to release us permanently from the stigma of being "Japs" before or after our registration is completed, is not mentioned. Whether or not it intends to clear our name to the country at large, is not admitted. What our actual status is, in terms of constitutionality, remains shrouded and vague. How our parents are to be treated in our absence (provided we enlist) is also a mystery.

These and other questions are not mere excuses offered by us to forestall further criticism of our actions, nor are they to be interpreted as a refusal to join the Army. But they are vital queries on which the future actions of our youth will depend, when they face actual combat. For how much emphasis does the

From a letter to the *Heart Mountain Sentinel,* 8 February 1943. Published by permission of the Director, The Bancroft Library, University of California, Berkeley. Material suggested by Douglas Nelson.

government place upon the moral of white Americans under arms? Quite a great deal, without doubt. Yet the American soldiers have no such problems confronting them [as] are facing those of Japanese extraction. Are the white parents being kept behind barbed wire fences, living in crowded quarters, facing a difficult and ominous future without their means of support guaranteed? Hardly. Then how well could any soldier fight with these truths steadily becoming reality day by day?

Is there, then, any wonder that there is a undercurrent of suspicion among us that we are being [v]ictimized again, sent to areas against our will, on the flimsy protest that we are doing our "duty". The whole Evacuation program was based on the principle that it was our solemn obligation not to interfere with the war program, and that we should quietly leave our homes, our friends, our jobs, and become wards of the government. That much we did, and admirable, for dissenters were in extreme minority.

Actually, however, the means by which the program was and is, being carried out, and especially in the light of certain recent events we are becoming more and more aware that our evacuation was not merely a matter of military necessity alone. Bills being submitted to the California legislature smack of economic dealings as well. For, granted that certain politicians in that state found it to their advantage to use us as a lever to raise themselves into prominence, why then is there the urgent necessity to keep us out permanently? Why the undiminished clamor to couple our citizenship with the land problem? Only a blind person could fail to see that there have been, and there are now, certain interested parties to whom the evacuation of Japanese from the West Coast was more than a fear of possible sabotage.

And is there any reason to believe other than that these same parties have been largely instrumental in keeping the loyalty and true feelings of we Nisei in the dark, smudged by the powerful newspapers who blared (totally without proof) the evil-doings of the Japanese? Why should there be, when even the foremost governmental agencies have been suspicious of our intentions—when the FBI itself had been delude to believe that every fishing boat carried radios and weapons with which to spy on, and possibly cripple the Pacific fleet!

And our pitifully few voices that were raised in the wilderness of public disapproval were woefully inadequate to prove our loyalty. Even our splendid public record was not enough to sway public opinion, for us in our battle for equality. There is no need here to pursue the endless statistics which prove beyond doubt our high moral, social, scholastic records. They are buried and forgotten by American as surely as our personal property, back deep in the archives of public opinion. Not because they have proved our disloyalty, but because they did not.

Even the investigating Congressional committees from Washington could find no fault with our behavior. Still, we are here, victims of whatever choice was forced upon us. And our future certainly is no brighter for our having evacuated. Nor is there any reason for hoping it will be bettered when we have joined the colors. The present plan to form a Japanese-American unit has proved that we are still regarded as unequal as still un-assimilable by the government.

Whatever angle we attack with reference to our future, we find the cards stacked against us. No amount of wishful thinking by idealists will better our lot now or after. Rather, what is needed now is hardheaded realism, and facing of facts.

One of the facts stands clear: There is left to we Nisei one opportunity to better our fate after the war; one means by which we can assure for ourselves and our people the treatment we so richly deserve after our mis-han[d]ling by the people of America; one remaining lever to pry off the veil of hypocrisy and greed, from the plain truth of our loyalty. That one last hope is the present volunteer plan submitted by the Army, which is now in the process of digestion.

The means we have at hand, the plan is simple. We should, we must *demand now* our true status in American life. We still have time to discover whether we are being used as we have been used in the past, or if this time, the government is really extending to us the opportunity we need to prove one and for all our unswerving loyalty to America. By our status, however, we should make clear that we mean the rights and privileges of full citizenship, and not merely the handouts of a tolerant society. *We must demand* that our name be cleared, and have it read to the world that there had never been a justification for our evacuation, and that we are fighting, not to *redeem* ourselves, or to clear our names, but for what we have always believed in.

Then, should we be put off with a pretext that the time is not ripe for such actions, we will know at least just where we stand. This much in itself will clear the air.

But there is reason to hope that the government will accede to our demands. Why should they keep back the truth—that we have proven our citizenship requirements far and above that demanded of ordinary citizen? We have given everything the American people have asked, and more. The government of this country has adopted a course which the world now looks forward to, a course which will rid the world of fear and persecution. Such a policy by such a government cannot be lightly followed at home, for the eyes of the world are focused here.

Surely, it is not un-American in demanding such clear, forceful measures now. The world is waiting for such a statement, on a much broader and more comprehensive basis. And could not this policy be an assuring factor abroad as well as at home? For what could be a greater blow to the Axis preaching of race-hatred than the news that the sons of the sons of Nippon are actually treated as equals in America? And what could be a greater blow than throwing 30,000 of us at their weakening lines?

Isn't it worth a little effort now to clear up our status? Isn't it worth a great deal of effort to become American citizens in fact as well as in name? Isn't it worth the yellow publicity we will surely invite, if we can stand and face an unenlightened public with the majority of clear-thinking, unprejudiced people behind us? For here are many such men and women today.

Then, now is the time to speak out, to act. For once we have been "volunteered" into the army, our rights to free speech will have been submerged for the duration—and perhaps longer. And those who hopefully cling to the dream of a more kindly-minded Congress and public opinion after the war, need only to ask themselves—"How easily does human nature change? How easily will those politicians and opportunists who have used us as tools to power, change their minds? And how easily can we re-educate the public in our favor, when it took from the Gentlemen's Agreement to Pearl Harbor to brand us slowly but surely as un-American, however untruthfully?"

A Volunteer

Saturday, Nov. 20, 1943
10:00 P.M.

Dear Dad,

Thanks a million for your very nice, heart warming letter. To tell you the truth, it was the best letter I've ever received in all my life. Before I forget, please tell Mom to write to me as I miss her very much. She could write to me in Japanese if it is easier for her. I'll probably have some trouble in reading it but I could ask one of my friends who is studying Japanese to help me out. . . .

Don't worry about us fellows because we are going to do our best in everything we do. I din't want to brag but this outfit is really tops. There's quite a number of Caucasian outfits stationed here but my infantry has them all beat. We made the best scores in the recent tests. Right now the whole outfit is training awfully hard. They're never in camp because they have to go out into the bivouac area for various military problems. Last week they went thru live machine gun fire with dynamite blowing up all around them. This week they had to eat and sleep in a fox-hole for about four days. When the company goes out they close the mess hall so we (recruits) have to eat at some other mess hall. . . .

From anonymous letters, collections of Topaz Volunteers. Published by permission of the Director, The Bancroft Library, University of California, Berkeley.

Sunday, Nov. 21, 1943

. . . This morning I went to church and Chaplain Yamada from Hawaii was the speaker. This infantry outfit has three chaplains now. The other two are Chaplains West and Higuchi. Chaplain Yamada spoke about the true meaning of Thanksgiving. Boy, I sure had a lot to be thankful for, Dad. Thanks a million for understanding my volunteering into the army. Boy, I sure tried like hell to make you understand how I felt towards volunteering. I guess if Mom had said "no", too, I probably wouldn't have volunteered. To both of you I'm greatly indebted and this is my way of showing how much I love my folks, so that we may be together again in a nice home.

Gee, Dad, I sure hated to go against your word but it was the one thing in my life that would have bothered me if I didn't. I guess if the Japanese from Hawaii could come all the way down here, I don't see why the mainlanders can't. They're Japanese just like me and any other niseis in the mainland. Some of them might never see their folks again but they are willing to take a chance and its a darn good gamble if we come out the way we wanted it to be. So, Dad, you can just about understand how prowd I am to serve in the Japanese American Combat Team. A month ago I saw a news reel which showed the Japanese Americans of the—Inf. fighting over in Italy. All of us fellas whistled and cheered because we were so proud of the fine record they are making.

No, Dad, I won't be coming home this Thanksgiving or Christmas as I haven't finished my basic training. Sure wish I could be there to enjoy the Christmas Holidays. But don't worry, I'm coming home on the first furlough I get. So, until that day comes, I'll always be thinking of you folks.

Again I want to thank you both, you and Mom, for understanding the way I feel. It just makes me feel glad all over when I can say: "Sure, my folks are backing me up 100 percent and more with all their love." Some of the fellas aren't as lucky as I am because their folks have gone to Tule Lake. But just the same they are training just as hard as anybody else and more. . . .

Your loving son,

Men in war

Soldiers, as usual, experienced the brunt of the horrors and terror of the war. The following survey of soldiers' observations offers a variety of responses. The first several letters are from an army lieutenant who was in the Philippines when the Japanese attacked in December 1941. The evolution of his attitudes from rage and callousness to a recognition of tragedy for both sides is especially poignant. Shortly after his last letter, the lieutenant was captured, survived the Bataan

"Death March," but was killed by American planes that bombed a Japanese prison ship. The next letter is from an army engineer who did not need propaganda to convince him of Nazi destructiveness. This soldier's comments on the Russians' role in the war, and future considerations for them, reflected the prevailing mood of cordiality and friendship toward the Soviets—an attitude that later became grounds for suspicion of one's loyalty. The final letter is a graphic, outraged account by an army sergeant who helped liberate a Nazi concentration camp.

December 9, 1941
PHILIPPINES

DEAREST FOLKS:

I wish there was some way to speed this letter on wings to let you know I am now on the front.

One day of war has passed. . . . We were eating lunch when the first heavy bombs hit. The Japs came over and knew exactly what they wanted. They bombed and strafed up the Clark Field area and strafed the upper post with heavy fire. Quite a few casualties, but I am O.K. We immediately moved out to the crater areas until nightfall, then moved to the jungle.

There were bombings, fires, and air battles all around and over us all night. I wasn't near a bed and it's now 7:30 A.M. the second day. Hope we don't move for a few hours, but I know we will. The whole battalion is dog-tired. . . .

It is now almost nightfall and we are in the same position. We've almost made ourselves at home. We have seen many planes today, but all ours, I guess. The news is very slow out here except by radio, and we do not know how much of that to believe. I went up the road to quiet down some white antitank groups who had nervous fingers and were firing on our own aircraft.

Later I found a pump and a bucket, and took a bath and shave. It does wonders for you, even in war. All the people have taken to the deep jungles, and it looks so funny to see open *bahis,* with chickens, pigs and carabaos around, but no people. Can't say I blame them. Awfully pitiful, though, to see them leave everything they have in the world behind.

My foxhole is very nice already. I have my bedding well in it, and it's very comfortable, except for mosquitoes.

From Howard Peckham and Shirley A. Snyder, *Letters from Fighting Hoosiers* (Bloomington: Indiana War Commission, 1948), pp. 11–15, 173–176, 203–207. Used by permission.

Dec. 10

Up at 4:30 A.M. today. The roosters around here just won't let you sleep. Very quiet all night. I had the 8-12 watch, and it was very boring. Nothing at all. . . .

I guess we know less about what's happening than anyone in the States. All we know is what we see and hear. . . .

Finally resting a moment again. Just had our first parachute scare. A Jap bomber was shot down over to our right about 4,000 yards, and the crew of five bailed out. Immediately they were filled with lead. All reached the ground dead. . . .

Jan. 5, 1942

Almost a month of war now. Still going strong and in perfect health. I've developed a slight case of jitters, but that's only natural, I guess, with so many bombs dropping every day.

I got my promotion over a week ago, but doesn't make much difference now. A little more money. . . . I have had no mail at all since the war. I've written about four times to you—hope you've received at least one. . . .

The days are hot and the nights cool and moonlit these past few nights. This is winter here, too, but you would never know it. I really enjoy the beauty of the huge forests and mountains around us, even when we know they (Japs) are coming closer each day. . . . I don't have time to write much any more. Just work, eat, sleep, and stay on the ball. . . .

There have been airplanes overhead constantly for four hours now, and the ground is always shaking from some bombing or another. Planes are so common they are not even scouted any more. We know whose they are. We just yell "cover" and jump into our foxholes. There are holes of all sizes all around. Some we have dug, and some, others have dug before us. They get deeper every time we are bombed.

Feb. 12

I know that I have not kept you informed of my well-being, etc., for the past six weeks, but I know that even had I written you probably would not get them for months, and also I haven't had time for writing.

I am well as can be, healthy and in good spirits. We have been through some very rugged times in these past weeks, with very little sleep, if any, and it becomes rather tiresome being on the constant alert dodging shells, bombs, and machine gun fire. You read enough of that in the papers I suppose, and anyway, I can't tell you anything about it, or my letters wouldn't stand a chance of getting through. . . .

We have gone through a lot of h—— in these few months, but have had surprisingly few casualties. One of my best friends from Richmond, Va., George Hardy, was killed by bombs. Gee, I hated to see him go. I've prayed to God each night to have great pity on the souls of those who are gone as they paid for their sins many times over in this h—— on earth.

I wonder if God is not only caring for ours, but for the thousands of young Japanese left lying in the jungles here in Luzon. We have taken a toll of lives many times what we have lost. I have seen what deadly effect my own firing has had among the ranks of the attackers in places where we have retaken the ground. They do not bury their dead except as an afterthought.

All my belongings are of course up in smoke. Even those I came into the field with were burned when my car was hit by a shell several weeks ago. The men gave me clothes and the officers gave me a razor and toothbrush and that's all I need, I guess.

I suppose this awful war has really just begun, but nine weeks has seemed an eternity. I'm so tired of killed men littering the jungle paths, of the stench of dead bodies being always in the air.

Will you please tell all the boys and girls I know that it's O. K. so far. Tomorrow isn't in our vocabulary.

Easter Sunday 1945
E.T.O., Somewhere in France

Dear Mother:

I thought I'd write you an Easter letter at least—in reply to two letters from you that descended in a heap a week or so ago—back February mail that had been eddying around in some backwater. We read that a mail ship had broken down in some out-of-the-way port and finally had limped in some place that had facilities for trans-shipping some millions of pieces of mail. It had broken down four times, probably some vital part like a main drive shaft that can only be fixed in a big dry dock. With shipping as vital as it is, towing a boat is out of the question, besides being very risky business.

The Krauts are dying by inches like a snake, but evidently the U-boat arm is still alive and vicious. Everything they are doing now in their death throes has *only one* redeeming feature, that is to my mind; the fact that they are constantly removing themselves farther and farther from the circle of civilized nations each time they prolong the fighting, and they are smearing themselves and alienating any friends or support they might have by their stupid continuation of a lost struggle. They insist on the last ditch struggle to prove a conclusion which has been foregone ever since they retreated from Moscow and lost the battle of Africa. In this way the only good I can see come out of it is that more and more of them are being destroyed and it is daily coming closer to *my* idea that the entire race should be wiped out. As long as any of them live they will never cease to dream of ruling the world and will stop at nothing to accomplish their aim.

I firmly believe they have a plan for the Third World War—that they anticipated losing this one on paper—but actually statistics show that they have systematically slaughtered enough of the cream of every other smaller nation in Europe that by 1960 Germany will once more have an overwhelming advantage in manpower. This advantage we are helping to accomplish by feeding and caring for hundreds of thousands of strong young German prisoners who are complicating our supply system and burdening our transport system, if only by eating and riding. The only fault in their plan, their only successful rival competitor, enemy, and conquerer, is Russia. They undoubtedly counted on beating Russia and failed. Since this is so, and also since Russia has done the bulk of the fighting—by which I do not mean to underestimate nor belittle what our own boys have done, but when you compare the Russian front of 2,500 miles with our own front and remember how many years the Russians have been absorbing the heaviest punishment the Germans could deal out and the tremendous destruction that has been wreaked on Russian soil and citizens—you realize how incalculably more difficult our own fighting would have been without them. I am in favor of giving the major part of Germany to Russia, who certainly has earned it and who can be counted upon to see to it that Germany will never again threaten the world with slavery.

I know you have never agreed with my deep hatred for the Germans and everything they admire and stand for. When I realize how much you personally have suffered, I am at a loss to understand your attitude. I don't doubt that in your case it is a miscarriage of a Christian virtue. I find it not only blind but positively dangerous to try to deal with these animals on any such basis. One might just as well read the Ten Commandments to a spotted leopard, walk into the cage and not expect to be eaten. The only reason I consider it important that you and everyone like you, who has no active opinion against these subhumans, should listen to me is that *we have not won the war even after the fighting ceases.* This is definitely only one step in their thousand-year plan to dominate the world. They are stubborn and absolutely unchanging in their ideas. They live forever and breed like rabbits and everywhere they emigrate they remain a hard, foreign, unassimilated element whose sole desire and ambition is to Germanize and brutalize the world into an exact replica of Germany. Each time they are allowed to proceed with the next step in their plan, it takes more and more blood, sweat, and tears to stop them, and the next war they have planned may very well destroy the entire world, *if they are allowed to proceed with it. It is possible.* Destruction of men, materials, wealth, resources and *brains,* which are the race's rarest and most precious possession, can reach such a rate that the world will revert to an uninhabited jungle. You have only to notice how difficult it is to operate the United States today with only 13,000,000 men missing to see it would not take too much more to wreck the place.

This is a strange kind of an Easter letter, I will admit, but in another way it is the best and only kind I feel will guarantee a more peaceful Easter in years to come—in fact the only kind that will guarantee that there will be any kind of an Easter when you remember the Nazi sacrileges against the Christian churches in Germany. You need no imagination to see the horrible little paperhanger enshrined in your own church this Easter, if his plan had not failed. I write this because the peace conference and the San Francisco meeting are the payoff on the tremendous debt the nation owes the dead and wounded. *This time there must be no slip up.* The world can not afford to fail, and civilians like you are the only ones who now have a voice to raise and see that justice is done and the sacrifices of millions are not in vain.

This does not in any way affect my love for you, but I have given you my reasons for what I think and I hope I have convinced you that these next few months in America are the most important months in the history of the world. We may not have another chance to find the right answer. I won't try to suggest what you can do, but if you do no more than talk to people, which I know you do constantly at the University, you can do a great deal of good with the *thinking* people if only helping to convince them that whatever else is done the Germans must not be allowed the slightest possible chance to make war on the world again. There is no way to punish them justly for the misery, torture, pain, death and destruction they have deliberately unleashed on helpless peoples, but *they must be stopped from doing it again in twenty years, as they have five times in the last one hundred years.* I will leave the means to you, ways will certainly present themselves.

I send you my best love, and hope that this finds you, as it leaves me, in good health and suffering only from the natural results of this German-inspired world tragedy. Once more my love to you.

BILL

April 20, 1945
GERMANY

DEAR MOTHER AND DAD:

This is one letter that won't be the ordinary "How are you? I am well" kind. I have seen and been through one of Germany's most famous institutions—the

Americans supervise German civilians burying the dead in a
Nazi concentration camp.

concentration camp—and I don't feel like writing a letter about the weather and the neighbor's babies, if you get what I mean. It took a strong stomach and a mind used to similar sights to view the results of the "New Order" and its "Kultur."

To begin with, this place had been captured or freed by the Americans only a few days when I visited the place, and so I was able to see the camp at near firsthand. The first thing we saw as we came up the driveway was a ten-foot high electrified fence, with about every hundred yards, a guard tower mounting a searchlight and machine guns (now dismounted).

We passed through a nice looking entrance into a stone-paved court filled with about thirty or forty buildings one story high, and about one hundred feet long by twenty-five wide. These buildings at one time held upwards of fifty thousand men and boys—no women. More about the women later. At the present time there are about ten thousand left in it.

As we walked along we were followed by a crowd of hobbling wretches that had once been men. Now their whole effort is to remain alive, to get a bite to eat, a cigarette to smoke, to catch a glimpse of these American soldiers—soldiers who don't beat and curse them but who feed them and give medical care to those who require it. I say "hobbled after us" literally. They were so thin their legs looked like my arms. They were emaciated by starvation, slavish labor and dysentery.

Here and there one of them would have the cunning, bestial glare of a madman, a monomaniac whose single thought was for food, food and more food! Most of them had sores where the points of bones, shoulder blades, etc., had lost their normal covering of flesh and had rubbed raw on their clothing, or rags, I should say, or their straw pile beds. I watched one poor fellow take about three minutes to get to an outdoor toilet seat, from a door about thirty feet away. There were signs on his clothing of failure at previous attempts to reach the seat. Yet, such signs of filth were not common here—the Germans made them wash everything. But all they had was water—no soap at all.

We went on walking, and once, looking back, I saw several of them in a feeble imitation of a fight. They were fighting over a cigarette butt one of us had thrown away. Some of the boys had chocolate with them—D-rations or Hershey Tropical that we get as part of our candy rations. They threw them over the fence around one of the huts, being careful to make sure that one person got it all, and not a disputed half. They thanked us in broken English or their own language, whatever it happened to be. I saw the flags of several nations flying, denoting the "residence" there of Russian, Polish, French, Belgian, Czech, and Dutch, but not English or American flags for the same reason. There were American flags flying alongside the others, but as in a place of honor and respect only.

I didn't have anything but a cellophane bag of C-ration bouillon powder to give them, but if I had had candy I would have been afraid to give it to them, as their stomachs are not used to much food, and it is too concentrated. They told us later that the American medics were feeding very lightly, but even then it was hard to keep it down, and what stayed down was passed through their bowels by dysentery too quickly to help them very much. But they are on the road to recovery, and that's what matters.

By the time we had walked around and seen all these things, it was getting on toward time for us to leave. So we headed for the thing we had mainly come to see. This was the torture room, the crematory and the place where bodies were kept before disposal. We had been told beforehand what to expect, and so we purposefully went to see it last. Even the pitiful things we had seen would have been anticlimax to this one overbearingly evil thing.

The building was a low, brick structure, with a squat brick smokestack on one side of it. It was surrounded by a seven-foot high board fence, so as to permit no one to see the things that went on behind it, I suppose. As we went through the gate, the first thing that met my eyes was a pile of about forty or fifty dead men, piled four or five deep, like cordwood. They were for the most part naked, and thus exposed the most hideous cuts, bruises and broken limbs that sub-human minds could inflict on them. They were even thinner than the live ex-prisoners. All these were the result of the Nazi delight in torture and, so a Jew told us, a few were cremated alive for the same reason. Their guards and torturers were the infamous SS troops, who are the elite Nazis.

This pile of bodies was by no means normal, the Jew told us. They killed more than they could burn because the Americans were coming, and they exceeded their quotas because of that. The day before the medics had taken away about the same amount as we saw for burial and the same amount the morning of the day we were there. Normally the output of the killers was about the same as the capacity of the crematory ovens. I took two pictures of this pile of bodies and then followed the rest of the bunch inside.

The building inside reminded me of a small, neat, old-fashioned bakery. There were two furnaces of brick and steel, with three doors each for the placing of the body and the removal of ashes, if any. When we saw the place there were bodies in various stages of cremation in the ovens, and I took a picture of the most recognizable of these. In the rest of the oven were things that couldn't be recognized as bodies. In the end of this room was an elevator entrance. It was of the type and size used in hospitals for the removal of patients from ward to surgery, etc. Only in this case, it was used to bring in the dead "patients" from the cellar room in which they had been tortured and killed.

We went down there next to view the instruments of torture and death that had silenced so many men. They were few—only a row of stout pegs about eight feet off the floor, a rubber hose, a hose connected to a water faucet, a rope, and last but not least, an oversized potato masher-like club. There was a stuffed suit of clothes hanging by the neck from one peg and beside it the club. It was rather splintered, as if it had been stirring concrete instead of mashing potatoes, and of a peculiar dark color, a sort of brownish red. Needless to say, this was the main means of the torture and death of hundreds if not thousands of men. The hose was only an extra tool; it wouldn't break bones or fracture skulls, it would only bruise and cut. The water hose was used to wash the bloodstains from the whitewashed walls and to revive the fainting. It was further used to torture by the forced introduction of water, under pressure, into the mouth or other openings of the person, being used to rupture internal organs. At one side of this room was the elevator to the crematory.

After seeing and passing through this mass-production disassembly line of human beings, we were all rather speechless with horror. We were thankful, too, that such things had been confined in a military sense of the word, to the European side of the Atlantic. This, then, was the "New Order" which was to breed a new "civilization"—to last for a thousand years and which was to be as superior to Christianity as Christianity is to the ancient paganism. This was Germany. Yet, to give the devil his due, there had been German army officers and men in this camp, and they received no better treatment than the Jews from the Ghetto of Warsaw. A Jew told us that, and he said that he had been there for seven years, so he should have known the truth of things.

Oh, yes, I promised to tell more about the women's side of the camp. I said that there were no women in the camp. There were more actually on the inside with the men, but the best looking of the women taken captive in the foreign countries were kept as prostitutes by the SS guards, until pregnancy resulted. After that they followed the same course as those whose bodies we saw in the pile and the crematories. The only crime of these women was that they happened to be better looking than ordinary, or happened to catch the eye of some lustful SS trooper.

The people of the surrounding towns, when questioned, said that they knew something was here, but they were afraid to try to find out what it was. So they were "surprised" to see such things when they were taken through. Some women fainted, some cried, and the mayor of one town hanged himself when shown what they had been living with since Hitler came to power.

As a bit of Teutonic irony (unconscious, of course), as we left I happened to look through a lane in the surrounding forest and down a little hill. Over the crest of the next hill, about a third of a mile from the camp fence, was the steeple and cross of a little village church.

Maybe some more people would like to read this firsthand account of what a concentration camp looks like. If they want to see this letter and think they can stand it, let them see it. Maybe if enough people understand what totalitarianism is, they will guard against it at home.

I'll try to write a normal letter soon.

Love,
BRYSON

Hiroshima: children in war

The necessity and wisdom of dropping the atomic bombs on Hiroshima and Nagasaki in August 1945, have been the subjects of lively, often bitter, debate. The issue has aroused questions of morality as well as military strategy. Did the bombings shorten the war? Or was Japan already on the verge of total collapse? Was there a failure of military intelligence? Was it necessary to deploy the bombs on populated areas? Would a demonstration of the bomb have been sufficient? But what if it had failed to work? Were the bombings necessary to "impress" the Soviet Union and thereby demonstrate our postwar supremacy? As usual, historical judgments will differ according to one's bias and selective use of evidence. But the terror and horror of the attacks represent a constant reality that cannot be ignored. Nor, as reflected by the following account of a Hiroshima school child, will it ever be forgotten by the survivors.

Iwao NAKAMURA
—11th grade boy.   In 5th grade in 1945 —

Ah, the wretched scenes of that time!—they come floating one after another like phantoms before my eyes as I set out today to write about my experiences, after so many months and even years have passed. And accompanying these phantoms I can clearly hear those pathetic moaning voices, those weeping, calling voices. That town of Hiroshima on the day which in an instant became pitch dark as a moonless night! The flames which blaze up here and there from the collapsed houses as though to illuminate that darkness. The child making a suffering, groaning sound, his burned face swollen up balloon-like and jerking as he wanders among the fires. The old man, the skin of his face and body peeling off like a potato skin, mumbling prayers while he flees with faltering steps. Another man pressing with both his hands the wound from which blood is steadily dripping, rushing around as though he had gone mad and calling the names of his wife and child—ah—my hair seems to stand on end just to remember. This is the way war really looks. If some outsider who knew nothing of what had happened had seen this state of the people of Hiroshima which was

From Dr. Arata Osada (comp.), *Children of the A-Bomb: Testament of the Boys and Girls of Hiroshima,* translated by Jean Dan and Ruth Sieben-Morgen (Tokyo, Uchida Rokakuho Publishing Co., 1959), 233-238. Used by permission. Material suggested by Tadashi Aruga.

so cruel even to look at, he could only have thought he was seeing a world of monsters, or else a glimpse of Hell. The fiendish devil called War snatched away the precious lives of hundreds of thousands of Hiroshima's citizens.

This time which I shall never forget was when I was in fifth grade. In order to escape the severe air raids, I had gone with my sisters to stay with our relatives in the country, but I had had summer complaint and become very weak, so I took advantage of the school vacation, which began on the 2nd of August, to return to my own home which was at Nakaka-machi (near the former Prefectural Building.) At that time the members of my family living there included my father and mother and my two little brothers (aged five and two), and when I came back and joined them that made five in our family. From then on, every morning at eight o'clock I used to go to the Prefectural Hospital as though I were dragging my weary body along. . . .

On the morning of August 6th a little after eight o'clock, as the midsummer sun was beginning to blaze down hotly on the streets of Hiroshima, breathing more freely with relief after the sounding of the all-clear, we surrounded the table and were eating breakfast a little later than usual. On an ordinary day my father, who worked in an office, would have left at eight o'clock, and I would have gone about the same time to the hospital, but . . .

It was just as I was putting my chopsticks to my second bowl of rice. It felt as though a magnesium flare of greenish-white light had hit my face and then there was an ear-splitting roar and simultaneously everything became so dark that I couldn't see an inch ahead. I dropped my chopsticks and rice bowl and stood up. After that I don't know what happened. I wonder how long I was unconscious. Suddenly I came to and found that below my neck I was pressed down by something heavy like stone. Everything was still pitch dark. Finally I figured out that I was pinned under the collapsed wall of the room. This was all so very sudden that I couldn't believe I wasn't having a dream—I doubted myself any number of times. I struggled frantically to slip out from under the wall. But the wall, pressing down on me like a great stone, did not move at all. From no place in particular a bad odor comes drifting; it stops up my nose and gradually tightens my chest. My breathing became rapid, my ears began to ring, and my heart was beating as though it would burst. It was at this time that I murmured in my heart, 'Ah, this is the end.' From somewhere a cool breeze passed sighing over me, and my surroundings became the slightest bit brighter. To this day I cannot forget the indescribably delicious freshness of that air. I breathed it in with all the strength I could muster. With the new energy that came to me from the tiny brightness and the fresh air, I made another mighty effort and at last managed to slip out from under the wall. My parents? . . . My little brothers? . . . Anxiously I peered around, and in the dim light I could just make out the shapes of my parents busily searching for us. I hurriedly went toward them. My parents' hair was all mussed up and their faces were pale, but when they saw my face, "Oh good, good!" they breathed with relief.

Fortunately neither my mother nor I had a single scratch, but the blood flow-
ing from a cut on Father's forehead had stained his shirt bright red. While I tore
up the shirt I was wearing to bind Father's wound, I looked around and saw
that there was not a trace left of what until now had been the city of Hiroshima;
the houses were demolished and only the flames blazing up from the dark desert
which the streets had become shone red against the midnight darkness of the
Hiroshima sky. Before we know it the demolished house next door has begun to
shoot out flames. We cannot find a trace of my two little brothers. Mother
weeps as she calls their names. Father, like a crazy person, is digging among the
smashed walls and heaped up roof tiles. You could almost say it was like a
divine miracle that he was able to rescue my two crying little brothers just
before the flames reached the place where they had been caught under the
house. Neither of them was injured at all.

The five of us, leaving our burning house behind us, hurried straight in the
direction of Koi. We were already surrounded by a sea of fire. The streets were
blocked with the fire and smoke of the ruined houses; and blazing telephone
poles fallen across our path plunged us any number of times into the depths of
despair. I don't know whether the people who lived there had already fled; at
any rate there was no one in sight, and only once in a while we heard a moaning
voice like that of a wild beast coming from out of nowhere. I had the feeling
that all the human beings on the face of the earth had been killed off, and only
the five of us were left behind in an uncanny world of the dead, and I had to
shudder. As we passed the Nakajima School and came to Sumiyoshi Bridge, I
saw several people plunging their heads into a half-broken water tank and
drinking the water. I was very thirsty too, and I was so happy to see some people again that without thinking I left my parents' side and went toward them.
When I was close enough to see inside the tank I said "Oh!" out loud and in-
stinctively drew back. What I had seen in the tank were the faces of monsters
reflected from the water dyed red with blood. They had clung to the side of the
tank and plunged their heads in to drink and there in that position they had
died. From their burned and tattered middy blouses I could tell that they were
high school girls, but there was not a hair left on their heads; the broken skin of
their burned faces was stained bright red with blood. I could hardly believe that
these were human faces. As we came out to the main street and crossed
Sumiyoshi Bridge, for the first time we met some living people of this world.
No, rather than humans of this world it might be more correct to say we met
humans of that other world, of Hell. They were all stark naked, their skin was
rust-colored with burns and blood, their whole bodies were swollen like
balloons. But to us who had fled forlornly through that stretch without meeting
a single shadow of a human being, there was something reassuring about
meeting even these people, and before we knew it we had joined their group and
were fleeing with them. The great wide street was nearly blocked by the burning
houses which had fallen into both sides of it, and there were barely three or four

yards in the center where we could pass. The two sides of this path were piled with people who could not walk because of their burns or deep wounds, and with the people who had died. There was no place for us to put our feet down and I don't know how many times, with apologies in our hearts, we callously stepped over their bodies. Among them we saw old people begging for water; youngsters crying for help; delirious students calling the names of their fathers and mothers, their brothers and sisters; a mother who lay face downward, tightly holding her dead baby with one arm and groaning painfully. Yet we who were not even sure of own own lives could do nothing for them.

Arriving at the refuge in Koi, we heard from the people there that we were the last refugees who escaped from the Sumiyoshi Bridge area. After having Father's wound treated at the Koi medical station we went as fast as we could over the Koi hills to the home of our relatives at [Tomo] Village in Asa County. As we were crossing Koi Hill at sunset, we looked down on the distant streets of Hiroshima which were all ablaze in one desert of fire. We quietly offered a silent prayer for the victims and went on down the hill to [Tomo].

VII

The American
People Since 1945

CHAPTER 17

Equality and ethnicity

Desegregation
in the public schools

The paradox of fighting World War II in part as a crusade against Nazi racism while Jim Crow laws persisted at home was all too apparent. In 1947, President Truman's Committee on Civil Rights called for an end to formal segregation in the United States. Truman supported equal voting rights and an end to military segregation, and his administration opposed segregation in briefs before the Supreme Court. Congress did nothing. But in a series of decisions beginning in 1938, the high court steadily chipped away at the legal props for segregation. Finally, in *Brown* v. *Board of Education* (May 1954), the Court, led by Chief Justice Earl Warren, declared segregated public school facilities unconstitutional. This decision which found segregation inherently unequal was used to justify subsequent rulings invalidating all segregation statutes, and also many forms of private discrimination. The impact and enforcement of desegregation, however, were not without lengthy legal struggles, harassment, and even violence. Black children had to literally run the gauntlet of frenzied white mobs bent on preserving the racial purity of school seats and desks. Once in the classroom, the children's experiences, as those described next, were difficult, demeaning, and, in their own way, violent.

. . . QUESTION: How did you go about deciding to go to the white school, and what were some of the experiences you had there?

BOY NO. 1: I heard it was a better school, and had better equipment and facilities than the Negro school that I was going to.

GIRL NO. 1: Well, I understood that you had a chance to get better prepared, a better education than at the Negro school.

BOY NO. 2: Not only that, it was a better equipped and higher educated school, an all around better school than the Negro one. My parents asked me if I wanted to go, what did I think about going to this school, and I told them I would like to go and they said I could go.

GIRL NO. 1: I wanted to go and decided myself. My parents wouldn't make me go if I didn't want to. But I wanted to and then they let me go.

From Southern Regional Council, *In Their Own Words: A Student Appraisal of What Happened after School Desegregation* (Atlanta: Southern Regional Council, 1967), pp. 60–76. Transcript of interview with five black students who attended predominantly white schools in the South (August 1966). Used by permission of the Southern Regional Council.

QUESTION: Did they call you any names?

BOY NO. 2: Well not the first day, but later they called us names such as Niggers and all that.

GIRL NO. 1: They would stare at you and look at you hard and they wouldn't say too much.

BOY NO. 1: Most of the first day if the teachers asked you a question and you answered they mostly laugh.

QUESTION: How were the teachers compared to the teachers you had at the Negro school?

GIRL NO. 1: I would say they were more prepared than some of the Negro teachers. I would say that most of them were nice, most of them. Some of them, about two or three, would always make a spectacle of Negroes, you know, would say something about Negroes. Especially one teacher would always try to say something to the kids and they would get a conversation up and all they would do is talk, look back at us and laugh.

BOY NO. 1: Yeah, the first day of class I walked in the room and she said, "Have a seat." She said today we have a new student, today, today all day. It was different and that's all.

BOY NO. 2: They are not better than Negroes. Most Negroes wear dresses but they are no better here. They may wear better things because they're more able because they've taken all the Negroes' money and stuff from them.

BOY NO. 1: Some of the teachers will try to be funny. When they get to a word like Negro, they call it Nigger or else try to make fun. When my father got a ticket for driving or something they talked about that and made wisecracks about it and asked how come they have to pay a ticket and he didn't have to pay out.

BOY NO. 3: And again there is the problem of overcrowding classrooms in the Negro school; especially in the seventh grade there'd be about 60 students in the classroom. Over here our home-room teacher got mad at me the day after the election. The children started talking about the election and so we told them that we would have a colored sheriff and all that. We started talking about how many Negroes there were and the black camouflage and he got mad. The next day didn't nobody go to school but me and he told me he didn't want to hear no more about the election and no other kind of party, not in his room.

BOY NO. 2: The same day the election was, he brought the same things up in his classroom while I was in it. He wanted to find out who was running for offices and things like that. He wanted to make out that he was now kind of intending to go with the Black Panther movement. And so that's why he is trying to find out everything—he's saying he might want to come down and decide if he'll vote in the party.

BOY NO. 3: The history teacher had a little election in her room and the children voted. But we didn't vote because we didn't want to.

GIRL NO. 2: During the election the children would take stickers and stick them on our seats on the bus and when we got up off the bus they would start clapping their hands and stuff like that.

BOY NO. 3: And they would trade their stickers for Black Power or Black Panther stickers.

BOY NO. 2: I just gave him one and they would trade them. Except they won't trade with us.

GIRL NO. 3: In history class it was very bad. There were always conversations going on between the teacher and the students about the Governor and integration and the President and the federal government and all such that. They were talking against the federal government because the government was for integration and like they were talking against integration because they don't see any sense to it. And the teachers was always saying some kind of wisecrack just to hurt your feelings and like that. He was always praising the Governor. The students acted the same as the teacher did in their class; you know, there was always something that they could say and try and hurt my feelings. They said anything, like how they was 'feared of all of us, what they thought of the way things were running about integration, or anything like that. They would come right out and say it, especially in that class, because they knew that nothing could be done to them in that class.

GIRL NO. 4: You asked why did I go to the white school. Well, I don't see why I shouldn't go there since we don't have a school that big to attend and they don't have anything in the Negro school for equipment. My parents were getting taxed and they planned to use most of that money in the white school and they get all that equipment. I don't see why I shouldn't go there and get some benefit from it. You know, that's the primary reason for going over there, to get a accurate education. But the students weren't friendly at all and I didn't have any white friends.

QUESTION: What about your friends in school, do you have any white friends in school? Do any of them try to be friendly with you?

BOY NO. 3: If they try to be friendly then a gang of them get up and talk to that one and then they try and push him. Then he tries to be funny or smart, too.

BOY NO. 2: And, you don't never have anything to say regardless of what he's doing.

BOY NO. 1: I was in the bathroom one day and a boy pushed me down, I mean pushed me. He went running down the hall and I went to the principal. I also told you one day I was walking down the hall and a boy tripped me and my friend told the assistant principal. I got tripped and he told the assistant principal and he just didn't do anything about it and when the principal came the assistant told the principal.

BOY NO. 2: The assistant just jumped me once and then told the principal that I would have killed him. I didn't want to fight him. He said I told him I'd kill his damn head and was cussing him or something. But I didn't cuss him. He made it much worse the way he told it to the principal. But he's a dirty man anyway. He told my friend straight out, "Nigger you go to the office for chewing gum." Another friend of mine went to this class he taught and she said that he was always trying to bring on all of this stuff about Negroes and stuff just so they could talk against us.

GIRL NO. 2: Right after you got tripped in the hall that day I went to the bathroom and a lot of girls was talking. They said "You know this Nigger got knocked down in the hall." And some of them said "Yeah, somebody ought to knock all of them down." And one day, two of them went and told the principal that they were fighting in the hall but he didn't do anything about it. They came in the bathroom and said: "Two of the Negroes were in the hall trying to fight and we told the principal about it but you know he didn't do anything about it, because they are privileged characters, I don't care if I could paint my face black so I could be a privileged character too." Then they started talking, "You know we'll be going to the Negro schools this year" and the other girl said, "Yeah and I'm going to get myself one of those Negro boyfriends too." They didn't know I was there.

QUESTION: How did the principal seem? Did he seem fair toward you?

GIRL NO. 1: He was nice.

BOY NO. 1: The trouble was he was just as strict on the white children as he was on us.

GIRL NO. 2: I think that he was more strict on them than on us.

BOY NO. 2: That's what made it worse. See if something happened during the school hour a group of them would go to the office and tell him something, tell something was stolen and try to trip us all up. He didn't know what to believe most times so he just never paid any attention. . . .

QUESTION: Now you've told us about your schools, why don't you tell a little bit about your association with the white students?

BOY NO. 2: Some people think that white people are higher class than Negroes but from the way the children did behave they are lower class people than the Negro. We went in class one day and everybody sat down and when the teacher went out of the room some of the students had spit in the vacant seats that nobody sits in. And they put chewing gum all over the desks. I mean you didn't find too much chewing gum over at the Negro schools, they threw it out the window or trash can. But over there you find the desk packed with chewing gum and stuff like that.

GIRL NO. 2: My association with the white students, you know you can get along with them as long as they didn't have anything to do with us, until they called us names or something like that. They always pick at you and whenever they do something to you they always dare-devil you with a crowd behind you

Black children march for desegregation, 1960s.

or something like that. Personally they never did anything to me. When all the Negroes was out together standing out in the hall, when they saw that none of us was looking they would throw something at us and like that. I remember once going to class and somebody put stickers all over my desk. When I got in there I found them all over the place, one down where I sit and one about where I write at and then I took it off and put it in the trash can. You know they are always putting something on my desk or doing something like that.

BOY No. 1: Well, they usually stay away and just like she said if they are going to do anything they do it in a crowd just about. She told you about it, but one day in the halls just before the spring holidays in March I got off the school bus one Friday and I was a janitor in a church and was going to clean the church up. I saw two boys in the car and they had a girl friend of theirs with them and they stopped and asked me if I wanted to fight. I told them "Yeah I'll fight," if they fight why not? I had another friend with me too, and he picked up some rocks and started throwing them across the street. They said that they ain't playing with no rocks and so those kids talked and then they wouldn't get out. So I told them "Let's go" and the other reached for his seat and gave him a shotgun. He pointed it at us and all that. When we got back to school they didn't say anything about it. But on Tuesday or Wednesday they said, "We could have killed you." I said, "Yeah, you all say if you all meet one of us in the road you'll blow our brains out but that's one you all missed." (LAUGHTER) You see I was brave after they missed me. The sheriff came over to the school to see about it and so they got so worried one of them just didn't say nothing after that. He kept quiet.

GIRL No. 1: There weren't too many friends but we were in gym class where we dress up every day. We took our shoes off and left them in the gym and we were playing. They hid them so we couldn't find but one of them, and they had the other one hid on their feet, and they pretended that none of them knew anything about it. The principal came over, finally, he must have talked to them about it. Another afternoon we were going to our history class. We would usually come up to the room everyday and start studying before classes began and one day they had spread some crayon dust in the seats that we sit in. I told the teacher and she didn't say anything to them, but she gave me this old nasty rag to clean it with and told us that that was all right. I got some tissue from my pocketbook to clean it with. I wanted to tell her about it before I said anything to anyone else. One morning we were standing in the hall and some of the boys brought some bee-bees, you know, shots, and we were standing by the lockers and they threw them all over the hall and mostly to the front by the principal's office. All the teachers came running down the hall and I think they found out who did it though . . . some of the boys.

BOY No. 1: I wouldn't exactly call them friendly but there was a sister and a brother that would ride our bus. They went to school in December. But when we came back they weren't there any more. The girl was in the same class we were in and the boy was a senior. But they were just about the only children that would try to talk to us and try to have anything to do with us. After they stopped nobody else did. One day they shipped all these clothes down to our place and I found an old hat and I sewed up the rim. I wore it to school. I just wore it for the devil of it. The teacher honked her horn and she got mad and she told me to leave it in my locker. So I put it in my locker and when I went to eat lunch and came back somebody had stolen the hat. I reported it to the principal and none of them wanted me to wear the hat to school. The principal told me he couldn't be responsible for it, the hat, because it was something that you weren't supposed to wear to school. He told me if I could get the hat all well and good, but if I couldn't there wasn't anything that he could do about it. And another day I went to school I was wearing a pin, it wasn't a "Black Panther" pin, it was an "End the War in Vietnam" pin. My teacher read what was on it and I think he didn't like what was on it, so he went and told the principal. The principal had been reading the pin for about five days every time when I went to lunch. Later that day I was in study hall and he called me into the office and told me not to wear the pin to school no more. He couldn't fine me for wearing the pin but he said he could punish me for not obeying him. Around the last part of school, when these boys say something we would say it back to them so they started cussing us. One day we started cussing them back and they thought we were going to fight, at least the teacher did, and he went and told the principal and the principal called us to the office and he told us if he had any more trouble he would had to put us out of school.

QUESTION: Before you came to the white school did you think that most of the white students would be smarter than you? Tell me why and what about now?

BOY NO. 1: Well, I didn't have too much thought about it myself, some of them are smarter but they ain't all that smart. Some of them are real dumb.

GIRL NO. 1: You know, I thought some of them would be smart and some of them would be dumb and that's just the way it was. Some of them are smart and try to get the lesson and some of them are dumb just like the Negroes. I think that anyone could go over there if they studied and they could do just as well as the white children do.

BOY NO. 2: I did think at least the majority would be pretty smart except for one or two of them in the classroom. But in the class I was in about half of them was pretty bad.

GIRL NO. 2: Well I thought I could do just as well as most of them if I tried and I did try. Some of them are smarter and some of them are just as dumb as some of the Negroes are. I guess most of them just don't try. I think I did do just about as well as some of them did.

BOY NO. 3: Well, the teachers are very hard about the lesson because they would try to flunk you all they could and if a white person had the same answer as you had and it wasn't a full answer they took five points off your paper and like took off two off his paper. . . .

QUESTION: Have any of your ideas changed any since you've been going to that school?

BOY NO. 2: At least some of mine have because I thought they were all pretty close and clean, but the way the children act they are nasty. They're not trustful. If you turn your back you get knocked in the head or something and then you don't see some of them so you have to keep on the watch for some of them and find out who did it or what. I heard people say that Negro children don't act their age but the white children is the children that don't act their age. White boys in the eleventh and twelfth grade will be riding around playing and hollering and kicking like children in the first and second grade. . . .

QUESTION: Were you allowed to participate in the organizations at school?

GIRL NO. 3: For most of the organizations they had in school you had to maintain a certain grade to be on it. I think if you had a high enough grade you could be on it.

BOY NO. 2: Most of the plays and that they had at night and you know, it wouldn't be too neat to go because you'd need a lot of bodyguards.

QUESTION: Did any of you ever go back to the Negro high school for anything? How did you feel?

ALL: Same way.

BOY NO. 1: Yeah, I went over there about four times.

BOY NO. 2: Well, you could go over there and sit in the classroom and the teacher probably wouldn't even know it.

BOY NO. 1: Most of them knows you and asks you how you are doing and they say get the best of it and do the best you can.

QUESTION: Suppose some friends at the Negro school asked you for some suggestions about the white school, what would you tell them?

BOY NO. 1: It probably be all in their favor because there ought to be a hundred Negroes or more going.

GIRL NO. 3: I think that for myself I'd tell them something about the students, and the way the teachers treat them. I'd tell him maybe some of the teachers would treat him ordinary the way they treat the white students, but some of them try all they could to fail you. I'd encourage them to do the best they could and to study hard. There are many of these affairs or certain incidents, such as throwing paper at you, or calling you Nigger or talking from gossip, but they wouldn't do anything really big to you besides throwing paper or something at you. They wouldn't really hurt you in a big way.

BOY NO. 1: I don't even believe in that this year myself. There will be about as many colored children going to school as white. Last year they did things because they outnumbered us about twenty to one, but I think now it will be a different story.

BOY NO. 2: I wish I was going back; I just want some of them to pick at me like they did last year so I can get them back. When we have about an equal number of students we'll see if we can get in a fight over there. We will have the same number in our color as they got in their color so we probably have a better chance fighting, if they're looking for fight this year then I'm going to fight. . . .

QUESTION: Now you said the white kids would always do things behind your back but did any of them come up to your face and tell you things or call you names?

GIRL NO. 2: They may call you names to your face but they wouldn't hit you when you could see them. You know, they call you a Nigger or curse you or something like that.

BOY NO. 2: At least, every time one of them call me something I call him something back. When they call me Nigger I call them a cracker or something. You're not white, you're red.

GIRL NO. 2: Most times they call you something, you know, they curse you and call you old damn Nigger or something, anything they want to call you.

BOY NO. 2: Yeah, they made a sling shot one morning and they shot pecans here on the bus. They actually shot pecans off a sling shot.

GIRL NO. 2: But you know in the hallways you would hardly ever see any boys their size come up to them and say you want to fight. You see these great big boys that are about this wide and all around are these great big old boys. Way bigger than you so they looking down on you asking you if you wanna fight.

BOY NO. 2: Even in the class and on the bus we didn't have no big boys that size. Well, in the cafeteria one day one big boy did ask me for my ice cream. Now sometime they will beg in the cafeteria, some of them. I gave it to him that day but they won't get nothing else from me though. (LAUGHTER)

GIRL NO. 3: Sometimes we be going down the hall and if any of the white students was standing in the hall and they see us coming they say here come a black Nigger, you better stand back, or something. They would get back up against the wall. In the morning sometime we'd be standing by our locker and they would get off the bus and come in and try to walk close up by the wall or something pretending that they didn't want to get close to touch us or anything.

BOY NO. 2: And when they did walk up side close to the wall we'd begin laughing and everything. They think they're so much that they can't walk beside us, but when they go down to the cafeteria they're standing and they'd be eating and the Negro cooks could be putting their hand all over the rolls, especially. And they'd be eating out of their hands. . . .

"We shall overcome"

The struggle against racial inequality in the South involved desegregating all public facilities and securing the right to vote for blacks long disfranchised. In the early 1960s, idealistic, mostly northern, white youths played a prominent role in this struggle. The activists operated from a broad range of motives, and with varying degrees of commitment. But most accounts, particularly for the first half of the decade, acknowledge the sincerity, the toughness, and the effectiveness of their work. The basic strategy of the "movement" was to implement the "law of the land" that guaranteed racial equality. As such, the primary weapons were education, voter registration drives, nonviolence, and if necessary, filling the jails to embarrass public authorities. The following letters from a young woman, then a recent graduate from Swarthmore College, eloquently describe the horror of her experiences as well as her ability to frustrate the "system." The remark about prison stationery in the first letter refers to the fact that it was written on toilet paper and smuggled out of jail.

Port Allen Jail, Sept. 5, 1963
Dear Danny,

This is the finest of prison stationery—nothing but the best for you—

I trust my mother phoned you, as I told her to and informed you that there had been a change in my plans; I am being temporarily detained in the finest of Port Allen hotels, which boasts free room and board and pink cells with bathtubs. What more could one ask for?

Seriously, though, I have never seen such hell and such terror as we witnessed in Plaquemine [Louisiana] Sunday evening. By the end of it, everyone was involved—it was impossible to escape. I'm sure you've heard the story by now, so I'll just describe it briefly. There had been a march on the sheriff's home Sat. evening, protesting arrests made in sit-ins earlier in the day. The marchers were deliberately detained several blocks from the sheriff's home until horses could be brought to the scene, then horses and tear gas bombs simultaneously attacked the crowds. State troopers on the horses carried electric cattle prods, which they used with great abandon. In the massive attack on the fleeing marchers, one girl, about 12 years old, was trampled by a horse. I was just informed by a note from Spiver [?], who is at the other end of my cell block, that

From Miriam Feingold Papers (Madison: State Historical Society of Wisconsin). Used by permission of Miriam Feingold Stein.

The death-knell of segregation: Blacks registering for the vote in southern county courthouse, 1960s.

the girl died last night in Charity Hospital. Oh God, Danny, dues are high. I had spoken with the girl's parents Sunday morning when they came to the office to complain that she wasn't being treated at the Plaquemine Sanitarium—the hospital demanded a deposit of $75.00 before they'd touch her. HOW CAN PEOPLE BE SO CRUEL?? HOW LONG MUST THIS GO ON???

Sunday night another march was organized and this time we had the reluctant ministers with us. As the march began, the federal marshal arrived with one more [injunction]. . . . We marched anyhow. The line was stopped on Railroad Ave. by horses, tear gas, electric prodders, and again the marchers fled. The horses followed the demonstrators back to the church, as did the white mobs. They tear gassed all around the church, rode the horses into the churchyard, and when the marchers packed into the church, they broke down the door and windows and threw tear gas inside. There were many seriously injured, but by this time it was impossible to get anyone to the waiting ambulance. The injured were carried inside Rev. Davis' house but by this time, the crowds from the church, jumping through windows and doors had packed Rev. Davis' house with a mass more solid than the N.Y. City subway at rush hour (I was inside the house, attempting to nurse the injured.) The crowd was hysterical—injured women screaming and kicking on the beds, everyone crying and screaming. Eventually the police and the mobs broke into the front of the house and tear gassed it. When the crowd scattered across the row of backyards, the police tear gassed them, then turned high pressure hoses on the demonstrators in front of the church. What followed was mob rule. Bands of vigilantes roamed through the neighborhood breaking into homes overturning furniture and dragging out everyone with a black face. If they had prodders they used them to hurry the process. They pulled down one girl's pants and prodded her between her legs; they prodded an 8 month pregnant lady until she dropped from pain. They found me, with a 15-year old panic-stricken girl clinging to me, in a shed behind the church, where we had listened for over an hour to the mobs. For a while, we heard gunfire. The girl was released as a juvenile and I was arrested and carried to the stockade (the fair grounds) where, ironically, I integrated the women's section. Practically all the task force is now in jail, including Vic, who came back from Clinton to see what was going on. Monday a bunch of us were moved to Port Allen, where I was promptly segregated from everyone else. . . .

Demonstrations will resume as soon as the injunction is overturned. Something has to be done to get the people over their fear so they won't panic so much when they see horses, but how can you tell someone not to run, and have their kids trampled to death. . . .

Peace and take care———

Love,
M.

Baton Rouge, La.
March 10, 1964

Dear Parents,

Oh me, oh my. You'll never guess where I'm off to. Seems we rather upset the public officials around here with the library action as well as by CORE generally. We've been keeping the fires burning under their seats pretty high recently. Anyhow, in retaliation, their town officials are trying to get rid of the CORE leadership, and have, consequently, invited me up to a lovely white building where I get 3 free meals a day and all the rest I want. In other words, there is a warrant out for my arrest, and I shall turn myself in tomorrow morning. I won't be in for more than 2 weeks, however, so I don't think this should have much bearing on your visit, except that my trip to New Orleans will be a much-needed vacation.

One of the reasons they're mad at us is that we recently set the FBI on the trail of our registrar of voters, who has refused to register anyone since last November. He claims that because the Supreme Court is now considering whether one part of the registration form is unconstitutional and designed to keep Negroes off the rolls, he can't register because he doesn't know what he should do: use the form in question (which he wants) or not use it (which is what the state's attorney general recommends.) So in 2 parishes (East & West Feliciana) we have, virtually, no registrars.

Since registration is now impossible here, we've turned our attention to economic matters: extending to farmers info. on gov't. programs, and building interest in coops. What is needed, basically, are not desegregated libraries, but decent farm income and decent jobs for non-farm people. If CORE wants to get anywhere, it's got to address itself to this problem. What we hope to do is reach the farmers, through this sort of program, and gradually work them into the movement. This is the general direction work is taking all over this area: Louisiana and Mississippi.

By-the-by, I saw Jean Fairfax, a friend of O's, at a National Sharecropper's Fund conference in Mississippi. She carried multitudes of messages back to you all.

The brownies haven't made it yet—probably they're busy poisoning the sheriff. Actually, I haven't been in Clinton for several days (I'm in Baton Rouge), so I can't say for sure where the b's are—but rest assured that they'll arrive soon.

I'll try to write from jail, if I can. We're having trouble with the local P.O., so I'm trying an experiment. . . .

Love,
Me,

A portion of hell

However substantial the contributions made by white volunteers in the civil rights struggle, blacks themselves ultimately assumed the burden of the struggle. In the early days of the movement, the seeming passivity and lack of involvement by the blacks disturbed many white volunteers. But the pattern of white repression was deeply embedded in the fabric of southern life and blacks had real cause for fear. They, after all, were a permanent part of the community with much more at stake than transient activists. The following oral reminiscence by John McFerren from Fayette County, Tennessee, indicates the special personal risks for blacks. McFerren was a charter member of a group that sought to register black voters in a predominantly black county in which they had been denied the franchise. The white community retaliated by refusing bank loans and credit, cutting off the sale of groceries and other necessities, and, finally, evicting many of the blacks who occupied tenant farms. The blacks eventually secured Justice Department intervention to aid their cause. But before the ultimate victory, many participants in the struggle lost most of their worldly goods, and some, their lives. McFerren himself was badly beaten and nearly murdered.

My name is John McFerren. I'm forty-six years old. I'm a Negro was born and raised in West Tennessee, the county of Fayette, District 1. My foreparents was brought here from North Carolina five years before the Civil War and since then we have a very good history of stayin in Fayette County. My people was brought here in covered wagons because the rumor got out among the slaveholders that West Tennessee was still goin to be a slaveholdin state. And my people was brought over here and sold. And after the Civil War my people settled in West Tennessee. That's why Fayette and Haywood counties have a great number of Negroes.

Back in 1957 and '58 there was a Negro man accused of killin a deputy sheriff. This was Burton Dodson. He was brought back after he'd been gone twenty years. J. F. Estes was the lawyer defendin him. Myself and him both was in the army together. And the stimulation from the trial got me interested in the way justice was bein used. The only way to bring justice would be through the ballot box.

In 1959 we got out a charter called the Fayette County Civic and Welfare League. Fourteen of us started out in that charter. We tried to support a white liberal candidate that was named L. T. Redfearn in the sheriff election and the local Democrat party refused to let Negroes vote.

We brought a suit against the Democrat party and I went to Washington for a civil-rights hearing. Myself and Estes and Harpman Jameson made the trip. It took us twenty-two hours steady drivin. We met John Doar who took us over to the Justice Department canteen where you eat. While we were walkin down the street and goin over there to eat, I was lookin all up—lotsa big, tall buildins. I had never seen old, tall buildins like that before. After talkin to him we come on back to the Justice Department building and we sat out in the hall while he had a meetin inside the attorney general's office. And when they come out they told us they was gonna indict the landowners who kept us from voting. That night we were so poor with finance that three of us slept in one bed and four of us slept on the floor at a friend of ours house up there cause we wasn't able to go to a hotel. And when we came back we drove a Chrysler nonstop twenty-one hours back to Memphis—only stopped for gas and oil check.

Just after that, in 1960, in January, we organized a thousand Negroes to line up at the courthouse to register to vote. We started pourin in with big numbers—in this county it was 72 percent Negroes—when we started to register to vote to change the situation. In the followin September an article came out in the editorial of the Fayette *Falcon* that they would evict a thousand Negroes offa the land. So in October and November they started puttin our people offa the land. Once you registered you had to move. Once you registered they took your job. Then after they done that, in November, we had three hundred people forced to live in tents on Shepard Towles's land. And when we started puttin em in tents, then that's when the White Citizens Council and the Ku Klux Klan started shootin in the tents to run us out.

Tent City was parta an economic squeeze. The local merchants run me outa the stores and said I went to Washington and caused this mess to start. The first store I went in after I come back from Washington in 1959—I had been tradin there many years—was Farmer's Hardware. And I went in that day and went on back and done my buyin. The colored fellow who's been there for years waited on me—and when I started out the door the store owner called me and said, "John, come here." I went on back to the cash register. He says, "That mess you went to Washington on, that Democratic primary. You started somethin. I can't sell you nothin. I can't. I can't. I don't want you to come in my store anymore." So I come on out. They had a blacklist—once you registered and your name appeared on the registration books, your name would appear on the blacklist. And they had the list sent around to all merchants. Once you registered you couldn't buy for credit or cash. But the best thing in the world was when they run me outa them stores. It started me thinkin for myself. . . .

After six or eight months I found some friends in New Orleans to lend me the money to build a bigger grocery store. And when I got my buildin about 90 percent finished, their office was raided and they were called Communist, and I had three lawsuits against me in about three weeks' time. And one of the men that was in the Small Business Administration told me that the Small Business Administration let my record out for the local authorities to frame lawsuits. The Justice Department has this on record and yet the Justice Department has done nothin. In many other instances they hadn't did nothin. They brought suit against the big landowners, but yet and still they did not break the boycott against me. They did somethin and then left and did nothin no more.

And at the same time the inspectin engineer of the Small Business Administration, he got the word indirectly not to pass the buildin that I had built and constructed. But when he went down here for a final inspection he passed the buildin. They didn't fire him, they eliminated him. That's the way I see it. They cut back to cut him out because he passed the loans to me. Back then I didn't know that when a Negro in the South goes into business and tries to make substantial gains he is violatin the white man's civil rights. I didn't know that at the time. The engineer said I had one of the best-constructed buildins that he know'd of. Durin one of the trumped-up lawsuits that they had me in court on, the lawyer for the other side told the judge that I don't need a buildin that good. Out in open court. I'm convinced that the Negro or any other minority group has to be economically strong. That's the only way the Negro can have his civil rights.

Durin the time that the squeeze was put on me the Coca-Cola Bottling Company, they didn't sell to me until the Tennessee Council of Human Relations threatened to file a suit against them. The worst part was the big oil companies. They put the national screws on us. I tried to buy from major oil companies all over America. They would not sell to me The first shipment of gas I bought, the deputy sheriff put a gun on the driver and made him carry the shipment back to Memphis. It was six months again before we had gasoline in our tanks. . . .

Anytime a Negro stands up and be a Negro leader for his people he meets the thugs put up by the power structure to fight you and put up traps for you. Back in 1962 I had a lady claim she was sightseein on my buildin—claimed she fell and turned around and sued me for fifteen thousand dollars. Claimed she got hurt on a scaffold. Later, durin that same time, her daughter and her boyfriend's daughter gave affidavits that it was trumped-up charges to get me in trouble. Anyhow, the day I got beat I went down to the courthouse with Mr. Reed to cover a voter-registration drive, and when I started to approach the courthouse steps five thugs started to closin in on me. One had his knife out and I knocked one down and run and the five of em chased me and caught me about a quarter of a mile away from the courthouse steps. Durin the time I was approachin the courthouse steps—the highway patrol, I stopped him and told him there was five men chasin me and the highway patrol told me that he was on another detail, that he couldn't give me no aid. When they got after me at the courthouse steps, they chased me about a quarter of a mile. They caught me and beat me. They knocked, hit me on the head and legs with a bar. They knocked my teeth out and gave me other bodily harm. When the police came they carried me into the City Hall, they carried me into the back, and when John Thomas ran around to see what they had me for, the five thugs jump on him and beat him up. . . .

The southern white has a slogan: "Keep em niggers happy and keep em singin in the schools." And the biggest mistake of the past is that the Negro has not been teached economics and the value of a dollar. Negroes in West Tennessee still buys big fine cars—the schoolteacher buys big fine cars and especially the preacher—and the average child come up, he sees em with big fine cars and he think that's the thing for him to do. But in the long run they should buy cheap cars and channel their money to what will help em. Back at one time we had a teacher—we used to call him Bilbao because he come from Mississippi—and he pulled up and left the county because he was teachin the Negroes to buy land, and own land, and work it for hisself, and the county Board of Education didn't want that taught in the county. And they told him, "Keep em niggers singin and keep em happy and don't teach em nothin."

When my children started in the integrated schools—they were the first children in the county to start in their school—when they sit side by side with the white child they receive and learn that the white child does not have a superior intelligence because his skin is white. The Negro has the same portion of brains as the white child and he learns how the white people think and he learns exactly what they believe and he learns much more by experience of what the white person thinks and reacts than he do when he's separated. And I'm in favor of any integrated schools because your child, when he comes up in an integrated school, knows exactly what life's all about. When he gets out to facin life, it makes a much stronger child. You take, for instance, my children got the equivalent of education at twelve years old as I had when I was thirty.

Any nation regardless of what nation or nationality cannot live alone in the world by itself. In this county at the present time the white people have put up private schools tryin to keep their children isolated from the public. China made its mistake a million years ago tryin to keep its people isolated from the world. Anytime you isolate your people from the world then your people become like you cut your arm off—you die. When you mingle and pick up ideas from other nationalities and other people and put em all together in your own brain and make it work for yourself, you make much more progress than from isolation. With the Negroes in West Tennessee, when the white man cut him off and put him to thinkin for hisself, the white man done him a favor. The white man say he can replace the Negro with more machinery, but I want you to know that chemical farmin has already begun to fade because the chemicals are hurtin the earth. There are bare fields where nothin grows. He's gonna bring a starvation on his own self. This country is too poor to afford this big high-priced machinery when the machinery price is gettin higher and the farm produce products is gettin lower. Back in 1960 and '61 the big bankers told the big farmers, "We'll furnish you, get the niggers offa the land." Now he got the land and now he don't know what to do with it. And it's only a period of time that the big bankers will have to build a big parkin lot for the machinery and stuff they got to pay for.

Negroes in this county have made much progress in ten years and also have much progress yet to go. Durin this ten-year period I reached the opinion that the Negroes, while they are fightin for their rights, must enter into businesses of their own and study economics, because you cannot be free when you're beggin the man for bread. But when you've got the dollar in your pocket and then got the vote in your pocket, that's the only way to be free. The Negro race now is just enterin to the money stream. Business and economics is the money stream. And until Negroes can do that—what is votin to civil rights when a man can buy your rights from his pocket? You cannot have civil rights when you beggin for bread. You gotta be independent in economics. It's the only way you can demand your civil rights. And I have been successful and made good progress because I could see the only way I could survive is to stay independent.

Down through the years the Negro in West Tennessee—Fayette County, especially—this county has been controlled and dominated by two sets of families. They been controllin the county since the Civil War. It's been handed down from one generation to the next generation. And through the years the Negro has been the white man's shade tree in the summer and his wood pile in the winter. The Negro has woke up and the white man, more than ever, is drivin tractors for himself. But in the West Tennessee section the land do not produce enough to afford this high-priced equipment. It's only a matter of time when the white man—who's payin six hundred dollars for private schools and collectin food stamps at the same time—it's only a matter of time when all this will come to pass because the economics will automatically force him in line. The Negro is no longer goin back. He's goin forward.

The right to counsel

From 1953 to 1969, the Supreme Court under the leadership of Earl Warren asserted a deep commitment toward advancing the civil rights and liberties of individuals in areas such as freedom of speech and assembly, desegregation, reapportionment of legislative bodies, and the rights of the accused in criminal proceedings. The Court spectacularly instilled a positive substance in the First,

Fourth, Fifth, Sixth, and Fourteenth Amendments, particularly the latter's guarantee of "equal protection of the laws." Some decisions, such as those related to reapportionment, generally evoked acclaim and compliance; in criminal justice decisions, however, the Court became increasingly vulnerable to shrill outcries that it was "soft" on "law and order." Law enforcement officials and opportunistic politicians, exploiting public fears of increased crime and violence, found the Court a convenient target. One exception to the general reaction to these decisions was evoked by *Gideon* v. *Wainwright* (1963) in which the Court extended the right to counsel in all criminal cases. Most Americans believed that the Constitution assured the individual's right to a lawyer in a criminal proceeding, but actual practice long had held the Sixth Amendment guarantee inapplicable in state cases. The next document reproduces Clarence Gideon's handwritten petition to the Supreme Court. It is printed with Gideon's spelling and syntax errors which contrasted sharply with his self-taught legal knowledge.

In the Supreme Court of the United States, Washington D.C.

Clarence Earl Gideon   )
   Petitioner   )   Petition for a writ of

       vs.   Certiorari directed to the

H. G. Cochran, Jr. as Director   )   Supreme Court
   Divisions of corrections,   )
   State of Florida   )   State of Florida

                              No.   890   Misc.

                              OCT. TERM 1961
                              U. S. Supreme Court

to the Honorable Earl Warren, Chief Justice of the United States.

Comes now the petitioner, Clarence Earl Gideon, a citizen of the United States of America, in proper person, and appearing as his own counsel. Who petitions this Honorable Court for a Writ of Certiorari directed to the Supreme Court of the State of Florida. To review the order and judgement of the court below denying the petitioner a writ of Habeus Corpus.

Petitioner submits that the Supreme Court of the United States has the authority and jurisdiction to review the final judgement of the Supreme Court of the State of Florida the highest court of the State . . . because the "Due

From U. S. Supreme Court, Clerk's File, No. 890 Miscellaneous, October Term, 1961.

process clause" of the fourteenth admendment of the constitution and the fifth and sixth articales of the Bill of rights has been violated. Furthermore, the decision of the court below denying the petitioner a Writ of Habeus Corpus is also inconsistent and adverse to its own previous decisions in paralled cases.

Attached hereto, and made a part of this petition is a true copy of the petition for a writ of Habeus Corpus as presented to the Florida Supreme Court. Petitioner asks this Honorable Court to cosider the same arguments and authorities cited in the petition for Writ of Habeus Corpus before the Florida Supreme Court. In consideration of this petition for a Writ of Certiorari.

The Supreme Court of Florida did not write any opinion. Order of that court denying petition for Writ of Habeus Corpus dated October 30, 1961, and attached hereto and made a part of this petition.

Petitioner contends that he has been deprived of due process of law[.] Habeus Corpus petition alleging that the lower state court has decided a federal question of substance in a way not in accord with the applicable decisions of this Honorable Court. When at the time of the petitioners trial he ask the lower court for the aid of counsel. The court refused this aid[.] Petitioner told the court that this court had made decision to the effect that all citizens tried for a felony crime should have aid of counsel. The lower court ignored this plea.

Petitioner alleges that prior to petitioners convictions and sentence for Breaking and Entering with the intent to commit petty larceny, he had requested aid of counsel, that, at the time of his conviction and sentence, petitioner was without aid of counsel. That the Court refused and did not appoint counsel, and that he was incapable adequately of making his own defense. In consequence of which he was made to stand trial. Made a Prima Facia showing of denial of due process of law. . . . Counsel must be assigned to the accused if he is unable to employ one, and is incapable adequately of making his own defense. . . .

On the 3rd of June 1961 A.D. your petitioner was arrested for foresaid crime and convicted for same. Petitioner recieve trial and sentence without aid of counsel, your petitioner was deprived "due process of law."

Petitioner was deprived of due process of law in the court below. Evidence in the lower court did not show that a crime of Breaking and Entering with the intent to commit petty larceny had been committed. Your petitioner was compelled to make his own defense, he was incapable adequately of making his own defense. Petitioner did not plead nol contender. But that is what his trial amounted to.

Wherefore the premises considered it is respectfully contented that the decision of the court below was in error and the case should be review by this court, accordingly the writ prepared and prayed for should be issue.
It is respectfully submitted

Clarence Earl Gideon

Born Italian

The idea of America as the great "melting pot" for various ethnic and racial groups worked for some groups or individuals; for others it starkly contrasted with reality. That notion, however, ran deep in American life and accounts for the drives of first- and second-generation ethnics to Americanize themselves in order to suit the dominant cultural norms. But succeeding generations often found themselves "different" and somewhat apart from the prevailing values and customs. No matter how hard they tried to assimilate, people were still "Jews," "Italians," "Japs," "Chicanos," and so on. Such responses, plus growing psychic and material security, rekindled the ethnics' understanding and awareness of their origins—often accompanied by strong feelings of pride and militancy. In short, ethnics realized the limitations of assimilation, and found virtues and compensations in those limitations. The following essay relates the experiences of a young man, born of Italian immigrants, who had tried hard to "make it" in the WASP world but found the results not entirely meaningful or satisfactory given his own past. Instead, he has sought to utilize the knowledge of his heritage and has devoted himself to ethnic studies and the realities of pluralism in American life.

Ethnicity, which for some is a recent discovery, has been for me a lifelong preoccupation. The current dialogue over ethnic identity is something I have been carrying on with myself for almost half a century. I have always known that I was born Italian and that this circumstance profoundly affected my life. Even when I pretended to be one of "them" at an Ivy League university or in the Department of State, I knew that beneath my vested grey flannel suit there beat the heart of an Italian boy.

My life has been a journey through cultures and institutions far removed from my immigrant home; mine has been the career of the mobile, rootless academic. Yet through it all, despite university education, travel, and marriage to a non-Italian, and even when I wished otherwise, my ethnic identity has retained a powerful grip on me. My autobiography thus has been a prime source for my exploration of the meaning of ethnicity. If my story were truly singular, there would be little point in discussing it; but this biography is in some ways common to over three million second-generation Italian Americans.

From Rudolph J. Vecoli, "Born Italian: Color Me Red, White, and Green," *Sounding Spring*, 1973, pp. 117–123. Used by permission of the author.

This is what makes the experience ethnic and not merely idiosyncratic. I bring to this subject, then, not only the discipline of the historian, but also hopefully the "intelligent subjectivity," to use Michael Novak's term, of an ethnic American.

To be born in America of Italian parents, speak Italian as one's first language, and be raised on *polenta* (not spaghetti, since we were *Toscani*) is still not to be an Italian. My first given name was Calvin, after the illustrious president in whose term of office I was born. Thank heaven, it was changed to that of the famous movie star; not because the priest objected, but because my father's friends said that to them Calvin sounded like *cavolo* (cabbage). I was raised in a factory town in Connecticut, and my first memories are of the grim Depression years. My father was a construction laborer and there were long stretches of unemployment. My mother worked in a dress factory, a sweatshop, to eke out the family budget. There were breadlines that my sisters and I stood in to receive rations of flour, milk, and canned beef from Argentina. And yet we never suffered real privation; I don't remember once going to bed hungry. My mother was and is a fabulous cook; I didn't realize until much later that I was eating gourmet meals throughout my childhood. I remember the worry and anxiety as our parents strove mightily to keep us clothed and fed, but they did it. My father came home many nights with his shoulders broken open from carrying the hod. These are memories with which many of my generation of Italian Americans live, but of which we seldom speak. Our immigrant parents were the exploited proletariat of the 1920's and '30's, the factory workers, the miners, the laborers. Not only exploited, but despised to boot as foreigners, as "Dagoes" and "Wops." The insecurity and shame of those years throw a long shadow over the psychic landscape of my generation. No wonder we are anxious to protect our gains, however modest; they are hard won.

My parents, like most Italian immigrants, came from peasant stock. A heritage of centuries of unremitting toil on the land taught them to accept life as it came, a fatalism unrelieved by illusions. Life was a pilgrimage; everyone had a cross to bear. Still, all the more reason to enjoy the good things, especially food and wine, and the companionship of relatives and friends. The children were imbued with the virtues of obedience and respect. If the teacher punished a child for misbehavior, the parent did not protest; rather he administered a second punishment for good measure. Strict discipline, sometimes moderated by affection, was the rule in the Italian American household. No wonder that those of us raised under such a regimen despair at the willfulness of our children. Hard work was the lot of man, at least of the *contadini* if not of the *signori*. We were expected to contribute to the family income as soon as we were of working age. For my sisters this meant leaving school for the factory at fourteen. Being the youngest and coming of age during the war, I was able to continue in high school while working a shift in a factory.

But the "Protestant ethic" and high ambition were not part of our heritage.

My father aspired for me to become a barber or shoemaker. After all, he was a laborer all of his life; from his point of view, to become an artisan was a significant step upward. More than most other ethnic groups, the Italian Americans have persisted in the ranks of blue-collar workers. It is only in the third and fourth generations that a significant number are entering the professions, the academic careers, the corporate and government bureaucracies. This was due not only to restricted opportunities, though the barriers of prejudice were real enough, but also to the ethnic values which prized family solidarity over individual advancement. Though there were exceptions, education was often viewed as an alien influence which eroded parental control—as in fact it did. Sociological studies suggest that Italians were less characterized by the "achievement syndrome" than were, say, Jews, Greeks, or Japanese. This helps to explain the relatively more limited occupational and spatial mobility of the Italians. The converse of this is the higher degree of stability of the Italian American family and neighborhood.

Formal religion was not an important influence in my youth. Although a devout Catholic, my mother seldom attended church. Like many Italians she found the church of the Irish (there was no Italian priest or parish in our town) alien and cold. A few years ago I visited the church in which my mother worshipped as a girl in a small town in Tuscany. A Romanesque church a thousand years old, it was dark and cool even in mid-July. Banks of votive lamps, the smell of incense, statues of saints and martyrs, the offerings of the faithful for special graces covering the walls—all these had been lacking in America. So she preferred to pray at home. It was the experience of many Italians that the Catholic Church they found in America was strange and sometimes hostile. Like politics, it was dominated by their major antagonists, the Irish. Only in dense settlements where the Italians could have a national parish with Italian priests, venerate the saints of their villages, and celebrate their feast days, were they able to maintain their religious traditions. Although in recent decades many Italian Americans have become more integrated within the Church, religious institutions did not provide the Italians an organizational structure for community life as they did the Poles and Irish.

Like many of the Italian immigrants, my father was a sojourner in this land. He had come with the intention of working for a few years, saving money, and returning to his village. But he remained for a half-century. It was only after he had retired that he returned as an *Americano* to live the last years of his life comfortably on his social security. My father resisted Americanization, although he became a citizen when it was necessary to qualify for the W.P.A. He continued to live like the peasant he was. Rising at daybreak to tend his gardens which produced more vegetables than we could consume, raising rabbits which my mother prepared *alla cacciatora,* making and drinking a hundred gallons of wine a year, setting snares for birds which we ate with *polenta,* playing boccie and cards at the *Società Libero Pensiero* (the Americans did not know it, but this was the Free Thought Society). A man of great physical strength, he worked under driving bosses. He was ill used, and he knew it. One of his favorite expressions, said with bitterness, was, "America biznis" ("America is business").

This too is a memory which lurks in the recesses of the Italian American psyche. This land was not hospitable to the Italians. Our hearts are not full of gratitude, because we know the price that was paid for that which we enjoy today, a price paid in sweat, tears, and blood; the cliché is nonetheless true. How many thousands of Italian immigrants were killed and mutilated in industrial accidents and mine disasters God only knows. They along with the Slavs were the dung, as Louis Adamic put it, which fertilized the growth of America's industrial might. To the wounds of the flesh were added the hurts of the spirit, because they knew only too well that in the view of many Americans they were considered less than dirt. It is not surprising that in moments of despair an imprecation came to their lips: *"Accidenti all' America i a quell Colombo che la scoperta"* ("Curses on America and that Columbus who discovered her"). My father endured; he would not be bent or broken. When I was a child I was ashamed of him because he was not "American." This too we remember, that America has taught children to be ashamed of their parents. As I grew older I came to respect him for his integrity. . . .

Ours was a mixed neighborhood. We lived among Germans, Irish, Hungarians, and Poles. I also attended an integrated school, not racially integrated, since there was only one Black family in the town, but including all ethnic and socio-economic groups, from the Yankees who lived in the big houses on the hill to the "Hunkies" and "Dagoes" from the valley. These contacts did not dilute our ethnic consciousness, rather they sharpened it. The pattern of ethnic relationships reflected a hierarchy of groups, with the new immigrants occupying the bottom stratum. As I grew older I became aware of other spheres of American society far removed from the immigrants' world. A prestigious prep school was located in my home town, and Yale University was only a few miles away. These became, in my imagination, symbols of another world, a world of wealth and privilege far beyond the reach of an Italian boy of working-class background. Yet they stimulated my ambition to gain access to that WASP world (as I imagined it) of cultural refinement and cool confidence. More boys from my neighborhood went to reform school than to college, but I early set my sights on higher education as the ladder to that world.

It has been a long journey, psychologically as well as physically. My educational experience was totally alien to my family and ethnic background. In eighteen years of schooling, the only instance in which my Italian origins were recognized as a possible source of pride occurred in kindergarten! Curious how well I remember the teacher commenting to my mother, after I had painted a picture of an ocean liner with red smokestacks, that I might become another Michelangelo. Actually I have never been able to draw, but that comment did wonders for my morale. We now know how important it is that schools give positive reinforcement to a child's self-image. Erik Erikson and others have pointed out the necessity for continuity between self-identity in childhood and adulthood if an individual is to experience wholeness. How deficient our schools have been in this respect, and how deficient they remain. My schooling served to inculcate within me only negative feelings regarding my origins. By omission, and at times explicitly, I was made to feel that there was nothing of value, nothing worthy in my Italianness. Never once, from elementary through graduate school, was the fact that I was fluent in Italian remarked upon as an asset.

This, we know, has been a common experience of immigrant children, as it has been of black, brown, and red children. What a cruel commentary upon the inhumanity and stupidity of the American educational system! No wonder it has failed so many generations of the children of the outsiders, the poor, the alien, the racially and culturally different. But what should one expect? American schools were designed to assimilate, to standardize, to wipe out diversity. Being an obedient, ambitious Italian boy, I tried diligently to assimilate. I embraced the liberal creed of progress and enlightenment; I decried the benighted outlook of working-class ethnics; I sought to model myself after the cosmopolitan, sophisticated intellectual. I succeeded in part, and I did learn a great deal in the process. Yet I could never completely forget who I was. I gradually came to realize that much of what I was trying to be and to believe was at odds with my true self, with my sense of reality, my values, my loyalties. Not only could I never be an authentic WASP; I did not want to be one.

When I went to graduate school, responding to some inner compulsion, I chose to write my dissertation on the Italian immigration, at that time hardly an "in" subject. I have since specialized in immigration and ethnic history. The questions raised by my own autobiography—questions of identity, group life, assimilation, and social policies—have become the issues to which I have sought to address myself in my historical studies. Perhaps it is not surprising that my researches have tended to confirm my autobiographical insights. Another way of putting it would be that by accepting and affirming my own ethnicity I acquired a new perspective on American history, one which liberated me from the conventional interpretations based upon progressive and consensus assumptions. This, of course, is not a unique discovery on my part. Perhaps moved by similar personal as well as scholarly insights, a school of "new pluralists" is emerging to challenge traditional views of American society.

"The Rediscovery of Ethnicity," we must understand, has been a rediscovery on the part of the intellectual community. The ethnic groups, as well as the politicians, priests, and realtors who deal with them, have known about ethnicity all along. What has been termed a resurgence of ethnicity is rather the eruption into public view of passions and attitudes which have long existed submerged in the private worlds of ethnic life. . . .

Traditional Lenten party, American Slovak Home, Milwaukee, 1967.

Black awareness

The desegregation movement of the 1950s and early 1960s largely was an interracial effort. But blacks increasingly sought to assert leadership and, at times, exclusive participation in the battle for their equality. The heightened awareness of their own roles combined with rising militancy in the black communities. At times, rage and despair led to ghetto riots and bloodshed. Beneath the surface of public behavior, blacks emphasized inner feelings of racial pride, consciousness, and, at times, hate. These poems were written by high school students and stress that newly asserted sense of self and pride. Interestingly, however, a senatorial investigating committee used them to illustrate aspects of subversion in American life.

A Revolution of Mind

(By Gladys Smith, Yonkers, N.Y.)

I don't ask you to love me,
    Or like what I say
I don't want your charity
    Or to marry your brother one day
I don't want your friendship
    If it's not sincere
I don't want you on my picket line
    Just to say you were there
    When you know deep down
    you really don't care
For I'll say in a minute
    and repeat loud and clear
    I'm Black and I belong here
This is my Country,
    My People made it what it is
And if I can't get my part
    I'd rather die than live
I won't be slapped and
    simply turn the other cheek

From U.S. Senate, Hearings before the Subcommittee to Investigate the Internal Security Act . . . , Committee on the Judiciary, 91st Congress, 1st session, 1969, part 1, pp. 267–269.

I won't ride the back of the bus
    Or give up my seat
I won't take or accept
    less than my share
    Because when it comes to giving
    to this land I've always been there
For I'll say in a minute
    and repeat loud and clear
    I'm Black and I belong here
This is my country,
    My People made it what it is
And if I can't get my part
    Maybe no one will live
No longer will I listen
    to The Man say "Wait"
No longer will I use Love
    to fight Prejudice and Hate
No more grinning at Mr. Charlie
    as he stabs me in the back
    Cause I'm ready Now Brother
    and I'm gonna stab him back

"Leave Pig"

(By Rasheed Abdul Ali)

Come on Mister, leave us alone
    America is also our dog-on home.
Don't lynch our people to bring us fear
    If your folks didn't kidnap us we would have never come here
Get out of here and mess with them others!!!
    You always picken on us, you stupid, dirty mothers!
Leave us alone you dirty bums
    And let us run our nasty slums.
You bombed our churches and thought We'd be silent
    Well you thought wrong. We've all turned violent
Are you picken on us cause our skin is brown?
    Well we built America up and we'll burn it back down
You better get the hell out of our dog-on community.
    For we've all joined together and achieved black unity.

On Becoming

(By Ali Sadiki)

The blackness within me
    is my soul
    is my strength.
Now look at me beast
Check me out!
Yesterday you came in my back yard
You took my woman
    Pride, Culture
Today you refuse to free me
But I am determined, know that now!
I'll attend your schools, and wash your floors
    to survive
But tomorrow, Yes tomorrow with your "Education",
    Your weapons
And my determination for freedom
I'll be free
Think about that,
Just think about that

La Raza

Mexican- or Spanish-Americans, particularly those living in the Southwest, long had suffered the pains of discrimination and second-class citizenship. But they, like blacks, developed a movement for equality and for a recognition of their ethnic culture. Even in areas where they constituted a majority, Spanish-speaking people found themselves dominated politically, socially, and economically by Anglo elites. The schools especially became a prime area of concern. In Crystal City, Texas, where Mexican-Americans comprised eighty percent of the population, the movement sponsored a school boycott to protest Anglo domination and discrimination within the school system. The boycott was successful, and ultimately the Raza Unida party gained control of the school board and the city council. The following document reproduces some of the students' demands and petitions.

A. HIGH SCHOOL STUDENT DEMANDS, SPRING, 1969

  1. No punishment for students involved in demonstrations for better education.

  2. Teachers should stop taking political sides and preaching them to students.

  3. Twirlers should be elected by band members, instead of faculty.

  4. Students should select most popular, most beautiful and handsome, etc., boy and girl, and cheerleaders, instead of faculty.

  5. The school should have bilingual and bicultural programs, recognizing that Spanish is just as good as English.

  6. Pave the school parking lot.

  7. Provide the band with new uniforms.

B. SETTLEMENT REACHED WITH SUPERINTENDENT JOHN BILLINGS, SPRING, 1969, AND NULLIFIED IN THE SUMMER BY THE SCHOOL BOARD

  1. Any infractions must be dealt with by school officials.

  2. Teachers should not be derogatory about Mexican-American achievements, and teachers have been ordered to treat all students equally.

  3. The selection of twirlers should follow the general rule of most schools in the area.

  4. Concerning the election of class favorites, there should be a Spanish-surnamed student and Anglo student selected for each position, and two more Mexican-American cheerleaders should be selected.

  5. Teaching in classrooms could not be in Spanish, however, the librarian has been instructed to order as many books as possible on Mexican culture.

  6. and 7. Fiscal limitations were the reasons for the unpaved parking lot and old band uniforms.

C. HIGH SCHOOL STUDENT PETITION TO SCHOOL BOARD, NOVEMBER 1969 (Reproduced Exactly as Written)

  1. Homecoming Queen Regulation done away with. Regulation: (Girl eligible only if one of her parents graduated from high school. We do

From John Staples Shockley, *Chicano Revolt in a Texas Town* (South Bend, Ind.: University of Notre Dame Press, 1974), pp. 232–238. Used by permission of the author.

not want Homecoming Queen to be presented before game or announced.

2. Elections of Cheerleaders held by the Student Body.
   (1) Twirlers by (Band)
   (2) Most Handsome & Beautiful
   (3) Most Representatives

3. Same regulations applied to Fly Jr. High School in the elections of cheerleaders.

4. Mr. Harbin retire as principal because he is unfair and discriminates.

5. Teachers should not call students names like, animals, stupid idiots, ignorants,

6. Teachers should not discrimination and if they do they should not be allowed to teach.

7. Have Sept. 16, recognized as a Mexican-American holiday. (We don't mind going to school one more day.

8. Have a Mexican-American counselor a long with Mr. Moore. A Mexican-American will understand us better.

9. Have Bilingual education. Have Texas History books revised. We want new textbooks with the history of Los Mexicanos. (A course with the history of the Mexicanos and be valued as one credit.

10. Students not punished for organizing peacefully and demanding what is right.

11. Have a student organization within school. Goal is to help people within our community that need help in clothing, money and food.

12. Publish a newspaper and sell it at noon hour. Everybody will have a say in this newspapers.

13. Dress-Code-Pants can be worn by girls during the cold weather.

14. Showers to be put in girls and boys dressing room.

D. REVISED PETITION PRESENTED BY HIGH SCHOOL STUDENTS TO THE SCHOOL BOARD, DECEMBER, 1969 (Reproduced Exactly As Written)

1. That all elections concerning the school be conducted by the Student Body such as:

   a. Class Representatives

1. The qualifications such as personality, leadership, and grades be abolished. These factors do not determine whether the student is capable of representing the student body. The students are capable of voting for their own representatives. The representatives are representing the students, not the faculty. All nominating must be done by the student body, and the election should be decided by majority vote.

   b. Cheerleaders should be elected by the Student Body not judges from out of town.

   c. Twirlers should be elected by the BAND MEMBERS.

   d. The present method of electing Most Handsome, Beautiful, Most Popular, and Most Representative is done by the faculty. This is not fair. The method of cummulative voting is unfair.

   e. National Honor Society—The grades of the students eligible must be posted on the bulletin board well in advance of selection. The teachers should not have anything to do with electing the students.

   f. No other favorites should be authorized by School School Administrators or Board Members unless sumitted to the Student Body in a referendum; for example; Homecoming Queen, Who's Who, and Mr. and Miss CCHS.

2. We want immediate steps taken to implement bilingual and Bi-cultural education for Mexican-Americans. We also want the school books revised to reflect the contributions of Mexicans and Mexican-Americans to the U. S. society, and to make us aware of the injustices that we, Mexican-Americans, as a people have suffered in an "Anglo" dominant society. We want a Mexican-American course with the value of one credit. These are some books which will be educational;;;;;;;;

   1. *NORTH FROM MEXICO* by Carey McWilliams. First printed in 1948.

   2. *LATIN AMERICANS in TEXAS* by Pauline R. Kibbe. First printed in 1946.

   3. *AN AMERICAN-MEXICAN FRONTIER* by Dr. Paul S. Tayor. First printed in 1934.

   4. *CONQUISTADORS in NORTH AMERICAN HISTORY* Paul Horgan Printed in 1963.

   A list of many other books may be accquired by writing the DEPARTMENT of SOCIAL RELATIONS, University of Texas,

Austin. and asking for the ANNOTATED BIBLIOGRAPHY ON THE MEXICAN-American which they compiled.

3. We want any member of the school system who displays prejucide or fails to recognize, understand, and appreciate us Mexican Americans, our culture, or our heritage removed from Crystal City's schools. TEACHERS SHALL NOT CALL STUDENTS ANY NAMES.

  1. Mr. Ruthledge, a civics teacher, calls students animals, carpet-baggers, aliens bananas, fruits, and vegetables.

     a. Lydia Maltos was told last week not to speak SPANISH during the 5 minute break. This was outside of class. Yet the School Supertindent says there is no rule prohibiting SPANISH.

     b. During October when the armband were being worn; he told Lucy Ramirez that she should not write on white paper but on brown paper. He was making fun of our skin tone.

     c. He is constantly putting the students down with remarks such as those mentioned above.

  2. Mr. Lopez uses some of the techniques:

     a. In this class during Sept. in front of Cleofas Tamez, he told the students "he wished they were all dead before the age of 21. He stated that it was for their own good because they were too stupid to survive in this world.

     b. Armando de Hoyos was literally kicked out of class by Mr. Lopez. This happened last school year.

     c. A student does not like to attend a class where he is constantly called an idiot.

  3. Mrs. Harper is not qualified to teach students because of her RACISM and BIGOTRY.

     A. Ten Years Ago, the Freshman Class of 1958–59. Irma Benavidez was told by Mrs. Harper that it was a previliage to be sitting next to an anglo.

     B. Mario Trevino was told by Mrs. Harper, "You have been acting so dam smart alecky this period." She was angry at the class because she was corrected on one of her mistakes. She grabed Mario by the arm and told him the above.
       Students can not learn with Mrs. Harper. The students do not like her. We can not learn because she has built up a bad and fearful attitude toward her. Since Jr. High most Mexican-

American students are warned of the RACISM and BIGOTRY of the Red Headed Ant.

9. Our classes should be smaller in size, say about 20 students to one teacher to insure more effectiveness.

   A. We want parents from the community to be trained as teacher's aides.

   B. We want assurances that a teacher who may disagree politically or philosophically with administrators will not be dismissed or transferred because of it.

   C. Teachers should encourage students to study and should make class more interesting, so that students will look forward to going to class.

10. There should be a manager in charge of janitorial work and maintenance details and the performance of such duties should be restricted to employees hired for that purpose. IN OTHER WORDS NO MORE STUDENTS DOING JANITORIAL WORK.

   EXAMPLE: P.E. Boys should not be made to pick up paper at the football field.

11. RIGHTS—STUDENT RIGHTS

   1. We want a free speech area plus the right to have speakers of our own.

   A. We would like September 16 as a holiday, but if it is not possible we would like an assembly, with speakers of our own.

   We feel it is a great day in the history of the world because it is when Mexico had been under the Spanish rule for about 300 years. The Mexicans were liberated from the harsh rule of Spain. Our ancestors fought in this war and we owe them tribute because we are Mexicans too.

   Yes, you will say that the students from Irish descent will want St. Patricks Day. In Boston and New York where there is a heavy population of Irish students; they have St. Patricks day as a Holiday.

   When we have the Stock Show we have a day or half off too. So we are entitled to September 16.

12. Being civic minded citizens, we want to know what is happening in our community. So, we request the ritht to have access to all types of

literature and to be able to carry suffient information. It carries things like the gossip column, which is unnecessary.

13. The dress code should be abolished. We are entitled to wear what we want. This includes Jr. High which the code is very strict there. The girls cannot wear a short dress because they are suspended or are given three (3) licks.

14. We request the buildings open to students at all times.

15. We want Mr. Harbin to resign as Principal of Fly Jr. High School. He openly shows his RACISM and BIGOTRY.

16. We want a Mexican-American counselor fully qualified in college opportunities.

17. We need more showers in the boys' and girls' dressing rooms. They should be enlarged.

18. No reprisals against students participating in the walk out.

19. That an Advisory board of Mexican-American citizens, chosen by the citizens, to be established in the school board in order to advise the school board on needs and problems of Mexican-Americans.

The WASP: a vanishing species?

The zealous movements for racial equality and ethnic recognition inevitably produced a variety of counterattacks. Open manifestations of bigotry, legal resistance, and violence characterized the responses of the "majority." But in a nation that encouraged pluralism and diversity, the so-called majority became harder to identify. Indeed, as the struggle for equality escalated with demands for preferential treatment, many white Americans now believed themselves to be victims of discrimination in reverse. This letter to the United States Commission on Civil Rights came from a Texas woman who claimed that the Commission's excessive concern with the status of Mexican-Americans jeopardized *her* civil rights.

December 12, 1963

Dear Sir;

I have been following the current controversy on civil rights in the San Antonio area with a great deal of interest, and I sincerely hope you will read my letter, and perhaps return any comments you may have.

Let me preface my comments by stating that I hold no social or racial prejudices toward Mexican Americans. Quite the contrary; some of my dearest friends are Mexican American.

I sincerely believe in equality for all men, and I am most willing to help those less fortunate than I in any way I can. It is my understanding that civil rights means equal opportunity for all, without infringing on anyone's rights as guaranteed by the Constitution of the United States. That is to say, that all persons in minority groups deserve social, economic, and educational opportunities in equality with those in the majority. However, it is also my understanding that, in allowing these opportunities to the minority groups, it is the purpose and duty of civil rights to see that none of the rights of the majority are revoked or violated.

In my estimation, the true meaning of civil rights has been misinterpreted by the minority groups, as pertaining only to them, at the sacrifice of those of us in the majority. I submit that majority groups have civil rights as well, and when my rights are violated, in order to give a Mexican American, or anyone else preferential rights, I shall stand up for my rights, and call attention to the fact that I am not being treated fairly.

I was greatly impressed by the testimony given by Mayor McAllister, as shown on television, December 11. His was the first testimony I have seen which brings the other side of this hearing to light. As the mayor said, investigation is a good and healthy commodity, if applied in its proper prospective, and used to see all sides of a problem. But when only one side of the discord is heard, the investigation becomes a vehicle of demagogory and prejudice. I feel that just such a distortion has occurred in San Antonio. The hearings have become a one-sided exercise in propaganda, which can only cause more disturbance and unrest in the Southwest, and indeed, throughout the country. It is no longer a sincere and realistic probe into the facts when only one side is heard, and there is no room for compromise. It is now left to the majority to do all the giving. This Civil Rights Committee has gone to the extreme with minority groups, and seems to be forgetting the majority. When this situation occurs, it is no longer civil rights. I do not believe that our entire social, economic, and educational structure should be done away with completely, in order to satisfy any minority group. This is precisely what the Mexican Americans are asking.

I would suggest that you focus a committee hearing on Eagle Pass, Texas, or any other Rio Grande border town, if you are interested in seeing discrimination in reverse. You are giving more and more to the minority groups, and neglecting to investigate what effect all this giving is having on the majority. The Anglo American is, in fact, a minority group in these areas. That, in itself,

From *Hearings before the United States Commission on Civil Rights,* San Antonio, Texas, 9–14 December 1968, pp. 1218–1219. Mrs. A. L. Pellegrin to Chairman, 12 December 1968.

means little or nothing to me, as I have lived most of my life in border towns, and have acclimated myself to such areas. I would hazard an estimate that better than 50% of the population of Eagle Pass, Texas does not speak English. In accordance with this estimated statistic, one is required to have a working knowledge of the Spanish language in order to secure employment, but as stated by a prominent figure in local politics, there is no requirement whatsoever regarding knowledge of English. Upon making application for employment here, one major deciding factor in acceptance is whether or not the applicant can speak Spanish. It has been the experience of several of my friends, as well as myself, that the applicant is refused employment despite his educational background, and or his job qualifications if he does not speak Spanish.

It is a common occurrance to be approached by non-English speaking clerks in the department stores, as well as restaurants, service establishments, and virtually every business concern in this area. In fact, it is more common than not.

The situations in these areas has always bee a sourse of irritation and concern to me, as well as many others. But not until recently has this been a problem truly needy of bringing to the attention of your Committee. When an Anglo American cannot shop in his own country without benefit of a foreign language, and when he cannot secure employment for the same reason, I submit that the civil rights of the majority are being violated, and that it is time to take a look in the other direction.

When the Mexican Americans complain of discrimination because school classes are not taught in Spanish, and when they say that they are discriminated against in job opportunities, I submit to you, Mr. Chairman, that the Mexican American has a better chance than I, a native born American.

I am anxious for minority groups to have equal rights, as it should be, but I am most emphatic in stating that I am not willing to relinquish my rights as an American to satisfy a desire in them for preferential rights. America is rapidly becoming a country tailored to the wishes of minority groups, and a country where its native born must relinquish their rights to those who are in the minority. I ask you; is this a democracy, and am I being given equal opportunities? What has happened to my rights?

CHAPTER **18**

The Vietnam war
and social unrest

ᴱarly warning

The United States militarily intervened in Korea (under United Nations's auspices) following North Korea's invasion of South Korea in June 1950. It was a limited war, fought with certain restraints on both sides, and limited in both sides' perception of goals. As the conflict dragged on, the American people grew increasingly disenchanted with a war that neither promised nor delivered victory. The war concluded with a truce agreement in 1953. A year later, reports circulated in Washington (attributed particularly to Secretary of State John Foster Dulles and Vice President Richard Nixon) of possible American intervention in behalf of the embattled French who were trying to retain their Indochina colony. President Dwight Eisenhower, however, refused to act, primarily for military reasons. He also realized the American people were in no mood for another land adventure in Asia, given the Korean experience. The following letter, printed exactly as written to Senator William Langer of North Dakota, represents fairly both the frustration and cynicism that had developed toward the idea of an American role as policeman for liberty and freedom throughout the world. If the writer were alive a decade later, he must have felt a sense of satisfaction with his analysis—but also a sense of outrage over the course of events.

Joplin, Mont.
April 25—54.

Dear Sen. Langle,
Washington, D.C.

I am sending you a write up, would you please read it, and do all you can to stop all these trouble-makers.

We are going to git in an other world war. These leaders of ours, are just looking for trouble all over the world, not for pease what so ever. its nothing but lies, and propaganda. just like they started out with in the fall of 1952. As well as befor, missleading the people, more and more.

What in the world have we got to do over there in Indochina. Those people wanted to get rid of them French, and these leaders of ours, want to forse them native, to take what they don't want. Thats this freedom they are always telling us about. so good luck to you. with best regards,

Yours truly,
[B.J., Sr.]

From [B. J., Sr.] to William Langer, Langer Papers, Orin G. Libby Manuscript Collection (Grand Forks: University of North Dakota). Material provided by Robert Griffith.

Intervention: the conflict over dissent

After the Geneva Accords of 1954 carved the new state of South Vietnam out of Indochina, President Eisenhower offered its government vague assurances of security. The United States subsequently provided substantial military and economic assistance, but when Eisenhower left office in 1961, there were merely a few hundred military advisers. By the time of John F. Kennedy's death in November 1963, there were 16,000 military personnel, some of whom had engaged in combat. Our participation escalated dramatically as local guerrillas and the North Vietnamese stepped up their activities in the South. By the end of 1965, we had nearly 200,000 troops in Vietnam, and three years later, there were over 500,000. All this occurred after the presidential election of 1964 in which Lyndon Johnson appeared to be the "dovish" choice given the "hawkish" postures of his opponent, Barry Goldwater. The growing American presence in Vietnam correspondingly increased dissent over the war at home. As often is the case, the dissenters at first constituted a minority as public opinion polls showed support for the administration's policies. The following documents offer a capsule of the early conflict at home. The first selection is from an antiwar street flyer distributed in Chicago in 1965, and it is followed by two letters written in response to the protest.

A True Message from Vietnam

(From a Mother with Two Sons There)

I had one son . . . in Viet Nam at the time the Diem regime was terminated. At that time the corrupt regime was supported in virtual luxury by the U.S. simply because it was non-communistic. Also, at that time, the Diem army was carrying out midnight raids on the temples of Viet Nam's predominant religious faction, the Buddhists—with American-supplied armament wielded by American-trained troops.

This went on under the nose of Washington who refused to grasp the political

From Pamphlets and Letters, Chicago Committee to End the War in Vietnam (Madison: State Historical Society of Wisconsin). Used by permission of the director.

Ronald Haberle.

Helicopters that brought American Company C soldiers to
Mylai for assault.

aspect of this triangular civil war. The military had access to the press at this time but the copies were recently cut to two issues (a military and V. govt press) in which Saigon published slanted . . . news and the military issue fills the boys with anti-communist paranoia.

At that time (1963–4) there was no talk of infiltration from the North and the Saigon press coined the dreisive name "Vietcong" onto a labor party (National Liberation Front) which emerged to protect the rights of the farmer against the inroads of the govt. This kind of derision, and not much of anything else, left the young unionists (VC guerrillas) no place to turn. Even today the villagers consider him their protector & provide aid and recruiting priviledges for him—lying to the govt and to our army. His weapons, a year ago, were water-pipe shotguns and tin can grenades; today his equippment is 80% (captured) American weapons for which he can buy ammo at any post or turn in the road. He still holds two-thirds of Viet Nam (in spite of govt reports to the contrary) and uses terrorism to rid the provinces of the headmen to rescue his people of more—supposed or real—tyranny. He gives the rice farmers bonds in return for rice and the govt, in turn, collects (or confiscates) these bonds as "invaluable payment from the enemy) leaving the farmer with no material security. The farmer blames the govt., not the VC guerrilla.

Heads Chopped Off—U.S. Orders!

This son recently returned to the States with nothing more than leg wounds and a shattered idealism of our committment-policy; he sees the pitiful need to the Vietnamese for political and economic help and is concerned over our continual destruction of that country and its people. He is sending home pictures of beheaded VC's and states that any suspect is grabbed and beheaded publicly—by orders from U.S. officers—but carried out by Vietnamese officers. According to his story, anyone even suspected of hoarding or VC participation is beheaded on the spot. . . .

History speaks of our undisputed supremacy of the air and the Pacific which our boys won through much bloodshed in W.W. II. Must we believe the barefoot, emaciated liberators of Viet Nam will permeate our beaches, our universities, our very doorsteps? Their communism is a socialized farming in an attempt to feed their starving people. We need never fear that the poor people of Viet Nam will ever make inroads on our country as they greatly fear and hate China. Hanoi does not take its order from Peking but if we pressure them into the hands of the Chinese, what independence they may have hoped for will end as vassal states to China. Or is our floundering in Viet Nam only an excuse to provoke China into an incident? If we dismember China, it will be a feat no other nation in history has ever been able to perform.

Freedom to Vote Withheld

We who are concerned over the course of our government and what it once proudly stood for are appaled that the administration is using our splendid military to support reactionary governments in Viet Nam and in Santo Domingo in order to beat down the oppressed people's desire for national freedom and independence and abusing our capitalistic theory which is buried by monopolistic gains. In Viet Nam we withheld the freedom of free elections for the reason that the people would surely have voted communistic. Instead, we supported one unpopular and corrupt govt after another—just as we did the bloody Trujillo in Santo Domingo—until the desperate people murdered both rulers in an attempt for freedom.

Gov. Rockefeller owns billion dollar monopolies both in Asia and S.D.—he is only one example—and our President owes his election debts to these monopolists—thus his mad escalation of the war. He knows little of foreign affairs and turns our military over to the discretion of a cold-blooded millionaire war general—to be used at his discretion. The young draftees do not owe these men their lives, nor does the young guerrilla.

Another son who landed in Saigon with the army engineers, writes . . .

"The average V. is emaciated-looking; no teeth, starved, scarred or covered with sores—bubonic plague, they say. I'm almost afraid to breathe the air here when I look at the people. Guess I'm not very international if this country is an example of what we're supposed to die for. There's nothing here. They say Hanoi has some factories and a little industry but not here. Saigon looks oriental and attractive at a glance, but it is filled with corruption. Little kids who should be in school are hawking phornographic photography in the streets; mothers with babies sleeping on the streets their bodies with open sores. You wouldn't believe all the people who are without arms and legs. They say 10,000 of them. You think you've seen poverty and filth? Well, you haven't—it's all here.

"An old hag came into the camp yesterday begging cigarettes. It turns out she's really selling information.—"A baby-san put a bomb in the cement mixer under the sand. A five-yr-old girl put it there, the hag said. None of these people like us, they only want to beg. We have a feeling when we see the starving little kids; 8 & 9-yr. olds—always carrying a baby around—he says 'Gotta dolla, Joe?—baby-san no eat three days." We do what we can but hell we can't feed them all. Makes us feel like we shouldn't complain about our rations. We've got money but nothing to buy. These people want food, not candy—course every kid likes candy, but———What do the millionaires do with their money? Maybe they never see this stuff. It sure makes you think. These people work from sun-up til after sun-down to give their families a handful of rice and (if they're lucky) a third of a head of cabbage once a week and a small piece of fat is a delicacy. The next time you trim the fat off a pork chop, remember it will feed two kids for a week over here. No wonder they eat grasshoppers.

"I'm beginning to think you couldn't believe any of this. I think we become dependent-thinkers in the army. I can hardly believe I am writing this as because I noticed, but immediately forgot, what I had seen until you keep asking me specific questions. Sort of like I had forgotten how to think for myself. Now, I am learning to keep my eyes open so I can tell you what you ask for. Somehow, I still have the feeling that you don't believe it, tho. Well, maybe it will help me because I'm telling you, we feel wasted over here. There's nothing to do. Sometimes we pity the poor gook in the jungle then sometimes we envy him. It's the monotony that's the worst for our outfit. Better come on over here and exploit your 45 years. They don't believe it when I tell them as they die at 35 or 40.

"I can tell you why your other son wouldn't tell you the true facts over here—about jungle fighting—it's too subversive for anyone's talk. Just don't try to get the picture. But I will tell you one thing. Our outfit is leaving Uncle Sam after this hitch because this isn't our idea of fighting for democracy. Maybe you won't go along with me but the whole outfit couldn't be wrong, you just don't know. We would welcome the job of protecting you and our country—we're trained that way and have been on alert for years—but this is complaining and we're not supposed to.

"Sometimes I think I won't send even this but then if I go back and re-read or add to I'll never get up the nerve to send it for sure and you won't quit plaguing me."———

As my son said, I asked for information and this is what I got. We know this is an immoral war upon innocent people but what do I write to my sons? A copy of the Army Press shows how they are indoctrinated with anti-communism. They have to have some idealistic reason for fighting in a war 10,000 miles from our shores.

I saw a picture of the "enemy" last night on tv. Two young American folk-song singers were winning them over . . . "Charley just sat there—a young, barefoot, emaciated, cold-eyed kid; quietly listening to these young American who sought to win them over. It makes me wonder why our President sends Conrad & Cooper on goodwill tours at our expense . . . these young men are doing more on their own. My eyes stung with tears for "Charley." Maybe he will kill my sons. I hope not. And I hope they never kill him.

[1965, Oct 13]

May I call to your attention several facts related to United States involvement in the war in Viet Nam. You state that 200,000 people have been killed in the fighting in Viet Nam. If you had asked each and every one of those 200,000 people whether they would rather die as a slave of a socialist and communist society or be killed trying to perpetuate the idea that all men have the right to live as they please and earn their living in the manner they best see fit, what would their reaction have been? No man likes to face death, but I would destroy my own life rather than deliver myself to be a slave in a socialistic society.

Socialism destroys everything in a man that is honorable, everything he can believe in. His pride in his creative ability, his will to produce, even his desire to live. What honest man can stand by and watch the profit of his labor being given to a less productive person just because the other person has more children. I have nothing against children except the belief that any two people who concieve a child and bring it into the world should be willing and able to accept all the responsibilities connected.

You may ask "Does the US have the right to go into South Viet Nam?" I believe that the United States not only has the right, but has the obligation to fight the danger of spreading communism wherever it exists. Does any socialist nation have rights? How can any government which does not recognize the rights of its individual people have any rights among the free nations of the earth. A society as a whole has no rights, there is no such animal as the collective rights, only the rights of the individual. If these are denied and suppressed, then there is a need for a free government, one where the rights of its citizens are recognized and defended to send in soldiers to liberate the people, not to exploit and colonize, but to liberate, such as the United States troops are doing in South Viet Nam.

Yes, I agree it is time to hold teach-ins, but to teach the people the dangers of spreading socialism.

Yes, I agree it is time to picket, time to picket the embassies of the free nations of the world and demand their nations' support in stamping out the spreading evils of communism. Unless they pitch in to do their part, communism truly will bury us: Unless the free nations of the world awaken to the danger, the United States will be put in David's position when he fought Goliath, and this time he may not have the five stones.

In closing, I ask you to check your premises before you try to get the United States out of Viet Nam, where our soldiers are desperately needed.

[G. T. C.]

[1965, Oct 19]

Dear Americans: ?

I read your propaganda in Saturday's Sun Times. Is that all you MORONS have to do is protest & demonstrate against people who are fighting so that you can go to any school you want to or work at the job of your choice? I'm a 19 year old Marine. I wasn't drafted, I enlisted. I'M proud to serve a country that has given me all the freedoms you AMERICANS take for granted. Most of you are probably college students. The future leaders of our country they call you. I hope to GOD I'm not here under your leadership. If you don't like it here GET OUT!! Go live in Cuba or some other Soviet controlled country where people think like you do. You people aren't fit to live here. You've had so much. Now when your support is needed you forget what you've got. You forget about your fathers or relatives who fought, some died, in World War II so that *you could be free.* Go ahead you chicken shits burn your draft card, demonstrate all you like. When we win and YOUR liberty is preserved, your kind of people will be around to collect all the spoils. Your kind always is.

[Pvt. W. L. P. USMC]

Dissent on campus

The most sustained, dramatic protests against the Vietnam War occurred on college campuses throughout the late 1960s. Beginning first in the larger universities such as the University of California, the University of Wisconsin, Columbia, and Harvard, demonstrations spread to virtually every kind of campus and in every region. The protests began because of the threat of military service, but soon responded to the larger political and moral implications of the war. Street parades, classroom disruptions, and, finally, violence by both police and demonstrators characterized the heightened protests. The ultimate tragedy came at Kent State University where four students were killed during protests over the Cambodian invasion in May 1970. One prominent, early conflict occurred at the University of Wisconsin in October 1967, when students attempted to prevent interviews by recruiters for Dow Chemical Company, prime manufacturers of napalm. The following documents chronicle the call for a demonstration, and various reactions to the violence that ensued when campus administrators called in outside police forces.

[October 15, 1967]

From Tuesday to Friday of this week, Dow Chemical Company will be recruiting on this campus. On Tuesday, this fact will be brought to the attention of the entire campus. On Wednesday, students will block Dow from recruiting.

From materials collected by Professor Stanley N. Katz (Madison: State Historical Society of Wisconsin). Used by permission of the director.

Why Pick on Dow?

Like other large corporations, Dow is a political institution. 75% of its business is with the military. Dow makes the napalm used in Vietnam. Recruiting for Dow is recruiting for the war.

The Administration says it invites all corporations to recruit here, why stop Dow? Thus, it brags of its part in the war and sees no conflict between "sifting and winnowing" and "Let the corporations come!" We get the point. By "sifting and winnowing," the Administration means "Think and espouse good causes, but forget everything when you begin the serious business of production."

The Faculty argues, if Dow goes then all corporations go. We agree. But they decide Dow should stay. We think it should go.

Why This Week?

This is Vietnam week. On Friday, hundreds of thousands of Americans will travel to Washington to confront the warmakers. The Mobilization on Saturday is a crucial part of the worldwide movement to stop America's war against the Vietnamese.

But the work of the government cannot be separated from the daily operations of American corporations or universities. To end the war, it is necessary to comprehend its true nature, to understand the extent to which major institutions such as this university and Dow Corporation are committed to its continuation. We pick this week to demonstrate against Dow, against the university as a corporation and against the war because they are all one.

Being Against the War is Not Enough!

Last year 61% of the students on this campus indicated they opposed the war. National polls show more than 50% of the American people oppose the war. But opposition is not enough. Even on this campus, opposition has become "in": Not one faculty member in a hundred will defend the government. But the government. But the war effort has not even slowed down. Opposition must move against the forces which under[lie] the war.

Many oppose the war as "citizens," but refuse to do so as "faculty," "Administrators" or "students." The chancellor opposes the war as "citizen" but invites Dow and the other corporations to recruit our students. To those who make this separation, we say, what does Washington care what you do on your own time so long as you continue to work for this economy and support its corporate institutions? As student-citizens, we must act as whole human beings.

From Protest to Resistance

Mass opinion has it that all we need is a new president, or ten years to mend our broken image. According to those who would keep demonstrations "peaceful," the aim of protest is education. Protest leads to a change in public opinion which in turn ends the war. But publicity will not stop Dow or the war. Both the Administration and the faculty know the true nature of Dow and yet they invite it to return. What the Administration here and in Washington cannot say is that they are undemocratic to the core, that they willingly defend the status quo which they control against all of the individuals who make it up.

Two years ago, thousands of students demonstrated against class rank. The Faculty laughed. Class rank was finally eliminated because it was an inefficient way to recruit men for Vietnam. Even on this campus, protest has become a much publicized spectacle without any effect.

We must move from protest to resistance. Before, we talked. Now we must act. We must stop what we oppose.

Stop Dow From Recruiting—Grind Dow to a Halt

Ou[r] Tuesday picket will not stop Dow from recruiting. The picket is purely educational. We are not appealing to the men in power to make a change. A picket is a waiting for. The time for waiting is done.

Everyone talks about the revolt of youth. Sociologists and psychologists study it. It is a spectacle like a football game or a movie. Soon there will be so much talk about the revolt of youth, that people will forget to participate in it. We must stop looking at events as pictures on a wall and enter the arena of action to make the kind of history we want.

On Tuesday we will meet at commerce, demonstrate our opposition to Dow and to the war in Vietnam. On Wednesday morning, we will meet on Bascom Hill, enter a building in which Dow is recruiting and stop them. We will not beg the Administration or Faculty to do our work for us. Corporations do not disappear upon request. Neither will the war. If Dow is to be removed from this campus and if the war is to be ended, all of us must do it.

The Dean Has Threatened Us

Dean Kaufman threatens to discipline us as "students" if we disrupt Dow's recruitment. The Dean sees that the revolt against Dow as a corporation producing napalm is a revolt against American as a corporation producing mass murder of social revolution in Vietnam, in our ghettos and elsewhere. He is therefore correct to see that our revolt is also against this unversity, against its sterile academic assembly lines and against its fight, "peaceful" until someone steps out of line, to make us an integrated part of the corporate economy.

We also revolt against Dean Kaufman's conviction, shared in Washington, that autonomy means obedience to administrative fiat. The Dean has sent us "Rules for [P]rocedure." Naturally, he thinks he can design our resistance the way the administration designs our minds in the classrooms. He would make the resistance a spectacle so that those who oppose the war and Dow will stand by and watch. But the Dean will not stop us.

A First Step

Stopping Dow will not end corporate imperialism. It is merely a first step in that direction. Like those fighting tyranny throughout the world, we must build as we resist. If we did not know how to make this university and this society a better place, we would sit with the vast majority of faculty and preach "neutrality." By punishing us educationally for what we do politically, the Administration points to the unavoidable fact that our education has become totally political in precisely the same way as Dow's recruitment. To those who plead neutrality, we say there are no neutrals. We are not neutral. Not only do we oppose the war and the corporations that make it and the university that feeds it, we are also *for* a society in which men control their own products and in which men make themselves and are not designed by other men.

Out of this demonstration and resistance, we will form a radical student union, a cohesive organization of resistance in which all students may learn the true nature of their society and to change it, in which they may set their dreams within the framework of a sensible critique of this society and those who would keep in this way.

Join us on Tuesday and Wednesday. Join the trip to Washington to confront the warmakers. Let us break through the spectacle and become people who act!

Statement by Members of the Faculty of the School of Business

October 19, 1967

The undersigned members of the School of Business faculty were in the School of Business building and most of the time in the main floor offices or corridor where the student riot occurred. The following is what we witnessed.

The student protest group blocked the corridor to classrooms and offices from mid morning until the order to remove them was given. It was out of the question to conduct classes or carry on normal work in this area of the building due to their disruptive activities.

The student protest group was not the typical, "normal" student group which alumni and public may visualize getting into trouble with police. These students were a belligerent group; they deliberately defied public authority and sought forcible ejection from the building.

The police, Madison and University, carried out the ejection order with noticeable restraint. They had the nasty task of removing from the building several hundred cursing, spitting, hitting and kicking men and women. Those who would walk were permitted to do so. Those who would not walk were dragged. The police used considerable and commendable restraint in the use of their sticks. Police officers used their sticks to prod when they might have hit; they hit at legs or buttocks when they might more easily have hit heads. A less well disciplined group of officers could readily have broken a hundred heads. Cries of "police brutality" are sheer propaganda in the face of all that we saw both in and outside the building.

Excerpts from Students' Statements: Eye Witnesses

[W.A.W.]

. . .the police crossed the street in a group, the large crowds of students outside clearing way for them. The police entered through the front doors, and without waiting, moved into the group of students and began to use their nightsticks. The police poked, clubbed, shoved and wrestled with the students inside the building, attempting to pull them outside. As the police moved into the area between the double doors, I heard the window in from of me break, and I moved back away from it. A policeman then broke the window away from its frame using his stick.

The police shoved students through the doors into the group outside, and a group of police cleared an area in front of the doors. Students were being shoved out between the two lines of police that had formed inside the doors, and the police shoved them into the crowd, clubbing them as they went past.

The crowd, infuriated by the police actions, wrestled with them and were clubbed in return. People were being pressed into the police line by those behind them, and were clubbed back.

[L.S.]

I am a third year la[w] student at the University of Wisconsin. The events I am about to describe occured between 10:15 A.M. and 2:30 P.M. on Wednesday, October 18th, 1967. I am dictating this statement ten minutes to four of that day.

At 10:15 A.M. I left the Law Review office to observe the protesting of the presence of Dow Chemical Corporation on the University of Wisconsin campus. I entered the building and stood in a doorwell three feet from the office in the School of Commerce. Subsequently I was surrounded by other observers and protesters. I in no way participated in the speech-making, in the singing of songs, or in any actual obstruction. The protesters filled the hallway which goes in an east-westerly direction. They also filled the hallway that goes in a north-south direction. The halls were packed. I could not lift my arm to see my watch because of the crowd. There was obstruction. Some people tried to get through. At times it was conscious obstruction, at other times obstruction occured because the place was simply packed. Prior to noon, the three University policemen stationed at the door to the School of Commerce office, grabbed three students, with no warning, in an attem[pt] to pull them into the office. These three students, with some help of others, shook loose. One would not characterize the resistance as violent, but just an attempt to avoid someone pulling them by surprise. When they shook loose, they did not run (they couldn't), they just stood there, but the police left them alone. Approximately at 12:30 Chief Hanson asked to see some of the leaders of the demonstration. He knew them by name. He talked to them and then they said over a loud-speaker that there was going to be a deal: If Dow would leave, the demonstrators would leave. The question was put to the crowd. Every one cheered with approval. There was no desire to stay once Dow was gone. The goal of the demonstration apparently, from my view, was to get Dow off the campus. The protesters talked among themselves—if Dow would leave, then they would leave. As far as I could observe there was no dissent from this position. Many protesters announced that if the interviewers from Dow were to come down the halls, no one was to molest them in any way. The protest leaders then left the scene of the demonstration to get confirmation of this offer from Chancellor Sewell. They returned. They announced that their meeting with Chancellor Sewell did not produce this result, and that Dow would not leave. At this point, Chief Hanson took the loudspeaker and addressed the noisy demonstrators: "This is an unlawful assembly. If you wish to avoid arrest, leave now." The halls were so packed that there was no possibility of emptying the halls in less than ten minutes. Within one minute of Chief Hanson's "arrest warning," at least twenty riot police, helmeted, with clubs swinging, charged the crowd. I could see several assaulted protesters falling. As they fell, police continued to beat them. It was clear beyond a doubt that the force being used was not for the purpose of arrest, but to beat the demonstrators. I saw no provocation during any time that I was there of the riot police. There was immediate panic among the protesters. There was no place to go. They were forced to face the police lines. When people tried to leave, voluntarily, they were clubbed, tripped and clubbed some more. I saw a girl who had been pushed over on to the floor. She wanted to get out. She tried to get up, but the police clubbed her again to the floor with blows to the head and shoulders. At this point of the pandemonium, I was pushed back by the crowd which was trying to avoid the riot police. I pleaded with a University policeman guarding the office to the School of Commerce "Please let me in. I'm an observer. Let me out of this." This red-haired policeman answered, "You fink, go out like the rest of them." He then pushed me over the heads of several demonstraters who were on the floor. The University policeman kicked the people on the floor, and kicked with vengeance. The front line of the riot police continued to club the people around me. Another group had formed two lines which led to the exit. To leave, I had to run the gauntlet of the riot police. I was hit four times as I went through the gauntlet. As I got to the front entrance of Commerce there were fragments of broken glass which came from a window which the riot police had broken. Many of the riot police, without badges, tried to knock down, or trip, students who were attempting to leave by the front exit. Outside of Commerce police were continuing their assault on demonstrators who had fallen in their attempt to leave. As I left, I saw people with blo[o]dy faces; people holding different parts of their bodies.

A soldier in the quagmire

Unlike previous wars, the Vietnam intervention inspired little idealism and sense of purpose for ordinary soldiers. It was a war only vaguely understood by them, and the domestic debate over the legitimacy of the conflict only heightened their bitterness. The high rate of desertion, the breakdown in morals and discipline, the incidence of the use of narcotics, the frustration of fighting a well-concealed enemy without clearly drawn battle lines, and even the hostility from supposedly allied Vietnamese—all reflected feelings of despair and cynicism. While media reporters in the field and domestic critics described the war as a quagmire for the United States, soldiers in the field, although less articulate, knew first-hand the enormity, indeed the futility, of their role. The following letter by a twenty-six-year-old draftee to his former college professor is a striking, sensitive narrative of the military effort and the daily hardships experienced by such soldiers.

Dear Pete,

Got your two letters yesterday at mail call, or I should say a buddy did who later brought them to me. Can't understand why your first letter was returned. . . .

I've been keeping a day-by-day diary since 15 May 68. Hope I can successfully smuggle it out of the country since it's a court martial offense to be keeping one. My buddies are very amused about it all.

Since I've been here, I have acquired the nickname of "professor." This is probably due to my great learning & education, or at least in reference to that of my comrades.

Unfortunately your advice about going to a military hospital to seek possible reassignment is not possible. Am now on a new work schedule whereby I work a half day every day. Certainly, in comparison to the other GI's, we cooks have quite a bit of leisure-time.

Two weeks ago I had off for two whole days & flew down to the huge military-naval complex at Da Nang. Flew down & back in one of our coptors; my first ride in one.

While in Da Nang I had a most unusual & interesting experience. A nine year old youth, or there abouts, approached me while I was waiting for the navy bus & begged me to have my boots polished. I resisted but finally gave in after he started to polish 'em. Initially, the fee agreed upon was 25¢ which is enough to support one Vietnamese for approximately three days. Midway thru, he changed his price to one dollar & later to two & five dollars. When I handed the youth a 25¢ note, he screamed & demanded five dollars. After this I became stubborn & insisted on paying him only 25¢. He took the bill & picked-up two large rocks & approached me in a most threatening manner, especially for a youth of his age. As I began to board the bus, he threw both rocks at me hitting me in the knee & leg. I chased him & naturally caught him. A strong verbal admonishment was being administered by me when a US army truck pulled-up & three South Vietnamese military policemen approached me. They demanded that the youth be paid the full five dollars & that they would accept it since it had "to be registered" at the police station. To me this was nothing but "highway robbery." Suddenly, I saw a shore patrol jeep appear & I dashed onto the highway for help. I attempted to explain the situation to the sailors but the Vietnamese police attempted to interfere. One sailor stopped a truck loaded with armed Marines & then the senior sailor abruptly advised everyone to "shut-up." My story was told & the Vietnamese police suddenly remembered that they "needed gas" & suddenly disappeared. The youth's shoe shine box was found by a Marine & contained a small plastic bomb. I was told to "move out" & to keep my mouth shut. Certainly, I moved out in a very fast hurry. What became of the youth I'll never know. Also, how he gained entry into the post is hard to understand.

Perhaps I advised in my previous letter that I'd subscribed to *The Christian Science Monitor*. My issues usually are two weeks late & come in bunches, but

From David L. Sartori to Edward M. Peterson, July 1968 (Madison: State Historical Society of Wisconsin). Used by permission of David L. Sartori.

it sure is worth the $1.00 per month fee charged servicemen.

Last week we began to move into our own new company area. This is situated on a small hill about a mile from our old area we borrowed from the 131st aviation. I'm still "cooking" in the 131st mess hall as are all the men in our company. Our mess sgt told me this afternoon that next Monday our own mess hall goes into operation.

Despite the fact that we have only 200 soldiers & airmen to feed this will be a real bitch since we have only three actual cooks at present, not counting the mess sgt.

My mess sgt is a negro from North Carolina. So far he has treated me straight but I still like the 131st mess sgt better.

One thing that I really like about my mess sgt is that he told me never to be forced by another NCO into going on any "shit details." This came in handy when a sgt ordered me this afternoon to participate in digging a bunker. I explained that my mess sgt had ordered me not to participate in any non-messing details & that I was to tell any one who "tried to 'fuck' with me to go to hell or try to 'fuck' my mess sgt." Upon hearing of our solidarity, he simply told me to move out.

Our CO is a major. First time that I had a field grade commander & also my first commander older than myself.

I live in the cook's hooch (barracks) which is shared at present with five other men. We got beds just a few days ago. Prior to this, we were sleeping on cots & air mattresses. This certainly was a welcome change. All hooches have a hooch-maid, a Vietnamese cleaning woman. Initially, our hooch-maid was one in her fifties & extremely unattractive. This has all been changed since our mess sgt had his old hooch-maid brought up today. She must be about eighteen. Not only does her talents include being our hooch-maid & sgt's mistress, she has also offered to bestow upon all other cooks her favors for additional rations.

Since my sister-in-law is Japanese, I have met many Japanese "war brides" back in the states. They sure are a world apart from the Vietnamese. The Japanese are so clean, polite, & considerate.

One would seem to think that a man of my education would understand & tolerate the dynamics of "cultural relativity" but I find it so hard to tolerate these people. Intolerance certainly runs contrary to my general personality, but I simply have so little tolerance for these people. . . .

Going back to the "gooks;" they seem to have—both the north & south alike—one thing in common besides their Roman Catholicism & that is their hatred of foreign domination. Among the south Vietnamese, we seem to have become what the Chinese were traditional[ly] to the north.

No doubt you've heard about the "pull out" (evacuation) of the South. It's amusing that the Joint Chiefs of Staff issued a statement three months ago that post could be & must be held at all cost. What insanity!

Have heard Hanoi Hannah's broadcast three times since I've been here. If one could only ignore the "hundreds of American GI's were killed & thousands wounded" it would be a fairly accurate broadcast—or as accurate at least as ours. Last time she broadcasted names of downed pilots over . . . [North Vietnam]. She also played a tape of an American pilot's evaluation . . . of the war. It was so rational and logical to me.

Lately, have been plagued by the Wis. Council for Higher Ed. Loans & the National Defense Loan program for payment of my loans despite by military service. Finally got a deferment form filled-out for my national indebtedness.

. . . Might as well tell you a military secret. Lately, there has been increased NVA copter activity in the. . . . [area]. The Army denies it all but it's true. Our own radar has picked up 'copters right outside our perimeter. Rumor has it that about twelve have so far been shot down.

I wrote my Selective Slave Board back in . . . [Fond duLac] & requested the names of the members of the board. Was expecting some "chicken-shit" reply but surprisingly they gave me the board member names.

Last night we had a live entertainment group from Korea. They sang songs, etc. The last time we had a live performance we had a full strip tease. Now I fully can understand the phrase's definition.

dls

Conscience and the war

While there were massive public demonstrations against the war, individual resistance also played a prominent part in the mounting protest. Some refused induction and went to jail; others fled to Canada or other countries rather than submit to the draft or jail; and others already in service, deserted. Captain Dale Noyd, a teacher at the Air Force Academy, attempted to resign because of conscientious objections to the Vietnam War specifically. The Air Force refused to accept his resignation and ordered him transferred to serve as an instructor to train pilots for Vietnam duty. According to the records, Noyd's resignation was rejected because it was "not considered to be in the best interest of the Air Force." Noyd refused to accept his new assignment, was court-martialed, found guilty, and sentenced to one year in jail, which he served in the form of house arrest. Noyd's subsequent appeal to the federal courts failed. This statement is from Noyd's original letter offering his resignation.

8 Dec. 66

1. I, Dale Edwin Noyd, Captain, FR28084, under paragraph 16m, AFR 36–12, hereby voluntarily tender my resignation from all appointments in the USAF. . . .

2b. I am opposed to the war that this country is waging in Vietnam; and for the past year—since it has become increasingly clear that I will not be able to serve out my obligation and resign from the Air Force—I have considered various stratagems that would obviate my participation in, and contribution to, that war. Among other alternatives, I have considered grounding myself or seeking an assignment other than in Southeast Asia. But these choices were not an honest confrontation of the issues and they do not do justice to my beliefs. The hypocrisy of my silence and acquiescence must end—I feel strongly that it is time for me to demand more consistency between my convictions and my behavior. Several months ago I came to a decision that would reflect this consistency and sought counsel on what alternatives I might have. This letter is a result of that decision. . . .

2c. Increasingly I find myself in the position of being highly involved and *caring* about many moral, political, and social issues—of which the war in Vietnam is the most important—and yet I cannot protest and work to effect some change. Not only may my convictions remain unexpressed and the concomitant responsibilities unfulfilled, but I am possibly confronted with fighting in a war that I believe to be unjust, immoral, and which makes a mockery of both our constitution and the charter of the United Nations—and the human values which they represent. Apart from the moral and ethical issues, and speaking only from the point of view of the super-patriot, it is a stupid war and pernicious to the self-interest of the United States. I am somewhat reluctant to attempt an analysis of the role of this country in the affairs of Southeast Asia for two reasons: First, I have nothing to say that has not been eloquently stated by men such a Senators Fulbright and Morse, U Thant, Fall, Sheehan, Morgenthau, Goodwin, Scheer, Terrill, Raskin, Lacouture, and, of course, the spokesmen for most of the nations of the free world; and secondly, any brief statement almost of necessity will hazard the same defects that have been characteristic of our foreign policy and its public debate—simplistic and obfuscated by cliches and slogans. Nevertheless, because of the gravity of my circumstances and the unusual nature of my resignation, I shall state some of the observations and premises from which I have made my judgments. First of all, in a nation that pretends to an open and free society, hypocrisy and subterfuge have pervaded our conduct and policy in Southeast Asia at least since 1954. This is not only in relations with the Vietnamese and in our pronouncements to

From U.S. District Court, Denver, Colorado, *Noyd* v. *McNamara,* Secretary of Defense, et al., 1967, Records and Briefs. Material suggested by B. Alan Dickson.

the other nations of the world, but also with the American people. One need look no further than our public statements in order to detect this. I insist on knowing what my government is doing and it is clear that this right has been usurped. Although I am cognizant that an open society may have its disadvantages in an ideological war with a totalitarian system, I do not believe that the best defense of our freedoms is an emulation of that system. . . .

2g. It is an immoral war for several sets of reasons. It is not only because our presence is unjustified and for what we are doing to the Vietnamese—as I have discussed above—but also because of our "sins" of omission. This country is capable of achieving for its people, and encouraging in other nations, enormous social advancement, but we are now throwing our riches—both of material and of purpose—into the utter waste of the maelstrom of increasing military involvement. If we as a nation really care about people, then we had best make concepts like freedom and equality *real* to all our citizens—and not just political sham—before we play policeman to the world. Our rightousness is often misplaced. Our behavior in Vietnam is immoral for another set of reasons which concern our conduct of that war. As many newsmen have witnessed, time and again we have bombed, shelled, or attacked a "VC village" or "VC structures" and when we later appraise the results, we label dead adult males as "VC" and add them to the tally—and fail to count the women and children. Our frequent indiscriminate destruction is killing the innocent as well as the "guilty." In addition, our left-handed morality in the treatment of prisoners is odious—we turn them over to the ARVN for possible torture or execution with the excuse that we are not in command but are only supporting the South Vietnam government. Again, this hypocrisy needs no explication. Also frighteningly new in American morality is the pragmatic justification that we must retaliate against the terrorist tactics of the VC. Perhaps most devastatingly immoral about the war in Vietnam are the risks we are assuming for the rest of the world. Each new step and escalation appears unplanned and is an attempt to rectify previous blunders by more military action. The consequences of our course appear too predictable, and although we as a people may elect "better dead than red," do we have the right to make this choice for the rest of mankind?

2h. I am not a pacifist; I believe that there are times when it is right and necessary that a nation or community of nations employ force to deter or repel totalitarian agression. My three-year assignment in an operational fighter squadron—with the attendant capacity for inflicting terrible killing and destruction—was based on the personal premise that I was serving a useful deterent purpose and that I would never be used as an instrument of agression. This, of course, raises the important and pervasive question for me: What is my duty when I am faced with a conflict between my conscience and the commands of my government? What is my responsibility when there is an irreparable division between my beliefs in the ideals of this nation and the conduct of my political and military leaders? The problem of ultimate loyalty is not one for which there is an easy solution. And, unfortunately, the issues are most often obscured by those who would undermine the very freedoms they are ostensibly defending—by invoking "loyalty" and "patriotism" to enforce conformity, silence dissent, and protect themselves from criticism. May a government or nation be in error? Who is to judge? As Thoreau asked, "Must the citizen ever for a moment, or in the least degree, resign his conscience, to the legislator? Why has every man a conscience, then? I think that we should be men first, and subjects afterward. It is not desirable to cultivate a respect for the law, so much as for the right. The only obligation which I have a right to assume, is to do at any time what I think right. . . . Law never made men a whit more just; and, by means of their respect for it, even the well-disposed are daily made the agents of injustice." The individual *must* judge. We as a nation expect and demand this—we have prosecuted and condemned those who forfeited their personal sense of justice to an immoral authoritarian system. We have despised those who have pleaded that they were only doing their job. If we are to survive as individuals in this age of acquiescence, and as nations in this time of international anarchy, we must resist total enculturation so that we may stand aside to question and evaluate—not as an Air Force officer or as an American, but as a member of the human species. This resistance and autonomy is difficult to acquire and precarious to maintain, which perhaps explains its rarity. Camus puts it succinctly: "We get into the habit of living before acquiring the habit of thinking." We must not confuse dissent with disloyalty and we must recognize that consensus is no substitute for conscience. As Senator Fulbright has stated, "Criticism is more than a right; it is an act of patriotism—a higher form of patriotism, I believe, than the familiar ritual of national adulation. All of us have the responsibility to act upon this higher patriotism which is to love our country less for what it is than for what we would like it to be." . . .

2j. I have attempted to sincerely state the values and beliefs that are both most meaningful in my life and relevant to my present dilemma. It would appear that I am no longer a loyal Air Force officer if this loyalty requires unquestioning obedience to the policies of this nation in Vietnam. I cannot honestly wear the uniform of this country and support unjust and puerile military involvement. Although it may be inconsistent, I have been able to justify (or rationalize) my position here at the Academy by my belief that my contribution in the classroom has had more effect in encouraging rationalism, a sense of humanism, and the development of social consciousness than it has had in the inculcation of militarism. My system of ethics is humanistic—simply a respect and love for man and confidence in his capability to improve his condition. This is my ultimate loyalty. And, as a man trying to be free, my first obligation is to my own integrity and conscience, and this is of course not mitigated by my government's permission or command to engage in immoral acts. I am many things before I am a citizen of this country or an Air Force officer; and included among these things is simply that I am a man with a set of human values which I will not abrogate. I must stand on what I am and what I believe. The war in Vietnam is unjust and immoral, and if ordered to do so, I shall refuse to fight in that war. I should prefer, and respectfully request, that this resignation be accepted. . . .

The agony of amnesty

As direct American military participation in the Vietnam War ended, bitter controversies erupted over the question of amnesty for those who had deserted or refused induction. President Richard M. Nixon steadfastly refused to consider amnesty and claimed that only "a few hundred" resistors had failed to serve. An estimate published in the *New York Times* on January 30, 1973, however, contended there were 10,000 draft resistors in jail or on probation; 80,000 draft resistors underground in the United States; between 60,000 to 100,000 draft resistors or deserters in exile; and nearly 400,000 veterans with less-than-honorable discharges. Nixon and Vice President Spiro Agnew continually insisted that these people were criminals and must fully pay the penalty for their actions. Agnew's disgrace and resignation, coupled with President Gerald Ford's pardon of Nixon for all his Watergate-related crimes, finally forced the government to introduce a limited amnesty policy in September 1974. A sample of the national disunity over amnesty appears next, taken from congressional hearings in March 1974.

Testimony of Fred E. Darling, Executive Coordinator, Military and Veterans Affairs, Noncommissioned Officers Association of the United States of America. . .

Mr. DARLING. Mr. Chairman and members of the distinguished subcommittee.

The Non-Commissioned Officers Association of the United States of America, NCOA, and the Marine Corps League welcome the opportunity to testify in opposition to any and all legislative proposals introduced in Congress that will grant amnesty or earned immunity to draft evaders and armed forces deserters of the Vietnam conflict.

From U. S. House of Representatives, Hearings before the Subcommittee on Courts, Civil Liberties, and the Administration of Justice of the Committee on the Judiciary, *Amnesty,* 93rd Congress, 2nd session, 8, 11, 13 March 1974, pp. 394–396, 527–531.

The positions of the NCOA and the Marine Corps League were unanimously mandated by their membership assembled in convention. The association, representing 160,000 plus members, is the world's largest enlisted military association, and its mandate was ratified on the 20th day of April 1973, at San Antonio, Tex. The league, congressionally chartered and composed of 16,000 active, retired, reserve and veteran Marines, ratified its resolution in August 1973, at Miami, Fla.

The NCOA's and the Marine Corps League's viewpoints are contained in the attached position paper available for the subcommittee's perusal at its earliest convenience. The paper was prepared by Mr. "Mack" McKinney, a retired sergeant major of Marines, who is the NCOA director of legislative affairs and the league's national legislative officer.

The comments contained therein expand somewhat on a commentary delivered by Mr. McKinney on a recent television newscast originating from WTOP–TV, Channel 9, Washington, D.C. Mr. McKinney offered these remarks on February 5, 1974, in rebuttal to a previous "News 9" commentary by Mr. Hugh Sidey on January 27, 1974, advocating amnesty. It is also an exhibit to the attached position paper.

With your kind permission, the commentary will be read at this time.

The Non-Commissioned Officers Association of the United States of America, composed of 160,000 plus noncommissioned and petty officers of the U.S. Armed Forces, 85 percent of which are on active duty as career-enlisted military members, is opposed to granting amnesty to those men who avoided the draft or deserted the armed forces during the Vietnam conflict.

We have listened to many appeals, everything from, "They were too young to realize the error of their ways," to, "It has been done before, so let's do it again." But to any and all please, we can only say, "Humbug."

These men are criminals, just as certain as one who commits or contributes to murder, or at least homicide. Their refusal to be drafted, or to go into or remain in combat, caused others to be drafted, sent into combat as their replacements, and possibly wounded, maimed, or killed.

There is only one way to deal with these men, and that is through due process of the law. They may return and lend their pleas of extenuating circumstances—if there are any—to their cases before a competent judge and jury. If the latter feels they are or are not criminally liable, then justice has been accomplished.

But to let them return to the country they have shunned, and possibly serve in the armed forces when there is little or no chance of being shot at by an enemy, is a slap in the face to the millions of men who were drafted, who were wounded, who were maimed, or who were killed in a bloody, unpopular war.

To further excuse these men because of youthful age bears no rationale to recent congressional action allowing 18-year-olds the right to vote. If they are old enough to vote, they are old enough to serve their Nation.

The good God calls upon us to be merciful—to forgive our trespassers—but he did not mention amnesty. Our mercy and our forgiveness can be granted through the present judicial system.

In conclusion the NCO Association and the Marine Corps League respectfully extend their appreciation for the Chair's indulgence and sincerely hope that the distinguished subcommittee will uphold the honor and dignity of our Nation's military and veteran patriots. . . .

Testimony of Mrs. Peg Mullen, State Chairman, Iowa Gold Star Families. . .

Mrs. MULLEN. Thank you. My son, Michael Mullen, was killed 4 years ago in Vietnam by our own artillery. He was killed, in military terminology, by "friendly fire" and was, therefore, a "nonbattle casualty" because of an artillery incident officially referred to as a "misadventure" in a war that was undeclared. He was 25 years old.

Now, we are a very ordinary family, we are just simple Iowa farmers, and we are not hampered or confused by the political considerations, nor the political motivations, nor political expediences that you are, so we can speak plainly. We know and can accept what you politicians are still simply unwilling to admit and that is that the war in Vietnam which took our son was a senseless, terrible, tragic blunder and now we see that you want to compound this mistake by punishing further those young men who refused to be deluded by your war from the beginning.

Gentlemen, the whole Vietnam war was a misadventure. We are all its nonbattle casualties. Only those who have lost sons and husbands and brothers in Vietnam can understand the depth of the anguish and the bitterness my son's death makes me feel. I want to believe—I desperately need to believe that my son's life was not wasted, that he died for some higher ideal, but what comfort have you given me?

If Congress is going to insist on misinterpreting "amnesty" as meaning to pardon, then the amnesty issue will remain too emotionally charged ever to be resolved. A pardon implies guilt, and I would no more expect a young man who refused to kill in Vietnam, whose profound moral and spiritual opposition to that war left him no alternative but to leave the country, to admit that he was guilty of a crime, than I would expect Congress, than I would expect you, whose support of that war permitted it to endure for so long, at so dreadful a cost in young lives, to admit that it, too, was guilty of a crime.

Amnesty, in its original Greek, meant forgetfulness. Forget that these young men left rather than serve. Forget the draft inequities that forces them to leave. Forget the lies—and I repeat the lies—told you by the Presidents, the generals, the spokesmen for the State Department and the Pentagon. Forget all the moral and philosophical dilemmas posed by the war in Vietnam which tore this Nation apart for over a dozen years. Remember only this: the American people have suffered enough because of this war and we want our children home.

Vietnam's dilemmas cannot be resolved, but only a fool still believes "My Country, right or wrong." We all now understand that if our country is wrong, we, as citizens, have an obligation to correct it. Who is the more loyal citizen: the one who agonizes over his Nation's policies and attempts to change them? Or is docile acceptance of governmental policy—no matter how immoral and misguided—the more acceptable, the truer mark of a loyal citizen? If it is the former, then you cannot and must not punish those young American citizens whose unwillingness to take part in the war in Vietnam was based on a higher sense of allegiance and responsibility to America's ideals. If it is the latter, if the mark of good citizenship is docile submission to governmental policy, then all those convicted and imprisoned and executed at Nuremberg for war crimes should have been freed.

In 1964 the American people voted for that Presidential candidate whom they believe would most swiftly bring that war to a close. Six years, 6 long years, before my son's death an overwhelming majority of the American people expressed by that vote they wished no further involvement in the Vietnam war. If you interpret these young men who refused to serve in Vietnam as having abandoned America in her time of need, then I ask you—did you not, yourselves, as the duly elected representatives subject to the will of the American people, by allowing that war to go on and on and on, abandon us in our time of need?

What difference is there between a government which forces its dissidents to seek exile, and a government which exiles its dissidents? Today, Canada, Sweden, and Europe, the world is filled with a generation of young American Solzhenitsyns. If I am to believe that my son sacrificed his life for some higher ideal, if I am to receive any comfort from my son's death, then let me believe that he died so that some other mother's son, somewhere, might now come home. . . .

Mr. MEZVINSKY. Mrs. Mullen, in telling us of the circumstances surrounding your son's death, you made a very eloquent statement. As you ended your testimony you said that you hope he died so that some other mother's son somewhere might now come home.

Would you care to elaborate on that ending and why you feel so deeply that there is a connection between your son's death and the question of amnesty?

Mrs. MULLEN. Well, I feel that almost everyone that testified against amnesty continuously talks about the mothers and fathers who lost sons and how they feel.

How many of you know how we feel? How many of you talked to fathers and mothers that actually lost sons?

We really know the anguish of a son being gone and in my heart I feel that these men that died in Vietnam, when they died, they are not thinking of dying for their country. They are dying and fighting to save their own lives. They kill. My son became a killer because he did not want to die there. He did not become a killer in Vietnam because of his country.

And this is what all of you seem to forget. There are no heroes in a foxhole in Vietnam. There are none as far as this country is concerned.

And they are just as unpatriotic at that stage as the man who ran away.

And I think if the dead could come back from their graves, the issue could be settled immediately. . . .

Mrs. MULLEN. Could I say one more thing? May I please?

Mr. KASTENMEIER. Yes.

Mrs. MULLEN. I was hoping someone would ask me about the inequities of the draft system. This is the basis of the whole thing. It has always been interesting to me in following the war—and I had been following it long before my son died—that not a Senator lost a son in Vietnam, not a Congressman lost a son in Vietnam, not a President lost a son in Vietnam, no Ambassador in Vietnam. Where did they come from, these citizen soldiers?

He came from the farm. He came from the ghetto. He came from the mountains of West Virginia.

I visited a lady in West Virginia whose son died with my son. They lived outside of Pittsburgh. It was 32 miles from the hill to his home. The boy probably had not even heard of Vietnam. When I visited with her, she told me three of those boys on the hill had died in 90 days.

A month later I was in Washington lobbying for 609 and I spent quite a lot of time trying to see Senator Hugh Scott. I was unable to see him, but I did visit at length with a great many of his aides, who were all very young and asked each and every one why they were not in the service and they quickly said they had CO's.

The boys on the top of the hill did not even know what the word CO meant. Do you know that in the State of Pennsylvania that if you were employed by a large industry, like Bethlehem Steel, Inland Steel, Alleghany, that if you were sweeping the floor, you had an automatic deferment?

I think these are the things that you must realize. If you are asking a handful of boys to give 2 more years to their country, how about the millions of people who knew somebody?

Thank you. . . .

CHAPTER 19

Tensions of the 1970s: still looking for the promised land

Prosperity for whom?

The needs of World War II and the release of consumer demands in the postwar period produced nearly thirty years of unparalleled prosperity for most Americans, interrupted only by several recessions touching isolated segments of the society. But by the early 1970s, the steady, rapid growth of the gross national product stalled, and the economy reflected alarming signs of distress and sluggishness. High prices, high interest rates, rising inflation, and most significant, the scarcity of jobs unleashed growing concern for the future. The effects of the slowdown have had a special impact on young people hopeful of professional careers or a place in the work force. The first two selections offer a statement by a recently organized labor coalition outlining its views on the necessity for shortening the work week to increase jobs. The third selection relates the difficulties of those attempting to find a place as industrial workers and who have found their opportunities restricted by both reduced demand and priorities assigned to senior workers and special minorities. The author was a former staff worker for the United Automobile Workers.

A Shorter Work Week

Greetings:

On October 25, 1977, Local Union Leaders representing a quarter million members founded the All Unions' Committee to Shorten the Work Week and decided to call the First National All Unions' Conference to Shorten the Work Week. . . .

[A] shorter work week with no cut in pay is not an idle dream. New technology has changed it into an idea whose time has come, as across the country, in shop after shop and in union after union, a mighty demand for shorter hours is developing. Because a new rash of plant and business closings, coupled with cutbacks in public employment, have added to the alarming loss of jobs and declines in membership that affect local union after local union in industry after industry. No worker's job is safe, as even the strongest unions have been unable to fully protect their members from the massive slaughter of jobs.

Despite thirty years of collective bargaining and legislative effort, nearly 10

From "All Unions' Committee to Shorten the Work Week," Pamphlet File, State Historical Society of Wisconsin. Used by permission of the director.

million workers are unemployed or underemployed while our nation suffers from inadequate housing, poor schools and deteriorating health. Long-term unemployment, falling most heavily on those whose living standards are already the lowest, places an intolerable burden on our nation's economy and an unnecessary load on working taxpayers. It is destroying the moral fabric of our nation, the mental and physical health of millions and eroding the base of both private and public retirement programs.

These jobs cannot be found elsewhere, as the continued introduction of new machinery and new processes perpetuates the stagnation that has marked the job market for a quarter of a century.

Thus the labor movement faces a new challenge: To create and preserve jobs for all who need and want them.

Historically, organized labor has fought for shorter hours as the best means of creating jobs and reducing unemployment. Our labor movement was born in the battle for shorter hours. It grew to maturity in the campaigns that reduced the work week by thirty-five percent in the first forty years of the twentieth century. But for all intent and purpose, the movement for shorter hours has lain dormant. There has been no significant decrease in the hours of labor for forty years and, worse yet, the companies have increased the eight hour day, forty hour standard through a concerted campaign of compulsory overtime.

Many International Unions—AFL-CIO and independent—have taken convention action in support of a reduction in hours. All of this activity must be continued. It must be multiplied and re-enforced at every opportunity.

But something more is necessary if the desire and demand of millions of workers is to be transformed into legislative and collective bargaining campaigns to reduce the hours of labor. New ways must be found and new movements must be built to fire the imagination and unleash the strength of the entire labor movement.

The Founders of the All Unions' Committee to Shorten the Work Week has accepted that challenge. We have begun to build a national movement to carry on the educational, economic, legislative and electoral activities necessary to reduce the hours of labor. We have committed ourselves and the resources of our local unions to building that movement.

We call upon every local union—upon the leaders of labor and union members without regard to craft, industry or affiliation, to pick up the torch. We call upon all of organized labor to join us on April 11, 1978 at the First National All Unions' Conference to Shorten the Work Week. We invite your local union to join this campaign.

Fraternally,
FRANK RUNNELS, President
For the Officers, Sterring Committee and Founders
of the All Unions' Committee to Shorten the Work Week

Unemployment and Jobs

The Problem

The following statistics reflect the great challenge that each of us face in helping create jobs for the millions of people who desperately need them: (Figures taken from U.S. Government Sources):

At the end of World War II, the "official" rate of unemployment stood at somewhere around 2%. The rate has gone up and down but, since 1970, it has never dropped below 5%. In November 1977, the official rate of unemployment stood at 6.9%.

An official 6.9 rate means that approximately 7 million people were out of work. Of those nearly 7 million workers, 5,226,000 were white and 1,599,000 were "black and others"; 3,459,000 were men and 3,359,000 of them were women.

Although census shows that the number of men and women in this country is roughly equal, the RATE of unemployment for women was 8.2% and for men it was 5.9%. This disproportionate rate of unemployment is reflected in other categories also. The official unemployment rate for white workers last November was 6.0% and for "blacks and others" it was 13.8%. The same holds true for young workers. Although there are three times as many white youth between the ages of 16 and 19 out of work, the unemployment rate for white youth is "only" 14.5% while the rate of unemployment is 39.0% for "blacks and other" youths.

The Answer

An idea whose time has come—how shorter hours create jobs

As of August 1977, there were 34,500,000 full-time workers who worked 40 hours and 20,500,000 workers on longer work weeks for a total of 55,000,000. (U.S. BLS, Employment and Earnings, September 1977.)

If the work week of the 55,000,000 working 40 hours or more was cut by one hour, 1,400,000 new jobs would be added.

If the work week of these 55,000,000 workers was reduced by 5 hours, 7,850,000 new jobs would be created.

If the work week was reduced by 8 hours, then 13,700,000 new jobs would be created.

Up Against the Wall You Old Etcetera

. . . [Y]oung workers are acting up. . . . But the gratuitous suggestion that young workers are talking back to their elders and betters because they do not know any better and won't listen to the voice of men who have been there is the expression of an attitude that is the source of the grievances of young people across the society, students, workers, blacks, and for that matter Democrats. It is also an elegant evidence of the . . . observation that young people are a minority with the usual minority grievances, unfair discrimination in the matter of rewards and priviliges, a denial of representation in the government of their society, and finally unwilling audiences to the traditional declarations of the people in power that those who are demanding representation are too young, too inexperienced, too ignorant, too unprepared, and in general too damned insolent to merit serious consideration, young people, black people, female people, and working people.

Against the claim that young workers strike to the embarrassment of their elder betters because they have never met a payroll or walked a picket line in the winter of 1938, there is clearly visible in the work situation and in available economic data evidence that young workers have serious causes for complaint.

Within the union structure itself, neither the local unions nor the national and international unions begin to give young people the representation in the rule of the union they are entitled to on the basis of their numbers, the basis for feminine and black claims to additional representation. No one on the Executive Council, . . . no one on the International Executive Board of the UAW [United Automobile Workers] qualifies as a youth anywhere except perhaps in the Young Democrats where the cutoff age is 45.

Seniority, the increasing tenaciousness of the aged, the instinct of people who have jobs in a bureaucracy account for the fact that the labor movement has become a presbyterian society or perhaps what might be called a gerontocracy. The movement which rejects the view that seniority qualifies superannuated Dixiecrats for chairmanships in the key Congressional committees might turn its attention to the problem of trade union arteriosclerosis.

On the job, young workers understandably, especially in their earliest days in the plant, resent the operation of the seniority system, and frequently claim that the local union leadership and plant management, are an establishment in league against them in the matter of the distribution of overtime, promotions, desirable transfers, and in the understanding of grievances connected with low seniority, for example work on the second and third shift. Unquestionably the history of the trade union movement is a powerful argument for the strongest possible seniority protection, except that other security provisions, and full employment conceivably might make it possible for new provisions in the plant which might give young people an opportunity under some circumstances, that are clearly set down, to bypass seniority restraints to make possible the utilization of a particular talent, to facilitate an education program, or when older

From Lewis Carliner, "Illegal to Discriminate against Blacks, Jews, Catholics, Women, and the Old, but It Is Still Legal to Deny Young People Equal Incomes, Equal Opportunities, Equal Rights, and Equal Privileges. Short Title——Up against the Wall You Old Etcetera" (unpublished hectograph typescript), Archives of Labor History and Urban Affairs, Wayne State University, Vertical File, ca. 1973. Used by permission of Mr. Carliner.

workers might want to swap places in the layoff scheme as the result of the SUB [Supplemental Unemployment Benefits] operation.

An important discontinuity in plants which mock the pretention of older workers to knowing more and being wiser than younger workers is the disparity in education as between the young and aged. In 1940 for example the average American over 25 had completed 8.6 years of schooling, by 1950 years of schooling had risen to 9.3 years, by 1960 it had reached 10.6. At the present time the greater number of new hires are high school graduates, many have university training, and in general they are substantially better educated formally than the people who deny them representation in the union.

Both the statistics compiled by the UAW and BLS [Bureau of Labor Statistics] figures demonstrate the importance of what might be called these demographic facts to unions and the situation among workers, young and old. Each year now some three million people enter the labor force and of these one third of the men and about one fifth of the women go to work in factories. In 1960 there were slightly more than 13 million people in the labor force under 25, by 1970 this figure will have increased to almost 20 million. Workers over 45 will increase about 18.5 percent in the same period, while workers in the 35 to 44 age group will decline. In a sense the leaders of the labor movement will have to deal very soon with a constituency that is relatively old and relatively young, with the relatively young in the majority.

The testimony everywhere in the society, especially in the political society where the raw materials are the sense of grievance, is that young workers are subject to an intense agitation on the question of pensions and social security.

In the plant they are told, very often by foremen, but it is in the air, for in many ways the plant is the most intense forum for political ideas that exists in the country, that young workers are taxed out of wage increases to provide pensions for the older workers in the plant, many of them will never receive.

Outside the plant, Chambers of Commerce, employer organizations, right wing political organizations rain literature on the work place which insists that the social security program is a fraud on young workers, that payments equivalent to theirs simply deposited in a savings bank would pay them far more than they will ever receive in social security benefits, that the social security fund is bankrupt, and that they are being taxed to pay pensions to the aged today because of the bankruptcy of the social security fund. All these allegations are demonstrably untrue but increases in taxes for social security have evoked workers especially because their own economic situation is not well-understood by the labor movement, the government, or for that matter the young worker himself.

Apart from the poor, no group in the society is under greater economic pressure than young workers.

When a young worker is told by the older workers in the plant that things have never been so good, wages are higher, conditions are better, vacations are more satisfactory, the rest rooms cleaner, and life more beautiful for workers than ever before, and they the older workers won all this by their sacrifices and why don't these young punks show gratitude for what has come to them for nothing, the reply is often so what else is new, things are not all that good now. The truth is, for the younger worker things are not very good at all.

He spends on the average more than he earns and goes into debt each year. At the beginning of the 1960s he was going into debt on the average of $100 a year. The chances are he is going more deeply into debt now. He sees the money he is taxed for pensions and for social security as a wage deduction which would enable him to pay his bills and keep even.

Wealth and financial wellbeing in the American society are closely related to the age of the worker and to the age of his wife and children. In part this is because workers under 35 for the most part are married to women whose full-time occupation is raising children. In this period they are under the heaviest economic burden most Americans have to bear, at one time they are buying a home, often paying off the down payment on the house they borrowed, they are buying a car, furniture, appliances, paying for their children, hardly knowing from one payday to the next where they are going to get the money to keep the electric current on and the phone active.

As the children get into their teens their situation suddenly changes. The wife returns to work, the family income almost doubles, the house is substantially paid for, the installment accounts are paid off, bills are under control, and suddenly instead of pressure there is affluence, but by then the man is no longer a young worker, instead he is telling young workers they do not know how good they have it. . . .

The changing situation of the young worker growing old is revealed in Federal Reserve System statistics.

Familes headed by persons under 35 had total assets valued at $6,304 in 1963. This presents equity in the car, in the house, investments, insurance, and all the other miscellaneous ways people accumulate assets. Scaled down by age, it is obvious that the assets of a family with the head of the family aged 25, one baby born and another on the way, come to very nearly nothing. Families with heads in the 35 to 44 age group are better off, total average assets of $16,008 with some $3,541 invested, and with liquid assets of almost $5,000. Things are even better, financially for the 55 to 64 year old group, essentially the men who are to be the beneficiaries of the social security tax and the pension deduction the hard up young worker is making. The resources of the people who are about to retire averaged $32,527 in 1963 and they had, among other valuable assets, some $12,212 in investments, and $6,401 in liquid assets.

The grievance is double in this case, the young worker is under an impossible financial burden, and part of it due to the fact that he is told he must forego pay to provide for the far more well-to-do older worker. Moreover this grievance in recent years has been compounded by the operation of inflation, which on the whole has benefitted American workers, but which in this case constantly presents to the young worker the evidence of a house that sold two years ago for three-four-or-five thousand dollars less than he is being asked. In addition the mortgage he must undertake exacts a usurious seven and seven and a half per-cent in comparison with the four and five and six percent mortgages the older workers are paying off. No wonder it seems to him that the entire society is a seniority swindle designed to victimize the young worker.

Young workers in Sweden, Great Britain, Japan, and a number of other countries are not tied in a bind that compels them to resent the pensions paid older workers. They receive housing assistance, grants on marriage, family allowances, and a variety of services that help them surmount the mountainous costs of raising a young family.

Unions and political parties responsive to the needs of young constituents long ago should have brought in a program to meet these problems. Yet in fact the student loans offered today would in fact add a further burden to the weight of being a young father, worker, householder.

What could be offered might be very long term loans for young families with minimal payments in the first fifteen years, but with higher payments in the last twenty five years when inflation and the combination of economic factors which benefit the aged would operate to reduce the required payments to a nominal charge.

Possibly social security could be tied to family assistance programs for young people, down payments on a house, interest subventions, grants to buy fur-niture and appliances, allowances for each child, so that the social security tax, and pension deduction are combined with benefits to the young as well as the old.

The unions should explore collective bargaining ventures aimed at relieving the pressure on young people. But most important, the society and the labor movement should move to admit the young into the government of the society. Otherwise the establishment may be confronted from another direction in the Society by the cry, up against the wall you old gerontocrats. . . .

Preserving the family farm

From Thomas Jefferson's day, the glorification of the "yeoman ideal" has been an important element in American thought. The yeoman symbolized the virtues of independence, hardiness, and honesty that at once marked him as an individual and as a valued member of the community. Mechanization, increased capital costs, taxation, and large-scale competition, however, have made farming a precarious enterprise in modern America. As corporate-owned farms (agribusinesses) have multiplied, politicians and farmers' organizations have struggled for the means to preserve the "family farm." As the testimony below indicates, governmental attempts to rationalize the marketplace through crop control can have completely unanticipated side effects.

Mr. HERMES. I am J. C. Hermes, route 4, Hallettsville, near Sweet Home. I am not here for any gifts or handouts or anything like that. I want to work for what I have to make to support my family. There are four of us in the family and the fifth is expected. With a 4½-acre cotton allotment for 4 in the family, which was cut from 5 last year, and with, I believe, a three-tenths acre peanut allotment, and on land which I couldn't get a thresher on, 20 acres in cultivation, with 50½ acres on the farm, if any of you gentlemen could tell me how to make a living on this farm with a cotton allotment and peanut allotment like that, I would appreciate it very much and take your hand in doing so.

Thank you. . . .

Mr. BASS. Mr. Chairman, the gentleman asks us for a solution. The reason we are here is not to give you a solution, as to the problems on your farm, but we want your advice and for you to tell us what you think we can do and what kind of laws we can pass in answering your problem. So, as a farmer, as a man who is experienced in farming, can you tell us what you think the Congress should do, in order to make it better for people who are in your position?

Mr. HERMES. Well, my answer to that question would be that that was better than a 50-percent cut in my cotton allotment. I have a diversified farm, turkeys, no chickens, I raise turkeys for the market. I have 12 head of cattle, and on this farm, like in 1953, I had 8.16 acres of cotton, my peanut allotment never has been over an acre, my farm I purchased—which I have not paid for yet—and after the crop is harvested, I have to go to the bank to borrow money to make ends meet until I sell my turkeys in November. If I plant 8 or 10 acres of cotton, it would tide me over until when my turkeys come on, and I could make it on to next spring to plant another crop.

Mr. BASS. In other words, your answer to the problem then, that we have, is increased cotton acreage?

Mr. HERMES. Increased cotton acreage is right.

Mr. BASS. Thank you, Mr. Chairman.

From *Hearings on Family Farms*, Committee on Agriculture, House of Representatives, 84th Congress, 1st Session, pp. 13–16.

Mr. ABERNETHY. Mr. Chairman?

Mr. THOMPSON. Mr. Abernethy.

Mr. ABERNETHY. You have 4½ acres of cotton this year?

Mr. HERMES. Right.

Mr. ABERNETHY. How much did you have last year?

Mr. HERMES. Five.

Mr. ABERNETHY. That was in 1954?

Mr. HERMES. 1954.

Mr. ABERNETHY. How much did you have in 1953?

Mr. HERMES. 8.16.

Mr. ABERNETHY. How much did you have in 1952?

Mr. HERMES. In 1952 I believe I had 9 acres.

Mr. ABERNETHY. So you are now just about half of what you had in 1952?

Mr. HERMES. Fifty percent.

Mr. ABERNETHY. You have less than an acre in peanuts?

Mr. HERMES. Less than an acre in peanuts, which it doesn't pay me to plant.

Mr. ABERNETHY. That is right. How much acreage in peanuts had been planted on that farm last year?

Mr. HERMES. Last year? There haven't been any peanuts planted on there since 1950, when I moved on the place, because the allotment was so small it didn't pay me to fool with them.

Mr. ABERNETHY. The acreage you got for peanuts was taken out of the reserve because your farm did not have any?

Mr. HERMES. That is right.

Mr. ABERNETHY. I appreciate the fact—and I am sure everyone here does —that you have a problem, a serious problem, and particularly with regard to your peanut allotment. You appreciate the fact, however, that peanuts are one of those crops which has been overproduced.

Mr. HERMES. Right.

Mr. ABERNETHY. And, as a result of the overproduction, they had to cut the acreage back on those farms where it was already being produced—you understand that?

Mr. HERMES. Yes.

Mr. ABERNETHY. Now, if they gave an additional peanut acreage to you they would have to take it away from those people who have already been cut, would they not?

Mr. HERMES. That is right.

Mr. ABERNETHY. Whom would you suggest that they take it away from?

Mr. HERMES. I don't think they should take it away from anyone, because I have planted them. I have planted cotton, and that is my base. As far as peanuts, I never raised peanuts, and the allotment is so small—my place is not very big. If I could plant more cotton they wouldn't have to take peanuts away from anyone.

Mr. ABERNETHY. In other words, you do not feel that you have been discriminated against on your peanut allotment?

Mr. HERMES. No, sir.

Mr. ABERNETHY. Because you have not had any peanut history.

Mr. HERMES. No. The peanuts came out with a small allotment, and I forgot about them.

Mr. ABERNETHY. What is your feeling about reducing the price of cotton?

Mr. HERMES. Reducing the price of cotton? I don't know whether it should be reduced or not. If it were reduced, we wouldn't be getting the price for the cotton, and, as far as I can see, the places that are producing cotton by the hundreds of acres, say 100, 200, or 300 acres, they are the guys that are overdoing the markets. It is not the guy trying to make a living on the farm, producing 5, 6, or 7 or 10 bales. He is not hurting the market a bit.

Mr. ABERNETHY. How many acres could you work alone?

Mr. HERMES. Ten acres, with my wife and two children.

Mr. ABERNETHY. You know, we have a number of large farms throughout the country that have been cut. I do not know how it is out in Texas. I know in my State, but not particularly in my area, that is true. You just referred to a farm that had 100 or 200 acres of cotton. They have been cut, too, pretty badly, you know. They have been reduced in proportion. Well, they have been reduced in proportion to what you have been reduced. And the man that owns that farm could not work the whole hundred acres, or 200 or 300 acres himself. He had families living on the farm that worked it.

Now, if you took it away from him, what would become of those families?

Before you answer, I would like to call your attention that there were 55,000 tenant families put on the road this year as a result of the reduction in cotton, according to the estimates of the Department of Agriculture, that the committee furnished the Agriculture Subcommittee on Appropriations; 55,000 tenant families were put on the road this year as a result of reduction of cotton to the larger farmers.

Now, of course, if they took more acreage away from those people and gave it to the so-called family farmers there would be more tenant families put on the road. What are we going to do with them?

Mr. HERMES. Those tenant families are put on the farm, in my way of thinking—it is just like the farmer now being forced on the road by not being able to make it on the farm. They are all in the same boat.

Mr. ABERNETHY. That is right; they are. Since they are all in the same boat, naturally, some consideration has to be given to their status, do you not think?

Mr. HERMES. That is right. They should be given consideration.

Still, they could be, say, for instance, a family of my size, if I was a tenant farmer, if I was out and could get enough cotton to plant, I would be on my own. The big guy I would be working for, the man that plants from 500 to a thousand acres, he wouldn't be putting out that much, and these guys working for him would be able to get on their own, getting enough cotton to plant, and they would be on their own and wouldn't be working for the other man.

Mr. ABERNETHY. They would either be working for one man or another man somewhere else.

Mr. HERMES. It would be for theirselves. These guys working for these guys are probably working, to my way of thinking, for a salary. They are not working for a crop or acreage, or such as that. They are working for salary.

Mr. ABERNETHY. Can you tell me what the average cotton allotment per farm is in this county?

Mr. HERMES. No, sir; I have not read up on it that close.

Mr. ABERNETHY. Mr. Chairman, I ask for anyone here to answer that question.

Someone has an answer to that. What is the average allotment per farm?

Mr. THOMPSON. Yes. Stay right there where you are.

Mr. HANSLIK (Moulton, Tex.). I have an answer to what he just asked: "Why are they put out?"

Here is an article from a man in Mississippi. He raises over 1,800 acres of cotton, and right here he says that at the time land was producing 250 pounds of cotton to the acre it might have been profitable to split with the tenants, but now it isn't. With new practices, the soil produces $200 or more to the acre, so the owners would be paying the tenant $100 or more. For chopping and picking cotton on mechanized and day-labor setups, the chopping and picking is $35 an acre. These poor people raise that 100 acres of cotton producing a bale and a half an acre. They just can't afford to hold a tenant. That is why they put those renters on the road, because they are making too much money.

Mr. THOMPSON. We are trying to get a little different answer. We appreciate having that in the record. We are trying to get an answer to a different question.

Mr. ABERNETHY. I will pass it for the time being.

Mr. HERMES. This is your answer why the tenant is put on the road. The big producer is making too much money.

Mr. ABERNETHY. The gentleman may be correct. I do not know. I do not have that sized farmer in my section. The average cotton allotment in my area is about 8 acres per farm.

Mr. HANSLIK. The average is 13 acres in this county. . . .

Busing and Desegregation

After a decade of court-ordered school desegregation, largely in the South, *de facto* (as opposed to *de jure,* i.e., legally enforced) segregation remained, particularly in large northern cities. The situation reflected the reality of residential segregation practices in which there were clear, discernible ghetto lines. Proponents of desegregation argued that quality education for all could be achieved only by a breakdown of the neighborhood-school concept and the mixing of children from different areas. Opponents, acting from a variety of motives, focused their criticism on the use of busing as a tool to achieve racial balance. The following testimony presents both sides of the controversy to a congressional subcommittee considering a constitutional amendment to prohibit school busing for integration purposes.

Statement of Students for Quality Integrated Education, Pontiac, Mich.

Chairman CELLER. We welcome you here and would be glad to hear from your spokesman, Mr. Brad Jackson.

Mr. JACKSON. Thank you.

Chairman Celler and honorable members of the committee, we would like to thank you for the opportunity to appear and express our opinions regarding the integration of the Pontiac schools. We represent supporters of integrated education from Pontiac's two high schools and from three of the six junior high schools.

From our own personal experience we can say that we support integration as a means to equal opportunity in education and we recognize that without the Federal court order, Pontiac schools would still be segregated.

The opinions which we express are taken from our own experiences. We are speaking for oursleves and we do not claim to speak for all of the students of the Pontiac school district.

On the whole, the actual busing of students in Pontiac has been peaceful. To our knowledge, there have been no major incidents of violence as a result of intradistrict busing. Several of us have younger brothers and sisters who rather enjoy the ride to school with their classmates. To them it does not seem

From *School Busing,* Hearings, Subcommittee on Constitutional Amendments, House of Representatives, 92nd Congress, 2nd Session, pp. 707–08, 997–1000.

to be a significant inconvenience. Those of us in junior high school do not find the bus ride overly inconvenient, but on the contrary, worth the effort because it means better education and relationships for all of us.

Two unexpected advantages of additional busing include the availability of extra buses for extracurricular activities and the availability of transportation to some of us who previously had to arrange for our own transportation.

The inschool situation is much improved over previous years for blacks, whites, and Latin Americans. We believe that the academic atmosphere in each of our schools is generally challenging and interesting and plans are underway to strengthen the program. With the junior highs each having only one grade level per school, there is an opportunity to choose from a broader selection of curricular offerings. Programs offered under title I are also available to more students under the integration plan.

We feel that there have been many personal benefits to each of us from an integrated school program. Several misconceptions have been dispelled due to personal relationships with students from other areas of the city. The majority of students that we associate with and have spoken with have had positive experiences that they will carry with them for the remainder of their lives.

We all seem to agree that discipline in our respective schools this year has been more firm, more equitable, and more understanding. School administrators seem to feel more free to use one disciplinary standard for all students regardless of race. Some of us feel that in past years a double standard was frequently used in school discipline.

As far as inschool violence is concerned, we do not want to imply that there have not been troubles in some of our schools, but then that is not something new this year. Students, teachers, and administrators have told members of our group that the number of disturbances in the schools had dropped considerably since the beginning of the school year and that complaints are now no more frequent than in previous years.

Administrators of both of our high schools have stated recently that their schools are more peaceful and less tense than they have been in several years. Although high school students are not bused, we feel that the attitudes developed in the elementary and junior high schools will affect the atmosphere in the high schools as well.

Positive identification by police and others have confirmed that many of the disturbances outside the schools at the beginning of the school year were the result of outsiders—students from outlying school districts whose schools had not opened, out-of-school youth, picketing adults, even agitators from several miles away. As the school year progresses, tension in our schools continues to decrease notably.

We conclude, therefore, that:

First. The integration plan is providing more equal educational opportunities.

Second. The integration plan is succeeding in creating a better understanding among Pontiac students.

Third. The majority of the students, teachers, and administrators directly affected are working for the success of quality integrated education in Pontiac. In short, integration is working, and we won't want to go back to the old way.

Chairman CELLER. Do your parents know that you are down here and that you are making these statements?

Mr. JACKSON. Yes.

Chairman CELLER. Do they approve?

Mr. JACKSON. They discussed it with me, and I think they do.

Chairman CELLER. Was this statement that you have just read written by you?

Mr. JACKSON. Yes; it was written by a party of four students. . . .

Statement of Mrs. Larnell A. Cleveland, Rochester, N.Y.

I live at 566 Hayward Avenue in Rochester, a neighborhood which is thoroughly integrated. We do not own our house and cannot afford to buy. I have two daughters and a son, all teenagers, attending schools in the Rochester School District.

My husband and I voluntarily bused our youngest daughter for 3 years under the open enrollment plan to an integrated school. We do not belong to any antibusing organization or school organization although we sympathize with their cause.

I am here on behalf of myself and many, many parents and children of Rochester who are undergoing hardships and anxiety brought on by compulsory busing. This busing program separates brothers, sisters, and friends, and takes children long distances from their homes.

I am in favor of voluntary busing and voluntary transfer, but vehemently opposed to compulsory busing to achieve racial balance in our schools. Compulsory busing has polarized our cities. Mothers of children in bloth black and white schools do not want their children bused.

The ultraliberal or left is sympathetic to the cause of the anarchist whose goals are to demolish the social structure and undermine our Government which appears to be succeeding by the mere fact that I am here pleading for my constitutional right of freedom of choice guaranteed under our Constitution.

These inntercity parents are against busing when they see their children short-changed in education in order to pay $11 million this year alone for busing. Next year as more loans are implemented the busing costs will be greater. See exhibit 1 and 1-A, please.

And then also the cost of monitors who are actually riding shotgun. The citzenry of Rochester has been fighting this fight against the compulsory busing since 1967, at which time Superintendent Herman Goldberg introduced his park plan which included compulsory busing at a school board meeting at East High School.

The programs proposed by Mr. Goldberg were defeated and it was then the open enrollment and voluntary transfer program was born. The racial problems started in our schools thereafter.

After boycotts by both teachers and parents, violent outbreaks in the schools, the board still voted in the reorganization plan. In 1970, two elementary organization plans, A and C zone consisting of seven schools were implemented under the first phase of this plan.

All children involved in these zones were within walking distance. Under the reorganization plan, elementary schools were broken down into categories K–3 and 4–6, 7 through 8, and 9 through 12.

In reorganizing in this fashion, it compelled children to walk farther distances from home and at the same time pass their neighborhood school on their long journey to reorganized schools.

It was explained to the community by Commissioner Thomas Frey that this was an experimental program that had to be evaluated before implementing further zones. Exhibit 2. But in 1971, the following year, they implemented the junior and senior high schools and one more elementary zone.

Rochester consists of 36.44 square miles and a school population of over 44,000 children. Due to its peculiar geographical shape, the bus runs up to 45 minutes one way in good weather, so gentlemen, you can imagine the time involved in rainy or snowy weather. Under poor conditions and good conditions buses run late and children are left standing in rain or snow and zero temperature.

In view of this fact and the fact that oftentimes children miss a bus, truancy has spiraled upward. Parents and children are underoing hardships because of busing due to the early hour a child has to arise in the morning. He gets home late and he is therefore unable to participate in extracurricular activities.

Parents who have more than one child often find their program in as many as five different schools. Reorganization's prime function was to integrate our schools through busing. It has failed miserably. Our schools were never segregated. Racially imbalanced, yes, but never segregated.

Today we have "segregated" integrated schools. Blacks remain with blacks, whites with whites, Puerto Ricans with Puerto Ricans, on the buses, in classes, assembly, and in the cafeteria.

Coercion in any program will lead only to failure. Where we used to have a student union, now we have black, white, and Puerto Rican student unions. Many in Rochester came into existence during violent times.

In my opinion we have three armies in school, white, black, and Puerto Rican. They were formed out of fear. Our youth is frightened. The hatred is kindled by the school's double standard set up by teachers and administrators. Unity, gentlemen, the word unity is dead as long as we are talking color and making laws in color.

As soon as the statement has to be prefaced with a word, white, black, or Puerto Rican, you imply that white, black, or Puerto Rican cannot trust each other and this has happened in our school.

In September the Rochester schools expected 45,000 children but they lacked 1,500. The dropout situation has spiraled. 1,500 in the first 2 months. The Rochester School District has been involved for many years in many federally funded and locally funded experimental programs.

The children in our community have been guinea pigs tested with programs that cannot be evaluated. Quality integrated education is education in which all children of all people go to first-rate schools. . . .

In speaking of desegregation and integration, we often lose sight of what these mean within the context of a free, open, pluralistic society. We cannot be free and at the same time be required to fit our lives into prescribed places on a racial grid, whether segregated or integrated and whether by some mathematical formula or assignment.

An open society does not have to be homogeneous or fully integrated. Especially in a Nation like America it is natural and right that we have Italian or Irish or Negro or Norwegian neighborhoods. It is a natural and right thing that members of these communities feel a sense of group identity and group pride.

The right and ability of each person to decide for himself where and how he wants to live, whether as part of the ethnic enclave or as part of a larger society or, as many do, share the life of both.

I have a quote in here by Robert Kennedy or words to that effect but I would like to say over 150 years ago President Thomas Jefferson said that if our Republic ever falls, it will be the fault of the Federal judiciary.

The time has come for you, the legislature, to realize that now is the time for you to assert yourself and live up to your responsibilities and desires of your constituents, the purpose for which you were elected. Any further usurpation of your prerogatives by the Supreme Court would be complete capitulation on your part. The end result would well be the disruption of our Republic.

An amendment to the Constitution is needed to prevent capricious and arbitrary decisions by appointed state and federal officials from overruling locally elected officials. . . .

Consumer activism

In the early twentieth century, the federal and state governments assumed an active role in consumer protection. The Pure Food and Drug Act of 1906 represented the first notable attempt to inspect, regulate, and approve the quality of products for consumers. Through the years, however, consumer-oriented lobby groups have complained that inadequate financing and inadequate administration too often has permitted impure, harmful products to enter the market. The exposure of the dangerous effects of the drug thalidomide in 1961 highlighted the value of effective evaluation by independent government agencies. In the sixties and seventies, consumer lobbies, largely led by "public interest" lawyers such as Ralph Nader, exerted increased pressure for more product-safety legislation. Perhaps the most notable achievements have been in the area of automobile regulation. Still, administrative efforts seemed inadequate; consequently, volunteer groups have proliferated to publicize and police dangerous products or misleading advertising. The following selections offer examples of such activities.

December 6, 1972

Dear Toy Store Owner:

You are probably aware of the growing concern of parents and consumers over the manufacture and widespread sale of dangerous toys. In the past this concern has been sporadic and short-lived, o brief flurry of protest which dies out immediately after Christmas and does not revive until the following year. The Central New York Public Interest Research Group intends to make this periodic focus on dangerous toys a year-round concern. Toward this end, CNY-PIRG, together with a number of concerned parents from the Syracuse area, has formed a Dangerous Toy Committee to insure that all those connected with the toy industry share in the joint responsibility of protecting our children from serious and occasionally fatal toy-related injuries.

The concern for dangerous toys is not to be taken lightly. Every year, an estimated 40,000 children are maimed or crippled and another 29,000 blinded by their seemingly harmless playthings. As a retailer, you are in a position to

From Wisconsin Public Interest Research Group Papers, State Historical Society of Wisconsin. Used by permission of the director.

exercise considerable influence over the manufacturers who have put financial gain before the public interest. If enough storeowners decide to act, and to act forcefully, we can begin to pressure the marginal manufacturers who are producing dangerous and deceptively packaged toys, and at the same time provide strong economic incentives to the makers of safe toys.

At the federal level, the Food and Drug Administration's Bureau of Product Safety has been shown to be grossly negligent in enforcing toy safety laws. We hold the FDA ultimately responsible for the current situation, and intend to work for stronger legislation and better enforcement, but it is clear that government cannot and will not solve the problem. Your active efforts can make a difference in convincing manufacturers to concern themselves with better design and construction of toys.

We have found what we believe to be FDA banned toys on your store shelves. If you find some of these toys to be revised, safe models of the originally banned toys, then please inform your customers by clearly labeling these as safe models. We trust you share our concern and will permanently remove FDA and other dangerous toys from your store shelves.

Thank you for your cooperation. If you wish to discuss further steps which can be taken to eliminate dangerous toys, please feel free to call us at 476-5541 ext. 4534.

Sincerely,

Suzanne Reade
for the Dangerous Toys Committee
123 Stadium Place
Syracuse, New York 13210

William R. Tincher, President
Purex Corporation, Ltd.
5101 Clarke Ave.
Lakewood, California 90712

May 3, 1972

Dear Mr. Tincher,

While reading the Sunday magazine of a Wisconsin newspaper recently I came upon a large, colorful ad for what I at first took to be a new fruit beverage. I was shocked to find, upon closer inspection, that the product pictured was your Bo Peep brand liquid ammonia, dyed bright shades of yellow and green to draw attention to your new lemon and pine-mint fragrances.

One of our researchers, as a child, drank uncolored ammonia cleanser which he mistook for grapefruit juice, and was fortunate to have his stomach pumped in time to avoid serious injury. It seems to me that your marketing of brightly colored ammonia in transparent containers similar in size and shape to 28-ounce soft drink bottles with nursery rhyme characters pictured on the label is certain to increase this danger. It is true that parents should take precautions to keep such products out of the reach of children who are too young to read the warning on the label, but the fact is that few homes are equipped with locked cleaning closets.

As the enclosed letter from state hazardous substance Investigator Charles Ahlgrim indicates, the appropriate state and federal agencies have been contacted for possible action in this case. Mr. Ahlgrim shares my concern over the danger your product poses for children.

I hope that you, too, share our concern, and that your prompt attendance to this matter will make federal action unnecessary. I respectfully request that you immediately halt distribution of this product in its present form. The transparent container is unneeded and I am sure the colors add nothing to the agent's cleaning power.

We await your response.

Sincerely yours,

Robert W. Park, Research Coordinator
Wis. Public Interest Research Group
420 North Lake St.
Madison, Wis. 53706

Women and equality

By the mid-1960s, the status of women provided another front in the general struggle for equal rights. The Nineteenth Amendment prohibited discrimination in voting on account of sex, but public and private discrimination against women pervaded the society, particularly in the area of employment. Protests by women followed patterns—demonstrations, legal suits, and political lobbying for new laws. As with most movements seeking social change, feminists operated on diverse levels and with varying means. One important activity focused on the drive for the Equal Rights Amendment (ERA) to the Constitution. The proposed amendment provided that "equality of rights under the law shall not be denied or abridged by the United States or by any State on account of sex." The amendment cleared the House of

Representatives in 1971 and finally received Senate approval the next year. By 1979, however, the amendment still lacked the approval of the thirty-eight states necessary for ratification. The first selection below is testimony taken from hearings on the ERA and illustrates women's difficulty in employment, especially because of so-called protective legislation that, notwithstanding original good intentions, actually compounded their difficulties. The second selection offers a farm woman's understanding of the advantages of "women's liberation" for men and women alike.

Equal Pay for Equal Work

I am Georgianna Sellers of Clarksville, Ind., speaking on behalf of the Indiana and Kentucky unit of the League for American Working Women, known as LAWW

I am acting chairman of this organization. LAWW is a new organization. Its basic purpose is to work for and achieve equality of rights for women. While our organization is not confined to working women, most of our members are employed as factory workers.

The members of our organization wholeheartedly support the equal rights amendment—and for many reasons. It would eliminate injustices to women in employment, educational opportunities, and other areas.

Since our major efforts have been directed toward achieving equality for women in employment, one of our strongest reasons for supporting the equal rights amendment is that it would nullify all State restrictive laws that limit women as to what work they can do, how long they can work, and what they can lift.

It is an insult to women that such laws or rules are referred to as "protective" when their sole function is to exclude women from the higher paying jobs.

The experience of the women employees at the plant where I am employed, demonstrates the urgent need for the equal rights amendment.

Most of us working women are employed in factories on high-speed production lines. Some of us—including myself, are working for the Colgate-Palmolive Co. which has arbitrarily refused to concede that there is a Civil Rights Act of 1964, which prohibits discrimination in employment on the basis of sex.

The union supposedly representing the employees at this plant fails to see why it should recognize the minority group—women—and has made contracts

From U. S. Senate, Hearings before the Subcommittee on Constitutional Amendments, Committee on the Judiciary, *The "Equal Rights" Amendment*, 91st Congress, 2nd session, 7 May 1970, pp. 575–592.

Women demonstrating for abortion rights.

since the advent of Title VII of the Civil Rights Act of 1964 that were just as discriminatory as were the previous contracts.

The women working for Colgate were denied the right to work on the better-paying jobs to which their seniority entitled them, simply because they were women and the jobs might occasionally require the lifting of over 35 pounds.

As a matter of fact, some women employees on the low-paying jobs lifted as much as 17 tons per day while men employees thumped buttons on automatic machinery. While Indiana has no so-called "protective" laws prohibiting women employees from lifting 35 pounds, the mere existence of such laws in other States was used as a phony excuse for this discrimination.

"Oh, no", our employer would say, "you are a woman. You can't do this job. You have to lift 35 pounds. Let George do it."

We were kept off of higher paying easier jobs for years because the company wanted to "protect" us. I say it did not protect, but exploited women. Used their hard labor for low pay, just as employers treated the Negroes for years. Keep them under foot, not on top.

Incidentally, the record that we sent to the Seventh Circuit Court of Appeals weighed 38.6 pounds. We did not have a man to carry it for us.

As a result of the employment discriminations practiced by the company and union at the Colgate plant, some other women employees and I filed a class action under Title VII of the Civil Rights Act against the Colgate Palmolive Co. in the U.S. district court, and then we had to appeal the district court's decision against us to the Court of Appeals for the Seventh Circuit before we won our case.

However, we are still being discriminated against because we are women although our complaint against this type of discrimination was filed with the Equal Employment Opportunity Commission in 1965.

The officials of Local No. 15, International Chemical Workers Union—our union—tell us that we should not fight for our rights because we are a minority. There are about 1,100 men employees and only 145 women employees at this plant. We need the equal rights amendment to eliminate restrictive laws and practices and to give us quicker and surer relief against both employers and unions.

The male representatives of the AFL–CIO who have appeared before the committee and argued that women should not be given their equality, should not be heard—they have no right to claim they represent working women.

[Applause.]

. . . There is not one single woman in the AFL–CIO executive council. Even the predominantly women's unions are governed and controlled by men. It is insulting for these males to use State restrictive laws as a gimmick for exploiting us by claiming they are protecting us. These males running the labor unions are merely trying to monopolize better jobs for themselves.

The women union representatives who testified yesterday that they preferred the State restrictive laws to equality are obviously sick.

Any human being who has no desire for equality has lost his or her self-respect. Women who have lost the urge to be free individuals have no right to speak for those who still are willing to fight for their human and civil rights.

American working women have learned the lesson that the black people have learned. There is no such thing as separate but equal. We do not want separate little unequal, unfair laws and separate little unequal, low-paid jobs. We want full equality.

I say that if a woman has to spend her time, her money, and give of herself to defend herself in court through long, drawn-out litigation, that there is no law that we now have that protects us or will do anything to protect our rights.

Therefore, we further support the equal rights amendment because it would have a restraining effect on those who abuse and discriminate against women. It would help to dispel the myth of women's inferiority.

We are meeting in public life and public offices the male of the species who refuses to recognize a woman as an individual with her own peculiar sense of values, freedoms, and faults.

Even the most docile female in the United States has her "weaker" moments when she'd much prefer to stand on her own two feet and say, "I have my rights, too, you know!"

Who she tells this to is not important. The important thing is that she is an individual wanting her ideas respected and her abilities recognized. This does not mean that because a woman wants equal rights she is a "man hater," nor a radical who wishes only her own rights to be recognized.

On the contrary, there is no stronger advocate of equal rights than I, and yet I have raised five wonderful sons, one lovely daughter, and have a devoted husband.

All my family respect and believe in me as an individual person with every right to say for whom my vote shall be cast and how I will live my own life.

I realize that the fifth and 14th amendments should have been enough to give women equal rights, but these amendments have been in effect over 100 years, and women are still discriminated against in every important phase of human life.

We need the equal rights amendment to further implement the present constitutional provisions and to strengthen the language so no one, no how, nowhere, can ever misinterpret the correct language which says that women as individuals must have equal rights.

It is my own personal viewpoint that any Senator or Congressman that wants to be elected or reelected must support the equal rights amendment. There is another unit of LAWW in California, and we intend to establish other units throughout the United States.

In Indiana we have gone from door to door during the past 6 months, and I still say that women are well enough organized to give anyone pussyfooting around with the amendment or dragging his feet and delaying passage a run for his money.

There is no one more aware of the power of woman than women—especially working women.

We are knowledgeable enough to know who is for us, who is against us, and who is using delaying tactics. There will be no acceptable alibi for failure to pass the amendment this term of Congress.

We are determined to fight for passage of the amendment on a day-by-day, week-by-week, and if necessary, year-by-year basis until we have won the passage of the equal rights amendment, and achieved complete equality.

Thank you. . . .

Women's Liberation

If you want to stir up a hornet's nest, just bring up the subject of Women's Liberation at the neighborhood coffee klatch, as I did. When the movement started two years ago, I already considered myself among the liberated. Yet I must admit to a short-sighted sense of amusement at the hullabaloo militant feminists were raising. Mine was a quiet revolution—and only as a result of reading and reflection do I now realize it took place.

Perhaps my case is extreme. I was born into a family of men. I married into a family of men, and I am rearing a family of men. Logic says that my rage at the basic inequalities between the sexes should be directed at men. But for me that is almost impossible.

I am surrounded by men who love and respect me and are as innocent of malevolent intent as my wonderful mother who tried her darndest to make me a paragon of womanhood. And, in the eyes of the world at least, I am a happy, satisfied, reasonably independent woman.

The idea of female inferiority is ingrained in our culture, sometimes in subtle and seemingly insignificant ways. Inequalities range from property rights to business, professional and political opportunities; from sex symbol debasement to attitudes of superiority which have caused many women to accept the status of second-class humans.

I have labored toward liberation through 20 years of marriage. I was born into a family of five boys, one girl. For Father, paternal dominance was an assumption enforced by screaming silence. His bigoted insistence on it was almost the only source of unhappiness in our seemingly well-ordered home.

My sister and I grew up never questioning the "fact" that male word was law.

From Patricia Leimbach, *A Thread of Blue Denim* (Englewood Cliffs, N.J., Prentice-Hall, 1974). Material originally published in *Farm Journal* 28 (November 1971): 28*ff*. Used by permission.

When I married, I moved into a situation of male dominance more destructive of my identity than the one I had left. My mother-in-law was a strong, capable woman who could have built and ruled an empire had she not submitted to the prevailing opinion that woman's place was subservient to man. I feel certain she died an unfulfilled human being in spite of a string of laudable accomplishments.

From her example, I learned not to buck the tide—I submitted completely to being a farm wife. I went to the fields; did what was asked of me always. I drove a truck and did chores when called upon, and learned to enjoy the work. Though I often seethed in disagreement, I never tried to intercede in the decision-making between my husband and father-in-law—they weren't conditioned to respect the opinions of women in their business.

Then gradually, I began to need help in the house to compensate for time spent in the fields, time off to attend conferences or retreats, to take part in activities where bit by bit I unearthed my identity as a person beyond wife, mother and farm hand.

My husband is a gentle man, well-schooled in the household arts by that mother of three sons.

We came to share responsibilities for the house, the farm and the children; I grew to understand that if I thought of myself as chattel it was a preconception I alone harbored; he had outgrown it.

Considering the happy balance of responsibility that he and I have achieved through 20 years, I see that "women's liberation" is a misnomer. What really is involved is *human* liberation. When women cease to be shrinking violets, they unburden men of a great deal of responsibility, both foolish and real.

Perhaps it is true that farm women as a class feel more liberated than others. While many farmers do realize the true economic value of working with their wives as partners, I know a lot of farm women who feel that the wrath of God would descend upon them if they did not have lunch on the table at the stroke of noon.

A farmer's infringements upon his wife's time and schedule are seldom questioned, but don't ask him to rattle the pots and pans. A wife gets little consideration for a workday extended by farm responsibilities until bedtime, while her husband usually relaxes after chores. On an economic level, his 10 hours may be of more value; on a human level, she is left just as weary.

For all their quiet submission, these are not unhappy women. Many of them, like my neighbors of the coffee klatch, are enraged by talk of Women's Lib.

Men who think Women's Lib is a big joke have no conception of how much more wholesome and fulfilling a marriage can be when a woman shoulders her share of the big problems and decisions, and he takes on a share of the small ones.

It is not enough for husband and wife to "do their own thing." They have to learn to do each other's thing. And a liberated woman is going to end up doing a lot more of "his thing" than she had expected! But experience has also taught me that when husband and wife operate on equal footing, life can be richer, fuller, more satisfying.

Surely our children do not see their father as less of a man because he can iron his own shirts and sometimes does; nor do they think me less of a woman because I go off on a potato delivery with a two-ton truck which I am capable of unloading. I think they see us as a team working for mutual satisfaction.

I do not advocate a reversal of roles or even a realignment in situations where freedom and harmony obviously exist, but I feel every marriage should be open to constant appraisal by the parties involved. Whether we approve the trend or not, it's a fact that nearly 50% of American women work outside the home. When a couple agrees that she should go out to work, it follows that they should share the responsibilities for physical care of house and family. Too often, children are losers in the equality business.

If I am in fact a "liberated woman," what then is all the beefing about? Perhaps it is directed hit and miss at fate—at culture, religion and society in general—for perpetuating the myth of inequality.

I suspect much of the anguish is directed inward. The scars are within *me* —so deep that I can never *fully* accept the truth that woman is not less than mankind.

I weep that I have no daughters to whom I can pass the truth. But, oh, my sons shall know!

The graying of America

The most striking demographic change of the seventies has been the rise in the percentage of the population over thirty years of age. An expanded life expectancy coupled with the declining birth rate has resulted in an increasing shift of social concern toward the problems of the elderly and aging. Numerous lobbying groups have emerged, but one of the most prominent has been the Gray Panthers, founded in the early 1970s by Maggie Kuhn. Coupling their special interests with ones attuned toward a broader appeal, they have criticized a variety of problems categorized under labels such as "sexism," "racism," and "ageism." For example, the Gray Panthers have advocated national health insurance, antipoverty measures, welfare reform, as well as educational opportunities for people of all ages and the abolition of age discrimination and compulsory retirement in employment. The following comment by an eighty-five-year-old woman was offered in response to a New York radio editorial defending the maintenance of compulsory retirement laws.

Aging in America.

. . . As you know, the age chosen by Bismarck about a hundred years ago was injurious to no one nor to the society of that time, because hardly anyone ever lived to the age of 65 anyway.

Today, with the advances in medical technology, the situation is far different. The age chosen in 1976 for the retirement of today's workers would have to be something above 100 to be equally appropriate and "reasonable."

. . . I simply do not understand your tender concern for the employing group, your assumption that "businesses and other institutions" need to have compulsory retirement so they can use it as a crutch to enable them to "deal with the inevitable decline of aging workers."

Do you know many employers, have you watched them operate? I have had many years of experience in the employment field, both as placement manager and as personnel worker, and I have observed that one of the prime requirements for a successful employer is that he must know of effective and seemingly reasonable ways of getting rid of unwanted workers at any time, at any age, and even when the employee is supposed to be protected by law, unless he has a strong organization to confront the employer and keep him in line. . . .

Another incentive for firing a worker . . . is likely to be purely financial. Since older workers, especially skilled ones, usually become more expensive with years of experience, and as a pension may be imminent, it is likely to be more profitable to dismiss the older person. . . .

At age 85, I work constantly with older people. I know how they feel and what happens to them when they are made to feel branded with the stigma of "no longer acceptable to normal society and its affairs. From now on you live on the fringes of the productive world," even though they know themselves to be as valuable as producers at age 66 as they were at age 64 and earlier. . . .

People who are discriminated against in employment because of age go through many stages: fear of loneliness . . . loss of confidence in oneself and one's society, which can behave so callously; self-doubt—could it be that "they" are right? . . .

There is the loss of dignity . . . loss of status. There is a hatred of feeling useless, a fear of being unwanted, a dread of becoming a burden on others instead of a support. . . .

Where social involvement of any kind remains, life then becomes a struggle to avoid sources of further humiliation. At first one may report for jury duty as ordered by the court. But one soon learns that the rights of citizenship in this area are closed to him after he reaches the age of 70.

Or suppose an aged person (as the government designates those over 65) applies for credit at a bank, or a credit card. His credentials will not even be examined to see if he is eligible. His age is enough to prove to the bank his incompetence to handle money—unless he is rich enough already that he does not need money or credit. . . .

From Hope Bagger, "Mandatory Retirement Is Death to Personality," *Gray Panther Network*, Philadelphia. Copy in State Historical Society of Wisconsin, Pamphlet Collection.

And so the more fortunate of the newly deprived and recently impoverished . . . take refuge in the centers set up for them. There they can find companionship of others similarly deprived and uncompensated; often meals which help out in the budget department, whether essential or not; perhaps arts and crafts; and meaningless games, games, games, which serve principally to kill the no longer wanted time. . . .

Of course these fates do not happen to all of the retirees. Many of them find satisfaction in hobbies or in voluntary work. Thirty percent find other jobs after retirement, where they are usually exploited, and seldom receive the compensation that would be due to the worth of their labors if it could be sold on the open market without legislative interference. . . .

The rich, of course, manage nicely, as they always have. . . . The poor, the poorest, and the nearly poor are in the vast majority of the enforced retirees.

These are the most unfortunate, destitute poor, scrounging around for food and protection against the elements—or doing without—and the almost destitute poor, kept going by welfare. . . . Then there are those who just made do when they had incomes from work, but are plunged into poverty when that possibility is withdrawn or reduced. Even Social Security is not adjusted properly for these people. Because their wages were never high enough to permit them to set aside a source of supplementary income for their old age, they are rewarded (?) by being allowed (of course as they deserve!) the most inadequate of the always inadequate Social Security benefits.

And so what the pro-mandatory retirement at age 65 or 70 advocates are recommending is actually the death, not of a person, but of a personality: the core and the worth of a human being.

During this last decade a rapidly growing number of these devastated personalities have been revived, and hope is spreading for the salvation of all. . . . The unwilling retirees are no longer accepting the fate of their personalities, they are using their leisure to unite, to organize, to study and think, and to become active for social change.

These recycled, reconstituted old people no longer believe it when they are told that it is their duty to make way for the young—they can see for themselves that this system does not take care of the young any better than it cares for the old. Regaining their self-respect, their courage and their momentum, they are preparing for battle against the unseen but powerful forces that require so many sacrifices from them.